DICTIONARY OF ITALIAN LEGAL TERMS
and Relevant Definitions

Dictionary of
Italian Legal Terms
and Relevant Definitions

by

JOSEPH THOMAS GENCO, J.D., J.S.D.

Professor of Law Emeritus
Pace University
New York

R
453
G 324

DICTIONARY OF ITALIAN LEGAL TERMS
AND RELEVANT DEFINITIONS

All Rights Reserved
Library of Congress Catalog Card No. 81-80354
ISBN 0-9605780-0-5

PRINTED IN THE UNITED STATES OF AMERICA BY
Theo. Gaus, Ltd., BROOKLYN, N.Y.

To:
ELEANOR, EMILY LYN
THOMAS KARL
and
JOSEPH MICHAEL

PREFACE

This work is a basic English dictionary of Italian legal terms and relevant definitions.

The caveat is issued that we are dealing with terms from a legal system based on the Civil Law and are attempting to make them comprehensible to those accustomed to one derived from the Common Law. Consequently, legal interpretations should be avoided by the uninitiated and left to those competent to make them. Where appropriate, citations have been furnished to insure further research, and should be examined under the latest available statutory enactments to assure accuracy, in view of possible changes and amendments.

Credit should be given to the works consulted in preparing this book. Among them are: "The American College Dictionary," "Black's Law Dictionary," Osborn's "A Concise Law Dictionary," Webster's "New International Dictionary" and "American Commercial Law" by Kassoff, Genco and Baum.

Consulted for Italian terms were: "Istituzioni di Diritto Civile" by Roberto de Ruggiero and Fulvio Maroi, "Dizionario dei Termini Giuridici" by Angelo Favata, "Titoli di Credito" by Angelo Asquini, "La Cambiale e L'Assegno" by Dr. Mario Levi, "A Short Italian Dictionary" by Alfredo Hoare, "A New Pronouncing Dictionary of the English and Italian Languages" by Arthur Enenkel and J. McLaughlin, as well as "Novissimo Dizionario della Lingua Italiana" by Fernando Palazzi.

Extensive reference was made to the Civil Code, the Code of Civil Procedure, the Penal Code and the Code of Penal Procedure of Italy. Examined were the Preliminary Dispositions which precede the Civil Code; the Usual Laws appended to the Civil Code, the Code of Civil Procedure and the Code of Penal Procedure; the Enabling Rules and Transitory Dispositions for the Civil Code and the Code of Civil Procedure; the Coordinating and Transitory Dispositions for the Penal Code; the Enabling Rules, Coordinating and Regulatory Dispositions for the Code of Penal Procedure, as well as the Constitution of the Italian Republic.

To facilitate pronunciation of the words and terms used, the standard Italian accents have been employed. Nouns have been identified as masculine (m.) or feminine (f.).

It is hoped that this dictionary may serve as a handy guide to Italian legal terms and relevant definitions and that it prove useful to those engaged in legal, commercial and international affairs. It will be beneficial to college and university students and those attending undergraduate and graduate Schools of Commerce and Business Administration and Schools of Law.

ACKNOWLEDGMENTS

The principal sources for the citation of authorities noted in the various terms and definitions are hereinafter set forth.

Constitution of the Italian Republic	Costituzióne della Repúbblica Italiàna
Preliminary Dispositions	Disposizióni sulla Légge in Generàle (D.P.)
Italian Civil Code	Còdice Civíle (C.C.)
Enabling Rules and Transitory Dispositions	Disposizióni per l'Attuazióne del Còdice Civíle e Disposizióni Transitòrie
Usual Laws, Appendix to Italian Civil Code	Léggi Usuàli, Appendíce al C.C.
Italian Code of Civil Procedure	Còdice di Procedúra Civíle (C.P.C.)
Enabling Rules and Transitory Dispositions	Disposizióni per l'Attuazióne del Còdice di Procedúra Civíle e Disposizióni Transitòrie
Usual Laws, Appendix to Italian Code of Civil Procedure	Léggi Usuàli, Appendíce al C.P.C.
Italian Penal Code	Còdice Penàle (C.P.)
Coordinating and Transitory Dispositions for the Penal Code	Disposizióne di Coordinaménto e Transitòrie per il Còdice Penàle
Italian Code of Penal Procedure	Còdice di Procedúra Penàle (C.P.P.)
Enabling and Regulatory Rules	Nòrme di Attuazióne e Regolamentàri; Disposizióni di Attuazióne
Coordinating Dispositions for the Italian Code of Penal Procedure	Disposizióni di Coordinaménto
Regulatory Dispositions for the Execution of the Italian Code of Penal Procedure	Disposizióni Regolamentàri per la Esecuzióne del C.P.P.
Usual Laws, Appendix to Italian Code of Penal Procedure	Léggi Usuàli, Appendíce al C.P.P.

DICTIONARY OF ITALIAN LEGAL TERMS
and Relevant Definitions

A

abàte m.—abbot.

abbadìa f.—abbey; monastery. Also **abbazìa**.

abbandonàre—to abandon; to renounce.

abbandonàto—abandoned; foundling.

abbandóno m.—abandonment.

abbandóno del domicílio coniugàle—abandonment of the conjugal home. Now, allontanaménto dalla residènza familiàre (departure from the family residence). The right of moral and material assistance is suspended from the spouse who, without just cause, is absent from the family residence and refuses to return. Art. 146, Italian Civil Code.

abbandóno di persóne minóri o incapàci—abandonment of minors or incompetents. Whoever abandons a minor of age fourteen, or an incompetent who cannot take care of himself by reason of mental or physical illness, advanced age or other reason, and of whom he has custody or should have care, is punished with imprisonment. Subject to the same punishment is the person who abandons abroad, an Italian citizen under eighteen years of age, who had been entrusted to him within the territory of the State for reasons of labor. The penalty of imprisonment is increased if personal injury flows from the act or death ensues. The penalties are augmented if the act is committed by a parent, son, guardian, spouse or an adopted or adopting party. Art. 591, Italian Penal Code.

abbaruffàre—to fight; to embroil; to come to blows.

abbaruffàta f.—a fight; a tumult.

abbassàre—to lower; to let down.

abbazìa f.—abbey; monastery.

abbigliàre—to adorn; to dress with elegance.

abbonàre—to subscribe to a publication; to improve.

abbondànza f.—abundance; plenty.

abbonìre—to cultivate; to improve.

abbozzàre—to sketch; to trace; to draft.

abbòzzo m.—sketch; draft; outline.

abbracciàre—to embrace; to contain.

abbreviàre—to abbreviate; to shorten.

abbruciàre—to burn; to consume with fire. Also, **bruciàre**.

abdicàre—to abdicate.

abdicazióne f.—abdication.

abigeàto m.—theft of cattle; cattle rustling. Abigeàto Usual Laws, Appendix to Italian Code of Penal procedure.

abígeo m.—cattle thief; the crime of cattle stealing.

àbile—able; skillful in a particular field; fit; apt.

abilitàre—to render able; to admit to the practice of a profession, art or right.

abilitazióne f.—admission to practice a profession, art or right; also, the document admitting one to such practice.

abitànte m.—inhabitant.

abitàre—to inhabit; to live in; to dwell.

abitazióne f. dwelling; home; habitation. One having the right of habitation in a house (of another) is limited to inhabit same, only for his needs or use and that of his family. The latter include children born after the right of habitation began as well as adopted, recognized natural children, and affiliated children together with those who live with him to render services to him or to his family. Art. 1021-1026, Italian Civil Code.

àbito m.—clothes; garment; vestment.

1

abituàle—customary; usual; habitual.

abituàre—to accustom; to acclimate; to familiarize.

abitúdine f.—habit; inclination; usage.

abolire—to abolish; to annul; to abrogate; to cancel.

abolizióne f.—abolition.

abortíre—to abort; to expel the fetus before its natural time.

abòrto m.—act and effect of aborting.

aborzióne f.—abortion.

abrogàre—to abrogate; to abolish; to annul; to revoke.

abrogazióne f.—the act of abrogating or annuling; abrogation.

abusàre—to abuse; to misuse; to use excessively; to waste.

abusívo—abusive; improper; unlawful; wrongful.

abusívo esercízio di una professióne—unlawful practice of a licensed profession. Art. 348, Italian Penal Code.

abúso m.—abuse; misuse; excessive use.

abúso d'autorità—abuse of authority.

abúso dell'immàgine altrúi—misuse of another's image or likeness. Art. 10, Italian Civil Code.

abúso di fidúcia—breach of trust.

abúso di sostànze stupefacènti—abuse of narcotic substances. Whoever, in a public place or one open to the public, or in private groups or clubs of whatever kind, is caught in a state of grave psychic change through abuse of narcotic substances, is punished with arrest or fine. Art. 729, Italian Penal Code.

accadèmia f.—academy.

accadèmico—academic; academician.

accafàre—to take away by force; to snatch.

accagionàre—to accuse; to impute; to attribute.

accagionatóre m.—accuser; informer.

accantonaménto m.—the quartering of troops; allocation or holding of funds for specific use.

accantonàre—to quarter troops; to allocate or hold funds for specific use.

accaparraménto m.—the act of cornering the market of a specific commodity or goods with the intent of reselling same at a higher price. See, also, bagarinàggio and incètta.

accaparràre—to give a deposit on merchandise to hold it for the prospective buyer.

accaparratóre m.—one who corners the market of a specific commodity or goods with the intent of reselling same at a higher price. Also, incettatóre and bagaríno.

accapigliàre—to grasp another by the hair; to come to blows; to affray; to discuss in violent and vulgar terms.

accasàre—to wed.

accatastàre—to register property in the office which maintains records of real property; to tax; to heap up; to pile up.

accattabríghe m.—a quarrelsome person; one who takes upon himself the burdens of others.

accattàre—to take; to borrow; to beg; to collect alms.

accàtto m.—act of borrowing or receiving; begging; amount collected; extraordinary tax levied by the Republic of Florence.

accattonàgio m.—the act of soliciting alms. See mendicità.

accèdere—to accede; to approve; to consent; to approach; to yield; to enter upon an office or post; to become a party to a pact.

acceleraménto m.—acceleration.

acceleraménto del pàrto—hastening child-birth; a violation listed under lesióne personàle. Art. 582, 583-585, Italian Penal Code.

acceleràre—to accelerate; to hasten.

acceleratóre m.—accelerator.

accelerazióne f.—acceleration.

accèndere—to light; to set fire; to turn on a light or the radio.

accendíbile—that which can be lighted.

accendiménto m.—act of lighting.

accenditóre m.—one who lights; a lighter.

accennàre—to hint; to indicate.

accénno m.—slight hint or trace of something.

accensióni ed esplosióni pericolose—dangerous lightings and explosions. These are part of unlawful acts prohibited in inhabitated places without license of Public Security Authorities. See ràzzi (làncio abusívo). Art. 703, Italian Penal Code.

accertaménto m.—act of ascertaining; confirmation; the act whereby the treasury determines a taxpayer's income subject to taxation.

accertàre—to ascertain; to assure; to determine; to verify.

accessíbile—accessible; approachable.

accessióne f.—accession; addition; augmentation; increase; adherence to a pact stipulated by others; one of the methods of acquiring property. Art. 922, 934-947, 1146, Italian Civil Code.

accèssit m.—honorable mention accorded to a student who came closest to the winner of a prize.

accèsso m.—access.

accèsso coatívo—compulsory access to land. It is the right of passage over neighboring land to repair a wall or building or to retrieve a strayed animal or property which accidentally finds itself on the adjoining land. Art. 843, Italian Civil Code.

accèsso giudiziàle—a method of proof requiring the personal inspection or examination of a thing or place by the court. Art. 118, 258, 262, Italian Code of Civil Procedure and Art. 309-313, 457, Italian Code of Criminal Procedure.

accessòrio m.—accessory.

accètta f.—hatchet.

accettànte—acceptor; one who accepts a draft or contract.

accettàre—to accept; to accept a draft or bill of exchange by the drawee signing or accepting it to make himself primarily liable on the instrument.

accettazióne f.—acceptance. Re contracts, Art. 1326-1330, 1335, Italian Civil Code. Also, a check-in point at an airport.

accettazióne dell'assègno bancàrio—acceptance of a bank check. It is considered void. Art. 4, Asségni (Checks), Usual Laws, Appendix to Italian Civil Code.

accettazióne della cambiàle—acceptance of a draft. It must be made in writing on the instrument. Art. 26-34, Cambiàle (Drafts), Usual Laws, Appendix to Italian Civil Code.

accettazióne dell'eredità—acceptance of inheritance. It can be unqualified and simple or with benefit of inventory. In the first instance, the acceptance results in the mingling of the assets of the estate with that of the successor who becomes personally liable for the decedent's liabilities. In the case of acceptance with benefit of inventory, it prevents commingling of the decedent's estate assets with those of the successor who becomes liable only to the extent of that which he has received and not personally. Art. 470-511, Italian Civil Code.

accettazióne dell'eredità col benefício d'inventàrio—acceptance of inheritance with benefit of inventory. It must be made by declaration before a notary or the Clerk of the Praetor in the judicial district where the estate is being administered. In this instance, there is no commingling of the estate's assets with those of the successor, who becomes liable only to the extent of that which he has received and not personally. Acceptance with benefit of inventory is compulsory for minors, those under interdiction, emancipated minors, those who are disqualified from managing their own affairs, and also, juridical persons. Art. 484, 471-473, 485-511, Italian Civil Code; Art. 778-780, Italian Code of Civil Procedure.

accettazióne per intervènto—acceptance of a commercial instrument by an intervenor. It is an acceptance by one who, acting as an intervenor and before maturity, accepts the instrument and makes himself primarily liable. He is in the position of an accommodation party. Art. 74-82 Cambiàle (Drafts), Usual Laws Appendix to Italian Civil Code.

acciàco m.—illness; habitual physical indisposition.

acciacòso—suffering from or having many illnesses.

acciaríno m.—a small piece of steel employed to strike a flint to start a fire.

accidènte m.—accident; the happening of an unforeseen event.

acciuffàre—to seize with violence; to seize by the hair; to scuffle.

accollàre—to place on the neck or back.

accollàrsi—to take upon one's self.

accollàrsi un débito—to take on a debt.

accollàrsi un lavóro—to undertake a job.

accollàrsi una spésa—to undertake an expense.

accollatàrio m.—one who has assumed a work, burden or obligation; a contractor.

accollatúra f.—opening of a dress at the neck; collar of a dress; mark left by the yoke on a beast's neck.

accòllo m.—burden; forward weight of a load in an animal drawn wagon which rests on the beast's back; the overhang on a building or structure; the assumption by a third party of a debtor's obligation; convention; agreement; pact. See accòllo di débito.

accòllo di débito—the assumption by a third party of the obligation of a debtor. Art. 1273, Italian Civil Code.

accomandànte—a partner in an accomàndita who contributes capital but does not participate in the management of the partnership. He is the equivalent of a limited partner. See società in accomàndita sémplice.

accomandatàrio—a partner in an accomàndita who contributes capital and has unlimited joint and several responsibility. He participates in

management and is the equivalent of a general partner. See società in accomàndita sémplice.

accomàndita f.—a corporation or partnership where shareholders or partners have limited responsibility. See società accomàndita per azióni and società accomàndita sémplice.

accomodàre—to put in order; to arrange; to settle; to seat oneself.

accòmodo m.—settlement of a suit at law.

acconciàre—to fix; to adorn; to arrange; to dress.

accónto m.—part payment of a debt or obligation.

accòrdo m. — accord; harmony; an agreement between nations.

accreditaménto m.—extension of credit to someone; act of accrediting.

accreditàre—to accredit; to open or extend credit; to render credible; to issue credentials to diplomatic officials for accreditation.

accréscere—to augment; to grow; increase of land by natural addition to the soil by natural deposits in a gradual manner; to increase by accretion.

accumulaménto m. — accumulation; mass; heap.

accumulàre—to accumulate; to amass; to heap.

accúsa f.—accusation; a formal charge against a person.

accusànte m.—accuser.

accusàre—to accuse; to bring a formal charge against a person before a magistrate or court in connection with a criminal offense.

accusàto m. (accusàta f.)—accused; an accused person subject to criminal trial; a criminal defendant. See imputàto.

accusatóre m. (accusatríce f.) — accuser; informer; a public official who brings criminals to trial.

àcqua f.—water.

acquàta f.—shower (rain).

acquàtico—aquatic.

acquedótto m.—aqueduct. An aqueduct is considered part of the public domain. Art. 822, Italian Civil Code.

acquedótto coattívo—compulsory passage of water; the obligation to allow the passage of a neighbor's waters over one's land. Art. 1033-1043, Italian Civil Code.

acquiescènza f. — acquiescence; tacit renunciation of a right; silent submission.

acquietaménto m.—the act of acquiescing.

acquietàre—to acquiesce; to agree; to consent to; to submit silently.

acquisíre—to acquire non-material things; to acquire a skill, a habit, a right, etc.

acquistàre—to acquire; to purchase; to obtain possession of a thing.

acquísto dell'eredità—acquisition of inheritance. The inheritance is acquired with its acceptance. Its effect is to relate back to the opening of the succession which occurs at the moment of death. Art. 459, Italian Civil Code.

acquísto della proprietà—acquisition of property. It is acquired by: (a) occupation or dominion; (b) finding ("invenzione", Lat., inventio); (c) accession; (d) "specificazióne" (Lat., specificatio), where one has transformed the property or materials of another into something new; (e) commingling; (f) prescription ("usucapióne", Lat., usucapio); (g) contract; (h) succession, and (i) by other modes prescribed by law. Art. 922, Italian Civil Code.

acquísto di còse di sospètta provenìenza—acquisition of things of suspicious origin. It involves the purchase or receiving of things without ascertaining their legitimate origin when because of their quality, the condition of the seller or the nature of the price, it would lead to suspicion that they are the fruits of a crime. Commonly called incàuto acquísto. Art. 712, Italian Penal Code.

addaziàre—to assess taxes.

addebitàre—to debit; to charge some-one with an action or characteristic.

addébito m.—attribution of a debt; accusation.

addétto—assigned to some use or function; an attaché in an embassy.

addí—dated this day; e.g. used in dating letters, the word addí is followed by the date.

addizióne f.—addition.

adempiménto m.—performance; execution; fulfillment or satisfaction of a debt, promise or obligation.

adempíre—to perform; to maintain or fulfill a promise or obligation; to satisfy a promise.

adescàre—to entice; to lure.

adescàto—enticed; lured.

adíre—to apply to a court for relief.

adíre un'eredità—to accept an inheritance.

àdito m.—entrance; access; right of access.

adolescènte—adolescent.

adolescènza f.—adolescence.

adontàre—to affront; to offend; to disdain. Also aontàre.

adottaménto m.—act of adopting; adoption.

adottànte—the one who adopts.

adottàre—to adopt.

adottàto—the person adopted.

adottívo—adoptive.

adozióne f.—adoption. Art. 291-314; 314/2-314/28, Italian Civil Code.

adulteràre—to adulterate; to falsify; to alter; to adulterate foods and beverages.

adulterazióne f.—adulteration.

adulterazióne e contraffazióne di sostànze alimentàri—adulteration and fraudulent imitation of food-stuffs. Art. 440, Italian Penal Code.

adulteríno—a child born of parents one of whom was married to a third party.

adultèrio m.—adultery.

adúltero m.—adultery.

adúlto m.—adult.

adunaménto m.—meeting; act of assembling.

adunàre—to assemble; to meet together to discuss public or private affairs.

adunàta f.—meeting; assembly.

aeròdromo m.—airdrome. It is considered part of the public domain if established by the State; likewise, every State construction or installation destined to serve aerial navigation. Art. 822, Italian Civil Code; Art. 692, Italian Navigation Code.

aeromòbile m.—aircraft in general, whether lighter than air or utilizing dynamic action.

aeronàve f.—airship; lighter than air, self-propelled aircraft; dirigible.

affàre m.—affair; undertaking; business; e.g., man of affairs; affair of state; business deal.

affidaménto dei minóri—entrusting of minors. Art. 404, 401, Italian Civil Code.

affidàre—to confide; to trust; to commit.

affidàvit m.—a written statement or declaration under oath.

affiliàre—to affiliate; to associate.

affiliazióne f.—affiliation; a legal status whereby a person takes an abandoned minor under his care for a period of three years and precedes filial status. Distinguished from adoption. Art. 404-413. Italian Civil Code.

affinità f.—affinity; relationship which exists between one spouse and the parents of the other. Art. 78, Italian Civil Code.

affittacàmere m. or f.—one who rents furnished rooms.

affittaiuòlo m.—farm tenant. Also fittaiuòlo.

affittànza f.—rent; rental contract or lease.

affittàre—to let; to rent; to hire. Properly refers to farm lands and productive things. Commonly, it is also used for rental of homes, shops, etc. However, for the latter type of rentals, see appigionàre and pigióne; locazióne di fóndi urbàni.

affìtto m.—a lease of productive things, be they personal or real property. The lessee must undertake its management in conformity with the economic destination of the thing and in the interest of production. He is entitled to the fruits and other benefits of the thing. Art. 1615-1627, Italian Civil Code. See locazióne.

affitto di fóndi rústici—lease of rural lands. Such lease may be destined to reforestation, cultivation of crops, raising of animals and other agricultural activities. Art. 1628-1654, Italian Civil Code.

affituàle m.—farm tenant. Also, fittuàrio.

affituàrio m.—farm tenant. Also, fittuàrio.

affocàre—to set afire; to burn.

affocàto — burned; inflamed; fire-colored.

affogàre—to choke; to suffocate; to drown.

affogàto—one who is choked or suffocated; drowned.

affondàre—to sink; to submerge.

affrancàre—to free; to liberate; to release property from a legal servitude.

affrancatúra f.—prepayment of postage.

affrancazióne f.—to free an estate from a canon (annual charge or rent). Art. 971 Italian Civil Code.

afrodisíaco—aphrodisiac.

agènda f.—agenda; list of matters to be considered.

agènte m.—agent.

agènte—acting; functioning; operating.

agenzía f.—agency. The contract whereby one party assumes the firm commitment to negotiate and conclude contracts in a specific area on behalf of another in return for compensation. Art. 1742-1753, Italian Civil Code. See mandàto.

agenzía con rappresentànza—agency with representation. It is an agency in which the agent is empowered to enter into a contract for his principal with third parties. Art. 1752, Italian Civil Code.

agevolàre—to facilitate; to aid.

àggio m.—discount; brokerage; exchange; premium placed on some currency over others, such as gold over paper currency; a percentage compensation given to public officials on monies collected.

aggiornaménto m. — adjournment; bringing up to date.

aggiornàre—to adjourn; to postpone.

aggiotàggio m.—the crime involving illegal and fraudulent variations of prices in the marget; it can consist of the publication of false or exaggerated information regarding prices on the stock exchange or the prices of goods. Art. 501, 518, Italian Penal Code; Art. 2628, Italian Civil Code.

aggiotatóre m.—one who commits aggiotàggio.

aggiudicàre—to adjudge; to decree; to sentence; to award.

aggiudicazióne f.—adjudication.

aggiúnto m.—adjunct; assistant.

aggiúnto giudiziàrio—judicial adjunct; a starting rank in the Italian judiciary.

aggravànte—aggravating. See circostànze aggravànti.

aggravànti (circostànze)—aggravating circumstances; circumstances accompanying a criminal act which increase or aggravate the penal responsibility and its punishment. Art. 61, 576, 577, Italian Penal Code.

aggravàre—to aggravate; to increase.

agguàto m.—ambush.

agiàto—comfortably well off financially, but less than rich.

àgio m.—comfortable; convenient.

a giórno—up-to-date; current; illuminated as though it were day.

agíre—to act.

agitàre—to agitate.

agrària f.—agriculture; agronomy; the art and science of agriculture.

agràrio—agrarian.

agrícola m.—agriculturist.

agricoltóre m.—farmer.

agricoltúra f.—agriculture.

agronomía f.—agronomy; the science of cultivation of the soil.

agrónomo m.—agronomist.

aizzaménto m.—incitement; provocation.

aizzàre—to incite; to provoke; to set a dog or other animal upon someone.

aizzatóre m.—provocator.

alabàrda f.—halberd; a medieval arm.

alalía f.—impossibility of pronouncing words; mutism; aphasia.

alambícco m.—still. See lambícco.

albergatóre m.—hotel or inn-keeper. Art. 1783-1786, Italian Civil Code.

albèrgo m.—hotel; inn.

àlbo pretòrio—a register located at the municipal headquarters on which are posted legal notices.

àlea f.—from the Latin, a game of dice; game of chance; hazard; risk.

aleatóre m.—one who plays a game of chance.

aleatòrio—aleatory; a contract involving gains and losses which depend on an uncertain event.

alfière m.—ensign.

àlias—alias; one known by another name.

àlibi m.—alibi; being elsewhere at the time of the commission of a crime, thus tending to prove that the person charged could not have committed it. See negatíva coartàta.

alienàbile—alienable; capable of being sold or transferred.

alienabilità f.—alienability.

alienaménto m.—alienation.

alienànte—one who disposes of his property by selling or transferring the same.

alienàre—to alienate; to convey; to transfer title to property.

alienazióne f.—alienation; the transfer of title to property from one person to another.

8

alienísta m.—alienist; one who specializes in diseases of the mind.

alièno—alien; a foreigner; one born in a country outside of the one in which he finds himself and is not naturalized therein.

aliménti al fallíto e alla famíglia—subsistence to the bankrupt and to his family. If the bankrupt lacks means of subsistence, the bankruptcy judge, upon hearing the trustee and the creditors' committee, if one has been named, may grant a subsidy for subsistence to the bankrupt and his family. Art. 47, Falliménto (Bankruptcy), Usual Laws, Appendix to Italian Civil Code.

aliménti (òbbligo dègli)—right to nourishment and sustenance; a reciprocal right and duty imposed on certain relations by blood and marriage. Art. 433-448, Italian Civil Code.

aliménto m.—food; meal; nourishment; that which is necessary to sustain life; subsistence; sustenance.

alimònia f.—alimony.

alleànza f.—alliance.

alleàre—to ally; to contract an alliance.

alleàto m.—ally.

allegaménto m.—allegation; affirmation.

allegàre—to allege; to cite; to testify; to affirm; to assert.

allegàto—enclosed (document).

allegazióne f.—allegation; collection of proofs.

allodiàle—allodial.

allòdio m.—all free; not subject to restriction or obligation; not held of any lord or superior; opposite of feudal.

allogàre—to place; to rent; to find employment; to marry.

allogatóre m.—one who rents or undertakes to find employment.

alloggiaménto m.—lodging.

alloggiàre—to lodge; to dwell.

alloggiatóre m.—host; inn-keeper.

allòggio m.—dwelling.

allontanaménto dalla residènza familiàre—departure from the family residence. Art. 146, Italian Civil Code. See abbandóno del domicílio coniugàle.

allopiàre—to put to sleep with opium.

allòpio m.—opium.

allucinàre—to hallucinate; to talk without sense; to dream.

allucinazióne f.—hallucination.

allungaménto m.—allonge; act of lengthening; a piece of paper annexed to commercial paper or negotiable instruments so that additional indorsements may be added when the instrument itself contains no further space for such indorsements.

alluvióne f.—alluvion; increase or deposit of soil left by receding waters of a stream or of the sea; inundation; the gradual increase of earth along the shore or bank of a river or stream brought about by the force of the waters. The union of land and the increments which are formed successively and imperceptibly in lands situated along the banks of rivers or streams, belong to the owner of the land, except as provided by special laws, Art. 941-943, 947, Italian Civil Code.

almiràglio m.—admiral. See ammiràglio.

almirànte m. — admiral. See ammiràglio.

alopecía f.—lack of hair in a part of the body which may be congenital or acquired. See atrichía.

alteràre—to alter; to change; to vary; to misrepresent; to render a thing different from its original state or condition; to falsify.

alterazióne f.—alteration; act of changing; falsification.

alterazióne del testaménto—alteration or falsification of the testament. A person so doing is excluded from the succession. Art. 463, subd. 4, 5, 6, Italian Civil Code.

alterazióne di stàto—alteration of civil status. Whoever alters the civil status of a new-born child by substituting one child for another, is punished with imprisonment. An increased punishment is applied to anyone altering the civil status of a new-born child by supplying data relative to a birth certificate by means of false affirmations, attestations or other falsity. Art. 567, Italian Penal Code. See **supposizióne o soppressióne di stàto.**

àlveo abbandonàto—abandoned river bed. If a river or stream forms a new bed, abandoning the old, the new bed belongs to the owners of the land of the confining river banks to the middle thereof. Also, **lètto del fiúme,** Art. 946, Italian Civil Code.

ambóne m.—pulpit; tribune, podium.

ammazzagàtti m.—worthless gun or pistol. See **mazzagàtti,** a pocket pistol or snub-nose revolver.

ammazzàre—to kill with a club or by violent means.

ammazzatóio m.—abattoir; slaughterhouse.

ammazzolàre—to gather in a bunch; said of flowers and playing cards.

ammènda f.—a penalty in the form of a fine, imposed for committing the violation of the Penal Code, known as contravvenzióne. Art. 17, 18, 26, 66, 75, 78, 135, 136, 173, 196, 197, Italian Penal Code; Art. 31, 122, 123, Italian Code of Penal Procedure; Art. 40, Enabling Rules, Appendix to Italian Code of Penal Procedure.

ammènde (càssa delle)—bank receiving funds derived from fines and penalties imposed by law.

amministràre—to administer; to govern; to manage; to dispense.

amministrativaménte — administratively.

amministratívo—concerning administration; administratively.

amministràto—administered.

amministratóre m. — administrator; manager.

amministratríce f. — administratrix; manager.

amministrazióne f. — administration; management; government.

amministrazióne controllàta — controlled management. A legal proceeding available to businesses having temporary difficulty in meeting their obligations. It is available to those who have not declared bankruptcy in the preceding five years or entered a composition of creditors. Control of the management of the business is under judicial supervision. Art. 187-193, **Falliménto** (Bankruptcy), Usual Laws, Appendix to Italian Civil Code.

ammiragliàto m.—admiralty; office or jurisdiction of the admiralty; headquarters of admiralty administration.

ammiràglio m.—admiral.

ammissíbile—admissible; allowable.

ammissibilità f.—possibility of being admissible; admissibility.

ammissióne f. — admission; admittance; access; act of admitting or being admitted.

ammoniménto m.—admonition; warning. Also, see **ammonizióne.**

ammoníre—to admonish; to warn; to caution; to reprove for a fault or shortcoming.

ammoníto—one who has been warned.

ammonizióne m.—admonition; warning. It is an admonition given by a judicial official to witnesses to tell the truth when they are sworn under oath. It is, also, a warning given by the Quaestor to persons who endanger public security and morality. Also, **ammoniménto.** Art. 238, 251, Italian Code of Civil Procedure; Art. 142, 143, 316, 329, 357, 359, 449, 458, Italian Code of Penal Procedure. See **diffída.**

ammortaménto m.—extinction of a debt. Art. 2016-2020, 2027, Italian Civil Code; Art. 69-74, **Asségni** (checks) and Art. 89-93, **Cambiàle** (Drafts), Usual Laws, Appendix to Italian Civil Code.

ammortàre—to extinguish; to gradually extinguish a debt; gradual return of capital.

ammortiménto m.—complete extinguishment of the sensibility of some part of the body.

ammortíre—to extinguish; to deprive of animation or efficacy.

ammortizàre—to ammortize; to gradually extinguish a debt by installment payments.

ammutinaménto m.—mutiny.

ammutinàre—to mutiny.

amnistía f.—amnesty. Art. 151, Italian Penal Code; Art. 79, Constitution of the Italian Republic.

amnistiàre—to amnesty; to pardon.

amnistiàto—one who has been amnestied.

amputàre—to amputate.

amputazióne f.—amputation.

anàgrafe f.—anagraph; register; record; inventory; register of population. It is the duty of everyone to register himself and the persons over whom he has parental authority or guardianship in the Municipal Register at the place of his usual residence. Foreign diplomatic and consular personnel and their dependents are not subject to registration. The mayor, as official of the government, is the official of the Register. Anàgrafi (Registers), Usual Laws, Appendix to Italian Civil Code.

anàgrafe tributària—register of taxes. It is the office which gathers and maintains nationwide records of tax declarations filed in the offices of financial administration. Other data, relative to imposition of taxes and having relation thereto, are also kept. Decréto del Presidènte della Repúbblica (Decree of the President of the Republic), 29 September 1973, n. 605.

analfabèta or analfabèto m.—illiterate.

analfabetísmo m.—the state of illiteracy.

anàlisi f.—analysis.

analísta m.—analyst.

analogía f.—analogy; the process used by judges in deciding a case that is without legal precedent. See Interpretazióne analògica.

anarchía f.—anarchy.

anàrchico m.—anarchist.

anatèma m.—anathema.

anatematizzàre—to anathematize.

anatocísmo m.—compound interest. Art. 1283, Italian Civil Code.

anatomía f.—anatomy.

anatomicaménte—anatomically.

anatòmico—anatomical.

anatomísta m.—anatomist.

ancèlla f.—maid servant.

ancípite — uncertain; ambiguous; doubtful.

àncora f.—anchor.

ancóra—again; still; yet; even; more; too.

ancoràggio m.—anchorage.

ancoràre—to anchor.

andicappàre—to put in a state of inferiority (from the English, handicap).

anemía f.—anemia.

anèmico—anemic.

anèmio m.—one who is anemic.

anestesía f.—anesthesia

anestesísta m.—anaesthetist.

anestètico—anesthetic.

anestetizzàre—to anaesthetize.

aneurísma m.—aneurism.

aneurismàtico—aneurismal.

anfiartròsi f.—adherence of diseased tissues around the skeletal structure; limited movement of the skeletal structure.

anfíbio—amphibious.

anfiteàtro m.—amphitheater.

anfitrióne m.—host; one who furnishes hospitality.

angaría—See anghería.

angariàre—to tyrannize; to oppress; to extort.

anghería f.—an odious tax; an overbearing abuse; violence against another without cause.

ànima f.—soul. See disposizióne a favóre dell'ànima — disposition in favor of the soul.

animàle m.—animal.

animàli (garanzía nella véndita di)—guarantee in the sale of animals. It is a guarantee against defects. Art. 1496, Italian Civil Code.

animàre—to animate; to encourage.

animosità f.—animosity.

animóso—livley; courageous.

animus m. (Lat.)—intention of one who acts or does something; mind; design; disposition.

animus cancellandi (Lat.)—the intention of cancelling or destroying (a will).

animus defamandi (Lat.)—the intention of defaming someone.

animus donandi (Lat.)—the intention of giving or making a gift. Art. 769, 2034, Italian Civil Code.

animus nocendi (Lat.)—the intention of causing damage, annonyance or trespass to the property of another. Art. 833, 844, Italian Civil Code.

animus revocandi (Lat.)—the intention of revoking a will.

animus testandi (Lat.)—the intention of making a will.

annàle m.—yearly record of events. pl., annals.

annalìsta m. — recorder of yearly events.

anniversàrio m.—anniversary; yearly recurrence of an event; celebration or commemoration of a notable event.

ànno m.—year.

annotàre—to annote; to note; to comment.

annotazióne f.—annotation; notation. A notation placed by a creditor at the bottom, in the margin or on the back of a document in his possession, is proof, though unsigned by him, if it tends to verify the release of the debtor. The annotation has the same value if similarly placed on a discharge or copy of the document of debt possessed by the debtor. Art. 2708, Italian Civil Code.

annotazióne dell'ipotèca — annotation on a mortgage. It must be entered on the margin of the recorded instrument. Art. 2843, Italian Civil Code.

annotazióni degli àtti dello stàto civíle —annotations to the records of the Civil Registry. No annotations or notes may be made upon an act or document of the Civil Registry unless permitted by law or ordered by the judicial authorities. Art. 453, Italian Civil Code.

annuàle—yearly; annual.

annuàrio—annuary; yearbook; a book recording useful facts which occurred the preceding years; almanac.

annullabilità del contràtto — annullability of the contract. Art. 1425-1446, Italian Civil Code. See nullità del contràtto.

annullaménto m.—annulment. It presupposes that the marriage was invalid from its inception. Art. 117-129, Italian Civil Code.

annullàre—to annul; to abrogate; to rescind.

annunziaménto m.—advertisement; announcement.

annunziàre—to announce; to predict.

annúnzio m.—announcement; presage; prediction of future event.

ànnuo—annual; yearly.

anomalía f.—anomalous; irregular; deviating from the common rule.

anòmalo—that which is anomalous.

anònima f.—See società anònima, a corporation.

anònimo—anonymous.

anormàle—abnormal.

anormalità f.—abnormality.

anseàtico—Hanseatic; a league of North German towns during the Middle Ages to foster and protect commerce.

antagonísmo m.—antagonism.

antagonísta m.—antagonist; adversary.

antecedènte—antecedent; that which precedes.

antecedenteménte—previously.

antecedènza f.—antecedence; precedence.

antecèdere—to precede.

antedétto—aforesaid.

antenàto m.—ancestor; forefather.

antichità f.—antiquity.

anticipàre—to anticipate; to advance (funds).

anticipataménte — beforehand; ahead of time.

anticipazióne f.—anticipation; an advance of funds.

anticipazióne bancària — an amount loaned by a bank which is secured by the borrower depositing securities or merchandise as pledge for repayment. The bank cannot dispose of the property pledged if it issues a document in which they are enumerated. Art. 1846-1851, Italian Civil Code. See pòlizza di anticipazzióne.

anticipazióne delle spése—advance of (trial) costs. The costs of penal proceedings are advanced by the State, except those relating to documents to be made at the request of private parties not receiving free defense counsel. Art. 611, Italian Code of Penal Procedure. See anticipazióne di spése, re payment for citations, interpreters, witnesses and experts. Also, see ricúpero delle spése processuàli anticipàte dallo stàto and spése di esecuzióne delle condànne e di manteniménto in càrcere.

anticipazióne di spése—advance of costs. Private parties, not provided with free counsel, must advance the costs for the citations and for the payment of the interpreter and witnesses and for the costs of citations which they request for technical advisers or experts. Art. 419, Italian Code of Penal Procedure. See anticipazióne delle spése—advance of (trial) costs.

antìcipo m.—anticipation; something in advance; deposit.

antìco—ancient.

anticostituzionàle—that which is contrary to the constitution; anti-constitutional; unconstitutional.

antìcresi f.—antichresis; an hypothecation of immovables (real property) whereby a debtor or third party permits a creditor to acquire the income of the hypothecated property. The income derived is applied toward interest due on the debt and to the reduction of the capital sum of the obligation. The contract of antichresis lasts till the extinction of the obligation but cannot exceed ten years. Art. 1960-1964. Italian Civil Code.

antidàta f.—antedate; precede in time.

antidiluviàno—antediluvian; before the flood.

antidinàstico—antidynastic.

antidotàrio m.—collection of antidote prescriptions.

antìdoto m.—antidote.

antifebbrìle—a remedy against fever.

antiflogìstico—antiphlogistic; a remedy which checks inflammation.

antifúrto—relating to an antitheft apparatus.

antinomìa f.—antinomy; a contradiction in the law whereby it can be interpreted in conflicting ways; a real or apparent inconsistency between two laws or its interpretation.

antipirètico—antipyretic; a fever preventative.

antipirìna f.—antipyrene; a medicine used to reduce fever or neuralgia; a sedative.

antisèpsi f.—medical process which combats infection in wounds.

antisèttico—antiseptic.

anulàre—annular; pertaining to or in the form of a ring; fourth finger of the hand on which a ring is worn.

anzianità f.—being old; seniority in service in a position.

anziàno m.—one of advanced years; elder; senior in years or position.

aontàre—to affront; to offend; to disdain. Also, adontàre.

apatìa f.—apathy; insensibility; indifference.

apertúra f.—aperture; opening.

apertúra della successióne—opening of the succession; the succession opens at the time of death in the place of the last domicile of the decedent. Art. 456, Italian Civil Code.

apertúra del testaménto—opening of the will or testament; the manner of the publication of holographic and secret wills before a notary is prescribed by law. Art. 620-623, Italian Civil Code.

apertúra di crédito bancàrio—opening or establishing bank credit. It is a contract whereby a bank obligates itself to hold a sum of money at the disposition of the other party for a specified period or for an indeterminate time. Art. 1842-1845, Italian Civil Code.

apiressía f.—apyrexia; apirexy; absence of fever.

apirètico—apyretic; without fever.

apòcrifo—apocryphal; not authentic; of doubtful authenticity; false; spurious.

apògrafo m.—apograph; transcript; copy.

apòlide m.—stateless person; one who is not a citizen of any nation. In that event, the laws of the place where he resides apply in all cases in which the national law must be applied. Art. 29, Preliminary Dispositions.

apolítico—one who is not a member of any political party.

apologètica f.—apologetics; a branch of theology concerned with the defense of religion.

apologia f.—a writing or speech in defense of someone or something.

apologísta m.—apologist; one who writes or speaks in defense of Christianity and religion.

apoplessía f.—apoplexy; break or rupture of a blood vessel in the brain.

apoplèttico—apoplectic.

apostasía f.—apostasy; renunciation of a religion by embracing a false one or none at all.

apòstata m.—an apostate; one who forsakes his church or party.

appaciaménto m. — act of making peace; pacification.

appaciàre—to make peace; to placate; to reconciliate.

appacificàre—to make peace; to placate; to reconciliate.

appagàbile—capable of being satisfied or contented.

appagaménto m.—act of satisfying; satisfaction.

appagàre—to content; to please; to satisfy.

appaltànte m.—one for whom a contract to perform work or render services is intended, be it a private party or public agency.

appaltàre—to rent; to lease; to take a subscription to the theater; to enter into a contract with a public agency or private party to perform work or render services.

appaltatóre m.—one who enters into a contract with a private party or public agency to perform work or render services at a determined price; a concessionaire; an impresario; manager; contractor; leaseholder.

appàlto m.—a contract whereby one party assumes the obligation to perform certain work or to render services at a determined price, and to provide the organization of the means necessary to complete the undertaking together with its management, all at his own risk. Art. 1655-1677, Italian Civil Code.

appanàggio m.—appanage; provision for the younger members of a royal family by way of funds, grants of lands or offices; a territorial dependency; that which appertains by custom or right.

apparàto m.—apparatus; that which is necessary to achieve a given purpose; ornament; fitting.

apparentàre—to marry into; to become familiar.

appartaménto m.—apartment.

appartàre—to go away; to separate; to put aside.

appellàbile—appealable.

appellabilità f.—possibility of being appealed.

appellànte m.—appellant.

appellàre—to appeal; to name.

appèllo m.—appeal. Civil appeals are governed by Art. 339-359, Italian Code of Civil Procedure. Criminal appeals are governed by Art. 511-523 and Art. 190-218 (impugnazióni), Italian Code of Penal Procedure.

appendíce f.—appendix.

appendicíte f.—appendicitis.

appiccàre—to hang; to attach; to suspend.

appicciàre—to light; to illuminate; to attach.

appiccicàre—to unite things together with mucilage or glue; to attach together.

appigionaménto m.—the act of renting a house or apartment.

appigionàre—to let a house or apartment on rental.

appoderàre—to take possession of land for cultivation.

appoderàrsi—to settle on a farm for cultivation.

appoderazióne f.—the taking possession of land for cultivation.

apportàre—to carry; to transfer something from one place to another.

apportatóre m.—one who brings; messenger.

appòrto m.—contribution; the contribution of a partner to partnership capital.

apposizióne dei sigílli — attaching seals; a procedure followed to prevent the removal of personal property belonging to a decedent, bankrupt or a minor without a guardian. Art. 752-761, Italian Code of Civil Procedure.

apposizióne di tèrmini—the fixing of boundaries of contiguous properties. Art. 951, Italian Civil Code; Art. 8, subd. 2, Italian Code of Civil Procedure. See azióne per apposizióne di tèrmini.

appòsta—with determination; knowingly; for a stated purpose.

appostaménto m.—ambush.

appostàre—to ambush; to spy.

apprendísta m.—apprentice; novice. See Art. 2130-2134, Italian Civil Code for provisions relative to duration of apprenticeship, compensation, certification and rules applicable. Also, tirocínio m.—apprenticeship.

appresellàre—to divide land in parcels for cultivation.

apprestàre—to prepare; to put together.

approdàre—to reach shore; to land; to disembark; to flourish (plants); to plant vines along banks of earth.

appròdo m.—landing; landing place; port of call.

approffitàre—to profit; to turn to one's advantage.

appropiàre—to appropriate; to take.

appropiazióne f.—appropriation.

appropiazióne indébita—unlawful appropriation; the crime committed by one having possession of another's personal property or money who uses it to acquire an unlawful gain for himself or a third party. Art. 646, Italian Penal Code.

approvàre—to approve; to acclaim; to ratify; to confirm; to pass (an examination).

approvazióne f.—approval.

appuntaménto m.—appointment.

appuntàre—to point at; to make a point (to a pencil); to attach; to make notes; to accuse.

appuntàto—noted; registered; precise; affected.

appuntatúra f.—a fine imposed for dereliction of duty in office; censure.

appúnto m.—a note to assist the memory; accusation.

appúnto—at the opportune moment; precisely.

a prónti—in commercial jargon, cash on delivery of the merchandise.

aquiliàna (cólpa)—Aquilian wrong; a wrong that does not arise out of a contractual obligation; it arises from the failure to exercise due care and is tortious in nature. Art. 2043-2059, Italian Civil Code.

aràre—to plow.

aràtro m.—plough.

arbitràggio m. — arbitrage; financial transaction involving the purchase and sale of commodities, securities or monies in different markets to assure profits from differing prices.

arbitràle (claùsola) — arbitration clause. See claùsola compromissòria.

arbitràre—to arbitrate.

arbitrària invasióne e occupazióne di aziènde agrícole o industriàli—arbitrary invasion and occupation of agricultural or industrial plants and businesses. Art. 508, Italian Penal Code. See sabotàggio.

arbitràrio—arbitrary.

arbitràto m.—arbitrator's award; office of an arbitrator. See compromésso. Art. 806-831, Italian Code of Civil Procedure.

àrbitro m.—arbitrator.

arcàno—arcane; hidden; mysterious; secret.

arcàrio m.—custodian of a treasure.

archívio m.—archive.

archivìsta m.—archivist.

ardènte—ardent; burning; impetuous; fiery.

ardènza f.—ardor; burning.

àrdere—to burn; to consume; to inflame.

ardíre—to dare; to risk; to try dangerous things with excess of zeal.

arditaménte — without care; with daring.

ardíto—brave; valiant; assault trooper.

arèngo m.—Medieval popular assembly of the Italian communes.

àrgano m.—crane (mechanical).

argentàto—silvered; silver-plated.

argentatóre m.—silversmith.

argentería f.—silverware.

argentière m.—silversmith.

argènto m.—silver.

arginaménto m.—embankment; dike.

arginàre—to embank; to enclose; to

confine; to protect with a mound or dike.

àrgine m.—a work of earth or masonry to prevent inundation of land; dike. See spónde e àrgine (riparazióne di), Art. 915, Italian Civil Code.

aridità f.—aridity.

àrido—arid.

àrma f.—a branch of military service, such as infantry, artillery, etc.

armaménto m.—arming; armament.

armàre—to arm.

armàta f.—fleet of warships.

armàto—armed.

armatúra f.—armature; armor.

àrme f. (àrmi pl.)—arms; weapons. Art. 585, 704, 53, 55, 242, Italian Penal Code.

arménto m.—herd.

àrmi da fuòco—fire-arms. See àrme.

arnése m.—tools; equipment.

arpènto m.—ancient agricultural measure indicating the amount of land which could be ploughed in one day (about 3,000 square meters).

arpióne m.—hinge.

àrra f.—deposit; a pledge or promise. See capàrra.

àrra confirmatòria—See capàrra confirmatòria.

àrra penitenziàle—See capàrra penitenziàle.

arredaménto m.—act of equipping or adorning; furnishing.

arredàre—to equip; to adorn; to furnish and decorate.

arrèdo m.—articles which serve to furnish.

arrèndere—to surrender; to submit; to yield. See résa.

arrestàre—to arrest; to capture; to detain; to stop.

arrestàto m.—one who has been arrested or detained.

arrèsto m.—arrest; detention; a punishment inflicted by incarceration for the crime of contravvenzióne. It may last from five days to three years.

Art. 17, 18, 25, 26, Italian Penal Code. See contravvenzióne and ammènda.

arrèsto illegàle—illegal arrest. It is committed by a public official abusing the inherent powers of his office. Art. 606, Italian Penal Code.

arretràto—arrears; backward.

arrichiménto m.—enrichment.

arrichiménto sènza càusa—unjust enrichment. See azióne di arrichiménto sènza càusa. Art. 2041, 2042, Italian Civil Code.

arrichíre—to enrich; to embelish.

arriffàre—to raffle; to dispose by lottery.

arrínga f.—harangue; a speech made in public; a lawyer's summation or final argument before the case goes to the jury.

arringàre—to harangue; to address.

arrischiàre—to risk; to put in peril; to venture.

arrischiataménte — perilously; with risk.

arrischiàto—full of risks; perilous; imprudent.

arrisicàre—to risk; to put in peril.

arrogàre—to arrogate; to assume or appropriate without right; under the Civil Law, to adopt a person of full age or sui juris.

arrogazióne f.—arrogation; the Civil Law adoption of a person of full age or sui juris.

arruffamatàsse m.—an intriguer; deceiver. See imbroglióne.

arruffàre—to deceive in such a manner as to cause confusion.

arruffóne m.—deceiver; confounder.

arsenàle m.—arsenal.

arsènico m.—arsenic.

arsióne f.—excessive heat; dryness; heat from fever.

arsíre—to dry.

àrso—burned.

artefàre—to falsify with artifice; to adulterate.

artefàtto—artifact; made by artifice.

artéfice m.—artificer; craftsman.

artèria f.—artery.

arteriàle—arterial.

arterioscleròsi f.—arteriosclerosis.

artícolo di fóndo—editorial. See editoriàle.

artière m.—artisan; soldier in the corps of engineers.

artificiàle—artificial.

artificière m.—a member of the military who prepares and is charged with the custody of explosives and arms.

artifízio m.—artifice.

artigianàto m.—the craft of artisans.

artigiàno m.—artisan; craftsman.

artiglière m.—artilleryman.

artiglería f.—artillery.

artríte f.—arthritis.

artrítico—arthritic.

ascendènte m.—ascendant; a person with whom one is related in an ascending line such as a grandparent.

ascendènza f.—ascendance.

ascéndere—to ascend.

ascensóre m.—elevator. See elevatóre.

ascèta m.—an ascetic.

ascètica f.—asceticism.

ascetísmo m.—ascetism.

ascóndere — to abscond; to remain hidden.

asèpsi f.—absence of infection in wounds or organisms that produce sepsis.

asèttico—aseptic.

asfissiàre—to asphyxiate; to suffocate.

asfissiàto—asphyxiated.

asílo m.—refuge; asylum.

àsma f.—asthma.

asmàtico—asthmatic.

aspettàre—to wait for; to await; to expect.

aspettatíva f.—expectation; the condition of an employee temporarily on leave due to illness or family obligations.

aspirína f.—aspirin.

asportàbile—transportable.

asportàre—to carry away; to transport.

asportazióne f.—asportation; removal of goods from one place to another.

assagiàre—to try; to taste; to try in small quantity to distinguish the taste.

assaliménto m.—assault; attack.

assalíre—to assault; to attack.

assalitóre—assailant.

assaltàre—to assault with force.

assaltatóre m.—assailant.

assàlto m.—assault; attack.

assassína f.—assassin.

assassinaménto m.—assassination.

assassinàre—to assassinate.

assassínio m.—assassination.

assassíno m.—assassin.

àsse m.—axle; axis.

àsse m.— the Roman coin which weighed a pound (also called *libra*) and was divided into twelve parts called *unciae*; axis.

àsse demaniàle—all the immovable (real) property of the State.

àsse ecclesiàstico—all the property of the church.

àsse ereditàrio—the entire inheritance.

àsse patrimoniàle—the entire estate.

assecondàre—to second; to favor.

assediànte—besieger.

assediàre—to besiege.

assediàto—besieged.

assediatóre m.—besieger.

assèdio m.—siege.

assegnàbile—assignable.

assegnaménto m.—assignment.

assegnàre—to assign.

assegnàto—assigned; a moderate person with regards to spending.

assegnazióne f.—assignment.

asségno m.—an assignment; a sum which is paid periodically; an order of payment; check. See **asségno bancàrio.**

asségno bancàrio—check; a bill of exchange or draft drawn by a drawer-depositor upon a drawee bank where he maintains funds on deposit and which draft is payable on demand. Asségni (Checks), Usual Laws, Appendix to Italian Civil Code.

assègno bancàrio garantíto—certified check.

asségno bancàrio sbarràto or asségno sbarràto—crossed check. It has two parallel lines on its face. The crossing is general if it is payable to a bank or banker. It must be paid by the drawee only to a bank or banker or a client of the drawee. If the crossed check is payable to a specified bank or banker, it is a special crossing and must be paid by the drawee to the designated bank or banker. If the drawee is the bank designated, it may pay to its client. Art. 40, 41, Asségni (Checks), Usual Laws, Appendix to Italian Civil Code.

asségno circolàre—cashier's check. It is a bill of exchange drawn by a bank upon itself and payable to the payee. It is considered accepted by the bank by reason of its issuance. Art. 82-86, Asségni (Checks), Usual Laws, Appendix to Italian Civil Code. See **vàglia postàle.**

asségno turístico—tourist check. Art. 44, Asségni (Checks), Usual Laws, Appendix to Italian Civil Code.

assemblèa f.—assembly; meeting.

assemblèa della società per azióni—corporate meeting. It is ordinary in the following instances: (1) when approving the budget; (2) when nominating officers, managers, directors and chairman of the board of directors; (3) when fixing the compensation of officers and directors if not set out in the charter; (4) when considering other matters relative to management. The ordinary meeting must be held at least once a year. The extraordinary meeting is convoked to consider modifications of the charter, issuance of obligations and determination of the power of liquidators. Notice of extraordinary meetings must be published in the Official Gazette at least fifteen days prior to the meeting. When the rights of one of various classes of stock have been prejudiced at a meeting, a special meeting of shareholders of that class must be held to pass thereon. The rules of extraordinary meetings apply to these. Art. 2363-2379, Italian Civil Code.

assemblèa delle associazióne—meeting of associations or unincorporated groups. An annual meeting for the approval of the budget is required. A meeting must also be called when necessary or when requested by, at least, a tenth of the members. Resolutions are passed by a majority with the attendance of at least half the membership. Art. 20, 21, Italian Civil Code.

assemblèa del condomínio—meeting of condominium (members). Art. 1130-1139, Italian Civil Code for powers of a condominium.

assemblèa delle cooperatíve—meeting of cooperatives. Art. 2516, 2532-2534, Italian Civil Code.

assembràglia f.—a meeting of militia; affray; clash; fight.

assembraménto m.—open air meeting; crowd; demonstration.

assembràre—to gather; to meet.

assennàre—to advert; to instruct; to hint.

assennataménte — with good sense; judiciously; wisely.

assennatézza f.—having good sense; being judicious.

assennàto—one who is judicious; one with good sense.

assènso m.—assent; consent; approval.

assentaménto m.—absence.

assentàre—to retire; to absent oneself; to consent.

assènte—absent.

assenteísmo m.—absenteeism.

assentiménto m.—act of absenting.

assentíre—to consent; to approve.

assènza f.—absence. For absence of a

person, see Art. 48-57, Italian Civil Code. Also, see **scompàrsa.**

asseríre—to affirm; to assert; to declare; to sustain.

asserràre—to enclose; to pack.

assèrto m.—assertion; confirmed opinion.

assertóre m.—one who asserts or sustains vigorously.

asservíre—to subjugate; to render or to render oneself subject.

asserzióne f.—assertion.

assessoràto m.—grade and office of an assessor; commission.

assessóre m.—assessor; an advisor or assistant; an adjunct to a superior judge who assists him; member of an administrative commission; a municipal official who assists the mayor; a consultant.

asseverànza f.—asservation; emphatic assertion.

asseveràre—to asseverate; to affirm or declare positively.

asseverataménte—affirmatively.

asseverazióne f.—affirmation; assurance.

assicuràbile—insurable.

assicuraménto m.—assurance; security; insurance.

assicuràre—to insure.

assicuràto—insured.

assicuratóre m.—insurer.

assicurazióne f.—insurance; the contract of insurance whereby an insurer, upon payment of a premium, undertakes to indemnify the insured for damages sustained through accident, or to pay a sum or annuity upon the happening of an event contingent on human life. Art. 1882-1932, Italian Civil Code. See **pòlizza d'assicurazióne**—policy of insurance.

assicurazióne cóntro i dànni—insurance against loss. The contract of insurance against loss is void, if at the moment of its inception, the insured does not have an insurable interest to receive compensation for damages. Art. 1904-1918, Italian Civil Code.

assicurazióne sulla víta—life insurance. It can be taken on one's own life or on the life of a third party. In the latter event, it is not valid unless the third party or his legal representative consents in writing. A policy of life insurance in favor of a third party is valid. The beneficiary may be named generically. Art. 1919, 1920-1927, Italian Civil Code.

assísa f.—uniform; livery.

assíse f.—a tribunal or legislative assembly; Court of Assize. See **córte d'assíse.**

assistènte m.—assistant.

assistènza f.—assistance; help; succor.

assistenziàle—helpful; beneficial; in the sense of werks of welfare or aid. See **patronàto assistenziàle.**

assistenziàrio m.—institute which provides social assistance.

associaménto m.—a contract of agistment. See **sòccida** and **associàre.**

assocciàre—to enter into a contract of agistment whereby one party turns over a quantity of livestock to another to care and feed, and then divide the profits or losses derived. See **sòccida.**

associàre—to associate; to join as a partner or ally; to unite.

associàto—a subscriber to a book or publication; partner.

associazióne f.—association; partnership.

associazióne in partecipazióne—association in participation; a limited partnership; the special partners share in the profits and losses but the losses cannot exceed the amount of capital contribution. Art. 2549-2554, Italian Civil Code.

associazióne per delínquere—association of persons for a criminal purpose. When three or more persons associate themselves for the purpose of committing many crimes, those who promote, or constitute, or organize the association are punished, for that sole reason, with imprisonment. Art. 416, Italian Penal Code.

assoggettaménto m.—submission; subjection.

assoggettàre—to subject.

assolcàre—to plough; to furrow. See **solcàre.**

assoldaménto m.—enlistment; pay; soldier's compensation.

assoldàre—to enlist; to enroll; to enroll in a militia.

assolutaménte — absolutely; without doubt.

assolutézza f.—the quality of being absolute.

assolutísmo m.—absolutism; a form of government with unlimited powers.

assolutísta m.—absolutist.

assolúto—absolute; free of restriction or limitation; imperious.

assolutóre m.—one who absolves.

assoluzióne f.—absolution; acquittal.

assòlvere—to absolve.

assommàre—to sum up; to conclude; to comprehensively express; to come afloat.

assopíre — to induce sleepiness or lethargy; to put to sleep.

assopíto—sleepy; drowsy.

assorbènte—absorbent; engrossing.

assorbiménto m.—act of absorbing.

assorbíre—to absorb.

assordaménto m.—act of deafening

assordàre—to deafen.

assordàto—deafened.

assortiménto m.—assortment.

assortíre—to sort; to choose; to furnish.

assortíto—assorted; well furnished.

assòrto — absorbed; engrossed; preoccupied.

assúmere—to assume; to take office; to undertake a task; to receive testimonial proof.

assúnto m.—task; undertaking.

assunzióne f.—assumption.

assunzióne del débito—assumption of debt. See **accòllo di débito**, the assumption by a third party of the obligation of a debtor. Art. 1273, Italian Civil Code.

assunzióne delle pròve—assumption of the burden of proof.

àsta f.—staff; pole; auction.

àsta desèrta—a public sale or auction with no bidders.

àsta (véndere all')—to sell at auction.

astànte—assistant; present; stand-by; a physician or surgeon on duty in a hospital.

astantería f.—receiving ward of a hospital.

astèmio m.—abstemious; temperate.

astenére—to abstain.

astenía f.—asthenia; debility; want or loss of strength.

astensióne f.—abstention.

astèrgere—to dry; to clean; to purge.

astigmatísmo m.—astigmatism.

astinènte—one who abstains.

astinènza f.—abstinence.

astràrre—to abstract; to separate with the mind; to draw away; to take away; to remove.

astrattàgine f.—abstraction.

astrattaménte—abstractly.

astràtto—abstract.

astrazióne f. — abstraction; abstract concept.

astringènte—astringent.

astríngere—to compress; to construct.

àstro m.—celestial body; star.

astrochímica f.—the science which studies the chemical composition of the stars.

astrofísica f.—astrophysics.

astronomía f.—astronomy.

astronòmico—astronomical.

astrònomo m.—astronomer.

astrúso—abstruse.

astúccio m.—case; jewel box; instrument case.

astúto—astute; shrewd; cunning.

astúzia f.—cunning; guile.

atassía f.—ataxia; loss of muscular coordination.

atàssico m.—one having ataxia.

atavísmo m.—atavism; reappearance in an individual of the characteristics of a remote ancestor.

àtavo m.—great-great grandfather.

ateísmo m.—atheism.

ateísta m.—atheist.

ateístico—atheistic.

àteo m.—atheist.

atermàno—body which prevents the passage of heat radiation.

atèrmico—a chemical reaction which is not influenced by temperature.

atipía f.—functional or morphological deviation from the usual or normal type.

atípico—atypical; not conforming to type; abnormal.

atmosfèra f.—atmosphere.

atmosfèrico—atmospheric. See **inquinaménto atmosfèrico**.

atòllo m.—atoll.

atòmico—atomic.

àtomo m.—atom.

atonía f.—atonia; atony; lack of tone or vital energy; weakness of the system or a contractile organ; weakness from lack of stress.

àtono—weak; without accent; that which is unaccented.

atrepsía f.—an illness of infants characterized by progressive deterioration and due to insufficient nutrition or gastrointestinal atrophy.

atresía f.—occlusion of a natural passage or channel in the body; lacking perforation.

atrichía f.—congenital lack of hair. See **alopecía**.

atróce—atrocious; cruel; ferocious; terrible.

atroceménte—atrociously.

atrocità f.—atrocity.

atrofía f.—atrophy.

atropína f.—atropine; a poisonous alkaloid extracted from belladonna and other solanaceous plants.

atropísmo m.—chronic poisoning produced by misuse of atropine.

attaccabríghe m.—one who seeks quarrels.

attacalíte m.—one who quarrels or starts litigation; barrator; one who commits barratry.

attacàre—to attach; to attack.

attacàto—attached.

attàcco m.—attack; assault.

atteggiaménto m.—attitude; posture.

atteggiàre—to express with acts or actions.

attempàre—to grow old.

attempàto—one grown old before his time.

attendaménto m.—encampment.

attendàre—to encamp.

attendàto — encamped; provisional lodging; lodged as well as possible.

attendènte m.—attendant.

attèndere—to await; to attend; to listen and observe attently.

attendíbile—that which merits faith; to be considered.

attenènte—related; that which belongs.

attenènza f.—pertaining; related to.

attenére—to belong to; to be related; to concern; to keep one's promise.

attentàre—to attempt; to make an attempt at an act which may be criminal in nature.

attentàti alla sicurézza degli impiànti di energía elèttrica e del gas ovvéro delle púbbliche comunicazióne—attempts against the security of electric energy and gas plants, or against public communications. Whoever attempts acts against the security of the workshops, the works, the machinery or other means destined to the production or to the transmission of electric energy or gas for illumination or for industries, so long as the act may cause danger to public safety, is punished with imprisonment. The same penalty is applicable to anyone who makes attempts against the security of public telegraph or telephone communications, so long as the act may cause danger to public safety. If a disaster follows the act, the punishment is increased. Art. 433, Italian Penal Code.

attentàti alla sicurézza dei trraspòrti—attempts against the security of transports. Whoever places in danger the security of public transports by land, sea or air is punished with imprisonment. The launching of bodies which cause damage or projectiles against vehicles in motion which are destined for public transport by land, sea or air is also punished with imprisonment. If a disaster follows the act, the punishment is increased. Art. 432, Italian Penal Code.

attentàto m.—criminal attempt; crime.

attentatóre m.—one who attempts to commit an act which may be criminal in nature.

attenuànte—attenuant; a mitigating circumstance. Art. 62-70; Italian Penal Code.

attenuàre—to attenuate; to weaken; to lessen; to mitigate.

attenuateménte—with attenuation; in a mitigating manner.

attenuàto—diminished; weakened.

attenuazióne f.—attenuation.

attergàre—to write on the back of a document or letter.

atterràggio m.—to land with an airplane; to dock.

atterraménto m.—act of landing.

atterràre—to land; to cast down; to prostrate.

atterríre—to terrify; to frighten.

attestàre—to attest; to sign as a witness.

attestàto—written testimony; certificate; proof.

attestazióne f.—attestation.

attestazióne fàlsa—false attestation. It concerns that made by a public official or employee or private person. Art. 476-493, Italian Penal Code.

àtti d'emulazióne—acts of competition. The owner of property cannot commit acts which annoy or damage others. Art. 833, Italian Civil Code.

àtti del govèrno—acts of government; acts of the executive power or its ministers in the form of decrees, instructions, and regulations.

àtti dello stàto civíle—civil status documents or acts. They are kept in each commune in the civil status office. They are: (1) register of citizenship; (2) register of births; (3) register of weddings; (4) register of deaths. Art. 449-455, Italian Civil Code; Art. 1, 14, **Stàto Civíle** (Civil Status), Usual Laws, Appendix to Italian Civil Code.

àtti di notorietà—verified acts or declarations attesting to matters of fact made by four or more witnesses. Art. 4, **Documentazióne Amministratíva** (Administrative Documentation), Usual Laws, Appendix to Italian Code of Civil Procedure.

àtti di tollerànza—tolerated acts. The acts performed with the toleration of others may not serve as the basis for the acquisition of possession. They are presumed to have been performed without intention of exercising a right to acquire possession over neighboring land, but to have been done for reasons of maintaining good relations as a neighbor or friend. Art. 1144, Italian Civil Code.

àtti giudiziàri—judicial acts or documents. These comprise citations and summonses, complaints and petitions, the appearances of the parties, the proceedings before the Court and the orders, decrees and judgments thereof.

attíguo—attiguous; contiguous; that which is in contact.

attinoterapía f.—cure through ultraviolet rays; radiotherapy.

attivàre—to activate; to hasten.

attívo—active; assets (m.).

attizzaménto m.—incitement; provocation.

attizzàre—to rake a fire; to incite; to provoke.

attizzatóre m.—one who rakes; one who incites.

àtto—apt; qualified.

àtto m.—act; expression of the will; a deed or instrument of a transaction; a writing or a certificate attesting to a public or private record; document; the writing presented by a party to the court or judge; the order or ruling of a judge.

àtto amministratívo — administrative act or ruling.

àtto d'accúsa—an accusation of criminal offense similar to an information.

àtto del parlaménto—act of parliament.

àtto di mòrte—death certificate.

àtto di nàscita—birth certificate.

àtto di nazionalità—certificate of nationality.

àtto púbblico—public or official document. It is an official, public document written in accordance with prescribed legal formality by a notary or other public official giving the document authenticity. Art. 2699-2701, Italian Civil Code.

attóre m.—actor; plaintiff in a civil case. See **convenúto.**

attribuíre—to attribute; to ascribe; to consider as belonging; impute.

attribuzióne f.—attribution; authority or function of a public official.

attuàre—to actuate; to execute.

attuariàle—actuarial.

attuariàto m.—position of actuary; office of a court clerk or registrar.

attuàrio m.—actuary; a public official who is custodian of public documents; registrar.

auditóre m.—a judge of certain tribunals. See **uditóre,** the first grade of a career magistrate in Italy.

audizióne f.—a hearing; hearing the testimony of witnesses.

àula f.—great hall; meeting place; court room.

aureomicína f.—aureomycin.

auricolàre—pertaining to the ear; *testimòne auricolàre*—one who has heard with his own ears; a witness testifying to facts he heard himself.

auscultàre—auscultate; to examine by auscultation.

auscultazióne f.—auscultation; the act of listening to sounds within a body by the use of a stethoscope or other instrument.

ausílio m.—aid; defense; help.

autèntica f.—authentic.

autenticaménte—authentically.

autenticàre—to authenticate.

autenticazióne f.—authentication.

autenticazióne della scrittúra privàta —authentication of a private document. The subscribed signatures are attested by a notary or other public official empowered to give them authenticity. The authentication consists in an attestation of the public official that the subscribed signatures were affixed in his presence after first ascertaining the identity of the subscribers. Copies thereof may also be authenticated. Art. 2703, 2712, 2715, 2716, 2719, Italian Civil Code. See sottoscrizióne autenticàta della scrittúra privàta.

autenticazióne di àtti púbblici—authentication of public documents. They are attested by a notary or other official empowered to give them authenticity. Copies thereof may also be authenticated. Art. 2699-2701, 2712, 2714, 2716, 2719, Italian Civil Code; Art. 743-745, Italian Code of Civil Procedure.

autenticazióne di sottoscrizióne—authentication of subscribed signatures. They are attested by a notary or other official authorized to give them authenticity. See autenticazióne della scrittúra privàta and autenticazióne di àtti púbblici.

autèntica f.—authentication.

autenticitá f.—authenticity.

autèntico—authentic.

autière m.—a soldier in the automobile corps.

autísmo m.—autism; daydreaming; fantasy; a condition where one is lost in his own thoughts and loses interest in the world of reality.

autísta m.—one who drives an automobile for a living; chauffeur.

àuto—a prefix derived from the Greek, meaning by itself.

àuto f.—auto; automobile.

àutobus m.—autobus; omnibus.

autocàrro m.—truck which transports freight.

autogíro m.—autogyro; helicopter.

autografía f.—autography.

autògrafo—handwritten; holographic.

autòma m.—automaton.

automàtico—automatic.

automèzzo m.—generic name comprising every type of motor driven vehicle. Also, autoveícolo.

automòbile—moving by self propelled means.

automòbile f.—automobile; motor vehicle.

autonomía f.—autonomy; political independence; faculty of governing oneself according to self-imposed laws.

autònomo—autonomous.

autoparchéggio m.—automobile parking space; auto parking area.

autopómpa f.—fire truck equipped with a water pump to extinguish fires.

autopsía f.—autopsy.

autóre m; autríce f.—author; authoress.

autorévole—one who has authority and is held in high respect; accredited; esteemed; important.

autorevolménte—with authority.

autoriméssa f.—garage.

autorità f.—authority; person or persons invested with public authority; legitimate power to command; force; power; the Public Security Authorities, the head of which is the Questóre. Sicurézza Púbblica (Public Security), Tèsto Único (Unified

Text), Usual Laws, Appendix to Italian Code of Penal Procedure.

autoritàrio—authoritarian.

autorizzàre—to authorize.

autorizzazióne f.—authorization; permission.

autoscàfo m.—motorboat.

autostràda f.—super-highway.

autosuggestióne f.—autosuggestion.

autotrèno m.—tow truck.

autoveícolo m.—generic name comprising every type of motor driven vehicle. Also, **automèzzo.**

àva f.—grandmother.

avallànte m.—guarantor; surety.

avallàre—to guarantee.

avallàto—one for whose benefit a guarantee has been made.

avàllo m.—guaranty; surety. Art. 35-37, Cambiàle (Drafts), Usual Laws, Appendix to Italian Civil Code.

avanguàrdia f.—vanguard.

avanguardísta m.—one who has extreme ideas.

avanzaménto m.—advancement; promotion.

avanzàre—to advance; to present; to place before; to succeed to a higher grade.

avanzàta f. — advance forward by troops.

avanzàto — advanced in years; advanced season.

avànzi m.—ruins; remnants; residue.

avànzo m.—remnant; residue; remainder; profit; gain.

avaría f.—loss or damage to persons or things transported by land, sea or air; loss or damage suffered by a vessel or its cargo; ship's average; generally, damage to goods in transit. Art. 1678-1702, 1787, Italian Civil Code. Art. 302, 469-481, 489-500, 502-504, 981-984, Italian Navigation Code.

avariàre—to sustain loss or damage.

avariàto—damaged.

avarízia f.—avarice.

avàro—miserly; stingy; avaricious; miser (m.).

avèllo m.—tomb; sepulchre.

avènte càusa—assignee. opp. **dànte càusa**—assignor.

avioriméssa f.—hangar.

avíto—hereditary; ancestral.

àvo m.—grandfather.

avocàre—to appeal; to remove a case from an inferior judge.

avocazióne f.—an appeal.

avogadóre, avvogàdore m.—one of three Patrician magistrates of the Venetian Republic charged with watching over the interests of the Republic.

àvola f.—grandmother.

àvolo m.—grandfather.

avulsióne f.—avulsion; a sudden removal of a quantity of soil from the land of one owner which is deposited upon the land of another by the action of the water. The owner of the land on which the soil is deposited acquires the property. He must, however, pay the other owner indemnification within the limits of the greater value brought to the land by the avulsion. Art. 944, Italian Civil Code.

avvelenaménto m.—poisoning.

avvelenàre—to poison.

avvelenatóre m.—poisoner.

avveniménto m.—event; occurrence.

avventàre—to launch; to throw with violence; to assail.

avventatàggine f.—rashness; imprudence; precipitation.

avventízio — adventitious; acquisition of property which is not derived through heredity.

avveraménto m.—averment; positive statement.

avveràre—to aver; to affirm; to allege as a fact.

avversàre—to oppose; to be against; to resist.

avversàrio m.—adversary; opponent; opposing lawyer or defense counsel.

avvertènza f.—attention; consideration; cautioning; warning; preface
to a book.

avvertiménto m.—counsel; warning;
caution; admonition. See **ammoniménto.**

avvertíre—to admonish; to warn; to
advise.

avvíso m.—news; announcement; opinion; advertisement; notice; advice;
counsel.

avvíso al púbblico—notice to the
public.

avvíso di depòsito—a notice sent by
the clerk of the court in a criminal
case to the prosecutor regarding
decisions and orders of the court. See
comunicazióne (del cancellière).

avvíso di procediménto—notice of proceeding. A notice in a criminal case
sent to the accused, the injured party
and other parties in interest setting
forth the law which was infringed
and calling upon them to retain counsel. Also, **comunicazióne giudizària.**
Art. 304, Italian Code of Penal Procedure.

avvocàti iscrítti nell'àlbo speciàle—
lawyers inscribed in the special roll
(of attorneys). These are lawyers
who have been admitted to practice
before the Court of Cassation, the
Council of State, the Court of the
Exchequer, the Superior Tribunal
for Public Waters and the Central
Commission for Direct Taxes. Art.
4, 33, **Avvocàti e Procuratóri**
(Lawyers and Procurators), Usual
Laws, Appendix to Italian Code of
Civil Procedure.

avvocàto m.—lawyer. He is admitted
to practice the legal profession before all the Courts of Appeals, the
Tribunals and Praetorships in the
Republic. Art. 2, 4, 27, **Avvocàti e
Procuratóri** (Lawyers and Procurators), Usual Laws, Appendix to Italian Code of Civil Procedure. See
avvocàti iscrítti nell'àlbo speciàle
(lawyers inscribed in the special
roll).

avvocatúra f.—legal profession; membership in the Bar.

azlènda f.—business; concern; man-

agement. Art. 2555-2562, Italian Civil
Code.

azionàrio—pertaining to a share of
capital stock.

azióne f.—action; institution of a legal
action or proceeding; operation;
gesture; share of capital stock.

azióne cambiària—action on commercial paper. It is brought by the holder
of such paper to obtain payment.
The actions are: (1) **"arrichiménto,"**
(2) **"causàle,"** (3) **"dirètta,"** and (4)
"regrèsso." See individual definitions, and Art. 49-82, 94, 95, **Cambiàle**
(Drafts), Usual Laws, Appendix to
Italian Civil Code.

azióne cambiària causàle—causal action on a draft. This is an action
with direct causal connection between the immediate parties to the
action. It is based on the underlying
obligation which gave rise to the
draft or commercial paper. Art. 58,
Assègni (Checks) and Art. 66, **Cambiàle** (Drafts), Usual Laws, Appendix to Italian Civil Code.

azióne cambiària dirètta—direct action
on a draft. This is an action brought
by the holder directly against the
party primarily liable such as the
acceptor and his guarantors. A protest is not required in this case. The
action is prescribed in three years
from maturity. Art. 49, 94, 95, **Cambiàle** (Drafts), Usual Laws, Appendix to Italian Civil Code.

azióne cambiària di regrèsso—action of
regression on a draft. This is an
action brought by the holder against
prior endorsers and other co-obligors.
Unless bankruptcy of the obligor has
been declared, a Protest is required.
The action is prescribed in one year
of the Protest or of maturity when
Protest has been excused. See Art.
49, 50-60, 94, 95, **Cambiàle** (Drafts),
Usual Laws, Appendix to Italian Civil
Code.

azióne civìle—civil action. Art. 24,
Constitution of the Italian Republic;
Art. 2907, Italian Civil Code; Art.
99-111, 69, Italian Code of Civil Procedure. See **udiènza civíle** and
**azióne civíle trasferíta in procèsso
penàle.**

azióne civíle trasferíta in procèsso penàle—civil action transferred to a penal trial. These involve damages sustained during the commission of a crime. Art. 22-28, Italian Code of Penal Procedure; Art. 185, Italian Penal Code. See **azióne civíle** and **udiènza civíle.**

azióne confessória—an action to enforce a servitude on real property. Art. 1079, Italian Civil Code and Art. 15, 21, Italian Code of Civil Procedure.

azióne del pagaménto indébito—action for restoration of a payment not owed. Whoever has made a payment which he does not owe, has the right to demand restoration of that which he has paid. Also, **azióne di ripetizióne,** Art. 2033-2040, Italian Civil Code.

azióne di annullaménto del contràtto—action for annulment of a contract. Art. 1441-1446, Italian Civil Code.

azióne di arrichiménto cambiàrio—action for (unjust) enrichment on a draft. Where the holder has lost his right of action against all those liable on the draft as well as the right to a causal action, he may proceed against the drawer or acceptor or endorser for the sum whereby they were unjustly enriched. See Art. 67 **Cambiàle** (Drafts); Art. 59 **Asségni** (Checks), Usual Laws, Appendix to Italian Civil Code. Also, **azióne per indébito arrichiménto.**

azióne di arrichiménto sènza càusa—action for unjust enrichment. Where one, without just cause, has enriched himself at the expense of another, he must, to that extent, indemnify the other party for the diminution of his estate. Art. 2041, 2042, Italian Civil Code.

azióne di contestazióne della legittimità—action to negate legitimacy. It is an action granted to those who would be named a parent of the child or to whomever has an interest therein. There is no prescription to this action. Art. 248, Italian Civil Code. See **azióni di stàto.**

azióne di dichiarazióne giudiziàle della

paternità e della maternità naturàle—action for the judicial determination of natural paternity and maternity. Art. 269-279, Italian Civil Code.

azióne di disconosciménto di paternità—action to disavow paternity. Also, see **disconsociménto di paternità** and **azióni di stàto,** Art. 235, 244-249, Italian Civil Code.

azióne di legittimazióne dei fígli naturàli—action for the legitimation of natural children. Art. 280-290, Italian Civil Code.

azióne di manutenzióne—an action for continuance in possession. It is available to one who has been injured in possession of real property, of a real right therein, or in an aggregate of personal property considered as a whole. He may, within a year of the injury, maintain such action for continuance of possession. Art. 1170, Italian Civil Code.

azióne di nunciazióne—declaratory action. One maintained by an owner of real property or one having the right of ownership or possession thereof to restrain any damage to his property or restrain any new work. See **denúncia di dànno temúto** and **denúncia di nuòva òpera,** Art. 1171, 1172, Italian Civil Code.

azióne di reclàmo dello stato di fíglio legíttimo—action to reclaim the status of legitimate child. It is an action granted to the child. If he has not instituted the action and has died a minor or five years after reaching majority, it may be instituted by his descendants. The action must be against both parents or in their stead against their heirs. The action cannot be prescribed against the child. Art. 249, Italian Civil Code.

azióne di regolaménto di confíni—action to establish boundaries. When the boundary between two lands is uncertain, each of the property owners may request that it be established judicially. Every means of proof is admitted. In the absence of other data, the judge will conform to the boundaries set out in the maps of the office of valuation of property. Art. 950, Italian Civil Code.

azióne di regrèsso—action of regression—An action brought by the holder of a right against his assignor for having been legitimately deprived of the right by a third party. The gist of the action is to recover back from the assignor the loss sustained. Art. 1299, 1797, 1950, Italian Civil Code. See azióne cambiària di regrèsso.

azióne di reintegrazióne—action for reintegration. It is an action for restoration of possession to the owner where he has been violently or secretly deprived of possession of property and demands possession of the same. The action must be commenced within a year and the restoration must be ordered by a judge without delay. Also, azióne di spòglio. Art. 1168, 1169, Italian Civil Code.

azióne di rescissióne del contràtto—action for rescission of a contract. Art. 1447-1452, Italian Civil Code.

azióne di rescissióne per lesióne—action of rescission for damage resulting from the division of the inheritance. Where a co-heir receives less than a quarter of the portion to which he is entitled from the estate, he may abrogate the division. See rescissióne per lesióne, Art. 763, Italian Civil Code.

azióne di riduzióne—action of reduction or diminution. This is an action granted by law to those whose portion of the inheritance has been reserved by statute. When their portion has been diminished by the decedent during his lifetime or by will, the portions alloted to others must be proportionately reduced to restore the quota reserved by statute. Art. 553-565, 536, 735, Italian Civil Code.

azióne di ripetizióne—action for restoration (of payment). Whoever has made a payment which he does not owe, has the right to demand restoration of that which he has paid. Also, azióne del pagaménto indébito. Art. 2033-2040, Italian Civil Code.

azióne di risoluzióne del contràtto—action for dissolution of a contract. In contracts with corresponding obliga-

tions, when one of the contracting parties does not perform his obligations, the other party may demand its performance or its dissolution. Grounds for excuse are impossibility of performance due to a supervening cause and unusually onerous burdens due to extraordinary and unforeseen events. Art. 1453-1467, 1372, Italian Civil Code.

azióne di rivendicazióne—action to recover possession of property. The action can be barred by adverse possession but not by prescription. Art. 948, Italian Civil Code.

azióne di spòglio—action for deprivation of possession. See azióne di reintegrazióne and Art. 1168, 1169, Italian Civil Code.

azióne estimatòria—an action to rescind a purchase contract because of hidden defects. The purchaser has the option of rescinding the contract or to take it at a reduced price. The choice is irrevocable when the demand has been made judicially. If the goods delivered perished because of the defects, the buyer has the right to rescind; if by accident or fault of the seller, or if the goods have been sold or transformed, only a reduction in price may be demanded. Art. 1492, 1491, Italian Civil Code. Also, azióne quanti minoris.

azióne generàle di arichiménto—general action for (unjust) enrichment. See azióne di arrichiménto sènza càusa. Art. 2041, 2042, Italian Civil Code.

azióne generàle di rescissióne per lesióne—general action for recission due to damage. If there is a disproportion of legal obligations between one party and the other, and it arises out of the state of need of one party of which the other took advantage to gain profit, the damaged party may seek rescission of the contract. The action may not be maintained unless the damage exceeds one-half the value of the performance rendered or promised by the damaged party at the time of the contract. Art. 1448, Italian Civil Code.

azióne imprescrittíbile—an action without prescription or statute of limitations. See **imprescrittibilità dell' azióne di nullità**—imprescriptability of an action to annul a contract, Art. 1422, Italian Civil Code.

azióne negatòria—negatory action; one where the owner seeks to declare the inexistence of rights claimed by others on his property and to abate annoyances and disputes as to possession. Art. 949, Italian Civil Code.

azióne Pauliàna—Paulian action; a revocatory action. Art. 2901, 2904, Italian Civil Code. See **azióne revocatòria.**

azióne penàle—penal action. It is public and is initiated by the public prosecutor or the Praetor for crimes within the latter's jurisdiction. Art. 112, 24, 27, Constitution of the Italian Republic; Art. 1-21, 74, 125, 185, 522, 571-574, Italian Code of Penal Procedure. See **udiènza penàle.**

azióne per apposizióne di tèrmini—action to fix boundaries. If the markers between contiguous lands are missing or have become unrecognizable, each of the owners has the right to demand that they be placed or be reestablished at common expense. Art. 951, Italian Civil Code; Art. 8, subd. 2, Italian Code of Civil Procedure.

azióne per indébito arrichiménto—action for unjust enrichment (on a draft). See **azióne di arrichiménto cambiàrio.**

azióne petitòria—a petitory action; an action to establish and enforce a right to property or title thereto. Art. 948-951, Italian Civil Code and Art. 705, Italian Code of Civil Procedure. See **azióne di rivendicazióne.**

azióne possessòria—possessory action. It is one to obtain or recover actual possession of property. The two possessory action are: reintegrazióne and manutenzióne, Art. 1168-1170, Italian Civil Code; Art. 703-705, Italian Code of Civil Procedure. Other actions for the protection of property rights are: rivendicazióne, Art. 948; negatòria, Art. 949, and azióne di nunciazióne, Art. 1171, 1172, Italian Civil Code.

azióne quanti minoris—an action to rescind a purchase contract because of hidden defects. The purchaser has the option of rescinding the contract or to take it a reduced price. The choice is irrevocable when the demand has been made judicially. If the goods delivered perished because of the defects, the buyer has the right to rescind; if by accident or fault of the seller, or if the goods have been sold or transformed, only a reduction in price may be demanded. Art. 1492, 1491, Italian Civil Code. Also, **azióne estimatòria.**

azióne reàle—real action (involving the power to enjoy and dispose of property).

azióne redibitòria—redhibitory action to rescind a contract because of latent or hidden defects in the property sold. In case of rescission of the contract, the seller must return the purchase price and reimburse the buyer for the expenses and legitimate payments made in the sale. The buyer must make restitution of the article if it has not been destroyed as a result of its intrinsic defects or vices. Art. 1490-1497, Italian Civil Code.

azióne revocatòria—revocatory action; one maintained by a creditor against a debtor to annul his disposition of assets to the detriment of the creditor. Also, **azióne Pauliàna.** Art. 2901-2904, Italian Civil Code.

azióne revocatòria fallimentàre—revocatory action in bankruptcy; an action brought by a Trustee to set aside various acts committed by a debtor during insolvency and prejudicial to the creditors. Art. 67-71, Falliménto (Bankruptcy), Usual Laws, Appendix to Italian Civil Code.

azióne riconvenzionàle—action of counterclaim. In a civil suit, the defendant who is being sued, may in turn present a claim against the plaintiff based upon the same cause of action and seek appropriate relief. Art. 36, 167, Italian Code of Civil Procedure.

azióne surrogatòria—surrogate or substitute action. A creditor in order to preserve his rights, may exercise the rights and actions of his debtor against third parties, which his debtor has failed to exercise. The rights invoked must involve assets and does not include rights or actions which by their nature or by law can only be exercised by the debtor. Art. 2900, Italian Civil Code.

azióni di stàto—actions to determine filial status. The actions are to establish legitimacy or illegitimacy. See **azióne di disconosciménto di paternità; azióne di contestazióne della legittimità**, and Art. 235, 244-249, Italian Civil Code.

azionísta m.—a stockholder or shareholder.

azotémia f.—azotemia; excess of nitrogenous bodies in the blood.

azzardàre—to risk; to imperil; to endanger; to venture.

azzàrdo m. — risk; peril; danger; chance; hazard. See **giuòco d'azzàrdo** —game of chance.

azzuffaménto m.—fight; quarrel; a coming to blows.

azzuffàre—to fight; to come to blows; to combat.

B

babórdo m.—the port side of a vessel; the side of the ship to the left of a person looking forward towards the bow. See **tribórdo**—starboard.

baccalàre m.—bachelor, said derisively of a person who pretends to have a bachelor's degree and to be learned.

baccalaurèato m. — baccalaureate; bachelor's degree.

baccàno m.—uproar; tumultuous noise.

bacellieràto m.—baccalaureate.

baccellière m.—bachelor.

bacchétta f.—rod; staff; stick; an orchestra conductor's baton.

bacchettóne m. (bacchettóna f.)—one who is completely devoted to religious observances with great zeal and often for ostentation or superstition; bigot; hypocrite. See **baciapíle.**

baciapíle m.—one who is an exaggerated "bacchettóne"; bigot; hypocrite.

bacíllo m.—bacillus.

bagagliàio m.—baggage storage place; baggage car.

bagaglière m.—baggage master.

bagàglio m.—baggage.

bagagliúme m.—mass of baggage or confused things.

bagarinàggio—the act of cornering a market, as performed by a bagaríno.

bagaríno m.—one who acquires all the available quantity of certain goods with the intention of selling same at a higher price; one who corners a market. Also referred to as incettatóre.

baldòria f.—bonfire; large fire set to celebrate public occasions; an occasion for feasting, drinking and eating.

balèstra f.—crossbow.

bàlia f.—nurse; wet-nurse.

balía f.—power; authority; absolute sovereignty; at the mercy of.

balísta f.—balista; ancient military machine used to catapult stones, darts and flaming materials.

balística f.—the science which deals with the motion and direction of projectiles; ballistics.

balívo m.—a title of dignity; judge.

ballòtta f.—boiled chestnut; a small ball once used for voting.

ballottàgio m.—balloting; voting; a vote to break a tie, or a previous vote where no majority was reached.

ballottàre—to ballot; to vote.

balzàre—to jump; to bounce.

balzatóre m.—jumper; leaper.

bànca f.—bank; credit institution.

bancàrio—pertaining to a bank. See **asségno bancàrio**—a check.

bancarótta f.—bankruptcy. See **falliménto.**

bancarótta frauduolènta — fraudulent bankruptcy. It is a crime. Art. 216, 219, 223, Falliménto (Bankruptcy),

Usual Laws, Appendix to Italian Civil Code. See sottrazióne in bancarótta fraudolènta. See reàti comméssi dal fallíto.

bancarótta sémplice — simple bankruptcy. It is a crime when the debtor has performed acts of insolvency or has violated obligations assumed under a prior preventive accord. Art. 217, 219, 224, Falliménto (Bankruptcy), Usual Laws, Appendix to Italian Civil Code. See reàti comméssi dal fallíto.

banchière m.—banker.

banchíglia f.—iceberg.

banchína f.—platform on a railway station or between tracks; quay; wharf; small bench; settee. See panchína. dirítto di banchína — wharfage; charges imposed for loading or unloading from a wharf.

bànco m.—bank; bench.

bancogíro m.—clearing of accounts. See stànza di compensazióne—clearing house.

banconòta f.—banknote.

bànda f.—band; company of soldiers; gang of thieves; group of musicians; heraldic band of color.

bandíre—to banish; to expel; to proclaim; to exile.

bandísta m.—one who belongs to a musical band.

bandíta f.—a place where hunting, pasture or fishing is prohibited; a privileged place.

bandíto m.—bandit; brigand; exile.

banditóre m.—auctioneer at an auction sale; crier.

bàndo m.—an order of the authorities; proclamation; ban; banishment; a public notice issued by a judge and entered in the records of the court clerk's office as well as published in a daily newspaper. It relates to the execution upon property for public sale. Art. 490, 534, Italian Code of Civil Procedure.

bandolièra f. — bandolier; cartridge belt.

bar m.—bar; a place where alcoholic drinks or coffee is sold.

bàra f.—coffin; wooden bed used to transport cadavers.

baràcca f.—barracks.

baraónda f.—a disorderly crowd which comes and goes; confusion.

baràre—to cheat at games of chance.

barattàre—to change or substitute.

barattière m.— one who traffics in public offices.

baràtto m.—barter; the exchange of two things of equal value; trade by the exchange of goods rather than the use of money; the exchange of one thing for another done deceitfully or through error.

bàrbero m.—a Barbary horse.

barbétta f.—small beard; emplacement for cannon on warships; a tow rope.

barbière m.—barber.

barbiería f.—barber shop.

barbitúrico—barbiturate.

barbugliaménto m.—act of stuttering.

barbugliàre—to stutter.

bardàssa f., m.—young white slave; street urchin.

bardòsso—bareback as riding a horse bareback; without saddle.

bardòtto m.—small mule; a young apprentice boy.

barèlla f.—hand-barrow; stretcher.

barèna f.—a strip of land which emerges in a lagoon during low tide; sand-bar.

bargèllo m.—an officer of foreign nationality who commanded a body of soldiers in the Florentine Republic in time of danger or rebellion; the place where the bargello resided and which contained the prison; the head of police agents.

bàrio m.—barium.

barísta m. or f.—bar-keep; one who tends or serves in a bar; bartender.

bàro m.—one who cheats at games of chance; a card-sharp.

barògrafo m.—an automatic recording barometer.

baròmetro m.—barometer. An instrument for measuring atmospheric pressure.

bàrra f.—barrier; bar; division in a court which separates the judges and lawyers from the public.

barricàta f.—barricade.

barrièra f.—barrier; impediment.

barúffa f.—a fight with great confusion; an altercation; a row.

basàre—to base; to ground; to institute.

basìlica f.—basilica; a great church having special privileges; in ancient Rome a spacious public building where law courts met or the Senate convened.

bassofóndo m.—the inferior stratum of society; a place where criminal elements congregate; shallow waters where a ship may run aground.

bastàgio m.—porter. See facchíno.

bastàrda f.—illegitimate daughter; a large sailing vessel or galley; a type of metal file that is larger than the ordinary one.

bastardèlla f.—saucepan; cooking pot.

bastardèllo m.—a style of writing between the round and medieval chancery style used in public writings.

bastàrdo m.—illegitimate child; bastard.

bastía f.—bastion; fortification around a city or encampment.

bastiménto m.—a ship or vessel of large dimension; freighter.

bastionàre—to fortify with bastions.

bastióne m.—bastion; rampart; fortification.

bastíre—to construct; to build; to mend.

bastonàre—to beat; to cudgel; to beat with a stick.

bastonàta f.—a blow with a stick or cudgel or similar weapon.

bastóne m.—cane; baton; staff; club; truncheon.

bastóni (pl.) m.—clubs in a game of cards.

batacchiàre—to beat; to cudgel.

batacchiàta f.—a blow with a large stick or cudgel.

batàcchio m.—large stick; cudgel.

batòcchio m.—any stick or cane; the clapper of a bell.

bàtolo m.—a silk rosette or gown worn as a sign of ecclesiastic dignity; a shoulder knot on a barrister's gown.

batòsta f.—blow or shock; shock resulting from illness; serious damage to one's interests.

battàglio m.—large, metal bell clapper.

battàna f.—small flat-boat propelled by one oar which is used in the Venetian lagoons.

battèllo m.—a small vessel utilizing sail or motor power.

bàttere—to knock; to strike; to beat; to touch with force.

batterìa f.—battery; a unit of artillery pieces; electric battery; kitchen utensils; percussion instruments.

battèri (pl.) m.—bacteria.

battèrio m.—bacterium

batterísta f.—a player of percussion instruments.

battesimàle—pertaining to baptism; baptismal.

battésimo m.—baptism.

battezzàre—to baptize; to christen.

battezzatóre m.—one who baptizes; baptizer. Also, battezànte.

battibécco m.—a dispute over an insignificant matter; altercation; dispute; argument.

batticuòre m.—palpitation of the heart caused by fear or strong emotion.

battifòlle m.—rampart built of logs in the form of a tower.

battifóndo m.—a billiard game in which one challenges many who compete with the challenger in turn.

battifrédo m.—a log watch tower containing a sentinel and a bell to sound alarms.

battifuòcco m.—a small piece of steel used to strike a light.

battígia f.—the water mark of a shore or river.

battilàno m.—wool carder.

battilòro m.—gold worker.

battimàno m.—applause created by clapping hands.

battipàlo m.—pile driver.

battistràda m.—outrider; one who precedes another to announce his arrival; guide; one who has led the way in some endeavor.

battología f.—battology; needless repetition in writing or speech.

baúle m.—travelling trunk.

baussíte f.—bauxite.

bauxíte f.—bauxite.

bàzzica f.—a card game; also a type of billiard game.

bazzicàre—to frequent a place; to associate with certain people, usually of bad character.

beccamòrti m.—grave digger; one who buries the dead.

becchíno m.—undertaker.

bèffa f.—a joke or trick performed with words or actions in a derisive fashion.

beffàre—to ridicule; to deride.

bèlla f.—beautiful woman; fiancee; the decisive game after each party has won a game apiece.

bellétto m.—a lotion or cream used by women to smooth the skin.

bellòcchio m.—a gem displaying opalescent reflections like the eye of a cat; catseye.

belzuíno m.—benzoin. Also, benzoíno.

bènda f.—bandage used to cover wounds or a part of the body.

bendàre—to bind; to cover.

bendàto—bandaged.

bendatúra f.—bandage.

bène, bèni (pl.) m.—things which may become the object of rights and property. They are distinguished as movables (mòbili) and immovables (immòbili). Art. 810-819, Italian Civil Code.

beneducàto—well-mannered.

beneficàre—to do good to others; to assist; to be charitable.

beneficènza f.—act of assisting someone in need.

beneficiàre—to benefit from; to give advantage to.

beneficiàrio m.—beneficiary.

benefício m.—a work or institution established for the benefit of others; benefit; advantage; acceptance of an inheritance subject to an inventory of the property.

benefício d'inventàrio—benefit of inventory. An heir or successor who accepts the estate of a decedent with benefit of inventory, succeeds to the estate but there is no commingling of the assets of the estate with those of the successor. The latter becomes liable only to the extent of that which he has received, and not personally. See accettaziòne dell'eredità col benefício d'inventàrio. Art. 484-511, Italian Civil Code; Art. 778-780, Italian Code of Civil Procedure.

benemerènte—meritorious.

benemerènza f.—merit; the act which renders one deserving of recognition for having done well.

benemèrito — well deserving; well merited.

beneplàcito m.—consensus; approval; convenience; option.

benèssere m.—well being.

benestànte—well off; comfortable, but less than rich.

benestàre m.—approval of an account or a proposal.

bèni consumàbili—consumable things. Those things or goods which can be used only once and are consumed. Art. 995, Italian Civil Code.

bèni fungíbili—fungible goods. Art. 812, 995, Italian Civil Code.

bèni inconsumàbili — inconsumable things or goods Those things which can be used more than once.

bèni infungíbili—non-fungible goods.

bèni mòbili—movable things; personal

property. Art. 810-819, Italian Civil Code.

bèni personàli del còniuge—personal property of the spouse. The following personal property of a spouse is not considered community property: (a) property of which the spouse was the owner before marriage or of which he had a real right of enjoyment; (b) property acquired after the marriage by gift or succession, when the Act of donation or the testament does not specify the same to be community property; (c) property which is of strictly personal use, and its accessories; (d) property serving the professional use of the spouse, except that destined to the conduct of a business which is part of the community property; (e) property obtained as damages for injuries sustained, as well as a pension related to partial or total loss of work capacity; (f) property acquired with the price obtained for the transfer of property above enumerated or its exchange, provided it is declared in the Act of acquisition. Also excluded from community property are real property and personal property enumerated in Art. 2683, when acquired as provided above under (c), (d) and (f) when the exclusion results from the Act of acquisition even if the other spouse participated. The property includes vessels, aircraft and automobiles. Art. 179, 210, 211, 215, Italian Civil Code.

beniamíno m.—favorite, derived from Benjamin, the youngest son of Jacob, who was his favorite.

benígno—benign; mild.

bensérvito m.—testimonial of good service given to one who has performed well; a testimonial given upon severance from service.

benzína f.—benzine; gasoline.

benzoíno, m.—benzoin. Also, belzuíno.

beóne m.—heavy drinker; tippler.

bernòccolo m.—protuberance; bump; knob.

bersàglio m.—target.

bestémmia f.—blasphemy.

bestemmiàre—to blaspheme.

béstia f.—beast; animal.

bestiàio m.—one in charge of animals.

bestiàle—bestial.

bestiàme m.—cattle.

béttola f.—tavern frequented by working class people.

bibliotèca f.—library.

bidèllo m.—beadle; messenger; school custodian.

bigamía f.—bigamy. Art. 556, Italian Penal Code.

bígamo m.—bigamist.

bígamo—bigamous.

bigliétto m.—note; ticket; bank note.

bigliétto di cancellería. A Notice sent by the Clerk of the Court in a civil case. See communicazióne (del cancellière).

bigliétto di viàggio—trip ticket; ticket for a journey. The traveler pays for his transportation and his payment is evidenced by the trip ticket, representing the contract of carriage.

bigliétto di vísita—calling card.

bilàncio m.—a budget of income and expense.

bilàncio consuntívo—a definite budget of income and expense for a period of time.

bilàncio preventívo—a budget of an estimate of expected income and expense.

bilàncio di verificazióne—trial balance. fàre il bilàncio—to prepare accounts. fòglio di bilàncio—balance sheet.

bilateràle—bilateral; two sided; a contract in the Civil law in which both parties assume reciprocal obligations; a synallagmatic contract. See sinallagmàtico.

binàrio m.—railway track.

binùbo—one who is legitimately married a second time.

birbóne m.—rogue.

bírra f.—beer.

bírro m.—police agent; a police agent of former times who was despised for his brutal actions—generally used in a pejorative sense. The word sbírro is in more general use. See sbírro.

blasfèma or blasfèmia f.—blasphemy.

blasfemàre—to blaspheme.

blasfèmo m.—blasphemer.

blòcco stradàle—road block. — Whoever, for the purpose of impeding or obstructing free circulation, places or abandons apparatuses or other objects of any kinds whatsoever on a railroad or ordinary road, or in any manner obstructs or encumbers the road itself for the same purpose, is punished with imprisonment. The same punishment is applied if the act is committed in a port zone or on the waters of rivers, canals or lakes, for the purpose of impeding or obstructing free navigation thereon. The penalty is doubled if the act is committed by more than one person, even if not in combination, or if the act is committed by the use of violence or threats to persons or violence on things. Blòcco stradàle (Road block) Usual Laws, Appendix to Italian Code of Penal Procedure.

bócca f.—mouth.

bócca (a)—by word of mouth.

bócca d'altrúi—from the mouth of others; orally; by word of mouth; hearsay. See vóci corrènti.

bocciàre—to fail an examination; to flunk; to strike away an adversary's ball with one's own at bowling.

bòia m.—hangman.

boicottàgio m.—boycott; a refusal to deal with another for coercive purpose, so called after Capt. Boycott, a land agent in Ireland in 1880, its first victim. Whoever, for the purpose of instituting a lockout or strike, avails himself of the force and authority of parties, leagues or associations, and induces one or more persons not to agree to a labor contract or not to supply materials and instruments necessary to work or not to acquire the agricultural or industrial products of another, is punished with imprisonment. Art. 507, 502-505, Italian Penal Code.

bólla f.—bull (Papal); bubble; blister.

bollàre—to stamp; to brand.

bollàrio m.—collection of Papal bulls.

bollétta f.—certificate; receipt; ticket stub.

bollettíno m.—bulletin.

bóllo m.—seal; stamp; proprietary mark; post-mark; mark.

bordèllo m.—house of ill-fame; uproar. Also, postríbolo; càsa di cartèlla; lupanàre.

borghése m. — civilian; middle-class. àbito borghése—civilian dress as opposed to military dress.

borghesía f.—the middle class; bourgeoisie.

bórsa f.—purse; pouch; exchange.

bórsa di commèrcio—commercial exchange.

bórsa di mèrci—commodity exchange.

bórsa di stúdio—scholarship.

bórsa di valóri—securities exchange.

bòzza f.—rough hewn stone; rough draft; printer's proof sheet; galley proof. Also, stampóne.

bòzze (pl.) f.—printer's proof sheets; galley proofs. See stampóne.

bozzétto m.—rough sketch; outline of work.

bréccia f.—breach in a wall; gravel; small stones used in mending a road.

bredindíno m. — tackle for stowing cargo in a ship's hold.

brefotròfio m.—foundling asylum or hospital.

brevétto m.—brevet; commission of appointment; patent.

brevétto d'invenzióne—letters patent of an invention; a privilege granted by a government to an inventor for the exclusive use of his invention for a term of years. Art. 2584-2594, Italian Civil Code.

brevi manu—from the Latin, indicating a transfer of personal property without any formality.

briccóne m.—rascal.

broccàrdo m.—a legal question which is difficult to resolve.

bruciàre—to burn; to consume with fire. Also, abbruciàre.

brutàle malvagità—perverse brutality. It is an aggravating circumstance in a homicide. Art. 575-578, 61, Italian Penal Code.

bucàto m.—laundry; wash.

bugía f.—lie.

buòn costúme—good custom or propriety. Relates to a provision in the Penal Code pertaining to crimes against public morality and good custom or propriety. Art. 519-544, Italian Penal Code.

buòn pàdre di famíglia (Lat. bonus paterfamilias)—a responsible father or master of a family. The degree of care required in handling various affairs, under the Civil Code, is the care that would be exercised by a responsible head of a family. See diligènza nell adempiménto and Art. 1176 et seq., Italian Civil Code.

buòna condótta—good conduct, referring to a citizen's deportment in his relations with others. A certificate of good conduct is generally required where licenses are sought, passports applied for or contests are entered.

buòna condótta (cauzióne di)—security for good conduct. It is a security measure to insure good conduct by depositing bail. Art. 236-239, Italian Penal Code.

buòna féde—good faith. The parties, during the development of the negotiations and the formation of the contract, must act in good faith. Art. 1337, Italian Civil Code.

buòno m.—good man; bond; commercial obligation; coupon; receipt; ticket; warrant.

burèlla f.—a narrow, dark place; subterranean corridor; prison; dungeon.

bússola f.—compass.

búzzo m.—paunch; belly of animals.

C

cablogràmma m.—cablegram.

càccia m.—hunt; chase; game.

cacciàre—to hunt; to chase; to pursue; to expel; to banish.

cacciatóre m.—hunter.

cacciatorpedinière m.—destroyer; torpedo-boat destroyer.

cacciavíte m.—screwdriver.

cadére—to fall.

cadétto m.—cadet; a student training for service as a military officer; a younger son or brother.

cadàvere m.—cadaver; corpse; dead body of a human being. See occultamento di cadàvere and soppressione di cadàvere. See vilipèndio di cadàvere.

cadàvere (úso illegíttimo di)—illegal use of a cadaver. Whoever dissects or otherwise uses a cadaver or a part of it for scientific or teaching purposes, in cases not permitted by law, is subject to imprisonment or fine. The penalty is augmented if the act is committed on a cadaver, or part of one, which the culpable person knew to have been mutilated, hidden or carried away by others. Art. 413, Italian Penal Code. See distruzióne, soppressióne o sottrazióne di cadàvere.

caducità f.—caducity; frailty; transitoriness; senility; legal invalidity; loss or lapse of a right; lapse of a legacy.

cadúco—caducous; tending to fall; transitory; fleeting; lapsed; subject to caducity.

cafaggiàio m.—head forester; custodian or manager of a farm; meddler.

calaprànzi m.—dumb-waiter. Also, tiraprànzi.

calàre—to lower.

calcàre—to tread; to trample; to be an actor or singer, fig., to tread the boards.

càlce m.—lower part or bottom of something; bottom of the page.

càlce f.—lime.

calía f.—gold or silver filings.

càlibe m.—steel.

calligrafía f.—calligraphy; the art of fine writing; penmanship.

callígrafo—of or relating to calligraphy.

callígrafo m.—one versed in the art of calligraphy or fine writing.

calmànte—sedative.

calmàre—to calm; to quiet; to placate; to sedate.

calúnnia f.—calumny; defamation; a false and malicious statement designed to injure the reputation of another; malicious prosecution; a crime which involves accusing another of a crime of which he is known to be innocent. Art. 368, Italian Penal Code.

càlvo—bald.

calzolàio m.—shoemaker.

camàuro m.—a red velvet cap worn by the Pope, covering the head and ears.

cambiàle f.—draft or bill of exchange. Art. 1992-2027, Italian Civil Code; Art. 1-99, Cambiàle (Drafts), Usual Laws, Appendix to Italian Civil Code. See vàglia cambiàrio and pagherò.

cambiàle agrària—agrarian draft; a draft used to obtain credit by those engaged in agricultural pursuits. This credit is restricted to be used during the current year. Art. 7-9, Crédito Agràrio (Agrarian Credit), Usual Laws, Appendix to Italian Civil Code.

cambiàle di favóre—accommodation draft. Drawn by a drawer as accommodation for another person, the current drawer having no primary responsibility but a secondary one in the event of dishonor.

cambiàle domiciliàta—a draft payable at the domicile of the drawee, a third person or elsewhere. Art. 4, Cambiàle (Drafts), Usual Laws, Appendix to Italian Civil Code.

cambiàle in biànco—a draft lacking one of the requisites of said instrument but signed by the person issuing it. It is often given as a guarantee. The missing required element of the instrument may be inserted and completed by the holder. Art. 14, Cambiàle (Drafts), Usual Laws, Appendix to Italian Civil Code.

cambiàle tràtta—a draft where the drawer orders another person, the drawee, to pay the instrument. Art. 1-3, Cambiàle (Drafts), Usual Laws, Appendix to Italian Civil Code.

cambiaménto m.—change; the act and effect of changing; mutation; alteration; exchange.

cambiamonéte m.—cambist; a dealer in money exchange.

cambiàre—to change; to exchange; to change one thing for another; to transform.

càmbio m.—exchange; change; rate of exchange between different currencies.

cambísta m.—money-changer.

càmera f.—chamber; room; deliberative body.

càmera di consíglio—a tribunal sitting in secret or in chambers; judge's chambers.

cameràle—a fee paid by members of a chamber of commerce or similar organization.

cameràta f.—dormitory.

cameràta m.—comrade; colleague.

camerièra f.—waitress; lady's maid; stewardess on a ship.

camerière m.—waiter; man-servant; steward on a ship.

camòrra f.—a secret criminal organization of Neapolitan origin. See Màfia.

camorrísta m.—a member of the camòrra.

campióne m.—sample; a standard for measurement or testing; a tax register; a ledger; champion.

campióne civíle—civil register; a register maintained by the clerk of the court relative to expenses incurred by those persons entitled by law to sue without paying court costs.

campióne penàle—penal register; a register maintained by the clerk of the court relative to criminal actions and fines imposed.

canàglia f.—rabble.

canagliàta f.—action of a rabble; despicable act.

canàle m.—canal; channel.

cancellàbile—erasable.

cancellaménto m.—erasure; repeal.

cancellàre—to cancel; to erase; to strike out; to annul. Also, **scancellàre.**

cancellatúra f.—cancelling; erasure; obliteration.

cancellazióne f.—cancellation.

cancellerésco—pertaining to the chancery or clerk's office.

cancellería f.—chancery; clerk's office.

cancellière m.—chancellor; register; clerk of an office maintaining public or judicial records. Art. 57, 58, Italian Code of Civil Procedure.

cancèllo m.—chancel; bar; lattice.

cancrèna f.—gangrene. Also, **cangrèna.**

càncro m.—cancer.

candéla f.—a wax candle; a surgical probe (bougie).

candèla vérgine—virgin or unlighted candle; a method employed in selling real property at auction under a forced sale. Where this method of sale is used, a candle is immediately lighted after each offer up to three in succession for a period of about one minute each. When the last candle is extinguished without a higher offer being made, the real property is struck down to the last offeror. Each offeror ceases to be held to his offer when it is surpassed by another, even though this last is declared null. The auction is held before the judge declaring the forced execution. Art. 581, Italian Code of Civil Procedure.

candidàto m.—candidate.

candidatúra f.—candidacy; presenting oneself as a candidate.

candóre m.—candor; sincerity.

càne m.—dog.

canèstro m.—basket; hamper.

cànfora f.—camphor.

canforàto—camphorated.

cangrèna f.—gangrene. Also, **cancrèna.**

canòne m.—canon; ecclesiastic rule of law; duty; tax; emphyteutic charge or rent. It may consist of a periodic sum of money or of a fixed quantity of natural products. Art. 960-963, Italian Civil Code.

cantière m.—dockyard; place where ships are built and repaired.

cantína f.—cool, subterranean place where wine is kept; place where wine is sold.

cantinière m.—wine-seller.

canúto—one who is gray haired; also, referring to gray hair itself.

capàce—ample; spacious; fit; able; capable.

capacità f.—capacity; power of receiving or containing; power and ability of doing something or learning; position; function; legal qualification.

capacità a delínquere—capacity and disposition to commit crime. In applying punishment discretionally, within limits prescribed by law, the judge also must take into account the capacity and disposition of the guilty party to commit crime, deduced from: (1) the motives to commit crime and the character of the crime; (2) the penal and judicial precedents and generally, the conduct and life-style of the guilty person before the crime; (3) the conduct contemporary to and subsequent to the crime; (4) the individual, family and social conditions of life of the guilty person. Art. 133, 108, 202, 203, Italian Penal Code. See **tendènza a delínquere.**

capacità di agíre—capacity to effect or perform legal acts and to personally acquire and exercise legal rights and obligations. This status is achieved with the reaching of the age of majority at eighteen years, unless a different age is established by law. Art. 2, Italian Civil Code. See **maggióre età.**

capacità di dirítto penàle—the capacity to be subjected to penal law and to be judged and condemned for having committed a crime. See **imputabilità penàle.**

capacità d'intèndere e di volère—the capacity to comprehend the nature and consequences of one's acts and the capacity to will and make free decisions. This capacity is normally acquired at majority. By law, however, a minor may make certain contracts and be held responsible for them. Penally, no one may be punished for an act anticipated as a crime by the law, if, at the moment he committed it, he was not imputable or chargeable. That person is imputable who has capacity of comprehending the nature and consequences of his acts and the will to make free decisions. No one may be punished for an action or omission anticipated by the law as a crime, if he has not committed it with conscience and free will. Art. 85, 42, Italian Penal Code. See sospensióne del procediménto; capacità di agíre; maggióre età, and imputabilità penàle.

capacità di testàre—the capacity to dispose of property by last will and testament.

capacità giurídica—legal or juridical capacity; it consists in being able to acquire rights and be subjected to duties. These rights and duties originate at birth and are completely enjoyed at reaching majority. Art. 1, Italian Civil Code.

capàrra f.—earnest money given in part payment of goods or property for the purpose of binding the contract; deposit.

capàrra confirmatòria — confirmatory deposit. Money or fungible goods given by one party to the other upon conclusion of the contract as earnest money. It must be returned upon performance or attributed or charged to the performance due. If the party giving the deposit does not perform, the other party may withdraw from the contract and retain the deposit. On the other hand, if the non-performing party is the one which received the deposit, the party which gave the deposit may withdraw from the contract and exact twice the amount of the deposit. If the party who is not in default prefers, he may elect to demand execution of the contract or its recission with indemnification for damages in accordance with the general rules of law. Art. 1385, Italian Civil Code.

capàrra convenzionàle—See clàusola penàle.

capàrra penitenziàle—deposit in a contract with penalty clause. It serves as liquidated damages in the event of default. If the contract stipulates the right of withdrawal to one or both parties, the deposit functions as compensation for the withdrawal. The party withdrawing, loses the deposit given, or must pay back twice the value of that received. Art. 1386, Italian Civil Code.

capèstro m.—halter; rope.

càpi (per)—by heads; as individuals; per capita (Lat.); in the distribution of an estate *per capita*, those in the same degree of kindred take in equal shares in their own right as principals, in contrast to taking by representation, or *per stirpes*. See rappresentazióne and stírpe. Art. 467-469, Italian Civil Code.

capitàle sociàle—the amount contributed by partners in a business partnership or the amount subscribed to and paid in by shareholders in a corporation; capital stock. See patrimònio sociàle.

capitanería f.—littoral land subject to the administrative jurisdiction of a maritime authority.

capitanería del pòrto—the office of the administrative maritime authority which directs the administration of the merchant marine in the maritime domain and under the charge of the Port Commander.

capitàno m.—captain.

capitazióne f.—head tax; poll tax.

capitolazióne f.—capitulation.

capítolo m.—chapter; part of an agreement or convention.

càpo m.—heading; chapter; beginning; chief; head.

capòccia m.—head of the household in a family of farmers; foreman.

capoconvòglio m. — train conductor. Also, capotrèno.

capodànno m.—first day of the year; New Year's Day.

capodepòsito m.—head of a depot or storehouse.

capodipartiménto m.—head of a department.

capodivisióne m.—head of a division of a public office.

capogíro m.—dizziness.

capoguàrdia m.—head of guards in a prison.

capolavóro m.—masterpiece.

capoluògo m.—the principal city or locality of a province, district or region somewhat similar to a county seat.

capolísta m.—one who heads the list of candidates on a ballot to gather the greatest amount of votes.

capomoviménto m.—an official who directs the movement of trains in a railroad.

caporióne m.—head of a region or neighborhood of a city; chief.

caposezióne m.—head of a section in a public office.

caposquàdra m.—head of a group of persons, workers or soldiers.

caposquadróne m.—commander of a squadron of cavalry.

capostazióne m.—station master.

capostípite m.—one from whom a noble family is descended.

capotàsto m.—peg in a stringed instrument used in tuning.

capotimonière m.—chief helmsman.

capotrèno m.—train conductor. Also, capoconvòglio.

capovèrso m.—beginning of a line of prose or poetry; paragraph.

cappellàno m.—chaplain.

cappèllo m.—hat; head cover.

cappòtto m.—cloak; overcoat.

cappúccio m.—hood; cowl; cabbage.

càpsula f.—capsule; cap; pod.

captàre — to capture; to intercept (radio waves).

captazióne f.—interception of radio waves. Captation; the use of fraud or illegal means to influence a testator. A testamentary disposition may be challenged by any interested party when it is the result of error, violence or fraud. Art. 624, 631, 463. Italian Civil Code.

captívo m.—captive; prisoner.

carabína f.—carbine.

carabinière m.—carabineer; a member of a select para-military group engaged in police work and maintaining public order. He is an agent of the judicial police. Art. 221, Italian Code of Penal Procedure.

carceraménto m.—incarceration; imprisonment.

carceràre—to imprison.

carceràto m.—prisoner. Art. 141-145, Italian Penal Code.

carcerazióne f.—the state of being imprisoned; imprisonment. Art. 581, Italian Penal Code.

carcerazióne preventíva — preventive imprisonment. Imprisonment suffered prior to the sentence becoming irrevocable is subtracted from the total sentence to be served. Art. 137, 138, Italian Penal Code; Art. 578, 581, Italian Code of Penal Procedure. See custòdia preventíva.

càrcere m.—prison; jail.

càrcere preventívo—preventive imprisonment; that suffered by the accused before and during the trial. See carcerazióne preventíva.

cardíaco—of the heart; cardiac.

cardiografía f.—cardiogram.

cardiògrafo m.—electro-cardiograph.

cardiologìa f.—cardiology; study of the heart and its functions.

cardiòlogo m.—cardiologist.

carènza f.—lack; scarcity; lack of capacity to perform legal acts.

carestía f.—lack of something, especially of food-stuffs; scarcity.

càrica f.—a public office of some importance; grade; dignity; honor; position; cavalry or infantry charge.

caricàre—to load; to burden; to charge; to encumber.

càrico m.—cargo; load; freight, responsibility. See pòlizza di càrico and lèttera di vettúra for bills of lading by sea and land.

càrie f.—caries; decay of teeth or bone or plant tissue.

carísma m.—charisma; a power or gift granted by divine grace.

carismàtico—charismatic.

carità f.—charity; a strong and sincere affection toward parents, one's country, etc.

caritévole—charitable; benevolent; philanthropist.

caritatívo—kind; charitable; pious.

carízia f.—scarcity; privation; insufficiency.

carminatívo m.—carminative; a drug which expels gas formed in the intestines or bowels.

carnàle—carnal; sensual.

carnalità f.—sensuality; carnal appetite.

càrne f.—flesh; meat.

carnéfice m.—executioner; one who executes a' death sentence.

carneficína f. — butchery; carnage; slaughter.

carnevàle m.—carnival.

carógna f.—carrion; body of a dead beast.

carèsi f.—a deep, abnormal sleep accompanied by insensibility to stimulants.

caròtide f.—carotid; artery on either side of the neck which carries blood to the head.

carpíre—to take with violence or with artifice; to seize; to snatch.

carreggiàta f.—rut in a road left by the wheels of a vehicle; a cart road.

carréggio m.—a convoy of cars or trucks; cartage.

carrièra f.—career; profession; course; race.

carriòla or carriuòla f.—wheel barrow.

carronàta f.—a cannon formerly used in warships and manufactured in Carron, Scotland, hence its name.

carròzza f.—carriage.

carròzza-lètto—railway sleeping car. The responsibility for liability of hotel keepers for a deposit or bailment of things left in their care applies to sleeping cars. Art. 1786, Italian Civil Code. See depòsito in albèrgo. Also see cuccétta.

carrozzàbile—a road which is fit for carriages, or today, fit for automobile travel.

carrozzería f.—carriage or automobile body works; body of a car, exclusive of chassis and engine, etc.

càrta bollàta—stamped or impressed paper authenticated with the governmental stamp for which a fee is paid as a tax under statutory provision. The stamp is required in connection with the issuance of commercial paper, documents relating to civil, commercial, judicial, extra-judicial transactions and on writings, documents and registers indicated by law. Regarding use on journal and inventory books employed in business, see Art. 2215, 2218, Italian Civil Code.

càrta filigranàta—paper with letters or figures which remain impressed and are visible, by transparency, in the paper; watermark.

cartacarbóne f.—carbon paper.

cartapècora f. — sheepskin used for diplomas, writing or book binding.

cartèlla f.—label; stone slab for an inscription; posted notice; printed form; lottery ticket; a certificate evidencing a State obligation; formerly, a prostitute's license or permit.

cartèlla (càsa di)—brothel. Also, bordèllo; postríbolo; lupanàre.

cartèlla d'incànto—posted conditions of a sale at auction.

cartèlla di rèndita—a certificate of

credit issued by the State or a municipality.

cartellàrio m.—archive.

cartellièra f.—file cabinet.

cartèllo m.—bill; placard; a large piece of paper upon which is written an announcement, insignia or inscription; sign; cartel; syndicate; trust.

cartèllo (artísta o attóre di)—artist or actor of renown.

cartèllo di sfída—a letter challenging one to a duel.

cartellóne m.—placard.

cartièra f.—paper-mill.

cartolàre—to number pages.

cartolàro m.—a folder to contain sheets of paper or designs; diary; appointment book.

cartúccia f.—cartridge; originally a piece of paper containing a powder charge for a rifle.

càsa f.—house; home.

càsa di cartèlla—brothel. Also, bordèllo; postríbolo; lupanàre.

càsa di cúra—health home; sanatarium.

càsa di salúte—health home; sanatarium.

casalíngo—domestic; home made.

casaménto m.—large house; one inhabited by many families; those who live therein.

càsco m.—casque; aviator's helmet.

casèlla f.—compartment; pigeon-hole; square on a chess board.

casellànte m. — railroad watchman; highway watchman and maintenance man.

cassellàrio m.—pigeon-hole for official documents; repository of court files.

casèrma m. — barrack; lodging for soldiers. It is part of the patrimony of the State. Art. 826, Italian Civil Code.

càso m.—case; chance; event; happening.

càso fortúito—accidental event; an event occurring independently of human will. For its effect in civil

and penal matters see, Art. 1218, 1256-1259 Italian Civil Code and Art. 45, Italian Penal Code.

càssa f.—box; case; chest; coffin; stock of a gun; gun carriage.
fóndo di càssa—cash reserve.
líbro di càssa—cash book.
píccola càssa—petty cash box.
vuòto di càssa—defalcation of funds by the cashier.

càssa di rispàrmio—savings bank.

cassafòrte f.—strong-box.

cassàre—to quash; to annul; to abrogate; to cancel.

cassazióne f.—act of annulling or reversing a decree or judgment.
córte di cassazióne—court of cassation; the highest court of appeal in Italy. See córte di cassazióne.

càsse rurale—rural banks. They are subject to the dispositions affecting cooperative associations. Art. 2517, Italian Civil Code. See società cooperatíve.

cassétta di sicurézza—safe deposit box. Art. 1839-1841, Italian Civil Code.

cassière m.—cashier.

castàldo m.—steward; administrator of the property of a prince; farm manager.

castràre—to castrate.

castràto—castrated; mutton (m.).

castratúra f.—castration.

castrènse—pertaining to a military camp.

catafàlco m.—catafalque; a structure on which the body of a deceased lies in state.

catalètto m.—stretcher to carry sick persons.

catapàno m.—the governor of Italian cities under Byzantine dominion.

catàsta f.—a pile of wood; a large quantity of things placed one upon another; great or abundant quantity of things.

catàsto m.—the register of assessed valuation of real property for tax purposes with the identity of the owner thereof; the public office which maintains the above records.

caténa f.—chain.

catenàccio m.—door-bolt; padlock.

catenàccio (decréto)—a decree which becomes effective unexpectedly, without advance notice. Generally, it relates to the rise in prices of monopoly merchandise to prevent purchases before the effective date.

catetère m.—catheter.

catràme m.—tar.

catramína f.—a substance extracted from tar which has expectorant properties.

càttedra f.—chair of a University instructor; principal seat of a Bishop or archbishop.

cattedràle—cathedral.

cattedràtico—professorial; doctoral.

cattivàre—to captivate; to win; also to take prisoner.

cattivèria and **cattivería** f.—wickedness; perversity; deviltry.

cattività f. — wickedness; imprisonment; captivity.

cattívo — captive; miserable; bad; malicious; ill-natured.

cattúra f.—arrest; capture. See **mandàto di cattúra**.

catturàre—to arrest; to capture.

càusa f.—cause; that which produces an effect; motive; reason; a cause of action; legal case; litigation.

càusa giusta—just cause.

càusa petendi—the legal basis for the relief demanded.

causàle—that which is the cause of; the efficient cause of a determined act; causal.

càuto—cautious; prudent.

cauzióne f.—bail; security. Art. 189, Italian Penal Code; Art. 84, 236-239, 241, 259, 282, 344, 618, 622, 654, Italian Code of Penal Procedure. See **malleverìa**.

cauzióne di buòna condótta—bond for good behavior. It is given by depositing the statutory sum in the Depository for fines. In lieu of deposit, the furnishing of a guarantee by giving a mortgage or a guarantee by a surety who is jointly and severally responsible with the individual under a measure of patrimonial security, is permitted. The duration of the security measure may not be less than one, nor more than five years, Art. 237, Italian Penal Code; Art. 654, Italian Code of Penal Procedure.

càva f.—cave; quarry; mine.

cavalière m. — knight; cavalier; mounted soldier; mounted gentleman; gallant.

cavallerìa f.—cavalry.

cavàllo m.—horse.

cavaménto m.—excavation.

cavàre—to excavate; to dig; to take out; to take off.

cavatóre m.—one who works in a stone quarry; miner.

cavatúra f.—cavity; digging; hole.

cavíllo m.—cavil; trivial and fallacious argument or objection.

cavità f.—cavity; hole.

cazzottàre—to give blows with a closed fist.

cazzòtto m.—a blow given with a closed fist; blow.

cedènte m.—cedent; assignor; transferror; one who cedes property. See **cessionàrio**.

cèdere—to cede; to transfer; to yield to pressure; to abandon; to release; to renounce; to assign.

cedíbile—assignable; cedeable; transferable.

cedibilità f.—that which can be ceded, transferred or assigned.

cediménto m.—the act of ceding, transferring or yielding; cession; renunciation; assignment.

cèdola f.—a coupon or slip detached from a booklet or matrix.

ceffàre—to catch; to take; to seize.

ceffàta f.—blow; slap.

cèffo m.—muzzle; snout.

ceffóne m.—blow on the face with open hand.

celebràre—to celebrate; to commemorate; to glorify; to praise greatly, orally or in writing.

celebràre un contràtto—to enter into a contract.

celebrazióne f.—celebration.

cèlebre — famous; renowned; well-known.

celebrità f.—a celebrity.

cèlere—swift; an express train (m.); a division of motorized police (f.).

celibàto m.—celibate; one who is unmarried.

cèlibe m.—unmarried man; an unmarried woman is said to be *nùbile*.

censiménto m.—census.

cènso m.—census taken every five years in Rome before the Censor; tax.

censóre m.—censor; a Roman magistrate who took the census of the citizens; an official who reviews books and writings, in order to authorize their publication; proctor.

censúra f.—censure; censorship; office of the censor.

censuràre—to censure.

centralíno m.—telephone switchboard.

ceremònia or cerimònia f.—ceremony.

ceremoniàle (cerimoniàle) — ceremonial.

ceremonière or cerimonière m.—master of ceremonies.

cervèllo m.—brains; mind.

cervicàle—cervical.

cervíce f.—back of the neck.

certificàre—to certify; to attest; to confirm.

certificàto m.—certificate; a written statement certifying to the truth of a matter stated; testimonial.

cerzioràre—certiorari; to make certain; in Anglo-American Law, a writ of review or inquiry.

cesàreo—Caesarean; Caesarian operation or section; imperial.

cesariàno m.—follower of Caesar; Caesarian.

cesèllo m.—chisel.

cessaménto m. — cessation; act of ceasing.

cessàre—to cease; to stop.

cessazióne f.—cessation; discontinuance.

cessionàrio m.—assignee; transferee; the one to whom an assignor or transferor cedes property. See cedènte.

cessióne f.—assignment; transfer; conveyance; giving title to goods to another; transfer of title; yield; give up; divestiture of property in favor of another.

cessazióne dei pagaménti—cessation or failure of payments. This is evidence of insolvency. Art. 5, Falliménto (Bankruptcy), Usual Laws, Appendix to Italian Civil Code.

cessióne dei bèni ai creditóri—assignment of assets to creditors. Art. 1977-1986, Italian Civil Code.

cessióne dei crèditi—an assignment of money due to creditor to a third party without the consent of the debtor. Art. 1260-1267, Italian Civil Code.

cessióne del contràtto—assignment of contract. Art. 1406-1410, Italian Civil Code.

cèsso m.—toilet; water closet.

cèto m.—class of persons; order; rank; condition.

chepí m.—kepi; a military cap with a flat circular top and a visor.

chèque m.—check. See asségno bancàrio.

chetaménte—silently.

chetàre—to silence; to appease.

chéto—quiet; noiseless; gentle.

chiàcchiera f.—small talk; chatter; false news.

chiacchieràre—to engage in light talk to pass time; to chatter; to prattle.

chiacchieràta f.—an idle talk; an inconclusive speech.

chiamàre in càusa—to sue.

chiamàre in giudízio—to sue.

chiamàta in càusa—bringing in a third party to intervene in a litigation between two others; similar to interpleading a third party defendant.

chiamàta in càusa del venditóre—interpleading a seller in an action. Where a buyer's title is disputed by a third party, he must vouch in or interplead the seller to defend or warrant his title or he will lose the seller's warranty. Art. 1485, Italian Civil Code and garanzía (chiamàta in).

chiappàre—to take by surprise or by force; to catch; to trap.

chiappíno m.—police agent.

chiarificàre—to clarify; to explain; to make clear; to elucidate.

chiaraménto m.—explanation; act and effect of making clear.

chiarificazióne f. — clarification; explanation.

chiassàta f.—uproar; boisterous noise; public scene.

chiàsso m.—uproar; shouting; clamor; tumult. Also, small village street.

chiedènte m.—petitioner; requesting or demanding party.

chièdere—to ask; to demand; to petition; to inquire.

chiedíbile—that which can be requested or demanded.

chílo m.—kilo; kilogram.

chilòmetro m.—kilometer.

chilowàtt m.—kilowatt.

chimèra f.—chimera; illusion.

chímica f.—chemistry.

chimòno m.—kimono.

chína f.—decline; China—more properly cína.

chinaménto m.—declining; lowering.

chinàre—to lower; to resign oneself; to bow; to stoop.

chinatúra f.—the act of bowing.

chiníno m.—quinine.

chiòsco m.—kiosk; small newspaper stand.

chirògrafo m.—a hand-written undertaking by a debtor.

chirurgía f.—surgery.

chirurgicaménte — according to the rules and practice of surgery.

chirúrgo m.—surgeon.

chiúsa f.—barrier; dam; enclosure; lock.

ciabàtta f.—old shoe; a person or thing that does not perform well.

ciabattíno m.—cobbler; bungler; one who performs his work badly; one who repairs old shoes.

ciampicàre—to walk slowly dragging the feet; to stumble; to work exceedingly slowly.

ciào—till we meet again; so long; farewell.

ciàrla f.—loquacity; nonsense.

ciarlàre—to talk vainly; to prattle.

ciarlatàno m. — charlatan; quack; cheat.

cibàre—to give food.

cibernètica f.—cybernetics; the scientific study of control and communication methods of living organisms and machines, particularly applicable to the analysis of machine operations such as computers.

cíbo m.—food.

cibòrio m.—ciborium; vessel containing consecrated wafers.

cicatríce f.—cicatrix.

ciceróne m.—Cicero, Roman orator, statesman and writer; a guide.

cicisbèo m.—a gallant of a married woman.

ciclotróne m.—cyclotron.

cièco—a blind person (m.); blind.

cífra f.—cipher; zero; any of the Arabic numerals or figures; something of no value or importance; a nonentity; a secret method of writing; an initial or monogram.

cifràre—to encipher or encode; to write by a specially devised code of symbols.

cifràrio m.—a book containing the key to a cipher or code.

címa f.—apex; summit; highest point.

cimitèro m.—cemetery.

cinegètica f.—art of the hunt or chase with dogs.

cinegètico m.—one who hunts with dogs.

cínta f.—circle of wall around a city or castle.

cínta daziària—a tax or impost on consumer goods imposed within a geographical area.

circolàre—to circulate; to move in a circle.

circolàre—circular; having the form of a circle; circuitous; a similar writing which is sent to a number of persons (f.).

circolazióne f.—circulation; movement; the movement of commercial paper, bank notes and coin.

circolazióne di veícoli—movement of vehicles. The driver of a vehicle not guided by tracks or rails, is obligated to compensate for damage caused to a person or to things by the circulation of a vehicle, unless he proves to have done everything possible to avoid damage. In the case of a collision between vehicles, it is presumed, till proof to the contrary, that each of the drivers had equally contributed to produce the damage sustained by the individual vehicles. The proprietor of the vehicle, or in his stead, the one using it or the purchaser under a conditional sales contract, is jointly and severally responsible with the driver, unless it is proved that movement of the vehicle was against his will. In every case, the persons above indicated are responsible for damages derived from faults of construction or defects of maintenance of the vehicle. Art. 2054, 2055, Italian Civil Code. Also, scóntro tra veícoli.

circoncisióne f.—circumcision.

circondàrio m.—an administrative subdivision of a province; the territorial jurisdiction of a tribunal. Art. 129, Constitution of the Italian Republic.

circonvallazióne f.—circumvallation; a road or railway that goes around a city; surrounded by a rampart.

circoscrizióne f.—circumscription; division of a territory with defined

limits; jurisdictional, territorial limits.

circostànza f.—circumstance; an attendant fact; an incident or occurrence; a particular accident or condition accompanying an act or deed which contributes to determining its nature, gravity and importance.

circostànze aggravànti — aggravating circumstances; circumstances accompanying a criminal act which increase or aggravate the penal responsibility and its punishment. Art. 61, 576, 577, Italian Penal Code.

circostànze attenuànti—extenuating or attenuating circumstances; circumstances which render a crime less serious and permit a judge to reduce the sentence. Art. 62, 62 bis, Italian Penal Code.

circostànze del reàto—circumstances of the crime; the elements of a criminal act which determine its seriousness and the imposing of a greater or lesser sentence. Art. 59-70, Italian Penal Code.

cistèrna f.—cistern.

citànte m.—one who sues; plaintiff.

citàre—to summon; to cite; to notify of legal process; to allege facts.

citazióne f.—citation; a summons to appear in court; the document containing said summons; a citation of documents or words óf an author or documents.

citazióne civíle—a civil summons.

citazióne penàle—a criminal summons or citation issued by the judicial authority.

città f.—city.

cittadína f.—female citizen; small city.

cittadinànza f. — citizenship. Citadinanza (Citizenship), Usual Laws, Appendix to Italian Civil Code.

cittadíno m.—citizen. Art. 13-28, Constitution of the Italian Republic.

ciùrma f.—rabble; galley-slaves who rowed the ship; gang of convicts. This term is not used for the crew of a ship which is known as the equipàggio.

ciurmatóre m.—rabble-rouser; charlatan; impostor.

civétta f.—little owl; screech-owl; coquette; a flirt.

cívico—civic.

civíle—civil; pertaining to citizens as members of the State; citizens distinguished from those in military or church organizations; pertaining to the social order of government; gracious; polite.
dirítti civíle—civil rights.
dirítto civíle—civil law.
funeràle civíle—civil funeral without religious participation.
govèrno civíle—civil government.
guèrra civíle—civil war.
lísta civíle—civil list.
matrimònio civíle — civil marriage without religious participation.
mòrte civíle—civil death; loss of civil rights.
pàrte civíle—civil party in a penal trial who seeks damages from an accused criminal.
pòpolo civíle—civilized people.
stàto civíle—civil status of a citizen regarding his birth, family, profession, etc.; office where such statistics are maintained.
tribunàle civíle—civil court.

civilísta m.—one learned in civil law; a lawyer specialized in civil law as distinguished from criminal law.

civiltà f.—civility; politeness; civilized.

civilizzazióne f.—civilization.

civilménte responsàbile — civilly responsible (person). See responsàbile civíle.

clan m.—clan; a group of people of common descent.

clandestíno—clandestine; secret.

clàsse f.—class; an order of persons distinguished by condition or social status.

classificàre—to classify.

classificaziòne f.—classification.

clàusola f.—clause.

clàusola compromissòria—arbitration clause. A clause stipulating that future controversies will be resolved

by arbitration. It must be in writing to be effective. Art. 808, 809, Italian Code of Civil Procedure; Art. 1341, Italian Civil Code. See compromésso.

clàusola limitatíva della proponibilità di eccezióni—clause limiting the interposition of defenses. A clause which provides that one of the parties cannot interpose defenses for the purpose of avoiding or delaying the performance due, has no effect against the defenses of nullity of the contract, annulability due to incapacity and rescission of the contract made under a state of peril. In cases where the clause is deemed effective, the judge, if he recognizes that grave reasons contributed thereto, may, nevertheless, suspend judgment and require the posting of security where necessary. Art. 1462, 1341, 1342, Italian Civil Code. See solve et repete (Lat.).

clàusola penàle—penalty clause. It is a secondary obligation added to the primary one for the purpose of enforcing its performance. It is in the nature of compensation in liquidated damages rather than a penalty as such. In the event of non-performance or delay in performance, one of the contracting parties is held to a stated performance. It has the effect of limiting indemnification for the promised performance unless compensation for further damages was stipulated. Art. 1382-1384, Italian Civil Code.

clàusole di esònero da responsabilità—exoneration clauses. An agreement which excludes or limits, in advance, a debtor's responsibility for fraud or lack of care is void. Likewise, agreements are void which exonerate or limit the responsibility of the debtor or his assistants where such acts violate duties derived from the norms of public order. Art. 1229, 1228, Italian Civil Code.

clemènte — clement; mild; compassionate; lenient; merciful.

clemènza f.—clemency.

cleptomanía f.—kleptomania; irresistible urge to steal without regard to need.

clèro m.—clergy.

cliènte m.—client; one who avails himself of the professional services of a lawyer; customer; one under the patronage of another.

clientèla f.—clientele.

clìma m.—climate.

climatèrico m.—climacteric; a critical or crucial period; a year in which important changes occur in health or fortune.

clìnica f.—clinic.

clìnico m.—a physician or surgeon who teaches in a clinic.

clistère m.—clyster; enema; syringe which introduces the liquid into the rectum.

cloàca f.—sewer; receptable of vice and moral filth.

clònico—violent, convulsive movement characterized by rapid muscular contraction.

cloràto m.—chlorate.

clòrico—chloric.

clorofòrmio m.—chloroform.

clorúro m.—chloride.

coabitazióne f.—cohabitation.

coaccusàto m.—one accused together with others.

coagulàre—to coagulate.

coagulazióne f.—coagulation.

coàgulo m.—coagulant.

coalizióne f.—coalition.

coartàre—to coerce.

coartazióne f.—coercion.

coassiàle—coaxial.

coattívo—coercive; compulsory.

coàtto—forced; imposed by force.
domicílio coàtto—enforced residence in a specific area with restriction of movement. See sicurézza detentíve (misúre di) and misúre di sicurézza personàli.

coautóre m.—co-author.

coazióne f.—violence; coercion; retriction; compulsion.

còca f.—coca; the dried leaves of this plant are used as a stimulant.

cocaìana f.—cocaine; alkaloid of the coca leaves used as an anesthetic.

codeìna f.—codeine.

còdice m.—code; compilation of laws and statutes.

còdice civíle—civil code.

còdice penàle—penal code.

codificàre—to codify; to reduce to a code.

codificazióne f.—codification.

coerède m. & f.—co-heir; one who is an equal heir with others.

coerènte—coherent.

coerènza f.—coherence.

coesistènza f.—co-existence.

coesístere—to co-exist.

coglióne m.—testicle; cullion; mean or base fellow.

cognàta f.—sister-in-law.

cognàto m.—brother-in-law.

cognazióne f. — relations by the mother's or feminine side.

cognizióne f.—cognition; knowledge; the act of examining and deliberation on a judicial matter.

cognizióne (giudízio di, procèsso di)— a proceeding under judicial consideration, involving the preliminary examinations, hearings, trial and judgment. Art. 163-466, Italian Code of Civil Procedure.

cognóme m.—surname; family name. See nóme (diritto al).

colàre—to strain; to filter; to make a metal casting.

colàre a pícco—to sink (of a vessel).

colàta f.—melting stage in refining metals.

colatóio m.—sieve; strainer; colander.

colazióne f.—breakfast; luncheon.
píccola colazióne, príma colazióne— breakfast.
secónda colazióne—luncheon.

colèra m.—cholera.

còlere—to honor; to venerate.

colèrico—choleric.

colesterína f.—cholesterol.

48

collaterále—collateral; side by side; parallel or diverging line, but not lineal; a security pledge for a loan (m.).

collazionàre—to collate; to compare; to conform.

collazióne f.—collation; return by an heir of property received by way of an advancement, so that all co-heirs may share equally in the estate. Art. 737-751, Italian Civil Code.

collazióne di còpie degli àtti púbblici—collation or conforming copies of public documents with the originals. A copy of the document is compared with the original on file with a public registry to determine if it conforms. Art. 746, Italian Code of Civil Procedure.

collazióne e imputazióne ereditària—This involves a return to the mass of the succession of all property received by an heir or descendant in advance of his share, so that such property may be divided by the heirs and descendants equally. Art. 724, 737-751, Italian Civil Code.

collèga m.—colleague.

collegaménto m.—act of uniting.

collegàre—to unite.

collegiàle—collegial; collegiate.

collègio m.—college; a group of persons having certain powers and functions, such as the College of Cardinals and the Electoral College.

collègio di difésa—defense counsel acting together.

collègio sindacàle—board of directors of a corporation. Art. 2397-2409, Italian Civil Code.

collètta f.—collection of money; harvest.

collettàre—to collect; to gather a contribution; to contribute to a charity or public use.

collettivísmo m.—collectivism; a social theory that the land and means of production should belong to the community or the State.

collettivísta m.—follower of collectivism.

còllo m.—cargo; freight; load.

collocaménto m.—arrangement; placing; placement.

agenzía di collocaménto—employment agency.

collocàre—to arange; to place.

collocàr denàri—to invest money.

collocàre a ripòso—to pension an employee.

collocàre una regàzza—to marry off a girl.

collocazióne f.—appointment; arrangement; classification of creditors according to their security. See crédito privilegiàto.

collotòrto m.—hypocrite; bigot; wryneck, a species of bird. See bacchettóne and baciapíle.

collusióne f.—collusion.

collusívo—collusive.

collutòrio m.—mouth wash.

colluttàre—to fight together.

colluttazióne f.—fight.

colònia f.—colony; a portion of a population sent to colonize or live in another country under the laws of their country of origin; the group of citizens of the same nationality who live in a foreign country; a contract for leasing a farm wherein the farmer agrees to cultivate the land and share profits and expenses as in mezzadria. The Italian name for the city of Cologne, derived from the Latin.

colòno m.—farmer; cultivator.

cólpa f.—blame; fault; neglect; negligence; violation of the legal right of another; violation of a legal obligation; a wrong committed without intent but done through negligence or lack of care. Civilly, it is the failure to excise due care. Penally, it connotes the commission of an illegal act or failure to act causing damage without intent. The consequence of the act leading to the damage may be foreseeable or not. See delítti cólpósi di comúne perícolo.

cólpa aquiliàna — Aquilian fault or wrong. It is one that does not arise out of a contractual obligation; it arises from failure to exercise due care and is tortious in nature. Art. 2043-2059, Italian Civil Code.

colpévole — culpable; blameworthy; guilty. The accused is not considered guilty until a definitive sentence is rendered. Art. 27, Constitution of the Italian Republic.

colpóso—culpable; a wrong or crime committed without intent but negligently and with lack of care.

coltellàta f.—wound inflicted with a knife.

coltèllo m.—knife.

coltivàre—to cultivate.

coltivatóre m.—cultivator.

coltivazióne f.—cultivation.

coltívo—cultivated land.

còlto—gathered.

cólto—learned; refined.

comàndo m.—command; act of commanding; the commander's headquarters.

comàre f.—god-mother; mid-wife; a neighborhood female friend.

comatóso—comatose.

combrícola f.—a group of intriguers operating more or less in secret for a non commendable purpose.

combútta f.—a disorderly gathering of people.

comitàgi m.—a band of armed irregulars.

comitàto m.—committee.

comitíva f.—a company of persons.

còmito m. — commander of galley-slaves; person who gives a measured beat to rowers.

comízio m.—comitia; assembly of Romans to exercise legislative power; meeting of citizens to vote or express their views.

còmma m.—comma; interval; clause of an article of law.

commerciàle—commercial.

commercialísta—one learned in the commercial sciences; a lawyer specializing in commercial law.

commerciànte—merchant.

commèrcio m.—commerce; exchange of goods or products.

commèrcio clandestíno o fraudolènto di sostànze stupefacènti—clandestine or fraudulent commerce in narcotic substances. Whoever, in a clandestine or fraudulent manner, carries on commerce in narcotic substances, or holds them for the purpose of carrying on clandestine or fraudulent commerce, or supplies or procures to others such substances clandestinely and fraudulently, is punished with imprisonment. Art. 446, Italian Penal Code.

commèrcio non autorizàto di còse prezióse—unauthorized commerce in precious objects. It is a violation punishable with arrest or fine to manufacture or place in commerce precious objects or engage in brokerage therein or to perform similar activities, arts or industries without license from the Authorities, or observing legal prescriptions. Art. 705, Italian Penal Code. Re sequestration, see Art. 18, Regulatory Dispositions, Italian Code of Penal Procedure.

commèrcio o somministrazióne di medicinàli guàsti—commerce in or supplying of spoiled medicines. Whoever holds for commerce, places in commerce or supplies spoiled or imperfect medicines, is punished with imprisonment. Art. 443, Italian Penal Code.

comméssa f. — commission; order; order for a particular action.

commésso — committed; done; performed.

commésso m.—clerk; employee.

commésso viaggiatóre — travelling salesman. Art. 2210-2212, Italian Civil Code.

commiàto m.—leave-taking.

comminatòrio — comminatory; threatening; punitive.

commissariàto m.—office of a commissioner.

commissàrio m.—commissioner; one entrusted with a public office; head of a police office.

commissionàre—to order goods.

commissionàrio m. — a person empowered to buy or sell goods.

commissióne f.—commission; charge given to someone to perform or provide something; order. It is a contract whereby one party obligates himself to buy or sell property on behalf of others. Art. 1731, 1703, Italian Civil Code.

commistióne f.—commixtion; commixture; mixture; a mixture or mingling. It is one of the methods of acquiring title to property. Art. 922, 939, Italian Civil Code. See unióne e commistióne.

commisto—mixed.

committènte m.—one who ships merchandise or sends goods to be sold on commission; employer; one for whom a contract to perform work or render services is intended. See appaltànte.

commoriènza f.—commorientes (Lat.); death occurring at the same time as a result of the same calamity or disaster. It is a legal presumption that those dying in the same incident are considered as having died at the same time irrespective of who was the first to die. Art. 4, Italian Civil Code. See premoriènza and sopravvivènza.

commutàre—to commute.

comodànte m.—the bailor who lends goods to a bailee without compensation, contemplating their return to the bailor. Also, comodatóre.

comodàre—to accommodate; to lend; to give property in a gratuitous bailment.

comodatàrio m.—the bailee who receives property without compensation with the understanding that the same must be returned.

comodàto m.—commodatum (Lat.), a loan for use. It is a contract whereby one party delivers to another, gratuitously, personal or real property to be used for a time or for a determined use, with the obligation of returning the identical property. Art. 1803-1812, Italian Civil Code. N.B.

The Anglo-American concept of a gratuitous bailment is similar except that it applies only to personal property. See dèposito (contràtto di).

comodatóre m.—a gratuitous bailor. See comodànte.

compaesàno m.—a person from the same country or area; fellow citizen.

companàggio (companàtico) m.—food eaten with bread.

compàre m.—god-father; an intimate.

comparizióne f.—appearance; coming into court as a party to a suit.

compàrsa f.—the appearance of the parties before a judge; in a civil case, the written document of the parties prepared on authenticated paper with the seal of State, to present their case; pleadings.

compatriòtta m.—compatriot.

compàtto—compact.

compèndio m. — compendium; an abridgment, digest or synopsis; extract.

compensàre—to compensate.

compensazióne f.—compensation; extinction of a debt by compensation. Art. 1241-1252, Italian Civil Code. stànza di compensazióne—clearing house. See that title.

compènso m.—compensation; indemnity; amends; expedient.

compratóre m.—purchaser.

competènte — competent; qualified; suitable; having capacity or qualification; sufficient.
giúdice competènte—a judge who has jurisdiction of a case to render judgment.
persóna competènte—a person in a position to know and judge.

competènza f.—competence; jurisdiction; legal capacity to adjudicate a cause of action; legal fee.

competènza civíle—civil jurisdiction; power to adjudicate a civil case.

competènza civíle per connessióne—civil jurisdiction by connection (of subject matter) or joinder of actions. Art. 39, 40, Italian Code of Civil Procedure. See connessióne.

competènza civíle per matèria e per valóre—civil jurisdiction by subject matter and by amount. The jurisdiction of the various civil courts by subject matter and amount is set forth. They are the courts of Conciliation, the Praetor and the Tribunal. Art. 7-17, Italian Code of Civil Procedure.

competènza civíle per territòrio—civil territorial jurisdiction. Unless the law provides otherwise, the judge in the place where the defendant has his residence or domicile has competence and jurisdiction, and if these are unknown, the judge in the place where the defendant is dwelling. If the defendant does not have residence, nor domicile, nor dwelling within the State, or if the dwelling is unknown, the judge in the place where the plaintiff resides, has jurisdiction. Art. 18-30, Italian Code of Civil Procedure.

competènza del pretóre—jurisdiction of the Praetor. He possesses jurisdiction over crimes for which the law establishes a detentive penalty not superior to a maximum of three years, or a pecuniary penalty alone or together with the detentive penalty. Art. 31, Italian Code of Penal Procedure. Civilly, Art. 8, 21, 434, Italian Code of Civil Procedure.

competènza del tribunàle—jurisdiction of the Tribunal. It possesses jurisdiction of crimes other than those tried by the Court of Assizes and which are granted to the Praetor. Art. 30, 29, 31, Italian Code of Penal Procedure. See tribunàle.

competènza del tribunàle fallimentàre—jurisdiction of the bankruptcy tribunal or court. The court which has declared the bankruptcy is competent to hear all the actions that derive therefrom, whatever their value may be, even if they relate to work contracts, except real property actions for which the ordinary rules of jurisdiction apply. Art. 9, 23, 24, Falliménto (Bankruptcy), Usual Laws, Appendix to Italian Civil Code.

competènza della córte d'assíse—jurisdiction of the Court of Assizes. Generally, it has jurisdiction over the

more serious crimes such as our felonies. Its jurisdiction is set out specifically by law. Art. 29, Italian Code of Penal Procedure.

competènza penàle—penal jurisdiction; the power to adjudicate a criminal case.

competènza penàle per connessióne—Penal jurisdiction by connection (of subject matter or territorial jurisdiction) and joinder of actions. Art. 45-50, Italian Code of Penal Procedure. See connessióne.

competènza penàle per matèria—penal jurisdiction by subject matter. The jurisdiction of the various penal courts by subject matter is set forth. They are the court of Assizes, the Tribunal and the Praetor. Art. 29-38, Italian Code of Penal Procedure.

competènza penàle per territòrio—penal territorial jurisdiction. The jurisdiction by territory is determined by the place where the crime was committed. With regards to an attempted crime, the jurisdiction lies with the judge of the place where the last act directed toward the commission of the crime was completed. In regards to a continuing or permanent crime, jurisdiction belongs to the judge of the place where the continuation or duration of the crime came to an end. If jurisdiction cannot be determined, as above set forth, that judge has jurisdiction in the last place where a part of the act or of the omission which constitutes the crime was verified. If this place is unknown, that judge has jurisdiction in the place where the arrest was made, or the judge who issued the mandate or decree of citation for trial and in lieu thereof, the judge of the place where the first act of the proceeding was completed. If the jurisdiction cannot be determined by one of the foregoing means, jurisdiction is, successively, in the judge of the place where the accused has his residence, dwelling or domicile. If the crime was committed, in part, in the territory of the State, and in part, abroad, the proceedings take place within the State, and jurisdiction is with the judge of the place where there occurred, in whole or in part, the act or the omission, or where the event was verified. If the crime was committed entirely in a foreign State, jurisdiction is determined, successively, by the place of residence, of dwelling, of domicile, of arrest or delivery of the accused. Art. 39-44, Italian Code of Penal Procedure.

compleànno m. — birthday; anniversary.

còmplice m.—accomplice.

complicità f.—complicity.

complottàre—to plot; to plot a secret plan or scheme to achieve some purpose, usually unlawful.

complòtto m.—plot; scheme; machination.

cómpera f. (cómpra)—purchase.

compravéndita—a contract of sale and transfer of a thing or right in exchange for a purchase price. Also, véndita. Art. 1470-1547, Italian Civil Code.

compravéndita (contràtto di)—a contract of sale and purchase.

compromésso m. — compromise; arbitration; an agreement between parties to submit a controversy for resolution to an arbitrator. Under Italian law the agreement must be in writing or it is void. Labor controversies and certain others are excepted. Art. 806, 807, Italian Code of Civil Procedure. Also, a promise to enter into a contract upon verification of certain conditions; a legal commitment. See clàusola compromissòria and transazióne.

comprométtere—to refer the decision of a controversy to someone.

compromissàrio—arbitrator.

compromissòrio — arbitrable matter. See clàusola compromissòria.

compropietà f.—property in common with others; condominium.

comproprietàrio m.—one who owns property in common with others.

comprovàre—to approve; to confirm.

computàre—to compute.

computazióne f.—computation.

computìsta m.—accountant.

computistería f.—accountant's office.

còmputo m.—computation.

còmputo dei tèrmini—computation of time. In computing time by days or hours, the initial day or hour is excluded. In computing time by months or years, the common calendar is used. Holidays are computed in the period of time. If the due date falls on a holiday, said maturity date is postponed to the following day which is not a holiday. Art. 155, Italian Code of Civil Procedure; Art. 14, Italian Penal Code; Art. 180-183 bis, Italian Code of Penal Procedure.

còmputo dei tèrmini di prescrizióne—computation of the limits of prescription. The limits of prescription contemplated by the present Code and other laws is computed according to the common calendar. The day on which the period of prescription starts is excluded from computation and the last day is included. If the period of prescription expires on a holiday, it is deferred to the following non-festive day. Prescription by months is determined in the month of expiration and on the day of the month corresponding to the day of the initial month. If the due month of expiration does not have such a date, then the termination of time is completed on the last day of that same month. Art. 2963, Italian Civil Code; Art. 155, Italian Code of Civil Procedure; Art. 14, Italian Penal Code; Art. 180, Italian Code of Penal Procedure.

comunàle—communal.

comunànza f.—community of things.

comúne—common; general; ordinary; usual.

comúne m.—commune; municipality. Like the province, it is an autonomous entity within the bounds of the general laws of the Republic which determine its functions. Art. 128, Constitution of the Italian Republic.

comunicàre—to communicate.

comunicazióne f.—communication.

comunicazióne (del cancellière)—communication from the clerk of the court. It is a Notice from the clerk in a civil case called *bigliétto di cancelléria*. In a criminal case, it is called *avviso di depòsito*. It is sent by the clerk to the prosecutor regarding decisions and orders of the court. Art. 136, Italian Code of Civil Procedure; Art. 151, Italian Code of Penal Procedure.

comunicazióne ed esibizióne di scrittúre contàbile—communication and exhibition for inspection of written records of account. The complete books and records of accounts and correspondence may be ordered by a judge only in controversies involving the dissolution of a partnership, community property and in matters of succession due to death. In other cases, the judge may order the inspection for reproduction of matters regarding the controversy. Art. 2711, Italian Civil Code. Also, esibizióne di scrittúre contàbile.

comunicazióne giudiziària — judicial communication. It is a Notice in a criminal case sent to the accused, the injured party and other parties in interest setting forth the law which was infringed and calling upon them to retain counsel. Also, *avviso di procediménto*. Art. 304, Italian Code of Penal Procedure.

comunióne f.—communion; property held in common; tenancy in common. Art. 1100-1116, Italian Civil Code. Also, see comproprietà and condomínio.

comunióne dei bèni tra còniugi—community property of spouses. The articles of the Civil Code relative to the above heading have been changed and repealed. The new heading substituted in its place is entitled: "separazióne dei bèni (regíme di)"—regime for the separation of property, thus changing the former rules pertaining to community property of spouses. See separazióne dei bèni (regíme di). Art. 215, 217-219, Italian Civil Code.

comunióne forzósa del múro—obligatory common or party wall. It is a form of enforced expropiation in favor of a private individual. The owner of land contiguous to another's wall may demand it be constituted into a common or party wall upon payment of one-half the value of the wall as well as one-half the value of the land on which it is constructed. Art. 874, 875, Italian Civil Code.

comunísmo m.—communism; a theory of government based on the State owning all property and means of production.

comunísta m.—communist; also used to indicate one who owns property or rights thereon together with others. See comunàza.

comunità f.— community.

concàusa f. — a preexisting cause whereby a crime acquires an effect more serious than would normally occur; concomitant cause; contributory cause. Art. 41, Italian Penal Code.

concausàle—referring to a preexisting cause which contributes to an effect.

concedènte m.—one who concedes; grantor. Also conceditóre.

concèdere—to concede; to admit as true; to grant.

concedíbile—that which may be admitted.

conceditóre m.—one who concedes; grantor. Also, concedènte.

concentraménto m.—concentration.

concentràre—to concentrate.

concentràto—concentrated.

concentrazióne f.—concentration.

concepiménto m.—conception.
presunzióne di concepiménto durànte il matrimònio — presumption of conception during the marriage. Art. 232, Italian Civil Code.

concepíre—to conceive.

concessionàrio m.—concessionaire.

concessióne f.—concession.

concilàre—to concilate.

conciliatóre m.—one who counsels or conciliates.

conciliatóre (giúdice)—judge of conciliation. An honorary post at the base of the Italian legal system. He is a conciliator and adjudicates small claims matters in civil and commercial disputes. Art. 7, Italian Code of Civil Procedure.

conciliazióne f.—reconciliation.

concílio m.—council; consistory.

concíme m.—fertilizer.

concistòro m.—consistory. Also, consistòrio and consistòro.

concittadíno m.—fellow citizen.

conclàve m.—conclave; meeting of cardinals for the election of a pope; the place of their meeting.

conclavísta m.—prelate or lay person attending a cardinal in conclave.

concordàre—to concord; to agree; to reconcile.

concordatàrio m.—party to an accord or agreement; party to a composition of creditors.

concordàto m. — concordat; accord; agreement; composition of creditors; a convention or agreement between two parties; a pact between the Holy See and a State to regulate relations between them.

concordàto fallimentàre—bankruptcy accord; composition in bankruptcy. The bankrupt, when his liabilities have been judicially determined, may propose a composition to the creditors by submitting it to the Bankruptcy Judge. It must contain the percentage to be repaid the creditors and the guarantees offered for their repayment as well as for the expenses of the proceeding and Trustee's compensation. The judge may suspend liquidation upon submission of the accord. Art. 124-141, Falliménto (Bankruptcy), Usual Laws, Appendix to Italian Civil Code.

concordàto preventívo—preventive accord or agreement. An insolvent businessman who has not been declared bankrupt, may arrange with his creditors to guarantee payment to them of at least 40% of his written debts within six months of the approval of the accord. Conditions precedent to the accord are that the insolvent party has not been declared a bankrupt during five years prior to the accord, or has been admitted to a composition; that he has not been convicted for a bankruptcy violation or for crimes against property, the public trust and economy or, industry and commerce. Art. 160-186, Falliménto (Bankruptcy), Usual Laws, Appendix to Italian Civil Code; Art. 2221, Italian Civil Code.

concòrde—in accord; in agreement; unanimous.

concòrdia f.—concord; agreement.

concorrènte—concurrent.

concorrènza f.—concurrence; competition.

concorrènza (límiti legàli della)—legal limits of competition. It must not injure the national economic interest and shall develop within the limits established by law. An agreement limiting competition must be proved by a writing. It is valid if limited to a specific area or to a specific activity. If the duration of the agreement is not specified or is for a period above five years, the agreement is only valid for five years. Art. 2595, 2596, Italian Civil Code.

concorrènza sleàle—unfair competition. Art. 2598-2601, Italian Civil Code.

concòrrere—to assemble; co-concur; to compete.

concórso — concourse; concurrence; crowd; competition.

concórso dei creditóri—meeting of creditors; right of unsecured creditors to share equally in the debtor's assets in satisfaction of their claims. Art. 2741, Italian Civil Code.

concórso delle pàrti—meeting of the litigating parties for an adjudication by judicial trial. See costituzióne delle pàrti in giudízio civíle and costituzióne di pàrte civíle.

concórso di cólpe—concurrence of wrongs. It occurs when damage has been produced by the wrongdoer himself or by others for whom he is responsible. Also, responsabilità civíle per fàtto illécito. See cólpa aquiliàna and risarciménto per fàtto illécito. Art. 2043-2059, Italian Civil Code.

concórso di persóne nel reàto—concurrence of persons in the crime. It involves the participation of more than one person in the same crime. Each person involved is subjected to the punishment prescribed for said crime, except for the dispositions contained in other articles. The punishments inflicted may vary. Art. 110-119, Italian Penal Code; Art. 45 et seq., Italian Code of Penal Procedure

concórso di reàti—concurrence of crimes. It occurs when a person, by a single action or omission, violates diverse dispositions of law or commits more than one violation of the same disposition of law, and is punished as prescribed. Art. 81, 74-80, 82-84, Italian Penal Code.

concretàre—to arrive at a definite conclusion; to effectuate.

concubína f.—concubine.

concubinàto m.—concubinage.

concussionàrio m.—extortioner.

concussióne f.—extortion; the abuse of a public office by extorting money or exacting other illegal profit. It is committed by a public official who abuses his office by compelling someone to unlawfully give or promise to him or to a third party, money or other thing of value. It is punished with imprisonment. Art. 317, Italian Penal Code.

condànna f.—condemnation; sentence for a crime or unlawful act; fine or penalty. Civilly, it is a judgment ordering a party to a controversy to pay a pecuniary penalty or perform something for the adversary. Penally, it is the infliction of detentive or pecuniary punishment or both. An accused is not considered guilty until a definitive sentence is rendered, nor is the death penalty permitted, except in cases allowed by Martial Law. Art. 27, Constitution of the Italian Republic; Art 179, Italian Code of Civil Procedure.

condannàre—to condemn; to sentence for a crime or unlawful act; to punish with sanctions, payment of a fine or penalty.

condannàto—condemned; sentenced.

condannàto m.—person condemned to punishment.

condizionàle f.—conditional; restrictive.
   condànna condizionàle—conditional sentence; more properly, liberazióne condizionàle, it is used for rehabilitation of the prisoner who is released conditionally. Art. 176, 177, Italian Penal Code.

condizióne f.—condition; a future and uncertain event upon the happening of which depends the existence of an obligation or liability. See condizióne nel contràtto, Art. 1353-1361, Italian Civil Code.

condomínio m.—condominium; property owned in common with others. Art. 1117-1139, Italian Civil Code.

condómino m.—one who owns property in condominium.

condonàre — to forgive; to condone; to remit a part or all of a debt or sentence.

condonazióne f.—condonation.

condótta f.—conduct; behavior; management; direction.

conduttóre m.—conductor; one who operates a vehicle; one who hires; lessee. See obbligazióni principàli del conduttóre.

confederazióne f.—confederation.

conferènza f.—conference.

conferiménto m.—conferring; act of conferring.

conferíre—to confer; to bestow; to grant; to collate. See collazióne e imputazióne ereditària.

conférma f.—confirmation; assent; approval.

confermàre—to confirm; to approve; to validate.

confermazióne f.—confirmation; the sacrament of confirmation.

confessàre—to confess; to admit as

true; to confess guilt; to acknowledge.

confessióne f.—confession. In a civil proceeding it is an admission or statement by one party as to the truth of facts that are adverse to it and which support the other side. In a criminal proceeding it is a voluntary admission of the crime. Art. 2730-2735, Italian Civil Code. Art. 228, 229, Italian Code of Civil Procedure; Art. 225, 389, 563, Italian Code of Penal Procedure.

confessióne giudiziàle—judicial confession. It is one made during the course of legal proceedings. Art. 2733, Italian Civil Code. Art. 228, 229, Italian Code of Civil Procedure.

confessióne stragiudiziàle—extra judicial confession. It is one made by a party otherwise than during the course of legal proceedings. Art. 2735, Italian Civil Code.

confèsso—acknowledged; confessed.

confessóre m.—confessor.

confidàre—to confide; to entrust.

confidènte m.—confidant; one to whom secrets are confided; a spy.

confidènte—confiding; trusting.

confidènza f.—confidence; trust.

confidenziàle—confidential.

confinàre—to be sentenced to the "confíno"; to banish; to confine; to border upon.

confinàto m.—one who has been sentenced to the "confíno".

confíne m.—confines; limits; border; frontier.

confíno m.—a preventive measure applicable to dangerous persons. One who is so condemned must leave his domicile to reside for a specified time in a designated area without leaving for the term of his sentence. See misúre amministratíve di sicurézza and misúre di sicurézza personàli.

confirmatòria—See capàrra confirmatòria.

confísca f.—confiscation; forfeiture. The penalty by which the goods and fruits of the crime are turned over to the public treasury. Also, confiscazióne. Art. 240, Italian Penal Code.

confiscàre—to confiscate.

confiscazióne f.—confiscation. See confísca.

conflagràre—to burn; to inflame; to burn quickly and nosily; to take fire.

conflagrazióne f.—conflagration.

conflìtto m.—conflict; combat; opposition; contention.

conflìtto di attribuzióne—conflict of authority. Conflicts between the State and Regions and between Regions are resolved by the Constitutional Court. Conflicts between judges, as to whether a matter comes within their respective competence, are resolved by the Court of Cassation. Art. 134, Constitution of the Italian Republic; Art. 41, Italian Code of Civil Procedure. See regolaménto di giurisdizióne e di competènza.

conflìtto di competènza—conflict of authority over a subject matter. See regolaménto di competènza.

conflìtto di giurisdizióne—conflict of jurisdiction; a conflict between judges as to whether a matter comes within their respective competence. It is resolved by the Court of Cassation. See regolaménto di giurisdizióne e di competènza and conflìtto di attribuzióne.

conflìtto di interèssi—conflict of interests. Art. 320, 347, 360, 2373, 2391, 2464, 2487, 2516 and 1394, Italian Civil Code.

confluènte m.—confluent; flowing or running together; a tributary stream; one of two or more streams which unite into one.

confluènza f.—confluence; the flowing together of two or more streams; an assemblage; throng.

confóndere—to confound; to confuse; to throw into disorder; to bewilder.

confondiménto m.—confusion.

confórme — concords; corresponds; same as; in conformity.

còpia confórme—a copy corresponding to the original.

confrontàre—to confront; to compare.

confrontazióne f.—confrontation.

confrónto m.—act of confronting; placing a witness face to face with the accused for the purpose of recognition and to ascertain the accuracy of testimony.

confusióne f.—confusion; mixture; the extinction of an obligation where the character of debtor and creditor have been united in the same person. Art. 1253-1255, Italian Civil Code.

confutazióne f.—confutation; part of a speech in which the arguments and proofs of the adversary are refuted.

congedàre—to take leave; to discharge; to dismiss.

congèdo m.—leave; discharge; furlough.

congégno m.—apparatus; mechanism.

congènito—congenital.

congestióne f.—congestion; an unnatural accumulation of blood in the vessels of an organ.

congettúra f.—conjecture.

congiúngere—to join together; to unite.

congiúnto m.—kinsman; relation.

congiunzióne f.—conjunction.

congiúra f.—conspiracy.

congiuràto m.—one who conspires.

congiuratóre m.—conspirator.

congiurazióne f.—conspiracy.

conglomeràto m.—conglomerate.

conglomerazióne f.—conglomeration.

còngruo—congruous; convenient; fitting; opportune; proportionate.

conguagliàre—to balance; to equalize; to adjust accounts; to square up.

conguàglio m.—balancing; equalization; levelling.

conguàglio (fàre il)—to balance an account.

coniugàle—conjugal.

còniuge m.—spouse; consort.

còniugi m.—husband and wife. Relative to rights and duties, see Art. 143-148, Italian Civil Code.

connazionàle m.—fellow countryman.

connessióne f.—connection; joinder. The joining of actions or parties in a suit. For civil actions, see Art. 40, Italian Code of Civil Procedure. For criminal actions, see Art. 45, Italian Code of Penal Procedure.

connúbio m.—marriage; union in matrimony.

conoscènte m.—an acquaintance.

conoscènte—knowing.

conoscènza f.—the act of knowing; cognition; knowledge.

conóscere—to know; to discern; to recognize.

conquèsto m.—complaint.

conquísto m. (conquísta f.)—conquest.

consanguínei (fratèlli e sorèlle)—consanguineous brothers and sisters. They are born of the same father but different mothers. See unilateràli (fratèlli e sorèlle), germàni (fratèlli e sorèlle) and uteríni (fratèlli e sorèlli).

consanguineità f.—consanguinity.

consanguíneo—consanguineous; of the same blood; brothers and sisters born of the same father but different mothers. See consanguínei (fratèlli e sorèlle).

consanguinità f.—consanguinity.

consapévole—aware; informed (of a fact); knowing; conscious; having knowledge or information.

consapevolézza f.—cognizance; knowledge; notice (of a fact); acquaintance with a fact or possessing information.

consapevolménte—with knowledge (of a fact); knowingly.

conségna f.—consignment; orders; instructions; delivery; transmittal.

consegnàre—to consign; to hand over or deliver formally; to transfer; to transmit; to entrust.

consegnatàrio m.—consignee; depositary.

consegnatóre m.—consignor.

consènso m.—assent; consent; accord; approbation; a written document which contains assent. Re contractual element, See Art. 1362-1342, Italian Civil Code.

consènso dell'avènte dirítto—an exculpatory cause of a crime. Also, esimènte and scriminànte. Art. 50, Italian Penal Code.

consenuàle—consensual.

consentiménto m. — accord; agreement; consent.

consentíre—to consent; to approve.

consenziènte—consentient; acting in agreement.

conservàre—to conserve; to keep; to preserve.

conservatívo—conservative; apt to preserve or conserve.

conservatívo (sequèstro)—preventive sequestration; an attachment of goods by creditors to prevent the possibility of their disposal by the debtor.

conservatóre m.—conservator; keeper of archives; guardian; conservative (politics); custodian.

conservatóre dei regístri immobiliàri—registrar of immovable property (real property). Art. 2673-2682, Italian Civil Code.

conservatoría f.—office of the custodian or conservator.

conservatòrio m.—conservatory.

conservazióne f.—preservation.

conservazióne del contràtto—preservation of the contract. In case of doubt, the contract or its individual clauses must be interpreted in a sense in which they may have some effect rather than one in which they would have none. Ambiguous clauses must be interpreted according to the general practice in the place where the contract was concluded. Where one of the parties to a contract is an entrepreneur, ambiguous clauses are interpreted according to the general practice in the place where his headquarters are located. Art. 1367, 1368, 1419, Italian Civil Code. Also, see princípio di conservazióne.

conservazióne delle scrittúre contàbili—preservation of book-keeping records. Records must be preserved for ten years from the date of last entry. The originals of invoices, letters and telegrams received and copies of similar documents sent, must be preserved for ten years. Art. 2220, Italian Civil Code.

consèsso m.—a meeting of important people.

consigliàre—to counsel; to advise.

consigliatóre m.—one who advises.

consiglière m.—counselor; adviser.

consíglio m.—counsel; advice; a council.

consíglio comunàle—municipal council. It is elected for a term of five years by the citizens inscribed in the municipal register of population.

consíglio dell'órdine degli avvocàti e procuratóri—Council of the Order of Lawyers and Procurators. It maintains the register of those inscribed to practice the legal profession and has disciplinary powers over them.

consíglio di amministrazióne nelle società per azióni. Managing council or board of directors in corporations. Art. 2380, Italian Civil Code.

consíglio di patronàto — Council of Patronage. An organization which gives aid and assistance to freed prisoners and to the families of those who are incarcerated. Art. 149, 185, 188, 193-195, Italian Penal Code; Consígli di Patronàto (Patronage Councils), Usual Laws, Appendix to Italian Code of Penal Procedure.

consíglio di prefettúra—Council of the Prefecture. It is an organization with consultative and jurisdictional functions regarding the accounting of municipal treasurers and local charitable groups.

consíglio di stàto—Council of State. It is charged with safeguarding the administration of justice. Art. 100, 103, Constitution of the Italian Republic.

Consíglio nazionàle forènse—National Forensic Council. It is the elected organ of the Councils of the Orders of Lawyers and Procurators. It exercises the powers granted to it by the law regulating the Bar. It gives opinions on laws regarding the legal profession when requested by the Minister of Justice.

consíglio provinciàle—Provincial Council. It is elected on the basis of proportional representation for a period of five years and is a deliberative body.

consíglio superióre della magistratúra —Superior Council of the Judiciary. It is charged with the appointment, assignment, transfers, promotions and disciplinary proceedings regarding judges. Art. 104, 105, Constitution of the Italian Republic.

consíglio supremo di difésa—Supreme Defense Council. It is presided over by the President of the Italian Republic. It is empowered to declare a state of war following resolution by the Parliament. Art. 87, Constitution of the Italian Republic.

consiliàre—pertaining to a council.

consistòrio or consistòro m. — consistory.

consociàre—to associate; to take into partnership.

consociàto m.—associate; partner.

consociazióne f.—alliance; association; league.

consòcio m.—partner; associate.

consolàre—to console; to comfort; consular; pertaining to a consul.

consolàto m.—consulate. Title I-IV, Consolàti (Consulates), Usual Laws, Appendix to Italian Civil Code.

cònsole m.—consul.

consòrte m. & f.—consort; spouse.

consòrzio m.—consortium; an association of various persons or entities with equal rights and obligations for the purpose of undertaking a specific enterprise.

cònsta—is proved; consists of.
Non consta—a verdict of not proven.

constàre—to be composed of; to be clear; to be evident.

constatàre—to establish as a fact.

consuetúdine f.—constant use; a custom having legal force. Custom is not admissible in Italian Penal Law. The Penal Code states that no one may be punished for an act which has not been expressly anticipated as a crime by the law nor with punishments established by it. Art. 1, Italian Penal Code. Art. 8, Preliminary Dispositions; Art. 1368, 1374, Italian Civil Code. See úsi.

consulènte m.—one who gives professional or expert advice; expert.

consulènte tècnico—technical or professional expert. In a civil case, an individual called to testify as an expert is referred to as "consulènte tècnico" whether called by the judge or the parties to the action. In a criminal case, the expert called by the parties is named "consulènte tècnico", but when called by the judge is referred to as "perìto." Art. 61-64, 87, 191-201, Italian Code of Civil Procedure; Art. 13-27, 89-92, Enabling Rules, Italian Code of Civil Procedure; Art. 314-322; 323-325, 341, 351, 423, 452, 518-520, Italian Code of Penal Procedure; Art. 380, 381, 383, Italian Penal Code. Re compensation, see vacazióne. See perìto.

consúlta f.—consultation; council.

consultàre—to consult.

consultazióne f.—consultation.

consúlto m.—professional advice of physicians or lawyers.

consultóre m.—adviser; consulter.

consultòrio m.—place where advice is given; physician's office.

consumàbile—that which can be consumed.

consumàbili (bèni) — consumable things. Those things or goods which can be used only once and are consumed.

consumàre—to consume; to waste; to commit (a crime).

consúmo m. — conusmption; (econ.) use of goods and services having a value.

dàzio cónsumo—a tax on consumer goods.

consunzióne f.—consumption.

contàbile m.—accountant.

contabilità f.—accounts; bookkeeping.

contabilità (tenúta della)—keeping of accounts. See tenúta della contabilità.

contadíno m.—farmer; farm worker; rustic.

contàdo m.—the countryside around a city.

contàgio m.—communication of a disease by contact; plague; contagion.

contagióne f.—contagion. See contàgio.

contagióso—contagious.

contaminàre—to contaminate.

contaminazióne f.—contamination.

contànte—cash; money on hand.

contàre—to count.

contèndere—to contend; to dispute; to question; to controvert.

contenzióso—contentious; litigious.

contenzióso m.—office which handles legal controversies.

contenzióso amministratívo—administrative justice between the public and private sectors.

contenzióso diplomàtico — a council which renders opinions on international law.

contestàre—to contest; to controvert; to deny; to dispute; to declare; to notify.

contestazióne f.—the act of contesting; notification in a peremptory manner.

contèste m.—a fellow witness; witnesses who are in accord in a deposition.

contèsto m.—context; content of a speech or writing.

contestuàle—relating to the context; contextual.

contíguo — contiguous; in contact; touching; in close proximity without actually touching.

continènza di càuse—pending actions comprising the same subject matter. See litispendènza e continènza di càuse.

contingènte—contingent.

contingènza f.—contingency.

continuità f.—continuity.

cónto m.—account; bill; calculation; check; explanation; itemized list for payment.
far di cónto—to make up an account.

cónto apèrto—open account.

cónto corrènte—current account. Art. 1823-1833; 1852-1857, Italian Civil Code.

contrabandière m.—smuggler.

contrabbándo m.—contraband.

contracchiàve f.—false key; a second key for double locking. See grimaldèllo and possèsso ingiustificàto di chiàvi alteràte o di grimaldèlli.

contraccífra f.—a cipher key.

contraccúsa f.—an accusation made by the accused against his accuser.

contràda f.—country region; section or quarter of a city.

contraddittòrio—contradictory; asserting the contrary or opposite; a political debate.

contraddizióne f.—contradiction.

contraddòte f.—a husband's settlement on his wife over and above the dower which she brings.

contraènte m.—contracting party.

contraffàre—to counterfeit; to imitate; to forge.

contrafattóre m. — counterfeiter; forger.

contraffazióne f.—counterfeiting; falsification.

contramàstro m.—ship's mate.

contrammiràglio m.—rear-admiral.

contràrre—to contract; to conclude; to establish.

contrassegnàre — to countersign; to mark.

contrasségno m.—countersign; a sign to recognize a thing or a person. See contromàrca.

contrastàre—to oppose; to resist; to contest.

contràsto m.—contrast; opposition; quarrel.

contrattàbile—open to an offer; subject to negotiation.

contrattàre—to contract; to negotiate.

contràtti m.—contracts. For requisites. See Art. 1325, Italian Civil Code.

contràtti a contànti—cash payment contracts.

contràtti a mercàto férmo—firm market price contracts. Those where the parties have defined their obligations from the beginning.

contràtti a mercàto líbero—free market contracts; contracts on exchange markets where one of the parties may withdraw from the contract upon payment of a premium. Also, contràtti a prèmio.

contràtti a prèmio—premium contracts; contracts on exchange markets where one of the parties may withdraw from the contract upon payment of a premium. Also contràtti a mercàto líbero.

contràtti a tèrmine—time contracts: contracts on exchange markets where payment is due at a certain time, usually the end of the current month or the following one. See contràtti di bórsa.

contràtti agràri—agrarian contracts.

contràtti bancàri—bank contracts. For bank deposits and savings bank deposit book, see Art. 1834, 1835, Italian Civil Code. For safety deposit boxes, see Art. 1839, 1840, Italian Civil Code.

contràtti bilateràli—bilateral contracts. These contracts contain reciprocal obligations of the parties towards each other, such as in a sale of property, where the seller obligates himself to transfer the property and the buyer obligates himself to pay the purchase price. Art. 1470, 1325, Italian Civil Code. See contràtti sinallagmàtici—contracts which create obligations on both parties thereto.

contràtti con prestazióne corrispettíve —contracts with corresponding obligations. See contràtti corrispettívi.

contràtti corrispettívi—contracts with corresponding obligations. These contracts contain reciprocal obligations or performances by both parties. Also, contràtti con prestazióni corrispettíve. See contràtti

sinallagmàtici and Art. 1406, 1453, 1460, 1461, 1463, 1467, Italian Civil Code.

contràtti dello stàto—state contracts. Such contracts may be awarded by public bidding, private closed bidding or by private negotiation.

contràtti di bórsa—exchange contracts. It includes sales of shares and merchandise generally, whether on the stock exchange or privately. Art. 1474, 1531-1536, 1515 and 1735, Italian Civil Code.

contràtti innominàti—innominate contracts. These are atypical or unclassified contracts not belonging to types having a particular discipline under the Civil Code. Art, 1322, 1323, Italian Civil Code.

contràtti nominàti—nominate, typical or classified contracts such as those of sale or rental which are disciplined by particular provisions of the Italian Civil Code.

contràtti sinallagmàtici—bilateral contracts which create obligations on both parties.

contràtti stellàge—contracts on exchange markets whereby the party paying a premium reserves the right to buy or sell a stated quantity of specified shares of securities. See contràtti di bórsa.

contràtti unilateràli—unilateral contracts. These contracts contain an obligation or promise of performance on one side only.

contràtto m.—contract; agreement by two or more parties to undertake legal obligations. Art. 1321-1986, Italian Civil Code. Re contracts required to be by public Act or private writing, see Art. 1350, Italian Civil Code. See requisíti del contràtto — requisites of a contract.

contràtto aleatòrio—aleatory contract. It is an agreement whereby the gains and losses depend upon an uncertain event. See contràtto con prestazióni corrispettíve.

contràtto (offèrta di modificazióne del) —offer to modify a contract. The contracting party against whom rescission is sought, may avoid it by offering to modify it sufficiently to restore its provisions equitably. Art. 1450, Italian Civil Code. See also, Art. 1432 and Art. 1467.

contràtto con prestazióni corrispettíve —contract with mutual performances. In contracts of a continuing nature or periodic or deferred execution, if the performance of one of the parties has become excessively burdensome due to extraordinary or unforeseen events, the party who must perform may demand the rescission of the contract. Rescission may not be obtained if the supervening burden inheres in the normal risk of the contract. The party, against whom rescission is sought, may avoid it by offering to modify, equitably, the terms of the contract. Art. 1467, Italian Civil Code. See **rebus sic stantibus.**

contràtto condizionàle — conditional contract. The parties may subordinate the effectiveness or rescission of the contract or of a single agreement, to a future and uncertain event. Art. 1353, Italian Civil Code.

contràtto d'òpera—work contract. It is a contract for work and services for compensation. Art. 2222-2228, Italian Civil Code.

contràtto di prestazióne d'òpera intellectuàle—contract for intellectual work and services. Art. 2230-2238, Italian Civil Code.

contràtto di somministrazióne—an output, requirements and exclusive dealings contract. Art. 1559-1570, Italian Civil Code. Cf. Art. 2-316, Uniform Commercial Code.

contrattuàle—contractual.

contravvenzióne f.—contravention; offense; an infraction or violation of the Penal Code which results in a crime with damage to another. It is punishable by arrest, which may last from five days to three years and the payment of a fine called ammènda or both. Art. 17, 18, 25, 26, 39, 40, 650-734, Italian Penal Code. See arrèsto and ammènda.

contribuènte m.—contributor; one who pays taxes.

contribúto m.—contribution; share; portion.

contributóre m.—contributor.

contribuzióne f.—contribution.

controdichiarazióne f. — a statement made after an agreement whereby the contracting parties annul or modify the contents of the agreement.

controfuòco (dàre il)—to undertake counter-measures against a fire.

controllàre—to control; to verify; to audit; to inspect; to review; to check; to regulate.

contròllo m.—control.

controllóre m.—controller.

contromàrca m.—a theater ticket stub for identification to permit re-entry to a performance. See contrasségno.

contropàrte f.—the adversary side in an action.

contropartíta f.—one side of entries in a double entry ledger.

controproducènte—counterproductive.

contropròva f.—evidence presented by one side in opposition to that presented by the adversary side on the same matter in issue.

controquerèla f.—a complaint against the original complaining party; counter-complaint; counter-claim.

contrórdine m.—counter order.

controreclàmo m.—counterclaim.

controricórso m.—counterclaim.

controspionàggio f.—counterespionage.

controstallía f.—the period of time a vessel is detained in excess of the normal period required to load and unload a vessel and for which extra compensation is given in proportion to the period of delay. Also, soprastallía. See stallía—demurrage.

controstallía straordinària — extraordinary demurrage. The period of time a vessel is detained for loading and unloading in excess of the contrastallia. Also, extrastallía. See stallía—demurrage.

controvèrsia f.—controversy.

controvertíre—to controvert.

contumàce—contumacious.

contumàcia f.—contumacy; wilful failure of a person duly summoned by a court to appear and defend himself or to obey a lawful order or direction of the court. Art. 497-501 Italian Code of Penal Procedure; Art. 290-294, Italian Code of Civil Procedure.

contusióne f.—contusion.

convalescènte m.—convalescent.

convalescènza f.—convalescence.

convàlida f.—act of validating. An annullable contract may be validated by the contracting party who has the right to institute an action of annulment by a writing referring to the contract, the reason for annulability and the statement that he intends to validate or confirm it. This confirmation is ineffective if the party requiring it is able to validly perform the contract. Art. 1444, Italian Civil Code.

convalidàre — to validate; to prove true; to prove certain; to ratify; to corroborate.

convalidazióne f.—act of validating.

convégno m.—meeting of persons for the purpose of discussion; the place where they meet.

conveníre—to come together for a meeting; to be in accord; to convene; to summon; to be proper; to be convenient.

conventícola f.—a secret meeting.

convenúto—having been agreed upon by common accord.

convenúto m.—defendant in a civil case.

convenzionàle—conventional.

convenzionàle (péna) — a penalty clause. See clàusola penále.

convenzióne f.—convention; covenant; agreement.

convenzióni matrimoniàli — nuptial agreements. These must be reduced to writing in an "àtto pùbblico," an official document by a notary or public official in accordance with legal requirements. They are invalid unless so prepared. Art. 161-164, Italian Civil Code.

conversióne f.—conversion.

conversióne del contràtto nùllo—conversion of invalid contract. An invalid contract may produce the effect of a diverse agreement containing the necessary requirements of substance and form, so that considering the objective sought by the parties, it may be held that they would have desired it, had they known its invalidity. Art. 1424, 1367, Italian Civil Code.

conversióne del débito pùbblico or conversióne della rèndita—conversion of public obligations. The substitution by the State of new bonds or obligations with different conditions.

conversióne di péna—conversion of punishment. When a defendant has been fined and cannot pay because he is insolvent, the prosecutor or Praetor may cause the fine to be converted into detention.

convertíre—to convert, to change; to transform.

convertíto—converted.

convertitóre m.—one who converts.

convinzióne f.—conviction; confutation.

convitàre—to invite to dinner.

convíto m.—banquet.

convítto m.—boarding school. An action to recover the charges for board and tuition by the operator of a boarding school is prescribed after a year. Art. 2955, subd. 3, Italian Civil Code.

convocàre—to convoke.

convocazióne f.—convocation.

convogliàre—to convoy; to escort.

convòglio m.—convoy; cortège.

coonestàre—to palliate; to extenuate; to cause an offense to appear less grave; to find an excuse for.

cooperatíva f.—cooperative.

cooptazióne f. — cooptation; election of a person to fill a vacancy by the votes of the existing members of the board of directors. Art. 2386, Italian Civil Code, for corporations and Art. 2516, idem, for cooperatives.

64

còpia f.—copy; transcription. Copies of public or private instruments deposited in public offices and issued by public officials under legally prescribed forms, have the same force as the original. Photographic copies have the same force as the original if attested by the competent public official. See duplicàti and Art. 2714, 2715, 2719, Italian Civil Code.

copiafattúre m.—invoice book.

copialèttere m.—letter copier.

copiàre—to copy; to reproduce; to transcribe; to imitate.

còpie f. (pl.)—copies. See còpia.

coprifuòco m.—curfew.

corazzière m.—cuirassier; in Italy, a mounted soldier with a cuirass or metal breastplate in the service of the head of State, the President of the Republic.

corbàme m.—timbers of a ship; also referred to as the ossatúra of the ship.

corbellàre—to deride; to make fun of.

corbellería f.—bizarre or extravagant words; nonsense.

còrbona f.—box where religious offerings were collected; box for gratuities.

cordòglio m.—grave moral pain; anguish.

còrpi moràli—juridicial bodies. See persóne giurídiche.

còrpo m.—body; mass.

còrpo-frànco m.—a body of volunteer, irregular troops; partisans.

còrpo di reàto—body or instrument of the crime; fruits of the crime.

corporazióne f.—corporation.

corrèdo m.—trousseau; bride's outfit of clothes and linens which she brings with her when she marries; necessary articles and furnishings of a soldier, sailor, student or of a traveler.

correlazióne f.—correlation.

correntísta f.—one with a current account at a bank; depositor.

corrèo m.—co-defendant; one who has committed a crime together with another; accomplice.

corresponsàbile—responsible together with others; co-responsible; accountable.

corresponsióne f.—a sum paid in return for a service, or to extinguish a debt.

correzionàle — correctional; reformatory (m.).

correzióne f.—correction.
càsa di correzióne or istitúto di correzióne—correctional home or institute.

corrispondènza f.—correspondence. For proof against the writer. See Art. 2707, Italian Civil Code. Re secrecy, see Art. 15, Constitution of the Italian Republic.

corrispóndere—to correspond; to be convenient; to suit.

corrispósta f.—a sum paid in return for a service.

corroboraménto m.—corroboration.

corroborànte—corroborating.

corroboràre—to corroborate.

corroboratóre m.—corroborator.

corroborazióne f.—corroboration.

corrómpere—to corrupt; to spoil; to contaminate.

corrompitóre m.—one who corrupts.

corrótto—corrupted.

corruttóre m.—corrupter.

corruzióne f.—corruption.

corruzióne di minorènni—corruption of minors. It consists in the commission of libidinous (lustful or lewd) acts upon the person of, or in the presence of a minor of age sixteen, or in inducing said minor to commit libidinous acts on himself, on the person of the one charged with inducing such acts, or upon others. Art. 530, Italian Penal Code.

corruzióne del cittadíno da pàrte dello stranièro—corruption of a citizen by a foreigner. The citizen, who, even indirectly, receives or obtains promises from a foreigner, of money or other things of value for himself or for others, or only accepts such promise for the purpose of committing acts contrary to the national interests is punished with imprisonment and fine, unless the act constitutes a graver crime. The foreigner who gives or promises money or other things of value is subject to the same punishment. The penalty is augmented if the act is committed in time of war, or, if the money or other thing of value is given or promised for propaganda by means of the press. Art. 246, Italian Penal Code.

corruzióne di persóna incaricàta di un púbblico servízio—corruption by a person in charge of a public service. This crime is committed by a public employee, who, to omit or delay an act of his office, or to perform an act contrary to the duties of office, receives for himself or a third party, money or other thing of value, or accepts a promise thereof. Art. 320, Italian Penal Code.

córsa f.—race.

corsàro—corsair; armed vessel of war.

corsía f.—aisle; gangway; current; stream; side-scene in a theater.

córso—run; past-due.

còrso m.—Corsican; principal thoroughfare of a city; the course of a stream.

còrso legàle—legal tender. Debts are paid in legal tender of the State. Art. 1277, Italian Civil Code. See obbligazióni pecuniàrie.

córte f.—court; court of law or justice; court of a king or prince.

córte costituzionàle — Constitutional Court. This court adjudicates the constitutionality of laws or Acts having the force of law. It is composed of fifteen judges and may function with the participation of eleven judges. The hearings are public, but may be held behind closed doors when its president deems that publicity may disturb the security of the State, or the public order or morale, or when there are public manifestations which may disturb tranquility. Their decisions are deliberated in chambers by the judges who were present at all the hearings and are arrived at by an absolute majority of the votes cast. In case of a tie, the vote of the president of the court prevails. The jurisdiction, composition and powers of the Constitutional Court are set forth in Art. 134-137, Constitution of the Italian Republic and Córte Costituzionàle, Usual Laws, Appendices to the Italian Codes of Civil and Penal Procedure. See leggitimità costituzionàle.

córte dei cónti—Court of the Exchequer or accounts. It has jurisdiction in matters relating to accounting of public revenues and other matters specified by law. Art. 100, 103, 111, Constitution of the Italian Republic.

córte d'appèllo—Court of Appeals. This court is the first appelate court in civil and penal matters. Art. 339-359, Italian Code of Civil Procedure; Art. 52-59, Ordinaménto Giurisdizionàle (Jurisdictional Ordinance of the Judiciary), Usual Laws, Appendix to Italian Code of Civil Procedure.

córte di assíse—Court of Assize. It is a court which has jurisdiction over the trial of serious crimes, Art. 29, Italian Code of Penal Procedure; Art. 1 et seq., Córti di Assíse (Courts of Assize), Usual Laws, Appendix to Italian Code of Penal Procedure.

córte di assíse di appèllo—Appellate Court of Assize. It reviews judgments of the Courts of Assize. Art. 29, Italian Code of Penal Procedure; Art. 2, et seq., Córti di Assíse (Courts of Assize), Usual Laws, Appendix to Italian Code of Penal Procedure.

córte di cassazióne—Court of Cassation; the highest appellate court in Italy with jurisdiction over civil and criminal matters; also, known as Córte Suprèma di Cassazióne. Art. 101-113, Constitution of the Italian Republic; Art. 41, 360-394, Italian Code of Civil Procedure; Art. 524-574 bis, Italian Code of Penal Procedure; Córte di Cassazióne, Usual Laws, Appendices to Italian Codes of Civil and Penal Procedure; Art. 65-67, Ordinaménto Giurisdizionàle (Jurisdictional Ordinance of the Judiciary), Usual Laws, Appendix to Italian Code of Civil Procedure.

córte suprèma di cassazióne—Supreme Court of Cassation. See córte di cassazióne.

corteggiàre—to court.

cortigiàno m.—courtier.

cortíle m.—court yard.

cortína f.—curtain.

cortisóne m.—cortisone.

cortometràggio m.—short length film, usually documentary.

còsa (còse pl.) f.—thing; chose in action; incorporeal and corporeal rights.

còsa giudicàta—res judicata (Lat.); an adjudicated matter; the findings contained in a judgment or sentence are binding on the parties, their heirs and assignees. Art. 2909, 2953, Italian Civil Code; Art. 324, 395(5), Italian Code of Civil Procedure; Art. 124, Enabling Rules, Italian Code of Civil Procedure. Also, regiudicàta.

cosciènza f.—conscience; internal recognition of good and evil; the faculty of perceiving the motives and moral qualities of one's actions. See consapevolèzza.

coscrítto m.—conscript.

coscrizióne f.—conscription.

còse consumàbili—consumable things. Quasi usufructs. See quàsi usufrútto.

còse mòbili assolutaménte impignoràbili—personal property absolutely not subject to attachment. See impignoràbili (còse mòbili assolutaménte).

cospiràre—to conspire; to plot.

cospiratóre m.—conspirator.

cospirazióne f.—conspiracy.

costàre—to cost; to be worth.

costatàre—to certify; to verify; to ascertain; to establish as factual.

costituènte—constituent; component. assemblèa costituènte — constituent assembly.

costituíre—to constitute; to establish; to form; to settle.

costitúto m.—an interrogatory or examination of the accused by a judge.

costituzionàle—constitutional.

costituzióne f.—constitution; composition; structure; to present or appear for trial.

costituzióne delle pàrti in giudízio civíle—appearance of the parties in a civil case. The plaintiff files with the clerk a "nòta di iscrizióne a ruòlo," and his complaint and other papers. The defendant files his appearance and answer together with his other pleadings. Art. 163-168, Italian Code of Civil Procedure.

costituzióne di pàrte civíle—appearance as a civil party (in a criminal action). Where a party has sustained damages arising out of a criminal act, he may appear as a civil party during the trial of the penal action so as to be indemnified for the damages sustained as a result of the criminal act. Art. 91-106, Italian Code of Penal Procedure.

costituzióne in mòra—declaration of default. A debtor is declared in default by means of formal notice or demand in writing. Art. 1219-1229, 1308, Italian Civil Code.

costringiménto físico—physical constraint. One is not punishable if he has committed an act by reason of having been constrained by others, by means of physical violence which he could not resist or from which he could not withdraw in any manner. In such case, the author of the violence is responsible for the act committed by the constrained person. Art. 46, Italian Penal Code. Also, violènza física.

costruíre—to construct.

costruzióne f.—construction.

costumànza f.—habit; custom; usage.

costumatézza f.—politeness; civility; good manners.

costumàto—accustomed; civil; polite.

costúme m.—custom; habit; usage. See buòn costúme—good custom or propriety. A provision of the Italian Penal Code relating to crimes against public morals and good custom or propriety. Art. 519, 544, Italian Penal Code.

cotidiàno—daily.

còttimo m.—a work contract at a fixed price; piece-work. Art. 2099, 2100, 2101, 2127 and 2131, Italian Civil Code.

coúso m.—the use of a right together with others.

coutènte m.—one who uses a right together with others.

crài—tomorrow.
compràre a crài—to buy on credit.

creànza f.—good breeding; education; politeness.

creanzàto—well-bred; civil; polite.

credènza f.—belief; faith; credit; sideboard.
compràre a credènza—to buy on credit.

crédito m.—credit; good financial reputation; money due from another; opposite of debt; belief; trust and reputation enjoyed by a person.

crédito privilegiàto — a privileged credit; one given preference by law over others. Art. 2745-2783, Italian Civil Code. Also, privilègi.

crédito immobiliàre—loan secured by a mortgage on real property.

creditóre m.—creditor; one to whom money is due and owing.

cremàre—to cremate.

crematóio m.—crematory.

cremazióne f.—cremation.

crícca f.—a group of intriguers.

criminàle—criminal; guilty of crime (m.).

criminalísta f.—a lawyer who is an expert in criminal law.

criminalità f.—criminality.

crímine m.—crime.

criminología f.—criminology.

crumíro m.—strike-breaker; scab.

cuccàgna f.—imaginary land where there is great abundance of everything which is to be had free; life of happy delight and thoughtlessness.

cuccétta f.—sleeping-car berth. See carròzza-lètto.

cúlto—cultivated; learned; erudite.

cúlto m.—cult; rite; religious worship.

cultúra f.—culture; cultivation.

curatèla f.—curatorship; guardianship.

curatóre m.—curator; guardian of property; trustee; the person administering the property of a bankrupt, incompetent, minor or inheritor. Art. 28-39 Fallimónto (Bankruptcy), Usual Laws, Appendix to Italian Civil Code; Art. 166, 334, 392, 508, 528, 532, Italian Civil Code.

cúria f.—meeting place of the Roman Senate; place where cases were heard; forum; tribunal; assemblage of Cardinals of the Roman Catholic Church.

custòde m.—custodian; conservator; guardian; one who conserves and administers the mortgaged or attached property of a debtor. Art. 65-67, 520-522, 559, 560, 676, 679, Italian Code of Civil Procedure; Art. 171, Enabling Rules, Italian Code of Civil Procedure; Art. 344, 624, 626, Italian Code of Penal Procedure.

custòdia f.—custody.

custòdia preventíva—preventive custody or detention. It is the detention of a person who is suspected of a crime, or arrested in the very act of committing it, or apprehended by an Order or Warrant of Arrest. The detention is effectuated to assure proof of the crime or to protect the evidence. Art. 269-276, Italian Code of Penal Procedure. See carcerazióne preventíva.

custodíre—to conserve; to guard; to secure.

cúte f.—human skin.

D

dàdo m.—die.

dàdi m. (pl.)—dice.

danàro m.—money; a suit in an Italian deck of playing cards (diamonds). Also, denàro.

danneggiaménto m. — damage; loss. Art. 635, Italian Penal Code.

danneggiàre—to damage; to injure.

danneggiàto—damaged; deteriorated.

danneggiatóre m.—one who damages.

dànno m.—damage; harm; loss; prejudice; wrong. An act done criminally or culpably which causes unjust loss must be compensated by the one performing the damage. Art. 2043, Italian Civil Code; Art. 185, Italian Penal Code.

dànno emergènte—damnum emergens (Lat.); resulting damage. It is a real or definite diminution of one's property or estate.

dànno moràle—moral damage. Also, dànno non patrimoniàle; damages suffered to one's person or rights exclusive of his estate or property. See Art. 2059, Italian Civil Code.

dànno non patrimoniàle—damages suffered to one's person or rights exclusive of his estate or property. Also, dànno moràle, moral damage. See Art. 2059, Italian Civil Code.

dannosaménte—harmfully.

dannóso—harmful; hurtful· prejudicial.

dànte càusa—assignor. Opp. avènte càusa—assignee.

dàrsena f.—dockyard; wet dock.

dàta f.—date; a patronage or ecclesiastical benefice; act of dealing playing cards.

datàre—to date.

dataría or datería f.—Papal office which records the granting of dispensations and graces.

datariàto m.—the office of the Datario.

datàrio m.—the person who presides over the dataría; the one who dated the Pontificial letters.

datio in solutum (Lat.)—a giving in payment; similar to accord and satisfaction. A debtor cannot free himself of an obligation by offering a performance other than that due unless with the consent of the creditor. See Art. 1197, Italian Civil Code.

dattilografàre—to write by typewriting machine.

dattilografía f.—writing by typewriting machine.

dattilògrafo m. (dattilògrafa f.)—typist.

dattilología f.—the art of conversing by using fingers in conventional signs corresponding to the alphabet; sign language used by mutes.

dattiloscopía f.—examination of fingerprints in police work.

dàzio m.—an import or export tax; excise tax; impost; customs.

dàzio consúmo — tax on consumer goods.

dazióne in pagaménto—a giving in payment. See datio in solutum (Lat) and Art. 1197, Italian Civil Code.

debitaménte—duly; justly; according to right; according to justice.

débito m.—debt; that which is owed.

débito di sómma di danàro—pecuniary debt. See obbligazióni pecuniàrie.

débito púbblico—public debt; the totality of State obligations.

debitóre m.—debtor.

debòscia f.—debauchery; licentious behavior.

debosciàto m.—debauchee; one given over to debauchery.

dècade f.—decade; period of ten years.

decadènte—decadent.

decadènza f.—decadence; default; expiration; loss of the feasibility of exercising a legal right or cause of action due to failure to act within a prescribed period of time. Art. 2964-2969, 1186, Italian Civil Code. See tèrmine (decadènza del) and prescrizióne.

decadére—to become decadent; to decline; to default; to lose a legal right.

decàno m.—dean; senior.

decapitaménto m.—decapitation.

decapitàre—to decapitate

decapitazióne f.—decapitation.

decèdere—to die.

decedúto—defunct,

decennàle—decennial.

decènnio m.—space of ten years.

decèsso m.—death; decease used in a statistical sense.

decètto—defrauded.

decezióne f.—deception.

decifràre—to decipher.

decifratóre m.—one who deciphers.

dècima f.—tithe; a tax or impost on a proportional part of the products of the soil or animals raised by human labor which is paid periodically.

decimàle—decimal.

decimàre—to decimate.

decimàrio m.—register of lands subject to the tithe.

dècimo—tenth.

decína f.—units of ten; ten or about ten.

decisióne f.—decision; decree.

decíso—decided; resolved.

decisóre m.—one who decides.

decisòrio—a deciding oath; an oath required by one party to an action from the other to resolve totally or partially, the outcome of the case. See Art. 2736, Italian Civil Code. Also, giuraménto decisòrio.

declaràre—to declare.

declaratòria f.—a judgment whereby an accused is declared innocent of the charge.

decollàre—to behead; to decapitate.

decollazióne f.—decapitation.

decomposizióne f.—decomposition.

decorrènza f.—expiration; cessation.

decórrere —to run; to pass; regarding obligations and rights, the passing of time from a stated period of time.

decórso m.—expiration of time (on an obligation).

decòtto m.—decoction; extract.

decòtto (ajd.)—bankrupt.

decozióne f.—the operation of making a decoction; bankruptcy; state of insolvency.

decretàle—decretal; the decretals form

the second part of the body of canon law.

decretalísta m.—one learned in the decretals or canon law.

decretàre—to decree.

decréto m.—decree.

decréto légge—law or legal decree; a legal decree of law issued by the government in extraordinary cases of necessity and urgency with provisional force of law. It must be presented the same day to both houses of parliament for conversion into law. If they are adjourned, they must be convoked within five days. Such a decree loses efficacy if not converted into law within sixty days of its publication. Art. 77, Constitution of the Italian Republic.

decréto legislatívo—legislative decree or rule of law. The exercise of the legislative function cannot be delegated to the government except under fixed principles and determined guidelines and only for a limited time and for definite objectives. Also, légge dèlega; légge delegàta. Art. 76, Constitution of the Italian Republic.

decréto ministeriàle—ministerial decree. This decree emanates from ministerial or administrative powers. It need not be presented to parliament for approval but must be registered with the córte dei cónti (Court of the Exchequer) and thereafter published. Art. 100, Constitution of the Italian Republic.

decúbito m.—the position assumed when lying in bed; the position of a sick person in bed.

de cuius (Lat.)—from whom; the person from whom another claims (an inheritance). Art. 456-461, Italian Civil Code.

decumàni—the soldiers of the Tenth Legion.

decumàno—pertaining to the Tenth Legion; tenth.
pòrta decumàna—one of the principal entrances to a Roman camp opposite that of the Pretoria.
vía decumàna—the road, which in a Roman camp, ran between the De-

cumana and Pretoria entrances and hence the principal street in a city.

decúria f.—squad of ten mounted men in the Roman army; place of meeting of the decuria; group of ten men.

decúrio or decurióne m.—commander of a decúria.

decurtàre—to abbreviate; to diminish; to diminish a debt by paying something on account.

decussàre—to cross; to intersect; to make an X.

decússe f.—Roman numeral X which signifies ten; Roman coin.

dèdica f.—dedication.

dedicàre—to dedicate; to devote oneself to.

dedicazióne f.—the ceremony of dedicating; dedication.

dèdito—inclined to; given to (study).

dedizióne f.—surrender; voluntary submission.

dedótto—deducted; drawn.

deducíbile—deductible.

dedúrre—to deduct; to deduce; to infer; to subtract a sum from another.

dedútto—deducted.

deduzióne f.—deduction.

deduzióne di pròve—a statement of facts alleged to prove the civil party's case. Art. 244, 345, Italian Code of Civil Procedure.

defalcaménto m.—defalcation; setoff; diminution of a debt.

defalcàre—to subtract; to detract a certain amount from a larger sum; to diminish; to defalcate.

defalcazióne f.—defalcation.

defàlco m.—defalcation.

defenestràre—to throw out of the window; to chase away in a violent manner; to take a position from someone violently.

defenestrazióne f.—defenestration.

defènsa f.—defense. See difésa.

defensionàle—relating to the defense.

deferiménto m.—deferment; submis-

sion; administration of an oath; swearing in a witness.

deferíre—to defer; to submit; to conform or yield; to administer an oath; to swear in a witness.

defettíbile—possible defector.

defezionàre—to defect; to desert.

defezióne f.—defection.

deficiènte—deficient.
restáre deficiènte—to fail an examination.

deficiènza f.—deficiency.

dèficit m.—deficit.

deflagrazióne f.—deflagration.

deflazióne f.—deflation.

deflemmàre—to remove water from a liquid.

defloràre—to deflower; to deflorate; to deprive of virginity.

deflorazióne f.—defloration.

deformànte—that which deforms; deforming.

deformàre—to deform; to alter; to disfigure.

deformazióne f.—deformation.

defórme—deformed.

deformità f.—deformity.

defraudaménto m.—act of defrauding; cheating.

defraudàre—to defraud.

defraudatóre m.—defrauder.

defraudazióne f.—act and effect of defrauding.

defúnto m.—deceased; defunct.

degeneràre—to degenerate.

degeneràto m.—degenerate.

degenerazióne f.—degeneration.

degènere—that which degenerates.

degènte m.—one who is sick in a hospital.

degènza f.—period during which a sick person is in a hospital.

deglutíre—to swallow.

deglutizióne f.—act of swallowing.

degnàre—to deign; to condescend to grant; to believe worth.

degnità f.—dignity; decorum.

dégno—worthy; deserving; dignified.

degradaménto m.—degradation.

degradàre—to degrade.

degradazióne f.—degradation.

degustàre—to taste; to sample.

degustazióne f.—the act of tasting.

deicída—killer of God.

deícola m.—one who adores the true God; one devoted to God.

deificàre—deify.

deificazióne f.—deification.

delatóre m.—informer.

delazióne f.—delation; handing over; transference; accusation or information.

delazióne d'àrmi—wrongful bearing of arms.

delazióne dell'eredità—devolution or transfer of an inheritance. It occurs through force of law or by testament. Art. 457, Italian Civil Code.

delazióne ereditària—See delazióne dell'eredità.

delazióne di giuraménto—deferment of oath. See giuraménto.

del crédere—an agent for sale of goods, who for a higher commission, guarantees the solvency of the buyer and his payment of the purchase price. See stàr del crédere.

delèbile—that which may be cancelled.

dèlega f.—act of delegating.

delegàre—to delegate.

delegàto m.—delegate.

delegazióne f. — delegation; assignment; transfer of property or rights to another. Art. 1268-1276, Italian Civil Code.

deletèrio—deleterious.

delibàre—to taste; to try; to test to review.

delibazióne f.—tasting; trying; testing; reviewing; review.

delibazióne (giudízio di)—review proceeding; a proceeding to review civil and penal judgments imposed by foreign jurisdictions, to determine if they can be enforced in Italy. See sentènze stranière (efficàcia delle) for review of foreign civil judgments, Art. 796-805, Italian Code of Civil Procedure. For review of foreign penal judgments, see sentènze penàli stranière (riconosciménto delle), Art. 672-675, Italian Code of Penal Procedure.

delíbera f.—deliberation; to adjudge at auction or public sale when goods are sold to the highest bidder; distribution of work.

deliberàre—to deliberate; to resolve; to determine.

deliberataménte—deliberately.

deliberatàrio m.—the public at a public sale or auction where goods are sold to the highest bidder.

deliberazióne f.—deliberation.

delimitàre—to delimit; to demarcate; to circumscribe.

delineaménto m.—delineation.

delineàre—to delineate; to sketch; to outline.

delineazióne f.—delineation.

delinquènte m.—delinquent; offender. Art. 102-105, 108, Italian Penal Code.

delinquènza f.—delinquency; criminality.

delínquere—to offend; to commit a crime.
associazióne a delínquere—a meeting of persons for a criminal purpose. At least three persons are required. Art. 416, Italian Penal Code.

delirànte—delirious; raving.

deliràre—to be delirious; to rave.

delírio m.—delirium; madness.

delítti colpósi di comúne perícolo—crimes involving common danger through negligence. They cover acts such as carelessly and negligently causing fires and disasters, negligent failure to provide for, or the removal or rendering useless any apparatus designed to extinguish fire or for safe-guarding against disasters or work hazards. Included are negligent acts against the public health. Art. 449-452, Italian Penal Code.

delítti di comúne perícolo mediànte fróde—crimes of common danger by means of fraud. Included are: causing an epidemic by diffusion of pathogenic germs; the poisoning of water or food products and the adulteration and imitation of food products for consumption and putting the public health in danger by placing adulterated food products in commerce; also, placing in commerce and providing harmful medicinals and drugs. Art. 438-448, Italian Penal Code.

delítti di comúne perícolo mediànte violènza—crimes of common danger by means of violence. These are acts leading to massacre, fire, flood, landslide, avalanche, shipwreck, sinking, aviation disaster, railway disaster, endangering public transportation, electric and gas installations and public communications; also, fabricating, acquiring or illegal possession of explosive, toxic and inflammable materials or substances for their manufacture and removing, concealing or destroying any apparatus designed to counteract said disasters. Also, covered is the removal or negligent failure to supply safeguards or signals designed to prevent work hazards. Art. 422-437, Italian Penal Code.

delítti cóntro il patrimònio—crimes against property or the patrimony or estate of a person. Some crimes included are: theft; appropriating community or partnership property; robbery; extortion; deprivation of personal liberty for the purpose of robbery; or extortion; removing and altering boundary lines of real property for the purpose of appropriating same; invasion of public or private lands or buildings; violent disturbance of the possession of real property; deviation of public or private waters and modification of the state of places; destruction or damage to the personal or real property of another; introduction or abandonment of animals on the lands of another and unlawful pasturage; unlawful entrance on the lands of another; disfiguring and despoiling the personal or real property of another. Art. 624-639, Italian Penal Code.

delítti cóntro il sentiménto religióso e cóntro la pietà dei defúnti—crimes against religious sentiment and against the observance of piety for the deceased. Art. 402-413, Italian Penal Code.

delítti cóntro l'amministrazióne della giustízia—crimes against the administration of justice. Art. 361-391, Italian Penal Code.

delítti cóntro l'assistènza familiàre—crimes against family assistance and protection. It comprises failure to provide for the family as its head, the use of abusive disciplinary methods and the maltreatment of members of the family and children. Art. 570-574, Italian Penal Code.

delítti cóntro l'attività giudiziària—crimes against judicial action. Among the crimes covered are: failure of a public official or citizen to denounce a crime; failure to report a possible crime by a professional sanitary official; failure to comply with judicial obligations; simulation of a crime; falsely accusing another or oneself of a crime; false testimony by a party to a civil action; false testimony before judicial authorities; false expert testimony or interpretation; fraud during a trial, civil or administrative, committted to deceive a judge during an act of inspection or judicial proof, or false alteration by an expert of the state of places or persons; subornation of perjury; aiding to impede the investigation of a crime or aiding to dispose the fruits, profit or price thereof; disloyal legal defense or expert testimony; receiving money or anything of value by legal counsel boasting that he can influence a judge or public prosecutor or expert or interpreter. Art. 361-384, Italian Penal Code.

delítti cóntro l'economía púbblica—crimes against the public economy. Art. 499-512, Italian Penal Code.

delítti cóntro la famíglia — crimes against the family. Among those included are: bigamy; inducing another to matrimony through fraud; incest; crimes against family status by falsifying civil registers; violation of the obligation to aid the family; use of abusive means of discipline; maltreatment of members of the family or minor children; abduction of minors of age fourteen; abduction of persons lacking capacity. Art. 556-574, Italian Penal Code.

delitti cóntro la féde púbblica—crimes against the public faith and credit. Art. 453-466, Italian Penal Code.

delitti cóntro l'incolumità púbblica—crimes against public safety. Designated as delitti di comúne perícolo (crimes involving common danger), they are considered as follows: (a) delitti di comúne perícolo mediànte violènza; (b) delitti di comúne perícolo mediánte fròde; (c) delitti colpósi di comúne perícolo. See the respective titles. Art. 422-452, Italian Penal Code.

delitti cóntro l'indústria ed il commèrcio—crimes against industry and commerce. Art. 513-517, Italian Penal Code.

delitti cóntro la integrità e la sanità della stírpe—crimes against the integrity and physical soundness of the race. Art. 545-555, Italian Penal Code.

delitti cóntro la inviolabilità dei segréti —crimes against the inviolability of secrets. Included are: violation, abstraction and suppression of correspondence; fraudulently intercepting, interrupting or impeding telegraph and telephone communications; revealing the contents of another's correspondence; violation, abstraction, or suppression of correspondence by employees of the postal and telegraph service; disclosure of correspondence or communications by employees of the postal and telegraph service; unlawful disclosure of the contents of public or private documents; disclosure of professional secrets; disclosure of secret scientific and industrial documents. Art. 616-623, Italian Penal Code.

delitti cóntro la inviolabilità del domicílio—crimes against the inviolability of the domicile. Art. 614-615, Italian Penal Code.

delitti cóntro la libertà individuàle—

crimes against individual liberty. Art. 600-623, Italian Penal Code.

delitti cóntro la libertà moràle—crimes against moral freedom and customs. Art. 610-613, Italian Penal Code.

delitti cóntro la libertà personàle—crimes against personal liberty. Art. 605-609, Italian Penal Code.

delitti cóntro la libertà sessuàle—crimes against sexual freedom. It signifies the right to be free from sexual molestation as prohibited by law. Art. 519-526, Italian Penal Code.

delitti cóntro la moralità púbblica e il buòn costúme—crimes against public morality and good custom or propriety. Art. 519-544, Italian Penal Code.

delitti cóntro la persóna — crimes again the person. Among them are: homicide; unintentional homicide; homicide of a consenting person; homicide and wounding due to an offense to honor caused when surprising a wife, daughter or sister in the act of illicit carnal relation, and said killing or wounding occuring in a state of determined anger; infanticide due to a cause of honor; battery; instigating or aiding in suicide; negligent homicide; negligent wounding; death or wounding as a result of another crime; affray; abandonment of minors or persons lacking capacity; abandonment of a new-born infant by reason of offense to honor; failure to aid an abandoned or lost child of ten years of age or to help a person incapable of providing for himself because of mental or physical illness or other cause. Art. 575-593, Italian Penal Code.

delitti cóntro la personalità dello stàto —crimes against the jural personality of the State. Art. 241-313, Italian Penal Code.

delitti cóntro la personalità individuàle —crimes against individual personality or civil rights. Art. 600-604, Italian Penal Code.

delitti cóntro la púbblica amministrazióne—crimes against the public ad-

74

ministration of government. Art. 314-360, Italian Penal Code.

delítti cóntro l'onóre—crimes against honor. They include what are known in the common law as slander and libel. Art. 594-599, Italian Penal Code. See ingiúria and diffamazióne.

delítti cóntro l'órdine púbblico—crimes against public order. Art. 414-421, Italian Penal Code.

delítti cóntro lo stàto di famíglia—crimes against the family status. It includes the falsification of the public civil status records by reporting an inexistent birth, concealing a birth, alteration of status of a child by substitution of a new born child for registration, and concealing the status of a child already registered in the civil status records for the purpose of leaving it in a foundling home. Art. 566-569, Italian Penal Code.

delítto m.—delict; crime; offense; a violation of the Penal Code which results in a crime with damage to another. It is punishable by life imprisonment, incarceration (reclusióne) which may last from fifteen days to twenty four years and a fine called múlta, or both together. Art. 17, 18, 23, 24, 39, 40, 8-11, 642, Italian Penal Code; Art. 4-11, Coordinating Dispositions, Italian Penal Code. See reclusióne and múlta.

delítto colpóso—a crime resulting from lack of care or negligence. Art. 43, Italian Penal Code.

delítto dolóso—a crime with intent; one that is foreseen and willful. Art. 43, Italian Penal Code.

delítto preterintenzionàle—a crime resulting from an act of commission or omission that is graver than intended by the actor, Art. 43, Italian Penal Code.

delítto (quàsi)—quasi-delict. See quàsi delítto.

delítto tentàto—attempted crime—one which falls short of its accomplishment, although overt acts towards its commission were performed by the accused. Art. 56, Italian Penal Code. Also, tentàto delítto.

delittuóso—criminal; that which constitutes a crime.

delucidàre—to explain; to clear up; to elucidate.

delucidazióne f.—elucidation; clearing up; explanation.

delusióne f.—delusion.

delúso—deluded; deceived.

demagogía f.—demagogy.

demagògo m.—demagogue.

demandàre—to initiate a law suit; to delegate; to pass on.

demànio m.—domain; the sovereign right of the State in property; the totality of the property of the State and the administration of such property.

demànio púbblico—public domain; the totality of determined property of the State as defined by Art. 822 of the Italian Civil Code. See dirítti demaniàli su bèni altrúi and úsi cívici.

demarcàre—to demarcate; to limit.

demarcazióne f.—demarcation; limitation.

dementàre—to drive mad.

demènte—insane; mad.

demènza f.—insanity; madness.

demeritàre—to render unworthy; to be unworthy due to bad or poor conduct.

demèrito m.—demerit; blame.

demilitarizzàre—to demilitarize.

demilitarizzazióne f.—demilitarization.

deminútio f.—from the Roman deminutio capitis, which indicated loss of citizenship rights, liberty and family rights; loss of authority; loss of grade; loss of rank or position; a deprivation; taking away.

democràtico—democratic.

democratizzàre—to democratize.

democrazía f.—democracy.

democristiàno—abbreviation for Christian Democrat, a political party of Catholics having democratic tendencies.

demografía f.—demography; science of vital and social statistics.

demogràfico—demographic.

demolíre—to demolish; to dismantle.

demolitóre m.—one who demolishes.

demolizióne f.—demolition.

dèmone m.—demon.

demonetàre—to demonetize.

demònio m.—demon; devil.

demòtico — the popular writing of ancient Egypt as opposed to the sacred or sacerdotal writings.

demolizzàre—to demoralize.

demoralizzazióne f.—demoralization.

demorfinizzàre—to break the habit of taking morphine.

denàro m.—money; a suit in an Italian deck of playing cards (diamonds). Also, danàro.

denegàre—to deny; to refute.

denegatóre m.—one who denies; sceptic.

denegazióne f.—denial.

denigràre—to denigrate; to malign a person's good name.

denigratóre m.—denigrator.

denigrazióne f.—denigration.

denominàre—to denominate; to name.

denominatóre m.—one who names; that which denominates or from which a name is derived; a divisor placed under a dividend; denominator.

denominazióne f. — denomination; a name or designation for a class of things.

denominazióne sociàle—the commercial name and style of a stock corporation (società per azióni) and a limited responsibility partnership (società a responsabilità limitàta). The name of such business may be assumed or fictitious and take any form, provided it specifies its nature. Art. 2326, 2463, 2473, 2515, Italian Civil Code. See ragióne sociàle.

denotàre—to denote; to signify.

dentàle m.—ploughshare.

dentàle—dental.

dentàme m.—denture.

dentàre—to cut teeth; to indent.

dentaruòlo m.—teething ring.

dentàta f.—tooth mark.

dentàto—toothed; notched.

dentatúra f.—set of teeth.

dènte m.—tooth.

dentièra f.—set of false teeth.

dentifrício m.—tooth paste or tooth powder.

dentísta m.—dentist.

denudàre—to denude; to expose; to divest.

denùncia (denúnzia) f.—complaint; denunciation. Every person having knowledge of a crime prosecutable by the Authorities, even though such person is not the offended party, may denounce it to the Procurator of the Republic, to the Praetor or an official of the judicial police. It may be made in writing and subscribed or orally to the above mentioned officials. Art. 7, 8, Italian Code of Penal Procedure.

denúncia del dànno (òbbligo di)—duty to complain about damage. Except in the case of serious negligence on the part of an innkeeper or his agents, the innkeeper's responsibility is barred if the guest does not complain of the damage as soon as he becomes aware of it. Art. 1785, Italian Civil Code.

denúnzia di dànno temúto—complaint of possible (feared) damage. The owner or one having right of ownership or possessor of realty who has reason to fear that his property is in imminent peril of grave and proximate danger from any building, tree or other thing may complain to the courts for relief from the peril. Art. 1172, Italian Civil Code. Also, azióne di nunciazióne.

denúnzia di nuòva òpera—complaint of new work on realty. The owner or one having a right of ownership or possession of realty who fears that another's new work may cause damage to his property, may complain to the courts to restrain such work, and if the court permits it, that bond be posted against possible damages. Art. 1171, Italian Civil Code. Also, azióne di nunciazióne.

denúnzia nella véndita di còse da trasportàre—complaint in the sale of goods to be transported. In the sale of goods to be transported from one place to another, the time to complain about apparent faults and defects commences from the time of their receipt. Art. 1511, 1495, Italian Civil Code.

denunciàre (denunziàre) — to denounce; to accuse; to declare; to complain against; to refer.

denunciatóre (denunziatóre) m.—one who denounces; informer.

denunciazióne (denunziazióne) f.—denouncement.

denutríto—one suffering from lack of nutrition.

denutrizióne f.—insufficient nutrition.

deodorànte—deodorant.

deontología f.—deontology; the science of studying moral obligations; ethics.

depauperàre—to impoverish.

depennàre—to strike out a word or phrase; to erase; to cancel.

deperíbile—perishable.

deperíre—to perish; to deteriorate; to waste away; to decay; to decline.

deponènte m.—deponent; one who deposes; one who deposits.

deponiménto m.—deposition.

depórre—to attest; to bear witness; to depose; to deposit; to lay down; to resign; to degrade.

deportàre—to deport.

deportàto—deported.

deportazióne f.—deportation.

depórto m.—a banking operation, which involves a purchase of securities for cash and a sale at a determined time for a lesser price; the reverse of ripòrto.

depositànte m.—depositor; bailor.

depositàre—to deposit; to bail.

depositàrio m.—depository; bailee.

depòsiti (pl.) m.—deposits; bailments; storehouses; warehouses.

depòsiti di danàro—money deposits. See depòsito bancàrio. Art. 1834, Italian Civil Code.

depòsiti frànchi — free-entry warehouses. They are duty-free warehouses, usually in port cities, outside the customs area, so that goods deposited therein are exempt from customs duty. The purpose is to allow such goods to be unloaded, stored and shipped without paying said duties. See pòrto frànco and púnti frànchi.

depòsito m.—deposit; bailment; storehouse; warehouse.

depòsito àlla rinfúsa—deposit or bailment of fungible goods. See depòsito di mèrce fungíbile. Art. 1795, Italian Civil Code.

depòsito bancàrio—bank deposit. Art. 1834-1838, Italian Civil Code.

depòsito (contràtto di)—contract of deposit. It is a bailment contract whereby one party receives personal property from another and undertakes to keep it in his custody and to return it in the same condition. It is presumed to be without compensation, unless a different intent may be deduced on the part of the parties from the professional quality of the depository (bailee) or other circumstances. Art. 1766-1782, Italian Civil Code.

depòsito di mèrce fungíbile—deposit or bailment of fungible goods. Art. 1795, Italian Civil Code.

depòsito di títoli in amministrazióne—deposit of securities for management. A bank which assumes the deposit of securities for management, must act as their cusodian, collect dividends or interest, and verify distributions of rights and premiums or return of capital and manage payments for the account of the depositor and in general provide for the protection of the rights in the securities. Art. 1838, Italian Civil Code.

depòsito (féde di)—warehouse receipt. Art. 1790, Italian Civil Code.

depòsito frànco—free-entry warehouse. See depòsiti frànchi.

depòsito in albèrgo—deposit or bailment in a hotel. Hotel keepers are liable as bailees for the things their guests have left in their care. A similar responsibility is cast upon comparable businesses, such as sanatoria, establishments for public spectacles, bathing pavilions, pensions (boarding houses), eating establishments and restaurants, sleeping cars and the like. Art. 1783-1786, Italian Civil Code.

depòsito nei magazzíni generàli—deposit or bailment in public warehouses. These warehouses are responsible for the conservation of goods deposited therein, except where it can be proven that the loss, diminution or damage is derived from an accidental cause or their inherent faults or from their packaging. Art. 1787-1797, Italian Civil Code.

deposizìòne f.—deposition.

deputàto m.—deputy; a member of the Chamber of Deputies; substitute.

deputazíóne f.—deputation; mandate to act for or represent others.

derelìtto—abandoned; derelict.

derìva f.—leeway; lateral movement of a ship to leeward due to currents; the movement of an aircraft off its course by cross winds; a vertical, fixed plane on the tail of aircraft to maintain its stability; stabilizer.

derìva (in)—adrift.

derivàre—to derive; to issue; to proceed; to drift.

derivatìvo—derivative.

derivàto—derived.

derivazíóne f.—derivation; origin.

dèroga f.—derogation; revocation.

derogàre—to derogate; to revoke a previous law, rule or contract.

derogazíóne f.—derogation; partial repeal or abolishment of a law by a subsequent act.

derràta f.—product of the cultivation of the soil which is used as food. See mèrce.

derubàre—to rob; to steal.

derubàto m.—robbed person.

descrívere—to describe.

descrizìóne f.—description.

desèrta (àsta)—a public sale or auction with no bidders.

desèrto—deserted; abandoned; derelict.

desèrto m.—desert; wilderness.

designàre—to designate; to appoint.

designàto—designated; appointed.

designazíóne f.—designation.

desinàre—to dine.

desistènza f.—desistence; to withdraw an action; non-suit.

desístere—to desist; to abandon; to withdraw.

dèspoto m. (dèspota)—despot.

destàre—to awake.

destinàre—to destine; to direct; to assign.

destinatàrio m.—addressee.

destinàto—destined; fated.

destinazíóne f.—destination; ultimate end or design; the purpose for which something is destined.

destinazíóne del pàdre di famíglia—establishment of a praedial servitude or easement by the owner of land. It is necessary that the proprietor of both parcels of land create the servitude on behalf of the dominant estate. See Art. 1062, 1027, 1072, Italian Civil Code.

destíno m.—destiny.

destituíre—dismiss; to remove from office.

destituíto (destitúto)—destituted; removed from office; destitute; poor.

destituzíóne f.—destitution; removal from office; dismissal.

desuetúdine (dissuetúdine) f.—desuetude; lack of use; disuse.

desúmere—to deduce; to conclude; to infer.

desumíbile—deducible.

desúnto—deduced; inferred.

detenére—to detain; to hold.

detentóre m.—detainor; possessor of contraband.

detentóre di azióni—shareholder.

detenúto—imprisoned; prisoner (m.).

detenzióne f.—detention; confinement; a punishment consisting in the deprivation of liberty; a modified form of possession such as custody. For the latter, see Art. 1140, 1141, Italian Civil Code. See possèsso.

detenzióne abusíva di àrmi—wrongful and unlawful possession of arms. Whoever possesses arms or ammunition without having declared same to the Authorities when declaration thereof is requested, is punished with arrest and fine. A fine is also imposed on whoever has knowledge that in a place inhabited by him there are arms or ammunition and he fails to denounce same to the Authorities. Art. 697, Italian Penal Code. See pòrto abusívo di àrmi.

detergénte—detergent; cleansing.

detèrgere—to clean.

deterioraménto m.—deterioration.

deterioràre—to deteriorate; to waste.

deteriorazióne f.—deterioration.

determinànte f.—determinant.

determinàre—to determine; to limit; to definitely establish.

determinataménte—in a resolute manner; precisely.

determinatívo—decisive.

determinàto—determined.

determinazióne f.—determination.

detonànte—detonator.

detonàre—to detonate.

detonazióne f.—detonation.

detràrre—to take away; to detract.

detrattóre m.—detractor.

detrazióne f.—detraction.

detriménto m.—detriment.

detríto m.—residue; breakage; debris.

detronizzàre—to dethrone.

détta f.—debt; saying.

dettagliàre—to detail; to describe minutely; to sell at retail.

dettagliataménte — minutely; specifically; at retail.

dettàglio m.—detail.

dettàme m.—dictate; rule of science.

dettànte—one who dictates.

dettàre—to dictate.

dettàto m.—dictation; common proverb.

dettatóre m.—one who dictates.

dettatúra f.—dictation.

détto—the above named; the said named person.

deturpaménto m.—corruption; dirt; filth; disfigurement.

deturpaménto e imbrattaménto di còse altrúi—disfigurement and soiling of another's property. Art. 639, Italian Penal Code.

deturpàre—to corrupt; to disfigure; to soil; to tarnish.

deturpazióne f. — disfigurement; fading; withering; brand or stigma.

devàllo m.—inscription in the Customs records of the transfer of the ownership of merchandise.

devalutazióne f.—devaluation.

devastaménto m.—devastation.

devastàre—to devastate.

devastàto—devastated.

devastatóre m.—one who devastates.

devastazióne f.—devastation.

devastazióne e sacchéggio — devastation and pillage. These are crimes against the public order and are punished with imprisonment. Art. 419, 421, Italian Penal Code.

devastazióne, sacchéggio e stràge—devastation, pillage and massacre. It consists in a criminal attempt against the security of the State. It is committed by an act calculated to cause devastation, pillage or massacre within the territory of the State or any part thereof. It is punishable by imprisonment. Art. 285, Italian Penal Code.

deveníre—to arrive at a conclusion.

deviaménto m.—deviation.

deviàre—to deviate.

deviazióne f.—deviation.

deviazionísmo m.—deviationism.

dèviazionísta m.—deviationist.

devolúto — devolved; transferred; transmitted.

devoluzióne f.—devolution; the transfer of a right from one person to another.

devòlvere—to devolve; to transfer a right from one person to another.

dì m.—day (poetic).

diabète m.—diabetes.

diabètico—diabetic.

diaconàto m.—deaconate.

diaconéssa f.—deaconess.

diàcono m.—deacon.

diàfano—diaphanous.

diafonía f.—dissonance; discordance of sounds.

diafràmma m.—diaphragm.

diàgnosi f.—diagnosis.

diagnòstica f.—the art and method of diagnosis.

diagnòstico—diagnostic.

dialettàle—dialectical.

dialèttica f.—dialectic; the art of logical reasoning.

dialètto m.—dialect.

diamànte m.—diamond.

diamantíno—adamantine.

diària f.—daily per diem allowance given for travel expenses.

diàrio m.—daily; diary; journal.

diarrèa f.—diarrhea.

diartròsi f.—diarthrosis; articulation which permits great motion such as in the knee joint.

diàstasi f.—diastase; a property contained in many plants which converts starch into sugars.

diàstole f.—diastole; dilation of the heart which alternates with the movement of contraction called the systole.

diatermía f.—diathermy.

dibàttere—to debate; to discuss; to dispute; to shake.

dibattiménto m.—debate; disputation; argument of counsel in a criminal trial. Art. 423-436, 437, Italian Code of Penal Procedure. See udiènza penàle.

dibàttito m.—debate; dispute; controversy; discussion of a question in a public or legislative assembly.

dicastèro m.—the office of a minister of state.

dichiaràre—to declare; to affirm.

dichiarazióne f.—declaration.

dichiarazióne di falliménto—declaration of bankruptcy. Art. 1, 5, et seq., Falliménto (Bankruptcy), Usual Laws, Appendix to Italian Civil Code.

dichiarazióne di mòrte presúnta—declaration of presumed death. Art. 58-68, Italian Civil Code.

dichiarazióne di volontà—declaration, or manifestation of determination and intent. It is an essential element of the juridical transaction. Art. 1321-1326, 1372, Italian Civil Code.

dichiarazióne giudiziàle della paternità e della maternità naturàle—judícial declaration of natural paternity and maternity. Art. 269-279, Italian Civil Code.

dièta f.—political assembly; diet; regimen of food intake.

dietètica f.—dietetic.

dies a quo (Lat.)—the day from which. The day from which an action commences to be calculated.

dies ad quem (Lat.)—the day to which. The day on which the commenced action is concluded. In computing days or time, the day on which the calculation starts is excluded and the last day of the term is included. Art. 2963, Italian Civil Code. See còmputo dei tèrmini di prescrizióne.

dies cedit (Lat.)—the day begins. In Roman law, it signifies the vesting of an interest. See dies venit.

dies fasti (Lat.)—propitious days. The days on which the Roman courts were open and justice was administered. On these days it was legal for the praetor to proclaim the words, "do, dico, addico." See **dies nefasti** and **do, dico, addico.**

dies feriati (Lat.)—ferial days. Holidays, during which the Romans suspended law suits and political transactions and slaves did not work. These days were considered dies nefasti. See **dies nefasti.**

dies nefasti (Lat.)—unpropitious days. The days on which the Roman courts were not open and justice was not administered. See **dies fasti.**

dies utiles (Lat.)—useful days. These were days under the Roman law when it was lawful to perform a specific act.

dies venit (Lat.)—the day has come. In Roman law, it signifies the vesting of an interest. See **dies cedit.**

difèndere—to defend; to protect.

difensibile—defensible.

difensóre m.—defender; protector; attorney-at-law; lawyer. Art. 82-87, Italian Code of Penal Procedure; Art. 124-136, Italian Code of Civil Procedure; See **patrocinatóre** and **procuratóre.**

difésa f.—defense; defense attorney.

difésa legittima—legitimate or justifiable defense. An act is not punishable if committed under constraint of necessity to defend a right of the person so acting or of another in peril of actual, unjust harm, provided that the act of defense was proportionate to the anticipated harm. Art. 52, Italian Penal Code; Art. 2044, Italian Civil Code. Also, **legittima difésa.**

difètto m.—defect; imperfection; flaw.

difettóso—defective; imperfect.

diffalcàre—to defalcate; to diminish. See **defalcàre.**

diffàlta f.—default.

diffamàre—to defame. Also, **disfamàre.**

diffamatóre m.—defamer.

diffamatòrio—defamatory.

diffamazióne f.—defamation. It is a crime committed against an absent person by communicating defamatory statements about him to a number of persons, orally or in writing. Increased penalties are provided when the defamatory statements concern a specific fact or are transmitted by means of the press or other means of publicity, or in a public document or before a political, administrative or judicial body or other Authority. Art. 595, Italian Penal Code. See **ingiúria** and **delitti cóntro l'onóre.**

differibile—deferable.

differiménto m.—deferment.

differíre—to defer; to postpone; to yield to another's judgment or opinion.

difficile—difficult.

difficoltà f.—difficulty.

difficoltà nell'esecuzióne dell'appàlto—difficulty in the performance of a work contract. When unforeseen circumstances cause a rise or diminution in the cost of materials or labor which is a tenth of the agreed price, either party to the contract may demand a revision of the price. See Art. 1664, Italian Civil Code.

diffída f.—admonition; warning; an instrument or document warning someone to perform or refrain from performing an act; a public warning issued by the Quaestor (head of Public Security) to persons who endanger public security or morality. Art. 1-3, Measures of Prevention, Usual Laws, Appendix to Italian Code of Penal Procedure. See **ammonizióne; ammoniménto.**

diffída ad adempíre il contràtto—warning to perform a contract. A fifteen day notice sent by one party to the contract to the defaulting side, that at the termination of that time, the contract will be deemed dissolved unless performed within a reasonable time. See Art. 1454, Italian Civil Code.

diffidàre—to admonish; to warn; to give public admonishment; to mistrust; to suspect.

diffidènte—diffident; mistrustful.

diffóndere—to diffuse.

difformàre—to deform.

diffórme—deformed.

difformità f.—deformity; defect.

difformità dell'òpera nell'appàlto—defects in a work contract. The party ordering the performance of the work (committènte) can demand that defects be cured at the contractor's expense or the price be proportionately reduced. Where the defects render the entire contract worthless, the party damaged may abrogate the contract. Art. 1668, 1667 and 2226, Italian Civil Code.

difteríte f.—diptheria.

digelàre—to thaw.

digeríre—to digest.

digestióne f.—digestion.

digèsto m.—digest; an abstract of some body of law.

digitàle f.—digitalis.

digitàle—digital.

digiunàre—to fast; to abstain from food.

digiúno—fasting; abstinence.

dignità f.—dignity.

dignitàrio m.—dignitary.

dignitosaménte—with dignity.

dignitóso—one who has dignity; dignified.

digradaménto m.—gradual descent.

digradàre — to degrade; to descend slowly; blending of colors.

digradazióne f.—the act and effect of light and color diminishing.

digrassàre—to remove fat or grease.

digredíre—to digress; to deviate from a route.

digressióne f.—digression.

diguazzaménto m.—the shaking or mixing of a liquid.

diguazzàre—to shake up; to mix.

dilacciàre—to untie; to unlace. See slacciàre.

dilaceràre—to lacerate; to tear; see laceràre.

dilagàre—to flood; to inundate.

dilaniàre—to tear to pieces; to calumniate.

dilapidàre—to dilapidate; to ruin; to waste.

dilapidazióne f.—dilapidation.

dilatòrio—dilatory; tending to delay.

dilazióne f.—deferment; stay; delay.

diligènte—diligent.

diligènza f.—diligence; care.

diligènza nell'adempiménto—care used in performance (of obligations). The Civil Code requires that in fulfilling his obligations, a debtor must use the same degree of care exercised by the master of a family. See buòn pàdre di famíglia and Art. 1176 et seq., Italian Civil Code.

diloggiàre—to evict; to decamp; to take off.

diluviàle—diluvial; pertaining to a flood or deluge.

diluviàno—diluvian; of the flood.

diluviàre—to rain incessantly.

dilúvio m.—deluge.

dimagraménto m.—emaciation; growing thin; impoverishment of land through lack of elements necessary to cultivation.

dimagràre—to emaciate; to make thin; to become lean.

dimandànte m.—claimant; petitioner.

dimandàre—to ask; to request; to claim.

dimàndo m. (dimànda, dimàndita f.)—question; request. See domànda.

dimàni—tomorrow. See domàni.

diméttere—to resign; to discontinue; to forgive (a wrong); to condone (an obligation).

diminuzióne f.—diminution.

diminuzióne della garanzìa — diminution of guarantee. Where the security is destroyed or deteriorates, making the creditor insecure, he may require other security to be posted. Failing that, the creditor may request immediate payment of the obligation. See Art. 2743, 1186, Italian Civil Code.

dimissionàrio—one who has resigned.

dimissióne f.—resignation (of an office).

dimissòrio m. (dimissòria f.)—letter of dismissal.

dimòra f.—abode; residence; dwelling; a place where a person is then residing, though not habitually or permanently. See distinction between domicílio (domicile) and residènza (residence). Art. 43, Italian Civil Code; Art. 18, Italian Code of Civil Procedure.

dimoràre—to dwell; to live; to stay; to reside.

dimòro m.—delay.

dimostràre—to demonstrate; to show; to make known; to prove.

dimostratóre m. — one who demonstrates; one who explains.

dimostrazióne f.—demonstration.

dinamíte f.—dynamite.

dínamo f.—dynamo.

dinamòmetro m.—dynamometer; a device employed in measuring force or power.

dinànzi—before; in front of; in the presence of; appearing before (a judge).

dinàsta m.—dynast.

dinastía f.—dynasty.

dinàstico—dynastic.

dinegàre—to deny; to contradict; to oppose.

diniègo m.—denial; refusal.

dinotàre—to denote; to indicate; to signify. See denotàre.

dintornàre—to outline.

dintórno—outline; outskirts of a city; suburb; vicinage.

diocesàno—diocesan.

diòcesi f.—diocese.

dipartènza f.—leave-taking; farewell; departure.

dipartiménto m.—department (administrative).

dipartíre—to divide.

dipartírsi—to depart.

dipartíta f.—departure.

dipendènte — subordinate; employee; dependent.

dipendènza f.—dependence.

dipèndere—to depend upon.

dipennàre—to cancel; to erase; to abolish.

dipíngere—to paint; to color; to represent with words.

dipínto — painted; embellished; depicted; represented.

dipintóre m.—painter.

diplòma m.—diploma; certificate.

diplomàtica f.—the art of deciphering ancient documents and diplomas.

diplomàtico m.—diplomat; diplomatist.

diplomàtico—diplomatic.

diplomazía f.—diplomacy.

diportaménto m. — deportment; conduct.

diportàre (diportàrsi)—to behave; to proceed in a given way; to conduct oneself.

dipòrto m.—amusement; diversion; recreation.

dipsomàne m.—dipsomaniac; one who has an irresistible craving for intoxicating beverages.

dipsomanía f.—dipsomania; an irresistible craving for intoxicating beverages.

diradàre—to thin out; to do something less frequently.

diragnàre—to clear out cob-webs.

diramàre—to prune; to cut away; to distribute.

diramazióne f.—separation; division; ramification; bifurcation.

dirazzàre—to degenerate; to lose a racial quality.

diredàre—to disinherit. Also, diseredàre.

direttàrio m.—one who has legal ownership in property such as the proprietor or trustee as opposed to the beneficial owner or beneficiary.

direttísimo—most direct. See giudízio direttíssimo—summary proceeding.

dirètto—direct; straight. See giudízio direttíssimo.

direttóre m.—director; administrator.

direttóre responsàbile—the responsible editor of a newspaper in the event of legal action. Also, sometimes referred to as gerènte responsàbile.

diretríce f.—directress; manager.

direttòrio m.—directory.

direzióne f.—direction; management.

dirigènte m. & f.—one who manages or directs.

dirígere—to manage; to direct; to oversee; to surveil.

diriménte—annulling; breaking; terminating. See impediménto dirimento—impediment which prevents a marriage.

dirímere—to annul; to break; to terminate.

dirítta f.—right (hand) (side). Also, drítta.

dirítti civíli—civil rights.

dirítti demaniàli su bèni altrúi—rights of domain over the property of others. Equally subject to the regime of the public domain are the real rights which belong to the State, the provinces and the communes over property belonging to others, when these same rights are constituted for the use of some properties under the regime of the public domain for the achievement of purposes of public interest corresponding to those which serve the properties themselves. Art. 825, 822-824, Italian Civil Code. See úsi cívici.

dirítti e dovéri recíproci dei còniugi—reciprocal rights and duties of spouses. Upon marriage, the husband and wife acquire the same rights and assume the same duties. Marriage imposes reciprocal obligation of fidelity, to moral and material assistance, to collaboration in the interest of the family and to cohabitation. Art. 143, Italian Civil Code.

dirítto—straight. Also, drítto.

dirítto m.—law; the science of jurisprudence; the right to dispose of something or to do or not do a certain thing; the power to legally perform or refrain from performing an act; privilege; legal title; prerogative.

dirítto àlla libertà personàle—right to personal liberty or freedom. It includes religious freedom, the freedom to work, and the right to inviolability of the domicile. Art. 2, 8, 13, Constitution of the Italian Republic; Art. 605-609, 614, Italian Penal Code. Compensation for damages caused by criminal or culpable acts may be recovered. Art. 2043, Italian Civil Code.

dirítto amministratívo—administrative law.

dirítto canònico—canon law.

dirítto civíle—the law which regulates social and family norms of conduct; civil law; private law.

dirítto consuetudinàrio — customary law.

dirítto commerciàle—commercial law.

dirítto costituzionàle — constitutional law.

dirítto delle gènte—law of nations.

dirítto di autóre—copyright; right of authorship—Objects of the right of authorship are intellectual works of a creative nature relating to science, literature, music, design or plastic arts, architecture, theater and cinematography, whatever be its mode or form of expression. Art. 2575, Italian Civil Code. Also, Art. 2579 for rights of performers. Autóre (dirítti di), Usual Laws, Appendix to Italian Civil Code.

dirítto d'entràre—right of entry; good will of a business.

dirítto d'entratúra—good will of a business.

dirítto di esclusíva—right of exclusion. Where agreed, the supplier in an output, requirements and exclusive dealings contract, may prevent the other party from receiving performances of the same nature from third parties. Art. 1567, 1568, Italian Civil Code.

dirítto di esclusivítà—right of exclusivity. The person who obtains a patent to an invention has the exclusive right to its use and disposal. Art. 2584-2594, Italian Civil Code.

dirítto di intèrpreti ed esecutóri—right

of performers. Performers of operas, musical compositions as well as dramatic and literary works, in addition to compensation for their performances are entitled to just compensation from whoever diffuses or transmits these performances by radio, telephone or other apparatus and records, films or otherwise. Art. 2579, Italian Civil Code.

dirítto di verífica—right of inspection. The party for whom work is being performed under contract, before receiving delivery, has the right to verify or inspect the completed work. The inspection must be made as soon as the contractor has it in condition to be done. If, notwithstanding the invitation to inspection by the contractor, the one for whom the work is performed fails to inspect without just reasons or fails to communicate the result of his inspection within a brief time, the work is considered to be accepted. If the one for whom the work is performed receives delivery of the work, this is considered acceptance even if there was no inspection. Except agreement otherwise, or contrary usage, the contractor has the right to payment when the work is accepted. Art. 1665, Italian Civil Code. Also, verífica e pagaménto dell'òpera.

dirítto ecclesiàstico—ecclesiastic law. The rules established by a State to regulate relations between Church and State.

dirítto internazionàle — international law.

dirítto naturàle—natural law. The "jus naturale" (Lat.) of the Romans. A concept of rules and principles for the guidance of human conduct independent of enacted laws or systems peculiar to any one people and discoverable by rational intelligence.

dirítto penàle—penal or criminal law.

dirítto processuàle—procedural law.

dirítto reàle—real right. It is a right which entitles the person vested with it to immediate dominion and possession of the subject. It is a right in property which imparts the power to enjoy and dispose of it.

disabilità f.—inability. Also, inabilità.

disabitàto—uninhabited.

disaccòrdo m.—discord; disagreement; dissension.

disàggio m.—unfavorable discount or rate of exchange; inconvenient; uncomfortable.

disàstro m.—disaster; calamity.

disàstro ferroviàrio—railroad disaster. Whoever causes a railroad disaster is punished with imprisonment. Art. 430, Italian Penal Code. See perícolo di disàstro ferroviàrio causàto da dannegiaménto.

disavànzo m.—deficit; damage; loss of money.

disbórso m.—disbursement.

disbrigàre—to dispatch; to extricate; to disentangle.

discàpito m.—loss; damage; loss of capital.

discàrica f.—voucher.

discaricàre—to unload.

discàrico m.—discharge; justification.

discendènte m.—descendant.

discendènza f.—descent; extraction.

discéndere—to descend.

dischiúdere—to disclose; to open.

disciògliere—to dissolve; to loosen; to undo; to resolve a question.

disciplína f.—discipline; maintenance of order and obedience; subject for study and learning.

disciplinàre—to discipline; to train; to punish; to accustom to rules of discipline.

discolàto m.—a practice of enrolling vagabonds and unemployed in the military.

díscolo—quarrelsome; malcontent.

discólpa f.—exculpation; justification; proof of innocence.

discolpàre—to exculpate; to justify; to adduce proof of innocence.

disconciàre—to disarrange; to spoil; to waste.

disconfessàre—to disavow; to recant.

disconfidènza f.—diffidence; distrust.

disconfortàre—to dissuade; to discourage; to lose spirit.

disconoscènte—ungrateful.

disconoscènza f.—ingratitude.

disconóscere—to refuse to recognize or admit; to be ungrateful.

disconosciménto di paternità — disavowal of paternity. See **azióne di disconosciménto di paternità** and **azióni di stàto**. Art. 235, 244-249, Italian Civil Code.

discontinuàre — to discontinue; to cease.

disconvenìre—to be inconvenient; to be unfitting or disagreeable.

discopèrto—to be in the open; to be uncovered; to be disclosed.

discoprìre—to discover; to uncover; to disclose.

discordànza f. — discordance; dissonance; disagreement.

discordàre—to be discordant; to be at variance; to disagree.

discòrdia f.—discord; dissension.

discórso m.—discourse; speech.

discòsto—separate; removed; far.

discrédere—to disbelieve.

discredérsi—to change one's opinion.

discreditàre — to discredit; to lose reputation or trust.

discrédito del concorrènte—discrediting a competitor. It is an act of unfair competition. Art. 2598, Italian Civil Code.

discrepànza f. — discrepancy; difference.

discrepàre—to disagree; to differ; to be in disaccord.

discretaménte—discreetly.

discretézza f.—caution; moderation; prudence.

discretíva f.—discernment; criterion; good sense; faculty of discerning true from false, good from evil and beautiful from ugly.

discréto—discreet; prudent.

discrezionàle (potère)—a discretionary power of a magistrate to decide according to law and administrative procedures which is not subject to review.

discrezióne f.—discretion; moderation.

discriminànte — attenuating circumstance; that which removes criminal responsibility.

discriminàre—to distinguish; to discern; to note.

discriminàre da crímine—to remove penal or criminal responsibility.

discussióne f.—discussion.

discútere—to argue; to discuss.

discutíbile—that which can be discussed; that which is uncertain; arguable; problematic.

disdegnàre—to disdain; to scorn.

disdégno m.—disdain; scorn.

disdétta f.—the act of terminating a contract of hire or a lease; notice to quit premises. Art. 657, Italian Code of Civil Procedure.

disdétto — forbidden; negated; prohibited.

disdíre—to deny; to retract; to give notice.

disebbriàre—to regain sobriety; to become sober again.

diseccàre—to desicate.

disegnàre—to draw; to design; to delineate.

diségni ornamentàli—ornamental designs; letters patent may be obtained for such designs. Art. 2593, 2594, Italian Civil Code.

diségno m.—design.

diseredàre—to disinherit. Also, **diredàre**.

diseredàto—disinherited.

disertaménto m.—desertion.

disertàre—to desert.

disertóre m.—deserter.

diserzióne f.—desertion.

disfaciménto m.—defeat; destruction; ruin.

disfamàre—to satisfy one's hunger; to satiate. Also, **Sfamàre**.

disfamàre—to defame; to discredit. Also, **diffamàre**.

disfàre—to undo; to destroy; to defeat.

disfàtta f.—serious defeat of an army or navy; rout; ruin.

disfattísmo m.—defeatism.

disfattísmo econòmico—economic defeatism. It is a crime against the jural personality of the State. Art. 267, Italian Penal Code. See personalità dello stàto (delítti cóntro la).

disfattísmo político—political defeatism. It is a crime against the jural personality of the State. Art. 265, Italian Penal Code. See personalità dello stàto (delítti cóntro la).

disfavóre m.—disfavor; disgrace.

disfída f.—challenge. Also sfída.

disfiguràre—to disfigure. See sfiguràre.

disfioraménto—defloration.

disfioràre—to deflower.

disformàre—to deform; to disfigure.

disfunzióne f.—malfunction.

disgradàre—to put to shame.

disgradévole — unpleasant; disagreeable.

disgradíre—to displease.

disgravaménto m.—discharging; exoneration.

disgravàre—to unload; to relieve from a burden; to ease.

disgràzia f. — accident; misfortune; disgrace.

disgraziàto — unfortunate; wretched; unhappy; sad.

disigillàre—to unseal.

disimballàre—to unpack.

disimbastíre—to unstitch.

disimpacciàre—to remove an obstacle or impediment; to clear away; to remove an embarrassment.

disimparàre—to forget; to unlearn.

disimpegnàre—to discharge; to release from an obligation; to perform a duty.

disimpégno m.—discharge; release.

disimpiegàre—to dismiss; to fire (from a job).

disincagliàre — to free or float a stranded ship.

disincantàre—to disenchant.

disincarnàre—to disembody.

disinfettànte m.—disinfectant.

disinfettàre—to disinfect.

disingannàre—to undeceive; to clarify.

disingànno m.—act of undeceiving; disappointment.

disintegràre—to disintegrate.

disintegrazióne f.—disintegration.

disinteressàre—to lose interest.

disinteressàto—disinterested.

disinvitàre—to contermand or cancel an invitation.

disinvòlto—free; easy; cool; self-possessed; nonchalant.

disinvoltúra f.—coolness; ease; impudence; self-possession; nonchalance.

disleàle—disloyal. Also, sleàle.

dislivèllo m.—unequal level.

dislivèllo dei fóndi—unequal level of lands. Where two separately owned parcels of real property are located in an inhabited area, the owner of the land above must bear the entire cost of constructing and maintaining a wall from its foundation to his property level to provide lateral support. Both he and the owner of the lower level must contribute for the remaining height of the wall. It must be built half on ground of the lower level and half on that of the higher level. Art. 887, Italian Civil Code.

dislocaménto m.—displacement; displacement; disposition of troops or ships in military operations.

dislocàre—to displace.

dislogàre—to dislocate. Also, slogàre.

dismemoràto—forgetful. Also, smemoràto.

disméttere—to cease; to abandon; to give up; to stop using.

dismontàre—to dismount; to descend.

disnaturàto—unnatural; cruel; inhuman. See snaturàto.

disnodàre—to untie; to unravel.

disnudàre—to denude.

disobbediénza f.—disobedience.

disobbedíre—to disobey.

disoccupàre—to take away an occupation; to be released.

disocuppàto—unemployed.

disoccupazióne f.—unemployment; impossibility of finding employment.

disonestà f.—dishonesty.

disonèsto—dishonest.

disonoraménte—dishonorably.

disonoràto—dishonored.

disonóre m.—dishonor.

disópra—above; on top; over.

disordinaménto m.—disorder. Also, disordinànza.

disordinàto — disorderly; disordered; confused.

disórdine m.—disorder; lack of discipline; disturbance of public order.

disorganizzàre—to disorganize; to spoil an organized thing; to disarrange.

disorganizzazióne f.—disorganization; disorder.

disorientàre—to lose orientation; to lose direction; to lose a train of thought.

disossidàre—to deoxidize.

dispacciàre—to despatch; to clear; to remove an obstacle.

dispàccio m.—a dispatch; correspondence.

disparàto — disparate; different; diverse.

díspari—odd (numbers); unequal; dissimilar.

disparità f.—disparity; inequality.

dispàrte—aside.

dispartíre—to distribute; to separate.

dispèndio m.—expense; cost; charge; excessive cost.

dispènsa f. — distribution; dispensation; pantry; store-room; portion; part of a book published serially.

dispènsa da impediménti nel matrimònio — dispensation from impediments to a marriage. Art. 87, 89, Italian Civil Code.

dispensàre—to dispense; to distribute; to exempt.

dispensière m.—steward.

disperàre—to despair.

disperàto—desperate.

disperazióne f.—desperation.

dispèrdere—to dissipate; to waste; to scatter.

dispèrgere—to scatter.

dispersióne f.—dispersion.

dispettàre—to affront; to disrespect; to scorn; to spite; to regard or treat without respect; to treat with contempt. See disprezzàre.

dispètto m.—affront; scorn; spite; offense.

dispettóso—spiteful; malicious.

dispiàcere—to displease.

dispiacére m.—displeasure; sorrow.

dispiccàre—to detach; to pull up.

dispicciàre—to despatch; to expedite. See spicciàre.

dispiegàre—to explain; to extend.

dispietàto—pitiless; merciless.

dispodestàre—to deprive of power; to deprive of one's property; to dispossess. Also, spodestàre.

dispogliàre—to undress; to deprive; to despoil; to divest; to plunder. Also, spogliàre.

disponènte m.—testator. Also, testatóre.

disponíbile—disposable; free; that part of an estate which a testator may leave to whomsoever he desires. This is in contrast to the legítitma, which is a non-disposable portion which the law reserves to descendants and ascendants. Art. 536, 564, Italian Civil Code. Also, porzióne disponíbile.

disponibilità f.—disposability; on the unattached list (as an officer); on half pay; state of a public employee who has been relieved from service due to administrative action as punishment or from reduction in force or abolishment of office; liquid funds available in a bank account.

dispopolàre—to depopulate.

dispórre—to dispose; to arrange; to prepare; to prescribe; to order.

dispositivo — dispositive; regulating; that which arranges or disposes of matters.

dispositívo m.—the operative part of a decision or judgment; judicial opinion.

dispositóre m. (dispositríce f.)—one who disposes or orders.

disposizióne f.—disposition; disposal; transfer of property; arrangement; inclination.

disposizióne a favóre dei póveri—disposition in favor of the poor. A testamentary disposition of this nature, which does not indicate its use or the public institution for whose benefit it is made, is deemed to be made in favor of the poor in the place where the testator had his domicile at the time of his death. Art. 630, Italian Civil Code.

disposizióne a favóre dell'ànima—disposition in favor of the soul. Such a testamentary disposition is valid. Art. 629, Italian Civil Code.

disposizióne testamentària—testamentary disposition.

disposizióni preliminàri — preliminary dispositions. These are pre-laws which precede the Civil Code and are abbreviated "D.P.". The actual title of the preliminary dispositions is, "Disposizióni Sulla Légge in Generàle" (Dispositions on the Law in General).

disposizióni sulla légge in generàle—dispositions on the law in general. They are pre-laws which precede the provisions of the Civil Code. They consist of thirty-one articles and generally, are referred to as "Disponsizióni Preliminàri" (Preliminary Dispositions), abbreviated "D.P.".

dispósito m.—a legal decree, disposition or order.

dispósto—disposed; inclined.

dispregiàre (disprezzàre) — to disrespect; to scorn; to spite; to regard or treat without respect; to treat with contempt.

disprèzzo m. — disdain; contempt; scorn.

disproporzióne f.—disproportion.

dísputa f.—dispute; disputation; debate.

disputàre—to dispute; to debate.

disputazióne f.—disputation.

disquisizióne f.—disquisition; inquiry; dissertation.

disradicàre—to eradicate.

dissacràre—to profane; to deconsecrate; to desecrate.

dissalàre—to desalt.

dissaldàre—to unsolder.

dissanguàre—to bleed.

dissecàre—to dissect.

disseccàre—to dry up.

disselciàre—to unpave.

disseminàre—to disseminate.

disseminazióne f.—dissemination.

dissennàre—to deprive of the senses.

dissennàto—senseless.

dissensióne f.—dissension.

dissentería f.—dysentery.

dissentiménto m.—dissidence.

dissentíre—to dissent.

disseppellíre—to exhume; to disinter.

disseràre—to unlock.

dissertàre—to reason; to discuss.

dissertazióne f.—dissertation.

disservíre—to injure; to render a bad service.

dissestàre—to injure financially.

dissestàto—full of debts.

dissèsto m.—insolvent. See insolvènza.

dissetàre—to quench the thirst.

dissezióne f.—dissection.

dissidènte m.—dissident.

dissidènza f.—dissidence.

dissídio m.—dissension; discord.

disigillàre—to unseal.

dissímile—dissimilar.

dissimulàre—to dissimulate; to conceal.

dissimulazióne f.—dissimulation; concealment.

dissipàre—to dissipate.

dissipazióne f.—dissipation.

dissociàre—to dissociate.

dissociazióne f.—dissociation.

dissodàre—to plough; to break ground.

dissolúbile—dissoluble.

dissolúto — dissolute; licentious; debauched.

dissolutóre—dissolvent.

dissoluzióne f.—dissolution.

dissolvènte—dissolvent.

dissolvère—to dissolve; to undo.

dissomigliànte—different; dissimilar.

dissomigliànza f.—dissimilarity; difference; disparity.

dissomigliàre—to differ; to be unlike.

dissonànte—dissonant.

dissonànza f.—dissonance.

dissonàre—to be dissonant.

dissonnàre—to wake; to awake.

dissotteraménto m.—disinterment; exhumation.

dissotterràre—to disinter; to exhume.

dissuadére—to dissuade.

dissuasióne f.—dissuasion.

dissuetúdine f. — desuetude; disuse; lack of use or habit.

dissugàre—to dry up.

disuggellàre—to unseal.

distaccaménto m.—detachment.

distaccàre—to detach; to disengage.

distaccàto—detached.

distàcco m.—detachment; separation.

distànte—distant.

distànza f.—distance.

distàre—to be distant.

distemperàre—to dissolve; to dilute.

distèndere—to draw out; to extend; to spread out.

distendiménto m.—distension; extension.

distensióne f.—distension; extension.

distésa f.—expanse; extent.

distésa (à and àlla)—constantly; continuously; without interruption.

distesaménte—continuously.

distéso—extended; spread out.

distillàre—to distill.

distillatóio m.—still.

distillatóre m. (distillatríce f.)—distiller.

distillazióne—distillation.

distillería f.—distillery.

distínguere—to distinguish; to discern; to separate; to divide; to perceive.

distínta f.—price list.

distintaménte—distinctly; in a special way.

distintívo m.—a distinguishing mark; sign of distinction such as a rosette worn by members of an Order.

distínto — separate; diverse; distinguished; clear.

distinzióne f.—distinction.

distògliere—to distract; to dissuade.

distòrcere—to twist; to wrench. Also, stòrcere.

distornàre—to divert; to hinder.

distorsióne f.—sprain; strain.

distràrre—to distract; to divert; to separate; to amuse; to entertain.

distràtto—distracted; diverted.

distrazióne f.—distraction; recreation.

distrétta f.—distress; imminent peril.

distrettézza f.—rigor; severity.

distrétto—pressed; tightly bound.

distrétto m.—district; division of a territory for administrative, military or judicial purposes and its headquarters.

distribuíre—to distribute.

distribuzióne f.—distribution; division.

districàre (distrigàre)—to unravel; to free from an intrigue.

distríngere—to tighten strongly; to constrain.

distrúggere—to destroy; to demolish.

distruggiménto m.—destruction.

distrútto—destroyed, annihilated.

distruttóre m. (distruttríce f.)—destroyer.

distruzióne f.—destruction.

distruzióne o sabotàggio di òpere militàri—destruction or sabotage of military installations. Whoever destroys or renders unusable, in whole or in part, even temporarily, ships, aircraft, convoys, roads, installations, warehouses or other military works or those destined to the use of the armed forces of the State is punished with imprisonment. Art. 253, Italian Penal Code. See sabotàggio.

distruzióne, soppressióne o sottrazióne di cadàvere—destruction, concealment or withholding of a cadaver. Whoever destroys, conceals or withholds a cadaver, or a part thereof, or withholds or scatters its ashes, is punished with imprisonment. The penalty is increased if the act is committed in cemeteries or other places of burial, deposit or custody. Art. 411, Italian Penal Code. See occultaménto di cadàvere.

disturbàre—to disturb.

disturbatóre m. (disturbatríce f.)—disturber.

distúrbo m.—disturbance; inconvenience; temporary upset.

disubbidiènte—disobedient.

disubbidiènza f.—disobedience.

disubbidíre—to disobey.

disuggellàre—to unseal.

disuguaglìànza f.—inequality; diversity.

disuguagliàre — to make uneven, diverse.

disuguàle—unequal; diverse.

disumanàre—to dehumanize.

disumàno—inhuman; cruel.

disumàre—to disinter; to exhume.

disumazióne f.—disinterment; exhumation.

disumidíre—to dry.

disúngere—to remove grease.

disunióne f.—disunion; discord.

disuníre—to disunite; to create discord.

disuníto—disunited.

disusànza f.—disuse.

disusàre—to disuse; to fall in disuse.

disusàto—obsolete; fallen in disuse.

disúso m.—disuse.

disútile—useless.

disvantàggio m.—disadvantage.

disvarìàre—to vary; to distract.

disvìàre—to deviate; to lead astray.

ditàle m.—thimble.

díto m.—finger; inch.

dítta f. — firm; commercial name; trade-name. See Art. 2563-2568, Italian Civil Code and inségna.

dítta socìàle—firm name.

dittatóre m.—dictator.

dittatúra f.—dictatorship.

diurèsi f. — diuresis; excessive discharge of urine.

diurètico m.—a medicine which increases the volume of urine.

diurnàle—daily.

diurnísta m.—a day laborer.

diúrno—diurnal; pertaining to the daytime; daily.

díva f.—goddess; female deity.

díva—divine.

divagàre—to stray; to wander; to amuse.

divallàre—to descend.

divampàre—to burn; to blaze; to flare up.

divàno m.—formerly the Council of State in Turkey; divan; sofa.

divàrio m.—variation; unessential difference.

divèllere—to uproot; to remove with force.

diveníre—to become; to transform; to become gradually.

diventàre—to become; to become suddenly.

divèrbio m. — altercation; dispute;

lively exchange of words and opinions.

divergènte—divergent.

divergènza f.—divergence.

divèrgere—to diverge.

diversificàre—to diversify.

diversióne f.—diversion.

diversità f.—diversity.

divèrso—diverse.

divertèvole—amusing; entertaining.

divertiménto m.—amusement; diversion.

divertìre—to amuse; to divert (a stream).

divestìre—to divest; to strip.

divezzàre—to wean.

diviàre—to deviate.

dividèndo m.—dividend.

divìdere—to divide.

divietàre—to prohibit; to forbid.

divièto m.—prohibition.

divinàre—to divine; to foresee.

divincolàre—to twist.

divinis (Lat.)—it is used in the phrase, sospèndere a divìnis, which signifies the suspension or prohibition of a priest from exercising the sacred ministry, as punishment.

divìsa f.—uniform; heraldic arms; parting of the hair; share of an estate.

divìsa èstera — foreign exchange; money or currency accepted as legal tender in a foreign state.

divisióne f.—division; partition; partition of an estate.

divisióne ereditària—partition or share of an estate.

divìso—divided; disunited.

divoràre—to devour.

divorziàre—to divorce.

divorziàto m.—divorced.

divòrzio m.—divorced.

divòrzio m.—divorce; dissolution of marriage by divorce. Marriage is dissolved by the death of one of the spouses and by divorce. Art. 149, Italian Civil Code. See sciogliménto del matrimònio.

divulgàre—to divulge; to disclose, to publish.

divulgazióne f. — disclosure; publication.

dizionàrio m.—dictionary.

dizióne f.—diction.

doccétta f.—catheter; small conduit.

dóccia f.—douche; shower bath; conduit; canal.

docciàre—to douche; to shower.

do, dico, addico (Lat.)—I give, I say, I adjudge. They indicate the ancient Praetor's jurisdiction. Do—he gave actions, exceptions and *judices*. The latter were private persons appointed to try and decide an action. They received written instructions from the Praetor as to the principles of law with which to decide the case. Dico—he pronounced judgment. Addico—he adjudged the property of the debtor to the plaintiff. See dies fasti.

do ut des (Lat.)—I give that you may give. A formula of the Roman Civil Law of innominate contracts.

do ut facis (Lat.)—I give that you may do. A formula of the Roman Civil Law of innominate contracts.

docènte m.—teacher.
libero docènte—university teacher.

docènza f.—teaching.
libera docènza—faculty and grade of a libero docènte, a university teacher.

dòcile—docile; tractable.

docilità f.—docility.

documentàre—to document.

documénto m.—document.

dóga f.—stave which is part of the side of a cask.

dogàna f.—custom house; office which imposes and collects taxes on imports and exports.

doganière m.—customs official.

dogàre—to place staves; to bind.

dogaréssa f.—wife of a doge.

dogàto m.—office and rank of doge.

dòge m.—chief magistrate of the Republic of Venice and the Republic of Genoa.

dògma m.—dogma. Also dòmma.

dólce—sweet; mild; soft.

dólce m.—sweet.

dolceménte—gently; softly; sweetly.

dolcézza f.—sweetness.

dólco—mild weather; humid weather.

dolènte—painful.

dolére—to feel pain; to feel sorry.

doli capax (Lat.)—capable of criminal intent or malice.

doli incapax (Lat.)—incapable of criminal intent or malice.

dòllaro m.—dollar.

dòlo m.—civilly, it connotes fraud, deceit, or artifice. Contracts which are entered into by means of fraud of one of the parties, may be annulled or set aside. Art. 1427, 1439, 1440, Italian Civil Code. Damages may be recovered for loss caused thereby. Art. 2043, Italian Civil Code. Penally, it connotes acts of criminality, criminal intent or malice by a person having the capacity to perform an act of commission or omission deemed by the law to be a crime. Art. 42, 43, Italian Penal Code.

doloràre—to feel pain.

dolóre m.—pain.

doloróso—painful.

dolóso—fraudulent; deceitful; intentional; criminal.

domàbile—tameable; malleable.

domànda f.—demand; complaint; petition; question; written petition or complaint; interrogation; price asked for merchandise.

domànda giudiziàle—judicial petition —a formal request of the judiciary to obtain relief.

domandàre—to demand; to ask; to request.

domàni—tomorrow.

domàre—to subdue; to subject; to tame.

domatóre m.—tamer; subduer; two wheel cart used to tame horses.

doménica f.—Sunday.

domenicàle—dominical; of Sunday.

domenicàno m.—Dominican.

domèstica f.—domestic; maid servant.

domesticàre—to tame.

domèstico—domestic; tame.

domiciliàre—to be domiciled; to settle.

domicílio m.—domicile; place of permanent residence or abode; the place where a person has established the principal site of his business affairs and interests. Art. 43, Italian Civil Code. See residènza and dimòra.

domicílio civíle—civil domicile. It refers to the place where a person conducts his principal business affairs.

domicílio coàtto—enforced residence in a specific area with restriction of movement. See confíno and sicurézza detentíve (misúre di).

domicílio dei cóniugi, minóre e dell' interdétto—domicile of the spouses, the minor and the interdicted. Each spouse has his own domicile where the principal place of his own affairs or interests has been established. The minor is domiciled at the place of family residence or that of his guardian. If the parents are separated or their marriage has been dissolved or if its civil effects have ceased or they do not have the same residence, the minor has the domicile of the parent with whom he lives. One interdicted for mental incapacity has the domicile of his guardian. Art. 45, Italian Civil Code.

domicílio elètto (domicílio elettívo)— elected domicile. One may select a domicile specially for the prosecution of specific acts or his business affairs. Art. 47, Italian Civil Code. Also, elezióne di domicílio.

domínio dirètto — immediate ownership; strict ownership.

domínio púbblico—public ownership. See demànio púbblico.

domínio útile—beneficial use of property owned by another.

dominànte—dominant.

dominàre—to dominate; to govern; to reign; to rule.

dominazióne f.—domination.

domínio m.—dominion; domain; ownership; right to property.

domínio riservàto—conditional sale; an installment sale where the title remains with the seller until final payment has been made by the buyer when title passes to him. Also, riservàto domínio, véndita con risèrva della proprietà and véndita con risèrva di domínio. Art. 1523-1526, Italian Civil Code.

dòmma m.—dogma.

dommàtico—dogmatic.

dómo—subdued; tamed.

dòmo m. — cathedral. From domus (Lat.)—house. Also, duòmo. in dòmo Petri—in prison.

don m.—title of respect and distinction given to priests, nobles and those of good family.

donànte—donor.

donàre—to give as a gift.

donàrio m.—the treasury of a temple.

donatàrio m.—donee.

donatóre m. (donatríce f.)—donor.

donazióne f.—donation; gift; a gift by contract or legal instrument. A contract made in a spirit of liberality, whereby one party enriches another by granting him one of his rights or assuming an obligation towards the other party. It must be made by formal, public document or it is void. Art. 769, 782, Italian Civil Code. See revocazióne per sopravveniènza di fígli.

dònna f.—lady; wife; woman. In a game of cards, the Queen.

dóno m.—gift.

dónora f.—gifts given to a bride other than the dowry or trousseau.

donzèlla f.—damsel.

donzèllo m.—young esquire to a knight; page; Municipal usher or messenger.

doppiaménto m. — the operation whereby a precious metal is applied over a less precious one, for example plating copper with silver.

doppiàre—to double.

doppiàto—metal which has plated a less precious one; the dubbing in of a sound film.

doppiatóre m.—the one who has performed the operation of doppiaménto. See above. In a sound film, the actor whose voice is dubbed over that of another.

doppiatúra f.—dubbing in a sound film.

doppière m.—candelabrum.

dóppio—double.

doràre—to gild.

doràto—gilt.

doratóre m.—gilder.

doratùra f,—gilding.

dorè—gold colored; golden.

dorería f.—gold objects.

dòrico—Doric.

dormentòrio m.—dormitory; sleep inducing. See dormitòrio—dormitory.

dormicchiàre—to doze.

dormiénte—sleeping.

dormiglióne m.—one who sleeps much.

dormiglióso—sleepy; drowsy.

dormíre—to sleep.

dormíta f.—act of sleeping; nap.

dormitòrio m.—dormitory.

dormivéglia m.—half-asleep.

dorsàle—dorsal.

dòrso m.—back.

dosàggio m.—dosage.

dosàre—to determine the proportion of ingredients in medicines; to distribute in a stingy or parsimonious manner.

dosatúra f.—dosage.

dossàle m.—cover of the missal.

dòsso m.—back.

dossología f.—doxology; a hymn containing words of praise to God.

dòta f.—dowry. Also, dòte. See comunióne dei bèni tra còniugi and separazióne dei bèni (regíme di).

dotàre—to give a dowry; to endow; to favor.

dotàto—gifted; endowed.

dotatóre m.—one who furnishes a dowry.

dotazióne f. — dotation; endowment; the aggregate of equipment, machinery and appliances and their replacements used in the operation of a farm, or military or naval units; also, the scenery and equipment of a theater. See scòrte mòrte and scòrte víve.

dòte f.—dowry. Also, dòta.

dòtto—learned.

dottóra f.—woman doctor. Also, dottoréssa.

dottoràle—doctoral.

dottoràto m.—doctorate.

dottóre m.—doctor.

dottoréssa—woman doctor. Also, dottóra.

dottrína f.—doctrine; teaching of a complex of related matters.

dottrinàle—doctrinal.

dóve — where; place; whereabouts (m.).

dovére—to owe; to be indebted.

dovére m.—duty; moral obligation.

dovére del fíglio verso i genitóri—duty of a child towards his parents. He must respect his parents and must contribute to the maintenance of the family so long as he lives in it, according to his means and income. Art. 315, Italian Civil Code.

dovízia f.—abundance; plenty.

dovutaménte—duly; justly. See debitaménte.

dovúto—that which is owed.

dozzína f.—dozen; board and lodging. stàre a dozzína—to board. tenére a dozzína—to keep a boarding house.

dozzinàle—common; ordinary.

dozzinànte m.—boarder.

draconiàno — Draconian; rigorous; severe.

dràga f.—dredge.

dragàggio m.—dredging.

dragàre—to dredge.

dràgo m.—dragon.

dragomànno m.—dragoman; an interpreter at Oriental Courts and their embassies and consulates; Oriental official interpreter.

dragóna f.—sword knot.

dragonário m.—a Roman legion's standard bearer.

dragonàto—animal with dragon's tail represented in heraldic designs.

dragóne m.—dragon; dragoon, a soldier in the light cavalry.

dràmma m.—drama.

dràmma f.—drachma.

drammàtico—dramatic.

drammatúrgo m.—playwright.

drappèllo m.—small troop of soldiers; a streamer or pennant.

drappéria f.—drapery or silk stuffs; a store which sells them.

drappière m. — draper; silk-weaver; cloth worker.

dràppo m.—silk material or other woven cloth.

drítta f.—right (hand) (side); starboard. See tribórdo.

drítto—straight.

drízza f.—halyard.

drizzàre—to straighten; to direct; to raise; to trim (a sail).

dròga f.—drug; spice.

drogàre—to drug; to spice.

dràstico—drastic; energetic.

drenàggio m.—drainage.

drenàre—to drain.

dribblàre—to dribble (from the English).

droghería f.—grocer's shop; pharmacy.

droghière m.—grocer; pharmacist.

drogísta m.—See droghière, above.

dròma f.—mast or spar on a sailing vessel.

dromedàrio m.—dromedary.

drómo m.—place where a race is held; a series of poles set to mark direction as in a channel.

drusciàre—to caress; to cajole.

dùbbio m.—doubt.

dubitàre—to doubt.

dùca m.—duke.

dùce m.—leader. From the Latin, dux.

duchéssa f.—duchess.

dùe—two.

duellànte—duellist.

duellàre—to duel.

duellìsta m.—duellist.

duèllo m.—duel.

duètto m.—duet.

dùna f.—sand dune.

dùo m.—duet.

duòlo m.—grief; pain.

duòmo m.—cathedral. Also, dómo.

dùplex m.—telephone party line.

duplicàre—to duplicate; to repeat.

duplicàti dell'asségno — copies of checks; with the exception of bearer checks, any check drawn in one country and payable in another, or overseas within the same country may be issued in duplicate. In that event, they must be numbered consecutively otherwise they are considered as individual checks. The payment of one check discharges them all. Art. 66, 67, Asségni (checks), Usual Laws, Appendix to Italian Civil Code.

duplicàti della cambiàle—copies of drafts; drafts may be drawn in a number of copies. Each must be consecutively numbered otherwise they are considered as individual drafts. The payment of one draft discharges them all. The drawee is obligated for every copy he accepted but has not withdrawn. The drawer and subsequent indorsers are responsible for all copies bearing their signatures which have not been withdrawn. Art. 83-85, Cambiàle (Drafts), Usual Laws, Appendix to Italian Civil Code.

duplicàto m.—duplicate; copy.

duplicazióne f.—duplication.

dùplice—double.

duplicità f.—duplicity.

dùplo—double.

duràbile—durable.

durabilità f.—durability.

duràcine (duràcino)—clingstone, such as a clingstone peach.

duralluminio m.—duraluminum.

duramàdre f.—dura mater, the tough fibrous membrane forming the outermost of the three coverings of the brain and spinal cord.

duràmen m. (duràme)—the hard central part of a tree which is harder and of darker color.

dudurànte—during.

duràre—to last; to endure.

duràta f.—duration.

durézza f.—hardness.

dùrium m. — plastic material from which various objects and phonographic records are manufactured.

dùro—hard.

dùttile—ductile; malleable.

duttilità f.—ductility; malleability.

duttóre m.—one who leads; conductor.

duùmviro m.—duumvir; one of two citizens who form a diumvirate.

E

ebanìsta m.—cabinet maker.

ebanisterìa f.—workshop of a cabinet maker; the art or craft of a cabinet maker.

èbano m.—ebony.

ebbrézza f.—drunkenness; intoxication.

èbbro—drunk.

ebdomadàrio—weekly.

ebefrenìa f.—hebephrenia; a form of dementia praecox incident to puberty.

èbere—to faint; to grow weak.

ebetàggine f.—bluntness; obtuseness.

èbete—dull; obtuse; weak-minded.

ebollíre—to boil over; to overflow.

ebollizióne f.—ebullition; overflowing; seething.

eboràrio m.—a sculptor in ivory.

ebraicísta m. & f.—one learned in the Hebrew language.

ebràico—Hebraic.

ebrèo—Hebrew; Jew.

ebrietà or ebbrèzza f.—state of inebriation; drunkenness.

ebúrneo—ivory.

ebúrno—of ivory.

ecatómbe f.—hecatomb; sacrifice of 100 oxen in honor of the Greek gods; a great slaughter.

eccedènte—excessive.

eccedènza f.—excess.

eccèdere—to exceed.

eccellènte—excellent.

eccellènza f.—excellency; quality of excellence.

eccèllere—to excel.

eccentricità f.—eccentricity.

eccèntrico m.—eccentric.

eccepíbile—that which may be opposed; subject to exception.

eccepíre—to oppose; to take exception.

eccessívo—excessive.

eccèsso m.—excess.

eccèsso colpóso—culpable excess. It is committed by someone who uses more than justifiable force in the exercise of a right or fulfilling a duty, in legitimate self-defense, in the legitimate use of arms, or acting under a state of necessity in saving himself or others from grave personal danger not intentionally caused by him and not otherwise avoidable. Art. 55, 51-53, Italian Penal Code.

eccèsso di difésa—excessive defense. A mitigating circumstance by one who has acted in self-defense even though he has exceeded the force necessary for self-defense.

eccèsso di potére—excess of power. It is a defect rendering void an administrative act.

eccètto—except.

eccettuàre—to except.

eccezionàle—exceptional.

eccezióne f.—exception; generally, a defense interposed by a defendant to the form or substance of a complaint. It also refers, technically, to the discharge of an obligation by performance due to fraud, violence or mistake. Penally, when interposed by the defense during final argument, the presiding judge or Praetor may allow the public prosecutor to answer. Part IV, Art. 5, Enabling Rules, Code of Penal Procedure.

ecchímosi f.—ecchymosis; a discoloration due to a forcible diffusion of blood through the surrounding tissues; bruise; contusion.

eccídio m.—extermination; slaughter.

eccipiènte — excipient; a substance used as the medium for the administration of an active medicine.

eccitàbile—excitable.

eccitaménto m.—excitation; instigation.

eccitànte—excitant; stimulant.

eccitàre—to excite; to instigate.

eccitazióne f.—excitation.

ecclèsia f.—the popular assembly of ancient Greece.

ecclesiàtico—pertaining to the Church. dirítto ecclesiàstico—the rules established by a State to regulate relations between Church and State.

ecclisàre—to eclipse. Also, eclissàre.

echeggiàre—to echo.

eclèttico m.—ecclectic.

eclissàre—to eclipse.

eclísse or eclíssi m. & f.—eclipse.

èco m. & f.—echo.

ecología f.—ecology.

economàto m.—stewardship.

economía f.—economy.

econòmico—economical.

economísta m.—economist.

economizzàre—to economize; to save.

ecònomo m.—steward.

ecumènico — ecumenical; universal; general.

eczèma m.—excema.

edàce—consuming; devouring; voracious.

èdema m.—edema; swelling.

edícola f.—little chapel.

edificàre—to build; to erect.

edifício m. — edifice; fabric; social order.

edifízio m.—building.

edíle m.—Aedilis (Lat.). A Roman magistrate in charge of buildings, streets, bridges and spectacles.

edilízia f.—the art of raising buildings, opening streets, etc.

edilízio—pertaining to an Aedile; concerning building and plans for construction.

èdito—published; printed; issued.

editóre m.—editor; publisher.

editoriàle—editorial. Also, artícolo di fóndo.

edítto m.—edict; decree.

edizióne f.—edition; publication.

edonísmo m.—hedonism; devotion to pleasure.

educànda f.—young girl attending a boarding school.

educàre—to educate.

educataménte — with good manners; politely.

educàto—well-mannered.

educazióne f.—education. Re duty of parents to educate children, see Art. 147, 148, Italian Civil Code.

efèbo m.—adolescent.

efemèride or effemèride f.—ephemeris; a table showing the positions of heavenly bodies in orderly sequence on various dates; astronomical almanac.

effeminàre or effemminàre—to make effeminate; to enervate.

effeminàto—effeminate.

efferàto—cruel; ferocious; inhuman.

effervescènte—effervescent.

effervescènza f.—effervescence.

effettivaménte—effectively; in fact.

effetívo—effective; real.
monéta effetíva—real or coin money as opposed to paper.
sòcio effetívo—real member as opposed to honorary.

effètto m.—effect; end; result.

effetuàle—effectual.

effettuàre—to effect; to realize.

effettuazióne f. — accomplishment; execution.

efficàce—efficacious.

efficàcia f.—efficacy.

efficàcia della légge nel tèmpo—efficacy of time on the law. The law applies to future events. It is not retroactive. Art. 11, Preliminary Dispositions; Art. 25, Constitution of the Italian Republic.

efficàcia delle léggi penàli e di polizía—efficacy of penal and police laws. The Penal Law and that relating to the police and public security are binding on all those who find themselves within the territory of the State. Art. 28, Preliminary Dispositions.

efficiènte—efficient; that which produces an effect.

efficiènza f.—efficiency.

effíge or effígie f.—effigy.

effímera f.—may-fly.

effímero—ephemeral.

efflorescènte—efflorescent.

efflorescènza f.—efflorescence.

effluènte — effluent; flowing out; a stream flowing out of another body of water.

efflússo m.—the flowing of liquid through an aperture.

efflúvio m. — emanation of invisible particles which excite the olfactory nerves.

effóndere—to pour out.

effrattóre m. — effractor; one who breaks through; one who commits burglary; a machine which breaks walls.

effrazióne f.—effraction; breaking in;

breaking open; forcible breaking; breach made by force.

fúrto con effraziόne — burglary; house-breaking.

effrenàto—unbridled.

effusiόne f.—effusion.

effusívo — effusive; volcanic rocks which were cast out during an eruption, and solidified, lie on the surface of the earth.

èforo m.—ephor; a Spartan magistrate; overseer.

egemonía f.—hegemony.

egènte—indigent; needy.

ègida f.—aegis; shield of Zeus; protection; sponsorship.

ègira f.—hegira; flight of Mohammed in 622 A.D. from Mecca to Medina.

egítto m.—Egypt.

egiziàno m.—Egyptian.

egízio—Egyptian of antiquity.

egoísmo m.—egoism.

egoísta m.—egoist.

egrègio—famous; well-known; distinguished; egregious.

egrèsso m.—egress; exit.

ègro—sick, infirm; weak.

eguàle—equal. See ugguàle.

egualità f.—equality.

egualizzàre—to make equal.

elaboràre—to make something with art and application; to elaborate.

elargíre—to give generously.

elargiziόne f.—the thing given generously.

elasticità f.—elasticity.

elàstico—elastic.

elatína f.—extract of the oil of tar.

elefantíasi f.—elephantiasis.

elegànte—elegant.

elegànza f.—elegance.

elèggere—to choose; to elect.

eleggíbile—eligible.

elementàre—elementary.

eleménto m.—element; principle.

elemòsina f.—alms; charity.

elencàre—to catalogue.

elènco m.—catalogue; register; list.

elètta f.—select group.

elettívo—elective.

elètto—elect; chosen; rare; elected.

elettoràle—electoral.

elettoràto m.—electorate.

elettóre m. (elettríce f.) — elector; voter.

elettricísta m.—electrician.

elettricità f.—electricity.

elèttrico—electric.

elettrificàre—to electrify.

elettrificaziόne f.—electrification.

elettrizzàre—to electrify.

elettrocardiògrafo m. — electrocardiograph.

elettrocardiogràmma m. — electrocardiogram.

elettrochímica f.—electrochemistry.

elettrochímico m.—electrochemist.

elèttrodo m.—electrode.

elettrodótto m.—a conductor of electricity.

elettrodótto coattívo—the right of passage of electricity over the lands of others. Art. 1056, Italian Civil Code.

elettròlisi f.—electrolysis.

elettròlitico—electrolytic.

elettròlito m.—electrolyte.

elettromotόre m. — electric motor; dynamo.

elettromotríce f.—a railway car or trolley car propelled by an electric motor.

elettróne m.—electron.

elettrònica f.—electronics.

elettroterapía f.—electrotherapy.

elettrotípia f.—electrotype.

elevaménto m.—elevation.

elevàre—to elevate; to exalt; to raise.

elevàto—elevated; lofty.

elevatόre m.—elevator. See ascensόre.

elevaziόne f.—elevation.

eleziόne f.—election.

elezióne di domicílio — election of domicile. A particular domicile may be chosen for the transaction of specific acts or business affairs. This election must be made in writing. Art. 47, Italian Civil Code; Art. 30, 139, 141, Italian Code of Civil Procedure; Art. 58, Enabling Rules, Italian Code of Civil Procedure.

èlica f. (èliche pl.)—propeller of a ship; propeller of an airplane; spiral object.

èlice f.—helix; a spiral.

elicòttero m.—helicopter.

elídere—to remove; to annul.

eliminàre—to eliminate; to exclude.

eliminatòrio—that which serves to eliminate; a preliminary game to choose final competitors after the elimination of the losers.

eliminazióne f.—elimination.

eliografía f.—heliography; the study of the sun; the art of transmitting messages by use of mirrors which reflect beams of light.

eliògrafo m.—heliograph; a device for signalling by means of movable mirrors which flash beams of light.

elisióne f.—elision; removal.

elisíre m.—elixir.

elísse f.—ellipsis; omission.

elíttico—elliptical.

ellènico—Hellenic.

ellenísmo m.—Hellenism.

ellenísta m.—one learned in Hellenic studies.

ellenístico—Hellenistic.

elmétto m.—helmet.

elmínti (pl.) m.—intestinal worms.

élmo m.—helmet.

elocuzióne f.—elocution.

elogiàre—to eulogize; to praise.

elògio m.—eulogy.

elongazióne f.—elongation.

eloquènte f.—eloquent.

eloquènza f.—eloquence.

elòquio m.—manner of speech.

élsa f.—hilt (of a sword).

elucidàrio—explanatory.

elucubràre—to work with care.

elúdere—to elude.

elvèzia f.—Helvetia—ancient name of Switzerland.

emaciaménto m.—emaciation.

emaciàre—to emaciate.

emaciàto—amaciated.

emaciazióne f.—emaciation.

emanàre—to emanate; to issue; to originate.

emanazióne f.—emanation.

emancipàre—to emancipate; to free a minor from parental ties. A minor is emancipated upon reaching majority and upon marriage. Art. 2, 390, Italian Civil Code. See Maggióre età; capacità di agíre.

emarginàre—to note in the margin of administrative papers.

emarginàto m.—administrative paper with notes in the margins.

ematòma m.—hematoma.

ematòsi f.—hematosis; formation of blood.

emblèma m.—emblem; symbol.

embolísmo m.—embolism.

èmbolo m.—embolus; undissolved material carried by the blood stream.

émbrice m.—flat tile. It is used in roofing.

embriología f.—embryology.

embrióne m.—embryo.

emblèma m.—emblem; a distinctive symbol of a business.

embrocazióne f.—embrocation; moistening and rubbing a diseased or bruised part of the body with liniment or lotion.

emènda f.—correction; emendation.

emendaménto m.—amendment.

emendàre—to amend; to correct; to purge.

emergènte—emergent; emanating; resulting.

emergènza f.—emergency.

emèrgere—to emerge; to come forth; to rise.

emèrito—emeritus; a retired person who retains the grade and honors of his office, e.g., Professor Emeritus.

emerotèca f.—library of newspapers and magazines.

emersióne f.—emersion; reappearance.

emètico m.—emetic; a medicine that induces vomiting.

emèttere—to emit.

emicìclo m.—hemicycle.

emicrània f.—headache which only affects part of the head.

emigrànte m. & f.—emigrant.

emigràre—to emigrate.

emigràto—one who has emigrated.

emigrazióne f.—emigration.

eminènte—eminent.

eminenteménte—eminently.

eminènza f.—eminence.

emiopìa f.—partial blindness in which a patient only sees the right or left side of an object he looks at.

emiplegìa f.—hemiplegia; paralysis of one side of the body caused by disease of the brain or spinal cord.

emìro m.—emir; Moslem governor of a province.

emisfèrico—hemispheric.

emisfèro or emisfèrio m.—hemisphere.

emissàrio m.—emmisary.

emissióne f.—emission; issuance (of money).

emittènte—the maker in a vàglia cambiàrio; the maker of a promissory note; transmitter; issuer.

emmetropìa f.—normal vision; normal refraction of the eye.

emofilìa f.—hemophilia.

emolliènte — emollient; a medicinal substance which softens and soothes tissues.

emoluménto m.—emolument.

emorragìa f.—hemorrhage.

emorròide f.—hemorrhoid.

emostàsi f.—hemostasia; an operation to halt hemorrhaging.

emostàtico — hemostatic; a remedy which arrests blood in hemorraging; styptic.

emotèca f.—blood-bank.

emottìsi f.—spitting blood.

emozióne f.—emotion.

empietà f.—impiety.

émpio—impious; irreligious.

empìre—to fill.

empìreo m.—empyrean; firmament; the highest heaven.

empìrico—empiric.

empirìsmo m.—empiricism.

émpito m.—impetus.

emporètico—filtering paper; blotting paper.

empòrio m.—emporium; market.

emulàre—to emulate; to compete.

emulatóre m.—emulator; competitor.

emulazióne f.—emulation; competition.

emulazióne (àtti di)—acts of competition. The owner of property cannot commit acts which annoy or damage others. Art. 833, Italian Civil Code.

emulsióne f.—emulsion.

emúngere—to dry; to exhaust. Also smúngere.

emúnto—emaciated; very thin.

emuntòrio—said of parts of the body which excrete liquid wastes.

encàustica f.—encaustic; painting with wax colors fixed with heat; art procss in which colors are burned in.

encefalìte f.—encephalitis.

encèfalo m.—the cerebral mass.

encìclica f.—encyclical; a letter sent by the Pope to the bishops and faithful to define matters of discipline and faith.

enciclopedìa f.—encyclopedia.

encomiàre—to praise.

encòmio m.—praise.

endemìa f.—endemic disease; a disease peculiar to a particular people or locality.

endèmico—endemic.

èndica f.—a warehouse of articles for resale.

èndice m.—an article saved for remembrance or recall; stone nest egg.

endocàrdio m.— endocardium; membrane which lines the interior of the heart and aids in forming the valves.

endocardíte f.—endocarditis; inflammation of the endocardium.

endòcrino—that which secretes internally in glands or organs.

endocrinologìa f.—endocrinology; the science of studying the function of endocrine glands.

endogamìa f.—endogamy; marriage within a tribal, social or racial unit.

endolìnfa f.—endolymph; fluid contained within the membranous labyrinth of the ear and produces the sensation of equilibrium and orientation.

endoplàsma m.—endoplasma; the inner portion of monocellular organisms.

energìa f.—energy.

energùmeno m.—one possessed by the devil; energumen.

ènfasi f.—emphasis.

enfiagióne f.—abnormal swelling of part of the body; tumor; swelling.

enfiàre—to swell; to blow up; to swell with pride.

enfisèma m.—emphysema; abnormal distention of an organ of the body with air or gas.

enfitèusi f.—emphyteusis; a contract by which an estate is leased to a tenant in perpetuity or for a long term of years. A temporary emphyteusis may not be constituted for a period less than twenty years. The lessee is obligated to improve the property and to pay an annual rent called a canon. The lessee may alien the estate or pass it on to his descendants. Art. 957-977, Italian Civil Code.

enfitèuta m.—emphyteuta; the person to whom an emphyteusis is granted.

enìgma or enimma m.—enigma.

enòfilo m.—a scientific wine producer.

enologìa f.—the science of producing wine.

enòlogo m.— one learned in wine making.

enòrme—enormous.

enormità f.—enormity.

enòtria f.—Virgil's name for Italy.

èntasi f.—entasis; the swelling or outward curve of the shaft of a column.

ènte m.—being; creature; a group of persons or an institution which is granted a juridical personality by the law.

ènte giurìdico—legal entity; an association or corporate entity recognized by law as a juridical personality; an artificial legal entity created to perform some social or public function. See **persóne giurìdiche.** Art. 11, 12 et seq., Italian Civil Code.

ènte moràle—a charitable corporation or group dedicated to the advancement of private or public welfare.

enterìte f.—enteritis; inflammation of the intestines.

entità f.—entity.

entomologìa f.— entomology; that branch of zoology which deals with the study of insects.

entrànte—that which is about to start.
settimàna **entrànte**—next week.
mése **entrànte**—next month.

entràre—to enter.
dirìtto d'**entràre**—right of entry; good-will of a business.

entràta f.—entrance; beginning of a performance; income.

entratùra f.—act of entering; admission; admission to a group.

éntro—within; during the course of (month, year).

entusiasmàre — to stimulate enthusiasm.

entusiàsmo m.—enthusiasm.

entusiàsta m.—enthusiast.

enucleàre—to extract; to remove; to enucleate.

enucleazióne f.—removal of a tumor or other abnormality by an incision in the skin; extraction of the ocular bulb.

enumeràre—to enumerate.

enumerazióne f.—enumeration.

enunciàre—to enunciate; to express or declare in a particular manner; to announce; to proclaim; to declare a theory.

enunciatíva f. — the proposal with which something is announced.

enunciazióne f.—enunciation.

eneurèsi f.—enuresis; bed-wetting; involuntary discharge of urine.

enzíma m.—enzyme.

eòo—oriental.

èpa f.—belly; paunch.

eparchía f.—eparchy; a province of ancient Greece or Byzantine Empire; an administrative subdivision of a modern Greek province.

epàrco m.—eparch; prefect or governor of an eparchy.

epàtico—hepatic; pertaining to the liver.

epatísmo m.—disturbance of the function of the liver in general.

epatíte f.—hepatitis; inflammation of the liver.

epicàrdio m.—epicardium; the inner layer of the pericardium which encases the heart.

epicèdio m.—epicedium; funeral chant or eulogy in honor of the dead.

epicèno—epicene; pertaining to either gender.

epidemía f.—epidemic disease.

epidèmico—epidemic.

epifanía f.—Epiphany; a Christian festival on January 6th, commemorating the visit of the Three Kings to the child Jesus.

epifonèma m.—an emphatic sentence which serves to terminate a discourse.

epigamía f.—the right of matrimony possessed by subjects of two different States.

equità f.—equity; a concept of natural right or justice which allows a judge to correct and supplement a law without modifying it so as to temper its rigor in specific cases.

erariàle—fiscal; pertaining to state finances.
avvocatúra erariàle—a branch of the legal representatives of the State in disputes with private parties.

eràrio m.—the public treasury; fisc; exchequer; State finances.

erède m.—heir; one who succeeds to all the rights and obligations of a decedent whether by operation of law or by testament. Art. 456-768, Italian Civil Code.

erède apparènte—heir aparent; one who appears to be the heir. A transfer of property to third parties by one holding same under title of heir or without title, may be set aside by the actual heir. Art. 534, Italian Civil Code.

erède fiduciàrio — fiduciary heir. An action máy not be maintained to determine that dispositions made in favor of a named person in the testament are merely ostensible and in reality made for the benefit of another person, even though provisions of the testament may indicate the presumption that it deals with an interposed person. Art. 627, Italian Civil Code. See persóna interpósta.

erède giacènte—expectant heir; one who has not been instituted as an heir. See eredità giacènte.

erède universàle—universal heir; heir to the entire estate. Art. 588, 637, Italian Civil Code.

eredità f.—inheritance. Art. 456-768, Italian Civil Code.

eredità (accettazióne dell') — acceptance of inheritance. See accettazióne dell'eredità.

eredità (acquísto dell')—acquisition of inheritance. The inheritance is acquired with its acceptance. Its effect is to relate it back to the opening of the succession which occurs at the moment of death. Art. 459, Italian Civil Code.

eredità (delazióne dell')—devolution or transfer of an inheritance. It occurs through force of law or by testament. Art. 457, Italian Civil Code.

eredità giacènte—abeyant or vacant inheritance. Art. 528-532, Italian Civil Code.

ergàstolo m.—life imprisonment; place of confinement for those condemned to life imprisonment. Art. 22, 17, Italian Penal Code.

erróre m.—error; a mistake of judgment or ignorance or mistaken belief as to the existence of matters of fact; false or mistaken conception as to the application of the law on a set of facts. Essential error is a basis for the annulment of a contract. Art. 1427-1433, Italian Civil Code. Penally, see Art. 47, 48 and 5, Italian Penal Code.

erróre, violènza e dòlo—error, violence and fraud. The contracting party whose assent was given in error, extorted by violence or obtained by fraud, may seek the annulment or rescission of the contract pursuant to dispositions of the Civil Code. Art. 1427, Italian Civil Code.

esalazióne f.—emanation; exhalation.

esalazióne dal fóndo vicíno—emanations from neighboring land. The proprietor of land cannot impede the introduction of smoke or heat, the emanations, noises, rumbles and similar disseminations derived from the neighbor's land unless they exceed normal tolerability. See immissióne di fúmo o di calóre nel fóndo vicíno and Art. 844, Italian Civil Code.

esàme m.—examination; interrogation of the accused or the witnesses by the judge.

esàme di testimòni a futúra memòria—examination of witnesses for future recollection. It is a deposition under oath taken before trial. The testimony may be obtained in civil and criminal cases where it is feared the witness may be unavailable or cannot appear due to illness or other serious impediment. Art. 357, 418, 462, Italian Code of Penal Procedure and procediménti di istruzióne preventíva, Art. 692-699, Italian Code of Civil Procedure. See, also, istruzióne preventíva and rogatòria.

esclusióne f.—exclusion.

esclusíva f. — exclusion; monopoly; right of veto; the right of veto possessed by certain governments over Papal elections.

esclusíva (dirítto di)—right of exclusion; exclusive right, Art. 1567, 1743, Italian Civil Code.

escussióne f.—examination or interrogation of witnesses.

escussióne dei testimòni—examination of witnesses.

escussióne del debitóre—examination of the debtor; the proceedings against the debtor to secure his property towards the satisfaction of the debt.

escútere—to examine or interrogate witnesses.

esecutívo m.—executive; person empowered to execute.

esecutívo—executive; suited to accomplish an order.

esecutívo (giudízio)—executive or summary proceeding used in the attachment and sequestration of the goods of a debtor. Also, procèsso d'esecuzióne. Art. 474-632, Italian Code of Civil Procedure.

esecutóre m.—executor; one charged or empowered by a testator to carry out the provisions of a will.

esecutóri testamentàri — testamentary executors. Art. 700-712, Italian Civil Code.

esecutòria f.—writ or warrant of authority.

esecutòrio—that which gives the force or effect to a judicial execution.

esecuzióne f.—execution; the attachment and sequestration of the goods of a debtor.

esecuzióne coattíva—forced sale. If the buyer fails to fulfill the obligation of paying the price, the seller may sell the goods without delay for the account and at the expense of the buyer. The sale is made at auction through a person qualified to do so, or by a judicial officer. The seller must give timely notice to the buyer of the day, place and hour in which the sale is made. If the goods have a current market price set by public

104

authorities or quoted on exchanges, the sale may be made without auction at the current market price by the persons above mentioned or by a commissioner named by the Praetor upon notice to the buyer. The seller is entitled to the difference between the agreed price and the net amount received besides compensation for greater damage. If the sale is of fungibles having a current market price and the seller does not fulfill his obligation, the buyer may acquire the goods without delay at the expense of the seller, upon notice and through the officials above mentioned. The buyer is entitled to the difference between the amount expended for the acquisition of the goods and the price agreed, besides compensation for greater damage. Art. 1515, 1516. Italian Civil Code. See **véndita in dánno.**

esecuzióne dell'ôpera—performance of a work. If the performer of a work does not proceed with its performance in accordance with the terms of the contract and in a satisfactory manner, the one ordering the work may fix a suitable time within which the work must conform to these conditions. If the period fixed for performance expires without fulfillment, the aggrieved party may withdraw from the contract without affecting his right to damages. Art. 2224, Italian Civil Code.

esecuzióne della péna—execution of punishment. It pertains to the mode of the execution of penal dispositions and judgments. The public prosecutor in the court or tribunal which has rendered the disposition, procures the execution and the Praetor executes his dispositions or orders. Art. 141-149, Italian Penal Code; Art. 575-589, Italian Code of Penal Procedure; Art. 37-52. Enabling Rules, Italian Code of Penal Procedure.

esecuzióne forzàta—forced execution. See **espropiazióne forzàta** and **espropiazióne forzàta in fórma specífica.** Art. 2910-2933, Italian Civil Code; Art. 483, et seq., Italian Code of Civil Procedure.

esecuzióne (procèsso d')—a sequestra-

tion proceeding. It is used in the attachment and sequestration of the goods of a debtor. Also, **giudízio esecutívo.** Art. 474-632, Italian Code of Civil Procedure.

esecuzióne provvisòria — provisional execution. At the request of a party, an appealable judgment may be enforced provisionally by execution, with or without bond, if the complaint is based on a public writing, a judgment, or if there is danger in delay. It must be granted when there is a judgment of provisional payment or subsistence. Art. 282, 283, 642, Italian Code of Civil Procedure; Art. 489 bis, Italian Code of Penal Procedure.

eseguíre — to effectuate; complete; realize; to put into effect.

esemplàre—exemplary; commendable; copy; model.

esercízio abusívo di attività commerciàle—wrongful exercise of commercial activity. Whoever conducts a commercial enterprise though restrained from doing so doing by a penal judgment (for fraudulent bankruptcy), may be punished with imprisonment and fine. Art. 234, 216, Falliménto (Bankruptcy), Usual Laws, Appendix to Italian Civil Code.

esercízio abusívo di attività professionàle—wrongful exercise of professional activity. When the exercise of professional activity is conditioned upon inscription in a professional roll, payment for services rendered cannot be recovered by action by one who is not inscribed. Art. 2231, 2033, Italian Civil Code.

esercízio arbitràrio delle pròprie ragióni—arbitrary use of power in obtaining self-help. This is a crime which encompasses arbitrary use of power over things or the use of violence and threats to the person. Art. 392, 393, Italian Penal Code.

esercízio di un dirítto o adempiménto di un dovére—exercise of a right or fulfillment of an obligation. These are justifiable or exculpatory causes of a crime. Art. 51, Italian Penal Code.

esercízio provvisòrio dell'imprésa del

fallíto—provisional management of the business of a bankrupt. Following declaration of bankruptcy, the court may order the temporary continuation of the bankrupt's business where its sudden interruption would cause grave and irreparable harm. Art. 90, Falliménto (Bankruptcy), Usual Laws, Appendix to Italian Civil Code.

esibizióne f.—exhibition.

esibizióne di scrittúre contàbile—exhibition for inspection of written records of accounts and correspondence may be so ordered by a judge only in controversies involving the dissolution of a partnership, community property and in matters of succession due to death. In other cases, the judge may order the inspection for reproduction of matters regarding the controversy. Art. 2711, Italian Civil Code. Also, comunicazióne ed esibizióne di scrittúre contàbile.

esígere—to exact payment; to collect payment; to require compliance with the law.

esigíbile—collectible.

esimènte—that which frees from an obligation or duty. Art. 51-54, Italian Penal Code.

esímere—to free from an obligation or duty; to exempt; to free from.

esímio—distinguished; excellent.

esoneràre—to exonerate.

esonerazióne f. — exoneration. Also, esònero.

esònero m.—exoneration. Also, esonerazióne.

esònero (clàusole di esònero da responsabilità) — exoneration clauses. An agreement which excludes or limits in advance a debtor's responsibility for fraud or lack of care is void. Likewise, agreements are void which exonerate or limit the responsibility of the debtor or his assistants where such acts violate duties derived from the norms of public order. Art. 1229, 1228, Italian Civil Code.

esònero nel depòsito in albèrgo—exoneration for loss of property brought into hotels. The innkeeper is liable, up to a statutory amount, for theft, loss or deterioration of guests' property brought into the hotel and not delivered to him. His liability is unlimited where loss is due to his gross negligence or that of his aides. He is liable for refusing to receive custody of guests' property without just cause. Just cause includes excessive value or unwieldy size. He is free of liability if loss is due to gross negligence of the guest, his employees, visitors or those accompanying him or if loss or deterioration is due to the nature or defect of the property or by accident. Art. 1784, Italian Civil Code. Also, responsabilità per le còse portàte in albèrgo.

esòso—odious; detestable; hateful.

espèrto—expert. See consulènte tècnico.

espromissióne f.—assumption of an obligation by a third party. When a third party voluntarily assumes the obligation of a debtor to a creditor, he becomes jointly and severally liable with the debtor. Art. 1272, 1292, Italian Civil Code.

espromissóre m.—one who guarantees payment of another's debt or obligation.

espropiàre—to expropriate.

espropiazióne f.—expropriation.

espropiazióne forzàta — forced expropriation. Art. 2910-2933, Italian Civil Code; Art 483, et seq., Italian Code of Civil Procedure.

espropiazóne forzàta in fórma specífica—forced expropriation of a specific thing. Where the obligation of delivering a specific thing, whether personal or real property, has not been performed, the party entitled thereto may obtain its forced delivery. Art .2930, Italian Civil Code; Art. 483, et seq., Italian Code of Civil Procedure.

espropiazióne immobiliàre — expropiation of real property. It is the attachment of real property pursuant to execution of judgment and its forced sale. Art. 555-598, Italian Code of Civil Procedure; Art. 170-179, Enabling Rules, Code of Civil Procedure; Art. 2912-2918, Italian Civil Code.

espropiazióne mobiliàre prèsso il debitóre — expropriation of personal property of the debtor. It is the attachment of personal property pursuant to execution of judgment and its forced sale. Art. 513-542, Italian Code of Civil Procedure; Art. 165-169, Enabling Rules, Code of Civil Procedure; Art. 2912-2918, Italian Civil Code.

espropiazióne mobiliàre prèsso i tèrzi —expropriation, after attachment, of obligations or credits of a debtor towards a third party or property of the debtor in possession of third parties. Art. 543-554, Italian Code of Civil Procedure; Art. 2919-2929, Italian Civil Code.

espropiazióne per púbblico interèsse— expropriation in the public interest. It is the right to take private property for public use in exchange for just compensation; similar to condemnation under the right of eminent domain. Art. 834, 838, 1638, Italian Civil Code; Art. 42, Constitution of the Italian Republic.

espulsióne f.—expulsion.

espulsióne dello stranièro dello stàto— expulsion of the foreigner from the territory of the State. It is ordered by the judge in cases involving crimes against the personality of the State, crimes against political rights of a citizen and crimes against foreign States where he is condemned to a penalty restrictive of personal liberty, or has been condemned to imprisonment for a period of not less than ten years. Art. 235, 312, 215, Italian Penal Code.

espúngere—to expunge.

espurgàre—to expurgate.

estensóre m.—one who compiles or writes.

estensóre (giúdice)—the judge writing an opinion to support a judgment. See **giúdice estensóre** and **redazióne della sentènza.**

estenuànte — extenuating; lessening. See **circostànze attenuànti.**

estenuàre—to extenuate.

estenuazióne f.—extenuation.

estimàre—to esteem; to appraise. Also, **stimàre.**

estimatóre m.—appraiser.

estimatório (contràtto)—a type of contract similar to a consignment to a factor for the sale of goods or a sale or return. The Italian Civil Code provides that, in this type of contract, one party may deliver personal property to another at a fixed price which he must pay unless he returns the goods at a determined time. The party receiving the goods is not liable for the price if return is impossible for a cause not attributable to him. Art. 1556, 1557, Italian Civil Code.

estimazióne f.—estimation; value; appraisal.

estimazióne (giuraménto di) — estimative sworn testimony. Art. 241, 243, Italian Cdoe of Civil Procedure. See **giuraménto estimatório.**

èstimo m.—appraisal of real property for tax purposes.

estínguere—to extinguish.

estinzióne f.—extinction; extinguishment.

estinzióne dei dirítti — extinction of rights. This can occur by loss of the exercise of a right or a legal action by limitation of time. It can occur, also, by renunciation of a right or by prescription. Art. 2934 et seq., Italian Civil Code.

estinzióne del procèsso—extinction or discontinuance of a civil cause of action. It comes about by failure to prosecute or by renunciation. Art 171, 181, 305, 306-310, Italian Code of Civil Procedure.

estinzióne del rappòrto di lavóro— termination or release of work contract. Art. 2118-2125, Italian Civil Code. Also, **licenziaménto del prestatóre del lavóro.**

estinzióne del reàto—extinction of the crime. Causes which produce the extinction of a crime are: (1) death of the accused before sentence; (2) amnesty; (3) remission of the complaint by the injured party; (4) granting of a conditional suspension of the punishment; (5) judicial pardon afforded a minor of 18 years in certain cases; (6) prescription. Art. 150-170, Italian Penal Code.

estinzióne della péna—extinction of punishment. This occurs by death of the culprit after conviction, by extinction of the charge through limitation of time, by grant of conditional liberty, or conditional suspension of punishment. Art. 171-181, Italian Penal Code.

estinzióne della persóna giurídica—extinction of the juridical (artificial) person. Besides the causes provided in its charter or in the statute, the juridical (artificial) person is extinguished when its objective has been reached or it has become impossible. Partnerships are extinguished when all the partners are missing. Art. 27, Italian Civil Code; Art. 10, Enabling Rules, Italian Civil Code.

estinzióne delle ipotèche—extinction (discharge) of mortgages. (1) by cancellation of the recorded instrument; (2) by failure to renew as provided by law (20 years); (3) by extinction of the obligation; (4) by destruction of the mortgaged property. Where insured, the proceeds are held for the creditors; (5) by renunciation of the creditor; (6) by expiration of the mortgage time limitation or its conditional resolution in which case, the parties are restored to their original position; (7) by judgment transferring title to expropiated property to the acquirer and cancellation of the mortgage. Art. 2878, Italian Civil Code.

estinzióne delle obbligazióni—extinction (discharge) of obligations. (1) by diligent performance, Art. 1176; (2) by novation, Art. 1230; (3) by remission of debt, Art. 1236; (4) by compensation, Art. 1241; (5) by "confusióne," when debtor and creditor become one, Art. 1253; (6) by impossibility of performance by a cause not imputable to the debtor. Art. 1256; (7) by assignment of rights by the creditor, Art. 1260;

(8) by assumption of obligation by third parties, Art. 1268-1273, Italian Civil Code.

estòrcere—to extort.

estorsióne f.—extortion; it is a crime committed with the use of violence or threats whereby someone is compelled to commit or omit an act for the purpose of conferring unlawful gain upon the extortioner or another. Art. 629, Italian Penal Code.

estradàre—to extradite.

estradizióne f.—extradition; the surrender of a person charged or convicted of a crime by one State to another. It is not permitted for political crimes whether the person involved is an Italian citizen or a foreigner. Art. 10, 26, Constitution of the Italian Republic; Art. 13, Italian Penal Code; Art. 661-671, Italian Code of Penal Procedure; Estradizióne, Usual Laws, Appendix to Italian Code of Penal Procedure. See **genocídio**.

estradizióne (trattàti di)—extradition treaties. Italy has extradition treaties with the following countries: Argentina; Bolivia; Brazil; Colombia; Costa Rica; Cuba; Czechoslovakia; Finland; Guatemala; Holy See; Honduras; Hungary; Israel; Jugoslavia; Malta; Mexico; Monaco; Panama; Paraguay; Peru; Portugal; Romania; Russia; San Marino; San Salvador; Spain; Switzerland; Tunisia; United States; Uruguay; Venezuela. Estradizióne, Usual Laws, Appendix to Italian Code of Penal Procedure. Art. 13, Italian Penal Code; Art. 661-671, Italian Code of Penal Proceduhe.

estràtto m.—extract; essence; summary; synopsis.

esulàre—to go into exile.

èsule m.—exile.

esumàre—to exhume.

esumazióne f.—exhumation.

età f.—age; majority is reached at age eighteen. Art. 2, Italian Civil Code. See **emancipàre** — to emancipate. Minors cannot contract marriage. The Tribunal, upon petition of the interested party, verification of the minor's psycho-physical maturity, the basis for the reasons presented, and having heard the public prosecutor, the parents or guardian, may issue a decree in chambers, based on serious considerations, permitting the marriage of one who has reached sixteen years of age. The decree is communicated to the public prosecutor, the couple to be married, the parents and the guardian. The decree may be appealed to the Court of Appeals within a period of ten peremptory days from the communication. The Court of Appeals' decision is not appealable, Art. 84, Italian Civil Code. See minóre.

eternità f.—eternity; infinite time or duration; lacking the element of time; timeless; immutable.

etèrno—eternal; without beginning or end; existing without relation to time or change; of infinite duration. See **perpétuo.**

evàdere—to evade; to escape.

evàdere del càrcere—to escape from prison.

evasióne f.—evasion; escape. Art. 385-388, Italian Penal Code.

evasióne del imputàto—escape of the accused. For manner of serving notices on him, see **renitènza del imputàto**, Art. 173, 174, 170, Italian Code of Penal Procedure.

evàso m.—an escaped prisoner; fugitive.

eventus damni (Lat.)—occurrence of loss—this is an element or condition for bringing the azióne revocatòria. See Art. 2901, Italian Civil Code and azióne revocatòria.

evizióne f.—eviction; the deprivation of a right or property by legal process; the total or partial loss of property by a buyer when same has been declared judicially to belong to another; an action to recover possession of property unjustly taken from one person by another. Art. 1483-1489, Italian Civil Code.

ex abrupto (Lat.)—unexpected.

ex càthedra (Lat.)—from the chair; used to indicate the proclamation

of a dogma by the Pope from his cathedra or chair; one who speaks ex cathedra is doing so dogmatically and professorially.

exequatur (Lat.)—let it be executed; a commission issued by one State to a consul or commercial agent of a foreign State which acknowledges his official character and authorizes him to perform his duties in the State to which he is accredited.

extrastallía f.—extraordinary demurrage. The period of time a vessel is detained for loading and unloading in excess of the contrastallía. Also, controstallía straordinària. See **stallía**—demurrage.

F

fàbbrica f.—building; factory; construction.

fabbricàre—to build; to construct; to manufacture.

fabbricazióne f.—fabrication; manufacture; building; structure.

fabbricería f.—the management of a chapel, church, monastery, etc., and their construction and maintenance.

fabbricière m.—an administrator of a fabbricería.

fàbbro m.—blacksmith; metal worker.

faccènda f.—something to do; housework; affair; business.

faccendière m.—a meddler; one who engages in many businesses for a profit.

facchinàggio m.—the work of a porter; the fee paid for such work.

facchinàta f.—trivial action or word; unworthy or undignified action or word.

facchíno m.—porter; a gross or vulgar person.

facciuòla f.—each of two starched white bands hanging from the collar which are the insignia of a magistrate, doctor of laws etc.

facilitàre—to facilitate; to expedite; to remove an obstacle; to make easy.

facilitazióne f. — facilitation; the diminution of price or making easy terms for the purchase of things.

facio ut des (Lat.)—I do that you may give.

facio ut facias (Lat.)—I do that you may do.

facoltà f.—faculty; ability; power.

facoltativo—optional.

fàida f.—feud; vendetta; a right of private vendetta which Medieval law permitted in certain cases.

falcídia f.—Falcidian Law, named after the Tribune P. Falcidius. The law prescribed that no testator could bequeath more than three fourths of his property in legacies to others than his heir. The latter would have the right, in that case, to have a proportional deduction from each legatee to assure that the heir received a fourth of the estate.

fàlda f.—skirt; plait or pleat; lappet of a coat or dress coat; loin of meat; flake (of snow).

falegnàme m.—carpenter; joiner.

fallàce—fallacious.

fallànza f.—fallacy; error; deceit.

fallàre—to commit an error or mistake.

fallíbile—fallible.

fallimentàre — pertaining to bankruptcy.

falliménto m.—bankruptcy; proceedings following insolvency when the assets of a debtor are judicially distributed among his creditors. It is restricted to those who undertake a commercial activity and small businessmen, among them being artisans. Art. 1, et seq., Falliménto (Bankruptcy), and Artigianàto (Craft of Artisans), Usual Laws, Appendix to Italian Civil Code; Art. 2082, 2083, 2195, 2196, 2201, 2202, Italian Civil Code.

fallíre—to fail; to become bankrupt; to fail to respond to expectations.

fallíto—bankrupt.

fàllo m.—error; fault; mistake.

falò m.—a great fire set on festive occasions; also one set to burn books; bonfire.

fàlsa attestazióne o dichiarazióne a un pùbblico ufficiàle sulla identità o su qualità personàli pròprie o di àltri—false attestation or declaration to a public official regarding the identity and personal status of himself or another. It consists of intentionally uttering a falsehood in a public document to a public official Art. 495, Italian Penal Code.

fàlsa dichiarazióne sùlla identità o su qualità personàli pròprie o di àltri—false declaration to a public official or employee regarding the identity and personal status of the person questioned or of another. It is committed by making a false declaration to the officials mentioned during the course of interrogation. Art. 651, Italian Penal Code.

fàlsa perízia o interpretazióne—false expert testimony or interpretation. The expert witness or interpreter, who, named by the Judicial Authorities, gives mendacious opinions or interpretations, or affirms facts not conforming to the truth, is subject to imprisonment. The sentence of condemnation imports, besides interdiction from public offices, interdiction from a profession or art. Art. 373, 375, 376, 384, Italian Penal Code; Art. 1968, Italian Civil Code.

fàlsa testimoniànza—false testimony; perjury. Whoever, while deposing as a witness before the Judicial Authorities, affirms that which is false or denies the truth, or remains silent, in whole or in part, concerning his knowledge about facts on which he is being interrogated, is punished with imprisonment. Art. 372, 375, 376, 384, Italian Penal Code; Art. 359, 458, Italian Code of Penal Procedure; Art. 256, Italian Code of Civil Procedure. See **spergiúro**—perjury.

falsamonéte m.—counterfeiter.

falsàre—to falsify.

falsàrio m.—counterfeiter; forger.

falsificazióne di monéte—falsification or counterfeiting of money. It is a crime punished with imprisonment and fine. It is committed by: (1) whoever counterfeits national or foreign money which is legal tender in the State or abroad; (2) whoever alters genuine money in any manner by giving it the appearance of a higher value; (3) whoever introduces into the territory of the State or holds or spends, or, in any manner, places in circulation counterfeit or altered money, even though not a party to the counterfeiting or alteration, but in concert with the one who executed it, or with an intermediary; (4) whoever acquires, or otherwise receives counterfeit or altered money from the counterfeiter or from an intermediary for the purpose of putting same in circulation. Art. 453, et seq., Italian Penal Code; Art. 21, Enabling Rules, Italian Code of Penal Procedure.

falsità f.—false affirmation.

falsità comméssa da púbblici impiegàti incaricàti di un servízio púbblico—falsity committed by public employees charged with performing a public service. Relates to acts of a public servant falsely rendered in the discharge of his duties. Art. 493, Italian Penal Code.

falsità ideològica—false deception. It involves deception or falsity in regards to public documents, certificates or administrative orders. It can be committed by public officials and private individuals. Art. 476-493, Italian Penal Code.

falsità in sigílli o struménti o ségni di autenticazióne, certificazióne o riconosciménto—falsity in seals or instruments or signs of authentication, certification or acknowledgement. Art. 467-475, Italian Penal Code.

fàlso—false; forged; altered.

fàlso giuraménto della pàrte — false swearing or testimony by a party to a civil action. It is punished with imprisonment, the guilty party being also barred from holding public office. Art. 371, Italian Penal Code. See **fàlsa testimoniànza**.

fàlta f.—error; failing.

famíglia f.—family.

famíglia colònica—a family of farm workers who cultivate the soil and divide the products of the soil, by contract, on a proportional basis. See **mezzadría**, Art. 2141-2163, Italian Civil Code.

famíglia (delítti cóntro la)—crimes against the family. Art. 556-574, Italian Penal Code.

familiàre (patrimònio)—family fund or estate. See **patrimònio familiàre**.

fanàle m.—lantern; headlight of an automobile; beacon.

fànte m.—infantry soldier; the Jack in a game of cards.

fantería m.—infantry.

fàra f.—a small farm or land holding. Derived from the Lombard term for family, tribe or place of abode.

farabútto m.—knave; rogue; scoundrel.

faraglióne m.—a large reef of rocks.

faraóne m.—pharoah.

farínge m.—pharynx.

faringíte f.—pharyngitis.

farmacèutica f. — pharmaceutic; pertaining to pharmacy.

farmacía f.—pharmacy.

farmacísta m.—pharmacist.

fàrmaco m. — medicine; medicament; remedy.

farmacología f.—pharmacology.

fàsti m.—annals; archives; records. Derived from the records in which the Pontifex Maximus of the Romans inscribed the principal events. The register in which the names of the Roman magistrates were inscribed. See **dies fasti**.

fàsto m.—ostentation. Also, propitious.

fatàle—fatal.

fatalísmo m.—fatalism.

fatalísta m.—fatalist.

fatalità f.—fatality; destiny.

fatíca f.—hard work; labor; toil.

fàtti giurídici—jural actions. Those events to which the law attributes the power of producing jural effects such as the acquisition, loss, or modification of a right. They are a result of natural events such as birth, death, floods, earthquakes and the voluntary acts of a human being.

fattispècie f.—the particular fact under judicial consideration.

fàtto m.—fact; an action performed; that which has occurred.

fàtto altrúi—action of another. It concerns the responsibility of parents, guardians, preceptors and teachers as well as employers, for the illegal acts committed by those under their supervision. See **responsabilità dei genitóri, dei tutóri, dei precettóri e dei maèstri d'àrte.** Art. 2048, 2049, Italian Civil Code.

fàtto illécito (risarciménto per)—compensatory damages for an illegal act. See **risarciménto per fàtto illécito.**

fattóre m.—factor; agent; steward.

fattoría f.—large rural possession of lands; the house in which the steward of lands resides; rural holdings; factory.

fattoríno m.—post-man; officeboy.

fattúra f.—the operation involved in making something; invoice; bill for work performed or goods sold.

fatturàre—to fraudulently alter a substance; to invoice; to bill .

fàusto—propitious.

fautóre m.—promoter; protector; instigator.

favoreggiaménto m.—the crime of aiding a person guilty of a crime to evade punishment or to obtain a benefit therefrom. It is divided into favoreggiaménto personàle and favoreggiaménto reàle.

favoreggiaménto personàle—the crime of aiding a person who has committed a crime punishable by life imprisonment or incarceration for a lesser term, to evade investigation or elude the authorities. Art. 378, Italian Penal Code.

favoreggiaménto reàle—the crime of aiding a person to enjoy the fruits of a crime; this crime falls short of the crime of ricettazióne which involves concealing or buying stolen goods. Art. 379, Italian Penal Code.

favoreggiàre—to aid; to favor; to commit the crime of favoreggiaménto.

fecàle—faecal; pertaining to feces or faeces; waste matter.

fèccia f.—dregs; sediment.

fèci (pl.) f.—excrement; human waste; feces.

féde f.—faith; credit; trust; a certificate or document attesting to certain facts.

fedecommésso m.—a testamentary disposition similar to a trust. It is made for the benefit of a mentally incapacitated person. See **sostituzióne fedecommissària.**

fedecommissàrio m.—the recipient of a fedecommésso. He is a trustee of property left by will for the benefit of an incapacitated person. Also, **fidecommissàrio.** See **sostituzióne fedecommissària.**

féde di depòsito—warehouse receipt. It is negotiable and transferable by indorsement. It is issued together with a nòta di pégno (notice of pledge) and can be detached from it. It is also negotiable and transferable by indorsement. Both instruments can circulate independently of each other or together. See **nòta di pégno** and Art. 1790-1797, Italian Civil Code.

féde di nàscita—birth certificate.

féde púbblica—public trust.

fedéle—faithful.

fedelménte—faithfully.

fedeltà f.—fidelity.

fedeltà coniugàle — conjugal fidelity. See Art. 143-148, Italian Civil Code.

fedeltà (òbbligo di)—duty of fidelity. The worker or employee shall not engage in business for himself or on behalf of others in competition with his employer, nor divulge information relating to the organization and methods of production of his firm or make use thereof so as to cause harm. Art. 2105, Italian Civil Code.

fèllo—wicked; perfidious.

fellóne—traitorous.

fellonía f.—treason; felony.

feneratízio — usurious; pertaining to feneration. See usuràrio.

feneratóre m.—usurer. See usuràio.

fèra f.—wild beast. See fièra.

feràle — funereal; mournful; gloomy. See funèsto.

fèria f.—day of rest; holiday.
le fèrie (pl.)—period of rest; holiday period.

feriàle—business day; work day; non-holiday.

feríre—to wound.

feríta f.—wound.

feríto m.—wounded person.

férma f.—a voluntary term of military enlistment.

fermàre—to halt; to stop; to resolve; to fasten.

fermàta f.—pause; stop; delay.

férmo m.—the detention, stopping or halting of a person; arrest or detention by the police. Art. 238, Italian Code of Penal Procedure; Art. 157, Sicurézza Púbblica (Public Security), Usual Laws, Appendix to Italian Code of Penal Procedure.

férmo—firm; steady.

férmo stànte—formula indicating that a thing or matter remains in effect.

feróce—ferocious.

ferragósto m.—August Holidays, the first of August; Feast of the Assumption, August 15th.

ferràio m.—blacksmith; ironmonger.

ferraménto m.—iron tool; iron work.

ferraréccia f.—iron objects; shop that sells iron tools.

ferràta f.—railroad.

ferrovía f.—railroad, generally.

feticídio m.—feticide; destruction of the fetus. It does not exist as an independent crime, but it is provided for under the caption "infanticídio." See Art. 578, Italian Penal Code.

fèto m.—fetus; embryo.

feudàle—feudal.

feudatàrio m.—owner of a fief.

fèudo m.—fief; a tenure of land subject to feudal obligations; feud.

fiàba f.—fable for children; an unlikely story.

fiammífero m.—match.

fiàto m.—breath.

fidànza f.—confidence; faith.

fidanzaménto m. — engagement; betrothal.

fidanzàre—to become betrothed.

fidanzàto—betrothed; engaged.

fidàre—to entrust; to confide.

fidàto—faithful; loyal; trustworthy.

fidecommésso m.—See fedecommésso.

fidecommissàrio m.—See fedecommissàrio.

fideiussióne f.—a contract whereby one undertakes to satisfy the obligation of another in the event that party fails to discharge the obligation. Guaranty; suretyship. Art. 1936-1957, Italian Civil Code.

fideiussóre m.—guarantor; surety.

fído—faithful; honest; loyal; trustworthy; commercial credit (m.).

fidúcia f.—confidence.

fiduciàrio—fiduciary.
crédito fiduciàrio—unsecured credit.
títolo fiduciàrio—bank note.
véndita fiduciària—sale with right to purchase.

fièra f.—wild beast; fair; market.

fíglia f.—daughter; child.

fígli m.—children. It is the duty and right of parents to support, instruct and educate their children, even though born out of wedlock. Art. 30, Constitution of the Italian Republic; Art. 147, 148, 261, Italian Civil Code. Re the duties of a child toward his parents and parental authority, see Art. 315-337, Italian Civil Code.

fíglio m.—son; child.

filiazióne f.—filiation; parentage; relation of parent and child; judicial determination of paternity. Art. 231-279, Italian Civil Code.

fílobus m.—electric trolley bus.

filovía f.—a street equipped with electric overhead wires to propel an electric trolley bus or car.

finànza f.—finance; the conduct of money matters generally; the receipt and management of the public revenues.

guàrdia di finànza—border customs officer; frontier guard.

finanzière m.—financier.

finèstra f.—window.

finèstre (pl.) f.—windows. They are of two kinds: lúci, which admit light and air but do not permit one to look out upon the neighbor's land, and vedúte or prospètti which permit one to look out and observe a view. See lúci, vedúti o prospètti, Art. 900-907, Italian Civil Code.

finíre—to finish; to accomplish.

finíto—finished; accomplished; also, a highly accomplished person or one highly skilled.

finzióne f.—fiction; pretense.

finzióne legàle—legal fiction.

florétto m.—little flower; a fencing foil.

fírma f.—signature; the name and surname of a person signing a document or letter.

fírma commerciàle — commercial name; firm name.

fírma fàlsa—false or forged signature.

firmàno m.—firman; decree or edict of an Oriental Potentate.

firmàre—to sign.

firmatàrio m.—signatory.

fiscàle—fiscal; pertaining to the public treasury or revenues or financial matters generally.

avvocàto fiscàle—the prosecuting attorney in military tribunals.

físco—the treasury; the public agency which imposes taxes; the department which handles the finances of the state.

fissàto-bollàto—a document evidencing the sale and purchase of securities.

fissazióne f.—fixation.

fissióne f.—fission.

físso—fixed; firm; permanent.

fístola f.—fistula; pastoral musical pipe instrument.

fitologìa f.—the science of plants in general; botany.

fittaiuòlo m.—farm tenant.

fittízio—fictitious.

fítto—crowded; dense; thick; thrust in.

fítto m.—rental, usually of rural land and its letting.

fittuàrio m.—farm tenant. Also, affituàrio.

fiúme m.—river. It is part of the public domain. Art 822, Italian Civil Code.

flagrànte—flagrant; notorious.

flagrante delicto (Lat.)—in the act of the commission of the crime.

flagrànza f.—the act of being flagrant; the act of being caught in the act of committing a crime. Art. 237, Italian Penal Code.

flagrànza di reàto—a crime actually in commission. Art. 237, Italian Code of Penal Procedure.

flàmine m.—a Roman priest dedicated to the cult of a special divinity.

flàngia f.—flange.

flàto m.—flatus; accumulation of gas in the stomach or intestines.

flatulènto—flatulent.

flatulènza f.—flatulence.

flèmma f.—phlegm.

flessíbile—flexible.

flessibilità f.—flexibility.

flessióne f.—flexion; motion of a joint.

flirtàre—to flirt.

flótta f.—fleet.

flottíglia f.—flottila.

flussióne f.—flux; flow; act of flowing.

flússo m.—flux; discharge; flow of the tide.

flússo e riflússo—flow and ebb of the tide.

fòca f.—seal.

114

focàtico m.—a tax on the hearth or on each family.

fóce f.—opening to the mouth of a river.

fóchista f.—maker of fire-works; fireman or stoker of a fire in a steam engine.

fóco m.—fire.

focolàre m.—hearth.

fòdera f.—cover; lining; scabbard.

fòdero m. — sheath of a sword or bayonet.

fòglio m.—sheet of paper.

fòglio di rótta—way-bill.

fòglio di vía—a document issued by the proper authorities in lieu of a passport or other instrument to persons generally considered dangerous to public security so that they may travel under certain conditions. See misúre di prevenzióne.

fógna f.—sewer; drain. See Art. 1045, 1046, Italian Civil Code on their use and operation.

fòlla f.—crowd; multitude.

fòlla in tumúlto—a riotous mob. A person acting under such circumstances may have his sentence reduced by the judge as a mitigating circumstance. Art. 62, Italian Penal Code.

fónda f.—holster; anchorage place.

fóndaco m.—warehouse; a dry goods shop.

fondàre—to erect; to establish; to found.

fondazióne f. — foundation; entity which has a jural personality and is created by a public Act or by testamentary disposition. In general, the purposes may be charitable, cultural, educational, religious or limited to benefit a specific class such as the descendants of a particular family. Art. 12-35, Italian Civil Code.

fondiària f.—a tax on land.

fondiàrio—pertaining to land.

fóndo m.—bottom; depth; profound; fund; capital; land assembled for agricultural use; realty.

artícolo di fóndo—editorial; leading article.

fóndo dominànte—a dominant estate. The land or tenement in favor of which a service is constituted.

fóndo interclúso—enclosed land without possibility of ingress or egress. In such a case, the owner of the land is given the right of passage over the lands of neighbors to gain access to a public highway. This is similar to an easement of access or easement by necessity. Art. 1015-1055, Italian Civil Code. See passàggio coattívo.

fóndo patrimoniàle — family fund or estate. It is created by one or both spouses by public Act or by a third party under a will. It is intended to provide economic assistance to the family. Such estate may consist of personal and real property and securities. Art. 167-171, Italian Civil Code. See patrimònio familiàre.

fóndo servènte—a servient estate— one burdened with a servitude. It is a burden imposed on land for the benefit of another land called the dominant estate and belonging to another owner. See servitú prediàli, Art. 1027-1031, 1069, Italian Civil Code.

fonògrafo m.—phonograph. Also, grammòfono. Phonographic recordings are recognized as proof. See Art. 2712, Italian Civil Code.

foràneo—that which is outside the city; foreign; alien.

forastière m.—stranger; guest; alien. Also, forestière and forestièro.

fórca f.—pitchfork; gallows.

fórche (pl.) f.—gallows; gibbet.

fòrcipe m.—forceps.

forènse—forensic; pertaining to courts of law and lawyers.

forèsta f.—forest. Forests are part of the public domain. Art. 826, Italian Civil Code.

forestière m.—alien; stranger; guest.

forestièro m.—alien; stranger; guest.

fórma del contràtto—form of contract. The Civil Code provides that certain contracts, therein specified, must be by public Act or in writing under pain of nullity. Art. 1350, Italian Civil Code. Also, fórma del negòzio giurídico.

fórma del negòzio giurídico—form of a legal transaction. Certain instruments as well as contracts must be by public Act or in writing or they are invalid. Art. 1350, Italian Civil Code.

formàle—formal; relating to matters of form.
procediménto formàle—formal proceeding; one following strict observance of form and terminology.

fòrmula f.—formula; a set form of words required by law or custom and required for an instrument to be valid.

fòrmula esecutíva—executive formula. A formula which must be attached to a self-executing instrument such as a judgment or execution in order to have validity. It is captioned: "Italian Republic—In the name of the Law." It commands judicial officials, upon request, and those concerned, to execute the instrument; it also commands the attorney-general or State's attorney to give assistance and all public security officers to cooperate upon request. Art. 475, Italian Code of Civil Procedure.

formulàri m.—forms (legal). When a contract is prepared on a form, clauses added to the form prevail over those in the form when they are incompatible, even though the clauses in the form have not been cancelled. If the added clauses have been inserted by only one of the contracting parties, they will be interpreted against him and in favor of the other party in case of dispute. Art. 1342, 1370, Italian Civil Code.

fornicàre—to fornicate.

fornicazióne f.—fornication.

fornitóre m.—one who provides goods, wares and merchandise.

fornitúra f.—merchandise.

fóro m. — forum; place where the courts are located; jurisdiction; the Bar or legal profession.

fòrte m.—fort; strong.

fortézza f.—fortress; firmness; force. Forts and fortresses are considered part of the national defense and are thus in the public domain. Art. 822, Italian Civil Code.

fortúito — fortuitous; accidental; by chance.

fórza f.—force; power; strength; the public security agents.

fòrza maggióre — vis major (Lat.) — force majeure (Fr.) — irresistible force depending on external causes.

fòrza púbblica — public force; the agents of public order and security.

forzière m.—a box to enclose precious objects such as jewels. Also, scrígno.

fòssa f.—ditch; hole; grave; trench; cavity.

fòssile—fossil.

fòsso m.—large ditch; moat.

fotocópia f. — photocopy. Mechanical reproductions of photographs, motion pictures, phonograph recordings and every other mechanical representations of facts and things, offer full proof of the facts and things represented, if the person against whom they are produced does not deny their conformity to the facts and things represented. Art. 2712, 2719, Italian Civil Code.

fotofobía f. — photophobia; morbid dread of light.

fotografía f.—photograph. Photographic copies of writings, if attested by a competent public official and are not denied, have the same value of authenticity as the originals. Art. 2712, 2719, Italian Civil Code.

fotògrafo m.—photographer.

fracassàre—to destroy; to smash; to splinter.

fracàsso m.—noise; uproar; tumult.

fràcche m.—tail coat.

fràdicio—humid; rotten; wet.

fradiciúme m.—a quantity of wet rotting clothing.

fràgile—fragile.

fràgola f.—strawberry.

frammentàrio—fragmentary.

framménto m.—fragment.

fràna f.—landslide. It is a crime punishable with imprisonment to cause a landslide or to damage protective works against it. Art. 426, 427, Italian Penal Code.

franàre—to slide down; to move down or roll down.

francàbile—that which may be franked or transmitted by mail.

francàre—to free; to exempt; to affix postage stamps; to prepay transport; to release.

franchígia f.—exemption; legal privilege; right to free entry of goods without duty; right to frank letters.

frànco—free; privileged.

frànco m.—Franc, French currency.

frànco di pòrto—carriage paid; its cost is borne by the shipper. Also, **pòrto affrancàto.**

francobóllo m.—postage stamp.

franóso — precipitous; soil liable to slide down.

fràsca f.—branch; bush; a foolish or giddy person; a flirt.

frascheggiàre—to rustle; to trifle; to flirt.

frastòno m.—uproar. Also **frastuòno.**

frastornàre — to disturb; to prevent something from being accomplished; to divert; to hinder.

frastuòno m.—uproar. Also **frastòno.**

fràte m.—brother; friar; monk.

fratellànza f.—brotherhood.

fratellàstro m.—step-brother.

fratèllo m. — brother. Marriages between brothers and sisters are prohibited. Art. 87, Italian Civil Code. See germàni (fratèlli e sorèlle), unilateràli (fratèlli e sorèlle), uteríni (fratèlli e sorèlle) and consanguínei (fratèlli e sorèlle).

fratricída m.—fratricide.

fratricídio m.—the crime of killing a brother or sister. Art. 575-577, Italian Penal Code.

frattúra f.—fracture.

fraudàre—to defraud. Also **frodàre.**

frèccia f.—arrow.

fregàre—to rub gently; to draw the line; to deceive or do harm to someone.

fregiàre—to decorate; to honor.

frenàre—to brake; to curb; to moderate; to restrain.

fréno m.—brake; bridle or bit.

frigorífero—refrigerator.

frodàre—to defraud. Also, **fraudàre.**

fròde f.—fraud. Art. 1343, 1344, 1418, 2901, Italian Civil Code; Art. 501, 514, 640-649, Italian Penal Code.

fròde in commèrcio—fraud in commerce. It consists in delivering one kind of personal property for another, or personal property different from that stated or bargained for, as to origin, provenance, quality or quantity. Art. 515, Italian Penal Code.

fròde in emigrazióne — emigration fraud. It consists in receiving or being promised by another, money or anything of value as payment for facilitating his emigration. It is accomplished by false statements or sending the defrauded party to a country other than the one desired. Art. 645, Italian Penal Code.

fròde processuàle—procedural fraud. In connection with a civil or administrative proceeding, it consists in tampering with the state of places, things or persons with relation to judicial proof or the performance of expert examination for the purpose of deceiving the judge. Art. 374, Italian Penal Code.

fròdo m.—smuggling; evading the payment of duties or imposts.

frodolènto—fraudulent.

frónte f.—forehead; front; a political union of various parties to present a united front to an adversary party.

fronteggiàre—to confront; to face; to oppose.

frontespízio m.—title-page.

frontièra f.—frontier; border.

frontísta m.—one who owns building or land facing a river or a street.

fròtta f. — large group; disorderly multitude; troop.

frugàre—to search carefully; to rummage.

frugàta f.—search.

fruménto m.—wheat.

frumentóne m.—corn.

frústa f.—whip.

frútta f.—fruit. See frútto.

fruttàre—to render; to produce; to fructify; to render interest on capital.

fruttàto m.—the fruits of a capital investment.

frútto (frútti pl.) m.—fruit; in a general sense, the profit received on an investment; interest. Art. 820, 821, Italian Civil Code.

frútti civíli—civil fruits. These are those drawn from the thing as compensation for its use by another. They are interest on capital, canons or taxes on emphyteusis, life-time income as well as every other type of income and rent paid as compensation for the use of property. Art. 820, 821, Italian Civil Code.

frútti naturàli—natural fruits. These are those produced directly from the thing, with or without the labor of man, such as agricultural products, lumber, parts of animals and the products of mines, quarries and peat bogs. Art. 820, 821, Italian Civil Code.

fucilàre—to shoot; to execute by gun-fire.

fucilàta f.—discharge of gun-fire.

fucilazióne f.—execution by gun-fire.

fucíle m.—rifle.

fucína f.—forge.

fúga f.—escape; flight; a polyphonic musical composition. Regarding the obligation of a driver to assist a person who has been run over, see investiménto (òbblighi del conducènte in càso di).

fúga del imprenditóre—flight of the contractor or manager of a business resulting in insolvency. Art. 7, Falliménto (Bankruptcy), Usual Laws, Appendix to Italian Civil Code.

fugàce—transitory; fugitive.

fugàre—to put to flight; to rout.

fuggènte—fleeing.

fuggiàsco—fugitive.

fuggíre—to flee; to run away.

fuggitívo—fugitive.

fumaiuòlo m.—chimney stack; chimney top.

fumaruòlo f.—fumarole; a hole permitting the emanation of volcanic gases.

fumicàre—to fumigate. Also, fumigàre.

fumicazióne f. — fumigation. Also, fumigazióne.

funàmbulo m. — equilibrist; rope dancer; tight rope walker; a politician who plays a double game.

fúnebre—funereal; dismal; gloomy.

funeràle m.—funeral.

funèsto—disastrous; fatal; lamentable. See feràle.

fúnga f.—mould.

fungàia f.—mushroom bed.

fungíbile—fungible; goods of the same nature, quality and condition which when mixed together retain their original qualities in the aggregate mass. Ex. corn, grain; wheat, liquids of the same nature.

fúngo (fúnghi pl.) m.—mushroom.

funzionàrio m.—functionary; a public official.

funzióne f.—function; a ceremonious, public, religious or social occasion; the acts of an office.

fuoribórdo m.—outboard motor on a boat.

fuorilégge m.—outlaw.

fuoruscíto m.—exile.

furàce—thievish.

furàre—to rob; to steal.

furbería f.—slyness.

fúrbo—sly.

furènte—furious; enraged.

furería f.—the office of the commander of a company of soldiers; quartermaster's office.

furfànte m.—rascal; rouge.

furgóne m.—baggage car; freight car.

furibóndo—furious.

furière m.—a non-commissioned officer charged with the administration of a company of soldiers; quartermaster.

fúrti puníbili a querèla dell'offéso—thefts punishable on complaint of the offended party. They are punishable by imprisonment or fine and include the following: (1) where the accused has acted for the sole purpose of making momentary use of the thing abstracted and the same was immediately restored after the momentary use; (2) where the act is committed on articles of slight value to provide against a serious and urgent need; (3) if the act consists in gathering wheat left over by reapers, by raking, or gleaning left over grapes on the lands of others which have not been entirely harvested. Art. 626, Italian Penal Code.

furtivaménte — furtively; secretly; stealthily.

furtívo—furtive; stealthy.

fúrto m.—theft of personal property. Art. 624-627, Italian Penal Code.

fúrto con effrazióne—burglary; housebreaking. Art. 625, subd. 1, 2, Italian Penal Code.

fúrto con stràppo—theft by snatching property from someone's hand or person. Art. 625, subd. 4, Italian Penal Code. Also, scíppo. See fúrto and rapína.

fúrto d'úso—theft by use or appropriation. It is the crime consisting of (1) the appropriation or taking away of personal property for temporary use, even though returned immediately thereafter; (2) appropriating things of small value in case of grave and urgent need; (3) gleaning, raking and collecting kernels of wheat, grain or corn from the lands of another before being completely harvested. Art. 626, Italian Penal Code.

fusióne f.—fusion; merger. See incorporazióne and Art. 2501, Italian Civil Code.

fusióne delle società—merger of associations or corporations. Art. 2501-2504, Italian Civil Code.

futúra memòria (esàme di testimòni a) — examination of witnesses for future recollection. It is a deposition under oath taken before trial. The testimony may be obtained in civil and criminal cases where it is feared the witness may be unavailable or cannot appear to testify due to illness or other serious impediment. Art. 357, 418, 462, Italian Code of Penal Procedure and procediménti di istruzióne preventíva. Art. 692-699, Italian Code of Civil Procedure. See, also, istruzióne preventíva and rogatòria.

futúro m.—future.

G

gàbbia m.—cage.

gabbióne m.—large cage or cell in which prisoners are enclosed in the courtroom while on trial in the Court of Assize.

gabèlla f.—gabel; a tax on consumer goods.

gabinétto m.—cabinet; closet; study.

gaèlico m.—Gaelic; Celtic language of ancient Ireland and Scotland.

gàggio m.—deposit; pledge; stipend.

gagliardétto m.—pennant; streamer.

galantuòmo m.—man of honor; honest man.

galatèo m.—a book of rules on polite manners.

galèa f. — leather helmet used by Roman soldiers; galley; ancient ship of war.

galeòtta f. — ancient warship with a sail and oarsmen.

galeòtto m. — galley-slave; convict; evil man.

galèra f. — galley; penitentiary; prison; incarceration at hard labor.

galèro m.—the winged cap of Mercury; the cap of a Roman priest.

gàlle—inhabitant of ancient Gaul, now France.

gallègo m.—one from Galicia, Spain.

gallería f.—gallery.

gallése m.—one from Wales.

gallétta f.—biscuit; hard-tack.

gallétta—a species of grape.

gallétto m.—young cock.

gàllico—Gallic; from France.

gallína f.—hen.

gàllo m.—cock.

gallóne m.—triming of lace or braid.

galoppatóio m.—a track for horsemen in parks.

galoppíno m.—an errand boy; one at the service of others who runs from place to place.

gàmba f.—leg; shank.

gambàle m. — boot-tree; stem of a plant.

gàmbero m.—crayfish; name of various crustaceans.

gàna f.—(from the Spanish, ganas) with great desire; avidly; eagerly.

gancière m.—one who helps to shove off a boat from shore with the aid of a hooked pole; one who aids a gondolier in Venice to push the gondola from the shore or mooring.

gàncio m.—a hook.

gànghero m.—hinge; pivot.

gàngola f.—gland; swollen gland.

gangrèna f.—gangrene. Also, cangrèna.

gànzo m. (gànza f.)—lover, in a deprecatory sense.

gàra f.—competition; rivalry; strife.

garànte m.—guarantor; surety.

garantía or garanzía f. — guarantee; suretyship; warranty. See Art. 1179 et seq., and Art. 2740-2744, Italian Civil Code.

garanzía (chiamàta in)—a buyer whose title is disputed by a third party must vouch in the seller to defend and warrant his title. Art. 1483-1491, Italian Civil Code. Also, see evizióne,

and chiamàta in càusa del venditóre, Art. 1485, Italian Civil Code.

garanzía per i vízi della còsa vendúta —warranty for defects in goods sold. This warranty is made by the seller to the buyer. Art. 1490-1497, Italian Civil Code.

gas .(emissióne abusíva) — wrongful emission of gas. See gètto pericolóso di còse.

gènero m. — son-in-law. See nuòra, daughter-in-law.

gènio m.—genius; natural ability or capacity; in the military, that branch of the service which constructs roads, bridges, etc., equivalent to the Corps of Engineers.

gènio civíle—civil engineering; the governmental office which is charged with responsibility for planning and executing public works.

genitóre m. (genitríce f.)—procreator; parent.

responsabilità dei genitóri per fàtto illécito dei fígli minóri—responsibility of parents for illicit act of minor children. The father, mother or guardian are responsible for damage caused by the wrongful act of minor, unemancipated children who live with them. Art. 2048, Italian Civil Code.

genocídio m.—genocide. It is a crime punished with imprisonment. Genocídio, Usual Laws, Appendix to Italian Code of Penal Procedure. The Constitutional prohibitions against extradition for political crimes do not apply to crimes of genocide. Art. 10, 26, Constitution of the Italian Republic. See estradizióne.

gènte f.—people of the same stock and the same name; people; persons; nation.

diritto delle gènti—Law of Nations.

gerènte m.—one who administers the affairs or business of another.

gerènte responsàbile—the responsible editor of a newspaper in the event of legal action. Now currently referred to as direttóre responsàbile.

gèrgo m.—jargon of a trade or profession understood by those engaged therein and not commonly understood by others; gibberish; slang.

germàni (fratèlli e sorèlle)—brothers and sisters german. These are brothers and sisters born of the same father and the same mother. See **unilateràli (fratèlli e sorèlle)**, **uteríni (fratèlli e sorèlle)**, and **consanguínei (fratèlli e sorèlle)**.

germàno—from Germany.

germàno m. — German; inhabitant of Germany.

germàno m. and adj.—german; one born of the same father and mother. See **germàni (fratèlli e sorèlle)**.

gerontología f.—gerontology; that part of medical science which deals with the physiology, pathology and therapy of old age.

gestazióne f.—gestation.

gestióne f.—administration and daily management of business.

gestióne di affàri — management of businesses. Art. 2028-2032, Italian Civil Code.

gestóre m.—manager of a business; manager of the traffic of goods.

gettàre—to cast; to throw; to toss; to cast molten metal into a particular shape by pouring it into a prepared mould; to jettison.

gettàta f.—throw; range of a gun; molten metal during the refining process; shoot of a plant.

gèttito m.—that which is thrown; jettison; things cast off a vessel in peril in order to lighten it.

gètto m.—casting; jettison; jet; throw.

gètto pericóloso di còse — dangerous throwing of things. It is committed by whoever throws or pours out things in a place of public passage or a private place used in common by others, which may be apt to offend or soil or molest persons, or in cases not permitted by law, brings about emissions of gas, steam or smoke apt to bring about such effects. Art. 674, Italian Penal Code. See **immissióne di fúmo, calóre, esalazióne, rumóri e scuotiménti**.

gettóne m.—a chip used in lieu of money in games of chance; a token.

ghísa f.—cast-iron; pig-iron.

giacènte—in a lying position; placed; situated.

capitàle giacènte—dormant capital.

denàro giacènte—dormant money.

lettèra giacènte — unclaimed letter lying at the post-office.

mèrce giacènte—undelivered freight.

giacènza f.—position; situation; capital lying idle; inactiveness.

giornàle (líbro) m.—journal of daily operations of a business. Art. 2214-2220, Italian Civil Code .

giornàle naùtico or giornàle di bórdo—log; log-book kept on every vessel containing a brief record of daily occurrences.

gistrànte m.—indorser.

giràre—to turn around; to go around something; to circulate; to rotate; to indorse.

giràta f.—turn; walk around; revolution. Indorsement; act of transferring property rights in a draft, promissory note or check in favor of another by indorsement or signature of the holder. Art. 2008-2015, 2023, 1995, Italian Civil Code; Art. 17-27, Assègni (checks) and Art. 15-25, Cambiàle (Drafts), Usual Laws, Appendix to Italian Civil Code.

giràta a título di pégno—indorsement by the way of pledge. If the indorsement contains a clause which imports the constitution of a pledge, the indorsee may exercise all the rights inherent in the instrument, but the indorsement is only valid as an indorsement by procuration. The issuer may not interpose against the indorsee for guaranty the defenses based on his personal relations with the indorser, unless the indorsee receiving the instrument had acted intentionaly to the damage of the issuer. The clause, payment guaranteed or payment in pledge, or another which implies a pledge, when attached to the indorsement, allows the holder to exercise all the rights inherent to the draft, but the indorsement made by him is valid only as an indorsement by procuration. Those liable on the instrument cannot interpose against the holder the defenses based on their personal relations with the indorser, unless the holder receiving the draft had acted intentionally to the damage of the debtor. Art. 2014, Italian Civil Code; Art. 23, Cambiàle (Drafts), Usual Laws, Appendix to Italian Civil Code.

giràta per incàsso o per procùra—indorsement for collection or by procuration. If the indorsement contains a clause which imports the conferring of an agency for collection, the indorsee may exercise all the rights inherent in the instrument, but cannot further indorse except by power of attorney. The issuer may only interpose against the indorsee by procuration those defenses that could be interposed against the indorser. Those liable on the instrument, in this case, cannot interpose defenses against the holder that they could have interposed against the indorser. The order contained in an indorsement by procuration is not extinguished by the death of the one inserting it, or by his supervening incapacity. Art. 22, Cambiàle (Drafts), Usual Laws, Appendix to Italian Civil Code. Re restrictive indorsement, Cf.—Arts. 205-206, Uniform Commercial Code.

giratàrio m.—a person in whose favor commercial paper is indorsed; indorsee.

girocônto m.—settlement of accounts. The transfers of credits and debits in the accounts of depositors in the same bank, to reflect the liquidation of obligations to each other.

giubilazióne f.—jubilation; pensioning of an employee.

giudicàbile — judiciable; capable of being judged; justiciable.

giudicàre—to adjudge; to adjudicate; to judge; to resolve a dispute; to pronounce judgment or sentence.

guidicàto m. (giudicàta f.)—adjudged; adjudicated; passed on judicially; sentenced.
  còsa giudicàta—res judicata (Lat.); an adjudicated matter; the findings contained in a judgment or

sentence are binding on the parties, their heirs and assignees. Art. 2909, 2953, Italian Civil Code; Art. 324, 395(5), Italian Code of Civil Procedure; Art. 124, Enabling Rules, Appendix to Italian Code of Civil Procedure. Also, regiudicàta.

giúdice m. — judge; magistrate; one who sits in judgment on criminal or civil cases.

giúdice conciliatóre—judge of conciliation. An honorary and non-paid post of limited jurisdiction which is the first rung in the Italian judicial system. This judge is empowered to consider causes relating to rental of real property, the termination thereof and dispossess proceedings. He has jurisdiction to a limited amount over rental contracts of real property. He, also, endeavors to conciliate parties and settle disputes. Art. 7, Italian Code of Civil Procedure.

giúdice delegàto—delegate judge. He is an officer of the court similar to a Bankruptcy Judge. Art. 25, 26, Falliménto (Bankruptcy), Usual Laws, Appendix to Italian Civil Code.

giúdice estensóre—drafting or reporting judge; one charged by the President of the Tribunal to prepare an opinion setting forth the reasons for the judgment. Art. 119, Enabling Rules, Italian Code of Civil Procedure. See redazióne della sentènza.

giúdice istruttóre—examining judge or magistrate. One who holds preliminary hearings and examinations. See istruttòria, istruzióne civíle and istruzióne penàle.

giúdice popolàre — popular judge; people's judge; citizen judge. Popular judges in the Courts of Assize must have the following prerequisites: (a) Italian citizenship and enjoyment of civil and political rights; (b) good moral conduct; (c) not less than 30, nor than 65 years of age; (d) graduation from a first grade middle school of any kind. Those of the Court of Assize of Appeals must, in addition to the foregoing, be graduates of a second grade middle school of any kind.

The popular judges of the Courts of Assize, during the time of the session in which they serve, are respectively comparable to judges of Tribunals and counsellors of the Court of Appeals, in the order of precedence at public functions and ceremonies. They are chosen from two separate lists of citizens residing in the territory of the Commune. Art. 9-36, Córti di Assíse (Courts of Assize), Usual Laws, Appendix to Italian Code of Penal Procedure.

giúdice relatóre—reporting judge.

giúdice tutelàre—guardianship judge. One charged with appointing guardians for minors and protecting their persons and property. Art. 344-389, Italian Civil Code.

giudiziàle — judicial; pertaining to a judicial proceeding.

giudiziàrio—judiciary; pertaining to a judge or the judiciary.

giudízio m.—action; judgment; proceeding; sentence; verdict; opinion; good sense; presentation of a legal case or argument; a matter which is *sub judice*, that is under judicial consideration.

giudízio arbitràle—arbitral or arbitration judgment. For arbitration, see Art. 806-831, Italian Code of Civil Procedure. Re International Commercial Convention on Arbitration, see Convenzióni Internazionàli (International Conventions), Usual Laws,, Appendix to Italian Code of Civil Procedure.

giudízio assuntívo—a proceeding where one party assumes the burden of furnishing evidentiary proof. See **assunzióne delle pròve**—assumption of the burden of proof.

giudízio civíle—civil proceeding.

giudízio di cognizióne—a proceeding under judicial consideration, involving the preliminary examinations, hearings, trial and judgment. Also, **procèsso di cognizióne**. See Art. 163-466, Italian Code of Civil Procedure.

giudízio di delibazióne—a proceeding to review civil and penal judgments imposed by foreign jurisdictions to determine if they can be enforced in Italy. Art. 797, Italian Code of Civil Procedure. The Penal Code refers to the proceeding as Riconosciménto delle sentènze stranière. See Art. 674, Italian Code of Penal Procedure. See **delibazióne (giudízio di)**.

giudízio direttíssimo — summary proceeding. It is a penal proceeding in certain cases which by-passes the preliminary hearings and examinations. Art. 502-505, Italian Code of Penal Procedure; Art. 59, Enabling Rules, Italian Code of Penal Procedure.

giudízio di revisióne—a proceeding to review a case based on newly discovered evidence. See **revisióne**.

giudízio di rinvío—proceeding to remand a case. It consists in sending a cause back to another judge or tribunal or adjourning the same. Art. 392-394, Italian Code of Civil Procedure and Art. 543, 544, 546, Italian Code of Penal Procedure.

giudízio esecutívo—executive or summary proceeding used in the attachment and sequestration of the goods of a debtor. Also, **procèsso d'esecuzióne**. Art. 474-632, Italian Code of Civil Procedure.

giudízio penàle—penal proceeding.

giudízio per decréto—judgment by decree. It is employed by the Praetor in trying certain cases and to proceed to judgment without summation by counsel. Art. 506-510, Italian Code of Penal Procedure.

giudízio petitòrio—petitory action. One in which a right to property or title is sought as distinguished from a possessory action where the right to possession is in litigation. See **azióne petitòria**.

giudízio possessòrio — possessory action. It is an action to obtain or recover actual possession of property. The two possessory actions are: reintegrazióne and manutenzióne. Art. 1168-1170, Italian Civil Code. Other actions for the protection of property rights are: rivendicazióne (Art. 948), negatòria (Art. 949) and the azióni di nunciazióne, Art. 1171, 1172, Italian Civil Code.

giudízio sommàrio—summary proceeding. Also, procediménto sommàrio.

giúnta f.—board; board of advisors; commission; council.

giuòco d'azzàrdo — game of chance; game of risk. These games are those where the outcome depends solely on chance and not on the skill of the players. It is a Penal violation. Also, giuòco di sòrte. Art. 718-722, Italian Penal Code.

giuòco di sòrte—See giuòco d'azzàrdo.

giuòco e scomméssa—game of betting or wagering. An action to recover payment on a wagering debt is not permitted. A loser who paid a wager cannot recover the same where no fraud was involved. Excepted are games which train in the use of arms and all kinds of races and sporting events. An action to recover on a lottery winning may be maintained if it has been legally authorized. Art. 1933-1935, Italian Civil Code. Also, scomméssa.

giuraménto m.—oath; sworn attestation of fact. Art. 2736-2739, Italian Civil Code; Art. 329, Italian Code of Penal Procedure.

giuraménto decisòrio — determinative sworn testimony. One required of the other party to an action to resolve, totally or partially, the outcome of the case. Art. 2736, subd. 1, Italian Civil Code; Art. 233-239, 243, Italian Code of Civil Procedure. Also, decisòroi

giuraménto estimatòrio — estimative sworn testimony; testimony taken under oath by the judge for the purpose of ascertaining the value of the subject matter in dispute when it is not otherwise determinable. See giuraménto suppletòrio, Art. 2736, subd. 2, Italian Civil Code; Art. 240-243, Italian Code of Civil Procedure.

giuraménto suppletòrio — supplementary sworn testimony; testimony taken under oath by the judge for the purpose of deciding the case when the proof is insufficient, or, sworn testimony taken for the purpose of ascertaining the value of the subject matter in dispute when it not otherwise determinable. This last is

also referred to as giuraménto estimatòrio. Art. 2736, sub. 2, Italian Civil Code; Art. 240-243, Italian Code of Civil Procedure.

giuràre—to swear; to take an oath.

giuràto—sworn.

giuràto m.—juror.

giuratóre m. — one who habitually swears.

giuratòrio—done on oath.

giúre m.—law; legal science; jurisprudence.

giureconsúlto m.—one learned in the law; jurist; skilled advocate.

giurí m. (Eng.)—jury.

giuría f.—jury.

giuridicaménte—judicially.

giurídico—juridical; legal.

giurisdizionàle—jurisdictional.

giurisdizióne f.—jurisdiction; the authority of courts to take cognizance of and decide cases.

giurisperíto m.—one learned in the law. See giureconsúlto.

giurisprudènte m.—See giurisperíto.

giurisprudènza f.—jurisprudence; the science of law.

giurísta m.—jurist; one learned in the law.

giúro m.—oath.

gius m.—right; justice; law.

giusdicènte m.—magistrate; judge.

giústa—just; according to justice. See giústo.

giústa càusa—just cause. See recèsso per giústa càusa and Art. 2119, Italian Civil Code.

giustaménte — justly; rightly; precisely.

giustézza f.—justness; exactness.

giustificàbile—justifiable.

giustificàre—to justify.

giustificazióne f.—justification.

giustízia f.—justice.

giustízia amministratíva—administrative justice.

giustízia (delítti cóntro l'amministrazióne della)—crimes against the administration of justice. Art. 361-401, Italian Penal Code.

giustiziàre—to execute.

giustizière m.—executioner.

giústo—just; fair; reasonable.

giústo m.—a just or upright man.

giústo prèzzo—just, fair or reasonable price. When a contract price is not set by the parties, the fair price is presumed to be that normally charged by the seller. If the sale concerns things having an exchange or market price, it is deduced from the daily market quotations in the place where delivery is to be made or from the nearest market. Art. 1474, Italian Civil Code.

glàdio m.—short sword; dagger.

glèba f.—glebe; clod; soil; turf.

glèba (sèrvo della)—slave of the soil; a serf under feudal law.

godiménto m.—enjoyment; exercise of a right. See Art. 1380, Italian Civil Code.

governàle m.—rudder. Also, timóne.

governaménto m.—government.

governànte—governing.

governànte m.—governor.

governànte f.—governess.

governatívo—of the government; pertaining to the government.

governatóre m.—governor.

governatríce f.—governess.

governatúra f.—care of animals.

governíme m.—fodder for animals.

govèrno m.—government.

gradazióne f.—gradation.

gradiménto m.—acceptance; approbation; approval; satisfaction. See véndita con risèrva di gradiménto—sale on approval or to satisfaction, Art. 1520, Italian Civil Code.

gradína f.—burin; dented chisel; the mark left by such tool.

gradinàta f.—flight of steps.

gradíno m.—step; chisel.

gradíre—to accept with pleasure; to approve; to please; to satisfy; to partake of (food).

gràdo m.—degree; grade; rank; step.

gràdo dell'ipotèca—rank of recorded mortgage. The first in time of two recorded mortgages on the same property takes precedence over successively attaching mortgages and liens. Art. 2852-2855, Italian Civil Code.

gràdo di giurisdizióne—grade or degree of jurisdiction. Three grades are involved. First grade, over subject matter, amount, territorial jurisdiction and over the charge. Second grade, over appellate jurisdiction pertaining to the controversy or charge; Third grade, on the jurisdiction of the Court of Cassation over appeals of law or right. Art. 34-44, 46-54, 211, 435, Italian Code of Penal Procedure.

gràdo di parentèla—degree of consanguinity or kinship. Art. 74-77, Italian Civil Code.

gràdo di péna—degree or measure of punishment as prescribed by the Penal Code.

graduàre—to graduate; to divide by degrees; to confer a grade; to distribute proportionately a bankrupt's assets among the creditors.

graduàto m.—graduate; the rank of a non-commissioned officer.

graduatória f. — list of graduates; graduated list of persons in order of merit, seniority or preference; list of a bankrupt's creditors in order of their proportionate rights. Art. 110-117, Falliménto (Bankruptcy), Usual Laws, Appendix to Italian Civil Code. Also, see esecuzióne forzàta and espropiazióne forzàta.

graduazióne f.—graduation; division into grades. Admission of a creditor into the list of a bankrupt's creditors in the graduatòria. Partitioning among creditors of the amount realized at a forced sale. See esecuzióne forzàta and espropiazióne forzàta, Art. 2910-2940, Italian Civil Code; Art. 510, 512, 596, 598, Italian Code of Civil Procedure.

gràfico—graphic; life-like.

grafítto 'm.—a scrawled mural inscription.

gramàglia f.—mourning clothes.

grammòfono m.—gramophone; phonograph. Also, fonografo. Phonographic recordings are recognized as proof. Art. 2712, Italian Civil Code.

gratificazióne f.—gratuity.

gràtis — gratis; free of cost; for nothing.

gratuitaménte—gratuitously; without expense; without reason; without proof.

gratúito — gratuitous; that which is done without expense.

gratúito patrocíno—free defense. It is a protection afforded to the indigent or poor so that they can be defended without cost. Also, patrocíno gratúito. Art. 1-43, Patrocínio Gratúito, Usual Laws, Appendix to Italian Code of Civil Procedure.

gravàbile—taxable.

gravàme m. — gravamen; burden; grievance; the burden or gist of a charge or accusation; The act of challenging or opposing a ruling or judgment of a judge by taking the legal steps to oppose it. See impugnazióne.

gravaménto m.—sequestration of the assets of a debtor.

gravàto—burdened with a tax.

gravidànza f.—pregnancy.

gràvido—pregnant.

gravità f.—gravity; dignity; seriousness; solemnity.

gravitazióne f.—gravitation.

gràzia f.—grace; favor; pardon; a favor or indulgence as distinguished from a right; dispensation. A pardon condones punishment either totally or partially or commutes it as provided by law. It is granted by the President of the Republic as Chief of State. Art. 174, Italian Penal Code, Art. 87, Constitution of the Italian Republic.

graziàbile—pardonable.

graziàre—to pardon.

graziàto—pardoned.

gregàrio m.—private soldier; follower.

gregàrio adj.—gregarious.

grégge f.—herd; flock.

gréggia f.—herd; flock; stable to which a herd returns.

grèmbo m.—that part of the body between the belly and knees upon which a seated person would place something given to him; bosom; lap; in the midst of (the family).

grída f.—proclamation; announcement made by a crier; report.

grída e manifestazióni sedizióse — seditious or riotous reports and public demonstrations. Art. 654, Italian Penal Code.

grída o notízie àtte a turbàre la tranquilità púbblica o privàta—news or reports which may disturb public or private tranquility. Art. 657, Italian Penal Code.

grigiovérde m.—gray-green color; the Italian Army uniform was of this color during World War I and the word had a special connotation.

grillétto m.—trigger.

grimaldèllo 'm.—a pick-lock; an instrument which opens locks without a key. See possèsso ingiustificàto di chiàvi alteràte o di grimaldèlli; see contracchiàve.

grónda f.—eaves.

grondàia f.—gutter.

grossería f.—work of gold and silver in large form.

grossière m.—one who works gold and silver in large forms; wholesaler.

grossísta m.—wholesaler.

grossolàno—course; dull; thick.

gru f.—crane (bird); crane (machine for lifting heavy weights).

grúa f. — crane for lifting heavy weights.

grúccia f.—a bar to hang clothes in a closet; a crutch. Also, stampèlla.

gruèra m.—Gruyere (cheese).

grúma f.—tartar left in wine casks.

grúppe m.—croup; an affection of the larynx.

126

gruppière m.—croupier; an attendant who collects and pays out money at gaming tables.

grùzzolo m.—a hoard of money accumulated a little at a time.

guadagnàre—to earn; to gain; to win.

guadàgno m.—earning; gain; winning; profit.

guadàre—to ford a shallow stream or body of water.

guàdo m.—the place where a body of water is fordable.

guaína f.—sheath (for a sword or dagger); cover (for a flag).

guàio m. — difficulty; predicament; trouble; woe; wailing.

guància f.—cheek; the part of a rifle's stock upon which a shooter rests his cheek when taking aim.

guanciàle m.—pillow.

guancialíno m.—pin-cushion.

guanciàta f.—slap on the face.

guantièra f.—silver tray to hold pastries, calling cards, etc.

guànto m.—glove.

guardabarrière m.—a railroad crossing watchman charged with opening and closing the barrier at level crossings.

guardabòschi m.—forest ranger.

guardacàccia m.—game warden.

guardacòste m. — coastguardsman; coastguard.
nàve guardacòste — coastguard vessel.

guardafíli m.—telephone or telegraph wire repairman.

guardapòrto m.—picket boat guarding the port.

guardasigíli m.—keeper of the seals.

guardatóre m.—guardian; custodian.

guàrdia f.—guard.

guàrdia doganàle—customs guard.

guàrdia di finànza—treasury guard.

guàrdia di pùbblica sicurézza—guard of public security; policeman.

guàrdia di questúra—guard of the questúra; policeman.

guardiamarína m.—ensign.

guardiàno m.—guardian; caretaker; warden.

guardína f.—temporary detention cell at the office of the Questúra and Command Posts of the Carabinièri.

guarantía or guarentígia f.—guaranty; surety; warranty.

guarentíre—to guaranty; to warrant; to defend.

guaríbile—curage; remediable.

guarigióne f.—cure; recovery.

guariménto m.—cure; recovery.

guaríre—to cure.

guarnigióne f.—garrison.

guastafèste m.—spoil-sport.

guastamestièri m.—bungler; scab.

guastàre—to spoil; to waste.

guatàre—to watch with suspicion.

guattèro m. (guattèra f.)—a kitchen help performing menial duties. Also, sguattèra and sguattèro.

guàzza f.—dew.

guazzabugliàre—to muddle up; to mix up; to confuse.

guazzabúglio m.—slush; a mixture of snow and water; confused mixture.

guazzabuglióne m.—a muddler.

guazzàre—to agitate; to shake; to stir.

guàzzo m. — ford; pool; splash of water.

guèrra f.—war.
in guèrra—at war.
stàto di guèrra—state of war.
teàtro di guèrra—war theater.
zóna di guèrra—war zone. Regarding the responsibility of an insurer for damages caused by war, see terrèmoto, guèrra, insurrezióne, tumúlti popolàri.

guèrra chímica—chemical warfare.

guèrra civíle—civil war.

guèrra econòmica—economic warfare.

guèrra frédda—cold war.

guèrra religiósa—religious war.

guerrafondàio m.—warmonger.

guerregiàre—to make war.

guerrièro m.—warriór.

guerríglia f.—guerrila war.

guerriglièro m.—guerrilla fighter.

gúglia f.—pinnacle; spire; obelisk.

guída f.—guide; conductor; leader.

guidàbile—that which may be guided.

guidàre—to guide; to lead; to govern; to drive.

guiderdóne m. — guerdon; reward or recompense given for one's merits.

guinzàglio m.—leash; restraint.

gustàre—to taste.

gústo m.—taste.

I

identità f.—identity; sameness; being the same as it is claimed to be.

ideografía f. — ideograph; grafic reprepresentation of an idea.

ideología f.—ideology.

idiòta m.—idiot; a person born without normal or ordinary mental powers.

idòneo—idoneous; able; fit; suitable; competent. See sui juris.

ieràtico — hieratic; pertaining to the priesthood; priestly; a form of Egyptian hieroglyphics written in abbreviated form by the ancient priests of Egypt.

iettatúra f.—a superstitious belief in the influence of persons or things; malign influence; evil eye.

ígneo—igneous; fiery.

ignizióne f.—ignition.

ignorànza f. — ignorance; lack or absence of knowledge.

ignorànza della légge — ignorance of the law. An act done in ignorance of a Penal or Civil rule of law or statute is not excused. See erróre.

ignorànza della légge penàle—ignorance of the Penal law. Such ignorance cannot be invoked as an excuse. Art .5, Italian Penal Code.

ignòto—unknown.
mílite ignòto—unknown soldier.

illécito—illicit.

illegàle—illegal.

illegalità f.—illegality.

illegittimità f. — illegitimacy; unconstitutionality of a law or Act having the force of law. Art. 134-137, Constitution of the Italian Republic; Title I, Art. 1, 2, Córte Costituzionàle (Constitutional Court) and Title II, Chapter II, Art. 23-36, idem., Usual Laws, Appendix to Italian Code of Civil Procedure. See córte costituzionàle.

illegíttimo—illegitimate.

illéso—unharmed; unhurt.

illibatézza f. — purity; chastity; candor; integrity.

illibàto—pure; immaculate; spotless.

illúdere—to deceive.

illúso—deluded.

illusòrio—illusory; unreal.

imballàgio m.—packing; packing material. For responsibility in cases of loss or destruction of packed goods in transport or in warehouses, see Art. 1693 and 1787, Italian Civil Code.

imballàre—to bale; to pack.

imballatóre m.—packer.

imballatúra f.—packing.

imbalordíre—to bewilder.

imbalordíto—bewildered; stunned.

imbalsamàre—to embalm; to preserve.

imbalsamatóre m.—embalmer.

imbalsamazióne f.—embalming.

imbandieràre—to deck with flags.

imbandíre — to prepare; to set the table.

imbaràzzo m. — embarrassment; obstacle.

imbarcàre—to embark.

imbarcatóio m.—landing dock.

imbarilàre—to place wine or liquids in casks or barrels.

imbastardíre—to degenerate; to corrupt; to adulterate.

imbaulàre—to pack in a trunk.

imbecílle m. — imbecile; mentally feeble.

Imbecillíre—to become an imbecile.

Imbecillità f.—imbecility.

Imbrattaménto m.—dirt; filth; stain; daub of mud, paint or other adhesive matter. See deturpaménto e imbrattaménto di còse altrúi.

Imbrattàre—to daub; to defile; to foul; to soil; to stain.

Imbrattatóre m.—dauber.

Imbrattatúra f.—daub; sketch; spot.

Imbrecciàre—to spread gravel on a road.

Imbreviatúra f.—minutes of the ancient notaries; protocol.

Imbriacàre — to intoxicate; to get drunk. Also, ubriacàre.

Imbroccàre—to hit the mark.

Imbroccàta f.—a downward thrust in fencing.

Imbrogliàre—to confuse; to deceive. See arruffamatàsse.

Imbròglio m.—an intrigue; a deception.

Imbroglióne m.—intriguer; deceiver; meddler; confounder.

imbúto m.—funnel.

imitàre—to imitate.

Imitazióne f.—imitation.

Imitazióne servíle—close and confusing imitation of a competitor's products. It is an element of unfair competition. Art. 2598 (1), Italian Civil Code.

Immagazzinàre—to place in a storehouse or warehouse.

Immàgine f.—image; figure; likeness. abúso dell'immàgine altrúi—misuse of another's image or likeness. Art. 10, Italian Civil Code.

immàgine (dirítto all')—right to one's image or likeness. Misuse of this personal privilege is protected whether the likeness is of one's self, his parents, spouse or children. When the likeness is displayed or published in a manner not permitted by law and causes prejudice to the decorum or reputation of the person involved, such misuse may be restrained and compensation for damages obtained. Art. 10, Italian Civil Code.

immàgini oscèni—obscene representations. See pubblicazióne e spettàcoli oscèni — obscene publications and performances.

immateriàle—immaterial; incorporeal.

immatricolàre—to enroll; to register.

immatricolazióne f.—enrollment; registration.

immedicàbile—incurable.

immemoràbile — immemorial; extending beyond memory.

immersióne f.—immersion.

imméttere—to allow to enter; to introduce; to admit.

imméttere in possèsso—to give possession.

immissióne f. — the act of allowing something to enter within or upon; admittance; introduction.

immissióne di fúmo, calóre, esalazióni, rumóri e scuotiménti—introduction of smoke, heat, vapors, noises and violent agitations. The owner of land cannot impede the introduction of smoke, heat, vapors, noises or violent agitations and similar propagations issuing from neighboring land, if they do not surpass normal tolerability, having regard for the condition of the places. Art. 844, Italian Civil Code. See gètto pericolóso di còse. See inquinaménto atmosfèrico and esalzióne dal fóndo vicíno.

immissióne di tràvi e caténi nel múro commúne (appòggio e)—support and introduction of beams and chains or metal supports in the common or party-wall. The co-owner of a party-wall may introduce beams or chains and metal supports therein, provided he does not cause damage thereto or endanger its stability. Art. 884, Italian Civil Code.

Immissióne nel possèsso temporàneo dei bèni dell'assènte — admittance into temporary possession of the property of an absentee due to disappearance. Art. 50, 52-57, Italian Civil Code.

immòbile—immovable; that which cannot be moved; fixed.

immòbile (bèni)—immovable things; real property. For distinction between movable and immovable things or property, see Art. 812, Italian Civil Code.

immobiliàre—pertaining to real property.

immobilitàre—to immobilize.

immobilizzàre—to immobilize.

immòto—immovable.

immúne—immune.

immunità f.—immunity.

immunología f.—immunology.

immutàbile—immutable.

immutazióne f. — change; modification; tampering. See fròde processuàle — involving tampering with evidence in civil and administrative proceedings, Art. 374, Italian Penal Code.

impaccàre—to pack.

impacchettàre—to package.

impacciàre — to embarrass; to embroil; to encumber; to interfere.

impadroníre—to appropriate; to occupy; to usurp; to master; to put in possession of.

impagàbile—priceless; matchless; inestimable.

impaginàre—to make up pages (printing).

impalàre—to impale; to stake vines, to impound.

impalizzàre—to fence in as a palisade or stockade; to enclose.

impaludàre — to become marshy or swampy.

imparentàre—to become related.

ímpari—unequal.

imparziàle—impartial.

impediénte — impedient; that which hinders. See impediménti al matrimònio.

impediménti al matrimònio — impediments to marriage. These are: minority; mental infirmity; unfree status (already married); relationship, affinity, adoption, affiliation;

crime of attempted or consummated homicide upon the spouse of the other; widow's period of mourning (300 days). Art. 84-90, 136, 139, Italian Civil Code.

impediménto m.—impediment.

impediménto diriménto — impediment which prevents a marriage. See impediménti al matrimònio.

impedíre—to prevent; to hinder.

impegnàre—to pledge; to bind; to engage.

impégno m. — pledge; engagement; promise; obligation.

impenitènte — impenitent; obstinate; unrepenting.

impenitènza f.—impenitence.

imperíto — inexperienced; unskilled; inept; incapable.

imperitúro—imperishable; indestructable.

imperízia f. — unskillfullness; ineptness. Where lack of skill has caused unjust damage, an action for damages will lie. Art. 2043, Italian Civil Code.

impetràre—to obtain by entreaty.

impetrazióne f. — entreaty; petition; supplication.

impiantàre—to found; to establish; to set up (a business, plant, account).

impiànto m. — installation or placement of equipment.

impiccàre—to hang.

impiegàre—to employ; to use; to invest.

impiegàto m.—employee.

impiègo m.—employment; occupation; post.

impignoràbile—not subject to attachment.

impignoràbili (còse mòbili assolutaménte) — personal property absolutely not subject to attachment. Besides those things declared to be not subject to attachment by law, the following cannot be attached: (1) sacred objects and those used in religious worship; (2) the nuptial ring, clothes, linens, beds, tables for eating food with the relative chairs, chests for linens, wardrobes, chests of drawers or bureaus, the refrigerator, stoves and kitchen ovens whether gas or electric, the washing machine, household and kitchen utensils together with a suitable piece of furniture to hold them, which are indispensable to the debtor and the members of his family residing with him; nevertheless, except beds, there are excluded furniture having considerable economic value, even for certified artistic or antiquarian value; (3) the foodstuffs and combustibles necessary for a month's maintenance of the debtor and the other members of his family residing with him; (4) the instruments, objects and books that are indispensable for the exercise of the profession, art or trade of the debtor; (5) the arms and objects which the debtor is obliged to keep for the fulfillment of a public service; (6) decorations for valor or merit, registers and in general, family correspondence as well as manuscripts, unless they form part of a collection. Art. 514, Italian Code of Civil Procedure.

implacàbile—implacable.

implicàto—implicated.

implícito—implicit.

impolítico—impolitic; injudicious.

impollinàre—to pollinate.

impollinazióne f.—pollination.

imponíbile—taxable.

imponiménto m.—imposition.

impórre—to impose; to command; to tax.

importàbile—goods and merchandise which may be imported into a country.

importàre—to import.

importazióne f.—importation.

impórto m.—amount; price; sum.

imposizióne f.—imposition; duty; tax.

impossessàre—to appropriate; to take possession.

impossíbile—impossible.

impossibilità f.—impossibility.

impossibilità sopravvenúta per càusa non imputàbile aí debitóre—impossibility (of performance) due to supervening cause not imputable to the debtor. The obligation is then extinguished. Art. 1256-1259; 1463-1466, Italian Civil Code.

impòsta f.—leaf of a folding door or shutter; the point where the formation of the arch originates.

impòsta f.—impost; duty; tax.

impòsta catastàle—tax on immovables (real property). It is imposed on the transfer of immovables.

impòsta comunàle sugli increménti di valóre degli immòbili (INVIM) — municipal tax on the increase in value of immovables (real property). It is paid by the grantor where there is consideration for the transfer and by the grantee where it is without consideration.

impòsta di bóllo—stamp tax. It is required on commercial paper, documents relating to civil, commercial, judicial and extrajudicial transactions, as well as on writings, documents and registers indicated by law. A statutory fee is charged for the stamp which may be purchased as such or on a stamped or impressed form or paper called càrta bollàta (stamped paper). Bóllo (Impòsta di), Usual Laws, Appendix to Italian Codes of Civil and Penal Procedures.

impòsta di regístro—registration tax. It is a tax on transfers of real property, rentals and creation of rights therein. It is imposed on transfers with or without consideration at the time of registration of the corresponding instruments.

impòsta ipotecària—mortgage tax. It is imposed on recording the mortgage, renewals and satisfactions thereof.

impòsta locàle sui rèdditi (ILOR) — local tax on incomes. It is a second tax, co-existent with the income tax on legal entities and the personal income tax. It is applicable to all incomes produced in the country with the exception of income from wages.

impósta sostitutíva sui rèdditi derivànti da obligazióni e da depòsiti bancàri e postàli—substitute tax on incomes derived from legal obligations and from bank and postal deposits. It is imposed on certain incomes excluded from the taxable total income, and is withheld at the source. See impósta locàle sui rèdditi (ILOR); Impósta sul rèddito delle persóne giurídiche (IRPEG), and impósta sul rèddito delle persóne físiche (IRPEF).

impósta sul rèddito delle persóne físiche (IRPEF) — personal income tax. It is a personal tax on the total net income of the taxpayer from all sources.

impósta sul rèddito delle persóne giurídiche (IRPEG)—income tax on legal entities. It is a tax on corporations and associations or unincorporated organizations.

impósta sul valóre aggiúnto (IVA) — value added tax. It is a tax on the sale of goods and services rendered by a contractor or businessman in the course business as well as on services performed by those in the arts and the professions.

impostàre—to post (an item, a letter, a sentry); to support an arch upon its piers.

impostóre m.—impostor.

impostúra f.—imposture; deceit.

impotènte—impotent.

impotènza f.—impotence. It is a ground for annulment of a marriage or denial of paternity. Art. 123, 235, Italian Civil Code.

impregiudicàbile—that which cannot or should not be prejudged.

impregiudicàto—not prejudged; a person who never has been subjected to a penal proceeding.

impregnàre—to impregnate.

impremeditàto—unpremeditated.

impremeditazióne f.—without premeditation.

imprèndere—to undertake; to start a business; to begin.

imprendíbile—impregnable.

imprenditóre m. — one who professionally conducts an organized economic activity for production and the exchange of goods and services; entrepreneur; businessman; contractor. Art. 2082-2093, Italian Civil Code.

imprenditóre agrícolo — one directly engaged in cultivation of land, in forestry, the breeding of cattle and activities related therewith. Art. 2135, Italian Civil Code.

imprésa f.—undertaking; enterprise; heraldic device; motto.

imprésa agrícola—agricultural undertaking. Art. 2135-2139, Italian Civil Code.

imprésa commerciàle — commercial undertaking. See Art. 2188-2202, Italian Civil Code regarding obligation of registration.

impresàrio m.—manager; stage manager; contractor.

imprescrittíbile—imprescriptible; not subject to prescription.

imprescrittibilità — imprescriptibility; quality of being imprescriptible.

imprescrittibilità dell'azióne di nullità—imprescriptibility of the action to annul a contract. The action to declare the nullity of a contract is not subject to prescription except in the case of adverse possession (20 Years) and in cases of "ripetizióne" (repetition) where a demand or action for restoration of money paid under mistake or an unperformed condition is involved (10 Years). Art. 1422, 2946, Italian Civil Code.

imprestàre—to lend.

impréstito m.—loan.

impreteríbile — indispensable; infallible.

imprevedíbile—unforeseeable.

imprevedibilità f. — unforeseeability. Regarding its effect on certain contracts, see Art. 1467, 1664, 1809, Italian Civil Code.

imprevedúto—unforeseen.

imprevísto—unforeseen.

improbabilità f.—improbability.

improbità f.—improbity; wickedness.

improcedíbile—not subject to prosecution.

improcedibilità f.—quality of not being prosecutable.

imprónta f.—impression; imprint.

imprónte digitàli—fingerprint impressions or projections of other useful signs for the identification of persons, are sent urgently, when necessary, to the appropriate police office, which, when the proper searches have been made, will communicate the findings to the examining magistrate. Art. 309, subd. 4, Italian Code of Penal Procedure.

improponibilità f.—that which cannot be proposed; that which does not give rise to an enforceable claim or cause of action. Its loss cannot be cured. Art. 2969, Italian Civil Code.

improvvidènza f.—improvidence.

imprudènte — imprudent; incautious; lacking prudence or discretion.

imprudènza f.—imprudence; being imprudent; lack of care or discretion. For recovery and indemnification for unjust loss caused fraudulently or negligently, see Art. 2043, Italian Civil Code.

impugnàbile—impugnable; capable of being challenged; contestable; disputable.

impugnabilità f. — impugnability; annulability. Re annulability of contracts, see Art. 1425-1446, Italian Civil Code.

impugnàre—to impugn; to contest; to dispute; to oppose; to take up arms.

impugnatíva f.—a petition for relief; a direct petition to annul a proceeding or judgment.

impugnatúra f.—handle of a sword or tennis racket.

impugnazióne f.—impugnation; challenge; contestation; opposition. A legal remedy to contest, modify or appeal a judgment. Art. 323-338, Ital-

ian Code of Civil Procedure and Art. 190-218, 511-569, Italian Code of Penal Procedure. In *Civil* cases, the procedures followed are: Appèllo, Art. 339-359, Italian Code of Civil Procedure; Ricórso per Cassazióne, Art. 360-391, idem.; Revocazióne, Art. 395-403, idem., and Opposizióne di Tèrzo, Art. 404-408, Italian Code of Civil Procedure. In *Penal* cases, the procedures followed are: Opposizióne al Decréto Penàle di Condànna, Art. 507-510, Italian Code of Penal Procedure; Appèllo, Art. 511-523 and Ricórso per Cassazióne, Art. 524-536. Also, see Revisióne, Art. 533-569; and Incidènte di Fàlso, Art. 215-218, Italian Code of Penal Procedure.

imputàbile — imputable; chargeable; attributable.

imputabilità f.—imputability.

imputabilità del fàtto dannóso—imputability for a harmful act. One who was without capacity at the time of its commission, is not responsible for the consequences thereof unless the state of incapacity is a result of his fault. Art. 2046, Italian Civil Code.

imputabilità penàle — penal imputability. No one may be punished for an act considered as a crime by the law, if, at the moment he committed it, he was not imputable or chargeable. That person is imputable who has the capacity of comprehending the nature and consequences of his acts and the will to make free decisions. No one may be punished for an action or omission considered by the law as a crime, if he has not committed it with conscience and free will. Art. 85, 42, Italian Penal Code. See sospensióne del procediménto; capacità di agíre; maggióre età, and capicità di intèndere e di volère.

imputàre—to impute; to accuse or charge with a crime; to attribute; to ascribe.

imputàto m.—one accused or charged with a crime. Art. 78-90, Italian Code

imputazióne—accusation; charge; imputation; attribution. See collazióne of Penal Procedure.

and collazióne e imputazióne eredi-tària.

imputazióne ereditària—See collazióne e imputazióne ereditària.

imputazióne del pagaménto — indication by a debtor to a creditor that a payment is being made to satisfy a specific debt out of many. Art. 1193, Italian Civil Code.

imputazióne del pagaménto agli interèssi—allocation of payment toward interest. A debtor cannot allocate a payment toward the principal sum due without the creditor's consent but it must be first allocated toward payment of interest and expenses. A payment on account of principal and interest is first allocated toward payment of interest. Art. 1194, Italian Civil Code.

inàbile—not able; unable; lacking the quality required by law to exercise a right; lacking capacity or competency.

inabilità f.—being unable; inability. Also disabilità.

inabilitàre—to disable; to render incapable; to disqualify; a disqualification to act due to mental infirmity but less than interdizióne.

Inabilitazióne f.—disqualification of a person to manage his affairs. Subject to it are: those who have reached majority with mental infirmity not so grave as to warrant interdizióne; those who through prodigality, wasteful extravagance or habitual use of alcoholic beverages or stupefying drugs, expose themselves or their families to grave economic damage; deaf-mutes and the blind from birth or early infancy who have received insufficient education, excepting the application of Art. 414, when it results that they are totally incapable of managing their own affairs. Art. 415, et seq., Italian Civil Code. See persóne che pòssono éssere inabilitàte and interdizióne.

inabitàbile—uninhabitable.

inaccessíbile—unaccessable.

inaccettàbile—unacceptable.

inaccusàbile—not accusable.

inacerbíre—to embitter; to exasperate; to irritate.

inadempíbile—impossible to perform.

inadempiménto m.—non-performance; non-fulfillment. Regarding non-performance of contracts. See Art. 1453-1462, Italian Civil Code.

inadequàto—inadequate.

inadopràbile—not useable; not workable; useless.

inalberàre—to hoist; to raise.

inalienàbile—inalienable; that which cannot be ceded or sold.

inalienabilità f. — inalienability; regarding the inalienability of the family patrimony. See Art. 167-169, Italian Civil Code. Re inalienability of the dowry, see Art. 187-190, Italian Civil Code.

inalteràbile—unalterable.

inalveàre—to allow water to pass into a channel.

inalzàre—to raise or erect; to elevate.

inammendàbile—not amenable to discipline; incorrigible.

inammissíbile—inadmissable.

inamovíbile—irremovable.

inamovibilità f. — irremovability. Judges are irremovable. They may not be exempt from performance, suspended, or transferred without the decision of the Superior Council on the Magistracy. Art. 107, Constitution of the Italian Republic.

inappellàbile—not appealable.

inapprezzàbile—inestimable; priceless.

inappuràbile—that which cannot be ascertained or demonstrated.

inattéso—unexpected.

inattività f.—inactivity.

inattívo—inactive.

inattuàbile—impracticable.

inaudíto—unheard of; incredible.

inavvedutaménte — inadvertently; by mistake.

inavvedúto — inadvertent; unintentional.

incagliàre—to run aground.

incalzàre—to follow closely; to follow in hot pursuit.

incameràre—to transfer private property to the government.

incamminàre—to set on the road; to push forward.

incanalàre—to channelize; to put forward.

incancellàbile—indelible.

incànto m. — auction; auction sale; sale to the highest bidder; charm; enchantment; fascination.

incànto pùbblico—public auction. Art. 537, 581, Italian Code of Civil Procedure. See turbàta libertà degli incànti — disturbed freedom of auctions and nuòvo incànto—new auction.

incapàce—incapable; lacking capacity.

incapacità f. — incapacity; lack of capacity; lacking legal qualification to act. See infermità di ménte.

incarceraménto m.—imprisonment.

incarceràre—to imprison.

incarceràto—imprisoned.

incaricàre—to charge; to entrust with a duty.

incaricàto — charged with; one entrusted with a particular office.

incaricàto d'affàri—chargé d'affaires; a diplomatic representative who safeguards his country's interests in the absence of an Ambassador to a foreign country.

incàrico m.—commission; duty; office; post; that with which one is charged or entrusted.

incassàre—to receive cash; to pack in a case; to place in a coffin; to place the works of a watch in a case; to mount the barrel of a gun on the stock.

incàsso m.—money or cash taken in or received.

incatenàre—to chain; to fetter; to shackle.

incàuto—incautious; unwary.

incàuto acquìsto—incautious purchase. It involves the purchase or receiving of things without ascertaining their legitimate origin when, because of their quality, the condition of the seller, or the nature of the price, it would lead to suspicion that they are the fruits of a crime. See acquìsto di còse di sospètta proveniènza, Art. 712, Italian Penal Code.

incavàre—to hollow; to scoop out.

incàvo m.—that which is hollowed out; chiselled aperture.

incàvi nel mùro—chiselled apertures in a wall used to support beams. Regarding party-walls, see Art. 881-885, Italian Civil Code.

incedìbile—not subject to being ceded; not transferable.

incedibilità f.—that which cannot be ceded or transferred. See Art. 447, 1260, 1261, 1624, 2149, 2169, Italian Civil Code.

incèndere—to burn; to light a fire.

incendiàre — to set on fire; to burn down.

incendiàrio m.—incendiary; one who maliciously sets fire to buildings or property.

incèndio m.—fire; conflagration; arson; burning. Whoever causes a fire is punished with imprisonment. This disposition also applies in the event of a fire to one's own home, if it endangers the public safety. Art. 423, Italian Penal Code. See incèndio dolóso.

incèndio colpóso—fire through negligence. The act of causing a fire negligently which may endanger public safety, is punishable with imprisonment. Art. 449, Italian Penal Code.

incèndio di càsa abitàta da piú inquilìni—burning of a multifamily house. In this case, all tenants are responsible to the lessor for the damage caused by the fire in proportion to the value of the part occupied by them. If the lessor resides in the house, the value of the part occupied by him is deducted. The foregoing disposition is not applicable if it is proven that the fire originated in the dwelling of one of the tenants or if one of them proves that the fire could not have started in his dwelling. Art. 1611, Italian Civil Code.

incèndio di còsa assicuràta—burning of an insured thing. If the thing destroyed by fire was insured by the lessor or his agent, the responsibility of the leasee towards the lessor is limited to the difference between the damages recovered from the insurer and the actual damages. In the case of personal property, where the insured object was appraised and the recovery was equal to it, all responsibility ceases. Art. 1589, Italian Civil Code.

incèndio dolóso—arson with criminal intent. It involves the burning of another's property, thereby endangering the public safety. See incèndio, Art. 423-425, Italian Penal Code.

inceneràre—to strew with ashes.

inceneríre—to reduce to ashes; to incinerate.

incensuràto—uncensored; one who has not been subjected to a penal proceeding.

incèsto m.—incest. Art. 564, Italian Penal Code.

incestuóso—incestuous. See filiazióne.

incètta f.—cornering a market; monopoly; the common term for the surreptitious acquisition of a considerable quantity of a specific commodity or goods with the intent of reselling same at a higher price by changing the market price. See riàlzo e ribàsso fraudolènto di prèzzi sul pùbblico mercàto o nelle bórse di commèrcio, Art. 501, Italian Penal Code.

incettàre—to acquire surreptitiously a considerable quantity of a specific commodity or goods with the intent of reselling same at a higher price by changing the market price; to corner a market; to monopolize.

incettatóre m.—one who performs the act of incettàre as above described.

inchiésta f.—inquest; investigation.

inciàmpo m.—stumbling block.

incidentàle—incidental.

incidènte m. — incident; procedural question which arises as a secondary issue during the course of a trial.

incidènti di fàlso — false, forged or altered Acts or documents impugned or challenged by the public prosecutor or the parties to an action. Such challenge may be made at any stage of a proceeding. Art. 215-218, Italian Code of Penal Procedure. See querèla di fàlso.

incídere—to incise; to cut into; to engrave; to become usbject to or liable to.

incídere in légem (Lat.)—to incur or become subject to penalty of a law.

incínta—pregnant.

incipriàre—to powder (the face).

incisióne f.—incision.

incitàre—to incite.

inclito—famous; illustrious.

incoàre—to start; to launch.

incoàto—commenced; begun.

incoercíbile—incoercible.

incoerènte—incoherent.

incola m.—inhabitant; resident; one who has transferred his domicile to another country; one who has the right to remain undisturbed in a country. (Also, Latin).

incolàto m.—a resident of a country who has immigrated there and has the right to remain undisturbed.

incolleríre—to grow angry.

incolpàbile—blameless; not blameable.

incolpàre—to accuse; to inculpate.

incolpàto—blameless; not guilty, used as a plea in a criminal action. Sometimes refers to the accùsed. See imputàto.

incolpatóre—accuser.

incolpévole—innocent; free of blame.

incòlume—safe; unharmed.

incolumità f.—quality of being safe unharmed.

incolumità pùbblica (delítti cóntro)—crimes against public safety and welfare. See Art. 422-452, Italian Penal Code.

incombènte—incumbent.

incombènte m.—the proof during the examination in the istruttòria phase of a trial.

incommerciàbile—not marketable.

incompatíbile—incompatible.

incompatibilità f.—incompatibility.

incompensàbile—not compensable.

incompetènte—incompetent.

incompetènza f.—incompetence.

inconfessàbile—that which cannot be confessed without shame.

inconfessàto or inconfèsso — unconfessed.

inconsapévole — not knowing; ignorant; uninformed.

incònscio—unaware.

inconsuèto—unaccustomed.

inconsúlto—unreflecting; thoughtless.

inconsumàbile—not consumable.

inconsumàbili (bèni) — inconsumable goods or things. Those things which may be used more than once.

incontestàbile—incontestable.

incontestabilità f.—incontestability.

incontinènte—incontinent.

incontrastàbile—incontestable.

incontrastàto — uncontested; undoubted.

inconvertíbile—unconvertible.

inconvertibilità f. — unconvertibility; immutability.

incorporàle — incorporeal; without body; not of a material nature.

incorporàre—to incorporate.

incorporazióne f.—incorporation; the establishment of one corporation out of several or many or a merger of several or many into one which continues in existence. See Art. 2501-2504, Italian Civil Code and fusióne.

incorpòreo — incorporeal; without body; not material.

incorreggíbile—incorrigible.

incorròtto—incorrupted.

incorrutíbile—incorruptible.

incorruttibilità f.—incorruptability.

incosciènte—without conscience; without moral sense or quality.

incostànte—inconstant; fickle.

incostituzionàle—unconstitutional.

incostituzionalità f. — unconstitutionality.

increménto m.—increment.

incriminàbile—liable to prosecution.

incriminàre—to incriminate.

incriminazióne f.—accusation; incrimination.

incrociatóre m.—cruiser; a class of warships of medium tonnage, high speed and long cruising range.

incruènto—bloodless.

íncubo m.—incubus; nightmare.

incúlto—uncultivated; rough.

incuràbile—incurable.

incurabilità f.—incurability.

incurànte—careless; heedless; negligent.

incursióne f.—incursion.

incustodíto—unguarded.

indagaménto m.—investigation.

indagàre—to investigate.

indagatóre m.—investigator.

indagazióne f.—investigation.

indàgine f.—investigation; inquiry.

indébita limitazióne di libertà personàle—unjust restriction of personal freedom. It is committed by a public official in charge of a penal institution when receiving a person without an order of commitment, or in disobeying an order releasing a person or unduly delaying execution of the sentence or taking appropriate security measures. Art. 607, Italian Penal Code.

indebitaménte—unduly; wrongfully.

indebitaménto m.—indebtedness.

indebitàre—to incur debt.

indébito—undue; unjust.

indébito oggettívo — objective undue payment. Whoever has made a payment which is not due, has the right to restitution of that which he has paid. He has, besides, the right to the gains and interest from the day of payment if the one who received it acted in bad faith, or if the latter acted in good faith, from the day of demand for restitution. Art. 2033, Italian Civil Code. See **pagaménto dell'indébito.**

indébito soggettívo—subjective undue payment. Whoever has paid the debt of another, believing himself to be a debtor on the basis of an excusable error, may have restitution of that which he has paid, provided that the creditor has not been deprived in good faith of title or guarantees of credit. The one who has received the undue payment is also held to make restitution of the gains and interest from the day of payment, if he acted in bad faith, or from the day of demand for restitution if he acted in good faith. When restitution is not allowed, the one who has made payment succeeds to the rights of the creditor. Art. 2036, Italian Civil Code. See **pagaménto dell'indébito.**

indebolíre—to weaken.

indecènte—indecent.

indecènza f.—indedency.

indecifràbile—undecipherable.

indecisióne f.—indecision.

indefiníbile—indefinable.

indefiníto—indefinite.

indegnaménte—unworthily.

indegnità f.—affront; mean action; indignity. See Art. 463, Italian Civil Code, which excludes from the succession a person who has committed certain specified crimes.

Indégno—unworthy.

indènne—free of damage; unharmed.

indecènza f.—indecency.

Indennizzàre—to indemnify.

indennízzo m.—indemnity.

inderogàbile—not subject to derogation; that which cannot be diminished or lessened.

inderogabilità f.—the quality of not being diminished or lessened. See

Art. 160, 1932, 2113, 2936, Italian Civil Code, for rights which cannot be diminished or relinquished.

indicàto—indicated; pointed out; suitable.

indicazióne f.—indication.

índice m.—index; second finger of the hand.

indifendíbile—indefensible.

indiféso—undefended.

indigènte—indigent.

indíre—to announce.

indirízzo m.—direction; guidance; address (of a letter); address of a public body to a notable person; dedication of a book; domicile of a draft or bill of exchange.

indirízzo della víta familiàre e residènza della famíglia—direction and guidance of family life and fixing of its residence. It is assigned to both spouses, acting in accord. Art. 144, Italian Civil Code.

indisciplinàbile—not subject to discipline; incorrigible.

indisciplinàto—undisciplined.

indispensàbile—indispensable.

indisponíbile — undisposable; unfree. See **disponíbile.**

indissolúbile—dissoluble.

indistruttíbile—indestructable.

individuàre—to individualize; to characterize; to specify.

individuazióne f.—specification; selection; identification (of property). See Art. 1378, 1465, 2659, 2809, 2826, Italian Civil Code.

indivisíbile—indivisable.

indiziàre—to point to; to give indication of a crime or fault.

indízio m.—circumstance; a suspicious circumstance tending to show guilt; indication; a sign; circumstantial evidence.

indizióne f.—indiction; a cyclical fifteen year period in the Roman Empire fixing property valuation as a basis for taxation.

indugiàre—to delay; to temporize.

indúgio m.—delay; defer; postponement.

indúlto—a dispensation granted by an ecclesiastic authority; condonation or remission of a penalty. It is granted by the President of the Republic. Art. 79, Constitution of the Italian Republic. Art. 174, Italian Penal Code; Art. 591-596, Italian Code of Penal Procedure.

induzióne f.—inducement.

induzióne al matrimònio mediànte ingànno — inducement to marriage through fraud. It is committed when there is an impediment to marriage which leads to an annulment because of the concealed impediment. Art. 558, Italian Penal Code.

inebriaménto m.—intoxication.

inebbriàre or inebriàre—to intoxicate; to inebriate.

ineccepíbile—that to which an exception cannot be taken.

inèdito—unpublished.

ineleggíbile—ineligible.

inelleggibilità f.—ineligibility.

ineluttàbile—inevitable.

inemendabíle—beyond correction; incorrigible.

inerènte—inherent.

inèrme—unarmed.

inèrte—inert; inoperative.

inèrzia f.—inertness; inertia.

inesaudíbile—that which cannot be heard or listened to.

inesauríbile—inexhaustable.

inescogitàbile—unimaginable.

inescusàbile—inexcusable.

inescusàto—inexcused.

ineseguíbile—impractical.

infamàre—to defame; to calumniate; to slander.

infamatóre m.—defamer; slanderer.

infamatòrio—defamatory; slanderous.

infàme—infamous.

infàmia f.—infamy.

infamità f.—infamy.

infanticídio m.—infanticide. Art. 578, Italian Penal Code.

infantilísmo m.—infantilism.

infànzia f.—infancy.

infàrto m.—infarct.

infàusto—inauspicious; unlucky.

infecondità f.—infecundity; sterility.

infecóndo—barren; sterile.

infedèle m.—infidel.

infedèle—unfaithful; disloyal.

infedelità f. — infidelity; unfaithfulness; disloyalty.

infelloníre—to commit cruel or felonious acts.

infènso—hostile.

infèrie f.—sacrifices offered by the ancients on the tombs of the departed.

infermàre—to render infirm; to fall sick; to weaken or nullify (a law).

infermería f.—infirmary.

infermière m. (infermièria f.)—nurse.

infermità f.—infirmity.

infermità di ménte—mental infirmity. See Art. 414-432, Italian Civil Code, and capacità and incapacità.

infèrmo—infirm; sick; weak.

inferriàta f.—iron grill over a window.

infértile—infertile; barren; unproductive.

infertilíre—to fertilize.

infertilità f.—infertility; barrenness.

infestàre—to infest.

infettàre—to infect.

infettívo—infectious.

infeudaménto m.—enfeoffment; the act of investing with a dignity or a possession.

infeudàre—to enfeoff.

infeudazióne f.—enfeoffment.

infezióne f.—infection.

infiammàre—to inflame; to ignite or set afire.

infiammazióne f.—inflammation.

inficiàre—to retract a confession, deposition, testimony or signature; to declare suspect or false; to deny.

infído—faithless; false.

infiltrazióne f.—infiltration.

ínfimo—basest; lowest; vilest.

infíngere—to pretend; to simulate.

infirmàre—to weaken; to invalidate; to confute.

infiscalíre — to use excessive fiscal measures; to make more severe or rigorous; to become a fiscal officer.

infissióne di chiúsa — placing of enclosure or dam on a waterway. Art. 1047, 1048, Italian Civil Code.

inflazióne f.—inflation.

inflíggere—to inflict; to impose a penalty.

inflizióne f.—infliction; imposition of a penalty.

influènza f.—influence; influenza.

infocàre—to inflame.

infondàto—unfounded.

informàre—to inform; to give form.

informazióne f.—information.

infórme—formless; shapeless.

infortúnio m. — disaster; mischance; accident.

infralíre—to become weak.

infràngere—to break; to crush; to shatter.

infrangíbile—unbreakable; inviolable.

infrangiménto m.—infraction; breaking.

infrascrítto—undersigned.

infrazióne f.—infraction (of law); violation; act of breaking.

infrenàbile—unrestrainable.

infrenàre—to restrain.

infruttífero or infruttuóso—fruitless; unfruitful.

infunghíre—to become mouldy.

infungíbile—not fungible.

infuriàre—to become furious; to rage.

infuriàto—enraged; in a furious hurry.

ingabbiàre—to cage; to enclose in a cage.

ingaggiàre—to engage; to enlist.

ingàggio m. — enlistment; earnest money; deposit.

ingannàbile—deceitful.

ingannàre—to deceive.

ingannatóre m.—deceiver; cheat.

ingannévole—deceitful.

ingànno m.—deceit; error; trick.

ingarbugliàre—to entangle; to involve in trouble.

ingarbuglióne m.—deceiver; meddler; intriguer.

ingegnère m.—engineer.

ingegneria f.—engineering.

ingégno m.—genius; talent; contrivance; lock mechanism.

ingiudicàto—unjudged.

ingiúngere—to command; to enjoin; to impose; to order.

ingiunzióne f.—injunction; a special, summary proceeding. See Procediménto di ingiunzióne.

ingiunzióne di pagaménto di spése, dirítti ed onoràri—order fixing payment of expenses, rights and honorariums. It is prepared by the court clerk in civil matters from the filed records. Fixing, taxing, or assessing costs. See prenotazióne a débito. Art. 43, Enabling Rules, Italian Code of Civil Procedure.

ingiúria f.—abuse; injury; insult; offense to a person's honor; defamation. It is a crime against a person who is present when defamatory statements are made concerning him. The same penalty applies when the statements are directed to him by telegraphic or telephonic communication or by writings or drawings. Art. 594, Italian Penal Code. See diffamazióne and delítti cóntro l'onóre.

ingiúrie (pl.) f.—abuses; injuries; insults. As a ground for separation where grave abuse, threats and injuries result, see Art. 151, Italian Civil Code. As a ground for revocation of a gift where serious injury to the donor results, see Art. 801, Italian Civil Code and ingratitúdine.

Ingiustízia f.—injustice.

ingiústo—unjust.

ingombràre—to encumber; to burden.

ingómbro m.—encumbrance; burden; hindrance; obstruction.

ingómbro della carreggiàta—obstruction of the road or highway.

ingovernàbile—ungovernable.

ingratitúdine f. — ingratitude. As a cause for the revocation of a gift, see Art. 800-803, 805, 808, Italian Civil Code.

ingràto — ingrate; unfruitful; unproductive.

ingraziàre—to ingratiate.

Ingrèsso m.—ingress; entrance.

Ingrèsso abusívo nel fóndo altrúi — wrongful entrance on the land of another. Art. 637, Italian Penal Code.

ingròsso (all')—wholesale.

Inguaríbile—incurable.

Inibíre—to inhibit.

inibitòria—an order inhibiting or suspending a judgment. See Art. 283, 351, 373, 401, 407, Italian Code of Civil Procedure.

inibitòrio—prohibitory. See inibitòria.

inidòneo—not idoneous; not able; unfit; unsuitable; incompetent. See idòneo and sui juris.

Iniezióne f.—injection.

inimicàre—to treat as an enemy; to make an enemy of someone.

inimicízia f.—enmity.

inimíco m.—enemy.

inflammàbile—inflammable.

iniquità f.—iniquity.

iníquo—iniquitous; wicked.

iniziàle—initial.

Iniziàre—to initiate.

Iniziatíva f.—initiative.

innavigàbile—unnavigable.

innegàbile—undeniable.

innestàre—to graft into a tissue or plant.

Innèsto m.—graft of tissue or plant.

innocènte m.—innocent; foundling.

innocívo—harmless.

innòcuo—innocuous; harmless.

innominàbile—unnameable; unspeakable.

innominàto — unnamed; anonymous. See contràtti innominàti.

innovazióne f.—innovation; renewal; addiction; See Art. 986, 1067, 1108, 1120, 1582, 1618, Italian Civil Code.

inoccupàto—not occupied; not taken; unemployed. For latter, see disoccupàto.

inofficióso—inofficious; not in accordance with moral duty; a will contrary to the dictates of natural affection; a will which may not be valid because it disinherits certain heirs of a portion of the estate to which they are legally entitled. See legíttima.

inondàre—to inundate; to submerge.

inondazióne f. — inundation. It is a crime punishable with imprisonment to cause an inundation or to damage protective works against it. Art. 426, 427, Italian Penal Code.

ínope—poor.

inòpia f.—poverty; need; want.

inopinàbile — unimaginable; unforeseeable.

inoppugnàbile—incontestable.

inosservànza f.—inobservance; violation.

inosservànza dei provvediménti dell'-autorità—inobservance or violation of the measures of the Authorities. Whoever fails to observe a measure legally issued by the Authorities for reasons of justice or public security or hygiene, is punishable with arrest or fine unless the act constitutes a more serious offense. Art. 650, Italian Penal Code.

inosservànza di péna—violation of a sentence. It is committed by a condemned person who violates the terms and obligations of a sentence.

inosservànza di péne accessòrie—violation of accessory penalties. Whoever receives a sentence which results in interdiction from public offices or interdiction or suspension from a profession or art, and violates the obligations inherent in such punishments is punished with imprisonment or fine. The same penalty is imposed on one who violates the obligations flowing from a temporary suspension of the exercise of public offices, profession or art. Art. 389, Italian Penal Code.

inquilíno m.—tenant.

inquinaménti—pollutions; contaminations; uncleanness. See **inquinaménto atmosfèrico.**

inquinaménto m. — act of polluting; pollution; contamination.

inquinaménto atmosfèrico — atmospheric pollution; air pollution. Inquinaménti (Pollutions), Usual Laws,, Appendix to Italian Code of Penal Procedure. See **immissióne di fúmo,** etc., Art. 844, Italian Civil Code.

inquinàre—to contaminate; to pollute; to soil.

inquinazióne m.—See **inquinaménto.**

inquirènte—researching; investigating.

inquisíre—to accuse; to charge; to examine; to investigate; to search suspected premises.

inquisitóre m.—inquisitor.

inquisizióne f.—inquisition; examination; search.

insalúbre — insalubrious; unhealthy; unwholesome.

insanàbile—incurable; irremediable.

insanguinàre—to stain with blood.

insània f.—insanity; madness.

insàno—insane; mad.

insaziàbile—insatiable.

inscenàre—to put on stage or prepare a scene for some action.

insediàre—to install.

inségna f.—insignia; an emblem or trade name representing a particular business. Art. 2563-2568, Italian Civil Code.

Insegnànte—teaching.

insegnànte m.—teacher; instructor.

insegnàre—to teach; to instruct.

inseguíre—to pursue.

insempràrsi—to perpetuate; to be perpetual.

insensíbile—insensible; unfeeling.

inseparàbile—inseparable.

insepólto—unburied..

insequestràbile—not subject to sequestration.

inseríre—to insert.

inservíbile—unserviceable.

inserzióne f.—insertion. For insertion of clauses in contracts, see Art. 1339, 1340, Italian Civil Code.

insígne—renowned; famous.

insigníre—to decorate; to honor.

insindacàbile—not subject to criticism; not reviewable.

insinuàre—to insinuate; to present a claim by a creditor in a bankruptcy proceeding.

insinuazióne f.—insinuation; presentation of a claim by a creditor in a bankruptcy proceeding.

insolúbile—insoluble.

insolúto—unresolved; unpaid; untied.

insolvènte—insolvent; inability to pay one's debts or creditors.

insolvènza f.—insolvency; inability to pay debts as they fall due or in the regular course of business. Art. 5-8, 16, 195, 202, 203, Falliménto (Bankruptcy), Usual Laws, Appendix to Italian Civil Code.

insolvíbile — that which cannot be paid; insolvent debtor.

insórgere — to rise up in arms; to rebel; to rise in insurrection.

insorgiménto m.—insurrection.

insosteníbile—not sustainable; indefensible.

installàre—to install; to accommodate.

installazióne f.—installation.

instàre—to insist.

instauràre—to instaurate; to renew; to find; to install.

institóre m.—institor; agent; deputy; incumbent of a post; representative;

a business representative or agent. He is appointed by power of attorney and can manage the business of which he has been charged with the exception of those things not authorized. He cannot alienate or mortgage real property unless expressly authorized. He may bring actions in the name of the principal in matters affecting the business he manages. See Art. 2203-2208, Italian Civil Code.

institòria (aziόne)—an action involving the institor.

institòrio—referring to the institor.

instituíre—to institute; to found; to establish; to appoint an heir in a will. Also, **istituíre**.

insurreziόne f.—insurrection. Regarding the responsibility of an insurer for damages caused by insurrection, see **terremòto, guèrra, insurreziόne, tumúlti popolàri.**

intangíbile—intangible.

integràre—to integrate; to complete; to make whole or entire.

integraziόne f.—integration.

integraziόne del contràtto — integration of the contract. The contract obliges the parties not only to what is expressed therein, but also to all the consequences derived therefrom according to law, or in its absence, according to custom or usage and equity. Art. 1374, Italian Civil Code.

integraziόne del giudízio—integration of the trial. It consists of joining a third party to the litigation in order to properly resolve and prosecute the action.

integrità f.—integrity; state of being entire or undiminished.

integrità personàle (dirítto all') — right to personal integrity and security. It consists in the faculty of each person to repel any attempt against the integrity and security of his own body. It is a right, independent of contract, to be free of unlawful interference with the person similar to a tort. See Art. 575-593, Italian Penal Code and delítti cóntro la persόna.

integrità psíchica e sociàle (dirítto all')—right to psychic and social integrity and security. It permits the redress of certain wrongs (torts) by means of the Penal Code. Such are every attempt against the good name, fame, reputation and credit of a person. They include the crimes of abuse and defamation (Art. 594-599); malicious prosecution (Art. 368), Italian Penal Code and infringement of the right of authorship, Art. 2577, Italian Civil Code; Autόre (Dirítto di), Usual Laws, Appendix to Italian Code of Civil Procedure.

íntegro — entire; complete; just; upright.

intelligènza f.—intelligence; information; knowledge.

intelligènza segréta — secret intelligence; gathering or distribution of secret information.

intelligènze col nemíco—intelligence with the enemy. See **disfattísmo econòmico, disfattísmo político** and **personalità dello stàto (delítti cóntro la).**

intelligènze con lo stranièro per impegnàre lo stàto Italiano alla neutralità o alla guèrra—intelligence with a foreigner to engage the Italian State to neutrality or to war. Art. 245, Italian Penal Code and Personalità dello stàto (delítti cóntro la).

intemperànza f.—intemperance.

intemperàto—intemperate.

intempèrie f.—inclement weather.

intempestívo—inopportune; unseasonable; untimely.

intendènte—understanding; attentive.

intendènte m.—intendent; one who has the direction and management of a public administrative department; the title of such official; superintendent.

intendènza f. — intendance; intendancy; the office of intendant who has the direction and management of a public department.

intèndere—to comprehend; to understand; to intend; to mean; to have a purpose of mind. See **capacità d'intèndere e di volére.**

intentàre—to bring an action.

intentàto—unattempted; unexplored; untried.

intènto m.—intent.

intènto—attentive; diligent; tense.

intenzióne f.—intention.

intenzióne dei contraènti — intention of the contracting parties. In ascertaining the meaning of a contract, the mutual intention of the parties must be examined without being limited by the literal meaning of the words. See Art. 1362-1371, Italian Civil Code.

intenzióne del legislatóre—legislative intent. See **interpretazióne della légge.**

interchiúdere or interclúdere—to enclose; to shut in; to close a passage; to impede.

interclusióne del fóndo—enclosure of land without passage. See **passàgio coatívo,** Art. 1051-1055, Italian Civil Code.

interdétto m.—interdict; interdiction; injunction; prohibition; prohibitory decree.

interdizióne f.—interdiction. Civilly, it is a judicial decree interdicting an incompetent from managing his own affairs and appointing a guardian to do so. Art. 414 et seq., Italian Civil Code. Penally, it connotes a number of accessory penalties attached to certain crimes, such as interdiction to hold office or to practice a profession or art. Legal interdiction applies to a life sentence. Art. 28-37, Italian Penal Code. See **inabilitazióne** and **persóne che dèvono èssere interdètte.**

interdizióne da una professióne o da un'àrte—interdiction from a profession or art. It deprives the convicted person from exercising a profession, art, industry, commerce or occupation during the period of the interdiction. Its duration is not less than one month nor more than five years. Art. 30, Italian Penal Code.

interdizióne dai púbblici uffíci—interdiction from public offices. This may be perpetual or temporary. *Perpetual interdiction* deprives a convicted person of the right to hold public office, of voting and of political rights. It also deprives him from acting as guardian or trustee and from receiving decorations, public honors and academic rank as well as from serving in the military services or from receiving certain State benefits. *Temporary interdiction* deprives the convicted person of acquiring or exercising the same rights during the period of interdiction. Temporary interdiction may not last less than one year nor more than five. A life sentence or one for not less than five years, incurs perpetual interdiction. A sentence to a period not less than three years, incurs interdiction (temporayr) for five years. Art. 28, 29, Italian Penal Code.

interdizióne legàle—legal interdiction. For those sentenced to life, it involves loss of parental and marital authority and capacity to make a will. A will made prior to conviction is null. One convicted to imprisonment for a period of not less than five years is, during imprisonment, in a state of legal interdiction with the suspension of the exercise of paternal and marital authority, unless otherwise ordered by the judge. He also loses the power to manage his property and estate. Art. 32-34, Italian Penal Code; Art. 587, Italian Code of Penal Procedure.

interèsse m.—interest; a right in the ownership of property; the payment for the use of borrowed money; the return on invested capital.

interèssi (pl.) m.—interest or return on capital. Art. 820, 1194, 1224, 1282, 1283, 1284, 1499, Italian Civil Code.

interèssi compensatívi—compensative interest. It arises, independently, out of the same transaction where two debts exist simultaneously and are both liquidated and demandable. Art. 1499, 1282, Italian Civil Code.

interèssi convenzionàli—conventional

interest. Where the rate of interest has not been fixed by the parties, the rate of interest is deemed to be the legal rate as set by law. Art. 1284, Italian Civil Code.

interèssi corrispettívi—corresponding interest. That which a user of capital must pay a creditor for the use thereof. Art. 1499, 1282, Italian Civil Code.

interèssi legàli — legal interest. The legal rate of interest is set by law. Interest rates above the legal rate must be reduced to writing to be enforceable. Art. 1284, Italian Civil Code.

interèssi moratòri—interest on default. The interest owed by the debtor on default in meeting fulfillment of his obligation. Art. 1224, Italian Civil Code.

interèssi usuràri—usurious interest. It consists of an excessive and usurious rate of interest, the rate not being specified. The legal rate is set by current law, and rates in excess may be charged if reduced to writing. Usury involves taking advantage of a borrower's needs by the lender and is a crime. Art. 644, Italian Penal Code; Art. 1284, Italian Civil Code. See interèssi legàli and usúra.

interlocutòrio — interlocutory; provisional; temporary; intermediate; not final; not definitive; pertaining to a provisional order, decision or judgment.

interlocuzióne f.—interlocution; conversation; conference; dialogue; an interlocutory order or judgment.

interloquíre—to intervene (in a discussion); to issue an interlocutory order.

internaménto m.—internment.

internàre—to intern; to restrict or oblige to reside within a prescribed area.

interpellànza f. — interpellation; a formal request for an explanation in Parliament by a member thereof of a minister regarding an act or policy of the government. It usually leads to a vote of confidence.

interpellàre—to interrupt; to present something in opposition; to interrogate someone in authority to obtain his opinion; to interpellate.

interpetràre or interpretàre—to interpret.

interpetrazióne or interpretazióne f.—interpretation.

interpretazióne analògica—analogical interpretation; the process used by judges in deciding a case that is without legal precedent. See interpretazióne della légge.

interpretazióne della légge—interpretation of the law. In applying the law, there cannot be attributed to it any other meaning than that made manifest by the proper significance of the words according to their context and the legislative intent. Art. 12, Preliminary Dispositions.

intèrpetre or intèrprete m. & f.—interpreter.

interposizióne f.—interposition.

interposizióne di persóna — See persóna interpósta.

interrégno m.—interval between the reigns of two monarchs; the vacancy which exists when there is no government.

interrogàre—to interrogate.

interrogatòrio—interrogatory. Art. 228-232, Italian Code of Civil Procedure and Art. 245, 365-368, 441-446, Italian Code of Penal Procedure.

interrogazióne f.—interrogation.

interrómpere—to interrupt.

interròtto—interrupted.

interruzióne f.—interruption.

interruzióne del procésso — interruption of the civil cause of action. Art. 299-305, Italian Code of Civil Procedure.

interruzióne della prescrizióne—interruption of prescription. Art. 2943-2945, Italian Civil Code. Re: interruption of prescription on a servitude, see Art. 1165, 1167 Italian Civil Code. Re: interruption of prescription on drafts, see Art. 95 Cambiàle (Drafts), Usual Laws, Appendix to

Italian Civil Code. See Art. 160, Italian Penal Code.

interveniènte m.—intervenor.

intervenìre—to intervene.

intervènto m. — intervention; the appearance of a third party in a pending suit between others. See accettazióne per intervènto.

intervenúto—intervened; one who has been brought in.

intervenzióne f.—intervention. See intervènto.

interversióne del possèsso—conversion of title by possession. It is similar in nature to title by adverse possession. Art. 1164, 1102, 1141, Italian Civil Code. See usucapióne.

intimàre—to intimate; to order with authority and peremptorily; to enjoin; to give notice of a process.

intimazióne—a judicial order or command.

intimazióne di licènza e di sfràtto per finìta locazióne—a notice to terminate a lease and to quit premises. See disdétta and licènza per finìta locazióne (intimazióne di).

intimazióne di pagaménto—notice of payment. It is sent by the creditor to the debtor in writing, through a judicial officer similar to a marshal, demanding payment of an obligation. Art. 1209, Italian Civil Code. See offèrta per intimazióne.

intimazióne di ricévere la conségna di un immòbile —. Notice to receive transfer of real property. Where the obligation is to turn over possession of real property, the offer consists in notice to the creditor to take possession of it. The notice must be made in the form prescribed by law. The debtor, after notice to the creditor, may obtain the appointment of a sequestrator from a judge. In this event, the debtor is discharged from the moment he turns over the property to the sequestrator. Art. 1216, Italian Civil Code. Also, offèrta per intimazióne di ricévere la conségna di un immòbile.

intossicazióne f.—intoxication.

intrallàzzo m. (Sicilian)—black market; contraband.

intramésso m.—entremets (Fr.); sidedish.

intraméttere—to interpose; to intervene.

intrapendènte—enterprising.

intraprèndere—to undertake; to engage in.

intraprenditóre m.—contractor; entrepreneur; undertaker of a project.

intrattenére—to amuse; to entertain; to engage.

intrigànte—intriguer; meddler.

intrigàre—to intrigue; to confuse; to embroil.

intrìgo m.—intrigue.

introméttere—to introduce; to insert.

intrugliàre—to mingle; to spoil; to waste; to mix; to make unclear.

inúlto—unavenged.

inumàre—to bury.

inumazióne f.—inhumation; burial.

invàdere—to invade.

invaghíre—to charm; to inflame with desire.

invalére—to become established.

invalidàre—to render invalid; to invalidate; to annul.

invalidità f.—invalidity; nullity.

invàlido — invalid; infirm; without legal effect or validity.

invasióne f.—invasion.

invasóre m.—invader.

invecchiàre—to grow old.

inveíre—to inveigh; to attack vehemently with words.

invelenìre—to embitter; to irritate.

invendíbile—unsaleable.

invendicàto—unavenged.

invendúto—unsold.

invènia (invènie pl.) f.—cajolery; affectation; humiliation; request for pardon.

inventàrio m.—inventory; where required, see Art. 52, 64, 302, 362-365,

484-511; 705, 1002; 2217, 2277, Italian Civil Code; Art. 87, 172 Falliménto (Bankruptcy), Usual Laws, Appendix to Italian Civil Code and Art. 769-777, Italian Code of Civil Procedure.

invenzióne f. — invention; finding (a lost article) from the Latin, inventio. It is one of the means of acquiring title to property. Art. 922, 927-933, Italian Civil Code.

inversióne f.—inversion; agreements are void which invert or modify the burden of proof regarding rights which cannot be disposed, or when the inversion or modification renders the exercise of a right by one of the parties excessively difficult. Art. 2698, Italian Civil Code. See pàtti relatívi all' ònere della pròva.

investíbile—that which can be invested (capital).

investigàbile—that which can be investigated.

investigàre—to investigate.

investigazióne f.—investigation.

investiménto m.—investment of capital; investment in office; accident; collision.

investiménto (òbblighi del conducènte in càso di)—collision (obligations of the driver in case of). The driver of a vehicle in case of a collision where a person is hit, has the obligation of stopping and offering necessary help to the person who was struck. Failure to stop involves the offense of contravvenzióne for the fúga or flight, and the crime of delítto for the omission to offer help or assistance. Art. 133, Còdice Stradàle (Code of the Road).

investíre—to invest; to invest into an office; to invest money; to surround with military forces; to besiege; to strike against someone or something as in an accident or collision; to vest.

investitúra f.—investiture; investment into office or dignity.

inviolàbile—inviolable.

invítto—unconquered.

involaménto m.—theft.

involàre—to steal; to take away furtively; to take flight.

invòlgere—to wrap up; to contain; to involve.

involgiménto m.—wrapper; container.

invòlto — package; that which is wrapped up.

ipnòsi f.—hypnosis.

ipnotísmo m.—hypnotism.

ipocrisía f.—hypocrisy.

ipòcrita m.—hypocrite.

ipotèca f.—hypothec; mortgage; security for the repayment of a debt; a lien by a creditor on property of his debtor which remains in possession of the debtor. The mortgage is placed on real property and specified personal property and is registered or recorded. Art. 2808-2899, Italian Cinvil Code.

ipotèca giudiziàle—judicial mortgage. This mortgage is the result of a judgment of a court such as a money judgment, or one that directs the fulfillment of an obligation or one for money damages. It becomes a lien on the debtor's property and can be registered or recorded. Art. 2818-2820, Italian Civil Code. Art. 2819 provides that an arbitrator's award may become a mortgage lien and be recorded.

ipotèca legàle—legal mortgage. It is granted by law to: (1) the alienor of real property transferred for the fulfillment of the obligations which proceed from the act of alienation; (2) co-heirs, partners and other co-sharers for the payment of their respective amounts based upon the real property encumbered; (3) a wife on the property of the husband to guarantee restitution of the dowry, notwithstanding any agreement to the contrary; (4) the State upon property of the accused or person civilly liable according to the provisions of the Penal Code and the Code of Penal Procedure. Art. 2817, Italian Civil Code; Art. 189-191, Italian Penal Code; Art. 616, 618-620, Italian Code of Penal Procedure. Art. 69, Falliménto (Bankruptcy), Usual Laws, Appendix to Italian Civil Code.

ipotèca volontària — voluntary mortgage. A mortgage may also be granted unilaterally. The grant must be made by public Act or by private writing or it is void. It cannot be granted by will or testament. Art. 2821-2826, Italian Civil Code.

irremissíbile—without remission.

irremovíbile—unmovable.

irreparàbile—irreparable.

irreperíbile—not to be found; undiscoverable.

irreprimíbile—irrepressible.

irrepugnàbile—irrefutable; not subject to contradiction.

irretroattività f.—the quality of not being retroactive.

irretroattività della légge—the non-retroactivity of the law. The law prescribes for the future; it has no retroactive effect. Art. 11, Preliminary Dispositions, Italian Civil Code; Art. 25, Constitution of the Italian Republic.

irreversíbile—irreversible.

irrevocàbile—irrevocable.

irrevocabilità f.—irrevocability.

irriconoscíbile—unrecognizable.

irriducíbile—irreducible.

irrilevànte—irrelevant.

irrilevànza f. — irrelevance; irrelevancy.

irrimediàbile—irremediable.

irrisarcíbile—not compensable.

írrito—void; null; without effect.

irrogàre—to inflict a penalty.

irruènte — rushing in; that which enters furiously.

irruzióne f.—irruption.

iscrívere—to inscribe; to enroll; to record a legal instrument; to register; to write into a register.

iscrizióne f.—inscription; recording of a legal instrument; registration; a memorial on stone or metal.

iscrizióne a ruòlo—inscription on the calendar roll. It is similar to placing a case on the calendar of causes to be heard.

iscrizióne ipotecària—recording of a mortgage on the appropriate legal register.

ísola f.—island. Art. 945, 947, 822, Italian Civil Code.

isolaménto m.—isolation.

isolàno m.—inhabitant of an island; islander.

isolàre—to isolate.

isolàto m. — block of houses surrounded by streets.

isolàto—isolated.

ispezióne f.—inspection.

ispezióne giudiziàle — judicial inspection. In both civil and criminal cases, it involves the inspection of places, of things, or persons relating to a specific crime or controversy. Art. 118, 258, 262, Italian Code of Civil Procedure; Art. 309-313, 457, Italian Code of Penal Procedure.

istànza f. — instance; request; demand; an action or judicial demand; a judicial process.

istànza (tribunàle di príma)—court of first instance.

istigàre—to instigate; to incite.

istigazióne f.—instigation.

istigazióne a delínquere—instigation or incitement to commit crime. Art. 414, Italian Penal Code.

istigazióne all'abòrto — instigation to abortion. Art. 548, Italian Penal Code.

istigazióne alla corruzióne—instigation to corruption. Similar to bribery, it consists in offering or promising money or other things of value to a public official or one in charge of a public service to induce him to commit or to induce him to omit or delay the performance of a public duty or service. Art. 322, Italian Penal Code.

istigazióne alla prostituzióne—instigation to prostitution. It consists in inducing a female of minor age to engage in prostitution. Law of Feb. 20, 1958, n. 75 (Official Gazette, Mar.

148

4, 1958, n. 55) Arts. 3-6, replacing abrogated Arts. 531-536, Italian Penal Code.

istigazióne o aiúto al suicídio—instigating or abetting suicide. Art. 580, Italian Penal Code.

Istituíre—to institute; to found; to establish; to appoint an heir in a will. Also, instituíre.

istitúto m. — instituted; institution; foundation; a civil, moral or religious organization established and recognized by law.

istitúto di dirítto — legal institution. The aggregate of rules which regulate a jural institution such as property, possession and marriage.

istitúto giurídico — jural institution. See istitúto di dirítto.

istituzióne f.—institution.

istituzióne d'erède—appointment of an heir by a testator. Art. 588, 624-648, Italian Civil Code.

istituzióne del matrimònio—the institution of marriage.

istruttóre (giúdice)—examining judge or magistrate. See giúdice istruttóre.

istruttòria f.—the process which regulates the formal steps in a judicial proceeding, be it civil or criminal.

istruzióne f. — instruction; the steps involved in the process of an action.

istruzióne civíle—civil proceeding. The formal steps in a civil case.

istruzióne penàle — criminal proceeding. The formal steps in a criminal proceeding.

istruzióne preventíva—a special proceeding to preserve facts and receive testimony. See procediménti di istruzióne preventíva, Art. 692-699, Italian Code of Civil Procedure and futúra memòria (esàme di testimòni a).

L

laceràre—to lacerate; to tear.

lacerazióne f.—laceration.

làdro m.—thief.

lagnànza f.—complaint.

lagnàre—to complain.

làgo m.—lake.

làghi (pl.) f.—lakes. They are part of the public domain. Art. 822, Italian Civil Code.

làghi e stàgni—lakes and ponds. The land covered by the water when it reaches the height of the outlet of the lake or pond, belongs to the owner of the lake or pond, even though the volume of the waters starts to diminish. The owner does not acquire any right over the land along the bank or shore which the water covers again in cases of an extraordinary flood of water. Art. 943, Italian Civil Code.

laíco—lay; secular.

laidézza f.—ugliness; obscenity; indecency; disgusting act or habit.

làido—dirty; foul; indecent.

làma f.—blade; tract of low ground which is flooded; metal strip.

lambiccàre—to distil.

lambícco m.—still; alembic.

lamétta f.—small blade; safety razor blade.

lampióne m.—street or carriage lamp.

làmpo m.—flash of lightning.

lampóne m.—rasberrry.

làna f.—wool.

lànca f.—low ground which is often covered with water.

lànce f.—balance; pan for a balance or scales.

lancétta f.—lancet; watch hand.

lància f.—lance; launch.

lància di salvatàggio—life-boat.

lanciabómbe m.—trench mortar.

lanciafiàmme m.—flame-thrower.

lanciasàgole m.—line launcher; an apparatus that can cast a line which is used in towing or lifesaving operations.

lanciasilúri m. — an aparatus which launches a torpedo.

làpida or làpide f.—stone slab; headstone; gravestone.

lapidàrio m.—a cutter and polisher of precious stones.

largíre—to give liberally; to grant.

lasciàre—to leave; to bequeath.

làscito m.—legacy; bequest.

làstra f.—flagstone; slate; sheet of iron, glass or stone; pavement for streets or balconies.

làstrici solàri — terraces; balconies; flat roofs. In a condominum, the one having its exclusive use must pay a third of its repair or reconstruction. The balance is charged to the other condominium owners of the building or those which it serves, in proportion to the value of the floor or portion of the floor that each owns. Art. 1126, Italian Civil Code.

làstrico m.—pavement.

làstrico solàre—terrace; balcony; flat roof. See làstrici solàri.

latèbra f.—a dark, hidden place; dark recess.

latènte—latent; concealed; hidden.

laticlàvio m.—band of purple worn by the ancient Roman senators; dignity of a senator.

latifóndo m.—a large estate; a large estate made up of smaller ones.

latitànte—one hiding from justice and in concealment.

latitànza f.—concealment; hiding from justice. Art. 268, Italian Code of Penal Procedure.

latitànza del imputàto—concealment of the accused. For manner of serving notices on him, see renitènza del imputàto, Art. 173, 174, 170, Italian Code of Penal Procedure.

latrína f.—latrine. There must exist a distance of three meters between the internal perimeter of the structure and the boundary line nearest thereto. The cleansing of latrines is at the expense of the lessor of the property. Art. 889, 1610, Italian Civil Code.

latrocínio m. — theft; larceny. See fúrto.

làtta f.—tinned iron or metal; can.

lattàio m.—milkman.

lattànte—nursing or suckling child.

lattàre—to nurse; to suckle.

làtte m.—milk.

laudàre—to laud; to commend; to praise.

làude f.—commendation; praise. Also, lòde.

laudèmio m.—a sum of money once paid by the one acquiring an emphyteusis (enfiteùsi). The sum was paid in acknowledgement of the title or dominion of the grantor and his acceptance of the grantee.

làudo m. — arbitrator's award. Also, lòdo.

làurea f.—doctoral degree; doctorate; laurel crown.

lavàgna f.—slate; blackboard.

lavína f.—avalanche; landslide.

lavorànte m.—workman. Also, operàio.

lavoràre—to work.

lavoratóre m. (lavoratríce f.)—worker. See Statúto del Lavoratóre.

lavorío m.—intense work.

lavóro m. — work; employment; toil. Art. 2060, 2096, 2098, 2099-2129, 2240-2246, 2108, Italian Civil Code.

lavóro autònomo—independent work. Art. 2222-2238, Italian Civil Code.

lavóro domèstico—domestic work. Art. 2240-2246, Italian Civil Code.

lavóro subordinàto — subordinate or dependent work. A worker of this nature may perform intellectual or physical work under the direction of the contractor or management. Dependent workers may be administrative or technical assistants, employees or workers. Art. 2094, 2095 et seq., Italian Civil Code.

lazzaróne m.—man of the lowest or dregs of society.

leàle—loyal.

lealtà f.—loyalty.

lèbbra f.—leprosy.

leccàre—to lick; to graze.

leccàto—licked; affected speech, literature or art.

leccúme f.—sweet tid-bit.

lécito—licit; permissable.

ledère—to harm; to hurt; to damage; to offend.

legàle—legal; lawful; lawyer.

legalità f.—legality.

legalizzàre — to legalize; to authenticate a writing, signature or document by a public official. See àtti di notorietà; autenticazióne della scrittúrà privàta; autenticazióne di àtti púbblici; autenticazióne di sottoscrizióne.

legatàrio m.—legatee.

legàto m.—legate; a diplomatic representative of the Pope; legacy. Concerning legacies, see Art. 649-673, Italian Civil Code.

legazióne f. — legation; embassy; a diplomatic minister and his suite or staff of secretaries, attaches, counselors and others assisting him. The residence or place of business of a minister.

légge f.—law; it includes administrative orders and legislative decrees in addition to laws enacted by the two houses of Parliament. Art. 70-77, Constitution of the Italian Republic.

légge comúne — common law. See dirítto consuetudinàrio.

légge dèlega or **légge delegàta**—legislative decree or rule of law. See decréto legislatívo. Art. 76, Constitution of the Italian Republic.

léggi vessatríce—oppressive laws.

legíttima f.—legitim; the share of a decedent's estate reserved by law to certain heirs which cannot otherwise be disposed whether the succession is testamentary or intestate. The persons so protected are: legitimate, legitimized, natural and adopted children; legitimate ascendants; descendants of legitimate and natural children who take the succession in place of their parents; the spouse. Art. 536-564, Italian Civil Code. Also, quòta di risèrva and porzióne leggíttima.

legíttima difésa—legitimate or justifiable defense. An act is not punishable if committed under constraint of necessity to defend a right of the person so acting or of another in peril of actual unjust harm, provided that the act of defense was proportionate to the anticipated harm. Art. 52, Italian Penal Code; Art. 2044, Italian Civil Code. Also, difésa legíttima.

legittimàre—to legitimate or legitimize one's illegitimate child; to justify.

legittimàri m.—persons entitled to the legitimates' portion of the estate. The persons in favor of which the law reserves a quota or portion of the inheritance or other rights in the succession are: spouse; legitimate children; natural children; legitimate ascendants. Legitimized and adopted children have equal rights with legitimate ones. If a parent leaves one child, legitimate or natural, one half of the estate is reserved to him. If there are more than one, two thirds of the estate is reserved to the legitimate and natural children to be divided by them equally. Art. 536, 537, Italian Civil Code. See porzióne legíttima; legíttima! porzióne disponíble and disponíbile.

legittimazióne f.—the act of making legitimate; justification.

legittimazióne dei fígli naturàli—legitimation of natural children. Art. 280-290, Italian Civil Code.

legittimità f. — legitimacy; constitutionality of a law or act having the force of law. Art. 134-137, Constitution of the Italian Republic; Córte Costituzionàle, (Constitutional Court), Art. 1, 2, re: Nòrme sui giudízi di legittimità costituzionàle (Rules on Constitutionality of Judgments) and Title II, Chapter II, Art. 23-36, idem, Usual Laws, Appendix to Italian Code of Civil Procedure. See córte Costituzionàle.

legíttimo—legitimate.

leníre — to mitigate; to soften; to soothe.

lenitívo — lenitive; softening; soothing; mitigating.

lenocínio m.—pandering. Whoever induces a woman in her majority to prostitution, or personally commits acts of pandering in public places or those open to the public, be it by means of print or other means of publicity, is punished with imprisonment and fine. Art. 531-536, Italian Penal Code, abrogated and replaced by Art. 3-6, Law of 20 February 1958, n. 75.

leoníno—leonine; a pact where the advantage is all on one side. See pàtto leoníno.

lésina f.—awl; stinginess.

lesinàre—to wound; to erode.

lesióne f.—damage; harm; hurt; injury; lesion; wound. Civily, the term connotes damage to property or estate. In contract cases, where serious damage affects one of the parties, see azióne generàle di rescissióne per lesióne, Art. 1448, Italian Civil Code. Regarding serious damage resulting from a division of an inheritance, see rescissióne per lesióne, Art. 763, idem. Criminally, see lesióne personàle; circostànze aggravànti and lesióni personàli colpósi, Art. 582, 583, 590, Italian Penal Code.

lesióne di legíttima—damage to the reserved portion due on a decedent's estate. When there has been a reduction or diminution of this legally reserved portion resulting in damage to an heir, he may bring an action for restoration of his quota. See azióne di riduzióne. Art. 553-565, 536, 735, Italian Civil Code.

lesióne enòrme — enormous damage arising out of disproportionate legal obligations in a contract. See azióne generàle di rescissióne per lesióne, and Art. 1448, Italian Civil Code.

lesióne personàle—personal injury or harm. Whoever causes personal injury to another resulting in physical or mental illness, is punished with imprisonment. When the personal injury is serious and there are aggravating circumstances, the penalty of imprisonment is increased. Art. 582, 583, 585, Italian Penal Code.

lesióni personàli colpóse—culpable or negligent personal injuries. Whoever causes culpable personal injury to

another is punished with imprisonment or fine. Where the injury is grave or most serious, the imprisonment and fines are increased accordingly. Art. 590, Italian Penal Code.

leticàre—to litigate. See litigàre.

lèttera anònima — anonymous or unsigned letter.

lèttera di càmbio—draft or bill of exchange. See cambiàle.

lèttera di pòrto—letter of carriage or transport. It is a bill of lading for goods shipped by slow freight on railroads. Art. 1683-1702, Italian Civil Code. See nòta di spedizióne and lèttera di vettúra.

lèttera di traspórto aèreo—air bill of lading. Art. 956-964, Italian Navigation Code. See pòlizza di càrico and lèttera di vettúra.

lèttera di vettúra—bill of lading; letter of carriage or transport by land; document attesting to the existence of a contract of carriage or transport by land. Upon request of the carrier, the shipper must issue a bill of lading subscribed by him with the conditions agreed for transport and the following data: (1) the name of the consignee; (2) place of destination; (3) the nature, weight, quantity and number of things to be transported, and the necessary essential conditions to execute the transport. Upon request of the shipper, the carrier must issue a duplicate of the bill of lading subscribed by him, or if the bill of lading is not issued, a freight receipt with the same data. Barring contrary dispositions of law, the duplicate of the bill of lading and the freight receipt, may be issued "to order." Art. 1683-1685, Italian Civil Code. See ricevúta di càrico; nòta di spedizióne; lèttera di pòrto; pòlizza di càrico and lèttera di traspórto aèreo.

lèttera minatòria—threatening letter; one containing serious threats or threats to extort money.

letteràle—literal; following the text as in translation; formal; textual.

lèttere f.—letters. Regarding their preservation in connection with busi-

152

ness affairs, see **conservazióne delle scrittúre contábili**, Art. 2220, Italian Civil Code.

lètto del fiúme—river bed. If a river or stream forms a new bed, abandoning the old, the new bed belongs to the owners of the land of the confining river banks to the middle thereof. Also, **àlveo abbandonàto**, Art. 946, Italian Civil Code.

leucemía f.—leukemia.

lèva f.—levy of soldiers; conscription.

levatríce f.—mid-wife.

levisíte f.—Lewisite; chemical warfare agent.

libèllo m.—libel; written defamatory statement.

liberalità f. — liberality; generosity; the quality of being liberal in giving.

liberàre—to free; to liberate; to release; to discharge; to extinguish; to satisfy.

liberazióne f.—liberation; deliverance; discharge; release.

liberazióne condizionàle — conditional freedom or release. It is similar to parole, the release of the prisoner being conditioned upon the observance of certain conditions. Art. 176, 177, Italian Penal Code.

liberazióne dalle ipotèche—redeeming or freeing from mortgages. It liberates the mortgaged property by paying the debt for which it stood as security. Art. 2889-2898, Italian Civil Code.

libertà personàle (dirítto alla)—right to personal liberty or freedom. It includes religious freedom, individual freedom, the freedom to work and the right to inviolability of the domicile. Art. 605-609, 614, Italian Penal Code. Compensation for damages caused by criminal or culpable acts may be recovered. Art. 2043, Italian Civil Code. Art 1, 2, 8, 13, Constitution of the Italian Republic.

libertà provvisòria—provisional or conditional liberty or release. It is the release of a person being held in preventive custody. It cannot be granted for a number of crimes set forth in the Penal Code. Art. 277-

294, Italian Code of Penal Procedure. See **custòdia preventíva**.

libertà vigilàta—supervised liberty or release. It is intended to rehabilitate a person who must adhere to restrictions imposed by a judge under supervision of Public Security officials. It may be ordered in case of imprisonment for more than one year and in cases in which the Penal Code authorizes a security measure for an act not deemed a crime by law. Supervised release must always be ordered if the term of imprisonment is not less than ten years, in which case such supervision may not last less than three years. It must always be ordered when a prisoner is admitted to conditional freedom or release. Minors and those in a state of psychic infirmity cannot be released unless they can be entrusted to parents or those under duty to provide for them and where not possible or opportune, remanded to a reformatory or sanatarium. Art. 228-235, Italian Penal Code; Art. 648, 652, Italian Code of Penal Procedure.

libídine f.—lust; lewdness.

libràio m.—book-seller.

libràre—to weigh; to poise.

librería f.—book shop. See **bibliotèca**, library.

librétto m.—text of an opera or musical composition; note-book; small book.

librétto colònico—farm-worker's notebook. In a contract of mezzadría, the grantor must enter from time to time on his notebook and that of the mezzàdro, the credits and debits relative to the contract with dates and pertinent facts. At the end of the agricultural year, the entries must be subscribed for acceptance by both parties. The note-book must be presented by the farmer for the annotation of the yearly balances. Art. 2161, Italian Civil Code. See **mezzadría** and **famíglia colònica**.

librétto di depòsito a rispàrmio — savings bank deposit pass-book. Art. 1835-1838, Italian Civil Code.

librétto di rispàrmio—savings bank pass-book. See above.

líbro m.—book.

líbro màstro—ledger of accounts.

licènza f.—license; permission; excessive freedom or liberty; dismissal.

licènza per finíta locazióne (intimazióne di) — notice to terminate a lease. Art. 137-151, 657-669, Italian Code of Civil Procedure; Art. 1603, 1612, 1613, Italian Civil Code. See sfràtto and procediménto per convàlida di sfràtto.

licenziaménto 'm. — dismissal; discharge; eviction; act of leaving or bidding farewell.

licenziaménto del prestatóre di lavóro — discharge of an employee or worker. Art. 2118-2125, Italian Civil Code; Lavóro (Duràta del Contràtto) — (Duration of Work Contract), Usual Laws, Appendix to Italian Code of Civil Procedure.

licenziàre—to dismiss; to discharge; to evict; to take leave; to bid farewell; to release or approve proofs for printing.

licenziàto—licensed; licentiate; graduate; on leave.

licitàre—to put up for auction; to bid at auction.

licitazióne f.—auction sale; bid at an auction sale; assigning a work contract to the lowest bidder where closed bids are employed.

licitazióne privàta—private bidding for State contracts.

lído m.—shore. The sea shore is considered part of the public domain. Art. 822, Italian Civil Code.

lignàggio m.—lineage.

líma f.—steel file. fàr líma—to mock.

limatúra f.—filing; filings.

limitazióne f.—limitation.

limítrofo—contiguous; bordering upon.

limòsina f.—alms.

línee della parentèla e dell'affinità—lines (degrees) of kinship and affinity. Art. 74-78, Italian Civil Code.

lingería f.—lingerie; women's underclothes.

linguísta m.—linguist.

linotipía f.—linotype.

liquidàre—to liquidate; to settle.

liquidàre la pensióne—to determine the amount of a pension.

liquidazióne f.—liquidation; realizing assets and discharging liabilities in winding up a business. Re associations and foundations, Art. 30-32, 33, 35, Italian Civil Code; re other business organizations such as partnerships, corporations, etc., see Art. 2275-2283, 2312; 2315; 2450-2475; 2464; 2497; 2516, Italian Civil Code.

liquidazióne coàtta amministratíva — compulsory administrative liquidation. It is used in place of bankruptcy where businesses have a serious impact on the national economy. Upon petition of one or more creditors, a tribunal declares the existence of a state of insolvency and appoints a liquidating commissioner to proceed with the liquidation. Art. 194-15, Falliménto (Bankruptcy), Usual Laws, Appendix to Italian Civil Code; Art. 1902, Italian Civil Code.

líquido—liquid; cash assets.

lísta f.—stripe; list.

lísta civíle—civil list.

lísta elettoràle—electoral or voters list; register of voters.

listíno di bórsa—stock exchange quotations.

líte f.—dispute; lawsuit; judicial controversy.

litigànte—litigant.

litigàre—to litigate.

litígio m.—dispute; quarrel.

litisconsòrzio—a controversy or lawsuit. involving two or more of either plaintiffs or defendants. Art. 102, 103, Italian Code of Civil Procedure.

litispendènza e continènza di càuse—pending actions comprising the same subject matter. If the same cause of action is presented to different judges, the last judge before whom the action appears, may order that case stricken from the calendar, at any stage of the proceeding. He may order a peremptory time within which the parties shall resume the case before the first judge. Art. 39,

154

40, Italian Code of Civil Procedure.

litoràle or littoràle—littoral; pertaining to the shore of a lake, sea or ocean.

litoràneo or littoràneo — extending along the shore.

livèllo m.—level; a contract of emphyteusis; a feudal instrument of alienation or conveyance; periodic payment of a portion of the products of the land or animals.

lízza f.—the area within which tourneys were held; lists; arena.

locàle m.—premises.

locànda f.—inn; lodging house.

locàre—to let; to rent.

locatàrio m.—lessee.

locatóre m.—lessor.

locazióne f.—a contract whereby an owner of property permits its enjoyment to another for a determined price and period of time; rental contract or lease. The property may be personal or real. Art. 1571-1606, Italian Civil Code. See affìtto; affìto di fóndi rústici; locazióne di fóndi urbàni.

locazióni di fóndi urbàni — lease of urban dwellings. The lease to a house may be granted for the lifetime of the tenant and two years beyond his death. Ordinary repairs for maintenance of the property, caused by its use, must be made by the tenant, but not those due to age and accidents. Said repairs, in the absence of agreement, are determined by local usage. The tenant under a lease contract is called inquilíno and the rental is called pigióne. Art. 1607-1614, Italian Civil Code. See affìtto di fóndi rústici.

lòculo m.—a niche in cemeteries or catacombs to contain a body.

locupletàre—to enrich.

locupletazióne f.—enriching.

lodàbile—laudable.

lodàre—to commend; to praise.

lòde f.—commendation; praise. Also, laùde.

lòdo m. — arbitrator's award. Also, laùdo.

lòdo arbitràle—arbitration award. Art. 820-826, Italian Code of Civil Procedure.

logoràre—to consume; to wear out.

lordàre—to dirty; to stain.

lórdo—dirty; filthy.
péso lórdo—gross weight.
péso nétto—net weight.

lòtta f.—struggle; contest; effort.

lottàre—to struggle; to strive; to fight.

lottería f.—lottery; the office which administers the lottery. Where legally authorized, an action will lie to recover the prize. Art. 1935, Italian Civil Code.

lòtto m.—lottery; allotment of a portion of a drawing by lot among those entitled to the division.

lubricàre—to lubricate.

lúbrico—slippery; indecent; obscene.

lúce f.—light.

lúci, vedúte o prospètti.—Windows or apertures overlooking a neighbor's land are of two kinds. They are called lúci when they admit light and air but do not permit one to look out upon the neighbor's land. They are called vedúte or prospètti when they permit one to look out and to look before him, obliquely or laterally. Art. 900-907, Italian Civil Code.

lúcro m.—gain; profit.

lúcro cessànte—lucrum cessans (Lat.) —loss of profit; ceasing profit. Compensation for damages for nonfulfillment or delay in performing an obligation, includes the loss sustained by the creditor such as loss of profits which are the immediate and direct consequence of the act. Art. 1223, 1226, 1227, 2056, Italian Civil Code.

luògo m.—place; site; room.
non fàrsi luògo a procèdere — dismissal of a penal action on various statutory grounds. See sentènza di proscioglimento.

lúpa f.—she-wolf.

lupanàre m.—brothel. Also, bordèllo; càsa di cartèlla; postríbolo.

lupàra f.—short-barrelled shot gun, which is sometimes used in the commission of assassinations; sawed-off shot gun.

lúpo m.—wolf.

lútto m.—mourning.

lútto vedovíle—widow's mourning. A widow cannot remarry for a period of three hundred days following the death of her husband or an annulment of the marriage. Exceptions are annulment for permanent impotence prior to the marriage or impotence for procreation. This follows the annus luctus (year of mourning) of the Romans. Art. 89, 102, 140, Italian Civil Code.

M

màcca f.—great abundance.

màcca (a)—in abundance.

maccheronèa f.—a rhyme or composition in pig Latin, containing Italian words with endings in Latin.

màcchia f. — blemish; blot; stain; dense undergrowth; thick hedge.

macchiàre—to blemish; to blur; to stain.

macchiétta f.—little spot; a theatrical personage, broadly outlined by the author; a sketch or caricature.

macchiettísta f.—one who designs or depicts broad sketches; an actor who plays a bizarre or comic part.

màcchina f.—machine. In a conditional sale of machines over a certain price, the reservation of title by the seller is a defense against the creditors of the buyer of the machine. Art. 1524, Italian Civil Code.

macchinàrio (macchinàri pl.) m.—complex of machinery; machinery; machinery used in manufacturing. Whoever plans to build furnaces, hearths, salt warehouses, stables and the like, and intends to place damp or explosive or otherwise noxious materials or manufacturing plants from which damage may ensue, must comply with distance requirements from the property line. In the absence of regulations, a reasonable distance must be observed to protect neighboring land from all damage to its stability, health and safety. Art. 890, 997, Italian Civil Code.

màdre f.—mother. She exercises parental authority in common accord with the father of the family. Art. 316, Italian Civil Code.

madrígna f.—stepmother. Also, matrígna.

madrina f.—godmother. Also, matrína.

maèstra f. — school mistress; school teacher.

maestràle m.—northwest wind.

maestrànza f. — master workmen; skilled workmen as opposed to apprentices.

maestrànze (pl.) f.—workmen collectively engaged on a job. Workmen's guilds or unions.

maèstro m.—master; teacher. Teachers are responsible for the damage caused by the illegal acts of those students who are placed under their care. Teachers are free of responsibility only if they prove that they could not have prevented the occurrence. Art. 2048, Italian Civil Code.

màfia or màffia f.—a secret criminal organization once difused in Sicily. Although, in isolated instances, some of its objectives may have had a positive purpose, it operates outside the law and it employs illicit means to attain its ends. See Misúre di Prevenzióne (Màfia) — (Preventive Measures—Mafia), Usual Laws, Appendix to Italian Code of Penal Procedure; Art. 378 379, 416, 435, 695, 696, 698, 699, 700, 701, Italian Penal Code. See camòrra.

mafióso m.—a member of the màfia.

magàgna f. — defect; imperfection; hidden flaw, also used in a moral sense.

magazzinàggio m. — warehouseman's charges.

magazzíno m.—warehouse; a building where goods and merchandise are received and stored.

magazzíni generàli—public warehouses for the reception and storage of goods, wares and merchandise. They are responsible for the protection of merchandise therein deposited unless it can be proved that the diminution or loss occurred accidentally, from the nature of the goods, their inherent defects or from the packing. Art. 1787-1797, Italian Civil Code.

maggioránza f.—majority; in an election, when one of two or more candidates, receives more than 50% of the total votes cast. It is called a plurality when more than two candidates are running, but one receives more votes than any other candidate, but not more than 50% of the total votes cast.

maggioránza assolúta — absolute majority; absolute majority of all those entitled to vote.

maggióre età — majority; full age; capacity to perform all acts upon reaching the age of eighteen, unless a different age is established by law. Art. 2, Italian Civil Code; see capacità di agíre. See minóre.

maggiorènne—of full age; no longer a mínor but having attained full age. See maggióre età.

magistràto m. — magistrate; dignity and power of one who exercises civil authority.

magistratúra f.—magistracy.

màglio m.—pile driver; a large two-headed wooden hammer to stun beasts; small, round wooden hammer with a long shaft to strike a ball.

malacreànza f. — impoliteness; rudeness.

malaféde f.—bad faith; fraud.

malagiàto—lack of means; ill at ease.

malagràzia f.—rudeness; lack of grace.

malandríno m.—brigand; rogue; ruffian.

malavíta f.—a criminal or underworld association.

malcàuto—incautious.

malcontènto — discontented; displeased.

malcontènto m.—malcontent; discontented.

maldicènte (adj.) m. & f.—speaking evil of others.

maldicènza f.—the habit of speaking evil of others.

maleficio m. — maleficence; damage; wicked or tortious act.

malfattóre m.—malefactor; criminal.

malízia f.—malice; cunning; evil disposition.

malizióso—malicious.

mallevadóre m.—guarantor.

mallevería f.—guaranty. See cauzióne.

malmenàre—to maltreat; to abuse; to ill-use or treat roughly.

malsàno—unhealthy; unwholesome.

malsicúro—insecure; uncertain.

maltrattaménti in famíglia—maltreatment of a family member. It is committed by maltreating a member of the family or a minor of the age of fourteen or a person placed under the offendor's authority or entrusted to him for the purpose of education, instruction, custody or for the practice of an art or profession. Art. 572, Italian Penal Code.

maltrattaménto m.—maltreatment; ill-treatment; ill-usage; rough treatment.

maltrattaménto di animàli—maltreatment of animals. Art. 727, Italian Penal Code.

malvàgio—wicked; evil.

malvagità f.—wickedness; malignity.

malversazióne f.—malversation; illegal use of funds under one's control; embezzlement. It is committed by a public official or one in charge of a public service who appropriates and diverts to his use or that of a third party, money or any personal property not belonging to the Public Administration which he has in his possession by reason of his office. Art. 315, Italian Penal Code. See peculàto, and púbblica amministrazióne (delítti cóntro la).

mancànza di qualità — lack or deficiency of quality. When an article sold does not have the promised qualities, or those essential for the use intended, the buyer has the right to obtain the rescission of the contract according to the general dispositions for non-fulfillment, provided that the defect of quality exceeds the limits of toleration established by usage. Art. 1497, 1453, 1495, Italian Civil Code.

mància f.—a tip for service rendered.

mandaménto m.—territory over which the Praetor has jurisdiction; territorial jurisdiction of the Praetor.

mandànte m. — mandator; one who gives to another a mandate to do something on his behalf; principal. Art. 1719-1721, Italian Civil Code.

mandatàrio m. — mandatory; one to whom a mandate is given to perform something on behalf of another; agent. Art. 1710-1718, Italian Civil Code. See sostitúto del mandatàrio.

mandàto—mandate; command; order; warrant; faculty to perform some act in the name of the party authorizing it. It is a contract whereby one party undertakes to perform one or more legal acts on behalf of the other. The contract may be with representation, under power of attorney, or without representation. In the first instance, the mandatory acts in the name of the mandator. In the last instance, the mandatory acts in his own name and acquires the rights and assumes the obligations deriving from acts performed with third parties, even though these had knowledge of the mandate. Art. 1703-1730, Italian Civil Code. See agenzìa.

mandàto (estinzióne del) — extinction of the mandate. Art. 1722-1730, Italian Civil Code.

mandàto alle lìte—retainer of an attorney to perform professional services. It must be made by a public Act or by authenticated private writing. It may be special or general. Art. 83, Italian Code of Civil Procedure. See procúra alle lìte.

mandàto di accompagnaménto—a mandate to produce a person charged with a crime for interrogation. It is issued by an examining magistrate or Praetor. The Procurator of the Republic (Attorney General) or Praetor sitting in a summary proceeding may issue an Order to Produce the person charged with crime for interrogation. Art. 251, 261-266, Italian Code of Penal Procedure.

mandàto di arrèsto—warrant of arrest. It is an order directed to the judicial police by a judge to place an accused defendant in jail to await the issuance of the mandàto di cattúra. The accused must be released if the mandàto di arrèsto is not converted into mandàto di cattúra within twenty days. Art. 235, 236, 238, 243, 359, Italian Code of Penal Procedure. See órdine di arrèsto and mandàto di cattúra.

mandàto di cattúra—warrant of arrest. It is an order of apprehension issued by a penal judge to deliver a person to jail in preventive custody. Art. 250-268 and 269-276, 429, Italian Code of Penal Procedure. See órdine di cattúra and custòdia preventíva. See órdine di carcerazióne.

mandàto di comparizióne—mandate of appearance. It is a citation issued by a penal judge, directing a person charged with crime to appear before the judge issuing it at a stated time and place with a warning that a mandàto di accompagnaménto will issue to the police to produce him if he does not comply. Art. 261, Italian Code of Penal Procedure. See órdine di comparizióne.

mandàto di crédito — credit order. Where a person obligates himself to another to extend credit to a third party in his own name on his credit or name, the one giving the charge or mandate is liable as a guarantor or surety for a future debt. The one accepting the mandate cannot renounce it, but the party conferring it may revoke it, subject to compensation for damages to the other party. Art. 1958, 1959, Italian Civil Code.

mandàto di pagaménto — payment

order. It is a written order authorizing the cashier of a legal entity or business to make a payment. In bankruptcy matters, it consists of a notice and order for distribution of funds in the hands of the curator (trustee) by way of dividends to the creditors in payment of their respective shares. Art. 110-123, Falliménto (Bankruptcy), Usual Laws, Appendix to Italian Civil Code.

mandàto in càlce—retainer of an attorney by written authorization at the bottom of a citation, complaint, counterclaim or appearance. It is also signed by the retained attorney as certification of the subscription of the party retaining him. See mandàto alle líte and procúra alle líte.

màndra or màndria f.—flock; herd; sheepfold.

manétta or manétte (pl.) f.—handcuffs.

manía f.—a form of insanity characterized by great excitement.

maníaco—maniacal.

manicòmio m.—insane asylum.

manifattóre m.—manufacturer; workman.

manifattúra f.—manufacture; also, the place where work is done.

manifestàre — to manifest; to make clear and open.

manifestazióne f.—manifestation; public demonstration.

manifèsto—manifest; evident.

manifèsto m.—manifesto; a public declaration of a government or group of persons taking important action; a printed or written document attached in a public place to make known its contents to all.

manifèsto di càrico—ship's manifest, carried by merchant vessels to account for its cargo to customs officials.

maníglia f.—handle.

manométtere—to manumit; to release from slavery or servitude.

manomissióne f. — manumission; the act of liberating a slave or releasing a person from the power or control of another.

manomòrta f. — mortmain; literally, dead hand, referring to possessions in the dead hand of an ecclesiastical corporation. These tended to be perpetual and became inalienable. This condition has been abolished. Present law states that a jural person (corporation) cannot acquire real property or accept donations or inheritances or bequests without government authorization. Art. 17, Italian Civil Code.

manovàle m.—mason's helper; workman.

mànso—gentle.

mànso m.—small piece of land.

mansuèto—gentle; docile (of domestic animals.)

manteniménto — maintenance. See manutenzióne.

manuàle—manual; pertaining to the hand.

manuàle m. — handbook; manual; laborer.

manufàtto—made by hand.

manutèngolo m.—accomplice; receiver of stolen goods. See ricettatóre.

manutenzióne f.—maintenance. Also, a possessory action. Art. 1170, Italian ivil Code. See azióne di manutenzióne and manteniménto.

marachèlla f.—an illegal act, though not serious, which is done by stealth; trick; deception.

màrca f. — march; the tract of land along the border of a country; frontier; mark; sign; stamp; a slip or check to reclaim an object. See contromàrca and contrasségno.

màrca di fàbbrica — trade-mark. See màrchio and màrchio d'imprésa.

màrchio m.—mark; brand; stamp affixed by public officials on weights. It is a trade mark which distinguishes the goods or other products of a business. Also, màrchio d'imprésa. Art. 2569-2574, Italian Civil Code. For trade-name, see ditta.

màrchio d'imprésa—trade mark. See màrchio and màrca di fàbbrica.

màre m.—sea; ocean; the sea coast

and shore are part of the public domain. Art. 822, Italian Civil Code.

marèa f.—tide; ebb and flow.

maréggio m.—rise and fall of the waves; rippling noise of the waves.

maremòto m.—tidal wave produced by an earthquake.

mariòlo m.—cheat; swindler, rogue. Also, mariuòlo.

maritàto—married.

marìto m.—husband. He is the head of the family. His wife follows his civil status, assumes his surname and is obliged to accompany him wherever he believes it opportune to establish his residence. The husband has the duty to protect his wife, to keep her with him and to provide her with all that is necessary of the needs of life in proportion to his means. Art. 144, 145, Italian Civil Code. See potestà maritàle and dovéri del marìto. See Art. 143, Italian Civil Code, on the reciprocal obligation of spouses to co-habitation, fidelity and mutual assistance.

mariuòlo m.—cheat; swinder; rogue. Also, mariòlo.

mascalzone m.—blackguard; rascal.

màschio—masculine; manly; male.

màschio m.—male; the highest part or tower of a castle, strongly fortified for a last ditch defense; the castle "keep".

masnàda f.—troop of armed soldiers; band of armed men; gang.

masnadière m.—highwayman; trooper.

màssa f.—bulk; mass.

màssa ereditària—a decendent's estate.

màssa fallimentàre attíva—bankrupt estate's assets subject to distribution.

massàia f.—housewife.

massàio m. — house holder; steward; good manager; farmer in charge of cultivation of land.

masserìa f.—the land placed in charge of a massàio for cultivation.

masserízia f. — household goods and utensils.

massimalísmo m.—political extremism advocating maximum socialist reforms.

massimalísta m.—one advocating or favoring extreme socialist reforms.

màsso m.—rock mass.

màstro m.—master (artisan); ledger of accounts. See líbro màstro.

matèria f. — matter; material; stuff; pus; subject; subject of a writing or of discussion; a subject studied at school.
indice delle matèrie—table of contents.

matèria príma—raw material.

materiàle—material.

materiàle m.—material; material of different kinds needed for a particular purpose.

maternàle—maternal.

maternità f.—maternity. It may be declared judicially. Art. 269, Italian Civil Code.

matríce f.—matrix; stub; counterfoil; womb.

matricída m.—matricide; the murderer of one's own mother. See parricída.

matricídio m.—the crime of matricide. Art. 575, 577, Italian Penal Code.

matrícola f.—register of names of persons inscribed in a certain class or category.

matricolàre — to matriculate; to inscribe on a register.

matricolàto—matriculated.

matrígna f.—step-mother. Also, madrígna.

matrimònio m.—matrimony; marriage; wedlock. Art. 29-31, Constitution of the Italian Republic; Art. 79, 148, Italian Civil Code.

matrimònio (annullaménto del) — annulment of marriage. Annulment presupposes that the marriage was invalid from its inception. Art. 117-129, Italian Civil Code.

matrimònio (condizióni necessàrie per contràrre)—conditions necessary to contract marriage. Art. 84-90, Italian Civil Code.

matrimònio dello stranièro nello stàto —marriage of the foreigner within the State. The foreigner who wishes to contract marriage within the State must present to the official of Civil Status a declaration from the competent Authority of his own country to the effect that, in conformance to the laws to which he is subject, there exists no impediment to the marriage. Art. 116, Italian Civil Code.

matrimònio (impediménti al)—impediments to marriage. Art. 84-90, Italian Civil Code. Also, matrimònio (condizióni per contràrre).

matrimònio (induzióne al, mediànte ingànno) — inducement to marriage through fraud and deception. It is a crime covered by crimes against the family. See famíglia (delítti cóntro la), Art. 558, Italian Penal Code.

matrimònio putatívo — putative marriage. It is one contracted in good faith by one or both parties without knowledge that impediments exist to make it unlawful. Until a judgment of nullity is rendered, it is considered a valid marriage and the validity inures to the benefit of children born or conceived during the marriage as well as to children born before the marriage and recognized before the judgment of nullity. If only one spouse acted in good faith, the effects of validity benefit only that spouse and the children. Art. 128, Italian Civil Code.

matrimònio (scioglimónto del) — dissolution of marriage. It is dissolved by the death of one of the spouses and by divorce. Dissolution presupposes that the marriage was valid from its inception. Art. 149, Italian Civil Code.

matrimònio (violènza ed erróre nel)— violence and error in marriage. See violènza ed erròre nel matrimònio.

mazzagàtti m.—a pocket pistol or snub-nose revolver. See ammazzazgàtti, a worthless gun or pistol.

mazzière m.—mace-bearer.

màzzo m.—bunch (of flowers, things, etc.); bundle; pack (of cards).

mecenàte m.—a patron of the arts and letters, after a counselor of Augustus.

mediatóre m.—mediator; broker.

mediazióne f.—brokerage; mediation. Art. 1754-1765, Italian Civil Code. prossenèta.

medicàbile—medicable; curable; susceptible of medical treatment.

medicaménto m.—medicament; curative; treatment; medicine.

medicazióne f.—medication; application of medicine; treatment.

medicinàle—medicinal; medicament; medicine; remedy.

mendicànte m.—mendicant; beggar.

mendicità f.—the state of being a mendicant or beggar. It is a crime which occurs when a person begs in a public place or one open to the public. Art. 670, Italian Penal Code.

mènsola f.—bracket; corbel; ledge.

ménte f.—mind; intellect; intelligence. sapére a ménte—to know by heart. tenére a ménte—to keep in mind.

mentíre—to lie.

ménto m.—chin.

menzógna f.—lie.

mercanzía f. — merchandise; goods; wares.

mercàto m.—market; market place.

mèrce f.—goods, wares; merchandise; product of industry. See derràta.

mèrce fungíbile—fungible goods. See depòsito di mèrce fungíbile—deposit of fungible goods. Art. 1795, Italian Civil Code.

mercéde f. — payment; recompense; pity.

mercuriàle f.—daily quotation of market prices of commodities and foodstuffs. Art. 750, 1474, 1515, 1735, Italian Civil Code.

mercuriàle—mercurial.

meridionàle—meridional; pertaining to

or situated in the South. See **mezzo-giórno.**

mèrito m.—merit.

mérito della càusa o controvèrsia — merit of the action or controversy. Pertains to questions relating to essence and substance rather than to procedure; merits of the case.

mèro—unmixed; pure.

mesàta f.—the period of a month; a month's wage or salary.

meschíno—being in great poverty; unfortunate.

méscita f.—a shop where wine or liquor is sold at retail and drunk standing at a bench or bar. A bar.

mésso m.—messenger; envoy; message-bearer.

mésso di conciliazióne—an officer in the court of conciliation. Méssi di Conciliazióne, Usual Laws, Appendix to Italian Code of Civil Procedure.

mestière m.—trade; occupation.

mèta f.—goal; point of arrival; finish line.

metà f.—half.

metíccio m.—mestizo; a person of mixed blood.

mezzadría f.—It is a contract whereby a grantor (concedènte) of land and the head of a family of farm workers associate for the purpose of cultivating land and dividing the products of the soil on a proportional basis. See **famíglia colònica** and Art. 2141-2163, Italian Civil Code.

mezzàdro m.—a farmer who cultivates the soil of another and divides the products grown on a proportional basis with the landowner. Also, **mezzaiuòlo.**

mezzaiuòlo m.—See **mezzàdro.**

mezzàno m.—broker; intermediary.

mezzería f.—See **mezzadría.**

mezzogiórno m.—mid-day; noon; the South. See **meridionàle.**

míccia f.—wick; a bundle or braid of soft threads prepared with saltpeter which when lighted burns slowly; it is used to ignite explosives.

micidiàle—deadly; murderous.

miètere—to mow; to reap.

mietitóre m.—mower; reaper.

mietitríce f.—mower; reaper; reaping machine.

miglioraménto m. — improvement; a valuable addition to real property or amelioration of its condition that goes beyond repairs.

millantàre—to boast; to exaggerate.

millantàto crédito—the crime of taking or receiving money or a promise thereof or anything of value for oneself or another, as a price for mediation with a public official or employee, by boasting one holds his trust and confidence. Art. 346, Italian Penal Code.

millantàto crédito del patrocinatóre—the crime of taking or receiving money or a promise of anything of value by legal counsel from his client, for himself or a third party, by boasting of the trust and confidence of a judge, public prosecutor before whom he is appearing, or the witness, expert or interpreter involved, with the pretext of procuring the favor of such persons. Art. 382, Italian Penal Code. See **prevaricazióne.**

minàccia f.—threat. It is the crime of threatening a person with unjust damage or injury. Art. 612, Italian Penal Code. See **violènza.**

minatòria (lèttera)—threatening letter; one containing serious threats or threats to extort money.

minatòrio—threatening.

minièra f.—mine; together with quarries and peat-bogs, a mine is part of the patrimony of the State. Art. 826, 820, 840, 987, Italian Civil Code.

mínima unità colturàle—minimal unit of cultivation. It is defined as the extension of land necessary and sufficient for the work of a farm family or group; and regarding land not yet reduced to cultivation, sufficient to undertake cultivation according to the rules of good agricultural techniques. Art. 846-856, Italian Civil Code.

minimalísta m.—a member of the conservative group advocating the minimum or less extreme of socialist reforms.

ministeriàle—ministerial.

ministèro m.—ministry.

público ministèro—the official who represents the Executive Power before the courts. See that title.

minístro m.—minister; a diplomatic representative; a high official, head of a government department and member of the Cabinet.

minorànza f.—minority; state or condition of a minor.

minóre m. & f.—minor; a person under the age of legal competence. Majority is reached at age eighteen, when capacity to perform all acts is acquired unless a different age is established by law. Minors cannot contract marriage. The Tribunal, upon petition of the interested party, verification of the minor's psycho-physical maturity, the basis for the reasons presented, and having heard the public prosecutor, the parents or guardian, may issue a decree in chambers, based upon serious considerations, permitting the marriage of one who has reached sixteen years of age. The decree is communicated to the Public Prosecutor, the couple to be married, the parents and the guardian. The decree may be appealed to the Court of Appeals within a period of ten peremptory days from the communication. The Court of Appeals' decision is not appealable. Art. 2, 84, 90, 165, 390, Italian Civil Code. See maggióre età.

minorènne m.—of minor age; one that has not yet attained majority. See minóre.

minorità f.—minority; being of minor age. See minóre.

minúta f.—rough draft; first draft.

minúte (pl.) f.—minutes (of a meeting).

minutànte m.—a secretary charged with making drafts of documents.

minutàre—to take minutes; to make drafts.

minutería f.—quantity of small objects or jewelry.

minutière m.—dealer in small jewelry.

minúto—minute; very small; slender; thin.

minúto (a—al)—retail.

minúto m.—minute of time.

minúto secóndo m.—a second of time; one sixtieth of a minute.

minúzia f.—minutia; trifle.

míra f.—aim; object; purpose; sight.

miràre—to aim; to take aim; to behold; to contemplate; to gaze; to view. See puntàre.

miratóre—one who takes aim; one who views or beholds. See puntatóre.

míschia f.—scuffle; hand to hand fight.

míschio m.—mixture.

miscúglio m.—confused mixture.

misfàtto m.—misdeed; crime.

mistióne f.—mixture.

místo—mixed.

místo m.—mixture; compound.

mistúra f.—mixture.

misúra f. — measure; measurement; dimension. See véndita a misúra.

misúre amministratíve di sicurézza—administrative security measures. The term is applied to the personal restraint of individuals sentenced for crimes. They are personal and patrimonial. The personal restraints are measures of detentive and non-detentive security. The patrimonial are the posting of bond for good behavior and confiscation of the fruits of the crime and the implements used or destined to commit it. Art. 199-240, Italian Penal Code. See misúre di sicurézza personàli and misúre di sicurézza patrimoniàli.

misúre di prevenzióne—measures of prevention. These are measures taken in regard to persons considered dangerous to public security and morality. Art. 1-13, Misúre di Prevenzióne, Usual Laws, Appendix to Italian Code of Penal Procedure.

misúre di prevenzióne cóntro la màfia—measures of prevention against the mafia. Art. 1-10, Misúre di Prevenzióne (Màfia), Usual Laws, Appendix to Italian Code of Penal Procedure.

misúre di sicurézza patrimoniàli — patrimonial or property security measures. Besides those established by specific dispositions of law, they consist of: (1) posting of bond for good behavior; (2) confiscation of the fruits of the crime and the implements used or destined to commit it. Art. 236-240, Italian Penal Code. See misúre amministratíve di sicurézza and misúre di sicurézza personàli.

misúre di sicurézza personàli — personal security measures. They consist of detentive and non-detentive measures. The detentive security measures are: (1) commitment to a farm colony or to a work house; (2) recovery in a house of care and custody; (3) recovery in a judicial insane asylum; (4) recovery in a judicial reformatory. The non-detentive security measures are: (1) supervised liberty or release; (2) prohibition to reside in one or more communes or in one or more provinces; (3) prohibition to frequent taverns and public places for the sale of alcoholic beverages; (4) expulsion of the foreigner from the State. When the law does not specify the security measure to be applied, the judge will impose supervised liberty or release unless it is the crime, delítto in which case the judge may commit to a work farm or work house. Art. 215, Italian Penal Code. See misúre amministratíve di sicurézza, Art. 199-240, Italian Penal Code.

mitigaménto m.—mitigation.

mitigàre—to mitigate.

mitigazióne f.—mitigation; alleviation.

mitràglia f.—grape-shot.

mitragliatríce or mitraglièra f.—machine gun.

mitténte m.—sender; dispatcher. In connection with the transportation of goods, see Art. 1683-1702, Italian Civil Code.

mòbile m.—piece of household furniture; that which is moveable from place to place.

mòbile—moveable; changeable; variable fickle.

mòbili (bèni) — moveable property; personal property. Anything other than real property is personal property. Art. 812, Italian Civil Code.

mobília f.—household furniture.

mobilitàre—to mobilize.

mobilitazióne f.—mobilization.

modàle—modal; pertaining to manner or form; formal.

modalità f.—modality; modal quality or state; manner of execution.

modèllo m.—model; pattern.

modèlli di utilità — practical models. The person who has acquired a patent for an invention has the exclusive right to produce it, and to dispose of it and to sell the products therein referred. Art. 2592, Italian Civil Code.

modèlli e diségni ornamentàli—models and ornamental designs. Whoever has acquired a patent for a new design or ornamental design (design patent), has the exclusive right to produce it and to sell the products referred in the design or model. Art. 2593, Italian Civil Code.

mòdi di acquísto della proprietà — methods of acquiring property. Property is acquired by occupation, by invention (finding), by accession, by specification (transformation), by union and commixtion, by adverse possession, by contract, by succession in the event of death, and in other ways established by law. Art. 922-947, Italian Civil Code.

modificazióne del contràtto (offèrta di) —offer to modify a contract. The contracting party against whom rescission is sought, may avoid it by offering to modify it sufficiently to restore its provisions equitably. Art. 1450, Italian Civil Code. See also, Art. 1432 and Art. 1467.

mòdo m.—mode; manner; means; custom; usage. A burden or restriction placed on a donation or legacy by the donor or testator. It may impose a duty on the recipient to perform a certain act. Failure to do so, may lead to rescission of the donation or legacy. Art. 647, 648, 793, 794, 662, 671, Italian Civil Code.

mòduli o formulàri—legal forms. See formulàri and Art. 1342, 1370, Italian Civil Code.

mòdulo m. (mòdula f.) — module; model; draft; formula; established unit of measurement; established form for certain documents. See formulàri, Art. 1342, 1370, Italian Civil Code.

mòdulo d'àcqua—unit of measurement of water; the established unit of quantity of water granted for irrigation or industrial use. It refers to a running body of water which discharges a constant quantity of one hundred liters a second. Art. 1081, Italian Civil Code.

mòglie f.—wife; consort; spouse. With matrimony, the spouses acquire the same rights and assume similar duties. They have the reciprocal obligation of fidelity and moral and material assistance. Both spouses, according to their professional or domestic work, must contribute to family needs. Art. 143-145, Italian Civil Code.

molestàre—to molest; to importune.

molèstia f.—molestation; disturbance.

molèstia o distúrbo alle persóne — causing molestation or disturbance to persons. It is a violation committed by molesting or disturbing someone in a public place or one open to the public, or by use of the telephone with provocative or reprehensible motives. Art. 660, Italian Penal Code.

molèstie f. — disturbances. When the right of possession to property is disturbed, a number of actions will lie. See azióne negatòria; azióne petitòria; azióne possessòria; azióne di manutenzióne; azióne di nunciazióne; azione di regolamento di confini; azióne di reintegrazióne; azióne di rivendicazióne.

mónco m.—one who is maimed or mutilated.

monéta f.—money; a medium of exchange and measure of value. Pecuniary debts are extinguished with money which is legal tender in the State, at its face value at the time of payment. Art. 1277-1284, Italian Civil Code.

monéta èstera—foreign money. If a check or draft is payable in money which is not legal tender at the place of payment, it may be paid within the period of presentment or payment in the money of the country on the date of payment or maturity. Art. 39, Asségni (Checks) and Art. 47, Cambiàle (Drafts), Usual Laws, Appendix to Italian Civil Code and Art. 1278, Italian Civil Code.

moníre—to admonish; to warn.

mònito m. — monition; admonition; warning. Also, monizióne.

monitóre m.—monitor; one who admonishes or warns; an ironclad warship.

monitòrio m.—monitory; admonition; warning; a monitory letter.

monitòrio—act of admonition.

monitòrio (procediménto) — monitory proceeding. See procediménti sommàri and procediménto di ingiunzióne.

monizióne f. — admonition; warning. Also, mònito.

monopòlio m.—monopoly; privilege; exclusivity; an exclusive privilege granted by the State to a person or group; exclusive privilege reserved by a State in the sale of certain goods. Whoever conducts a business as a legal monopoly must contract with anyone requiring the services which form the object of the business, on a basis of equality. Art. 2597, Italian Civil Code.

mòra f.—default; delay in satisfying an obligation.

mòra del creditóre — default by the creditor. The creditor is in default when, without legitimate reason, he fails to receive the payment offered him by the debtor in the manners specified by law or he does not perform what is necessary so that the debtor may fulfill his obligation. Art. 1206, Italian Civil Code.

mòra del debitóre — default by the debtor. The debtor who does not perform the required obligation exactly, is held liable to compensate the creditor in damages if he does not prove that the non-fulfillment of the obligation or delay was caused by impossibility of performance due to a cause not imputable to him. Art. 1218, Italian Civil Code. See **costituzióne in mòra.**

moralità f.—morality.

moralità púbblica (delítti cóntro la e il buòn costúme)—crimes against public morality and good custom. Art. 519-544, Italian Penal Code.

moratòria f.—moratorium; a delay or postponement in the payment of debts; a suspension of certain legal remedies against debtors authorized by law. See **concordàto preventívo,** Art. 160-186, Fallimménto (Bankruptcy), Usual Laws, Appendix to Italian Civil Code and Art. 2221, Italian Civil Code.

mòrte f.—death.

mòrte civíle—civil death; the status of a living person who has lost his civil rights and as to them is considered dead. It follows certain sentences of imprisonment. See **interdizióne legàle.**

mòrte o lesióni cóme conseguènza di àltro delitto—death or wounds as a consequence of another crime. It results when an intentional crime is committed which, in turn, causes an unintended death or wounding of a person. Art. 586, Italian Penal Code.

mòrte o lesióne della dònna—death or wounding of a woman. It follows the death or injury sustained by a woman in a non-consenting abortion or one to which she consents. Art. 549, 545, 546, Italian Penal Code.

mòrte (péna di)—death penalty. The death penalty is not permitted except in cases provided by military laws of war. When the Penal Code threatens the death penalty, life imprisonment is applied. Art. 27, Constitution of the Italian Republic; Art. 21, 22, Italian Penal Code.

mòrte presúnta (dichiarazióne di) — declaration of presumptive death. Following ten years from the date when news was last heard from the absent person, the competent tribunal, upon motion of the Púbblico Ministèro or the persons indicated in Art. 50 (Ital. Civ. Code), may have a person declared presumptively dead. Such declaration may not be made until nine years have elapsed if the absent person was a minor. Art. 58-73, Italian Civil Code and Art. 727-731, Italian Code of Civil Procedure.

mòrto—dead.

mortòrio m.—funeral procession.

mortuària (féde)—death certificate.

mortuàrio m.—pall-bearer; bearer of a coffin.

mortuàrio—mortuary.

móstra f.—display; show; exposition. The organizers and managers of funds for charitable and welfare committees and promoters of public works, monuments, expositions and celebrations are jointly and severally liable for the conservation of funds and for their destination to the announced purpose. Art. 39-42, Italian Civil Code.

móstro m.—monster.

motivazióne f.—motivation; the reasons set forth by a judge in his opinion to support the judgment.

motívo m.—motive; that which incites or stimulates a person to do an act.

movènte—moving; active.

movènte m.—motive; cause; impulse; reason.

movènza f.—graceful movement; in art it is the movement of the body.

mòvere—to move. Also, **muòvere.**

mózzo m.—cabin-boy; stable-boy.

múffa f.—mold; mildrew.

mulièbre—feminine; pertaining to a woman. Also, **muliébre.**

mulinèllo m.—capstan; windlass; reel; whirlwind; whirlpool; side-stroke in swimming.

mulíno m.—mill. Mills are considered real property. Art. 812, Italian Civil Code.

mulíno ad àcqua—water mill.

mulíno a vapóre—steam mill.

mulíno a vènto—windmill.

mulíno elèttrico—electric mill.

múlta f.—a penalty in the form of a fine, imposed for committing the violation of the Penal Code known as delítto. Art. 17, 18, 20, 24, 66, 78, 135, 136, 172, Italian Penal Code.

muníre—to provide; to supply; to fortify.

munizióne f.—munition for arms; provision.

munizionière m.—supply officer in the military.

muòvere—to move. Also, mòvere.

muràglia f.—a strong, high, external wall.

muràle—mural.

muràre—to wall in; to enclose; to surround with walls.

múro m.—wall.

múro comúne—common or party wall. For obligatory common or party wall, see comunióne forzósa del múro.

musèo m. — museum. Collections in museums are considered part of the public domain. Art. 822, Italian Civil Code.

múto—mute; dumb; speechless. Regarding testaments of persons who are dumb; deaf or deaf-mutes, see Art. 603, 605, Italian Civil Code.

mutualità f.—mutuality; reciprocity.

mutuànte m.—lender in a mutuum contract. See mútuo m.

mútuo m.—a contract whereby one party delivers a determined quantity of money or other fungible property to another party and the latter undertakes to return a like number of things of the same kind and quality. The things given in a mútuo pass ownership to the borrower. Unless otherwise agreed by the parties, in-terest must be paid by the borrower to the lender. Art. 1813-1822, Italian Civil Code.

mútuo—mutual.

mútuo cambiàrio—a mútuo contract based on obligations arising from commercial paper.

mútuo ipotecàrio—a mútuo contract secured by a mortgage.

N

nàilon m.—nylon; a synthetic material.

nàno m.—dwarf.

narceína f.—narceine; an alkoloid of opium; it has a muscle relaxing action and can be dangerous.

narcòtico—narcotic.

nascènte—nascent; coming forth.

nàscere—to be born; to arise.

nàscita f.—birth. Legal capacity is acquired at the moment of birth. Art. 1, Italian Civil Code.

nascitúro f.—one who is about to be born or is conceived. He has the right of succession and to the protection of a guardian. A posthumous child is entitled to share in his parent's estate even though not mentioned in the will because his existence was unknown, unless provision for such eventuality was made by the testator. A gift may be made to a child conceived but unborn or to a child of a specific person though the child was not yet conceived. Art. 462, 687, 784, Italian Civil Code.

nascóndere—to hide; to conceal.

nascósto—hidden; concealed.

natàle—natal; native.
giórno natàle—birthday.
tèrra natàle—birth place; country of origin.

natalízio—pertaining to the day of birth.
giórno natalízio—birthday.

natalízio m.—birthday.

natànte—floating.

natío—native.

natúra f. — nature; essence; disposition.

naturàle—natural; not artificial.

dirítto naturàle—natural law; the "jus naturale" (Lat.) of the Romans. A concept of rules and principles for the guidance of human conduct independent of enacted laws or systems peculiar to any one people and discoverable by rational intelligence.

fígli naturàli—natural children; children born out of wedlock. Art. 250-270, Italian Civil Code.

naturalità f. — right of citizenship granted to a foreigner by law or decree; political status.

naturalizzàre—to naturalize; to grant citizenship.

naturalizzazióne f.—naturalization; a manner of acquiring citizenship. Cittadinanzà (Citizenship), Usual Laws, Appendix to Italian Civil Code.

naufragàre—to be shipwrecked; to be wrecked; to go under as a business or a proposition.

naufràgio m.—shipwreck. It is a criminal act to cause it. Art. 428, 436, 449, 450, Italian Penal Code.

nàufrago m.—a shipwrecked person.

naumachía f.—a spectacle representing a naval battle.

naupatía f.—seasickness.

nàutica f. — naval science; art and science of navigation.

nàutico—nautical; naval.

navàle—naval.

navàta f.—nave; aisle.

nàve f.—ship. For a testament executed aboard a ship at sea, consult **testaménto a bórdo nàve.**

nazionàle—national.

nazionalísmo m.—nationalism.

nazionalísta f.—nationalist.

nazionalità f.—nationality.

nazionalizzazióne f.—nationalization of industry, utilities, etc.

nazióne f.—nation.

necessità (stàto di)—state of necessity. Civilly, when a person who has committed a damage, compelled by the necessity of saving himself, or

others, from actual peril of serious damage to the person and the danger was not wilfully caused by him and was otherwise inevitable, the injured party must be indemnified, the measure of which is left to the equitable assessment of the judge. Art. 2045, Italian Civil Code. Penally, a person is not punishable who has committed an act under compulsion of necessity of saving himself or others from actual peril of serious damage to the person, a peril not wilfully caused by him and otherwise inevitable, providing that the act was proportionate to the peril. Art. 54, Italian Penal Code.

necroscopía f.—necropsy; examination of a cadaver for scientific or pudicial purposes.

nefàndo—execrable; that which should not be spoken; profane.

nefàrio—nefarious; wicked; infamous.

nefàsto—unpropitious; ill-omened.

nefríte f.—nephritis; inflammation of the kidneys.

negàbile—deniable.

negàre—to deny.

negatíva—negative; negation; denial.

negatíva coartàta—proof of an alibi. See **àlibi.**

negatòria—negatory. See **azióne negatòria** — negatory action. Art. 949, Italian Civil Code.

negazióne f.—negation; refusal.

negligènte—negligent.

negligènza f.—negligence.

neglígere—to neglect.

negoziàbile—negotiable.

negoziabilità f.—negotiability.

negoziànte m.—merchant; trader.

negoziàre—to negotiate; to trade; to carry on a business.

negoziàto m.—negotiation.

negoziatóre m.—negotiator.

negoziazióne f.—negotiation.

negòzio m.—affair; business; trade; transaction.

negòzio giurídico — jural relation or

transaction. It may be defined as a declaration or manifestation of private determination to achieve a legal purpose. Art. 965, 1322, 1324, 1350, 1372, 1414, Italian Civil Code. See nullità del negòzio giurídico.

nemíco m.—enemy.

nemíco—inimical; hostile.

neòfito m.—neophite.

neonàto—newborn.

neonàto m.—newborn child. See alterazióne di stàto and supposizióne o soppressióne di stàto.

nepóte m.—nephew. Also nipóte.

nepotísmo m.—nepotism.

nequità or nequízia f. — iniquity; wickedness.

nerbàta f.—blow with a bullwhip.

nèrbo or nèrvo m.—whip; force; main strength of an army.

nésso causàle—causal connection; efficient producing cause; proximate cause. See rappòrto di casualità.

neutràle—neutral.

neutralísta m.—neutralist; one opposed to intervention.

neutralità f.—neutrality.

neutralizzàre—to neutralize.

neutralizzazióne f.—neutralization.

nichilísmo m.—nihilism.

nichilísta m.—nihilist.

nièllo m.—inlaid enamel work.

nipóte m.—nephew. Also nepóte.

nocuménto m.—annoyance; damage; wrong.

nòia f.—annoyance; nuisance; tedium.

noleggiaménto m.—the act of chartering, hiring or renting.

noleggiànte m.—the ship owner who charters his vessel.

noleggiànte—chartering.

noleggiàre—to charter; to hire; to rent.

noleggiatóre m.—the charterer.

noléggio m.—the rental price or fee for the hire of a vessel or vehicle; a shop where automobiles are rented;

a charter-party. Noléggio is a contract whereby a ship owner charters a vessel to another for one or more voyages. Art. 384-395, Italian Code of Navigation. Art. 939, idem, refers to the charter of aircraft. Art. 1571, et seq., Italian Civil Code.

noléggio (contràtto di)—charter-party. It must be in writing. Art. 377, 385, Italian Code of Navigation.

nòlo m.—the price paid for chartering a vessel or for passage or the shipment of goods; price paid for the rental of an automobile, carriage, bicycle and other articles to be used for a certain period of time.

nóme m.—name.

nóme (diritto al)—right to the protection of one's name. It includes the name and surname of a person and cannot be altered or changed except as provided by law. Art. 6-9, Italian Civil Code. See Art. 22, Constitution of the Italian Republic which states that, "No one may be deprived, for political reasons, of his legal capacity, citizenship or his name."

nòmina f.—nomination.

nominànza f.—fame.

nominàre—to nominate; to name; to appoint.

nominazióne f.—nomination.

nomología f.—nomology; the science of drafting laws.

non dovérsi procèdere—dismissal of a penal action on various statutory grounds. Also, non luògo a procèdere and non fàrsi luògo a procèdere. See sentènza di prosciogliménto.

non fàrsi luògo a procèdere. See non dovérsi procedère.

noncurànza f.—carelessness.

nònna f.—grandmother.

nònno m.—grandfather.

nòno—ninth.

nòria f.—irrigation wheel.

nòrma f. — norm; standard; order; rule; model; pattern.

normàle — normal; conforming to standard. Also, an administrative directive to define activities in branch offices which is binding on the employees but not the public.

nòrme corporatíve—corporate norms or rules of law. These are corporate ordinances or orders having legal effect. They comprise collective economic agreements, collective labor contracts and judgments rendered by labor courts in matters involving collective controversies. Art. 5-8, Preliminary Dispositions; Art. 2063-2081, Italian Civil Code; Art. 39, Constitution of the Italian Republic.

nostròmo m.—helmsman; on a merchantman, one in charge of a crew and its operation; in a ship of war, a petty officer who acts as helmsman.

nòta f.—note; sign; comment; bill; list; observation.

nòta di iscrizióne a ruòlo—note of inscription on the court calendar. It is a notice filed with the court clerk, containing the names of the parties (title of the case), the attorney's name, the object of the complaint, the date of service of the citation and the date set for the first appearance of the parties. Art. 71, 72, 134, Enabling Rules and Art. 314, 347, Italian Code of Civil Procedure.

nòta di iscrizióne di ipotèca—note or evidence of recording a mortgage. For the contents of this document, see Art. 2839, Italian Civil Code.

nòta di pégno—notice of pledge. It is negotiable and transferable by indorsement. It is issued together with a féde di depòsito (warehouse receipt) and can be detached from it. It is also negotiable and transferable by indorsement. Both instruments can circulate independently of each other or together. When attached, the nòta di pégno indicates that the property is free of security interest. Alone, it reflects a security interest guaranteeing repayment of the amount on the instrument. See féde di depòsito and Art. 1791-1797, Italian Civil Code.

nòta di spedizióne—note of shipment. It is a bill of lading for goods shipped by railroad. The term is used in shipping goods expeditiously by fast freight. For goods shipped by slow freight, the term used is **lèttera di pòrto.** Art. 1683-1702, Italian Civil Code. See **lèttera di vettúra.**

nòta di trascrizióne — note of transcription or registry. The demand for the transcription of a registered document must be presented to the Register of Deeds with a duplicate original, setting forth (1) name and surname, place and date of birth, domicile or residence of the parties; (2) title of the document to be transcribed and date of same; (3) name and surname of the public official who received the document or authenticated the signatures or the judicial authority who rendered judgment; (4) the nature and situation of the property referred to in the document with the data required by Art. 2826 (Civil Code) concerning the nature of the mortgaged real property, the comune where located, the number of the tax book or the tax maps when they exist, or of at least three of the boundaries. If there are terms and conditions involved, they must be mentioned. Art. 2659, 2643-2658, 2826, Italian Civil Code.

notàio or notàro m.—notary; a public official who authenticates documents and keeps a register of them.

notazióne f.—notation.

nòte di'udiènza—hearing memoranda. These are memoranda submitted after argument at a hearing with the presiding judge's approval. As a rule, not generally received, the judge may permit them when the public prosecutor submits findings and produces documents for final sentence. Art. 3, 117, Enabling Rules, Italian Code of Civil Procedure.

notificazióne f.—notification. The service upon the defendant of a complaint, citation, petition or order of a judge by delivery through a judicial officer. A conformed copy of the original, duly certified, must be served. In civil matters, it is served by the judicial officer at the instance of the public prosecutor, the court clerk or one of the parties. In penal matters, it is served by order of the judge, the public prosecutor or on request of the private party by delivery to the judicial officer of the original, so that copies may be served on those parties to be notified. Art. 137-159, Italian Code of Civil Procedure; Art. 166-179, Italian Code of Penal Procedure.

notificazióne all'imputàto latitànte, evàso o renitènte. Notification to a concealed, escaped, or recalcitrant accused. For manner of serving notices on them, see renitènza del imputàto, Art. 173, 174, 170, Italian Code of Penal Procedure.

notificazióni all'imputàto irreperíbile— notifications to an accused who is not to be found. Such notifications may be ordered to be made by depositing same in the office of the clerk or secretary of the court. They are effective for all purposes unless otherwise provided by law. Art. 170, Italian Code of Penal Procedure.

notiziàrio m.—newsletter; a collection of diverse news items.

notorietà f. — notoriety. See àtti di notorietà.

notòrio—notorious.

nottànte m. & f.—night nurse.

novàle f.—newly broken ground after lying fallow.

novazióne f.—novation; a method of extinguishing an obligation. An obligation is extinguished when the parties substitute a new obligation for the original one with a different object or title. The determination to extinguish the precedent obligation must be evident in an unequivocal manner. Art. 1230-1235, Italian Civil Code.

novèlla f.—news; story; intelligence.

novèllo—new; fresh; young.

nòzze f.—nuptials; marriage; wedding. See matrimònio.

núbile—nubile; an unmarried girl or woman; marriageable.

núda proprietà—general property. It may be charged with equitable estates and liens. Art. 550, 1060, 2814, Italian Civil Code.

núlla-òsta m.—from the Latin, nulla obstat, nothing impedes or opposes. It is a declarative formula by the authorities that there is nothing which is contrary to a certain action or impedes or hinders its performance.

nullità f.—nullity; invalidity.

nullità del contràtto—nullity or invalidity of a contract. A contract is invalid when it is contrary to imperative norms, except where the law disposes otherwise. Art. 1418-1424, 1325, Italian Civil Code; Art. 128, 156-162; 164, 221, 365, 366, 398, 480, 806, 829, 830, Italian Code of Civil Procedure; Art. 179, 184-189, 412, 475, Italian Code of Penal Procedure.

nullità del matrimònio—nullity of the marriage. Art. 117-129, Italian Civil Code.

nullità del negòzio giurídico—nullity of the jural relation or transaction. Art. 1418-1424, Italian Civil Code. See nullità del contràtto and negòzio giurídico.

nullità del testaménto—nullity of the testament. Art. 606, Italian Civil Code.

núncio m.—See núnzio.

nuncius m. (Lat.)—messenger; representative; agent. Art. 1387-1400, Italian Civil Code. See institóre. See núnzio.

nuncupatívo—nuncupative; oral rather than written.

nunziatúra f.—nunciature; the office and dignity of a nuncio; residence of the nuncio.

núnzio m. — nuncio; the permanent diplomatic representative of the Pope in a foreign country.

nuòcere — to annoy; to damage; to hurt; to prejudice.

nuòra f.—daughter-in-law. See gènero, son-in-law.

nuotàre—to swim.

nuòto m.—act of swimming.

nuòva f.—news; information.

nuòva òpera—new work. See denúnzia di nuòva òpera—complaint of new work on realty.

nuòvo—new,

nuòvo incànto—new auction. Following the attachment and sale of personal property at public auction, if same is not sold under terms required by law, a new public auction may be held by order of the Praetor and notice to the parties by the court clerk. Art. 538, 540, 587, 591, 595, 734, Italian Code of Civil Procedure.

O

obbediénza f.—obedience; compliance.

obediénza (rifiúto di)—refusal of obedience. It is a crime committed by a member of the military or an agent of public security who refuses or unduly delays to execute an order given to him by the competent Authority in the manner prescribed by law. Art. 329, Italian Penal Code.

obbligazióne f.—a legal link derived from law or contract; a duty imposed by law or contract; debt; obligation. Art. 1173-1320, Italian Civil Code.

obbligazióne civíle per le ammènde—civil obligation for fines. In contraventions (violations of the Penal Code) committed by one under the authority, direction or supervision of another, the latter person so charged, is obligated, in the event of the insolvency of the condemned person, to pay a sum equal to the fine inflicted on the condemned person. Art. 196, 197, Italian Penal Code; Art. 122, 123, 447. Italian Code of Penal Procedure.

obbligazióne ex delicto — obligation arising out of a crime. The person committing a crime must compensate the offended individual for damages caused to him. The offender is also liable to the persons answerable civilly for his act and for the expenses of the trial and of his incarceration. Art. 185-188, Italian Penal Code; Art. 2043, Italian Civil Code.

obbligazióne genérica—generic obligation. When the performance of an obligation has as its object the use of determined things of a particular genus or class, the debtor or obligor must perform by using things of a

quality not inferior to mean or average. The above is applicable to fungibles. Art. 1178, 1378, Italian Civil Code.

obbligazióni alternatívi — alternative obligations. The debtor or obligor of an alternative obligation is discharged by performing one of two performances, but he cannot compel the creditor to receive part of one performance and part of another. The power of choice rests with the debtor or obligor if it has not been attributed to the creditor or a third party. Art. 1285, 1286-1291, Italian Civil Code; Art. 81, Enabling Rules, Italian Civil Code. See obbligazióni facoltatívi.

obbligazióni ambulatòrie—ambulatory obligations. In these cases, the jural link in the obligation arises merely from the fact that one finds himself in a relation to property, its possession or some other real right to the thing. The obligation is joined to a determinate relation with a thing and is not linked to the person. Art. 882, 1030, 1104, Italian Civil Code.

obbligazióni cambiàrie — commercial paper obligations.

obligazióni cartolàre — obligations based on commercial paper and instruments of credit (see títolo di crédito). The party acqiring such obligations in good faith, acquires the property thereto by possession. Art. 1153, 1994, Italian Civil Code.

obbligazióni da fàtto illécito—obligations arising as a result of an illegal act. It calls for compensation for damages caused by it. Art. 2043-2059, Italian Civil Code.

obbligazióni di società — corporate bonds. These obligations of stock corporations may be issued to bearer or to a named individual and the holders are creditors of the corporation. Art. 2410-2420, Italian Civil Code.

obbligazióni divisíble—divisible obligations. Where there are many debtors or creditors in a divisible obligation and it is not a joint and several one, each of the creditors or obligees, may not demand satisfaction except for his portion and each debtor need not pay but the obligation due by him. Art. 1314, Italian Civil Code.

obbligazióni facoltatívi—optional obligations. This involves an obligation with one performance but with the option in the debtor or obligor of being discharged by executing a second or different performance. When the performance originally agreed upon becomes impossible of performance, the obligation is discharged, but the debtor or obligor cannot be compelled to perform the second. However, should the second have become impossible of performance, the first obligation remains to be performed since the right of discharge through the optional performance is lost. See obbligazióni alternatívi.

obbligazióni (fónti delle)—sources of obligations. Obligations arise from contract, from illegal acts or from any other action or deed sufficient to produce them in conformity with the body of the law. Art. 1173-1320, Italian Civil Code.

obbligazióni in sòlido — joint and several obligations. The debtors or obligors are bound to fulfill the same obligation. Each is bound severally or individually to discharge the entire obligation and all of them together are jointly or collectively bound for its discharge. Fulfillment of the obligation by any one individual discharges all. Likewise, a situation where one of many creditors, each of whom has the right to demand fulfillment of the entire obligation, receives performance from the debtor. Such performance received by one of the creditors, discharges the debtor as against all the creditors. Also, obbligazióni solidàle. Art. 1292-1313, Italian Civil Code.

obbligazióni indivisíbili — indivisible obligations. The obligation is indivisible when the performance required has as its object a thing or fact which is not susceptible of being divided due to its nature or the manner in which it had been considered by the contracting parties. Art. 1316, Italian Civil Code.

obbligazióni legàli—legal obligations.

obbligazióni naturàli—natural obligations. An action may not be maintained to reclaim that which has been voluntarily given or performed in discharge of moral or social obligations, unless the performance has been executed by an incompetent. Art. 2034, Italian Civil Code.

obbligazióni parziàrie—partial obligations. Each creditor has a right to a portion of the total performance and each debtor is obligated to a quota or portion of the performance. See solidarietà tra condebitóri.

obbligazióni pecuniàrie—pecuniary or monetary obligations. Pecuniary debts are discharged with money which is legal tender of the State at the time of payment in the amount of its face value. If the sum due was determined in money which is no longer legal tender, payment must be made in current legal tender according to the corresponding value of the former. If the sum due is determined in money which is not legal tender in the State, the debtor has the choice of paying by legal tender at the rate of exchange on the date of maturity and in the place agreed upon for payment. Art. 1277-1284, Italian Civil Code.

obbligazióni principàli del conduttóre—principal obligations of a leasee. The leasee upon receiving possession of property must use diligence and prudent care in its use as provided by contract or as otherwise presumed. He must pay the price determined under the agreed terms. Art. 1587, Italian Civil Code.

obbligazióni solidàli—joint and several obligations. See obbligazióni in sòlido.

òbbligo di rimbórso delle spése per il manteniménto del condannàto—obligation to reimburse for the cost of maintenance of the convicted prisoner. See rimbórso delle spése per il manteniménto del condannàto.

obiettàre—to object; to oppose.

obiettivísmo m.—objectivism.

obiettività f.—objectivity.

obiettívo—objective.

obiètto m.—object.

obiettóre m.—objector.

obiezióne f.—objection. Also oggezióne.

obitòrio m.—mortuary; a place where unknown bodies are kept for the purpose of autopsy or judicial investigation.

obituàrio m.—obituary.

oblàta f.—a lay brother who lives in a monastery observing its rules.

oblatóre 'm.—giver; bidder at an auction.

oblazióne f.—oblation; offering.

oblazióne nelle contravenzíoni — payment of a fine in violations. In violations of law, where a fine (ammènda) only may be imposed, the offender, prior to the hearing or sentence, may pay a fine corresponding to a third of the maximum fine plus court expenses, thus extinguishing the crime. Art. 162, Italian Penal Code.

oblazióne volontària — voluntary payment of a fine to avoid a hearing in a violation.

obliteràre—to obliterate; to cancel.

obliterazióne f.—obliteration; cancellation.

òbolo m.—obol, an ancient Greek silver coin; a small offering for charity.

obrettízio—a thing obtained by fraud and surprise. See orrettízio.

obrogàre—to abrogate. See abrogàre.

occhialàio m.—maker or seller of eyeglasses.

occhiàle — pertaining to the eye; ocular.

occhiàli m.—eye-glasses.

occhiàta f.—glance.

occhièllo m.—button hole.

òcchio m.—eye.

occultaménto m.—hiding; concealment.

occultaménto di cadàvere — concealment of a cadaver. Whoever conceals a cadaver, or a part thereof, or con-

ceals its ashes, will be punished with imprisonment. Art. 412, Italian Penal Code. See distruzióne, soppressióne o sottrazióne di cadàvere.

occultaménto di neonàto—concealment of new-born child. It consists in concealment of the new-born to avoid his Civil Status by the appropriate registration in the record. Art. 566, Italian Penal Code.

occultaménto di reàto—concealment of a crime. It is an aggravating circumstance to commit a crime for the purpose of executing or concealing another, or to obtain or assure to oneself or another, the product, the profit or price or exemption from punishment for another crime. Art. 61, Italian Penal Code.

occultàre—to hide; to conceal.

occultatóre 'm.—concealer; hider.

occupaménto m.—See occupazióne.

occupànte—occupying.

occupànte m. — first occupant who takes possession of a place or thing belonging to nobody.

occupatóre m. — occupier; one who takes possession.

occupazióne f. — occupation; occupancy; occupation of a place; taking possession. Property is acquired by occupation, invention, accession, specification (transformation), commingling, by adverse possèssion, by contract, by succession upon death and in other manners established by law. Likewise, personal property owned by no one, may be acquired by occupation. Such are abandoned things, and animals which are hunted, and fish. Mislaid or lost articles are not considered to be abandoned. Art. 922, 923-933, Italian Civil Code.

oclocrazía f.—ochlocracy; government by the mob; mob rule.

odalísca f.—a female slave in a harem.

odiàre—to hate; to detest.

òdio m.—hate; hatred.

odóre m.—smell; scent.

offèndere—to offend; to injure.

offensíva f.—an attitude of offense or attack; assault; attack.

offensívo — offensive; disagreeable; pertaining to offense or attack.

offèrta f.—offer. Re contracts, see **propósta** and Art. 1326-1330, 1335, 1336, Italian Civil Code.

offèrta al púbblico—public offer. It is a valid offer when it contains the essential elements of a contract. It may be revoked in the same manner in which the offer was made. Art. 1336, Italian Civil Code. See **proméssa al púbblico.**

offèrta contrattuàle—contractual offer. It is a proposal to enter into a contract which the party to whom it is made, must accept before it becomes legally binding and effective. Art. 1326, Italian Civil Code.

offèrta di modificazióne del contràtto —offer to modify a contract. The contracting party against whom rescission is sought, may avoid it by offering to modify it sufficiently to restore its provisions equitably. Art. 1450, Italian Civil Code. See also, Art. 1432 and Art. 1467.

offèrta di pagaménto—offer of payment. A creditor is in default, when, without legitimate reason, he does not accept the payment offered to him as required by law, or he does not perform what is necessary so that the debtor may discharge the obligation. Art. 1206, Italian Civil Code.

offèrta per intimazióne — notice of offer of payment. Where the obligation is to deliver personal property at a place other than the creditor's domicile, the offer of payment is made by notice of payment is made by notice of payment to the creditor to receive it through an act as prescribed by law. Art. 1209, 1217, Italian Civil Code; Art. 73, 75, Enabling Rules, Italian Civil Code; Art. 137 Italian Code of Civil Procedure. See **intimazióne di pagaménto.**

offèrta per intimazióne di ricèvere la conségna di un immòbile—notice of offer to deliver possession of real property. Where the obligation is to

turn over possession of real property, the offer to the creditor is to assume its possession. The notice must be made in the form prescribed by law. The debtor, after notice to the creditor, may obtain the appointment of a sequestrator from a judge. In this event, the debtor is discharged the moment he turns over the property to the sequestrator. Art. 1216, Italian Civil Code.

offèrta reàle—real offer of payment by debtor. If the obligation due is in money, instruments of credit or in personal property to be delivered to the creditor's domicile, the offer of payment must be real. Art. 1209, Italian Civil Code; Art. 73, 74, Enabling Rules, Italian Civil Code.

offèrta secóndo gli úsi e depòsito—offer according to usage and deposit. If the debtor has offered performance in accordance with usage instead of the manner prescribed by law (Art. 1208, 1209, Requisites for a Valid Offer and Real Offer and Notice of Offer), the effects of a default are determined from the day the debtor deposits the thing according to Art. 1212 (Requisites of a Deposit) if same is accepted by the creditor or declared valid by judgment. Art. 1214, Italian Civil Code.

offèrte segréte—secret offers or sealed bids. This system is utilized in connection with the awarding of State contracts. Art. 537, 581, Italian Code of Civil Procedure. See **incànto púbblico.**

offésa f. — offense; affront; wrong; transgression.

offésa all'Autorità mediànte danneggiaménto di affissióni—offense to the public Authorities by means of damaging bill-posters. Whoever, in contempt of the Authorities, removes, tears or otherwise renders illegible or useless, any writings or designs affixed or displayed by order of the Authorities is liable to a fine. Art. 345, Italian Penal Code.

offésa àlla bandièra o ad àltro emblèma di úno Stàto èstero—offense to the flag or other emblem of a foreign State. Whoever, within the territory of the State (Italy), expresses contempt for, in a public or open place or when displayed in public, to the official flag or other emblem of a foreign State, which is used in conformity with the internal law of the Italian State, is punished with imprisonment. This article is applied only if there is reciprocity with the foreign country. Art. 299, 300, Italian Penal Code.

offésa àlla libertà dei Càpi di Stàti èsteri—offense against the liberty or freedom of foreign Heads of State. Whoever, within the territory of the State (Italy), and besides the provisions of the preceding article (Art. 295—Attempts against foreign Heads of State), attempts to deprive of freedom and liberty a foreign Head of State, is punished with imprisonment. This article is applied only if there is reciprocity with the foreign country. Art. 296, 300, Italian Penal Code.

offésa àlla libertà del Presidènte della Repúbblica—offense to the liberty and freedom of the President of the Republic. Whoever, besides the provisions of the preceding article (Art. 276—Attempt against the President of the Republic), attempts to deprive of freedom and liberty the President of the Republic, is punished with imprisonment. Art. 277, 276, Italian Penal Code.

offésa àll'onóre dei Càpi di Stati èsteri—offense to the honor of foreign Heads of State. Whoever, in the territory of the State (Italy), offends the honor or prestige of a foreign Head of State is punished with imprisonment. This article is applied only if there is reciprocity with the foreign country. Art. 297, 300, Italian Penal Code.

offésa àll'onóre o al prestígio del Presidènte della Repúbblica—offense to the honor or prestige of the President of the Republic. Whoever offends the honor or prestige of the President of the Republic is punished with imprisonment. Art. 278, Italian Penal Code.

offése cóntro i rappresentànti di Stàti èsteri—offenses against the repre-

sentatives of Foreign States. The provisions of the three preceding articles, (Art. 295—Attempt against Heads of Foreign States; Art. 296—Offense against the liberty and freedom of Heads of Foreign States; Art. 297—Offense against the honor of Heads of Foreign States), are applicable when the offenses are committed against the accredited diplomatic Chief of Mission during the exercise of his duties. Art. 298, 300, Italian Penal Code.

offéso—offended; the offended or injured party.

officiàle—official. Also, ufficiàle.

officiàle m.—officer; official. Also ufficiàle.

officiàre—to officiate. Also ufficiàre.

officína f. — laboratory; workshop, particularly in an industrial plant with many workers performing mechanical operations.

officinàle — officinal; stock of drugs kept by pharmacists; prepared in a standard manner.

offício m.—office; charge; duty. Also ufficio and uffízio.

oggètto m.—object; aim; end.

oggètto del contràtto—object of the contract. It must be possible, lawful, determined or determinable. Art. 1346 1349, Italian Civil Code.

oggeziόne f.—objection. Also, obieziόne.

oleografía f.—oleograph; a mechanical reproduction of an oil painting in colors.

oligàrca m.—oligarch; one of the rulers of an oligarchy.

oligarchía f.—oligarchy; a government where power is in the hands of a few or dominant class.

olocàusto m.—holocaust.

ològrafo — holograph; holographic; a will which is entirely written by the testator himself, subscribed by him and containing the day, month and year it was executed. Art. 602, Italian Civil Code.

oltràggio m.—abuse; affront; insult; outrage.

oltràggio a un Còrpo político, amministratívo o giudiziàrio—affront to a
political, administrative or judicial
body. Whoever offends the honor or
prestige of a political, administrative
or judicial body or its representative, or a Public Authority collectively, in the presence of such body
or representative, is punished with
imprisonment. The same penalty
applies when the affront is committed by telegraphic communication or in writing or drawing,
directed to the body or its representative relative to its duties. Art. 342,
Italian Penal Code.

oltràggio a un magistràto in udiènza—
affront to a magistrate in session.
Whoever offends the honor or prestige of a magistrate while in session,
is punished by imprisonment. The
penalty is increased if the action is
accompanied by threats or violence.
Art. 343, Italian Penal Code.

oltràggio a un púbblico impiegàto—
affront to a public employee. Whoever offends the honor or prestige
of a public employee, in his presence, in the discharge of his duties,
is punished with imprisonment. The
same penalty applies when the action
is committd by telegraphic or telephonic communication or by writing
or drawing. The penalty is increased
if the action is accompanied by
threats or violence or when committed in the presence of one or
more persons. Art. 344, Italian Penal
Code.

oltràggio a un púbblico ufficiàle — affront to a public official. Whoever
offends the honor or prestige of a
public official, in his presence, in the
discharge of his duties, is punished
with imprisonment. The same
penalty is increased if the action
is accompanied by threats or violence or when committed in the
presence of one or more persons.
Art. 341, Italian Penal Code.

oltrànza f.—insult; excessively; to the
end.
oltrànza (a)—to the bitter end.

oltrapassàre or oltrepassàre—to exceed; to go beyond; to overstep.

oltremàre m.—overseas.

ombelicàle—umbilical.

ombelíco or ombellíco m.—umbilicus;
navel.

omertà f.—the code of silence followed
by the underworld and the Mafia,
which permits its members to thwart
investigations leading to their prosecution and punishment.

omicída m.—murderer.

omicídio m.—homicide; murder. Whoever causes the death of a person
is punished with imprisonment of
not less than twenty-one years. Art.
575, Italian Penal Code. See uxoricídio.

omicídio colpóso—negligent homicide.
It is punishable by imprisonment
from six months to five years. If
death is caused through violation
of vehicular rules or those made to
prevent work accidents, the penalty
is imprisonment from one to five
years. Where death involves a number of persons or the death of one or
more persons and wounds to one or
more, the penalty is tripled on the
more serious violation, but imprisonment shall not exceed twelve
years. Art. 589, Italian Penal Code.

omicídio del consenziènte—homicide
of a consenting person. Whoever
causes the death of a person with
his consent, is punished with imprisonment from six to fifteen years.
The penalty for murder (Art. 575-
577) is applied where the act is committed: (1) against a minor of the
age of eighteen; (2) against a person
of infirm mind, or in a weakened
physical condition, due to another
infirmity or by use of alcohol or
drugs; (3) against a person whose
consent was extorted by violence,
threats, suggestion, or artifice. Art.
579, Italian Penal Code.

omicídio preterintenzionàle—unintentional homicide. Whoever causes
death of a person as a result of
committing acts of battery or personal injury, is punished with imprisonment for a term of ten to
eighteen years. Art. 584, Italian
Penal Code.

omissióne di refèrto—failure to report
a crime. It is an offense punishable

by fine. It ccurs when a person, in the performance of his professional medical duties, has given his assistance or work in cases which may indicate evidence of a prosecutable crime, and fails or delays to report it to the Authorities within twenty-four hours. Art. 365, Italian Penal Code; Art. 4, Italian Code of Penal Procedure.

omologàre — to homologate; to approve; to confirm; to ratify.

omologazióne f.—approval; confirmation; ratification. It is the approval granted by judicial authorities to certain acts so that they may acquire legal effect.

omònimo—homonymous; having the same name; having the same sound but a different meaning.

óncia f.—ounce.

onciàle—capital letter of the Latin alphabet.

oncología f.—oncology; that part of medical science which deals with tumors.

oneràre—to burden; to encumber.

onerària (nàve) — ship of burden; freighter.

ònere m. — burden; charge; encumbrance.

ònere della pròva—burden of proof. Whoever wishes to enforce a right at a trial, must prove the facts which constitute the basis of said right. Whoever opposes the allegations, or contends the right has been modified or extinguished, must prove the facts upon which the opposition is based. Art. 2697, Italian Civil Code. See **pàtti relatívi all'ònere della pròva.**

onerèrio—burdensome.

onerosità eccessíva—excessive burden. In contracts of a continuing nature or periodic or deferred execution, if the performance of one of the parties has become excessivly burdensome due to extraordinary or unforeseen events, the party who must perform may demand the rescission of the contract. Rescission may not be obtained if the supervening burden inheres in the normal risk of the contract. The party against whom rescission is sought may avoid it by offering to modify equitably the terms of the contract. Art. 1467-1469, Italian Civil Code.

oneróso—onerous; burdensome; heavy.

onomàstico — pertaining to the day honoring the saint whose name one bears.

onomàstico m. — anniversary; feast day.

onoràbile—honorable.

onorànza f.—public honor or esteem.

onoràrio—honorary.

onoràrio m.—honorarium; fee; compensation.

onóre m.—honor; rank; respect; great reputation based on merit.

onorévole—honorable; title by which members of the Italian Parliament are addressed.

onorificènza f.—decoration bearing the ribbon or cross of an Order.

ónta f.—affront; insult; shame; offense.

òpera f.—opera; artistic production; composition; labor; work; an activity directed towards an end.

òpera pía—charitable work or institution.

operàbile — operable; feasible; practicable; admitting of surgical operation.

operàio m.—workman.

operàia f.—working woman.

operatóre m.—operator.

operatóre (chirúrgo)—surgeon.

operatòria (sàla)—operating room.

operatòrio—operative.

operazióni bancàrie in cónto corrènte —banking operations in a current account. When the deposit of a sum of money, the opening of a line of credit or other banking operations are governed by a current account, the depositor may, at any moment, transfer the sums placed to his credit, except as otherwise agreed. Art. 1852-1857, Italian Civil Code.

178

operazióni a fído—credit operations. In a commission bailment, the bailee is presumed to be authorized by the bailor, to grant postponements in payment in conformity with local usage where credit is extended, unless the bailor has otherwise disposed. Art. 1732-1736, Italian Civil Code.

òpere dell'ingégno ed invenzióni industriàli—intellectual works and industrial inventions. An author has a right of property over intellectual works of a creative character which are in the realm of science, literature, music, design arts, architecture, the theater and cinematography. The possessor of letters patent to an industrial invention has the exclusive right to its use and to dispose of it within the limits and conditions established by law. Art. 2575-2594, Italian Civil Code.

opifício m.—workshop; factory.

oplíta or oplíte m.—heavy-armed foot soldier of ancient Greek armies.

òppio m.—opium.

oppórre—to oppose.

oppórre a—to appeal against (a judgment).

opposizióne f.—opposition.

opposizióne al decréto penàle di condànna—opposition to the penal decree of sentence of punishment. Art. 506-510; 190-218, Italian Code of Penal Procedure.

opposizióne alla dichiarazióne di falliménto—opposition to the declaration of bankruptcy. Art. 18 Falliménto (Bankruptcy), Usual Laws, Appendix to Italian Civil Code.

opposizióne di contumàce—opposition to contumacy. It is an order to review and modify an order of contempt. See contumàcia.

opposizióne di tèrzo—opposition by a third party. In civil matters, it is a challenge by a third party to a judgment rendered in a dispute by others which prejudice his rights. In cases of forced execution of property, the third party is asserting his superior right to it. Art. 404-408; 615-622, Italian Code of Civil Procedure.

opprímere—to oppress.

oppugnàre—to assail; to attack; to combat; to dispute; to oppugn.

oppugnazióne f.—oppugnancy; assailing; attack; confutation; contradiction; objection; opposition.

optàre—to opt; to make a choice.

opzióne f.—option; choice; power of choosing.

opzióne (dirítto di)—right of option. This is a right of shareholders of a corporation to be preferred in the acquisition of new shares issued by the corporation. Art. 1532, 2441, Italian Civil Code.

ordinaménto m. — arrangement; disposition; governance; order; regulation.

ordinaménto della Repúbblica—governance of the Republic. Art. 55-139, Constitution of the Italian Republic.

ordinaménto giudiziàrio — governance and disposition of the judiciary. Justice, in both civil and penal matters, is administered by the following courts and judges thereof: (1) Conciliation; (2) Praetor; (3) Tribunal; (4) Court of Appeals; (5) Supreme Court of Cassation. Also included are the Public Prosecutors, assistants to the judges, officers and bailiffs. Art. 1, et seq., Ordinaménto Giurisdizionàle (Jurisdictional Ordinance of the Judiciary), Usual Laws, Appendix to Italian Code of Civil Procedure.

ordinaménto giurisdizionàle della magistratúra—jurisdictional governance of the judiciary. The jurisdictional function of the judiciary is discharged by regular judges and is regulated by the ordinaménto giudiziàrio. Art. 101-110, Constitution of the Italian Republic; Ordinaménto Giurisdizionàle (Jurisdictional Ordinance of the Judiciary), Usual Laws, Appendix to Italian Code of Civil Procedure.

ordinànza f.—ordinance; order; disposition; mandate; regulation.

ordinàrio—ordinary; usual.

ordinàrio m. — regular; common; normal; usual; according to accustomed order.

ordinazióne f. — ordination; medical prescription; order of goods or work.

órdine m.—order; array; class; discipline; disposition; rule; series; an order of persons enjoying a common distinction, be it medical, military, monastic, legal or in an honorary group such as a knighthood.

órdine degli avvocàti e procuratóri— order of lawyers and procurators. See consíglio dell'órdine degli avvocàti e procuratóri.

órdine di accompagnaménto—order to produce a person charged with a crime for interrogation. It is issued by the Public Prosecutor to the police authorities. Art. 251, 393, Italian Code of Penal Procedure. See mandàto di accompagnaménto.

órdine di arrèsto—order of arrest. It is an order issued by the Public Prosecutor in the summary phase of a penal proceeding. It is directed to the police authorities, so that an accused be jailed or placed in custody elsewhere, subject to the prosecutor's disposition. Art. 251, 252, 444, Italian Code of Penal Procedure. See mandàto di arrèsto.

órdine di carcerazióne—order of imprisonment. It is issued by the Public Prosecutor or Praetor to the authorities of Public Security for the detention of a convicted person if he is not already in custody. Art. 581, Italian Code of Penal Procedure. See mandàto di cattúra.

órdine di cattúra—order of arrest. It is an order of apprehension issued by the Púbblico Ministèro (Public Prosecutor) or Praetor. Art. 243, 251, 277 bis, 393, 397, Italian Code of Penal Procedure. See mandàto di cattúra.

órdine di comparizióne—order of appearance. It is issued by the Public Prosecutor ordering the accused to appear before him. Art. 251, 393, Italian Code of Penal Procedure. See mandàto di comparizióne.

órdine púbblico — public order. Acts against public order or good behavior are invalid. This includes contracts and testamentary dispositions. Art. 634, 1229, 1343, 1344, Italian Civil Code; Art. 797, 804, Italian Code of Civil Procedure.

órdine púbblico (delítti cóntro) — crimes against public order. Art. 414-421, Italian Penal Code. For violations, see Art. 650, 656, idem.

órdini di conségna—delivery orders; they are issued by the carrier so that the shipper may divide the shipment into a number of consignments to different consignees in different locations. Art. 466, Italian Navigation Code.

òrgani dello Stàto—organs of the State. Generally, these are those public offices through which the State administers its affairs.

órgano m.—organ; part of the body which has a specific function; a medium of communicating ideas or opinions.

oricàlco m.—brass; a mixture of brass and bronze; alloy of copper and zinc; a vessell of brass. See ottóne.

orientàre—to orient.

orientazióne f.—orientation.

originàrio — native of; of origin; original.

oriúndo—native of a place.

órma f.—foot-mark; scent; trace.

ormàre—to follow the tracks; to trace.

ormeggiàre—to moor a ship; to follow up.

orméggio m.—anchoring of a ship.

orològio m.—watch; time-piece.

orpellàio m.—leather gilder.

orpellàre—to cover with tinsel.

orpèllo m.—tinsel; an alloy of copper and zinc which has the appearance of gold.

orretízio—a thing obtained by fraud and surprise; surreptitious; obtained by subreption or obreption. See obrettízio.

orrezióne f.—obreption; a thing obtained by fraud, surprise or false representations.

òrto m.—vegetable garden.

òrto m.—rising of the sun or planets (poetic); birth.

ortografía f.—orthography; proper and correct spelling.

ortopedía f.—orthopedia; orthopedics; cure and correction of deformities and diseases of the spine, bones, joints or other parts of the skeletal system.

oscenità f.—obscenity.

oscèni (àtti)—obscene acts. Art. 527-538, Italian Penal Code.

oscèno—obscene.

òspite m.—host; guest.

òssa f.—bones of a living being.

ossàrio m.—ossuary; a place for the collection of human bones.

ossígeno m.—oxygen.

òsso m.—bone; pit of fruit.

ostàcolo m. — obstacle; impediment; obstruction.

ostàggio m.—hostage.

ostàre—to impede; to hinder; to oppose. See núlla òsta.

òste m.—host; inn-keeper.

ostèllo m.—hostel; refuge; lodging.

osteria f. — inn; modest restaurant which serves alcoholic beverages. A penal sentence may forbid a defendant from frequenting such a place for at least one year. Art. 234, Italian Penal Code.

ostíle—hostile.

ostilità f.—hostility.

òttica f.—optics.

òttico—optic; visual.

ottóne m.—brass; alloy of copper and zinc.

P

pàdre m.—father.

buòn pàdre di famíglia—literally, the good or responsible father of a family. It is used to signify the nature and degree of care that should be exercised by a prudent and judicious person in discharg-ing certain business, professional or legal obligations. Art. 1176, Italian Civil Code.

responsabilità del pàdre per fàtto illécito del fíglio minóre—responsibility of father for illicit act of a minor child. The father, mother or guardian are responsible for damage caused by the wrongful act of minor, unemancipated, children who live with them. Art. 2048, Italian Civil Code.

padrefamíglia m.—family man; father of a family.

padríno m.—godfather; second at a duel. See secóndo.

padronàggio m.—authority; command; mastery; the office of the master of a merchant vessel. See patronànza.

padronàle—pertaining to the master or owner.

padronànza f.—mastery; dominance.

padronàto m.—ownership; rural possession; estate; patronage; protection.

padróne m.—master; owner; patron; protector; master of a merchant vessel; a boss.

pàga f.—pay; salary; wages.

pagàbile—payable.

pagaménto m.—payment; extinguishment of a debt; satisfaction of an obligation. Art. 1176-1200, Italian Civil Code.

pagaménto con surrogazióne—payment with right of subrogation. When a third party pays a debtor's obligation to a creditor, the third party is subrogated to the rights of the creditor thereunder. The obligation is not discharged but continues to the benefit of the substituted third party. It occurs by agreement or by operation of law. Art. 1201-1205, Italian Civil Code.

pagaménto con surrogazióne legàle—payment with legal subrogation. It is a subrogation by operation of law. It occurs in the following cases: (1) for the benefit of a creditor who pays another creditor who has a prior lien; (2) for the purchaser of real property who, to the extent of the purchase price, pays a lien creditor of the property; (3) for the benefit of one who was bound with others, or for others, to pay the debt, and had an interest in satisfying it; (4) for the benefit of an heir with benefit of inventory, who pays the estate debts with his own money; (5) in other cases established by law. Art. 1203, Italian Civil Code.

pagaménto con surrogazióne per volontà del creditóre—payment with subrogation at the option of the creditor. A creditor who receives payment from a third party may subrogate him to his rights. The subrogation must be done expressly and contemporaneously with the payment. It is a conventional subrogation. Art. 1201, Italian Civil Code.

pagaménto con surrogazióne per volontà del debitóre—payment with subrogation at the option of the debtor. Here, the debtor borrows a sum of money or fungible goods under a contract of bailment to repay a debt. He may subrogate the lender or bailor to the rights of his creditor. It is a conventional subrogation. Art. 1202, Italian Civil Code.

pagaménto del débito prescrítto—payment of a barred debt. Restitution is not permitted of that which has been paid voluntarily in fulfillment of a barred or outlawed debt. Art. 2940, Italian Civil Code.

pagaménto dell'indébito—payment of a sum which is not owed. The law provides for the restitution of sums paid, which are not owed. These are (1) where a payment is made which is not owed, and (2) where a payment is made, through error, of another's debt. Art. 2033-2040, Italian Civil Code. See (1) **indébito oggettívo**; (2) **indébito soggettívo**.

pagaménto indébito (azióne del)—action for restitution of a payment not owed. See **azióne del pagaménto indébito** and **azióne di ripetizióne**. Art. 2033-2040, Italian Civil Code.

pagherò m.—promissory note. Also, referred to as **vàglia cambiàrio** and **cambiàle**. See **vàglia cambiàrio**, Art. 100-103, **Cambiàle (Drafts)**, Appendix to Usual Laws, Italian Civil Code.

pagnòtta f.—small loaf; wages, in a figurative sense.

pagnottísta m.—a hireling; one who serves in a job merely for pay; one who belongs to the party from which he gains material advantage.

palànca f.—stake; split-rail.

palancàre—to haul with a tackle.

palancàto m.—stockade.

palànco m.—block and tackle with ropes for hauling. Also, **parànco**.

palàncola f.—plank or board placed over a canal for crossing.

pàlchi (pl.) m.—antlers of a stag.

pàlco m.—platform; stand for display or for spectators; theater box; a scaffold; ceiling beam or frame.

pàlco scènico—theater stage.

palése—evident; manifest.

pàlla f.—ball; bullet.

pallòtta f.—small ball or bullet.

pallòttola f.—small ball; bullet; billiard ball; small ball used in voting, so that black indicates a negative, and white, a favorable vote.

pàlo m.—stake; pole; mast; lever.

pàlo di fèrro—crow-bar.

pàlo d'orméggio—mooring post.

palombàro m.—deep-sea diver, appropriately equipped to work under water.

panàtica f.—provision of bread; victuals; the food or its equivalent in money given to merchant seamen.

pànca f.—bench.
càssa panca—locker.
scaldàre le pànche—to warm the benches; bench-warming; to attend school and learn nothing; to take it easy.

panchína f.—a low platform; a stone or iron railing in a park; a stone edging for a gutter. See **banchína**.

pandétte f.—pandects; compilation of Roman law from the writings of the older jurists arranged methodically and also called the Digests.

pànfano m.—ancient warship, smaller than a galley.

panfílio or panfilo m.—an ancient warship; it also refers to a sporting boat called in English, a yacht.

pantàno m.—marsh; swamp.

pantògrafo m.—pantograph; a copying machine.

pàpa m.—Pope.

papàbile—a Cardinal who is eligible to the Papacy and has the probability of election to that dignity.

papàto m.—Papacy; dignity of that office; reign of a Pope.

papàvero m.—poppy.

parabórdo m.—a fender on a ship consisting of timber, ropes and the like, hung over the sides of a vessel to absorb shocks when docking.

paracadúte m.—parachute.

paracadutísta m.—parachutist.

parafàngo m.—mud-guard on a car; fender.

parafernàle—paraphernalia; personal effects and belongings. The separate property of a married woman, not included in her dowry, which remains under her control. This concept has been superseded by statutory enactment. See bèni personàli del còniuge.

parafúlmine m.—lightning-rod.

parafuòco m.—fire-screen.

paragàmbe m.—leg-shield; a metal protective screen on a motorcycle to prevent injury to the legs.

paràlisi f.—paralysis.

paralítico—paralytic.

paralúce m.—light shade for a camera.

paralúme—eye-shade.

paramàno m. — upturned cuff on a sleeve; hand-guard on a fencing foil.

parànco m.—block and tackle with ropes for hauling. Also, palànco.

paranínfa r.—bridesmaid.

paranínfo m. — paranynph; groomsman; in ancient Greece, a friend who accompanied the bridegroom when he brought home the bride.

parànza f.—a lateen rigged craft used for fishing.

parapíglia f. — great confusion; disorder; turmoil.

paràre — to adorn; to deck out; to check; to ward off; to catch (a ball); to stop.

parastatàle—to governmental authority or agency pursuing a public objective and under supervision of the State. Art. 11, Italian Civil Code.

paràta f.—defense; parry; in fencing, the deflecting or warding off a blow; parade; review.

paràto m.—ornament; drappery handings.

paràto—prepared; ready.

paratóia f.—damper; register in a fireplace; sluice gate in a channel.

paraúrto m.—bumper on an automobile to guard against damage from a collision.

paravènto m.—folding screen.

parcàre—to collect (a bill); to park (a car).

parcèlla f.—an item of an account; a note or bill for reimbursement and compensation; a bill for a lawyer's fee; parcel or portion of land. See particèlla.

parcèlla catastàle—the parcel of land, buildings and appurtenances subject to taxation. Also, particèlla catastàle.

parchéggio m.—automobile parking.

pàrco m.—park.

pàrco—frugal; thrifty.

pàrdo m.—leopard.

pareggiàre—to equal; to level; to make even; to compare; to settle an account. See parificàre.

pareggiàto—equalized; equalled; compared; balanced; comparison of a private school with a public school regarding its rights, obligations and certification. See parificàto.

parènte m.—relative; relation.

parentèla f.—the bond between persons who are descended from the same stock. Art. 74-77, Italian Civil Code.

parére—to appear to be; to have the

appearance; to appear; to estimate; to judge.

parère m.—counsel; judgment; opinion; written opinion of a lawyer.

parèsi f.—paresis; incomplete motor paralysis.

paréte f.—interior walls of a room.

parificàre—to render equal; to equalize; to compare. See **pareggiàre.**

parificàto—equalized; compared; specifically said of a private school in comparison with a public school as having the same rights and obligations; equalled. See **pareggiàto.**

parificazióne f.—comparison; equalization.

parità f.—parity; equality.

paritètico—said of a commission with jurisdictional powers to terminate or conciliate economic or labor disputes where the contending parties are equally represented.

parlaménto m.—parliament; the Italian Parliament consists of a Chamber of Deputies and a Senate.

parlatòrio m.—a room in a college or convent where visitors may visit and talk with the students or nuns.

parricìda m.—parricide; one who kills his own father. See **matricìda.**

parricìdio m.—parricide; the act of killing one's own father. Art. 575-577, Italian Penal Code.

pàrte f.—part; portion; party; the party to a legal proceeding. In a civil action, the parties are the **attóre** (plaintiff), **convenúto** (defendant) and **interventóre volontàrio** (voluntary intervenor). In penal actions, the parties are the **Púbblico Minis-tèro** (Public Prosecutor), the **im-putàto** (criminal defendant), the **pàrte civíle** (injured civil party) who appears to seek damages, the party who may be liable civilly for the damages and the party liable for a fine. Art. 75-81, Italian Code of Civil Procedure; Art. 73, 78, 91-123, Italian Code of Penal Procedure.

pàrte civíle—civil party. It is the civil party in a criminal trial seeking damages arising out of the criminal act. See **costituzióne di pàrte civíle.** Art. 91-106, Italian Code of Penal Procedure.

pàrte lèsa—injured party. It refers to a party damaged by acts arising out of a violation of a penal law. See **pàrte civíle.**

partecipazióne a giuòchi d'azzàrdo—participation in games of chance. Whoever, in a public place, or one open to the public, or in private clubs of any kind, is caught while taking part in a game of chance, is punished with arrest and a fine. Art. 720, Italian Penal Code.

particèlla f. — particle; small part; parcel or portion of land. Also, **parcèlla.**

particèlla catastàle — the parcel of land, buildings and appurtenances subject to taxation. Also, **parcèlla catastàle.**

partigiàna f. — halberd; partisan (female).

partigiàno m.—partisan.

partigióne f.—partition; discord.

partiménto m.—division; sharing.

partíre—to depart; to divide.

partíta f.—entry in a ledger; game; round; departure.

partíta dóppia — double entry book-keeping.

partitànte—partisan.

partitàrio m. — commercial book in which debits and credits are entered.

partíto m.—political party; bargain; resolution; match (matrimonial).

partíto—departed; divided.

partitúra f.—musical score; division of a crop between landlord and tenant; parting of the hair; a wheel which serves to separate the time mechanism in a clock from the chiming mechanism.

pàrto m.—childbirth; confinement.
dolóri di pàrto—labor pains.
sópra pàrto—in labor.

pàsco m.—pasture; poetic for **pàscolo.**

pascolàre—to pasture.

pàscolo m.—pasture. Art. 866, 2186, Italian Civil Code.

pàscolo abusívo—improper or wrongful pasturage. Art. 636, 649, Italian Penal Code. It is one of the crimes against property. See delítti cóntro il patrimònio.

pàscolo (dirítto di)—right of pasturage. See Úsi cívici.

passàggio coattívo — compulsory passage—similar to easement of necessity. The owner of land which is surrounded by another's lands and who does not have egress to or access to the public highway, and cannot procure same without excessive expense or hardship, has the right to obtain passage over neighboring land for the cultivation and convenient use of his own land. Access to the highway must be made by the shortest route with minimum damage. Art. 1051-1055, Italian Civil Code.

passàggio di conduttúre elèttriche—passage of electrical transmission installations. Every owner must allow passage over his lands of electrical transmission installations in conformity to the laws regarding the subject. This article creates a servitude on the land. Art. 1056, Italian Civil Code; Art. 119-130, Àcque Públiche—Eletrodótto (Public Waters—Electrical Transmission Installation), Usual Laws, Appendix to Italian Civil Code.

passàggio di víe funicolàri—passage of funicular railways. Every owner must allow passage over his land to the cables of funicular aerial railways for agrarian or industrial use and to tolerate on his land the works, mechanisms and the occupation necessary for such purpose in conformity to the laws regarding the subject. This article creates a servitude on the land. Art. 1057, Italian Civil Code.

passività f.—passivity; indebtedness.

passívo—passive; liabilities; debts.

pàsso coattívo—compulsory passage. See passàggio coattívo.

pastúra f. — pasture; pasturage. See pàscolo.

patàcca f. — a copper coin of little value.

patènte—patent; evident; manifest.

patènte f. — certificate; license (to drive a car; to teach; to carry arms); letters patent; a grant of a privilege or property.

paternità f.—paternity; the condition, state and relationship of a father. Art. 231-235, Italian Civil Code.

paternità (disconosciménto di) — disavowal of paternity. See azióne di disconosciménto di paternità and azióni di stàto and disconosciménto di paternità.

paternità intellettuàle (dirítto àlla)— right to intellectual authorship. See Art. 2577, Italian Civil Code.

patibolàre — patibulary; pertaining to the scaffold or execution.

patíbolo m.—gallows; gibbet; scaffold; torture.

pàtria f.—country of one's birth; native land; fatherland.

patria potestas (Lat.) — parental authority; parental power. Art. 315-337, Italian Civil Code. See potestà dei genitóri.

patrimònio m.—patrimony; estate; an estate, whether inherited or otherwise acquired; any kind of property, owned privately or publicly.

patrimònio familiàre—family fund or estate. It is now referred to in the Civil Code as fóndo patrimoniàle. See fóndo patrimoniàle.

patrimònio sociàle—partnership or corporate assets. See capitàle sociàle.

patrocinàre—to defend; to protect.

patrocinatóre m.—advocate; defender; protector; patron. See difensóre and procuratóre.

patrocinatóre legàle—legal defender. He is a practitioner who has not been licensed as a lawyer or procurator, but may practice before Praetors and Conciliators. See Patrocinatóri Legàli, Usual Laws, Appendix to Italian Code of Civil Procedure.

patrocínio m.—patronage; protection; defense; defense of a client.

patrocínio gratuíto—free defense. It is a protection afforded to the indigent or poor so that they can be defended without cost. Also, gratuíto patrocínio. Art. 1-43, Patrocínio Gratuíto, Usual Laws, Appendix to Italian ode of Civil Procedure.

patrocínio o consulènza infedèle—disloyal defense or expert testimony. It is a crime committed by dereliction of professional duties in defense of the party represented before the judicial authorities, which prejudice or damage said party. It is also a crime for the above, directly or indirectly, to represent adversary parties. Art. 380, 381, Italian Penal Code.

patronàto m.—patronage; defense; favor; encouragement; support; act or office of a patron; protection of the ecclesiastical rights in a benefice.

patronàto assistenziàle—a group rendering to others some form of aid, assistance, charity, protection or relief.

patròno m.—patron; protector; defense lawyer.

pàtti (pl.) m.—agreements; pacts; conventions.

pàtti relatívi all'ònere della pròva—agreements relating to burden of proof. Pacts are null and void which invert or modify the burden of proof, when they relate to rights which the parties cannot dispose, or when the inversion or modification makes the exercise of a right excessively difficult to one of the parties. Art. 2698, Italian Civil Code. See ònere della pròva.

pàtto m.—agreement; pact; convention.

pàtto angàrico—oppressive agreement; one which exacts a compulsory and vexatious service. It is not countenanced.

pàtto commissòrio—an agreement derived from the Roman Lex Commissoria which was abolished by Constantine. Italian law continues the prohibition and declares such agreements null and void, even if made subsequent to the conclusion of the contract. Prohibited are the passing of ownership in real property to a creditor on default in payment of the debt; also, the passing of ownership to hypothecated or pledged property to a creditor on default in payment of the obligation at the time agreed. Art. 1963, 2744, Italian Civil Code.

pàtto di esònero da responsabilità—exoneration of responsibility agreement. It is void. See clàusole di esònero da responsabilità. Art. 1229, 1228, Italian Civil Code.

pàtto di non concorrènza in càso di alienazióne—agreement of non-competition in event of a sale. The seller of a business must, for a period of five years of its sale, abstain from starting a new one whose aim, location or other circumstances may serve to keep customers from the business which had been sold. An agreement of non-competition is valid so long as it does not prohibit every professional activity of the seller. It is only valid for five years. Art. 2557, Italian Civil Code.

pàtto di riscàtto—agreement to redeem back property sold. The conventional agreement of redemption is one added to a sale contract, whereby the seller reserves the right to redeem the property sold upon repayment of the sale price, expenses incurred in the sale and the increased value of the property. Personal property must be redeemed within two years of the sale and real property within five years. It cannot be prolonged. Art. 1500-1509, Italian Civil Code.

pàtto di riservàto domínio—conditional sales contract. Art. 1523-1526, Italian Civil Code. See riservàto domínio. Also, véndita con risèrva del domínio.

pàtto leoníno — an agreement where one or more partners are excluded from sharing in the profits or losses. It is null and void. Art. 2265, Italian Civil Code. Also null is a contract of agistment where the soccidàrio bears a larger portion of losses than profits. Art. 2178, Italian Civil Code.

pàtto successòrio—agreement regarding a succession or inheritance. An agreement whereby one disposes of an expectant inheritance or succession is null and void. Likewise, any act disposing or renouncing rights one may acquire pursuant to a succession not yet opened, is null and void. Art. 458, Italian Civil Code.

pauliàna (azióne)—Paulian action. A revocatory action. See azióne revocatòria. Art. 2901-2904, Italian Civil Code.

peculàto m. — peculation; embezzlement. It is the crime committed by a public official or one in charge of a public service, who, by reason of his possession of public funds or personal property, appropriates and diverts it to his own use or that of a third party. Art. 314, Italian Penal Code. See malversazióne and pùbblica amministrazióne (delítti cóntro la).

pedàggio m.—toll paid to pass a certain place or street or to cross over a bridge.

pedàta f.—foot-track: foot-print; stair tread; kick with the foot.

pedonàle—pertaining to a street reserved for pedestrians.

pedóne m.—pedestrian; foot soldier; pawn.

pégno m.—pawn; pledge; that which is given as security for an obligation and which must be returned after the obligation is extinguished. Personal property is the object of a pledge. Art. 2784-2807, Italian Civil Code.

péltro m.—pewter; an alloy of tin and lead or tin and one of various constituents.

pèna f.—pain; penalty; punishment inflicted for violation of the law. Art. 17-38, Italian Penal Code.

péna convenzionàle—a penalty clause. See clàusola penàle.

péna di mòrte—death penalty. The death penalty is not permitted except in cases provided by military laws of war. When the Penal Code threatens the death penalty, life imprisonment is applied. Art. 27, Constitution of the Italian Republic; Art. 21, 22, Italian Penal Code.

péna di recèsso—See capàrra penipenziàle. Art. 1386, Italian Civil Code.

penàle—penal.

penàle (clàusola)—penalty clause. See clàusola penàle.

penalísta m.—criminal lawyer.

pendènte — pending; hanging; overhanging; pending law suit.

pendènza f.—pendency.

péne accessòrie — accessory punishments. For crimes known as delítti, they are: (1) interdiction from public office; (2) interdiction from a profession or art; (3) legal interdiction (for those sentenced to life); (4) loss of the capacity to make a testament and the nullity of one made prior to the sentence; (5) the loss or suspension of parental and marital authority. Accessory punishment for the crimes known as contravvenzióni is the suspension of the right to exercise a profession or art. The accessory punishment common to both delítti and contravvenzióni is the publication of the judgment of penal sentence. The penal law determines the other cases in which accessory punishments established for delítti are common to contravvenzióni. Art. 19, Italian Penal Code. See interdizióne.

pensionàto m.—pensioner.

pensióne f.—pension; annuity; boarding house.

pensióne alimentària m.—alimony. See alimònia.

percòssa f.—blow given by hand or stick; a battery.

percòsse—batteries. Whoever commits a battery on another which does not result in physical or mental illness, upon complaint of the offended person, may be imprisoned up to six months and fined. This disposition is not applicable when violence is an element of the act or is an aggravated circumstance of another crime. Art. 581, Italian Penal Code.

pèrdita f.—loss.

perdonàre—to pardon; to excuse; to forgive.

perdóno m.—pardon; forgiveness.

perdóno giuduziàle per i minóri degli ànni diciòtto—judicial pardon for minors of age eighteen. It can only be granted once. The judge dismissing the charge because of minority, shall state the reason therefor in his opinion and declare the dismissal by judgment "non dovérsi procèdere". Art. 169, Italian Penal Code; Art. 379, Italian Code of Penal Procedure; Art. 14, Tribnal for Minors, Usual Laws, Appendix to Italian Code of Penal Procedure.

perènto—extinguished; expired.

perentòrio — peremptory; decisive; final.

perenzióne f. — extinguishment of a right or action through passage of time. See estinzióne del procésso.

perequàre—to equalize.

perequazióne f.—equalization.

perequazióne tributària—equalization of the tax base.

perfezionaménto m.—perfecting; finishing; improvement.

perfezionàre—to perfect; to improve.

perícolo m.—peril; danger; risk.

perícolo comúne (delítti di)—crimes involving common danger. See delítti di comúne perícolo mediànte violènza; delítti di comúne perícolo mediànte fròde and delítti colpósi di comúne perícolo. Also, delítti còntro l'incolumità púbblica. Art. 422-452, Italian Penal Code.

perícolo di disàstro ferroviàrio causàto da danneggiaménto—danger of railroad disaster caused by damaging acts. Whoever, for the sole purpose of damaging a railroad, or machines, vehicles, instruments, apparatuses or other things which serve its operation, destroys them in whole or in part, causes them to deteriorate, or otherwise renders them useless in whole or in part, is punished with imprisonment, if from the act, there may arise the danger of a railroad disaster. If disaster arises as a result of the act, the penalty is augmented.

The penal law intends the word railroad to include, besides the usual railroad, every other road with metal rails upon which there circulate vehicles moved by steam, electricity or other means of mechanical traction. Art. 431, Italian Penal Code. See disàstro ferroviàrio.

periòdico m.—newspaper; news items issued at stated intervals.

periòdico—periodic.

períre—to perish.

peritàle—referring to an expert's opinion or report.

períto m. — expert. See consulènte tècnico. Re compensation, see vacazióne.

políto—perished.

perízia f.—skill; expertness; report of the expert expressing his opinion.

pèrmuta f.—a contract of exchange whereby property or rights in one thing are transferred for another thing; barter; exchange. Art. 1552-1555, Italian Civil Code.

perpètua f. — a priest's housekeeper, from the name of Perpetua, the housekeeper of Don Abbondio, in the novel "I Proméssi Spòsi" of Manzoni; a garrulous and irascible old woman servant.

perpetuàre—to perpetuate.

perpètuo — perpetual; continuous; never ceasing; unlimited in time. It is distinguished from eternal which exists without relation to time or change. See etèrno.

perquisíre—to search.

perquisizióne f.—perquisition; a thorough search usually by the police authorities to confiscate the instruments and fruits of the crime. It is forbidden unless authorized by the judicial authorities as provided by law. Art. 13, Constitution of the Italian Republic, Art. 332-336, 224, Italian Code of Penal Procedure.

perquisizióne e ispezióne personàli arbitràrie—arbitrary personal search and inspection. The public official who abuses the powers inherent in his office and conducts a personal search or inspection, is punished with incarceration up to one year. Art. 609, Italian Penal Code.

persóna f.—person; the physical person and his rights. Art. 1, 2, 4-10, Italian Civil Code.

persóna (delítti cóntro la) — crimes against the person. Art. 575-623, Italian Penal Code.

persóna interpósta — interposed person; one placed as an intermediary in lieu of a person who cannot or does not wish to appear. For those prohibited to do so, see Art. 323, 378, 396, 599, 627, 779, 1261, 1471, 2233, Italian Civil Code.

personalità dello stàto (delítti cóntro) —crimes against the jural personality of the State. Art. 241-313, Italian Penal Code.

persóne che dèvono èssere interdètte —persons who must be interdicted (from managing their affairs). Persons who have reached majority and emancipated minors who find themselves in conditions of habitual mental infirmity which render them incapable of providing for their proper interests, must be interdicted. Art. 414, Italian Civil Code. See **interdizióne** and **inabilitazióne.**

persóne che pòssono èssere inabilitàte —persons who may be disqualified from managing their affairs. Subject to it are: those who have reached majority with mental infirmity not so grave as to warrant interdizióne; those who, through prodigality, wasteful extravagance or habitual use of alcoholic beverages or stupefying drugs, expose themselves or their families to grave economic damage; deaf-mutes and the blind from birth or early infancy who have received insufficient education, excepting the application of Art. 414, when it results that they are totally incapable of managing their own affairs. Art. 415, et seq., Italian Civil Code. See **persóne che dèvono èssere interdètte** and **inabilitazióne.**

persóne giurídiche—jural persons or bodies. Art. 11-35, 2331, Italian Civil Code. Art. 2, Enabling Rules, Italian Civil Code. Also, **còrpi moràli.**

pertinènte — pertinent; applicable; suitable; relevant.

pertinènza (pertinènze pl.) f. — that which belongs to something else; adjunct; appendage. Such are considered things destined to serve in a durable way or to ornament another thing. The destination may be effected by the owner of the principal thing or by one who has a real right over the same. Art. 817-819, Italian Civil Code.

pesànte—heavy; grave; dull.

pesàre—to weigh; to ponder.

péso m.—weight.

péso lórdo—gross weight.

péso nétto—net weight.

pésta f.—beaten track; footstep; trace.

pèste f.—pestilence; contagion; stench.

petèndi (càusa)—the legal basis for the relief demanded.

petènte m. & f.—petitioner. Also, **petitóre.**

pètere—to ask; to demand; to petition; to request.

petitóre m.—petitioner. Also, **petènte.**

petitòria (azióne)—petitory action. See Azióne petitòria and Arts. 948-951, Italian Civil Code and Art. 705, Italian Code of Civil Procedure.

petitòrio—petitory; relating to a petitory action to enforce a right or title to property. See **azióne petitòria** and **giudízio petitòrio.**

petitòrio (giudízio) — petitory action. See **giudízio petitòrio** and **azióne petitòria.**

petizióne f.—petition; a written application to the appropriate authorities for relief.

petizióne (dirítto di)—right to petition for redress of grievances. All citizens may address petitions to the Houses of Parliament to request legislative measures or to present matters of common necessity. Art. 50, Constitution of the Italian Republic.

petizióne di eredità—petition of heirship. It is an action by the heir for the recognition of his right to heirship against anyone who possesses all or part of the hereditary property under title of heir or without title whatever, for the purpose of obtaining restitution of the property itself. The action is imprescriptable except in cases of adverse possession of individual property. Art. 533-535, Italian Civil Code.

petrolièra f. — tanker; a ship which carries liquid petroleum products.

piàno m.—plan; plane surface; floor or story of a building; piano, meaning a pianoforte, a musical instrument.

piàno—plane; flat; level.

piàno regolatóre — zoning plan. Art. 869-872, Italian Civil Code.

pianofòrte m.—a musical instrument operated by means of a keyboard.

piantagióne f.—act of planting; plantation.

piantàta f.—planting; a row of plants; a row of trees, vines and fruit bearing shrubs.

pianterréno m.—ground floor.

pianùra f.—plain; vast expanse of flat land.

piattafórma f.—platform.

piàzza f.—plaza; square; a public place where people gather for business or for sport; a market place.

piccionàia f.—pigeon house; dovecote; the highest gallery in a theater.

picciòtto m.—in Sicilian dialect, a boy or young man; one who joined the Garibaldi forces in 1860 during the war for Italian unification and the invasion of Sicily.

píccoli imprenditóri—small contractors or entrepreneurs. These are the immediate cultivators of the land, the artisans, the small businessmen and those who perform a professional activity primarily with their own work and that of the members of their family. Art. 2083, Italian Civil Code. See **imprenditóre**. To determine who are considered small contractors under the Bankruptcy Law, see Art. 1, Falliménto (Bankruptcy), Usual Laws, Appendix to Italian Civil Code.

pidocchiería f.—stinginess.

pidòcchio m.—louse.

pidocchióso adj. & m.—lousy; avaricious; sordid.

pievanàle—pertaining to the pievàno or parish priest.

pievanía f.—the parish, incumbency or rectory of a country parish.

pievàno m.—rector or parish priest. Also, **piovàno**.

pième f.—rural population centered around a church; country parish church; country parish.

pigionàle m.—tenant; lodger; a daily worker on a farm.

pigióne f.—rental paid for the use of a house or apartment. See **obbligazióni principàli del conduttóre**.

pignoraménto m.—attachment; it is the first step in a forced expropriation or levy of execution. Art. 491-632, Italian Code of Civil Procedure; Art. 2912-2918, Italian Civil Code. See **esecuzióne forzàta** and **espropiazióne forzàta**.

pignoraménto di stipèndi, salàri e pensióni—attachment and garnishment of wages, salaries and pensions. By statute, it is limited to certain percentages of a debtor's obligations. See **sequèstro e pignoraménto di stipèndi, salàri e pensióni**.

pignoraménto immobiliàre — attachment of real property. See **espropiazióne immobiliàre**.

pignoraménto mobiliàre prèsso il debitóre—attachment of personal property of the debtor. See **espropiazióne mobiliàre prèsso il debitóre and impignoràbili (còse mòbili assolutaménte)**.

pignoraménto mobiliàre prèsso i tèrzi—attachment of obligations or credits of a debtor towards a third party or property of the debtor in possession of third parties. See **espropiazióne mobiliàre presso i terzi**.

pignoraménto (tèmpo del)—time for attachment. See **tèmpo del pignoraménto**.

pignoràre—to attach real or personal property so that it can be transferred by judicial sale; to pledge; to pawn.

pinacotèca f.—pinacotheca; a picture gallery containing paintings of artistic merit. Such galleries are considered part of the public domain. Art. 822, Italian Civil Code.

pínque—fat; plump.

pínza f.—pincers.

pinzétta f.—small pincers.

pinzétta a tàglio—nippers.

pinzétta piàna—pliers.

pío — pious; compassionate; kindly; religious.
òpera pía—charitable work or institution.

piombàre—to fall plumb; to hang vertically; to fall suddenly and violently; to weight with lead.

piombàta f.—leaden ball or dart.

piombàto—heavy; leaded; plumbed.

piombatóio m. — machicolation; an opening in the parapet of a fortification for hurling and dropping missiles upon attacking assailants.

piombatúra f.—coating of lead; soldering; alloy of tin and lead applied to sheet iron as a coating.

piómbo m.—lead.

piovàno m.—rector or parish priest. Also, **pievàno.**

piovàno—rainy; of rain. See **scàrico delle àcque piovàne.**

piovàsco m.—rain shower.

piovènte—raining; rainy; showery.

piovènte m.—inclined roof; inclination of the roof to allow waters to run off. There is a presumption that a dividing wall between cultivated lands, courtyards, gardens or orchards belongs to the owner of the land towards which the inclined roof is placed. Art. 881, Italian Civil Code.

piròscafo f.—steamer.

píscia f.—urine.

pisciàre—to urinate.

piscína f.—pool; swimming pool; fish pond.

písta f.—race course; race track; land-

ing and take-off strip for airplanes, **pistòla f.**—pistol.

pístola f.—epistle; letter.

pitàle m.—chamberpot.

pitoccàre—to beg.

pitoccheria f.—miserly action.

pitòcco m. (pitòcca f.)—beggar.

placàbile — placatory; that which placates or tends to appease.

placàre—to placate; to appease.

plàcca f.—plaque.

placet (Lat.) m.—approval by Civil authorities of ecclesiastic conferral of minor benefices.

plàcido—placid; calm.

plàcito m.—a decree issued by the authorities.

plàgio m.—plagiarism (Lat. plagium, theft of slaves); the appropriation of another individual's artistic, literary or scientific work and passing it off as one's own. It is forbidden and carries a penal sanction by way of a fine. Art. 101, 102, 171, Rights of Authors, Usual Laws, Appendix to Italian Civil Code; The Crime of plàgio consists in subjecting a person to one's power, so as to reduce him to a total state of constraint and submission. Art. 603, 604, Italian Penal Code. See **schiavitú.**

platèa f.—the pit of a theater; the orchestra seats in the seating arrangement; a concrete floor upon which foundations are set.

plebiscíto m.—plebiscite; a vote of the people on a solemn constitutional measure. See **referèndum.**

pluralità f.—plurality; the greater number. See **maggiorànza**—majority.

plúrimo—the casting of more than one vote by a single voter; plural voting.

plus-valóre m. — unearned increment; good-will.

pluviàle—pluvial; rainy. Also, **piovàno.**

podére m.—farm; agricultural land used for cultivation. See **mezzadría.**

podestà m.—chief of an ancient commune or municipality involved in the administration of justice.

poliandría f.—polyandry; the practice of having more than one husband at one time.

polifagía f.—excessive eating of food; voracity.

poligamía f.—polygamy; the practice of having a plurality of wives or husbands; usually, the practice of one man having a number of wives at the same time.

poliglòtta m. — polyglot; one who knows, speaks or writes several languages.

poligrafía f.—poligraphy; the writing of many, varied books; a system of secret writing and deciphering; the use of a polygraph.

polígrafo m.—polygraph; an imitator; a prolific writer; a duplicating or copying machine; a collection of various works.

polisarcía f.—excessive obesity.

política f. — politics; the art and science of governing a state; policy; artifice; finesse.

politicànte m.—politician, in a derogatory sense.

político—politic; pertaining to politics; political; crafty; shrewd.

político m.—politician; statesman.

polizía f.—police.

polizía giudiziària — judicial police. They are under the direct disposition of the judicial authority. The officers and agents of the judicial police are under the orders and direction of the Procurator General in the Court of Appeals and the Procurator of the Republic. Art. 109, Constitution of the Italian Republic; Art. 219-230, Italian Code of Penal Procedure.

polizía giudiziària (qualità di ufficiàli od agènti di)—composition of the officers or agents of the judicial police. The officers are: (1) functionaries of Public Security; (2) superior, inferior and under officers of the carabinieri, finance guards and agents of Public Security; the non-commissioned officers of the corps of security agents or guards; (3) the mayor in such communes or municipalities where there are none of the foregoing officials of the judicial police. The following are also agents of the judicial police: the carabinieri, the finance guards, the agents of Public Security, the custody agents or guards and the provincial and communal guards. Officials of the judicial police also include those so designated by law within the limits of the powers conferred upon them. Art. 221, Italian Code of Penal Procedure.

poliziòtto m.—policeman; police agent; Public Security agent.

pòlizza f. — policy; receipt; ticket; voucher.

pòlizza di anticiuazióne—memorandum of deposit of securities or merchandise with a bank which are left to secure a loan. See anticipazióne bancària.

pòlizza di assicurazióne—policy of insurance. The instrument which contains the contract of insurance. It may be made payable to order or to bearer. Art. 1888, 1889, Italian Civil Code. See assicurazióne.

pòlizza di càrico—bill of lading. The document containing the contract of carriage by sea. It is issued by the carrier or the master of the vessel in his stead. Art. 450-465, Italian Navigation Code; Art. 1638-1702, 1996, Italian Civil Code. See lèttera di vettúra and lèttera di traspòrto aèreo.

pòlizza diretta—through bill of lading.

pòlizza ricevúto per l'imbàrco—receipt for shipment of goods consigned to the carrier. Art. 459, Italian Navigation Code.

polizzíno m.—ticket; ticket distributed for communion; customs ticket notifying the recipient of goods of the amount of duty to be paid.

pollicitazióne f.—pollicitation; an offer which has not been accepted by the person to whom made; an offer or promise without mutuality; a unilateral promise or offer. Art. 1987-1991, Italian Civil Code.

polluzióne f.—pollution. See inquinaménto.

pólvere f.—dust; powder.

polverièra f.—powder magazine or mill.

popolàre—of the people; popular; suitable to all; representing the people.

popolàre (giúdice)—people's or citizen judge. See giúdice popolàre.

pórre—to place; to fix; to establish.

portafòglio m. — portfolio; a file or folder containing securities, bank notes and valuable documents. It also refers to a ministerial portfolio or post.

portatóre m.—bearer; an instrument payable to bearer; carrier; holder.

portavóce m. — spokesman; megaphone; speaking trumpet.

pòrti m.—ports; harbors. They are part of the public domain. Art. 822, Italian Civil Code.

pòrto m.—port; harbor (See pòrti); carriage of goods or persons; portage; postage; cost of carriage; freight; freightage; deportment.

pòrto abusívo di àrmi—wrongful and unlawful carrying of fire-arms. It is committed by carrying same outside a dwelling or its appurtenances and failing to produce a license issued by the authorities when requested to do so. If the same facts occur in a place where there is a concourse or assemblage of people, or at night, or in an inhabited place, the punishment is augmented. Art. 699, Italian Penal Code. See detenzióne abusíva di àrmi.

pòrto affrancàto—carriage paid; the cost of carriage is borne by the shipper. Also, frànco di pòrto. Art. 1686, Italian Civil Code.

pòrto assegnàto—carriage paid by the consignee on delivery. Art. 1689, Italian Civil Code.

pòrto d'àrme—license to carry a fire-arm.

pòrto frànco — free port. A port in which goods enter without paying custom duties. A free-entry port. See depòsiti frànchi.

porzióne f. — portion; share; allowance; the share of an estate to which a person is entitled.

porzióne disponíbile—disposable share. That part of an estate which a testator may leave to whomsoever he desires. See disponíbile and Art. 536, 564, Italian Civil Code.

porzióne indisponíbile—a reserved portion of an estate which cannot be disposed by the decedent. See porzióne riservàta.

porzióne legíttima—legitimate portion. The portion, quota or share of a decedent's estate reserved by law to certain heirs which cannot be otherwise disposed whether the succession is testamentary or intestate. See legíttima and leqittimàri. Art. 536-564, Italian Civil Code. Also referred to as porzióne indisponíbile.

porzióne riservàta—reserved portion or quota of an estate. That share of an estate that a decedent must leave to certain heirs. See porzióne legíttima and legittimàri. Art. 536-564, Italian Civil Code. Also referred to as risèrva and porzióne indisponíbile.

positúra f.—manner in which a thing is placed; attitude; posture.

posizióne f.—position; situation.

possànza f. — power; force; might; strength.

possèsso m.—possession; the power over a thing by exercising a right of property or other real right over it. Possession may be held directly or through another person who has detention or custody of the thing. Art. 1140-1157, Italian Civil Code. See quàsi possèsso.

possèsso di bòna féde—good faith possession. The good faith possessor is one who has possession without knowledge he is harming the right of another. Good faith is no justification if lack of knowledge is based on serious fault. Good faith is presumed and it is sufficient that it existed at the time of acquisition. Art. 1147, Italian Civil Code.

possèsso di stàto—possession of status. Generally, it concerns the proof of marriage, birth, filiation, legitimization and the judicial declaration of paternity and maternity. Art. 130-

133, 236-243, 269, 270, Italian Civil Code.

possèsso ingiustificàto di chiàvi alteràte o di grimaldèlli—wrongful possession of falsified keys or pick locks. Art. 707, Italian Penal Code.

possèsso ingiustificàto di valóri—unjustified possession of valuables; a violation committed by one previously condemned for crimes involving motives of gain, violations concerning prevention of crimes against patrimony, for begging, or having been warned and placed under a measure of personal security or under bail for good conduct. If apprehended in possession of money or things of value or other things not in conformity with his station and whose origin he cannot justify, he is punished with arrest from three months to one year. Art. 708, Italian Penal Code.

possèsso precàrio—precarious possession; possession which one enjoys at the pleasure and will of another. Art. 1140, 1144, Italian Civil Code.

possessóre m.—possessor.

possessóri (procediménti)—possessory proceedings. Art. 703-705, Italian Code of Civil Procedure.

possessòria (azióne)—possessory action. See azióne possessòria and Art. 1168-1170, Italian Civil Code; Art. 703-705, Italian Code of Civil Procedure.

possessòrio—possessory. See azióne possessòria—possessory action.

possidènte m.—one who has a fixed and continuing income from which he lives; a landed proprietor.

possidènza f.—the state of possessing; right of possession; owners as a group or class.

pòsteri (pl.) m.—descendants; successors; posterity.

posterità f. — posterity; succeeding generations and descendants.

postílla f.—postil; a marginal note; annotation; a notation by a notary setting forth the nature of the demand.

postrèmo—last; hindmost.

postríbolo m.—brothel. Also bordèllo; càsa di cartèlla; lupanàre.

postulànte m.—postulant; applicant; candidate.

postulàre—to ask; to request; to petition; to ask for a grace or favor, a position or benefice or benefit.

postulàto m.—postulate; a proposition admitted as true without demonstration since it is assumed to be self-evident.

postulatóre m.—postulator; claimant; plaintiff; one who presents the claim for a candidate for canonization.

postulatório—postulatory; petitionary; partaking of the nature of an assumption or postulate.

postulazióne f. — postulation; act of postulating; in Roman Law, an application to the Praetor to institute an action; judicial demand.

pòstumo — posthumous; a child born after the death of the father; a publication after the death of the author.

postúra f.—posture; position; attitude; cabal; plot; a secret and fraudulent deliberation.

potàbile—potable; drinkable.

potagióne f.—pruning; topping; pruning season. See potaménto and potatúra.

potaménto m.—pruning; topping.

potàre—to prune.

potatóio m.—pruning knife; pruning hook.

potatóre m.—pruner.

potatúra f.—pruning; topping.

potazióne f.—potation; act of drinking.

potènte—potent; powerful; mighty.

potènza f.—power; capacity to produce an effect; legal authority, capacity or power.

potére—to be able.

potére m.—power; ability to do or not to do something; authority; power to command.

potestà dei genitóri—parental authority. The child is subject to the parental authority till majority or

194

emancipation. Parental authority is exercised by common agreement of both parents. Art. 316 et seq; Italian Civil Code. See **patria potestas.**

potestà maritàle—marital authority as head of the family. This concept has been altered. Formerly, the father possessed this power. Now, both spouses acting in accord, have the right to guide the family and choose its residence. See **indirízzo della víta familiàre e residènza della famíglia.** Art. 144, Italian Civil Code.

pozióne f.—potion.

pozióre—preceding; prior; that which is prior or superior in right.

pozioritá f.—precedence; priority in rank or time.

pózza f.—puddle; pool; pit; drain.

pózzo m.—well; spring; tank. Wells, cisterns, cesspools, manure piles and water mains must be placed at least three meters distant from the property line or dividing wall between the properties. Art. 889, Italian Civil Code.

pózzo néro—cesspool.

pózzo (spúrgo di)—purging or cleansing of wells and latrines are at the expense of the leasor. Art. 1610, Italian Civil Code.

P.Q.M.—"**Per quésti motívi**". It is the abbreviation meaning, "For these reasons". It precedes a judge's opinion explaining the decision or judgment.

pràssi f. — practice; procedure developed in certain offices for handling their operations and activities.

pràtica f.—practice; usual or habitual performance; practice of a profession; a business situation and the paper work involved therewith.

pravità f.—pravity; depravity; wickedness.

pràvo—wicked; perverse; depraved; vicious.

preaccusàre—to accuse beforehand, or before the fact has occurred.

preannunziàre—to announce beforehand; to predict.

preavvertíre—to admonish or warn in advance.

preavvíso m.—notice in advance of the formal one.

prebènda f. — prebend; a stipend granted to a canon or chaplain; figuratively, an earning which is received with little effort.

precàrio—precarious; dependent on the will of another or circumstances beyond one's control; something held at the pleasure of another. See **possèsso precàrio.**

precarium (Lat.) m.—In Roman Law, a loan subject to be returned at the discretion of the lender; in Civil Law, a gratuitous bailment contract, subject to revocation at the will of the bailor.

precauzióne f.—precaution; an action taken in advance to avoid mistake and secure favorable results.

prèce f.—prayer; prayers; entreaty.

precedènte m.—precedent; prior established facts and rules of law which serve as authority in subsequent cases.

precedènza f.—precedence; priority in time, rank, order or importance.

precettànte m.—preceptor; one who issues commands or legal orders or warrants; instructor.

precettàre — to issue commands or orders; to give notice of a process to pay an obligation.

precettàto m.—one who has received a legal process.

precètto m. — precept; command; order; mandate. It is a judicial notification to comply with an obligation to pay the amount of a sum legally due and owed. It precedes the forced execution or expropiation of property by legal process. Art. 479-482, Italian Code of Civil Procedure. See Art. 55-57 Asségni (Checks) and Art. 63-65 Cambiàle (Drafts), Usual Laws, Appendix to Italian Civil Code.

prediàle f.—a tax on rural land.

prediàle—praedial; relating to or pertaining to land.

predominànte—predominant; being of greater power, authority or influence than others.

predominàre—to predominate; to be of greater power, authority or influence than others; to prevail.

predomínio m.—predomination; state of predominating.

preferènza f.—the act of preferring or favoring one thing or person over another. See **prelazióne** and **privilègio.**

prefètto m.—prefect; the chief administrative official of a province under the jurisdiction of the Minister of Interior; in ancient Rome, a high official or magistrate placed in charge of a province or some civil or military command.

prefettúra f.—prefecture; the office, dignity and jurisdiction of the prefect.

pregiudicàre—to prejudge; to judge in advance; to prejudicate; to prejudice; to damage; to compromise.

pregiudicàto—prejudged.

pregiudicàto m.—one who has been previously condemned; recidivist.

pregiudiziàle—prejudicial.

pregiudiziàle f.—prejudicial.

pregiudiziàli (questióni Penàli)—procedural questions which arise during the course of a penal proceeding which cannot be resolved till the conclusion of another controversy. Art. 18-21, Italian Code of Penal Procedure.

pregiudízio m.—prejudice; injury or damage resulting from another's disregard of a person's rights; an anticipated judgment; a preconceived opinion.

prégna—pregnant; impregnated.

pregnànte—pregnant.

prégno—pregnant; full.

prègo m.—entreaty; prayer. The response given to a person who says, "Thank you"; it is the equivalent to our "You are welcome".

prelazióne f.—prelation; preference; priority; act of preferring or placing before. See **preferènza** and **privilègio.**

prelazióne (diritto di)—right of preemption; the right of buying before others; preemptive right. Art. 732, 2157, Italian Civil Code.

prelegàto m.—a legacy left by a testator to one of a number of heirs in addition to the portion or share to which he would have been entitled by law. Art. 661, Italian Civil Code.

prelèggi f.—pre-laws, the provisions which precede the articles of the Civil Code, entitled "Disposizióni Sulla Légge in Generàle" (Dispositions on the Law in General). They are referred to, generally, as "Disposizióni Preliminàri" (Preliminary Dispositions), abbreviated "D.P.". Herein reported as Preliminary Dispositions.

prelevaménto m.—advance deduction.

prelevàre—to deduct in advance; to deduct by way of commission; to withdraw from partnership funds.

prelezióne f.—introductory lecture.

premeditazióne f.—premeditation; the act of premeditating or deliberating beforehand; a design formed in advance of performing an act. It is an aggravating circumstance in a prosecution for homicide. Art. 577, 575, Italian Penal Code.

prèmi di nuzialità, òpere di assistènza e símili—rewards or donations for marriage, works of assistance and welfare and the like. Testamentary dispositions are valid for grants of periodic liberality in perpetuity or for a time, of definite sums for the above and for births, subsidies for training for a profession or art or for other works of public utility in favor of persons chosen from a determined category or descendants of a determined family. Art. 699, Italian Civil Code.

prèmio m. — prize; reward; recompense; premium; subsidy; bounty on exports.

prèmio d'assicurazióne — insurance premium. Art. 1882, 1901, 1923, 1924, 2952, 2754, Italian Civil Code.

prèmio dovúto al ritrovatóre—reward due a finder. The owner of a lost article must pay a reward to the finder, if the latter demands it, of one-tenth of the value of the article found. If the value exceeds 10,000 Lire, the reward on the excess is only one-twentieth. If the article has no commercial value, the reward will be fixed by the judge according to his prudent appraisal. Art. 930, Italian Civil Code.

premoriènza f. — predecease; prior death. See **commorièza** and **sopravvivènza.**

premoríre—to die before another.

premuníre—to premonish; to admonish beforehand; to forewarn; to fortify in advance.

premunizióne f. — premonition; forewarning; precaution; anticipating an event or objection.

premúra f.—eagerness; haste; solicitude.

prenditóre m.—payee; one who takes; an agent in the public lottery office.

prenditoría f.—lottery office.

prenóme m.—given or Christian name. See **nóme (diritto al).**

prenotàre—to reserve; to fix or note in advance; to obtain priority in registration by recording or filing a mortgage.

prenotazióne f.—reservation; act of reserving; the acquisition of priority rights by a recorded mortgage holder over subsequent recorded mortgages or unrecorded or unfiled instruments.

prenotazióne a débito—fixing, taxing or assessing costs in civil matters involving natural or legal persons. See **ingiunzióne di pagaménto di spése, diritti ed onoràri.** Art. 43, Enabling Rules, Italian Civil Code.

prepotènte—prepotent; very powerful; superior in force or authority.

prepotènte m.—one who abuses power or authority; one who wants his own way in determining things; arrogant.

prepotènza f. — prepotence; prepotency; state of being prepotent; abuse of power or authority; arrogance.

prepúzio m.—prepuce; foreskin.

prerogatíva f. — prerogative; preference; privilege; right of voting before others.

présa f.—the act of taking; seizure; catch.

présa d'àcqua—taking or collection of water; point at which water is collected or drawn. The taking, collection and distribution of water is regulated by Art. 1080-1093, Italian Civil Code.

présa d'orméggio—mooring post.

prescrizióne f.—prescription. Civilly, it is the extinguishment of rights caused by non-use during a legally determined period of time. Penally, it consists in the extinguishment of a crime and its punishment due to passage of a legally determined period of time during which there has been a lack of prosecution. Art. 2934-2963, Italian Civil Code. Art. 157-161, 171-173, 150, Italian Penal Code.

prescrizióne acquisitíva — acquisitive prescription. Acquisition of a right by long use and continuity of possession. Art. 1158, Italian Civil Code. See **usucapióne.**

prescrizióne (còmputo dei tèrmini di)— computation of the limit of prescription. See **còmputo dei tèrmini di prescrizióne.**

prescrizióne estintíva—extinctive prescription. Extinguishment of a right by prolonged failure to use it. Art. 2934, 2935, Italian Civil Code.

prescrizióne ordinària—ordinary prescription. Rights are extinguished in ten years unless otherwise provided by law. Art. 2946, Italian Civil Code.

prescrizióne penàle — penal prescription. Extinction of a criminal action due to passage of a determined period of time from its commission. Art. 157, Italian Penal Code.

presèlla f.—division of a piece of land for cultivation; allotment of reclaimed land; metal rivet.

presèllo m.—blacksmith's hammer.

presentàrsi—to run for office; to stand

for election; to propose one's candidacy; to present oneself.

presentazióne f.—presentation; introduction; presentment.

presentazióne della cambiàle per accettazióne—presentment of the draft for acceptance. Art. 26-34, Cambiàle (Drafts), Usual Laws, Appendix to Italian Civil Code.

presentazióne della cambiàle per pagaménto—presentment of the draft for payment. Art. 43-48, Cambiàle (Drafts), Usual Laws, Appendix to Italian Civil Code.

presenziàre—to be present in person; to assist; to intervene in; to participate.

presidiàre—to garrison.

presídio m.—garrison.

préso—taken.

prèssa f.—press; crowd; throng.

prèsso—near; nearby; almost.

prestàre—to lend; to render; to give (aid); to give (faith).

prestàre giuraménto—to take an oath.

prestatóre m.—lender; one who performs work.

prestatóre di lavóro subordinàto—subordinate performer of work. In payment for his services, he is obliged to collaborate in the undertaking, giving his own intellectual or manual services under the direction and dependency of the entrepreneur. The subordinate performers of work are divided into administrative or technical managers, employees and workers. Art. 2094, 2095, Italian Civil Code. See **imprenditóre.**

prestazióne f.—loan; duty; tax; personal service; furnishing of work, labor or services.

prestazióne d'òpera intellettuàle—performance of work of an intellectual nature. Such contracts are governed by Art. 2230-2238, Italian Civil Code. See **responsabilità del prestatóre d'òpera intellettuàle.**

prèstito m.—loan.

presunzióne f.—presumption; an inference as to the existence of one fact from proof of the existence of other facts. The conclusions which the law or a judge draws from a known fact to determine an unknown fact. Art. 2727-2729, Italian Civil Code.

presunzióne legàle — legal presumption; one established by law and against which evidence cannot be introduced unless permitted by law. Art. 2728, Italian Civil Code.

presunzióne sémplice — simple presumption; also, presumption of fact. Presumptions not established by law are left to the discretion of the judge who must not admit any but serious, precise and concordant presumptions. Presumptions cannot be admitted in cases where the law excludes their proof by witnesses. Art. 2729, Italian Civil Code.

presupposizióne f. — presupposition; the act of presupposing or supposing beforehand; conjecture; representation of a future and uncertain event. The principle is contained in the case of posthumous birth and in contract law. Art. 687, 803, 1467, Italian ivil Code.

preterintenzionàle—beyond intention; a crime which was not intended or has surpassed what was intended. Such a crime occurs when from an act or omission there ensues a damaging or perilous event more serious than that desired by the acting party. Art. 43, 41, 584, Italian Penal Code.

preterizióne f.—preterition; passing by or over; the passing over or omission by a testator of an heir entitled by law to a portion of the inheritance.

preterizióne di erèdi e lesióne di legíttima—passing over of heirs and prejudice to the legitimate share. It comprises a division of the inheritance by the testator which fails to include one legitimately entitled thereto or of designated heirs. It is void and the injured co-heir, prejudiced by not receiving his statutory reserved share, may institute an action against the other co-heirs.

See **azióne di riduzióne** and Art. 735, Italian Civil Code.

pretésa f. — pretext; pretension; an alleged right or claim; a cloak or cover to conceal a real purpose or reason.

pretésa temerària (transazióne su)— compromise based on a groundless claim. If one of the parties had knowledge of the groundless nature of his claim, the other may demand the annulment of the compromise. Art. 1971, Italian Civil Code.

pretése da pàrte di tèrzi—claims made by third parties. If third parties causing interference with possession, pretend to have rights over the leased property, then the leasee must notify the leasor, under penalty of payment of damages. If the third parties proceed by judicial action, the leasor must assume the litigation if he is joined in the action. The leasee must be eliminated upon the simple indication of the leasor, unless he has an interest to remain. Art. 1586, Italian Civil Code.

pretóre m.—praetor; a judge having limited civil and penal jurisdiction. Art. 8, 21, 434, 436, 437, Italian Code of Civil Procedure; Title II, Pretóre (Praetor), Art. 30-35, Ordinaménto Giurisdizionàle (Jurisdictional Governance of the Judiciary), Usual Laws, Appendix to Italian Code of Civil Procedure; Art. 31, 74, Italian Code of Penal Procedure.

pretòrio—praetorian; pertaining to the praetor.
  àlbo pretòrio—a register located at the municipal headquarter on which are posted legal notices.

pretòrio m.—praetor's court.

pretúra f.—office of the praetor; juristion of the praetor.

preúso del màrchio—prior use of a trade mark. Whoever has used a non-registered trade mark may continue its use notwithstanding a registration for the same mark obtained by others during the time in which he availed himself thereof. A reseller of a product may affix his own trade mark thereto, but cannot suppress the trade mark of the producer of the product. Art. 2571, 2572, Italian Civil Code.

prevaricàre—to prevaricate; to deviate from the truth; to equivocate; to collude; to conceal a crime.

prevaricazióne f.—prevarication; unfaithful conduct by legal counsel; it is the crime committed by counsel or professional expert, who being unfaithful to his professional duties causes damage to the interests of his client, or in the same cause aides adversary parties. Art. 380-383, Italian Penal Code. See **millantàto crédito del patrocinatóre.**

prevedére—to foresee; to anticipate.

prevedibilità del dànno—foreseeability of damage. If non-performance or delay is not due to fraud of the debtor, compensation for damages is limited to the damage that could be foreseen at the time when the obligation arose. Art. 1225, Italian Civil Code.

preventíva istruzióne—a special proceeding. See **procediménti di istruzióne preventíva.**

preventívo (concordàto) — preventive accord, or agreement. See **concordàto preventívo.**

prevenzióne f. — prevention; precaution; anticipation.

previdènte—precautionary.

previdènza f.—foresight.

previdènza ed assistènza obbligatòrie —obligatory provisions for social security. The employer and employee, the latter to a lesser degree, contribute to the fund to support social security institutions. Moneys due for obligatory insurance for disability, old age and survivors, as well as that for other forms of security and assistance, have a general preference on the personal property of the employer. Art. 2114-2117, 2753, 2754, Italian Civil Code; Art. 459-466, Italian Code of Civil Procedure.

previdènza sociàle—social security; the aggregate of laws, institutions and agencies safeguarding life, health and well-being.

previsióne dell'evènto—foreseeability of the consequences of an act. It is an aggravating circumstance in the commission of a culpable crime. Art. 61; subd. 3, Italian Penal Code.

prezióso—precious; of great value. See commèrcio non autorizàto di còse prezióse—unauthorized commerce in precious objects.

prèzzi (riàlzo e ribàsso fraudolènto di) —fraudulent rise and fall of prices in public markets or exchanges. It is a crime when done with the purpose of disturbing or altering the internal market on monetary values and commodities by means of publishing or disseminating false, exaggerated or slanted news, or by using other fraudulent acts to cause a rise or drop in the price of merchandise or commodities listed on stock exchanges or saleable on the public market. Art. 501, 518, Italian Penal Code.

prèzzo m.—price; the consideration or that ordinarily accepted in exchanging one thing for another; the money value for which an article is sold.

prèzzo corrènte—current price.

prèzzo físso—set price.

prèzzo giusto—just, fair or reasonable price. For definition, see giústo prèzzo and Art. 1474, Italian Civil Code.

prigióne f.—prison.

prigióne m.—prisoner; captive.

prigionía f.—imprisonment.

prigionière or prigionièro m.—prisoner.

primogènito m.—first born son.

primogenitóre m.—primogenitor.

primogenitúra f.—primogeniture; the state of being first born; the superior right of the first born son to succeed to the estate of his parent to the exclusion of later born sons.

principàto m.—principality.

príncipe m.—prince.

princípio m. — principle; beginning; source; rule; rule of law.

princípio di conservazióne—principle of preservation. Relative to con-

tracts, see conservazióne del contratto.

princípio di dirítto—principle of law. The Court of Cassation, when entertaining an appeal based on a violation or erroneous application of legal norms, declares the principle to which the remanded judge must conform. Art. 384, Italian Code of Civil Procedure; Art. 143, Enabling Rules, Italian Code of Civil Procedure.

princípio di pròva per iscrítto—rule of proof by means of a writing. The proof of fact is permitted when based on any writing made by the person sued or his representative. In cases involving proof of paternity, the above rule is invoked regarding family documents, registers, private papers of the parents, from public or private instruments of the parties in controversy and of any person, who, if living, would have an interest in the controversy. Art. 242, 2724, 2712, 2717, Italian Civil Code.

privatíva f.—an exclusive privilege; a privilege granted by the State to manufacturers or sellers of certain merchandise; monopoly; patent.

privilègio (privilègi pl.) m.—privilege; preference; priority; the right of priority given to some creditors' claims over those of another. Art. 2741, 2745-2783, Italian Civil Code; Art. 53, 54, Falliménto (Bankruptcy), Appendix to Italian Civil Code.

procèdere—to proceed; to go forward; to continue; to act.

procèdere (non dovèrsi)—the halting of penal proceedings. It is somewhat similar to a dismissal. Art. 378, Italian Penal Code.

procedíbile—that which can be prosecuted.

procedibilità f.—the quality of being prosecutable.

procedimènti di istruzióne preventíva —special proceedings to preserve facts and evidence. They serve to obtain testimony before trial and preserve same where it may be lost and which are necessary for the trial. Such proceedings may also be used to obtain opinions of experts and have a discovery and inspection of places and other things. Art. 692-699, Italian Code of Civil Procedure. See **istruzióne preventíva** and **futúra memòria** (esàme di testimòni a).

procediménti sommàri—summary proceedings. These are special proceedings. Art. 633-705, Italian Code of Civil Procedure. Also, **giudízio sommàrio.**

procediménto m. — proceeding; procedure; progress; conduct; the content of a trial before a judicial officer.

procediménto civíle—civil proceeding.

procediménto coattívo fiscàle — compulsory fiscal proceeding. See **riscossióne coattíva di pùbbliche entràte.**

procediménto di ingiunzióne—injunction proceeding. It is a special summary proceeding whereby a creditor of a liquidated amount due in money or goods based on written proof, upon proper application, may obtain a decree of injunction commanding the debtor to fulfill the obligation within twenty days of notification. Art. 633-656, Italian Code of Civil Procedure.

procediménto disciplinàre — disciplinary proceeding.

procediménto monitòrio—monitory proceeding. See **procediménti sommàri** and **procediménto di ingiunzióne.**

procediménto penàle—penal proceeding.

procediménto per convàlida di sfràtto —eviction proceeding. It is one of the special proceedings. Art. 657-669, Italian Code of Civil Procedure. See **sfràtto** and **licènza per finíta locazióne** (intimazióne di).

procediménto sommàrio — summary proceeding. Also, **giudízio sommàrio.** See **procediménti sommàri.**

procedúra f.—procedure; the manner and form of a judicial proceeding; practice; conduct.

processàbile — that which can be brought to trial; indictable.

processàre—to bring to trial.

procèsso m.—trial; proceeding; process; cause of action.

procèsso civíle—civil action.

procèsso di cognizióne—a proceeding under judicial consideration, involving the preliminary examinations, hearings, trial and judgment. Also, **giudízio di cognizióne.** Art. 163-466, Italian Code of Civil Procedure.

procèsso d'esecuzióne—a sequestration proceeding. It is used in the attachment and sequestration of the goods of a debtor. Also, **giudízio esecutívo.** Art. 474-632, Italian Code of Civil Procedure.

procèsso penàle—penal proceeding.

procèsso verbàle—minutes of a meeting; minutes of a trial; an official Act or document; a document drawn by a public official to give faith and credit to his transactions or to declarations received by him from another public official whom he assists. Art. 155-161, Italian Code of Penal Procedure.

procùra f.—power of attorney; procuration; appointment of an agent or attorney. It may be special or general and must be in writing or it is void. Art. 1350, 1351, 1392, Italian Civil Code.

procùra alle líte—retainer of an attorney to perform professional services. It must be made by a public Act or by authenticated private writing. It may be special or general. Art. 83, Italian Code of Civil Procedure. See **mandàto alle líte.**

procuràto abòrto—procured abortion. Art. 546, Italian Penal Code.

procuratóre m.—procurator; attorney; attorney in fact; solicitor; legal representative. See **difensóre, patrocinatóre legàle** and **procuratóre legàle.**

Procuratóre della Repubblica — Procurator of the Republic. He represents the Pùbblico Ministèro in the Tribunals and initiates and prosecutes criminal actions. He reports to the Procuratóre Generàle della Repùbblica who is under the jurisdiction of the Ministry of Justice. See

Púbblico Ministèro and Procuratóre Generàle della Repúbblica.

Procuratóre Generàle della Repúbblica —Procurator General of the Republic. He represents the Púbblico Ministèro in the Courts of Appeals, generally, and in the Supreme Court of Cassation. Art. 70, Title I, Ordinaménto Giurisdizionàle (Jurisdictional Governance of the Judiciary), Usual Laws, Appendix to Italian Code of Civil Procedure. See púbblico ministèro.

procuratóre legàle—legal procurator; a legal practitioner below the rank of avvocàto. He may practice before the Court of Appeals and all Tribunals and Praetorships comprised within the district of a Tribunal. In criminal cases before a Tribunal, Court of Appeals and Court of Assizes, the defense of accused persons is reserved to avvocàti. Procurators may represent a civil party seeking damages in such cases, Art. 2, 5, 6, 17, Avvocàti e Procuratóri (Lawyers and Procurators), Usual Laws, Appendix to Italian Code of Civil Procedure.

procuratóre (praticànte) — practicing procurator. A law graduate may be admitted to practice, for a period not exceeding four years from date of graduation, before the Praetorships in the district of the Court of Appeals where he was admitted to practice, including those of communes where Tribunals are located or the chief city of a province. Art. 2, 8, Avvocàti e Procuratóri (Lawyers and Procurators), Usual Laws, Appendix to Italian Code of Civil Procedure.

proditóre m.—one who betrays; traitor. See traditóre.

proditoriaménte — traitorously. See tradiménto.

proditòrio—treacherous.

profittàre—to profit.

profittatóre m.—profiteer.

profítto m.—profit; the gain realized in a business, investment or sale over and above expenses.

pròfugo m.—refugee; displaced person.

proibíre—to prohibit; to forbid.

proibíto—prohibited; forbidden.

proiettàre—to project.

proièttile m.—projectile.

prolàsso m.—prolapse; prolapsus; falling of a muscle or organ from its normal position.

pròle f.—offspring; children; issue.

proletariàto m.—proletariat; the class of unskilled workers without property or money.

proletàrio m.—proletarian; in Rome, a citizen so poor he could not serve the State with money but only by having children.

proméssa f.—promise.

proméssa al púbblico—promise to the public. It is a unilateral promise in favor of anyone who finds himself in a stated situation or performs a stated action. Unless an expiration date has been fixed, or follows from the nature or purpose thereof, the obligation of the promisor expires within a year. Art. 1989-1991, Italian Civil Code. See offèrta al púbblico and promése unilateràli.

proméssa di matrimònio—promise of marriage. It does not obligate the parties making it to contract it, nor in case of non-performance to execute that which was agreed. The restitution of gifts made under a promise of marriage must be made within a year of the refusal to celebrate the marriage. Mutual promises of marriage made by public Act or private writing made during majority or by a minor empowered to do so, will subject the breaching party to damages. Art. 79-81, 93-96, Italian Civil Code.

proméssa di matrimònio comméssa da persóna coniugàta (seduzióne con)— seduction with promise of marriage committed by a married person. See seduzióne con proméssa di matrimònio comméssa da persóna coniugàta. Carnal knowledge is an essential element of the crime.

proméssa di pagaménto e ricognizióne di débito—promise of payment and recognition of debt. The promise of payment and recognition of a debt exempts the one to whom it is made of the burden of proving the underlying legal relationship. Its existence is presumed until proof to the contrary. Art. 1988, Italian Civil Code. See **promésse unilateràli**.

promésse unilateràli—unilateral promises. A unilateral promise of a performance does not produce contractual obligations in the promisor except in those cases permitted by Law. Art. 1987-1991, Italian Civil Code. See **proméssa di pagaménto e ricognizióne di débito** and **proméssa al público**. Also, Art. 1323, 1324, Italian Civil Code.

promotóre m.—promoter.

promòvere—to promote. Also, **promúovere**.

promulgazióne f.—promulgation; official announcement. Laws are promulgated by the President of the Italian Republic within a month of approval or passage. If the Parliament, by absolute majority of each House, declares an urgent necessity therefore, the law is promulgated within the time established by them. The laws are published immediately after promulgation and take effect after the fifteenth successive day of their publication, unless the laws themselves set a different time. The President of the Republic, before promulgating the law, may send a message to the Houses of Parliament, requesting a new deliberation and reconsideration. If the Houses of Parliament again approve and pass the law, then it must be promulgated. Art. 73, 74, Constitution of the Italian Republic. See **vacatio legis**.

promuòvere—to promote. Also, **promòvere**.

pronunziàre — to pronounce; to declare; to utter.

pronunziàre úna sentènza — to pronounce a judgment.

pronunziazióne f.—pronunciation; pronouncement; utterance.

propagànda f.—propaganda.

propagànda ed apología sovversíva o antinazionàle—propaganda and sub-versive or anti-national apology or defense. Whoever, within the territory of the State, propagandizes for the violent installation of a dictatorship of one social class over another, or for the violent suppression of a social class, or, in any manner, for the violent overthrow of the economic and social order established in the State, or propagandizes for the destruction of every political and juridical order of governance of society, is punished with imprisonment. Art. 272, 302, Italian Penal Code.

propína f.—special compensation given to a professor for each examination in which he participates; a toast to someone's health.

propinàre—to drink a toast to someone.

proponènte m.—proponent; one who presents a will for probate.

propónere—to propose. See **propórre**.

proponíbile—proposable.

proponibilità f.—that which can be proposed; that which gives rise to an enforceable claim or cause of action.

propórre—to propose; to propound; to move for consideration or adoption, as in a motion before a body. Also, **propónere**.

propòsito m. — intention; purpose; question; reason.
a propòsito—with reference to.
con propòsito—intentionally; on purpose.
di propòsito—seriously; diligently.
fuòri di propòsito—out of order as regards a matter or proposition.

proposizióne f.—proposition; proposal.

propòsta f. — proposal; proposition; argument; motion; offer. Re contract offers, see Art. 1326-1330, 1335, 1336, Italian Civil Code.
fàre una propòsta—to make an offer; to present a proposal by motion or otherwise.

proprietà f.—property; the owner of property has the right to enjoy and dispose of things owned with full and exclusive use within the limits prescribed by law. Art. 832-839, Italian Civil Code; Art. 42, Constitution of the Italian Republic.

pròroga f.—prorogation; adjournment; deferment; postponement; suspension; discontinuance.

prorogàre—to prorogue; to adjourn; to defer; to postpone.

prorómpere—to break out; to burst out.

prorompiménto m.—breaking out or bursting forth with violence.

prosciògliere—to free from a promise; to absolve from or dismiss an accusation.

proscioglimёnto m.—the discharge or release from a criminal charge; dismissal of a charge. See **sentènza di proscioglimènto.**

proscioglimènto per difètto di una condizióne di procedibilità — dismissal due to defect in a procedural requirement. Also, see **riproponibilità della azióne penàle.**

prosciòlto—absolved; freed from an accusation; discharged.

proscrítto m.—one who is proscribed; banished; exiled or outlawed.

proscrívere—to proscribe; to banish; to exile; to outlaw.

proscrizióne f.—proscription; banishment; outlawry.

prosecuzióne f.—prosecution; the institution and continuance of a suit or action in a court of law.

prosecuzióne del giudízio—prosecution of the trial. With regard to the assumption of proof. See Art. 203, 204, Italian Code of Civil Procedure and **prosecuzióne del procèsso.**

prosecuzióne del procèsso — prosecution of trial. With regard to the interruption of the trial or proceeding, see Art. 302-307, Italian Code of Civil Procedure.

proseguiménto m.—pursuit; pursuit of happiness, occupation, profession, studies and the like; continuation.

proseguíre—to pursue; to continue something already started; to pursue a business or profession; to seek

remedy by judicial proceedings; to prosecute.

prosiéguo m.—continuation. See **proseguiménto.**

prospettàre—to prospect; to look out upon; to overlook a place.

prospettíva f.—perspective.

prospètto m.—prospect; view. See **lúci, vedúte o prospètti.**

prospiciènte—with a view of; overlooking a place.

prossenèta m.—intermediary; broker; marriage broker. See **mediazióne.**

prossenètico m.—marriage brokerage fee.

prossèno m. — a host; in ancient Greece, a citizen charged by the State to entertain ambassadors or other foreign dignitaries.

pròssimo—near; very near; next; contiguous; immediate; related.
parènte pròssimo—close relative.

pròssimo m.—fellow-man; neighbor.

pròssimo congiúnto — close relative; kin; relation by ties of consanguinity.

prostituíre—to prostitute.

prostituzióne f.—prostitution. See **lenocíno,** and **Prostituzióne,** Usual Laws, Appendix to Italian Code of Penal Procedure.

prostràre—to prostrate.

prostràto—prostrated.

prostrazióne f.—prostration.

protèsta f.—protest; public declaration; opposition to the ideas of others; assurance; promise.

protestàre — to protest; to declare firmly; formal expression of disapproval.

protèsto m.—protest; a formal declaration in writing by a notary public or other public official that a draft was dishonored by non-acceptance or non-payment. Art. 51, et seq., Cambiàle (Drafts), Usual Laws, Appendix, Italian Civil Code.

protocollàre—to register.

protocòllo m.—protocol; register kept by notaries of documents and transactions; formulary; form book for public documents; the minutes of a diplomatic or international conference.

protutóre m.—one who acts in place of the guardian when the latter has a conflict of interest with the ward. Art. 360, 345-355, Italian Civil Code. See **tutóre.**

pròva f.—proof; experiment; examination (school); rehearsal; printer's proof. For burden of proof, see **ònere della pròva** and **pàtti relatívi all' ònere della pròva.** Re manner of proof, see Art. 2699-2739, Italian Civil Code; Art. 115-118, 199-266, Italian Code of Civil Procedure; Art. 104, 306, 308, 402, 457, 469, 554, 557, Italian Code of Penal Procedure.
a pròva—contesting with one another.
a tútta pròva—as much as possible.
a pròva del fuòco—fire-proof.
mettère a pròva—to put to the test.

pròva testimoniàle—testimonial proof. Art. 2721-2726, Italian Civil Code; Artfl 244-257, Italian Code of Civil Procedure. Art. 348-359, Italian Code of Penal Procedure.

provàre—to prove; to try; to examine; to feel (pain, joy, grief); to taste.

pròve di stàmpa—printer's proofs.

proveniènza f.—provenance; the place of origin.

provenzàle m.—an inhabitant of Provence, a region of France.

província f. — province. Like a commune, it is an autonomous entity within the bounds of the general laws of the Republic which determine its functions. Art. 128, Constitution of the Italian Republic.

provocazióne f.—provocation; a mitigating circumstance in the commission of a crime. Art. 62, 599, Italian Penal Code.

provvediménti d'urgènza — urgent measures for relief. Where there is a well founded reason to fear that during the time required to enforce a right in regular course, that said right may be threatened by imminent and irreparable damage, the party so threatened may request the judge to take such urgent measure for relief as may, under the circumstances, appear more appropriate to assure, temporarily, the effects of a decision on the merits. Art. 700, Italian Code of Civil Procedure.

provvediménto m.—provision; precaution; disposition; regulation; a measure taken to meet a certain need. Generally, it refers to dispositions and measures taken by the authorities to fulfill a need for public order.

provvediménto di polizía—police measure or disposition. It is issued by police authorities to preserve public order and security.

provveditoràto m. — inspectorship or his office; the office of supply for a public agency.

provveditóre m.—purveyor; supplier; manager; steward; title of a public official such as a hospital manager or school inspector.

provveditúra m. — the office of the Governor of Dalmatia under the Venetians, who was called a Provveditóre or Provvisóre.

provvigióne f.—provision; award; compensation; the fee or compensation given to a mediator, broker or agent. Art. 1733, 1736, 1748, 1749, 1755, 1758, 2099, 2121, 2751, 2751 bis, Italian Civil Code. See **stàr del crédere** and **provvisióne.**

provvisionàle — provisional; an order to a debtor to make provisional payment of a sum within the proof adduced, pending final determination of the action. Art. 278, Italian Code of Civil Procedure; Art. 574, Italian Code of Penal Procedure.

provvisióne f.—provision; stock; commission; brokerage. See **provvigióne.**

provvíso—provided.

provvíso m.—impromptu.

provvisóre m.—the title of the Governor of Dalmatia under the Venetians. Also, **provveditóre.**

provvisòria esecuzióne — provisional execution. At the request of a party, an appealable judgment may be enforced provisionally by execution, with or without bond, if the complaint is based on a public document, an admitted private writing, a judgment, or if there is danger in delay. It must be granted when there is a judgment of provisional payment or subsistence. Art. 282, 283, 642, Italian Code of Civil Procedure; Art. 489 bis, Italian Code of Penal Procedure.

provvísta f.—provision; supply.

provvísta cambiària — provision inserted in a draft. It is an assignment or transfer to a bank or banker of the value of the merchandise delivered to a drawee and for which the draft was issued. It applies to non-accepted drafts thus transferred. In the event of the drawer's bankruptcy, the bank may repossess the goods rather than the drawer's trustee. Art. 1-4, Cambiàle (Drafts), Usual Laws Appendix, Italian Civil Code.

pseudònimo (tutèla dello)—protection of the pseudonym. It can be protected as well as the name where it has acquired an important significance in the artistic and literary world. Art. 9, Italian Civil Code.

pùbblica amministrazióne (delítti cóntro la)—crimes against public administration. These consist of crimes committed by public officials, such as malversazióne and peculàto, and crimes committed by private persons against the public administration. Art. 314-360, Italian Penal Code.

pùbblica sicurézza — public security. The authorities which preserve public order and security. See **sicurézza pùbblica.**

pubblicàre—to publish; to make public; to communicate; to proclaim; to promulgate.

pubblicazióne f.—publication; notification to the general public.

pubblicazióne del testaménto—publication of a will. Art. 620-623, Italian Civil Code.

pubblicazióni e spettàcoli oscèni — obscene publications and performances. It is a crime which consists in processing, acquiring, manufacturing, circulating, distributing or displaying in public, writings, drawings and obscene representations or objects of every sort. Art. 528, Italian Penal Code.

pùbblico demànio—public domain. See demànio pùbblico.

pùbblico domínio — public ownership. See demànio pùbblico.

pùbblico incànto—public auction. Art. 537, 581, Italian Code of Civil Procedure. See **turbàta libertà degli incànti**—disturbed freedom of auctions and nuòvo incànto—new auction.

pùbblico ministèro—public prosecutor. He is the official representing the Executive power before the courts and is under the jurisdiction of the Ministry of Justice. He prosecutes Crimes, defends the rights of the State and appears in certain civil cases. Art. 112, Constitution of the Italian Republic; Art. 73-77, Italian Code of Penal Procedure; Art. 69-74, 132, Italian Code of Civil Procedure; Title III, Art. 69-84, Ordinaménto Giurisdizionàle (Jurisdictional Governance of the Judiciary), Usual Laws, Appendix to Italian Code of Civil Procedure; Art. 32, Enabling Rules, Italian Civil Code.

pùbblico ufficiàle—public official. Under the penal law, public officials are: (1) employees of the State or of a public entity, which exercise permanently or temporarily, a public function, whether legislative, administrative or judicial. (2) every other person who exercises, permanently or temporarily, gratuitously or with compensation, voluntarily or by duty, a public function, whether legislative, administrative or judicial. Art. 357-360, Italian Penal Code.

pùbblico ufficiàle (delítti cóntro) — crimes against a public official. Art. 336-347, Italian Penal Code.

pubertà f.—puberty.

pudóre m.—decency; modesty; prudency; pudicity.

pudóre (offése al pudóre e all'onóre sessuàle)—offenses against modesty and sexual dignity and honor. Included are: obscene acts; obscene publications, performances and objects; corruption of minors; traffic in women (white slave) and minors committed abroad; the promotion of prostitution and maintenance of houses for its practice; recruitment for the purpose of prostitution or aiding same; inducing a woman of major age to commit prostitution, or personally committing acts of pandering in public places or those open to the public, be it by means of print or other means of publicity; inducing a person to go into the territory of another State, or to a place other than her habitual residence for the purpose of prostitution; participation in national or foreign associations and organizations designed to recruit persons for prostitution, or its exploitation in any manner. Art. 527-538, Italian Penal Code. See lenocínio.

puèrpera f.—a woman who has just been through childbirth.

puerperàle—puerperal; pertaining to childbirth.

puerpèrio m.—puerperium; the state of a woman following childbirth.

pugnalàre—to stab.

pugnalàta f. — dagger blow; dagger wound.

pugnàle m.—dagger.

pugnàre—to fight.

pugnàta f.—handfull.

púgno m.—fist; punch.
   di súo púgno—in his own handwriting.

puniménto m.—punishment. See punizióne.

puníre—to punish.

punizióne f.—punishment.

púnta f.—point.

puntàglia f.—combat; struggle.

puntàle m.—metal point; ferrule.

puntàre — to exert by all possible means; to point (a gun, weapon, telescope); to punch a card; to place a stake on a card; to stare at; to attempt to advance troops toward a given point.

puntatóre m.—pointer; a member of a gun crew who aims it by adjusting its elevation and lateral movements.

púnti frànchi—free entry points. See depòsiti frànchi.

púnto m.—point; period (sentence); spot; speck; stitch.

púnto frànco—free entry point. See depòsito frànco and depòsiti frànchi.

puntúra f. — puncture; pang; acute pain in the side or the shoulder.

pupílla f.—pupil of the eye; female ward.

pupíllo m.—ward; pupil; simple person. A ward must respect and obey the guardian. He cannot leave the house or institute wherein he has been placed without permission of the guardian. Art. 358, Italian Civil Code.

purgazióne f.—purgation; the act of purging; freeing.

purgazióne della ipotèche—freeing or redeeming from mortgages. See liberazióne delle ipotèche.

purgazióne (giudízio di)—proceeding to free from a mortgage. See liberazióne della ipotèche. Also, discharge from a crime.

putatívo—putative; reputed.

putatívo (matrimònio)—putative marriage. See matrimònio putatívo, Art. 128, Italian Civil Code.

Q

quàcquero m.—Quaker.

qualífica f.—title; designation.

qualificàre—to qualify; to characterize; to define.

qualificàto — qualified; of note; of quality.

qualificazióne f.—qualification.

qualità f.—quality; condition; nature; attribute; characteristic; property. See mancànza di qualità—lack of quality.

quanti minoris (azióne)—an action to rescind a purchase contract because of hidden defects. See azióne quanti minoris and azióne estimatòria.

quarantèna f.—period of forty days.

quarantína f.—series of forty; quarantine.

quàsi — about; almost; as if; like; nearly.

quàsi contràtto—quasi-contract. It is not reported in the present Italian Civil Code. It is an obligation arising, not by agreement, but from some relation between the parties. See Art. 1173, Italian Civil Code.

quàsi delítto—quasi delict. It is not reported in the present Italian Civil or Penal Codes. In the former Civil Code, it referred to a culpable act, done without malice, which caused damage. Such an act gave rise to an action to recover compensation for the damage. See Art. 1173, Italian Civil Code.

quàsi flagrànza—quasi flagrance. Procedurally, it comes within the purview of a flagrant crime by definition, which states that a person is also considered in a flagrant state, who, immediately after the crime, is pursued by the public security force, by the victim of the crime or other persons, and, in fact, is surprised with things or indications from which it appears that he may just have committed the crime. Art. 237, Italian Code of Penal Procedure.

quàsi possèsso—quasi possession. In the Roman Law, it signified a right to possession rather than actual corporal possession. It was called *juris possessio* or *quasi possessio.* This concept is contained in the broader one of the definition of possession in the present Italian Civil Code. Art. 1140, Italian Civil Code.

quàsi usufrútto—quasi usufruct. The Civil Law usufruct gave no right to the usufructuary to consume the thing being enjoyed, so that it was confined to inconsumable things. It was later extended to consumable things and the latter were designated quasi usufructs to distinguish them from true usufructs. The present Italian Civil Code adopts quasi usufructs under the title, còse consumàbili — consumable things. The usufructuary who has used the consumable things must pay their value at the end of the usufruct according to their agreed valuation. In lieu thereof, he must pay for them according to the value they have at the time the usufruct expires or to return other things of equal quality and quantity. Art. 995, Italian Civil Code. See **usufrútto.**

querèla f.—complaint; accusation. It is an accusation or information made by a person who has sustained a crime which is prosecutable on his complaint. It can be made by personal declaration or through the special prosecutor to the Authorities. The minutes of the oral declaration must be subscribed by the one complaining or the special prosecutor to be effective. Art. 120-126, Italian Penal Code; Art. 9-14, Italian Code Penal Procedure.

querèla di fàlso—complaint of forgery. It is a method to impugn or challenge an act or document at any stage of a civil or penal proceeding by a party or the public prosecutor. When commencing an independent civil action for forgery, a citation or summons is issued. The penal action is referred to as incidènti di fàlso. Art. 221-227, 318, 355, Italian Code of Civil Procedure; Art. 99-102, Enabling Rules, Appendix to Italian Code of Civil Procedure; Art. 215-218, 337, 480, 481, Italian Code of Penal Procedure. See **incidènti di fàlso.**

querèla (remissióne della)—remission or abatement of a complaint. In crimes punishable on complaint (querèla) of the person injured, remission extinguishes the crime. It may not contain limits or conditions and is permitted only before judgment. Remission is procedural or extra-procedural. The latter is express or tacit. It is tacit when the complaining party has committed acts inconsistent with the objective of pursuing the complaint. Art. 152-156, Italian Penal Code.

querelànte m.—the one who makes a complaint (querèla) in a penal proceeding.

querelàto m.—one who has been served

208

with a penal complaint (querèla).

quesíto m.—legal controversy under investigation; inquiry.

quesíto—search or investigation for legal rights.

questióne f.—question; examination towards a resolution of a point; interrogation; controversy under consideration by a legal, judicial or official body. It concerns the resolution of matters of fact or law necessary to reach a judgment.

questióni incidentàli—incidental questions. These are points of controversy arising during the course of taking proof. The judge who proceeds with the assumption of the manner of taking proof, resolves by order, all the questions that arise during the course of the proceeding. Art. 205, 819, Italian Code of Civil Procedure. Art. 438, Italian Code of Penal Procedure.

questióni preliminàri — preliminary questions. These must be resolved upon the opening of the trial and involve the appearance of civil parties in a criminal action, the citation or intervention of the responsible or answerable civil party, or the one chargeable with the fine. Other preliminary questions involve the nullity of the order remanding the cause to trial, as well as questions over territorial jurisdiction, the joinder or separation of actions, admissibility of witnesses, experts, interpreters or technical experts, the absence of witnesses, experts or interpreters, the presentation or request for documents and the exceptions or defenses permitted. Art. 439, Italian Code of Penal Procedure.

questóre m.—quaestor (Lat.); questor; in ancient Rome, the official who administered the public treasury; the head of Public Security in a Province; in the Italian Chamber of Deputies and the Senate, the member of such House charged with maintaining order, similar to a Sergeant at Arms.

quèstua f.—a collection for a charitable purpose.

questúra f.—the office and headquarters of the chief of public security—the Questóre.

questuríno m. — an agent of public security; guard; policeman.

quiescènza f.—quiescence; quiescency; the state of being quiescent; retirement of a public employee.

quietànza f.—written receipt of payment; discharge of a debt or obligation.

quietànza con imputazióne—discharge of a specific debt out of many. One who has many debts with the same creditor and accepts from him a discharge for a payment allocated to a specific debt, cannot claim a different allocation unless he was taken unawares or there was fraud on the part of the creditor. Art. 1195, Italian Civil Code.

quietanzàre—to give a written receipt of payment; to discharge a debt or obligation.

quietàre—to calm; to give a receipt.

quintàle m.—quintal; hundredweight; in the metric system, 100 kilograms.

Quirinàle m.—Quirinal Palace in Rome, the residence of the President of Italy; formerly the palace of the Popes and then of the Kings of Italy.

quisquília f.—mote; speck; scrap.

quòrum—quorum; number of members of a body required to vote or transact business legally.

quòta f.—quota; portion; share.

quòta ereditària—hereditary share.

quòta líte (pàtto di)—an agreement whereby an attorney-at-law promises to receive for his services a part of the sum or object in dispute if he wins; contingent fee. It is void. Art. 1261, 2233, Italian Civil Code. Also, quotalizio.

quotalízio m. — contingent fee. See quòta líte.

quòta di fàtto—the portion reserved to brothers and sisters of one who dies without leaving children or ascendants. Unilateral brothers and sisters receive, however, half the share received by brothers and sisters german. Art. 570, Italian Civil

Code. See germàni (fratèlli e sorèlle) and unilateràli (fratèlli e sorèlle).

quòta di risèrva—the portion of a decedent's estate reserved to certain heirs. Art. 537, 538, Italian Civil Code. See porzióne legíttima; porzióne riservàta and legíttima.

quotàre—to assess; to quote or name the current price on the exchange.

quotazióne f.—quotation; a quotation of current prices on the exchange.

quòte di partecipazióne—shares of a stock corporation. Art. 2325, Italian Civil Code.

quòte di società—partnership shares.

quotísta único—sole remaining shareholder in a limited partnership. In the event of insolvency, where it appears that the shares belong to a sole remaining partner, the latter is answerable for the partnership obligations without limitation. Art. 2497, Italian Civil Code.

R

rabùffo m.—rebuff; rebuke; reprimand. Also, ribùffo.

raccertàre—to reassure; to reconfirm.

raccettaménto m.—harboring; lodging.

raccettàre—to entertain; to harbor; to lodge; to shelter; to give refuge.

raccòlta f.—collection; harvest; harvest time.
suonàre a raccòlta—to sound a retreat; to sound to assembly.

raccòlta del sàngue — collection of blood. The Minister of Sanitation issues the technical directives for the organization, functioning and coordination of the services pertaining to the collection, preparation, conservation and distribution of human blood for use in transfusions. He also exercises supervision of the preparation of its derivatives. Art. 1 et seq., Raccòlta del Sàngue, Usual Laws, Appendix to Italian Civil Code.

raccomandàre—to recommend; to enjoin; to register (a letter).

raccomandàta f.—recommended; registered (a letter).

raccòrdi ferroviàri—railroad switching tracks. Part 2, Art. 1, Ferrovíe (Railroads) Usual Laws, Appendix to Italian Civil Code.

raccòrdo m. — accord; agreement; union; in railroads, a track equipped to switch trains from one track or route to another.

ràda f.—roadstead; a sheltered place for ships.

ràde (pl.) f.—roadsteads. They are part of the public domain. Art. 822, Italian Civil Code.

radènte—grazing; scraping.

radènza f.—scraping; grazing.

ràdere—to shave; to shear; to erase or efface; to graze; to skim.

radiàre—to radiate; to emit rays; to drop, cancel or erase from a list.

radiazióne f.—radiation; cancellation; erasure. A trial is interrupted from the day of death, cancellation or suspension of the Procurator of one of the parties. Art. 301, Italian Code of Civil Procedure.

radiazióne d'ipotèca—cancellation of a mortgage.

radíce f.—root; radish. The owner of land onto which the roots of his neighbor's trees extend, may cut them himself unless otherwise provided by local use and regulations. See recisióne di ràmi protèsi e di radíci. Art. 896, Italian Civil Code.

radunàta f.—an assemblage of persons. sonàre a radunàta—a call for troops to assemble.

radunàta sediziósa—seditious assemblage. It is composed of ten or more persons. Art. 655, Italian Penal Code.

raggiraménto m.—deception; subterfuge; trick; the act of encircling; circuitous talk for the purpose of deceiving. Also, raggiràta.

raggíro m.—deception; trick; artifice and circuitous talk for the purpose of deception. It may be ground for rescinding or annulling a contract. Art. 1426, 1439, 1440, Italian Civil Code. See trùffa.

ragguagliàbile—comparable.

raggualiaménto m.—equalization; the act of comparing or equalizing.

ragguagliànza f.—See raggualiaménto.

raggualiàre—to balance; to compare; to equalize; to level; to inform in detail.

ragguagliàre le partíte—to balance the ledger entries.

ragguagliataménte — on the average; proportionately; in relation to.

ragguagliatívo—tending to equalize or to advise.

ragguàglio m. — balancing; comparison; equalization; proportion; rate; notice; advice; detailed information.

a ragguàglio di—in accordance with the opinion of; in relation to.

al ragguàglio di 5%—at the rate of 5%.

tàvole di ragguàglio—tables of different measures.

ragguàglio fra péne divèrse—equalization among different penalties. It relates to equating monetary punishments with detentive punishments where allowable. Art. 135, Italian Penal Code.

ragióne f.—reason; judgment; right.

ragióne sociàle—firm name, title or style under which business is conducted by a partnership bearing a collective name (società in nóme collettívo) and a limited partnership (società in accomàndita sémplice). Art. 2292, 2314, 2564, 2567, Italian Civil Code. See denominazióne sociàle.

ragionería f.—the science of keeping books; accountant's office.

ragioniére m.—accountant; auditor.

ràme (pl.) f.—branches. See ràma.

ràma f.—branch of a tree; a branch which bears fruit. See ràmo.

ràme m.—the metal, copper. Slang for policeman, similar to "cop."

ràmi m.—branches. The owner of land over which a neighbor's tree branches protrude or extend, may, at any time, compel his neighbor to prune them. See recisióne di ràmi protèsi e di radíci. Art. 896, Italian Civil Code,

ràmo m.—branch; branch of a tree which produces leaves and flowers, such as an olive branch or a bunch or cluster of flowers; a branch of a family; a branch of an art, discipline or science.

rancía f.—the daily list of sailors present who will attend mess.

ràncido—rancid. Also, ràncio.

rancière m.—the soldier who distributes rations.

ràncio m. — a soldier's ration or a sailor's mess; a group of ten from a ship's crew who eat together.

ràncio—rancid. Also, ràncido.

ràngo m.—rank; condition; grade.

rapiménto m.—abduction; ravishment; act of rapine or pillage; kidnapping.

rapína f.—robbery; theft accompanied by violent acts. Whoever, to procure to himself or others an unjust profit or advantage by means of violence to the person or threats, takes possession of another's personal property by taking it from one in possession of it, is punished with imprisonment. Art. 628, Italian Penal Code.

rappòrto m. — report; relation; rapport; connection. Officials and agents of the Judicial Police must report every crime of which they become cognizant unless it is one punishable upon complaint of the person injured. The report is presented to the Procurator of the Republic or the Praetor. If, during the course of a civil trial, facts arise indicating a crime, the Judge must report same to the Procurator of the Republic. Art. 2, 3, Italian Code of Penal Procedure.

rappòrto di causalità—causal relation. No one may be punished for an act deemed a crime by law, if the damaging or perilous event, upon which the existence of the crime depends, is not the consequence of his act or omission. Failure to prevent an occurrence which one has the legal duty to prevent, is equivalent to causing it. Art. 40, Italian Penal Code.

rappòrto giurídico—jural relation that exists between men in their activities and the institutions such as marriage, family, property, etc. which are protected and disciplined by the law.

rappresàglia f.—reprisal.

rappresentànte m.—representative.

rappresentànza f.—representation. The power of representation is conferred by law or the party granting it. A power of attorney conferring representation is invalid if it fails to follow the forms prescribed by the Code for the type of contract which the representative must conclude. A contract concluded by a representative in the name of and on behalf of the party represented, within the limits of the power conferred, is binding on the represented party. Art. 1387-1400; 2203-2213, Italian Civil Code.

rappresentàre — to represent; to exhibit; to perform.

rappresentatívo—act of representing; representative.

rappresentàto — represented; performed.

rappresentazióne f. — representation. Representation permits legitimate or natural descendants to replace an ascendant and take in his stead and rank in all cases where he does not or cannot accept the inheritance or legacy. Representation in testamentary succession occurs when the testator failed to provide for the case where the inheritance or legacy cannot or will not be accepted. Taking by representation is *per stirpes*. Art. 467-469, Italian Civil Code. See **stírpe** and **càpi (per)**.

rappresentazióni teatràli o cinematogràfiche abusíve — unlawful theatrical or motion picture performances. It is a violation to give public performances without first advising the Authorities, or to exhibit motion pictures without first having them reviewed by the Authorities, that is by the chief of Public Security, the Questóre. Art. 668, Italian Penal Code; Title III, Art. 68, Unified Text on Public Security, Usual Laws, Appendix to Italian Code of Penal Procedure.

ràscia (ràsce, pl.) f.—black serge material hung together with white drapes on public buildings as a sign of mourning.

rasentàre—to pass close to; to brush by in passing.

rasènte—close by, almost touching.

rasóio m.—razor.

raspollàre—to glean the small bunches of grapes left after vintage.

raspóllo m.—small bunch of grapes left after vintage.

rasségna f.—parade; muster; military review; registration of university students for various courses.

rassegnàre—to review troops; to resign; to produce documents in court.

rassegnazióne f.—resignation (of the spirit).

rassicuràre—to reassure.

rassicurazióne f.—reassurance.

rastrellàre—to rake.

rastrèllo m.—rake.

ràta f.—quota; share; an installment payment.

rateàle—by installments.

rateàre—to divide into installments. Also, **ratizzàre**.

rateazióne f.—the division into installments.

ratífica f. — ratification. See **ratificazióne**. A contract made by a representative without power to do so, or exceeding the powers granted, makes him responsible for damages caused a third party. However, such a contract may be ratified by the principal and it has retroactive effect. The faculty of ratification is transmitted to heirs of the principal. Art. 1398, 1399, Italian Civil Code.

ratizzàre—to divide into installments. Also, **rateàre**.

ràtto—ratified; approved; confirmed.

ràtto m.—abduction; ravishment; kidnapping.

ràtto a fíne di libídine—abduction for lewd and lustful purpose. The crime of carrying off or detaining a minor or a woman who has attained majority, for lewd or lustful purpose, by means of violence, threats, or deception. Art. 523, Italian Penal Code.

ràtto a fíne di matrimònio—abduction for the purpose of marriage. The crime of carrying off or detaining an unmarried woman for the purpose of marriage, by means of violence, threats, or deception. Art. 522, Italian Penal Code.

ravvisàre—to recognize.

ràzzi (làncio abusívo) — unlawful launching of rockets. It is a violation to commit any of the following acts, without license of the Public Security Authorities, in an inhabitated place or adjacent thereto, or in a public street, or in its direction: to shoot firearms; ignite fireworks or launch rockets; to raise lighter than air balloons with flames; or, generally, cause dangerous ignitions or explosions. Art. 703, Italian Penal Code; Title II, Art. 57, Unified Text on Public Security, Usual Laws, Appendix to Italian Code of Penal Procedure.

reàti comméssi dal fallíto—crimes committed by a bankrupted businessman. Among these are: fraudulent bankruptcy, involving (1) diversion, hiding, concealment, destruction or dissipation of assets, in whole or in part, or, for the purpose of prejudicing creditors, exhibiting or acknowledging inexistent liabilities; (2) abstraction, destruction, or falsification, in whole or in part, of books and other documents of account, or keeping them in such manner as to render impossible the reconstruction of the property or the movement of the affairs. Crimes committed by a businessman under simple bankruptcy, involve: (1) making excessive personal or family expenses, considering his economic condition; (2) wasting a notable part of his property in speculative or manifestly imprudent operations; (3) committing operations of great imprudence to delay bankruptcy; (4) aggravate one's insolvency by abstaining from requesting his bankruptcy, or by

other serious wrong; (5) failure to satisfy obligations assumed in a previous preventive or bankruptcy accord. The businessman in simple bankruptcy, is punished with imprisonment for a lesser term than for acts of fraudulent bankruptcy. Art. 216-224, Falliménto (Bankruptcy), Usual Laws, Appendix to Italian Civil Code.

reàto m.—crime; it is distinguished into contravvenzióne (infraction or violation) and delítto (delict or criminal act). No one may be punished for an act considered a crime at law, unless the damage or peril upon which the existence of the crime depends, is not a consequence of one's act of commission or omission. Failure to prevent an act one has the legal duty to avoid is equivalent to causing it. Art. 39-58, bis, Italian Penal Code. See rèo.

reàto suppósto eroneaménte e reàto impossíbile — erroneously supposed crime and impossible crime. One who commits an act not constituting a crime in the erroneous supposition that it does constitute a crime is not punishable. Punishment is also excluded when, through the insufficiency of the action or the inexistence of its object, the damaging and perilous event is impossible. Art. 49, Italian Code of Penal Procedure.

rebus sic stantibus (Lat.)—at this instance in the matter; under these circumstances. An implied or express condition in a contract which permits a party whose performance has become excessively burdensome, due to supervening causes, to withdraw therefrom by way of rescission. See **contràtto con prestazióni corrispettíve.** Art. 1467, Italian Civil Code.

recèdere—to go back; to recede; to return or give up; to renounce; to abandon; to desist; to withdraw.

recèsso m.—act of receding; recession; withdrawal from an action; abandonment; depth; recess.

recèsso per giústa càusa—withdrawal from a work contract for just cause. Art. 2119, Italian Civil Code.

recèsso unilateràle del contràtto —

unilateral withdrawal from a contract. Art. 1373, Italian Civil Code.

recezióne f.—receipt; the act and effect of receiving; reception; admission into a position or office; admission or declaration of the receipt of a sum of money or similar thing.

recidíva f.—relapse; repetition of an offense. Whoever has been convicted of a crime and thereafter commits a subsequent one, will receive an augmented punishment for the new crime. Art. 99-101, Italian Penal Code.

recidíva genèrica—generic recidivism; the commission of a subsequent crime, different in character from a previous one which is committed by a person already convicted of the prior crime.

recidíva specífica—specific recidivism; the commission of a subsequent crime, of the same character as a previous one which is committed by a person already convicted of the prior crime.

recidività f.—recidivism.

recidívo—recidivous.

recidívo m. — recidivist; incorrigible criminal; second offender.

recínto m.—enclosure.

rècipe m.—prescription.

recipiènte m.—a vessel suitable to receive something; receiver; recipient.

recipiènte—adequate; suitable; useful.

reciprocàre—to reciprocate.

reciprocazióne f.—reciprocation; act of mutual giving giving and receiving.

reciprocità f.—reciprocity; mutuality; state of being reciprocal.

recíproco—reciprocal; mutually interchangeable.

recisióne f.—recision; act of cutting off or pruning; act of rescinding.

recisióne di ràmi protèsi e di radíci—recision of protruding or extending branches and roots. The owner of land over which a neighbor's tree branches protrude or extend, may, at any time, compel the neighbor to

prune them. He may, also, cut the roots which enter onto his land, unless otherwise provided by local use and regulations. Art. 896, Italian Civil Code.

reclamànte m.—reclaimant; appellant; one who appeals to reclaim.

reclamànte—appealing.

reclamàre—to reclaim; to publicly express a grievance; to lodge a complaint; to protest; to demand.

reclamazióne f.—reclamation; appeal. See reclàmo.

reclàme f.—advertisement.

reclàmo m. — a complaint against an unjust thing; protest. In civil cases, it is an attack against certain orders and decrees of a judge, to obtain from him or a superior judge, a reconsideration of the ruling. Art. 178, 179, Italian Code of Civil Procedure. In bankruptcy matters, when a petition in bankruptcy is rejected or disallowed, an appeal may be taken to the Court of Appeals. Art. 22, Falliménto (Bankruptcy), Usual Laws, Appendix to Italian Civil Code; Art. 739-742 bis, Italian Code of Civil Procedure.

reclusióne f.—reclusion; confinement; incarceration; imprisonment; punishment for the crime of delítto which may last from fifteen days to twenty four years. Art. 23, 17, Italian Penal Code. See delítto.

reclúso m.—one incarcerated as punishment.

reclusòrio m.—prison.

reclúta f.—recruit; conscript.

recriminazióne f.—recrimination.

rècto m.—the obverse side of a coin, medal or page; the reverse side is referred to as vèrso.

recuperàre — to recover. Also, ricuperàre.

recuperatòrio—a possessory action to regain possession of a lost object.

redàtto — compiled; drawn up; expanded; extended; written.

redattóre m.—editor; writer.

redattóre responsàbile — responsible

editor. Besides the responsibility of the author of the published material, the responsible director or vice-director of the newspaper or periodic publication is answerable for crimes committed as a result of failure to exercise necessary control over its content to prevent the publication of criminal material. Art. 57-58 bis, Italian Penal Code.

redazióne f.—editing; editorial staff or office; drafting of material for reporting or printing.

redazióne della sentènza—preparation of the opinion to support a judgment. It is written by the estensóre, the drafting or reporting judge, presented to the President of the Tribunal, subscribed by both and filed with the Clerk of the Court. Art. 119, Enabling Rules, Italian Code of Civil Procedure.

redde rationem (Lat.)—render the account or bill.

rèddito m.—income; return or income from capital, industry or professional employment; revenue.

rèddito agràrio—agrarian income; that part of the income belonging to the cultivator of the soil.

rèddito dominicàle—master's income; that part of the income belonging to the owner of the land.

redibitòria—redhibitory; a rescission of a contract because of hidden or latent defects in the property sold. See **azióne redibitòria.**

redígere—to draw up (a document); to edit.

redímere—to redeem; to liberate; to free from a mortgage.

redimíre—to wreathe; to crown.

rèdina (s.) rèdine (pl.) f.—reins of a bridle.

rèduce m.—returning veteran.

reductio ad aequitatem (Lat.)—reduction to equity. A party whose performance is excessively burdensome may ask for rescission of the contract or for a mitigation of its effect by asking for a reduction or modification of its terms of execution to bring it to an equitable state. Art.

1448, 1467, 1468, 1664, Italian Civil Code.

referendàrio m.—an official referee; a court officer who investigates petitions and reports thereon.

referèndum m.—referendum; a practice of submitting a measure to the electorate for approval or rejection; a communication by a diplomatic representative to his home government for further instructions. Art. 75, 123, 132, 138, Constitution of the Italian Republic; Art. 1-53, Referendum, Usual Laws, Appendix to Italina Code of Civil Procedure.

refèrto m.—report. It is the statement which a person must make to the Authorities, when in the performance of his professional medical duties, he has given assistance or work in cases which may indicate evidence of a prosecutable crime. It must be reported within twenty-four hours. See **omissióne di refèrto,** Art. 365, Italian Penal Code; Art. 4, Italian Code of Penal Procedure.

rèfolo m.—squall. Also, **rìfolo.**

refrattàrio m.—refractory; unmanageable; disobeyer of the law; a deserting conscript.

refurtíva f.—stolen property.

refúso m.—a misplaced type letter.

regalía f.—regalia; royal right.

regàlo m.—gift; present.

regèsto m.—a chronological register of ancient public or private documents.

règge f.—portal; gate through the altar rails.

reggènza f.—regency.

règgere—to administer; to manage; to support; to sustain; to hold (an object); to bear (an expense).

règgia f.—royal palace; court.

reggitóre m. — ruler; governor; administrator; head of an agricultural household. See **capòccia.**

regía f.—an organization which had the royal monopoly to sell certain goods or the contract to collect indirect taxes; a shop for the sale of goods subject to an excise tax. See **appàlto.**

regicída m.—regicide; the killer of a king; the killing of a king.

regicídio m.—the crime of killing a king.

regíme m.—regime; regimen; a system of ruling or governing; rules for administering an operation or agency.

regísta m.—director of a stage or theatrical performance as well as a film director.

registràre—to record; to inscribe in the office of Public Records; to record sound or voices with an appropriate apparatus.

registratóre f.—recorder; apparatus to record voices or sounds.

registrazióne f.—registration; mechanical reproduction of sounds or voices.

regístri delle tutèle e curatèle—registers of tutelage and guardianships. These are public registers maintained at the office of the Tutelary Judge. One register (tutèle) pertains to minors and those totally incapacitated. The other (curatèla) pertains to emancipated minors and those partially incapacitated. Art. 47-51, Enabling Rules, Italian Civil Code; Art. 389, 423, Italian Civil Code.

regístri dello stàto civile—civil status registers. These are public registers maintained in each commune. They are: (1) register of citizenship; (2) register of births; (3) register of weddings; (4) register of deaths. Art. 449-455, Italian Civil Code; Art. 1, 14, Stàto Civíle (Civil Status), Usual Laws, Appendix to Italian Civil Code.

regístri immobiliàri—registers of immovables (real property). The custodian of registers of immovables must issue a copy of recorded material to anyone requesting it. Inspection must be allowed of his registers during the hours fixed by the regulations. The custodian must release a copy of original documents deposited with him or of originals deposited with a notary or in a public archive outside the territory of the Tribunal where he has his headquarters office. Art. 2673-2683, Italian Civil Code.

regístri di cancellería—court clerk's registers. The registers to be maintained are listed for the following courts: (a) Conciliation; (b) Praetor; (c) Tribunal; (d) Court of Appeals; (e) Supreme Court of Cassation. Art. 28-33, Enabling Rules, Italian Code of Civil Procedure.

regístro m. — register; the book in which public records are inscribed and maintained.

regístro aeromòbili—aircraft register. It is a public register maintained under the provisions of the Navigation Code. Art. 752, Italian Navigation Code; Art. 2683, Italian Civil Code.

regístro aeronàutici — See regístro aeromòbili.

regístro automobilístico — automobile register. It is a public register of self-propelled vehicles maintained in the headquarters of the Automobile Club of Italy in each Province. Art. 2683, Italian Civil Code; Autoveícoli (Self-Propelled Vehicles) Usual Laws, Appendix to Italian Civil Code.

regístro dei condomíni — register of condominiums. It contains the rules for its management approved at a regularly constituted meeting. Such meeting requires the attendance of owners representing two thirds the value of the entire building and two thirds of the participants of the condominium. Deliberations are valid when approved by a vote representing the majority of those present and at least half the value of the building. The register contains the identity of the appointed administrator of the condominium and his termination from office for any reason. An administrator must be appointed when there are more than four condominium owners. If not appointed at a meeting, the Judicial Authority may appoint one at the request of one or more owners. The register is maintained in the office of the Professional Association of Building Owners. Art. 1129, 1136, 1138, Italian Civil Code; Art. 71, Enabling Rules, Italian Civil Code.

regístro dei fallíti—register of bankrupts. It is a public register maintained in the office of the clerk of each Tribunal. It contains the names of those declared bankrupt by the same Tribunal as well as those so declared elsewhere. Art. 50 Falliménto (Bankruptcy), Usual Laws, Appendix to Italian Civil Code.

registro dell'adozióne—adoption register. The decree of adoption must be recorded in the appropriate book which is in the care of the Tribunal's clerk. Within ten days, he shall transmit a copy thereof to the official of Civil Status so that an annotation may be made in the margin of the birth certificates of the adopted and adopting persons. Art. 314, Italian Civil Code.

registro delle càrceri—prison register. It contains the petitions, declarations and applications for relief and to appeal a judgment made by a detained person charged with a crime. Art. 80, 171, Italian Code of Penal Procedure.

registro delle imprése—register of enterprises. It is a public register of businesses and enterprises. Art. 2188, Italian Civil Code; Art. 99-101 bis, Enabling Rules, Italian Civil Code.

registro delle persóne giurídiche — register of juridical persons. It is a public register of juridical persons maintained in the clerk's office of a Tribunal in the principal city of each Province. Art. 33, 34, Italian Civil Code; Art. 22-30, 254, Enabling Rules, Italian Civil Code.

registro delle successióni—register of successions. It is a public register of the devolution of property of decedents. The registers are maintained in the clerk's office of each Praetor. They are numbered and each page is authenticated by the Praetor. Art. 52-55, Enabling Rules, Italian Civil Code.

registro di trascrizióne — register of recorded documents. Those required to be recorded are set forth in Art. 2643, Italian Civil Code. Recording must be made in the office of the registers of immovables (registri immobiliàri) in the Judicial district where the property is located. Art. 2663-2673, Italian Civil Code. See **trascrizióne**.

registro (impósta di)—registration tax. It is a tax imposed when registering certain documents required to be registered by law. Title I-IX, Registro (Impósta di) Usual Laws, Appendix to Italian Code of Civil Procedure.

registro navàle—naval register. It is a public register maintained under the provisions of the Navigation Code. Art. 146, Italian Navigation Code; Art. 2683, Italian Civil Code.

registro púbblico — public registry; office of the register; office in which public records are maintained.

regiudicàta f.—res judicata (Lat.); adjudicated matter; the findings contained in a judgment or sentence are binding on the parties, their heirs and assignees. Art. 2909, 2953, Italian Civil Code; Art. 324, 395(5), Italian Code of Civil Procedure; Art. 124, Enabling Rules, Italian Code of Civil Procedure. Also, **còsa giudicàta**.

règola f.—rule; norm; rule of performance or behavior; a monastic rule.

règola d'àrte—a rule of the art; in a satisfactory manner. See **esecuzióne dell'òpera**, Art. 2224, Italian Civil Code.

regolaménti m.—norms; regulations; rules or orders. The regulatory power of the Government is disciplined by laws of a constitutional character. It is exercised by diverse authorities within the limits of their respective jurisdictions and in conformity with specific laws. The President, as Chief of State, issues regulations by decree as well as Ministers within their jurisdiction. Art. 1, 3, 4, 10, Preliminary Dispositions; Art. 87, Constitution of the Italian Republic.

regolaménto m.—regulation; the norm, rule or order prescribed for management or government; precept.

regolaménto di competènza—norm to determine competence or jurisdiction. A judgment rendered in a civil matter, may be challenged by application of either party to the Court of Cassation. The Public Administration may also challenge the defect in jurisdiction at any stage of the proceeding. For conflicts in Penal matters, see risoluzióne dei conflitti. Civilly, see regolaménto di giurisdizióne e di competènza.

regolaménto di condomínio — condominium rules. When the condominium owners in a building are more than ten, rules of management and governance must be drawn to contain the norms for the use of the common property. They must be approved at a regularly constituted meeting with the attendance of owners representing two thirds the value of the entire building and two thirds of the participants of the condominium. Deliberations are valid when approved by a vote representing the majority of those present and at least half the value of the building. The rules of management of the condominium must be entered in the register. Art. 1138, 1136, Italian Civil Code; Art. 68-72, Enabling Rules, Italian Civil Code.

regolaménto di confíni—establishment of boundaries. See azióne di regolaménto di confíni. Art. 950, Italian Civil Code.

regolaménto di giurisdizióne e di competenza—norm for jurisdiction and competence. The provisions apply to both civil and penal cases. The proceedings are initiated civilly upon application of the State Prosecutor or one of the parties. Penally, the questions are resolved upon proper complaint. Art. 37, 41-50, 364, 368, Italian Code of Civil Procedure; Art. 51-54, Italian Code of Penal Procedure. See risoluzióne dei conflítti.

regolaménto giudiziàrio (trattàti di)— treaties on judicial regulation. A number of treaties and conventions have been signed to regulate the recognition of judgments, civil, penal and commercial matters between Italy and various foreign countries. They are: Argentina, Australia, Austria, Belgium, Bolivia, Brazil, Canada, Czechoslovakia, Chile, Colombia, Costa Rica, Finland, France, Germany, Great Britain and Ireland, Greece, Holland, Honduras, Hungary, Japan, Yugoslavia, Lebanon, Luxemburg, Norway, Panama, Romania, San Marino, Siam, Spain, Switzerland, Tunisia, Turkey and the United States. Trattàti di Regolaménto Giudiziàrio, Usual Laws, Appendix to Italian Code of Civil Procedure.

regolàre—to proceed according to rules or norms; to regulate; to adjust.

regolàre (adj.) — regular; normal; usual.

regolàto — disciplined; normal; that which follows good rules.

règolo m.—ruler for drawing lines.

regrèsso—regression; turn back; the right of an unpaid holder of commercial paper to seek payment from prior indorsers. See azióne cambiària di regrèsso and azióne di regrèsso.

reimpiegàre—to re-employ; to reuse; to reinvest.

reimpiègo m.—re-employment; reuse; reinvestment.

reimpiègo dei capitàli dei minóri—reinvestment of the funds of minors. Art. 301, 320, 376, Italian Civil Code.

reintegràre—to reintegrate; to reinstate; to make whole; to restore; to compensate.

reintegrazióne f. — reintegration; restoring of possession. See azióne di reintegrazióne, Art. 1168, 1169, Italian Civil Code.

reintegrazióne in fórma specífica— reintegration in specific form. See risarciménto in fórma specífica.

relatóre m.—relator; reporter; narrator; one who reports on a matter. relatóre (giúdice)—reporting judge.

relazióne f.—relation; account; report.

relegàre—to relegate; to banish; to exile; to consign to an obscure position; to remove; to transfer.

relegazióne f.—relegation; removal; banishment; in Roman law, a milder form of banishment, unlike deportation which entailed loss of property and civil rights.

relínquere—to leave; to abandon; to let go; to relinquish; to renounce.

relítti aeronàutici—aeronautic wreckage or remnants. Special laws apply to the recovery of aircraft and the wreckage of aircraft. Art. 933, Italian Civil Code; Art. 510-513, 993-995, Italian Navigation Code.

relítti di màre—flotsam of the sea. Rights over things thrown into the sea and over those which the sea rejects and over plants and grasses which grow along the sea shore are regulated by special laws. Art. 993, Italian Civil Code; Art. 510 et seq., Italian Navigation Code.

relítto m.—reliction; a leaving behind; remains or residue of a ship-wreck; land left uncovered by a recession of the sea.

relítto—relict; abandoned; left; survivor of a married couple.

remàre—to row.

rematóre m.—rower.

remissíbile—remissible; that which is capable of being remitted, forgiven or pardoned.

remissióne f.—remission; act of remitting or sending back; abatement; forgiveness; pardon; cancellation or release of a debt or claim. Also, **rimessióne** and **rimissióne**.

remissióne del débito—remission of debt. A declaration by the creditor to remit or cancel a debt, extinguishes the obligation when it is communicated to the debtor, unless the latter declares in an appropriate manner that he does not wish to take advantage of the remission. The renunciation of guarantees to the obligation does not give rise to a presumption of the remission of the debt. Art. 1236-1240, Italian Civil Code.

remissióne della querèla—remission or abatement of a complaint. In crimes punishable on complaint (querèla) of the person injured, remission extinguishes the crime. It may not contain limits or conditions and is permitted only before judgment. Remission is procedural or extra-procedural. The latter is express or tacit. It is tacit when the complaining party has committed acts inconsistent with the objective of pursuing the complaint. Art. 152-156, Italian Penal Code.

remozióne f. — removal; dismissal; change; demotion in grade. Also, **rimozióne**.

rèndere—to render; to return; to restore; to give back; to surrender; to compensate; to produce; to yield; to translate.

rendicónto m.—rendering of an account. See **resocónto**.

rendiménto del cónto—rendering of the account required by law. Art. 263-266, Italian Code of Civil Procedure; re guardianship, Art. 385-389, Italian Civil Code; re heir of an estate, Art. 496, 497; re curator of abeyant inheritance, Art. 531; re testamentary executor, Art. 709; re co-sharers of inheritance, Art. 723; re contract of mandàto, Art. 1713; re assignment of assets to creditors, Art. 1983; re administrator of a condominium, Art. 1130, Italian Civil Code; re trustee in Bankruptcy, Art. 116, 134, Falliménto (Bankruptcy), Usual Laws, Appendix to Italian Civil Code; re judicial commissioner in a business under controlled management, Art. 191, Bankruptcy, Usual Laws, Appendix to Italian Civil Code.

rèndita f.—income from capital, land, buildings, commerce or industry; interest; dividend; rent.

rèndita (conversióne della)—conversion of public obligations. The substitution by the State of State bonds or obligations by new ones with different conditions. See **conversióne del débito púbblico** and **conversióne della rèndita**.

rèndita fondiària—income from land. It is an income in perpetuity created under a contract whereby one party grants to the other the right to collect, in perpetuity, a sum of money or a certain quantity of fungibles, in exchange for the alienation of land. Art. 1863, 1861, Italian Civil Code.

rèndita perpètua—perpetual income. It is an income in perpetuity created under a contract whereby one party grants to the other, the right to collect in perpetuity, a sum of money or a certain quantity of fungibles, in exchange for the alienation of land or assignment of a stated capital Art. 1861-1871, Italian Civil Code.

rèndita púbblica—public income; the income from evidences of obligations of the State to pay money.

rèndita sémplice—simple income. It is income in perpetuity created under a contract whereby one party grants to the other, the right to collect in perpetuity, a sum of money, in exchange for the assignment of a stated capital. Simple income must be guaranteed with a mortgage over land. The capital is, otherwise, subject to restitution. Art. 1863, 1864, 1861, Italian Civil Code.

rèndita vitalízia—life-time income. It is income for the life of a beneficiary, or a third party or number of persons. It is created by contract whereby one party grants to another the right to collect, periodically, a sum of money or fungibles in exchange for a grant of real or personal property or capital. It may also be created by donation or by testament. Income terminates upon the death of the one upon whose life it is limited. Art. 1872-1881, Italian Civil Code; **Rèndite Vitalízie,** Usual Laws, Appendix to Italian Civil Code.

renitènte—renitent; recalcitrant; resistent; one who resists pressure and persistently opposes.

renitènte alla lèva—one who fails to respond to the call for military duty.

renitènza f. — renitency; opposition; recalcitrance.

renitènza del imputàto—renitence of the accused. When a person is recalcitrant, a fugitive or in concealment, or has not presented himself for interrogation without legitimate excuse, notices to him are served by depositing same in the office of the clerk or secretary of court. The Judge or Public Prosecutor names a defense lawyer for the accused who is without one. Art. 173, 174, 170, Italian Code of Penal Procedure.

renúnzia f.—act of renouncing; declaration renouncing or abandoning some right or claim. Also, **rinúnzia.**

renunziazióne f. — renunciation. See **renúnzia.** Also, **rinunziazióne.**

rèo m.—culprit; guilty of a crime; criminal defendant. No one may be punished for an act considered criminal by law, if at the moment of its commission it was not chargeable. That person is chargeable who has the capacity of comprehending and willing an act (intent or state of mind necessary to commit a crime). Art. 85-98, 133, 150, 171, Italian Penal Code. See **reàto.**

rèo—evil; wicked; criminal.

repentàglio m. — risk; danger; jeopardy; peril.

repènte—sudden; unexpected.

repènte (di)—unexpectedly; suddenly.

reperíbile—that which can be found; discoverable.

reperíre—to find out; to discover.

repertàto—found in a search related to a crime.

repèrto m.—the object found as a result of a search. See **perquisizióne.**

repertòrio m.—repertory; index; inventory; register required to be kept by court clerks, notaries and judicial officers which contain daily entries of documents subject to registration.

rèplica f.—copy of an original; reproduction; repetition of a performance. Also, answer; reply; rejoinder; answer to a defendant's plea; replication. Art. 180, 190, 379, Italian Code of Civil Procedure; Art. 117, Enabling Rules, Italian Code of Civil Procedure; Art. 438, 468, 536, Italian Code of Penal Procedure.

replicaménto m.—act of replying or answering; replication.

replicàre—to answer; to reply; to replicate; to answer an objection; to controvert a statement; to repeat again.

replicazióne f.—repetition. See **replicaménto.**

reprimènda f.—severe scolding; reprimand.

reprímere—to repress; to curb; to restrain.

repulisti (Lat.) m.—rejection; repulsion.

repulisti (fàr)—to carry everything off; to consume everything; to eat everything; to make a clean sweep.

reputazióne f.—reputation. Also, riputazióne.

requisíre—to requisition; to take under authority for public necessity or military use.

requisíti del contràtto—requirements of a contract. The elements of a contract are: (1) agreement of the parties; (2) a cause, motive or inducement for the contract (consideration; (3) lawful subject matter; (4) compliance with legal requirements that a certain contract be by public Act or in writing. The contract is binding when the offeror acquires knowledge of acceptance. Art. 1325, 1326, Italian Civil Code.

requisitòria f.—the presentation of the prosecutor's propositions and points in writing and orally, in a criminal trial. Art. 369, 468, 519, 536, Italian Code of Penal Procedure.

requisizióne f. — requisition. When there occurs a necessity of a grave and urgent nature regarding public, military or civil matters, the requisition of personal and real property may be ordered. The owner of such property shall receive appropriate indemnification. Art. 835, 1020, Italian Civil Code.

résa f. — surrender; yield; submit; render (an account, a service); restitution (of a book).

résa a discrezióne—unconditional surrender.

résa in méno—a short delivery of merchandise.

résa (tèrmine di)—delivery term, as used in the transportation of things. Art. 1688, Italian Civil Code.

rescíndere—to rescind; to annul; to abrogate.

rescissióne f.—rescission; the act of rescinding or annulling; abrogation.

rescissióne del contràtto—rescission of a contract. Art. 1447-1452, Italian Civil Code. See azióne di rescissióne del contràtto.

rescissióne per lesióne—rescission for damage resulting from the division of the inheritance. Where a co-heir receives less than a quarter of the portion to which he is entitled from the estate, he may abrogate the division. Art. 763, Italian Civil Code. Also, azióne di rescissióne per lesióne.

residènza f.—residence; residence is the place where a person has his habitual dwelling. Art. 43, Italian Civil Code. See domicílio and dimòra.

residenziàle—residential.

residuàle—residual.

resistènza f.—resistance.

resistènza a un púbblico ufficiàle—resistance to a public official. Whoever uses violence or threats to oppose a public official or one in charge of a public service while he discharges an act of office or service, or those assisting him at his request, is punished with imprisonment. Art. 337, 339, Italian Penal Code.

res nullius (Lat.)—things which have no owner. Immovable (real) property which belongs to no one, is part of the patrimony of the State. Personal (movable) property which belongs to no one, may be acquired by occupation. Personal property which is found must be returned to its owner, and if he is unknown it must be turned over to the mayor of the place where it was found, without delay, with an explanation of its finding. Art. 827, 923, 927, Italian Civil Code.

réso—rendered; delivered; returned.

resocónto — account; report; bank statement. See rendicónto.

respíngere—to reject; to drive back; to repel; to disapprove; to return.

responsàbile civíle—a person civilly responsible (in damages) for loss caused by a crime. He may be sued as well as the person charged with the commission of the criminal act. Every crime requires restitution or compensation according to the norms of the civil law. Where it has caused property damage or other, the culpable person is obligated to pay damages, as well as the person who must respond for the act with him. Art. 185, Italian Penal Code; Art. 107-123, 447, 489, Italian Code of Penal Procedure.

responsabilità civíle del giúdice—civil responsibility of a judge. The judge is civilly responsible only: (1) when in the exercise of his functions, he is chargeable with acts of criminality, fraud or extortion; (2) when, without just cause, he refuses, omits or delays to take measures on complaints or demands of the parties, and generally to discharge the duties of his office. Art. 55, Italian Code of Civil Procedure.

responsabilità civíle per fàtto illécito—civil responsibility for an illegal act. See **risarciménto per fàtto illècito.**

responsabilità dei genitóri, dei tutóri, dei precettóri e dei maèstri d'àrte—responsibility of parents, guardians, preceptors and teachers of the arts. Parents or guardians are responsible for damage caused by the illegal act of minor, unemancipated, children or persons under their tutelage who live with them. Preceptors and those who teach a trade or art are responsible for damage caused by the illegal act of their pupils and apprentices under their supervision. Art. 2048, Italian Civil Code. Also, **responsabilità per fàtto altrúi o indirètta.**

responsabilità dei padróni e dei committènti—responsibility of masters and employers. Masters and employers are responsible for damage brought about or caused by their domestics and employees in the performance of their assigned tasks. Art. 2049, Italian Civil Code. Also, **responsabilità per fàtto altrúi o indirètta.**

responsabilità del conducènte—responsibility of the operator (of a motor vehicle). The operator of a motor vehicle must compensate for damage caused to persons or things during the operation of the vehicle unless he proves that he did everything possible to avoid the damage. In case of collision between vehicles, it is presumed, till proved to the contrary, that each operator contributed equally to the damage sustained by each vehicle. Art. 2054, Italian Civil Code.

responsabilità del debitóre—responsibility of the debtor. The debtor who does not exactly fulfill the performance due, is held to respond in damages if he does not prove that the non-performance or delay was caused by impossibility of performance due to a cause not imputable to him. Art. 1218, 2740, 2741, Italian Civil Code. See **responsabilità patrimoniàle.**

responsabilità dei prestatóre d'ópera intellettuàle—responsibility of intellectual worker. The law determines the intellectual professions whose exercise requires inscription in appropriate registers. Failure to be inscribed prevents an action for compensation. Work performed must be done personally or with aides and assistants under the professional's direction and responsibility if such collaboration is permitted by the contract or usage and not incompatible with the object of the performance. Where work to be performed involves technical problems of special difficulty, the performer of the work is not responsible for losses incurred except in the event of a criminal act or gross negligence. The client may withdraw from the contract by repayment of expenses incurred and compensating for the work performed. The performer of professional services may withdraw from the contract for just cause without prejudice to the client. He is entitled to expenses incurred and compensation for services rendered to be determined by its utility to the client. Art. 2229-2238, Italian Civil Code.

responsabilità del tutóre e del protutóre—responsibility of the guardian and pro-guardian. They must administer the minor's property with the diligence of a good father of the family. They respond to the minor for every loss caused to him by violation of their duties. Art. 382, Italian Civil Code.

responsabilità obbiettíva—objective responsibility. Responsibility without fault. See **responsabilità oggettíva.**

responsabilità oggettíva—objective responsibility. Responsibility without fault. It is based on the equitable principle that loss of property must be compensated even when committted by one who is not personally responsible. Consequently, certain persons, such as parents, guardians, teachers and employers are responsible for damage caused by those under their supervision. Art. 2043-2059, Italian Civil Code. Also, **responsabilità obbiettíva.**

responsabilità patrimoniàle — patrimonial (property) responsibility. The debtor must account for the fulfillment of his obligations with all his present and future property. There are no limitations on this responsibility except in cases provided by law. Art. 2740, 2741, 1218, Italian Civil Code. See **responsabilità del debitóre.**

responsabilità penàle—penal responsibility. No one may be punished for an act of commission or omission deemed by law to be a crime, unless he has committed it with knowledge and will (intent). Art. 42, 43, Italian Penal Code.

responsabilità per le còse portàte in albèrgo — liability for property brought into a hotel. The innkeeper is liable for theft, loss or deterioration of guests' property brought into the hotel and not delivered to him, up to a statutory amount. His liability is unlimited where loss is due to his gross negligence or that of his aides. He is not liable for refusing guests' property with just cause including excessive value or unwieldy size. He is free of liability if loss is due to gross negligence of the guest, his employees, visitors or those accompanying him or if loss or deterioration is due to the nature or defect of the property or by accident. Art. 1784, Italian Civil Code. Also, **esònero nel depòsito in albèrgo.**

responsabilità per dànno cagionàto da animàli — responsibility for loss caused by animals. The owner of an animal or the one using him, during the period of its use, is responsible for loss caused by the animal whether under his custody and whether lost, strayed or a runaway, except in the event an accidental situation is proved. Art. 2052, Italian Civil Code.

responsabilità per dànno cagionàto da còsa in custòdia—responsibility for loss caused by a thing in custody. Everyone is liable for loss caused by the things which he has in his custody or care unless it is proved that the loss or damage was accidental. Art. 2051, Italian Civil Code.

responsabilità per fàtto altrúi o indirètta—responsibility for the action of another or indirect responsibility. See **responsabilità dei genitóri, dei tutóri, dei precettóri e dei maèstri d'àrte,** and **responsabilità dei padróni e dei committènti.**

responsabilità per l'esercízio di attività pericolóse—responsibility for undertaking dangerous activities. Whoever causes damage to others by undertaking an activity which is dangerous in its nature or by reason of the means employed, is held to make compensation, unless he can prove he adopted all necessary measures to avoid danger. Art. 2050, Italian Civil Code.

responsabilità precontrattuàle (trattatíve e)—negotiations and precontractual responsibility. The parties, during the development of the negotiations and the formation of the contract, must act in good faith. Art. 1337, Italian Civil Code.

responsabilità solidàle — joint and several responsibility. Where the action which causes loss is imputable to many persons, all are liable jointly and severally in compensating for the damage. Art. 2055, Italian Civil Code. See **obbligazioni in solido.**

responsióne f.—a payment or pension to be made at fixed periods. See **risponsióne.**

restituzióne f. — restitution; restoration; repayment.

restituzióne di còsa determinàta—restitution of a specific thing. Whoever has wrongfully received a specific thing, must return it. If it has perished, even though accidentally, the one receiving it in bad faith must return its value; if it only deteriorated, the one who gave it may demand its equivalent or restitution plus indemnification for its loss in value. Whoever received it in good faith does not answer for its loss or deterioration although responsible, except within the limits of his enrichment. Art. 2037, Italian Civil Code.

restituzióne in tèrmini—restoration to a legal right after default to exercise it within the prescribed period of time. Art. 183 bis, Italian Code of Penal Procedure.

restituzióni e riscarciménto del dànno —restitutions and compensation for loss. Every crime demands that restitutions be made in accordance with the norms of the civil laws. Every crime which has caused either property or non-property damage, obligates the guilty party and the persons who under civil laws must respond for his action, to render compensation for the damages. Art. 185, Italian Penal Code.

restituzióni (òbblighi del condannàto) —obligations of the condemned to make restitutions. The conditional suspension of punishment may be subordinated to the fulfillment of the obligation of making restitutions, to the payment of a liquidated sum by way of compensation for damages, or provisionally assigned as its amount, and the publication of the judgment, by way of reparation for the loss. Art. 165, Italian Penal Code.

restrizióne f.—restriction.

reticènza f.—reticence; state of keeping silent; failure to speak freely. The act of remaining silent, in whole or in part, while under oath concerning knowledge of facts about which one is being interrogated. See **fálsa testimoniàza.**

retràtto m.—portrait; picture; representation; likeness. Also, **ritràtto.**

retràtto—retracted; drawn back. Also, **ritràtto.**

retràtto successòrio—the preemptive right of a co-heir to purchase the other's share of the inheritance ahead of strangers. See **prelazióne (dirítto di)**, Art. 732, Italian Civil Code.

retrazióne f.—retraction. Also, **ritrazióne.**

retribuíre—to retribute; to pay back.

retribuzióne f.—retribution; requittal; that which is given in compensation; reward.

retroattività f.—quality of being retroactive.

retroattività della légge—retroactivity of the law. It refers to ex post facto or retroactive laws. No one may be punished for an act which, according to the law at the time of its commission, did not constitute a crime, nor, may anyone be punished for an act which, under subsequent law, does not constitute a crime. If the law at the time of commission of the crime and laws thereafter are different, those dispositions more favorable to the culprit will apply, unless they are exceptional and temporary in nature; Art. 2, Italian Penal Code; Art. 25, Constitution of the Italian Republic; Art. 11, Preliminary Dispositions.

retroattivo — retroactive; retrospective; looking backward.

retroazióne f.—retroaction; operating on something which preceded.

retrocàrica f.—a breech-loading firearm.

retrocèdere—retrocede; to go back; to turn back; to recede; to give back; to return to the assignor a right previously given to the assignee.

retrocessióne f.—retrocession; act of retroceding; recession; disappearance (of an illness); giving back a right previously acquired; demotion in rank.

retroguárdia f.—rear guard.

retrovéndita f.—resale; right of a purchaser to resell property to the vendor.

retrovía f.—rear lines in a military operation.

rettífica f.—rectification; correction.

rettífica del nóme—correction of name; change of name; additions thereto or corrections are not permitted except in the cases and with the formality indicated by law. Art. 6, Italian Civil Code.

rettificazióne f.—rectification; correction.

rettificazióne degli àtti dello stàto civíle — correction of civil status records. It is made by judgment of the Tribunal which is then transcribed in the civil status registers. Art. 449, 454, 455, Italian Civil Code.

revíndica f.—an action to recover possession of property. See **azióne di rivendicazióne.** Also, **rivendicazióne.**

revisióne f. — review; revision; re-examination; the review of a case based upon newly discovered evidence. See **giudízio di revisióne.**

revisióne del cànone nell'enfiteùsi—review of rent on land held in emphyteusis. See Art. 962, Italian Civil Code.

revisióne del cónto approvàto—review of approved account. See Art. 266, Italian Code of Civil Procedure.

revisióne del prèzzo nell'appàlto—review of cost in a public works contract. See Art. 1664, Italian Civil Code.

revisióne in matèria penàle—review in a penal case. It is based on newly discovered evidence and other circumstances specified by statute. Art. 479 and Art. 553-574 bis, Italian Code of Penal Procedure.

revisóre m.—auditor; reviser.

rèvoca f. — revocation. Also, **revocazióne.**

revocàre—to revoke.

revocatívo—revocatory; tending to or involving revocation.

revocatòria (azióne)—revocatory action. See **azióne revocatòria,** Art. 2901-2904, Italian Civil Code.

revocatòria fallimentàre (azióne) — revocatory action in bankruptcy. See

azióne revocatòria fallimentàre and Art. 67-71, Falliménto (Bankruptcy), Usual Laws, Appendix to Italian Civil Code.

revocazióne f. — revocation. Also, **rèvoca.**

revocazióne f.—revocation. It is used in civil matters to challenge judgments rendered therein. Those subject to challenge are: (1) where judgment is the result of fraud by one party to the injury of the other; (2) where the judgment was rendered on the basis of evidence declared to be false subsequent to judgment, or which the losing party was unaware to have been known or declared to be false prior to judgment; (3) where, following judgment, decisive documents were discovered which the party could not have produced at the trial by reason of *force majeure,* or action of the opposing party; (4) where the judgment is the effect of an error of fact resulting from acts or documents in the action. This error arises when judgment is based on the supposition of a fact, the truth of which is incontestably excluded, or when the inexistence of a fact is supposed whose truth has been positively established; (5) where judgment is contrary to a previous adjudication between the parties; (6) where judgment is due to fraud of the judge. Art. 395-403, Italian Code of Civil Procedure.

revocazióne per sopravveniènza di fígli —revocation (of gifts) made prior to the time a donor had knowledge of having children. Donations or gifts made by one who did not have or was unaware that he had children or legitimate descendants at the time of a donation, may be revoked for the benefit of an unexpectedly existing child or legitimate descendant of the donor. Besides, they may be revoked upon the acknowledgement of a natural child, made within two years of the donation, except when it can be proved, that at the time of the donation, the donor had knowledge of the existence of the child. Revocation may also be demanded if the child of the donor had already been conceived at the time of the donation. Art. 803, Italian Civil Code.

revòlver m.—revolver (English); a repeating pistol having a revolving chambered cylinder holding a number of cartridges which can be discharged successively without reloading. Also, rivoltèlla.

revolveràre—to hit with a revolver; to shoot someone with a revolver.

revolveràta f. — revolver shot. Also, rivoltellàta.

riabilitàre — to rehabilitate; to reinstate; to restore to former capacity; to invest again with a former right, authority and dignity; declaration by the court under which a bankrupt is released from the obligation of his debts; a discharge in bankruptcy.

riabilitazióne f.—rehabilitation. Under penal law, it is the act whereby a condemned criminal who has served his sentence, is reinstated to his personal rights and condition prior to his sentence. Rehabilitation extinguishes accessory penalties such as deprivation of the right to hold office, to vote, to be enrolled in professional registers, etc. Rehabilitation is granted by the Court of Appeals in the district where the sentence was imposed upon proof of constant good behavior for five years or ten years for recidivists. Art. 178-181, Italian Penal Code; Art. 597-602, Italian Code of Penal Procedure; Art. 44, Enabling Rules, Italian Code of Penal Procedure.

riabilitazióne civíle (del fallíto) — civil rehabiiltation of the bankrupt. It terminates the personal incapacity which attaches to the bankrupt by force of the judgment of bankruptcy. Rehabilitation is declared by the Tribunal on motion of the debtor or his heirs and judgment is rendered to that effect with order to cancel the bankrupt's name from the public register of bankrupts. Art. 142-145, Falliménto, Usual Laws, Appendix to Italian Civil Code.

riabilitazióne dei minorènni—rehabilitation of minors. The Tribunal pro-

vides the method for rehabilitation of minors by judgment issued in chambers without the assistance of defense counsel, after having heard the provincial public security authorities, the Public Prosecutor and the one exercising parental authority or guardianship of the minor. The provision for rehabilitation is entered on the judgments regarding the minor and is inscribed in the judicial records. No mention is made of the criminal antecedents in the minor's penal record. Art. 24, Tribunal for Minors, Usual Laws, Appendix to Italian Code of Penal Procedure.

riabilitazióne del'indégno — rehabilitation of the unworthy (person). Whoever has incurred the status of unworthy, is admitted to the succession when the person whose succession is involved, has expressly qualified him with a public Act or testament. Nonetheless, if mentioned in the will when the testator knew the cause of the unworthy status, the person not legally qualified as required by law, is admitted to the succession within the limits of the testamentary disposition. Art. 466, 463, Italian Civil Code. See indegnità.

riaccreditàre—to reaccredit; to accredit once more; to reacquire credit.

riacquistàre—to reacquire; to recover; to retake.

rialzàre — to raise again; to raise higher; to rise up again.

riàlzo m.—rise in price; a prominence or rise in the ground.

riàlzo e ribàsso fraudolènto di prezzi sul púbblico mercàto o nelle bòrse di commèrcio — fraudulent rise and lowering of priees in the public market or in commodity exchanges. It involves the surreptitious acquisition of a considerable quantity of a specific commodity or goods with the intent of reselling same at a higher price by changing the market price. Art. 501, Italian Penal Code.

riapertúra f.—reopening.

riapertúra del falliménto — reopening of bankruptcy proceeding. When there has been final distribution of assets or when it was impractical to continue the proceeding due to insufficient assets, the Tribunal, within five years of termination of the proceeding, may order its reopening if it appears that the bankrupt had sufficient property to make the proceeding practical or when the bankrupt guarantees payment of at least ten per cent of old and new creditors. Art. 121-123, Falliménto (Bankruptcy), Usual Laws, Appendix to Italian Civil Code.

riapertúra della istruzióne—reopening of the hearing (in a criminal case). Whoever has been discharged in the formal proceedings may be subjected to new proceedings for the same act, unless it is barred, upon the discovery of newly found evidence against him. The person discharged for insufficient evidence may ask for a reopening on the basis of new evidence in his favor. The reopening is made upon written request by the Public Prosecutor or written notice by the discharged person to the judge who ordered it. Art. 402-404, Italian Code of Penal Procedure.

riappaltàre—to subcontract; to sublease. Also, **subappaltàre**.

riappàlto m. — subcontract; sublease. Also, **subappàlto**.

riassicuràre—to reinsure.

riassicurazióne f.—reinsurance; a contract made by one insurer with another to protect him against loss or risk assumed by reason of the original insurance with an insured party. Contracts of reinsurance must be made in writing. They do not create a legal relationship between the insured and the reinsurer. Art. 1928-1931, Italian Civil Code.

riassociàre—to associate once again.

riassúmere—to reassume; to resume; to recapitulate; to summarize.

riassúnto m.—summary.

riassúnto—resumed.

riassúnto di contròllo—summary of a set of ledgers.

riassunzióne f.—resumption; resumption of an interrupted civil trial.

riassunzióne della càusa—resumption of the trial. It concerns the resumption of a trial which has been suspended, interrupted or annulled or resumed after failure of the parties to appear as required by law. Art. 181, 295-305, 309, Italian Code of Civil Procedure; Art. 125-126, Enabling Rules, Italian Code of Civil Procedure.

ribadíre—to clinch; to rivet; to beat down the point of a nail that has been driven through wood.

ribaditúra f.—clinching; riveting; the beaten down point of a nail that has been driven through wood.

ribàlta f.—flap; trap; flap of a trap door or writing desk; in the theater, that portion of the stage where the footlights are situated.

ribàlta (àlla)—to the footlights; the call to the footlights of an actor who is accorded applause.

ribàlta (lètto a)—folding bed which recedes into a wall and is concealed by a flap.

ribàlta (tàvola a)—folding table.

ribaltàre—to capsize; to overturn.

ribassàre — to lower the price; to diminish.

ribàsso m.—diminution or drop in price; discount; abatement.

ribellàre—to rebel; to revolt.

ribèlle m.—rebel.

ribellióne f. — rebellion; open and armed resistance to authority or government.

ribrézzo m.—shudder; disgust; chilliness.

ricadére—to fall back or down again; to hang down; to relapse; to transmit by legal right such as by right of inheritance.

ricaducità f. — lapsing of a lease or legacy; nullity of a donation or vote.

ricadúta f.—relapse.

ricadúto m.—lapsed.

ricambiàre — to re-exchange; to re-exchange or return greetings.

ricàmbio m.—to re-exchange; replacement of one thing for another; a gift given in return; exchange of greetings.

ricaricàre—to reload.

ricattàre—to extort; to ransom; to recover business expenses.

ricàtto m.—common term for extortion. See estorsióne.

ricavàre—to dig out; to draw out; to earn; to profit; to extract or obtain; to recover; to copy.

ricavàto m. — earnings; profit; recoveries.

ricavàto in contànti—cash proceeds.

ricàvo m.—earnings; profit. See ricavàto.

ricchézza f.—wealth.

ricchézza mòbile—movable (personal property) wealth; that produced by work, industry, commerce or income. The former tax on income was so denominated.

ricérca f.—research; inquiry; search.

ricérca della paternità e della maternità—inquiry to determine paternity and maternity. See dichiarazióne giudiziàle di paternità e maternità. Art. 269-279, Italian Civil Code.

ricérca delle còse da consegnàre—search for things to be delivered under attachment. Art. 606, Italian Code of Civil Procedure. See ricérca delle còse da pignoràre.

ricérca delle còse da pignoràre — search for things subject to attachment. Art. 513-524, Italian Code of Civil Procedure. See espropiazióne mobiliàre prèsso il debitóre.

ricercàre—to research; to investigate; to interrogate; to search out.

ricercataménte—with affectation or refinement; on purpose.

ricercatézza f.—excessive affectation or refinement.

ricercàto — investigated; wanted; sought for (merchandise); affected.

ricètta f.—prescription.

ricettaménto m.—harboring; providing a refuge; to shelter.

ricettàre—to harbor; to shelter; to receive and keep stolen goods.

ricettàrio m.—book of prescriptions.

ricettatóre m.—one who harbors or gives asylum or shelter; receiver of stolen goods. See manutèngolo.

ricettazióne f.—receiving stolen property. The crime of buying, receiving or concealing stolen money or property or becoming involved in having such property bought, received or concealed. Art. 648, Italian Penal Code. See favoreggiaménte reàle.

ricevúta f.—receipt. See quietànza.

ricevúta di càrico—freight receipt. Art. 1684, 1685, 1691, Italian Civil Code. See lèttera di vettúra. Cf. Art. 1-201 (15); 7-102(e), Uniform Commercial Code.

richiamàre—to recall (such as an ambassador); to call again; to reproach; to complain; to summon.

richiàmo m.—recall; reclaim; decoy; complaint; a reference mark in a book.

richiàmo alle àrmi—recall to arms. Art. 2111, Italian Civil Code; Lavóro (Servízio Militàre)—Work (Military Service), Usual Laws, Appendix to Italian Civil Code.

richiàmo di documénti—recall of documents. When submitting the list of witnesses to be called at the trial, the Public Prosecutor and the other parties may demand that documents be produced. Art. 416, Italian Code of Penal Procedure.

richièdere—to require; to request; to necessitate; to summon; to send for; to demand; to cite; to ask for.

richièsta f.—request; demand; petition; summons.

richièsta d'informazióne alla pùbblica amministrazióne — demand for information directed to the Public Administration. Except as provided otherwise by statute, the judge may demand that the Public Administration provide written data relative to Acts and documents of their administration which may be necessary to present at the trial. Art. 213, Italian Code of Civil Procedure; Art. 96, 97, Enabling Rules, Italian Code of Civil Procedure.

richiúdere—to enclose; to close or shut up; to heal (a wound).

richiusúra f.—enclosure.

riclàmo m.—claim; claim under an insurance policy.

ricognizióne f.—recognition; acknowledgement; recognizance; expression of appreciation; military reconnaissance; verification or identification of a fact in criminal matters.

ricognizióne di débito (proméssa di pagaménto e)—promise of payment and acknowledgement of debt. The promise of payment and acknowledgement of a debt exempts the one to whom it is made of the burden of proving the underlying legal relationship. Its existence is presumed until proof to the contrary. Art. 1988, Italian Civil Code. See promésse unilateràli.

ricognizióni di persóne e di còse e dei confrónti—recognition or identification of persons and things and confrontations. The procedure employed during preliminary hearings to identify persons or things and the confrontation of persons already examined and interrogated when there is discord between them regarding important facts and circumstances. Art. 360-364, Italian Code of Penal Procedure.

ricompènsa f.—recompense; compensation; reward.

ricomposizióne f.—recomposition; rearrangement.

ricómpra f.—repurchase; redemption.

riconciliazióne f.—reconciliation.

riconciliazióne tra i còniugi—reconciliation between spouses. It denotes the abandonment of the demand for personal separation already proposed. By common accord, spouses can terminate the effects of a judgment of separation without intervention of a judge, with an express declaration or with an unequivocal comportment which is incompatible with the state of separation. Art. 154, 157, Italian Civil Code.

riconduttóre m.—a leasee who renews

a lease on property after its original expiration.

riconduzióne f.—renewal of a lease on property. See rinnovazióne tàcita del contràtto (di locazióne).

riconfermazióne f.—reconfirmation.

riconoscènte—grateful; thankful.

riconoscènza f.—gratitude; acknowledgement; reward; admission; confession.

riconóscere—to recognize; to acknowledge; to admit; to confess; to reward; to reconnoiter.

riconóscere un govèrno—to recognize a government.

riconosciménto m. — recognition; acknowledgement.

riconosciménto della sentènze penàli stranière — recognition of foreign penal judgments. Art. 672-675, Italian Code of Penal Procedure. Re civil matters, see sentènze stranière (efficàcia delle), Art. 796-805, Italian Code of Civil Procedure. See delibazióne (giudízio di).

riconosciménto di débito — acknowledgement of debt. See ricognizióne di débito (proméssa di pagaménto e) and promésse unilateràli.

riconosciménto di fígli incestuósi—recognition or acknowledgement of incestuous children. Children born of persons between whom there exists a bond of kinship, even though natural in direct line without limit, or in a collateral line to the second degree, or a bond of affinity in direct line, cannot be recognized by their parents, unless at the time of conception, the parents were unaware of the relationship existing between them, or that the marriage from which the affinity arose, be declared null. When only one of the parents acted in good faith, the recognition may be made solely by that party. Recognition or acknowledgment is authorized by the judge, having consideration for the interests of the child and the necessity to avoid any prejudice to him. Art. 251, Italian Civil Code.

riconosciménto di fíglio naturàle—recognition or acknowledgment of a natural son or child. It may be accomplished by the father and mother, even if at the time of conception they were married to another person. Recognition may be made jointly as well as separately. If the child has reached age sixteen, recognition is not effective without his assent. If the child is under sixteen, recognition cannot be made without the consent of the other party who has already acknowledged the child. The recognition of a natural child is made in the birth document or in a declaration made for that purpose subsequent to birth or conception. It is made before a civil status officer or a tutelary judge, or in a public document, or in a testament in whatever form. Art. 250, 254, Italian Civil Code.

riconosciménto di paternità e maternità—recognition of paternity and maternity. See **dichiarazióne giudiziàle della paternità e della maternità naturàle.** Art. 269-279, Italian Civil Code.

riconosciménto di sentènze stranière—recognition of foreign judgments. See **giudízio di delibazióne.**

riconségna f.—reconsignment.

riconsegnàre—to reconsign; to return; to restore.

riconvalidàre—to revalidate; to reconfirm.

riconveníre—to counterclaim in a civil action (the defendant presents a claim against the plaintiff in the same action).

riconvenúto — the plaintiff against whom a counterclaim has been interposed.

riconvenzionàle (azióne) or **(domànda)** —action of counterclaim. In a civil suit, the defendant who is being sued, may, in turn, present a claim against the plaintiff based upon the same cause of action and seek appropriate relief. Art. 36, 167, Italian Code of Civil Procedure.

riconvenzióne f. — a counterclaim by defendant against the plaintiff in a civil action.

ricopèrta f.—covering; hiding; excuse; pretext.

ricopèrto—recovered; hidden; covered (book, metal, furniture).

ricordànza f.—remembrance; record; memorial.

ricordàre—to remember; to remind; to recall.

ricorrènte m.—petitioner.

ricorrènte—recurring.

ricorrènza f.—recurrence.

ricórrere—to rerun; to recur; to return; to appeal for assistance; to appeal to a higher court.

ricorrezióne f.—the act of correcting again.

ricorriménto m.—recourse; appeal for help; act of appealing.

ricórsa f.—appeal; a new loan contracted by a debtor to pay off the interest on a prior loan.

ricórsi amministratíva—petitions for administrative relief. They are: (a) ricórso geràrchico (hierarchical recourse), which is a petition to the higher administrative authorities to review the administrative acts of ministers, public entities and collegial bodies, (b) ricórso in opposizióne (petition in opposition) which is directed to the administrative body which issued the challenged administrative disposition; (c) ricórso straordinàrio al Presidènte della Repúbblica (extraordinary petition to the President of the Republic). It is allowed in cases of definitive administrative acts involving a question of legality. Art. 1-17, Ricórsi Amministratívi, (Administrative Appeals), Usual Laws, Appendix to Italian Code of Civil Procedure.

ricórso m.—recourse; appeal for help or protection. Generally, it is a written petition or appeal for relief to an administrative or judicial officer. In civil procedure, it refers to the written petition to the judge for relief in connection with a proceeding as well as a demand for relief by way of impugnazióne. See **impugnazióne.**

ricórso abusívo al crédito — abusive

230

recourse to credit; except where it constitutes a more serious crime, an entrepreneur engaged in a commercial enterprise is punished with imprisonment up to two years, if he has recourse to or continues to seek credit while concealing his own insolvency. Where considerable property loss has been caused, the punishment is increased up to half. Art. 218, 219, Falliménto (Bankruptcy), Usual Laws, Appendix to Italian Civil Code.

ricórso geràrchico — hierarchical recourse. It is a recourse to higher officials of administration by petition to review the administrative acts of ministers, public entities and collegial bodies. Art. 1-6, Ricórsi amministratívi, (Administrative Appeals), Usual Laws, Appendix to Italian Code of Civil Procedure. See **ricórsi amministratívi.**

ricórso in opposiióne—petition in opposition. It is a challenge to an administrative disposition which is directed to the administrative body which issued it. Art. 7, Ricórsi Amministratívi (Administrative Appeals), Usual Laws, Appendix to Italian Code of Civil Procedure. See **ricórsi amministratívi.**

ricórso per cassazióne—recourse to the Court of Cassation. It is an appeal to reverse a judgment of a lower court. In both civil and penal cases, the procedures follow those in appellate cases. Art. 360-391, Italian Code of Civil Procedure; Art. 524-552, 190-218, Italian Code of Penal Procedure.

ricórso straordinàrio al Presidènte della Repúbblica — extraordinary petition for relief to the President of the Republic. It is allowed in cases of definitive administrative acts involving a question of legality. Art. 8, Ricórsi Amministratíve, (Administrative Appeals), Usual Laws, Appendix to Italian Code of Civil Procedure. See **ricórsi amministratívi.**

ricostituzióne di àtti—reconstitution or re-establishment of documents. It is a procedure invoked following the destruction of judicial Acts or probative documents in possession of private parties, which, as a result of earthquakes, floods or other public calamities or popular tumults, may be destroyed or lost. Upon petition of the interested party, the President of the Tribunal, upon proof of destruction of the Acts or documents under the circumstances indicated, may order that necessary copies be made to substitute for the destroyed ones if the original or other copies are deposited in public archives, and that such copies be released without tax or duty. When the Acts and documents destroyed as above, or by fire, are in public archives, the necessary reconstituted copies are also exempt from tax. See **Ricostituzióne di Àtti,** Usual Laws, Appendix to Italian Code of Civil Procedure; Art. 89, Cambiàle (Drafts), Usual Laws, Appendix to Italian Civil Code; Art. 2007, 2714-2719, Italian Civil Code; Art. 162, 163, Italian Code of Penal Procedure.

ricóvero dei minóri in un riformatòrio giudiziàrio—asylum of minors in a judicial reformatory. Art. 215, 223-227, 232, Italian Penal Code; Art. 246, 301, 374, 400, 485, Italian Code of Penal Procedure. See **misúre di sicurézza personàli** and **misúre amministratíve di sicurézza.**

ricóvero in una càsa di cúra e di custòdia—asylum in a house of cure and custody. Art. 148, 206, 212, 215, 219-221, 232, Italian Penal Code. See **misúre di sicurézza personàli** and **misúre amministratíve di sicurézza.**

ricóvero in un manicòmio giudiziàrio—refuge in a judicial insane asylum. Art. 215, 222, Italian Penal Code; Art. 88, Italian Code of Penal Procedure. See **misúre di sicurézza personàli** and **misúre amministratíve di sicurézza.**

ricuperàre—to recover. Also, **recuperàre.**

ricúpero della spése processuàli anticipàte dallo stàto—recovery of trial expenses advanced by the State. Art. 613, Italian Code of Penal Procedure. See **spése di esecuzióne delle condànne e di mantenimènto in càr-**

cere and anticipazióne delle spése.

ricúsa f.—recusancy; nonconformity; refusal to obey; denial; objection.

ricusàre—to recuse; to refuse; to reject; to object; to challenge; to take exception.

ricusàre un giúdice—to take exception to, or challenge a judge to disqualify himself. See ricusazióne del giúdice.

ricusàre un testimónio—to take exception to, or challenge a witness' testimony and object to his testifying.

ricusazióne f.—recusation; refusal; objection; plea; a challenge to a judge, asking his disqualification because of interest or other incompetency; a challenge to a witness' testimony or to a juror.

ricusazióne del giúdice—exception to a judge. In both civil and penal cases, an exception may be taken challenging the judge's qualification to hear a case because of interest or other incompetency. Art. 52-56, 51, Italian Code of Civil Procedure; Art. 64-72, Italian Code of Penal Procedure.

ridúrre—to reduce; to bring back; to reduce or record in writing; to convert or change into; to diminish; to lower; to reduce or bring into possession.

riduzióne f.—reduction; diminution; discount; subjugation.

riduzióne delle ipotèche—reduction of mortgages. Art. 2872-2877, Italian Civil Code.

riduzióne in schiavitú—reduction to slavery. It is a crime punished with imprisonment. Art. 600, Italian Penal Code.

riedificàre—to rebuild.

rieducàre—to re-educate.

rieducazióne f.—re-education.

riesàme m.—re-examination.

rifaciménto m. — re-making; re-establishment; re-polishing; an indemnity for damages.

riferiménto m.—act of referring; reference; relation; regard.

riferíre—to wound anew; to refer; to relate; to report; to attribute.

riferitóre m. — one who reports on secret matters or things heard in private.

riférma f.—reconfirmation; re-closing.

rifèrto m.—report. See refèrto.

ríffa f.—violence; abuse; overbearing act; a lottery offering prizes to the winners; raffle. See lottería.

rifiutàre—to refuse; to renounce.

rifiúto m.—refusal; rebuff; refuse.

rifiúto di àtti da pàrte del giúdice—refusal of a judge to perform (his official duties). See responsabilità Civíle del giúdice. Art. 55, Italian Code of Civil Procedure.

rifóndere—to refund; to reimburse; to refinance; to indemnify; to recast (metal); to recast a document or a writing.

rifórma f.—reform; amendment; correction; modification; restoration to a former state or condition; discharge of invalid soldier from military service due to physical disability.

riformàre—to reform; to form again; to correct legal abuses by amendment or new laws; to discharge from military service because of physical disability; to put on half-pay.

riformàto — reformed; changed; improved; amended; restored; discharged from military service because of physical disability.

riformatòrio m.—reformatory; an institution for the correction and reformation of minors.

riformatòrio giudiziàrio—judicial reformatory. An institution for the correction and reformation of minors. See ricóvero dei minóri in un riformatòrio giudiziàrio. Art. 223, Italian Penal Code.

riformatòrio speciàle—special reformatory. A special institution or section of a judicial reformatory where socially dangerous minors are confined. Art. 227, Italian Penal Code.

riforniménto m. — refurnishment; supply.

riforniménti (pl.) m.—provisions.

rifornitóre m.—supplier; a water tank for locomotives.

rifràngere—to refract.

rifrangiménto m.—refraction.

rifugiàre—to seek refuge.

rifugiàto m.—refugee.

rifúgio m.—refuge.

rifusióne f.—refusion; restitution; reimbursement.

rigattière m.—second-hand dealer.

rigettàre—to reject; to throw back.

rigètto m.—rejection; refuse; sweepings.

rigovernàre—to wash again; to scour pots and pans; to finish off on the plate without leaving any.

rilasciàre—to liberate; to release; to release an arrested prisoner; to cede; to let go; to grant a passport; to give a receipt.

rilàscio m. — release; deduction (for pension or other benefit).

rilàscio dei bèni (dell'eredità) ai creditóri e ai legatàri—release of inheritance property to creditors and legatees or beneficiaries. The declaration of release is entered in the register of succession or inheritance and then transcribed in the registers of immovables where the immovables are located as well as in the registers of movable property. The heir must also turn over the property to the trustee. Art. 507-509, Italian Civil Code.

rilevaménto m. — act of raising up again; picking up again; projection; jutting out.

rilevànza f.—relevance; bearing upon; pertinence; raising up. See rilièvo.

rilevànza dell'erróre (nel contràtto)—relevance of error in a contract. It is a ground for annulment, when it is essential and is recognized by the other contracting party. Art. 1428, 1429, Italian Civil Code.

rilevàre—to raise up again; to set up again; to exempt; to release; to discharge; to receive a new born infant; to nurse; to raise children; to educate; to bring out clearly; to

notice; to show in relief (painting or sculpture); to buy out (contents of a business) to survey (the coast); to relieve; to bring into relief or prominence; to indemnify.

rilièvo m.—relief; release; discharge; emphasis; act of raising up or setting up; projection.

rilièvo del fideiussóre—discharge of the surety. Art. 1953, Italian Civil Code.

rimandàre—to remand; to send back; to return an object; to dismiss; to compel one to take another examination (student); to postpone; to refer one to another.

rimàndo m.—act of sending back or returning.
di rimàndo—promptly; quickly; as reprisal.

rimborsàre—to reimburse; to repay; to refund; to replace numbers or names in a bag for drawing.

rimbórso m.—reimbursement; repayment; refund.

rimbórso delle spése per il manteniménto del condannàto — reimbursement for the cost or expenses of maintenance of the convicted prisoner. He is obligated to reimburse the State treasury for the cost of his maintenance in penal institutions and is liable for such obligation with all his personal and real property, present and future according to the civil laws, Art. 188, Italian Penal Code; Art. 612, Italian Code of Penal Procedure; Art. 2740, Italian Civil Code.

rimediàbile—remediable; curable.

rimediàre — to remedy; to repair a damage; to provide; to cure.

remédio m.—remedy.

riméssa f. — remission; remittance; automobile repair shop; garage. See autoriméssa—garage.

rimessióne f.—remission; remand; act of remitting or sending back; abatement; forgiveness; pardon; cancellation or release of a debt or claim. Also, **remissióne** and **rimissióne.**

rimessióne dei procediménti—remand of proceedings. At any stage of the proceedings on the merits, upon grave reason of public order or for legitimate suspicion of bias, the Procurator General before the Court of Appeals or the Court of Cassation, may request said court to remand the hearings or trial to a different judge. The accused may propose a remand upon motion based on a legitimate suspicion of bias, only. This privilege does not inure to the benefit of private parties. Art. 55-60, Italian Code of Penal Procedure.

rimessióne in tèrmini del contumàce—remission of defaulting party to make timely appearance in a civil case. Art. 294, Italian Code of Civil Procedure.

riméttere—to remit; to send back; to remand; to send back a case for further action; to refer to arbitration; to remit (money); to send (an account); to replace; to put back.

rimissióne f.—remission. See **rimessióne** or **remessióne.**

rimorchiàre—to tow.

rimorchiatóre m.—that which tows; towboat.

rimòrchio m.—the act of towing; towline.

rimozióne f. — removal; dismissal; change; demotion in grade. Also, **remozióne.**

rimpatriàre—to repatriate.

rimpàtrio m.—repatriation.

rimpiàngere—to lament; to remember dolorously.

rimpiànto m. — to remember with regret.

rimproveràre — to reprove; to reprimand.

rimpròvero m.—reproof; reprimand.

rimuneraménto m. — remuneration. Also, **rimunerazióne.**

rimunerazióne f.—remuneration. Also, **rimuneraménto.**

rimutàbile—that which can be changed again.

rinasciménto m.—renaissance.

rinàscita f.—re-birth.

rinchiúdere—to enclose.

rincorporàre—to reincorporate.

rincréscere—to be sorry; to displease; to regret.

rinforzaménto m.—reinforcement.

rinforzàre—to reinforce.

rinfòrzo m. — reinforcement; fresh supply.

rinfúsa—mixed without distinction; bulk loaded cargo.

rinfúsa (àlla)—bulk cargo loaded in a mass without distinction.

rinnovaménto m. — renewal; renovation; restoration.

rinnovànza f.—renewal. See **rinnovaménto.**

rinnovàre—to renew; to renovate; to restore.

rinnovazióne f.—renewal.

rinnovazióne del cónto corrènte—renewal of current account. Art. 1823, Italian Civil Code.

rinnovazióne dell' ipotèca—renewal of mortgage. The recording of a mortgage is effective for twenty years and may be renewed by a new recording. Art. 2847-2851, Italian Civil Code.

rinnovazióne tàcita del contràtto di locazióne—tacit renewal of the lease contract. The lease is renewed, if at its expiration, the leasee remains and is left with the detention of the rented property, or if it is a lease for an undetermined time, without having given the notice to quit the premises as required by law. Art. 1597, 1596, Italian Civil Code.

rintegràre — to re-integrate; to integrate again; to reinstate.

rintegrazióne f.—reintegration.

rinúncia f.—renunciation. Also, **rinúnzia.**

rinúncia agli àtti del giudízio—renunciation of the proceedings of a trial; discontinuance of the proceedings. Art. 306, Italian Code of Civil Procedure.

rinúnzia f.—renunciation. Also, **rinúncia.**

rinúnzia all'eredità—renunciation of the inheritance. It is done with a declaration before a notary or the clerk of the Praetorship in the judicial district of the Praetor where the succession is being administered. Art. 519-527, Italian Civil Code.

rinunziaménto m.—renunciation.

rinunziànte—the person renouncing.

rinunziàre—to renounce.

rinunziatàrio m.—the person in whose favor a renunciation is made.

rinviàre—to remand; to send back; to adjourn; to return a case to the court where it originated for further action.

rinvío m.—remand; act of sending back; adjournment.

rinvío a giudízio—a remand for trial. Penally, when the examining magistrate determines that an act constitutes a crime, and there is sufficient evidence against the accused, he will order him remanded for trial in the court having jurisdiction. Art. 374-376, 386, 396, 397, Italian Code of Penal Procedure. For the trial of remanded cases in civil matters, see Art. 392-394, Italian Code of Civil Procedure.

río m.—brook; rivulet.

río—evil; wicked; cruel.

rióne m.—a quarter of the city.

rípa f.—river bank; shore.

ripagàre—to repay.

riparàre—to repair; to remedy; to shelter; to provide for; to restore.

riparazióne f.—repair; restoration.

ripàrio—riparian.

ripàro m.—repair; remedy; defense;

ripartíre—to leave again; to divide; to distribute; to share.

ripartizióne f. — repartition; distribution.

ripàrto m. — distribution; division of profits; apportionment of offices.

ripàrto d'avaría—apportionment of a general average loss proportionately, according to interests and losses, between the owner of the vessel, the freight and cargo. See **avaría**.

ripàtica f.—riparian rights.

ripàtico m.—river wharf.

ripésco m.—amorous intrigue.

ripetènte m.—a student who repeats a course.

ripetènte—repeating.

ripètere—to repeat; to demand back that which is due; to claim back.

ripetizióne f.—repetition; a demand or action for the restitution of money or goods given by mistake or under an unperformed condition. See **azióne del pagaménto indébito** and **azióne di ripetizióne.**

riportàre — to report; to relate; to carry back; to reproduce; to carry forward (an account or balance).

ripòrto m.—an amount brought forward; report; statement; ornament or embroidery. A premium paid on the day of settlement on the stock exchange as consideration by the buyer to the purchase price; contango.

ripòrto m.—a contract whereby the first party transfers title to specific securities for an agreed price to the second party, and the latter assumes the obligation to transfer at a determined time, to the first party, title to an equal number of securities of the same kind, the price being higher or lower than the original one as agreed by them. Art. 1548-1551, Italian Civil Code.

riposànte m.—a retired public employee.

ripòso m.—rest; repose; retirement.

ripòso (período di)—rest period. The worker has the right to a day of rest each week, usualy coincident with Sunday. Art. 2109, Italian Civil Code.

riprensióne f.—reprehension; rebuke; reproof; censure; admonition.

riprensióne giudiziàle—judicial admonition.

riprésa f. — resumption; recovery; repetition; underpinning (of a wall); reprise.

riprésa (a)—at intervals.

riprodúrre—to reproduce; to cause.

riproduzióni meccàniche—mechanical

reproductions. Photographic or cinematographic reproductions, phonographic recordings, and generally, every other mechanical reproduction of facts and things, constitute full proof of the facts and things represented unless the party against whom they are produced disclaims their conformity to the facts and things themselves. Art. 2712, Italian Civil Code.

riproponibilità della azióne penàle—reinstatement of a penal action. Where a penal action has been dismissed for a procedural defect, the case may be reinstated upon the same facts and against the same person, if it is subsequently presented in regular procedural form. Also, prosciogliménto per difètto di una condizióne di procedibilità.

ripropórre—to repropose.

risarciménto m.—the act of compensating; reparation; restoration.

risarciménto del dànno—compensatory damages for loss. Art. 1218-1229, Italian Civil Code. See lúcro cessànte.

risarciménto in fórma specífica—compensation for damages in specific form. Where the damage was caused by an illegal act, the damaged party may seek reintegration in specific form if it is possible in whole or in part. This may require reconstruction or reparation of the thing destroyed or damaged; public retraction of the affront caused; publication of a judgment. If reintegration in specific form is excessively burdensome, the judge may order equivalent compensation. Art. 2058, Italian Civil Code; Art. 120, Italian Code of Civil Procedure.

risarciménto per fàtto illécito—compensatory damages for an illegal act. Any criminal or culpable act which causes unjust damage to others, obligates the person committing such act to compensate and indemnify for the damage. Art. 2043-2059, Italian Civil Code.

risarcíre—to compensate; to restore; to repair; to amend; to indemnify; to satisfy; to reintegrate.

riscattàre—to redeem; to recover; to recover or buy back something sold; to free from a mortgage by paying the debt for which it served as security; to liberate a prisoner.

riscàtto m. — redemption; a buying back or repurchase; liberation of property from a mortgage. See pàtto di riscàtto.

ríschio m.—risk; hazard; peril.

riscontàre—to re-discount.

risconto m.—re-discounting.

riscontraménto m. — checking; collating; comparison; conforming.

riscontràre—to meet; to compare; to collate; to verify accounts; to verify merchandise or quotations.

riscontràta f.—the act of verifying; verification of accounts; reciprocal exchange and liquidation of credit instruments issued by various credit institutions.

riscontratóre m.—examiner.

riscóntro m.—examination of accounts for the purpose of verification; collation; comparison; conforming; meeting; counterpart.

riscóntro di càssa — verification of cash.

riscóntro (ufficio del) — controller's office.

riscòssa f.—insurrection; revolt; recovery of a military position.

riscossióne f.—collection (of a debt); exaction; receipt of funds or money; a day's cash receipts.

riscossióne coattíva di púbbliche entràte—compulsory collection of public revenues. Art. 200, et seq. Procediménto Coattívo Fiscàle, (Compulsory Fiscal Proceeding), Usual Laws, Appendix to Italian Code of Civil Procedure.

risèrva f.—reserve; the reserved portion or quota of an estate. See porzióne riservàta.

risèrva di proprietà—reservation of title. See riservàto domínio—conditional sale.

riservàto domínio — conditional sale; an installment sale where the title remains with the seller until final payment has been made by the buyer when title passes to him. Also, **dominio riservàto, véndita con risèrva della proprietà** and **véndita con risèrva di dominio.** Art. 1523-1526, Italian Civil Code.

risòlto—settled; solved.

risolutívo—resolutive; that which may annul or rescind a contract.

risolúto — resolute; determined; resolved; dissolved.

risoluzióne f.—resolution; annulment; dissolution. See **azióne di risoluzióne del contràtto** and **risoluzióne del contràtto.**

risoluzióne dei conflìtti—resolution of conflicts (of jurisdiction and competence). The Court of Cassation resolves conflicts between judges as to jurisdiction and competence over a crime. Its judgment therein has the authority of an adjudicated matter (res judicata). Art. 51-54, Italian Code of Penal Procedure. See **regolaménto di giurisdizióne e di competènza** and **regolaménto di competènza.**

risoluzióne del concordàto—annulment of bankruptcy accord or composition. If the promised guarantees are not established in conformance with the accord or the bankrupt fails to comply regularly with the provisions of the composition and the judgment of ratification, the Trustee may refer the matter to the Tribunal, which may order the annulment of the accord, Art. 137, Falliménto (Bankruptcy), Usual Laws, Appendix to Italian Civil Code.

risoluzióne del contràtto—annulment or dissolution of the contract. By mutual consent, Art. 1372, Italian Civil Code. For non-fulfillment, Art. 1453-1462, Italian Civil Code. For impossibility of performance due to supervening cause, Art. 1463-1466, Italian Civil Code. For excessive hardship caused by extraordinary and unforeseen events, Art. 1467-1469, Italian Civil Code. The above grounds are not applicable to aleatory contracts whose outcome depends on an uncertain event. Art. 1469, Italian Civil Code.

risoluzióne e annullaménto del concordàto — annullment of the composition of creditors. Art. 137, 186, 215, Falliménto (Bankruptcy), Usual Laws, Appendix to Italian Civil Code. See **risoluzióne del concordàto** and **concordàto preventívo.**

risòlvere—to resolve; to dissolve; to annul; to rescind; to untie.

risolvíbile—that which may be annulled, dissolved or rescinded.

risorgiménto m.—renaissance; rebirth; the rebirth of Italian unity and independence during 1831-1870.

risórsa f.—resource.

risparmiàre—to save; to economize; to put aside.

rispàrmio m.—savings; that which is put aside as savings against future contingencies.

rispàrmio (càssa di)—savings bank.

rispàrmio (librétto di)—savings bank pass-book.

rispedizióne f.—reshipment.

rispedizióne della mèrce (traspòrto con)—transport with reshipment of the merchandise. If a carrier undertakes to forward things under transport beyond his lines by use of successive carriers without receiving a through bill of lading to destination from the shipper, it is presumed that the carrier assumes the obligations of a forwarding agent beyond his own lines. Art. 1699, Italian Civil Code.

rispondènte—respondent; responding; corresponding; answering.

risponsióne f. — canon; impost; tax rate. See **responsióne.**

rispósta — response; answer; reply. During the formal hearing, the party examined must respond in person without using prepared writings, but the judge may permit the use of notes when referring to names or figures or when particular circumstances may so require. Art. 231, 232, 253, 256, Italian Code of Civil Procedure.

ríssa f. — affray; dispute; quarrel; strife. Art. 588, Italian Penal Code.

ristabilíre—to re-establish; to restore.

ritàrdo m.—delay.

ritégno m.—restraint; reserve; self-possession; moderation; restraining influence.

ritenère—to retain; to hold back; to repress; to detain; to regard; to maintain; to deduct (from a bill).

ritenitóre m.—one who detains; one who receives. See **manutèngolo** and **ricettatóre**.

ritenúta f.—retention; deduction (from wages or pensions); a withholding.

ritenzióne f.—retention; deduction.

ritenzióne a favóre del possessóre di buòna féde—retention in favor of a good faith possessor. He may retain the property so long as he does not receive repayment for improvement, maintenance and collection of the natural or civil fruits thereof even though an action to regain possession has been instituted. Art. 1152, 1149, 1150, Italian Civil Code.

ritenzióne (dirítto di)—right of retention (of property). The law grants to a creditor lawfully in possession of a debtor's property, the right to retain it until his obligation has been satisfied. Art. 1152, 748, 936, 975, 1006, 1011, 1502, 1593, 1689, 2235, 2756, 2761, 2794, 2864, Italian Civil Code.

ritiràre—to draw back; to pull back; to fire again; to withdraw; to retire (from a position); to receive (a pension or wages).

ritiràta f.—retreat; subterfuge; evasion; privy.

ritiràto — solitary; a retired person (pensioner).

ritíro m.—retirement; retreat; collection of a sum of money.

ritíro (in)—in retirement; on the retired list.

ritíro dei fascícoli di pàrte — withdrawal of files by the parties. Each party to an action may obtain the examining judge's permission to withdraw his file from the clerk's office, but it must be re-deposited each time as ordered. Art. 169, Italian Code of Civil Procedure; Art. 77, Enabling Rules, Italian Code of Civil Procedure.

ríto m.—rite; ceremony; custom; the procedure followed in a court appearance.

ritòrcere — to twist again; to wring again; to turn back.

ritòrcere un'accúsa—to turn an accusation against the person making it.

ritòrcere un argoménto—to turn an argument against the person making it.

ritornàre—to return; to send back; to come back; to rise (dough).

ritórno m.—return; gain; profit.

ritórno (bigliétto di)—return ticket.

ritórno dell'assènte — return of the person declared absent. Those who temporarily possessed his property must return it. Art. 56, Italian Civil Code.

ritorsióne f. — act of turning back; counter action.

ritorsióne e provocazióne — counter accusation and provocation. In cases of ingiúria (Art. 594), if the defamatory offenses are reciprocal, the judge may declare one or both offenders not punishable. Anyone committing acts of ingiúria and diffamazióne (Art. 594, 595) in a state of anger due to another's unjust act and immediately thereafter, is not punishable. Art. 599, Italian Penal Code.

ritràrre—to retract; to draw back; to deduce; to show.

ritrattàre—to treat again; to handle again; to renegotiate; to reproduce; to portray.

ritrattazióne f.—retraction.

ritrattísta m.—portrait painter.

ritràtto—retracted; drawn back. Also, **retratto**.

ritràtto m.—portrait; picture; representation; likeness. Also, **retràtto**. See **abúso dell'immàgine altrúi**—misuse of another's image or likeness, Art. 10, Italian Civil Code.

ritrazióne f.—retraction. Also, **retrazióne** and **ritrattazióne**.

ritrattazióne f.—retraction. Where a witness, expert or interpreter has given false testimony, he is not punishable if he makes admission of his perjury and retracts the false testimony before the hearing is terminated with a judgment of dismissal or remanded because of the falsity. In a civil action, the perjured party is not punishable if he retracts the false and admits the truth before judgment. Art. 376, 372, 373, Italian Penal Code.

ritròvo m.—resort place; a place where persons meet for diversion or for other purposes.

riunióne f. — reunion; meeting; assembly; joinder.

riunióni púbbliche—public meetings. It refers to public meetings and assemblies in public places. Those who promote them must give the Quaestor at least three days notice. The Quaestor, in the event the notice is not given, or for reasons of public order, morality or public health, may prevent the meeting from taking place, and, for the same reasons, may prescribe the circumstances of time and place of the meeting. Those disobeying the prohibition or prescriptions of the Authorities, are punished with arrest and fine. One who retires from the meeting, prior to the order of the Authorities, or to obey it, is not subject to punishment. The carrying of firearms to public meetings is forbidden even to those persons possessing permits. When, during the course of public meetings and assemblies in public places, there occur manifestations or seditious cries or those harmful to the prestige of the Authorities, or which, in any manner, may place in danger the public order or safety of the citizens, or when crimes are committed in said meetings and assemblies, they may be disbanded. The order to disband is issued by officers of the Public Security, or, in their absence, by officers or sub-officers of the Carabinieri. When the order to disperse is ineffective, the dispersal is ordered with three, separate, formal orders of the Authorities, each preceded by a blast of the horn. When said orders to disperse have been ineffective, or they cannot be made because of revolt or opposition, the officers of Public Security, or in their absence, the officers or sub-officers of the Carabinieri, will order the dispersal of the meeting or gathering with the use of force. The public force or the armed forces, under command of their respective chiefs, will execute said order. Art. 18-24, Sicurézza Púbblica (Public Security), Tèsto único (Unified Text), Usual Laws, Appendix to Italian Code of Penal Procedure; Art. 17, Constitution of the Italian Republic.

riuníre—to reunite; to bring together again; to assemble.

riuscíre—to succeed; to prosper; to result; to come out again.

ríva f.—river bank; shore; in maritime parlance, an emerged anchor is said to be "a ríva", and the command "a ríva", sends the men to the masts.

rivalère—to recover; to receive compensation from another for loss or damage.

rivàlsa f.—the right of compensation from another. The unpaid holder of a draft, who has a right of action against prior indorsers, may, with no provision to the contrary, issue a new sight draft (rivàlsa) drawn upon one of the prior indorsers. The rivàlsa includes the principal amount due plus interest and expenses and stamp tax. Art. 59, Cambiàle (Drafts), Usual Laws, Appendix to Italian Civil Code.

rivelazióne f.—revelation; disclosure.

rivelazióne del contenúto di corrispondènza—disclosure of the contents of correspondence. Whoever, except as provided by law, has wrongfully become cognizant of the contents of correspondence not directed to him, which should have remained secret, and discloses same without just cause, in whole or in part, shall be punished with imprisonment or fine. Art. 618, Italian Penal Code.

rivelazióne del contenúto di documénti segréti—disclosure of the contents of secret documents. Whoever, wrongfully, becomes cognizant of the public or private acts and documents of others, not constituting correspondence, which should remain secret and discloses it without just cause or uses it to the profit of himself or others, shall be punished with imprisonment or fine if the disclosure results in damage. Art. 621, Italian Penal Code.

rivelazióne di segréti scientífici o industriàli—disclosure of scientific or industrial secrets. Whoever, because of his position, office, profession or art, has become cognizant of information destined to be secret regarding scientific discoveries or inventions or industrial applications, discloses them or uses them to his profit or that of others, shall be punished with imprisonment. Art. 623, Italian Penal Code.

rivelazióne di segréti di stàto—disclosure of State secrets. Whoever discloses to anyone secret information relating to the security of the State, or in whatever manner relates to the internal or international political interest of the State, shall be punished with imprisonment for a period of not less than five years. If the act is committed in time of war or it has compromised war preparations or their effectiveness to the State, or compromised military operations, the penalty is a term of imprisonment of not less than ten years. If the guilty party has acted for the purpose of political or military espionage, he may be imprisoned for life. The above penalties are also applied to anyone who receives the information. If the act is committed through negligence, the punishment is reduced. Art. 261, 263, 256, Italian Penal Code.

rivelazióne di segréti di ufficio—disclosure of secrets of office. The public official or person charged with a public service who violates the duties inherent to his functions or the service or in any manner wrongfully uses his position to reveal information of his office which should remain secret, or facilitates, in any manner, its disclosure, is punished

with imprisonment. The penalty is reduced where the facilitation of disclosure was negligent. Art. 326, Italian Penal Code; Art. 230, 307, Italian Code of Penal Procedure.

rivelazióne di segréto professionàle—disclosure of professional secret. Whoever has notice of a secret because of his position, office, profession or art and discloses it without just cause, or uses it to his profit or that of others, if the act may result in damage, shall be punished with imprisonment or fine. Art. 622, Italian Penal Code.

rivéndere—to sell; to sell at retail.

rivendicàre—to vindicate anew; to reclaim; to recover possession of property. See azióne di rivendicazióne.

rivendicazióne f.—act of revindicating; the act of instituting an action to recover property. See azióne di rivendicazióne.

rivéndita f.—resale; retail sale; small shop selling at retail.

rivenditóre m.—re-seller; retail seller; small shop keeper.

riveníre—to come again; to return.

riveríre—to revere; to respect; to pay one's respects.

riversàre—to pour out; to overflow.

riversibilità f.—reversibility.

riversibilità (condizióne di)—condition of reversibility. The donor may stipulate the reversibility of things given, either due to the prior death of the sole donee, or the prior death of the donee, and his descendants. The pact of reversibility has the effect of annulling the alienation of all property and making it return to the donor free of every burden and mortgage. Art. 791, 792, Italian Civil Code.

riversibilità delle pensióni—reversibility of pensions. This is a right granted to widows and orphaned children of civil and military employees to receive a percentage of the deceased husband's or father's allowable benefits as a pensioner, provided he had completed a stated number of years of service.

riversióne f. — reversion; the act whereby certain property rights revert to one who had a right of possession before they were ceded.

rivertíre—to revert.

rivíncere—to reconquer; to re-win.

rivíncita f.—act of winning again; a return match.

rivísta f.—review; a military review or parade; a military inspection; revision; correction; a periodic publication.

rivívere—to relive; to come alive again; to revive.

rivivificàre—to revive.

rívo m.—stream.

rivòlgere—to turn; to turn to; to direct; to engage; to have recourse to.

rivolgiménto m.—turning; turning to; change; revolution; upset.

rivòlta f.—revolt; change; turn; rebellion; mutiny; folded over (gloves, sleeves); facing on a dress jacket.

rivoltèlla m.—revolver; a repeating pistol having a revolving chambered cylinder holding a number of cartridges which can be discharged successfully without reloading. Also, revòlver.

rivoltellàta f.—revolver shot. Also, revolveràta.

rivoluzionàrio m.—revolutionary.

rivoluzióne f.—revolution.

ròba f.—goods; wares; stuff; property in general; necessaries to live, dress or eat.

ròba andànte — goods of ordinary quality.

robàccia f.—poor stuff.

rogatòria f.—interrogatory; a proceeding in which a judge in one jurisdiction requests a judge in another to take testimony. The request can also be directed to a judge in a foreign jurisdiction or to Italian consuls in civil and criminal matters. Art. 203-205, 802-805, Italian Code of Civil Procedure; Art. 296, 392, 657-660, Italian Code of Penal Procedure;

Art. 53, Enabling Rules, Italian Code of Penal Procedure.

ròta f.—an ecclesiastic tribunal of the Roman Catholic Church at the Vatican in Rome; wheel. See ruòta.

rotàbile—suitable for wheeled traffic.

rotàia f.—wheel track; a rail in a railway track.

rotàre—to rotate.

rovína di edifíci o di àltre costruzióni —collapse of buildings or other constructions. Whoever has had part in the project or the works concerning a building or other construction which thereafter collapses through his fault, is punished with a fine. If danger to persons follows from the act, the punishment is a fine or arrest. Art. 676, Italian Penal Code.

rovína di edifício—collapse of a building. The proprietor of a building or other construction is responsible for damages caused by its collapse unless he proves that it was not due to defect in maintenance or fault in construction. Art. 2053, Italian Civil Code.

rúba f.—plunder; pillage.

rubbacchiàre—to pilfer.

rubaménto m.—theft. See fúrto.

rubàre—to steal; to appropriate someone's property furtively.

ruber ía f.—thefts; a series of thefts.

rubinétto m.—stop-cock.

rubíno m.—ruby.

rubríca f. — rubric; title; heading; rules for the celebration of divine services; the title of a statute formerly printed in red letters.

rúffa f.—scramble; scuffle.

ruffiàno m.—procurer; pimp.

rugiàda f.—dew.

rumóre m.—noise; rumor; rumble; murmur.

rumóri dal fóndo vicíno—noises emanating from neighboring land. See esalazióne dal fóndo vicíno and gétto pericolóso di còse, Art. 674, Italian Penal Code.

ruòlo m.—roll; list; register; calendar

of events; court calendar of cases to be tried. Art. 168, 168 bis, Italian Code of Civil Procedure; Art. 28-32, 71, Enabling Rules, Italian Code of Civil Procedure.

ruòta f.—wheel. Also, **ròta.**

ruscèllo m.—brook.

rúzza f.—dispute; quarrel.

rúzzo m.—frolic; playful.

S

sabotàggio m.—sabotage. Whoever, for the sole purpose of impeding or disturbing normal work operations, invades or occupies the agricultural or industrial plant or business of another, or takes over another's machines, live-stock, apparatuses or instruments destined for agricultural or industrial production, is punished with imprisonment. Also, **arbitrària invasióne e occupazióne di aziènde agrícole o industriàle**—arbitrary invasion and occupation of agricultural or industrial plants and businesses. Art. 508, Italian Penal Code. See **distruzióne o sabotàggio di òpere militàre.**

sacchegiàre—to pillage; to plunder; to sack.

sacchéggio m.—pillaging; plundering; sacking.

sacchéggio (devastazióne e)—devastation and pillage. These are crimes against the public order and are punished with imprisonment. Art. 419, 421, Italian Penal Code.

saccheggio (devastazióne, sacchégio e stràge) — devastation, pillage and carnage. It consists in a criminal attempt against the security of the State. It is committed by an act calculated to cause devastation, pillage or carnage within the territory of the State or any part thereof. It is punishable by imprisonment. Art. 285, Italian Penal Code.

sàggio—wise; prudent.

sàggio m. — assay; examination; sample; taste; rate of interest or discount. Also, **tàsso.** Art. 1284, Italian Civil Code. See **interèssi, interèssi compensatívi, interèssi con-**venzionàle, interèssi corrispettívi, interèssi legàle, interèssi moratòri, interèssi usuràri.

sàggio degli interèssi—rate of interest. The legal rate of interest is fixed by law. Where the rate of interest has not been fixed by the parties, conventional interest is applied, the rate of which is the same as the legal rate. Interest above the legal rate must be proved in writing. Art. 1284, 1815, 2725, Italian Civil Code. See **interèssi convenzionàli.**

sàggio di scónto—rate of discount.

sagrestía f.—sacristy.

salàrio m.—salary.

salassàre—to bleed or remove blood for curative purposes.

salassatúra f.—the act of bleeding for curative purposes.

salàta f.—the action of salting; salting food.

salàto m.—salted meat.

salàto—salted; salty.

sàldo m.—entire balance of an account due from a debtor; full payment of an account or debt.

sàldo — solid; sound; firm; robust; strong; valid; unbroken.

sàla f.—hall; room.

sàle (pl. f.)—halls; rooms.

sàle m.—salt.

sàle inglése—Epsom salt.

salíre—to ascend; to mount; to rise.

saliscéndi m.—a door latch; going up and down.

salíta f.—ascent.

sàlma f.—corpse; mortal remains; a heavy burden.

salpàre—to weigh anchor.

salutàre—to greet; to salute.

salúte f.—health; a toast.

salúte (delitti colpósi cóntro la salúte púbblica)—culpable crimes against public health. It is committed by causing an epidemic by means of the negligent diffusion of germs or the poisoning of waters and foodstuffs. Art. 452, 438, 439, Italian Penal Code.

See **delítti colpósi di comúne perícolo.**

salúto m.—salute.

sàlva f.—a salvo of gunfire; a discharge of firearms simultaneously; a volley of discharging firearms intended as a salute.

salvacondótto m.—safe-conduct. Safe-conducts cannot be granted to witnesses or other persons. Art. 355, Italian Code of Penal Procedure.

salvagènte m.—life preserver; a buoyant jacket or device to prevent persons from drowning; a safety island located in the center of a street to assist pedestrians in crossing and to avoid vehicles.

salvàggina f.—game.

salvaguardàre—to protect; to defend.

salvaguàrdia f.—safeguard.

salvaménto m.—saving; safety; preservation. See **salvatàggio.**

salvaménto (batèllo di)—life boat.

salvaménto (scialúppa di)—life boat.

salvàre—to save.

salvatàggio m.—salvage. An insured must do everything possible to avoid or diminish damage. Expenses incurred for this purpose by the insured are borne by the insurer in proportion to the insured value of the thing at the time of the accident. The insured who criminally fails to discharge the obligation of giving notice or of salvage, loses the right to indemnity. If it is done negligently, the insurer has the right to reduce indemnification by reason of the prejudice suffered. Art. 1914, 1915, Italian Civil Code. See **salvaménto.**

salvazióne f.—salvation.

sàlve (Lat.)—hail!

salvézza f.—safety; salvation.

sàlvo—safe; secure; unhurt; barring; excepting; without.

sàlvo erróre od omissióne — barring error or omission. It is a commercial formula appended to bills.

sanaménto m.—the act of curing or rectifying; act of correcting or remedying.

sanàre—to cure; to heal; to rectify.

sanatòria f.—the act of legitimizing or regularization of a condition which was performed irregularly or with nullity. The act of correcting and rectifying it. Art. 157, Italian Code of Civil Procedure; Art. 184, 187, 188, Italian Code of Penal Procedure. See **convàlida.**

sanatòrio m.—sanatorium.

sanità f.—health; soundness of health; soundness of body; moral soundness; board of health; medical corps of the army.

sanità (delítti cóntro la integrità e la sanitá della stírpe)—crimes against the integrity and physical soundness of the race. Art. 545-555, Italian Penal Code.

sanità púbblica—public health. Sanità púbblica, Usual Laws, Appendix to Italian Code of Penal Procedure.

sanitàrio—sanitary.

sàno—sane; sound; healthy; healthful.

sàno e sàlvo—safe and sound.

Sànta Sède—the Holy See. The State and the Catholic Church are, each within its own sphere, independent and sovereign. Their relations are regulated by the Lateran Pacts. Art. 7, Constitution of the Italian Republic; Sànta Sède, Usual Laws, Appendix to Italian Code of Civil Procedure.

sanzionàre—to sanction.

sanzióne f.—sanction; penalty.

sanzióni civili—civil sanctions. Every crime demands restitution in accordance with the norms of the civil laws. Every crime which has caused property damage or damage of another nature demands compensation from the guilty party and the persons who, by the norms of the civil laws, must respond for his action. Art. 185-198, Italian Penal Code.

sanzióni cóntro il difensóre dell' imputàto che abbandóna la difésa—sanctions against defense counsel who abandons the defense. Such counsel, whether retained by the accused defendant or appointed, may be suspended from exercising the legal profession and is liable for the expenses caused by his act. Art. 131, 129, Italian Code of Penal Procedure.

saracinésca f. — portcullis; a metal blind which can be raised and lowered, installed in front of shop windows and doors for security purposes.

saracinésco—pertaining to Saracen or saracinésca.

saracíno m.—Saracen.

sardégna f.—Sardinia.

sàrdo m.—Sardinian.

sàrta f.—dressmaker; seamstress.

sàrto m.—tailor.

sartoría f.—tailor shop.

sassàia m.—stone dam; stone mound; stony place or road.

sbadàto — inattentive; careless; listless; negligent.

sbadíre—to undo beaten down nails. See ribadíre.

sbafàre—to eat without paying; to eat at the expense of others.

sbagliàre—to make a mistake; to commit an error.

sbàglio m.—mistake; error; oversight.

sballàre—to unpack; to unbail; to invent tales.

sballatúra f.—the operation of unpacking.

sbandàre—to disband; to disperse; to careen a ship; regarding an automobile, to slide or move out of control.

sbandieràre—to unfurl a flag.

sbandíre—to banish.

sbarattàre—to disperse; to put to flight.

sbarazzàre—to remove impediments; to clear; to put in order.

sbarcàre—to debark; to disembark.

sbarcatóio m.—landing place; quay.

sbàrco m.—debarkation; disembarkation.

sbàrra f.—bar; barrier; cross-bar.

sbarraménto m.—barricading; barring.

sbarràre—to bar; to block; to open.

sbeffàre—to scoff; to mock; to ridicule; to deride; to jeer.

sbevezzàre—to drink habitually and to excess.

sbigottiménto m.—alarm; amazement; dismay.

sbigottíre—to alarm; to dismay; to terrify.

sbirràglia f.—a body of police agents —used in a pejorative sense. See bírro and sbírro.

sbirrésco—in a police agent manner —used in a pejorative sense.

sbírro m.—police agent; a police agent of former times who was despised for his brutal actions — generally used in a pejorative sense. See bírro.

scadènte—goods of inferior quality; imperfect; defective.

scadènza—due date; maturity; fixed time within which to perform an obligation or pay a debt. Art. 1182, 1183, 1193, Italian Civil Code; Art. 32, 34, 84, Asségni (Checks), Usual Laws, Appendix to Italian Civil Code; Art. 38-42, 100, Cambiàle (Drafts), Usual Laws, Appendix to Italian Civil Code; Art. 181, Italian Code of Penal Procedure.

scadére—to decline; to lose strength; to become due; to fall due; to mature.

scadiménto m.—decline; decay; decadence; ruin.

scadúto — due; expired; fallen; decayed.

scafàndro m.—a deep-sea diver's outfit.

scaffàle m. — book-shelves; shelves used to store merchandise or packages.

scàfo m.—the hull of a ship.

scagliàre—to hurl; to fling.

scàla f.—stairs; staircase; ladder; degree; grade; scale.

scàla mòbile—movable scale, referring to wages or salary which vary with the cost, price index.

scalèa f.—flight of steps, generally

leading to a church or to monumental buildings.

scàlo m.—landing place; wharf; port of call; loading platform in a railway station.

scalpellàre—to chisel.

scalpèllo m.—chisel; scalpel.

scàltro—astute; sharp; shrewd.

scalzàre—to remove shoes and stockings; to lay bare; to pump a person for information.

scàlzo—bare-footed; unarmed.

scambiàre—to exchange; to mistake one for another; to barter.

scambiévole—reciprocal; mutual.

scambievolézza f. — reciprocity; mutuality.

scàmbio m.—exchange; barter; mistaking one for another.

scambísta m.—one who favors free exchange or free trade; a switchman on a railroad.

scameràre—to release goods that have been confiscated or sequestered.

scamiciàre—to remove one's shirt; to remain in shirt sleeves.

scamiciàto m.—plebian; a vulgar person of rude manners; a person who follows dangerous political doctrines.

scamiciàto — without one's shirt; naked.

scampafórca m.—scapegallows; rogue.

scampàre—to escape; to get out of danger; to save; to deliver; to avoid; to preserve.

scàmpo m. — escape; deliverance; safety; shrimp.

scàmpolo m.—remnant.

scancellàre—to cancel; to erase; to strike out; to annul. Also, cancellàre.

scandagliàre—to take a sounding; to measure the depth of water or deep hole with lead and line.

scandàglio m. — a sounding line or plummet to determine depth of water or deep hole.

scannabécco m. — a knife with a twisted point.

scannafòsso m.—open drain.

scannàre — to cut the throat of; to slaughter; to butcher; to kill with ferocity.

scannàto—butchered; slaughtered.

scannàto m.—poor; indigent.

scansafatíche 'm.—one who has aversion to work; idler; lazy person.

scansàre—to avoid; to shun; to move out of the way; to displace.

scansía f.—bookcase.

scànso m.—avoiding; shunning.

scapestràto m. — unbridled person; rascal; libertine.

scapitàre—to suffer loss.

scàpito m.—loss.

scappaménto m.—escapement.

scappàre—to escape; to run away.

scappàta f.—the act of escaping.

scarabocchiàre—to scrawl; to scribble.

scarabòcchio m.—scrawl; scribble.

scaraceménto m. — release from prison.

scarceràre—to release from prison.

scarcerazióne f.—release from prison or confinement. Art. 246, 269, 280, 272, 272 bis, 275, 276, 375, 663, 665, Italian Code of Penal Procedure.

scàrica f.—discharge; discharge of firearms; volley.

scaricàre—to discharge; to unload; to unburden.

scàrico m.—unloading; discharge.

scàrico—unloaded; discharged; free.

scàrico coattívo — compulsory discharge (of water). A servitude imposed by law so that excess waters or those to be drained from land may be allowed to pass over neighboring drainage ditches and canals. Art. 1043-1046, Italian Civil Code.

scàrico delle àcque piovàne—discharge or drainage of rain waters. The owner must construct roofs in such a manner that rain waters will drain off to his ground and he cannot allow them to fall on the neighbor's land. If there exist public drains, he must arrange for the rain waters to be discharged therein with gutters and drains. In every case, local regulations and the laws on hydraulic policy must be observed. Art. 908, Italian Civil Code.

scarmigliàre—to ruffle; to rummage; to entangle.

scarmigliàto—uncombed.

scarnàre—to remove superficial flesh.

scarnàrsi—to grow thin; to lose flesh.

scàrno—thin; lean; emaciated.

scarrièra f.—out of course.

scarrièra (comperàre o véndere per)— to buy or sell out of course; to buy or sell smuggled goods or those out of the regular course of traffic.

scarrièra (gènte di)—people of evil affairs; vagabonds.

scarseggiàre—to have a scarcity of something; to be lacking in; to be short of; to be wanting.

scarsézza f.—scarcity.

scarsità f.—scarcity.

scàrso — scare; short; insufficient; lacking; niggardly; sparing.

scartabellàre — to glance through or skim through a book.

scartabèllo m.—waste paper; worthless papers; a book of little value.

scartaménto m. — rejection; discard; width between rails on a railroad; width of a vehicle from wheel to wheel.

scartàre—to discard; to set aside; to reject; to reject as unfit for military service.

scartàto m.—one who has been rejected as unfit for military service.

scartàto—discarded; rejected.

scàrto m.—that which has been discarded or rejected; refuse.

scasàre—to move from one lodging to another; to change lodgings; to turn out a lodger.

scassàre—to unpack; to break in; to break open; to break ground.

scassatóre m.—one who breaks in; housebreaker. See **effrazióne**.

scassatúra f.—the act of unpacking.

scassetàre—to empty the box; to make off with the money.

scassinàre—to smash; to break with force for the purpose of theft. See **fúrto con effrazióne**.

scassinatúra f.—the act of unpacking; cancellation.

scàsso m.—breaking of locks or boxes for the purpose of theft. See **effrazióne**.

scatenacciàre — to remove chains to open; to unbolt.

scatenaménto m.—unchaining.

scatenàre—to unchain.

scatenàto—unbridled; unfettered; unchained.

scàtola f.—box.

scattàre—to release; to spring up on release of tension; to go off (a gun); to escape.

scattatóio m.—detent; catch; trigger. See **grillétto**.

scàtto m.—the act of escaping or being released.

scaturígine f.—spring; source.

scaturíre—to spring; to rise; to issue.

scavàre—to excavate; to dig.

scavezzàre—to remove the halter; to lop off branches of a tree; to break; to overstrain.

scàvo m.—excavation.

scógliere—to choose; to select.

sceleràre or **scelleràre**—to commit evil deeds; to contaminate.

scelleràto — wicked; heinous; monstrous; villainous.

scélta f.—choice; option; selection; best.

scélto—chosen; preferred; best; one who has special merit.

sciògliere—to dissolve; to untie; to resolve; to adjourn (a meeting); to release from an obligation.

scèna f.—scene; stage; scenery.

scenàrio m. — scenario; outline or script of a play containing the parts of the players, situations and scenes.

scenàta f. — altercation; commotion; scene.

sceríffo m.—sheriff.

schèda f.—slip of paper; list; note.

schèda d'abbonaménto — subscription form.

schèda elettoràle—electoral ballot.

schedàrio m.—catalog; collection of lists; receptacle for catalogs and lists.

schéggia f.—splinter.

schèletro m.—skeleton.

schérma f.—fencing.

schérmo m.—defense; shield; motion picture screen.

schérmo m.—affront; derision; insult; scorn.

schiàffo m.—slap in the face; in a game of billiards, hitting the adversary's ball with a rebound shot after first striking the cushion.

schiamàzzo m.—noise; uproar. It is a violation of law to disturb the occupation or rest of persons or disturb exhibitions or performances or gatherings or public entertainments. Art. 659, Italian Penal Code.

schiantàre—to burst open; to shatter; to split.

schiàppa f.—chip of wood; bungler.

schiappíno m.—bungler.

schiariménto m.—clarification.

schiàtta f. — race; lineage; issue; breed.

schiattàre—to burst; to break.

schiattíre—to bark; to yelp.

schiavísta m.—slave trader.

schiavitú f.—slavery; servitude. It is a crime against personal liberty and is punished with imprisonment. The crimes include, reduction to slavery, forcible taking and commerce in slaves, as well as selling and acquiring them and subjecting a person to one's power by reducing him to a state of total submission. Art. 600-604, Italian Penal Code. See plàgio.

schiàvo m.—slave.

schiàvo di dàzio—unpaid duty.

schiavóne m.—Slav. Also, Slàvo.

schièna f.—back; back-bone.

schiètto — pure; genuine; unaltered; unmixed.

schífo m.—skiff; launch; small boat.

schífo m.—disgust; dirt; repugnance.

schífo—dirty; repugnant; disgusting.

schifóso — filthy; dirty; disgusting; disagreeable; loathsome; nasty.

schióppo m.—hunting rifle.

schiúdere—to open; to disclose.

scía f.—wake of a ship.

scià m.—Shah.

sciàbola f.—sabre.

sciacquàre—to rinse.

sciagúra f.—calamity; disaster; misfortune.

sciaguràto m. & adj. — unfortunate; miserable; wretched; unhappy; vile.

scialacquàre — to squander; to dissipate.

scialàre—to dissipate; to feast; to display great luxury; to show off.

scialúppa f.—launch.

sciàme m.—swarm; crowd.

sciàmi di àpi—swarm of bees. The owner of a swarm of bees has the right to pursue them upon another's land, but must indemnify for damage caused to the land; if he has not pursued them within two days or has ceased to pursue them within that time, the owner of the land may take and keep them. Art. 924, Italian Civil Code.

sciampàgna f.—champagne.

sciampagnóne m. — spendthrift; wastrel.

sciancàto m. & adj. — hipshot; dislocated hip; lame.

sciàre—to go astern; to ski.

sciàrra f.—noisy affray or quarrel.

sciattàre—to spoil; to ruin.

sciàtto—slovenly; careless; clumsy.

scíbile m.—knowledge; that which is knowable.

sciènte—learned; knowing.

scienziàto m.—scientist.

scilòma m. — tiresome speech lacking content; tiresome verbiage.

scimitàrra f.—scimitar.

scimunìto m. & adj. — silly; lacking good sense.

scìndere—to separate with force; to split; to divide.

scintìlla f.—spark; sparkle.

sciòcco m.—silly person.

sciòcco—inspired; silly.

sciògliere—to untie; to undo; to resolve; to dissolve; to release; to annul; to cancel.

sciogliménto m.—resolution; solution; dissolution.

sciogliménto della comunióne — dissolution of a tenancy in common or of property held in common. Art. 111, Italian Civil Code.

sciogliménto del contratto—dissolution of the contract. Art. 1372, Italian Civil Code.

sciogliménto della locazióne—dissolution of the rental contract. Where it had been agreed said contract could be dissolved in the event of the sale of the rented property, the buyer who wishes to avail himself of that right, must give notice to the leasee, honoring the term of notice to be given under the law. Art. 1603, 1596, 1574, Italian Civil Code.

sciogliménto del matrimònio—dissolution of marriage. It is dissolved with the death of one of the spouses or in the other cases provided by law. Art. 149, Italian Civil Code.

scioperàre—to strike (from work).

scioperàto—striker; one who does not work.

scioperìo m.—wasteful loss of time.

sciòpero m.—strike; collective cessation of work by employees. The right to strike is exercised within the limits of the laws regulating it. Art. 40, Constitution of the Italian Republic; Art. 502-512, Italian Penal Code.

sciovinìsmo m.—chauvinism.

sciovinìsta m.—chauvinist.

scìppo m.—in the Neapolitan dialect, it is a theft committed with the use of cunning, guile or snatching of personal property from the person of another. Art. 624, 625, subd. 4, Italian Penal Code. Also, stràppo, and fúrto con stràppo. See rapìna.

siròcco m.—sirocco; a hot, dry, dust-laden wind originating in northern African and affecting the northern Mediterranean coast, particularly in Malta, Sicily and Italy; a warm, moist, southeast wind.

scìsma m.—schism.

scissióne f. — division; separation; split.

sciupàre—to spoil; to waste; to dissipate; to ruin.

sciupàto — wasted; consumed (in health); used badly.

scivolàre—to slide; to slip.

sclamàre—to exclaim.

sclamazióne f.—exclamation.

scoccàre—to let fly; to shoot off; to strike (the hour in a clock).

scoccatóre m.—archer; shooter with a bow.

scoccatúra f.—springing of a catch.

scocciàre—to break the shell (of an egg); to annoy; to bother; to harass.

scocciatóre m. — one who annoys or bothers.

scocciatúra f.—the act of annoying or bothering.

scòglia f.—slough; the outer skin of a snake which it sheds annually.

scoglièra f.—reef of rocks or coral.

scòglio m. — rock near the shore; slough of a serpent.

scoglióso—rocky; reefy.

scolàra f.—schoolgirl. Also, scolàre.

scolàre m. or f.—schoolboy; schoolgirl.

scolàre—to drain; to filter.

scolàro m.—schoolboy. Also, scolàre.

scolatóio m.—drain; strainer; sink.

scòli (servitú attìva degli) — active servitude of draining waters. Running or draining waters originating in another's land may constitute the object of a servitude in favor of the land which receives them, which has the right to impede their diversion. Art. 1094, 909, Italian Civil Code.

scólo m.—drainage; drainage course or channel.

scólo delle àcque—drainage of waters. The lower land is subjected to receive the waters which drain naturally from the higher land without the intervention of human works. The owner of the inferior land cannot impede this drainage, nor can the owner of the superior land render it more burdensome. Art. 913, 915, Italian Civil Code.

scolpàre—to exculpate.

scolpíre—to sculpture; to carve; to engrave; to articulate; to pronounce distinctly.

scolpitaménte — clearly; distinctly; words which are articulated distinctly.

scolpitúra f.—sculpture; carving. Also, **scultúra.**

scombinàre—to disarrange; to discompose; to unsettle; to break up an affair; to distribute (type).

scombúglio m.—disorder.

scombussolàre—disperse; to rout; to cause utter disorder; to scatter; to lose one's bearings.

scomméssa f.—bet; stake; wager. An action to recover payment on a wagering debt is not permitted. A loser who paid a wager cannot recover the same where no fraud was involved. Excepted are games which train in the use of arms and all kinds of races and sporting events. An action to recover on a lottery winning may be maintained if it has been legally authorized. Art. 1933-1935, Italian Code. Also, **giuòco e scomméssa.**

scomparíre — to disappear; to fade away; to vanish; to decline by comparison; to cut a poor figure; to eclipse.

scompàrsa f.—disappearance; death; presumptive death. Art. 58, Italian Civil Code; Art. 726-731, Italian Code of Civil Procedure. See **assènza.**

scompartiménto m. — compartment; division; partition; alloting; sharing.

scompiacènte — disobliging; ungracious; unkind; rude.

scompíglio m. — confusion; disorder; turmoil.

scomputàbile—deductible.

scòmputo m.—deduction.

scomúnica f.—excommunication.

sconcatenàre—to unchain; to disconnect.

sconcertàre—to disconcert; to disturb; to perturb.

sconciàre—to break; to confound; to derange; to embroil; to spoil; to waste.

sconclúdere—to unsettle; to break (a treaty); to undo.

sconfermàre — to contradict; to disaffirm.

sconfessàre—to disavow; to renege.

sconfidàre—to distrust.

sconfíggere—to defeat; to discomfit; to ruin.

sconfinàre—to go beyond the limits (of one's territory).

sconfinàto — without bounds; having passed beyond the limits.

sconfítta f.—defeat.

sconfítto—defeated.

sconfóndere—to confound.

scongegnàre—to throw out of gear.

scongiuràre—to exorcise.

scongiúro m.—exorcism.

sconosciúto—unknown.

sconquassàre—to crush; to shatter; to smash.

sconsigliàre—to dissuade; to advise one to abstain from doing or saying something.

sconsolàto—disconsolate.

scontàbile—discountable.

scontaménto m.—act of discounting.

scontànte m.—one who discounts.

scontànte—discounting.

scontàre — to discount; to pay the penalty.

scónto m.—discount; abatement.

scónto bancàrio—bank discount. It is a contract whereby a bank, after deducting its rate of discount and taking a transfer of an instrument of credit which is not yet due, advances to a client the amount of a credit towards third parties, without prejudice to its interest in the credit. Art. 1858, Italian Civil Code.

scónto di cambiàli—discount of drafts or bills of exchange. If the discount occurs by indorsement of a draft or check, the bank, in the event of non-payment, besides the rights under the instrument, has also the right to restitution of the sum advanced. Art. 1859, Italian Civil Code.

scónto di tràtte documentàte — discount of drafts accompanied by documents of title. The bank which has discounted drafts accompanied by documents of title, has the same right over the merchandise represented by the documents as the agent so long as the documents representing title are in its possession. Art. 1860, Italian Civil Code.

scontríno m.—slip or check to reclaim an object; voucher.

scóntro m.—accident; collision; meeting; combat between adversaries; duel; catch in a mechanism.

scóntro tra veícoli—collision between vehicles. The driver of a vehicle not guided by tracks or rails, is obligated to compensate for damage caused to a person or to things by the circulation of the vehicle, unless he proves to have done everything possible to avoid the damage. In the case of a collision between vehicles, it is presumed, till proof to the contrary, that each of the drivers had equally contributed to produce the damages sustained by the individual vehicles. The proprietor of the vehicle, or, in his stead, the one using it or the purchaser under a conditional sales contract, is jointly and severally responsible with the driver, unless it is proved that movement of the vehicle was against his will. In every case, the persons above indicated are responsible for damages derived from faults of construction or defects of maintenance of the vehicle. Art. 2054, 2055, Italian Civil Code. Also, **circolazióne di veícoli.**

sconvòlgere—to upset; to overturn; to confound.

sconvolgiménto m. — confusion; disorder; overturning.

scoperchiàre—to uncover.

scopèrta f.—discovery.

scopèrto—uncovered; open.

scòpo m.—aim; design; intent; purpose; target.

scoppiàre—to burst; to explode; to uncouple.

scoppiatúra f.—explosion; crack in the skin.

scòppio m.—explosion; crash; burst.

scopriménto m.—uncovering; unveiling (a statue); disclosure; discovery.

scopríre—to discover; to uncover; to unveil; to perceive.

scopritóre m. (scopritríce f.) — discoverer.

scórrere—to run over; to run away; to pass (of time); to slip (of the pen); to run through (a book); to plunder; to raid.

scorrería f.—incursion; raid.

scórsa f.—incursion; slip of the pen; glance through a book.

scórso m.—involuntary error in writing or speaking; mistake.

scórso—run away; run over; passed (time); raided; plundered; past.

scórso (mése)—the past month.

scòrta f.—escort; convoy; provision; subsidy; accessory.

scòrte mòrte — inanimate accessories which are part of the land. They consist of such fixed accessories as machinery and appliances, as well as circulating accessories such as seeds, forage, manure and compost, which have been turned over by the lessor of the land to the lessee at the start of the leasehold and which must be returned at its termination. When the accessories have been turned over with a determination as to their species, quality and quantity, they must be returned to the lessor at the termination of the leasehold, in the same species, quality and quantity. If the fixed accessories which have been turned over by the lessor consist of machinery and appliances, they must be returned in the same condition. If there is an excess or deficiency, it will be adjusted or balanced in money according to its current value at the time of return. Art. 1640, Italian Civil Code.

scòrte víve—live accessories which are part of the land. They are constituted by working or breeding animals which have been furnished in whole or in part by the lessor. Whenever the animals turned over to the farm tenant have been determined with indication as to their species, number and sex, of their quality, age and weight, even though there has been an appraisal, the property in them remains with the lessor. However, the tenant farmer may dispose of individual heads, but must maintain the necessary complement of live accessories of the land. Art. 1641, 1642, Italian Civil Code.

scorticàre—to skin; to lacerate; to fleece; to extort.

scorticatóre—extorter; fleecer; skinner.

scorticatúra—scratch; extortion.

scoscéndere—to break with force; to tear asunder (branch or trunk of a tree); to crash down.

scòssa f.—shock; sudden shower; perturbation.

scostàre—to move away (one thing from another).

scostumatézza f.—a mode of living not in accord with the rules of morality and good manners; coarse manners; impoliteness.

scostumàto m.—ill mannered person.

scottàre—to scald; to scorch; to burn.

scòtto m.—meal at an inn; reckoning; share of a charge or payment; scot.

scòtto—over cooked.

scovàre—to ferret out; to dislodge; to discover.

scozzése—Scotch.

screanzàto—ill-bred; ill-mannered.

screditàre—to discredit; to lessen the reputation.

scréscere—to decrease; to diminish.

scríba m.—scribe.

scribacchiàre—to scribble.

scribacchíno m.—scribbler; one who pretends to be a writer.

scrígno m.—a box to enclose precious objects such as jewels. Also, **forzière**.

scriminànte — that which removes criminal responsibility; a cause which diminishes or excludes criminal responsibility; extenuating circumstance.

scriminàre—to absolve from a crime; to remove an accusation.

scriminatúra f.—parting of the hair.

scrítta f.—writing; written contract; inscription; nuptial contract; bond obligation.

scrittúra f.—written public or private document. See **scrittúra privàta** and **àtto púbblico**.

scrittúra dóppia—double entry bookkeeping.

scrittúra privàta—private writing or document. It is any document, not drawn by a public official, which is subscribed by the party issuing it. Art. 2702-2708, Italian Civil Code; Art. 214-220, Italian Code of Civil Procedure.

scritturàre—to engage in writing; to engage artists by the manager of a theater.

scrittúre contàbili—written books of accounts. Art. 2214-2220, Italian Civil Code; Art. 634, 635, Italian Code of Civil Procedure.

scrittúre offensive—offensive writings. Offensive matter contained in the writings presented by the parties or their advocates or in oral presentations by them before Judicial or Administrative Authorities are not punishable if they concern the object of the case or administrative recourse. Art. 598, Italian Penal Code.

scrivanía f.—writing desk.

scrivàno m.—scrivener; copyist; clerk.

scroccàre—to live parasitically at the expense of others; to cheat; to swindle; to sponge on others.

scròcco m. — cheating; swindling; sponging. See trúffa and fròde.

scroccóne m. — cheater; swindler; sponger.

scrutinàre—to scrutinize.

scrutínio m. — computation of votes; election by ballots; balloting.

scudería f.—large stable for horses, carriages and their equipment; in modern parlance, the establishment where motor cars are prepared for racing or otherwise.

scudisciàre—to whip.

scudíscio m.—whip.

scugnízzo m.—in the Neapolitan dialect, a street urchin; impudent boy.

scultóre m.—sculptor.

scultúra f.—sculpture.

scuotiménto m.—shaking; disturbance; shock.

scuotiménti dal fóndo vicíno—shocks from neighboring land. See immissióne di fúmo o di calóre nel fóndo vicíno.

scúre f.—axe.

scurétto m.—interior, folding window shutter.

scuríre—to obscure; to darken.

scúro—dark; deep color.

scurríle—scurrilous.

scúsa f.—excuse; pretext.

scusabilità f.—excusability; excusableness.

scusàre—to excuse; to justify.

scusàrsi—to apologize.

scússo—plain; stripped;

sdaziàre—to clear through customs by paying duty. See sdoganàre.

sdebitàre — to pay one's debts; to satisfy an obligation.

sdegnàre — to disdain; to scorn; to despise.

sdégno m. — disdain; scorn; indignation; wrath.

sdentàre—to break the teeth; to make toothless.

sdigiunàre—to breakfast.

sdoganàre—to clear customs; to take out of bond at customs. See sdaziàre.

sdrucciolàre—to slide; to slip.

sdrucíre—to unstitch; to unsew; to rip.

sécca f.—sandbar.

seccàre—to dry up; to drain; to importune; to annoy; to vex; to weary.

sécchia f.—bucket; pail.

sécchio m.—milk pail.

sécco—dry; lean; slender.

seccóre m.—drought.

secessióne f.—secession.

secessionistà m.—secessionist.

secónde nòzze—second marriage. See lútto vedovíle—widow's mounring.

secondína f.—secundine; afterbirth.

secondíno m.—the jailer who serves under the chief jailer.

secóndo m. — second at a duel. See padríno.

secóndo—second; that which immediately follows the first; according to.

secondogènito m.—second born son.

secondogenitúra f.—the legal. status of a second born son.

secretàre—to secrete.

secretàrio m.—secretary. Also, segretàrio.

secréto m.—secret. Also, segréto. The product of secretion. See secrezióne.

secrezióne f.—secretion.

secúra f.—safety bolt on a gun.

securità or securtà f.—security; assurance.

sedàre—to sedate; to calm; to quiet; to allay; to compose.

sedatívo—sedative; calmative.

sède f. — seat; residence; domicile; headquarters.

sède delle persóne giurídiche — headquarters of juridical persons. The residence or domicile of juridical persons or legal entities is determined by their charters. Art. 16, 46, Italian Civil Code. Art. 141, Italian Code of Civil Procedure.

sedére—to sit; to be seated; to be situated.

sedére (méttere a)—to remove an official from office.

sederíno m.—folding chair in a carriage or automobile.

sèdia f.—chair; seat.

sedicènte—self-styled; so-called.

sedíle m.—bench; seat; park bench; carriage seat; stand for a cask.

sediménto m.—sediment; dregs.

sedizióne f.—sedition; uprising.

sedizióso—seditious; rebellious.

sedótto—seduced.

seducènte—seductive; fascinating; attractive.

sedúrre—to seduce.

sedúta f.—meeting; session; sitting.

seduttóre m.—seducer.

seduttríce f.—seductress.

seduzióne f.—seduction.

seduzióne con proméssa di matrimònio comméssa da persóna coniugàta — seduction with promise of marriage committed by a married person. It involves the seduction of a minor female by promise of marriage and inducing her to error over the marriage status of the seducer. Carnal knowledge is an essential element of the crime. Art. 526, Italian Penal Code. See **violènza carnàle.**

séga f.—saw.

segàre—to saw; to cleave; to mow.

segatúra f.—the act of sawing; sawdust; harvest; harvest time.

sèggio m. — seat of a person in authority.

sèggiola f.—straw bottom chair.

segnalàre—to signalize; to communicate by signals; to do honor; to caution.

segnàle m.—signal; sign; omen. Whoever omits to place signals or shelters prescribed by law or the Authorities to prevent dangers to persons on a place of public passage, or removes said signals or shelters or extinguishes beacon lights placed as signals, is subject to arrest and a fine. Art. 673, Italian Penal Code.

ségni distintívi commerciàli—distinctive commercial marks. These include the firm name and insignia and the trademark and its emblem. Art. 2563-2574, Italian Civil Code.

ségni distintívi della personalità—distinctive personality marks. The rights to these include the right to one's name, surname and pseudonym; the right to one's portrait or picture and the right to privacy in written, telephonic and telegraphic communications. Art. 6-10, Italian Civil Code; Art. 15, Constitution of the Italian Republic; Art. 338-343, Italian Code of Penal Procedure.

ségno m.—mark; sign. The counterfeiting or alteration of distinctive signs or marks, national or foreign, of intellectual works or industrial products and their use is prohibited. The counterfeiting or alteration of letters patent, designs or industrial models, national or foreign, is also prohibited, as well as the sale and circulation of intellectual works and industrial products with deceptive names, marks or distinctive national or foreign signs. Art. 473-475, 517, 518, Italian Penal Code.

ségo m.—suet; tallow.

sgregàre—to segregate.

segregazióne f.—segregation.

segréta f. — secret place; dungeon; prayers recited in a low voice during a mass.

segretariàto m.—secretariat.

segretàrio m.—secretary.

segretería f. — secretary's office or room.

segréti (delítti cóntro la inviolabilità dei) — crimes against the inviolability of secrets. Art. 616-623, Italian Penal Code.

segréti dell'aziènda—business secrets.

The employee may not divulge information pertaining to the organization and methods of production of the enterprise or make use thereof in a manner to cause it prejudice. For its inobservance, the employee may be subjected to established sanctions according to the gravity of the infraction. Art. 2105, 2106, Italian Civil Code. Art. 97, Enabling Rules, Italian Civil Code.

segréti di stàto (rivelazióne di)—disclosure of state secrets. See rivelazióne di segréti di stàto.

segréti di stàto (utilizzazióne di)—utilization of state secrets. See utilizzazióne di segréti di stàto.

segréti di uffício (rivelazióne di)—disclosure of secrets of office. See rivelazióne di segréti di uffício.

segréti (rivelazióne del contenúto di documénti)—disclosure of the contents of secret documents. See rivelazióne del contenúto di documénti segréti.

segréti scientífici o industriàli (rivelazióne di)—disclosure of scientific or industrial secrets. See rivelazióne di segréti scientífici o industriàli.

segréto militàre—military secret. Art. 1-11, Segréto Militàre, Usual Laws, Appendix to Italian Code of Penal Procedure.

segréto professionàle (rivelazióne di)—disclosure of professional secret. See rivelazióne di segréto professionàle.

seguíre — to follow; to continue; to pursue.

séguito m. — retinue; adherents; continuation; following.

sèlla f.—saddle.

sélva f.—forest; wood; a multitude of things, figuratively.

selvàggio—savage; wild.

selvàtico—uncultivated; wild.

semàforo m.—semaphore; traffic signal.

sembràre—to appear; to seem; to look like.

séme m.—seed; origin; race.

seménta f.—the operation of sowing.

sementàre—to sow.

semènza f.—seed for sowing.

semenzàio m.—seed-bed.

semèstre m.—semester; half-year; six months.

seminàre — to sow; to scatter; to spread.

sèmita f.—footpath; narrow street.

semíta f.—Semite.

semítico—Semitic.

semiufficiàle—semi-official; a private notification sent by a high official which does not have the authority of his office.

sempitèrno—eternal; everlasting.

senàle m.—tackle; mechanism such as a rope and block for hoisting and lowering heavy objects.

sène m.—old; aged.

seníle—senile.

séno m.—bosom; breast.

sensàle m.—broker.

senseria f.—brokerage; brokerage fee.

sènso m.—sense; significance.

sensòrio m.—sensory organ.

sentènza f. — sentence; opinion; decision; a judgment in a civil or criminal case.

sentènza costitutíva—constitutive judgment. In the cases provided by law, the judicial authority may constitute, modify or extinguish legal relationships, with effect between the parties, their heirs and assignees. Art. 2908, Italian Civil Code.

sentènza di condànna—judgment ordering a party to a civil controversy to give or do something on behalf of the adversary party. Penally, it is the infliction of detentive or pecuniary punishment or both. Art. 132, 179, 474, Italian Code of Civil Procedure; Art. 148-151, 490, Italian Code of Penal Procedure.

sentènza di prosciogliménto — judgment of discharge or release from a criminal charge. The judge may dismiss such charge at any stage of the proceeding with the prescribed

254

formula, "sentènza non dovérsi procèdere," giving the reason for dismissal in his opinion. The grounds for dismissal are: (a) that the fact does not exist; (b) that the accused has not committed the crime alleged; (c) that the person is not chargeable or not subject to punishment as the facts alleged do not constitute a crime; (d) that the crime is barred or extinguished; (e) that the penal action should not have been initiated or prosecuted; (f) that there is insufficient evidence. Art. 378, 387, 152, Italian Code of Penal Procedure, Title II, Art. 62, Enabling Rules under Coordinating Dispositions, Italian Code of Penal Procedure. Also, "non dovérsi procèdere" and "sentènza non dovérsi procèdere".

sentènza non dovèrsi procèdere—judgment of dismissal of a penal action. See sentènza di proscioglimènto.

sentènza passàta in giudicàto — res judicata. See còsa giudicàta.

sentènze penàli stranière (riconoscimènto delle)—recognition of foreign penal judgments. Art. 672-675, Italian Code of Penal Procedure. Re civil matters, see sentènze stranière (efficàcia delle), Art. 796-805, Italian Code of Civil Procedure. See delibazióne (giudízio di).

sentènze stranière (efficàcia delle)—force of foreign judgments. Relative to civil matters, Art. 796-805, Italian Code of Civil Procedure. Relative to foreign penal judgments, see sentènze penàli stranière (riconoscimènto delle), Art. 672-675, Italian Code of Penal Procedure. See delibazióne (giudízio di).

sentenziàre—to adjudge; to condemn; to sentence.

sentièro m.—path.

sentire—to perceive by the senses, viz., hearing, tasting, smelling, feeling, but not the sense of seeing.

sentíta f.—the act of hearing, feeling, tasting, smelling or sensing.

sentíta (per)—hearsay.

sentíto—felt, heard, perceived. Also, sentúto.

sentíto díre—hearsay. That which is heard. See vóci corrènti.

sentóre m.—indication; hint; sign; information received in a roundabout way; scent, odor; noise.

sentúto—felt, heard; perceived. Also, sentíto.

separazióne f.—separation.

separazióne dei bèni—separation of properties (of the spouses) — The spouses may agree that each of them preserve the exclusive title to property acquired during the marriage. Art. 215, 217-219, Italian Civil Code.

separazióne dei bèni (regíme di)—regime for the separation of property (of spouses). This heading has changed the former rules of law governing the community property of spouses. See comunióne dei bèni tra còniugi.

separazióne dei bèni del defúnto da quélli dell'erède—separation of the properties of the deceased from those of the heir. It is a method of assuring the creditors and legatees of the deceased of the satisfaction of their claims in preference to the heir's creditors. The right to separation is granted to creditors and legatees of the deceased who have other guarantees over his property. Art. 512-518, Italian Civil Code.

separazióne dei còniugi—separation of spouses. It may be judicial or consensual. Art. 150-158, Italian Civil Code; Art. 706-711, 474, Italian Code of Civil Procedure. Also, separazióne personàle.

separazióne giudizìàle dei bèni—judicial separation of the properties (of spouses). It may be adjudged in case of interdiction (interdizióne), or disqualification to manage one's affairs (inabilitazióne) on the part of a spouse or bad administration of community property. Art. 193-197, Italian Civil Code.

separazióne personàle — personal separation of spouses. It may be judicial or consensual. Art. 150-158, Italian Civil Code; Art. 706-711, 474,

Italian Code of Civil Procedure. Also, separazióne dei cóniugi.

sepolcréto m.—place of burial.

sepólcro m.—sepulcher; tomb.

sepólto—buried.

sepoltúra f.—burial.

seppellíre—to bury; to inter.

sequestrànte m. — sequestrator; the one who initiates a sequestration.

sequestàre—to sequester; to remove property temporarily from the possession of the owner; to set aside; to seize property or a person; to detain; to abduct; to kidnap.

sequestratàrio m. — sequestrator; the one making a sequestration; one chosen to perform a sequestration.

sequèstro m.—sequestration. In civil matters, see Art. 670-687, Italian Code of Civil Procedure. In penal matters, see Art. 226, 337, 344, 347, 617, 626, Italian Code of Penal Procedure and Art. 189, 190, Italian Penal Code.

sequèstro conservatívo—conservative sequestration. In civil matters, it is granted by a judge on petition of a creditor who has reasonable fear of losing the guarantees or sustaining prejudice to the credit he has extended. Such sequestration may be authorized over real and personal property of the debtor or of sums due to him, within the limits in which the law permits their attachment. Art. 671, et seq., Italian Code of Civil Procedure. In penal matters, it is used to guarantee payment to the State of the costs of the trial and maintenance of the convict in jail. It also assures payment for hospital expenses of one injured by the crime and sums advanced by counsel and his fees. The property of the person civilly responsible is also subject to the preceding procedures. The State having a right to a legal mortgage over the property subject to sequestration, the Public Prosecutor makes application for the same. Art. 188-190, Italian Penal Code; Art. 616, 617, Italian Code of Penal Procedure; Art. 2817, Italian Civil Code; Art.

670-687, Italian Code of Civil Procedure.

sequèstro convenzionàle—conventional sequestration. It is a contract whereby two or more persons entrust something or a number of things to a third person, when there arises a dispute between them concerning the property, so that it may be conserved and then restored to the one entitled thereto when the controversy is resolved. Art. 1798-1802, Italian Civil Code.

sequèstro di persóna—kidnapping; abduction of a person. Whoever deprives someone of personal liberty, is punished with imprisonment. Art. 605, Italian Penal Code. See **persóna (delítti cóntro la)**.

sequèstro di persóna a scòpo di rapína o di estorsióne—abduction or kidnapping of a person for the purpose of obtaining for himself or others an unjust profit or advantage as the price for release or liberation of the seized person, is punished with imprisonment. Art. 630, Italian Penal Code.

sequèstro e pignoraménto di stipèndi, salàri e pensióni—attachment and garnishment of wages, salaries and pensions. By statute, it is limited to certain percentages of a debtor's obligations and it is imposed on his wages, salaries and pensions. Stipèndi, salàri e pensióni (Wages, salaries and pensions), Usual Laws, Appendix to Italian Code of Civil Procedure.

sequèstro giudiziàrio—judicial sequestration. It is authorized by a judge over real and personal property, businesses or other universality of property, when there is a dispute over property or its possession and it is opportune to provide for their custody and temporary management. Art. 670, Italian Code of Civil Procedure. See **sequèstro conservatívo**.

seràta f. — evening; evening party; soiree; evening benefit performance at a theater.

serbàre—to put aside; to reserve; to save.

serbatóio m.—reservoir. Its owner has

a servitude on land. Whoever has the right to derive waters from rivers, torrents, streams, canals, lakes or reservoirs, may, when necessary, construct an enclosure or dam at the shores with the obligation, however, to pay indemnity and to make and maintain the works properly to insure the lands against every damage. Art. 1047, 1048, Italian Civil Code.

serràta f.—enclosure around a building; lock-out (in a labor dispute). Art. 502-506, Italian Penal Code.

serràto—closed; locked; shut; close; thick; pressed together.

serratúra f.—lock. See **grimaldèllo**—a pick lock and Art. 707, 710, 711, Italian Penal Code.

servígio—service; favor; employment. Also, **servizio.**

servíto m.—service for the table.

servíto—served.

servitóre m.—servitor; servant.

servitú f. — servitude; a limitation, charge or burden placed on real property for the benefit of another, be it a person or other land; household servants as a group.

servitú prediàli—servitude on land. A burden imposed on land for the benefit of another land called the dominant estate and belonging to another owner. Art. 1027-1031, 1069, Italian Civil Code.

servízio m.—service, domestic or public; service for the table. Also, **servigio.**

sèsso m.—sex.

sessuàle—sexual.

séta f.—silk.

séte f.—thirst.

setería f.—silk factory or store.

sètta f.—sect; faction.

sètte—seven.

settimàna f.—week; a week's work or wage.

settóre m.—sector; dissector; one who prepares cadavers for examination.

settóre (períto)—expert dissector.

sevízia f.—cruelty. It is ground for a judicial separation. Art. 151, Italian Civil Code.

sezióne f.—section; division or part of a thing; a section or part of a court or tribunal.

sfaccendàto m.—a do nothing; loafer.

sfacciatàggine f.—effrontery; shamelessness. See **sfrontatàggine.**

sfamàre—to satisfy one's hunger; to satiate. Also, **disfamàre.**

sfàre—to unmake; to undo.

sfàrzo m.—pomp; ostentatious luxury.

sfasciàre—to undo; to remove a bandage; to dismantle; to break; to collapse; to ruin.

sfavóre m.—disfavor.

sfavorévole—unfavorable.

sferràre—to unshoe (a horse); to remove fetters or shackles; to remove a weapon from a wound; to attack with force and violence; to throw a blow or kick suddenly and with force.

sfèrza f.—whip; lash.

sferzàre—to whip; to lash.

sfída f.—challenge. Also, **disfída.**

sfída a duèllo—challenge to a duel. Whoever challenges another to a duel, even though the challenge is not accepted, is punished with a fine if the duel does not take place. The same penalty is applicable to the one who accepts the challenge, provided that the duel does not take place. Those who carry the challenge are punished with a fine which is diminished if the duel does not take place. Whoever uses arms in a duel, is punished with imprisonment even though he fails to cause personal harm to his adversary. Imprisonment for the dueller is increased if the adversary receives a serious or very serious wound, or death result. The seconds and persons who have facilitated the duel are subject to fines. Art. 394-396, Italian Penal Code.

sfiguràre—to disfigure; to make a bad impression.

sfilàre—to unthread; to file past; to march past.

sfilàrsi—to sprain one's back; to become unravelled.

sfilàta f.—a long series of persons or things passing by; a marching past of guests, troops or ordinance.

sfilàto m.—filigree work.

sfilàto—unstrung; unwound.

sfiníre—to faint. Also, sveníre.

sfioríre—to fade.

sfittàre—to terminate a lease; to give notice to quit.

sfítto—unleased; unrented.

sfogàre — to release something enclosed; to give vent.

sfòggio m.—pomp; ostentatious luxury.

sfortúna f.—misfortune; bad luck.

sforzàre—to force; to constrain.

sfòrzo m.—effort; strain; stress.

sfracassàre—to break; to shatter.

sfratàre—to unfrock; to leave a religious order.

sfrattàre—to evict; to expel.

sfràtto m.—eviction; expulsion. Art. 657-669, Italian Code of Civil Procedure. See licènza per finíta locazióne (intimazióne di) and procediménto per convàlida di sfràtto.

sfregiàre—to disfigure; to gash; to disgrace.

sfrègio m.—gash; discredit; affront; dishonor; gash on the face.

sfrègio permanènte—permanent gash or disfigurement. It is an aggravating circumstance when a very serious disfigurement has been inflicted. Art. 583, subd. 4, Italian Penal Code.

sfrenàre—to unbridle; to throw off restraint.

sfrenatézza f. — dissoluteness; licentiousness.

sfrontatàggine f.—effrontery; shamelessness; impudence. Also, sfrontatézza and sfacciatàggine.

sfrontatézza f.—effrontery. See sfrontatàggine.

sfruttàre—to misuse; to abuse; to drain; to exploit; to derive profit.

sfruttatóre m.—exploiter.

sfuggíre—to avoid; to elude; to escape from; to flee.

sfuggíta f.—hasty trip to a place.

sfuggíta (alla)—hastily.

sfuggíto—fugitive.

sgabellàre—to pay the tax or duty. See sdoganàre and sdaziàre.

sgabèllo m.—stool or bench.

sgarbatàggine f. — impoliteness; incivility; rudeness.

sgarbàto—rude; impolite; awkward.

sgàrro m.—mistake; error.

sghèrro m.—hired assassin; cutthroat.

sgovernàre—to misgovern.

sgovèrno m.—bad government.

sgozzàre—to cut the throat; to bleed by usury.

sgozzíno m.—usurer.

sgravàre—to alleviate; to discharge; to lighten a burden; to reduce taxes.

sgravàrsi—to be delivered of a child.

sgràvio m.—alleviation; discharge; relief (from taxes); justification.

sgraziàto—awkward; clumsy; ungraceful.

sgrillettàre—to pull the trigger.

sgrínfia f.—claw; thieving hand.

sguaiàto — without good manners; graceless; disagreeable.

sguàttero m. (sguàttera f.)—kitchen help performing menial duties. Also, guàttera and guàttero.

sicàrio m.—assassin; cut-throat; one who kills at the bidding of others.

siccità f.—siccity; aridity; dryness.

sicofànte m.—sycophant; informer; spy.

sicúra f.—safety-catch.

sicurézza f.—safety; assurance.

sicurézza (cassétta di)—safety deposit box.

sicurézza detentíve (misúre di)—measures of detentive security. They are: (1) assignment to a farm colony or to a work house; (2) recovery in a house of cure and custody; (3) recovery in an insane asylum designated by the judiciary; (4) recovery in a judicial reformatory. Art. 215-227, Italian Penal Code. See misúre amministratíve di sicurézza.

sicúrézza non detentíve (misúre di)—non detentive measures of security. They are: (1) supervised liberty; (2) interdiction from sojourning in one or more Comunes or in one or more Provinces; (3) interdiction from frequenting taverns and public shops selling alcoholic beverages; (4) expulsion of a foreigner from the State. Art. 215, 228-235, Italian Penal Code. See misúre amministratíve di sicurézza.

sicurézza púbblica — public security. The Authority of Public Security preserves the maintenance of public order and the security of the citizens and protects their safety and property; it is concerned with the observance of the laws and the general and special regulations of the State, provinces and communes as well as the orders of the Authority; it furnishes aid in case of public or private disasters. The Authority of Public Security is provincial and local. It is headed by the Prefètto and Questóre. Sicurézza Púbblica, Tèsto único (Unified Text), Usual Laws, Appendix to Italian Code of Penal Procedure. Also, púbblica sicurézza.

sicurtà f.—safety; security; commercial and legal security; insurance; surety.

sicurtà (vàlvola di)—safety valve.

sièro m.—serum; whey.

sièrra f.—from the Spanish, sierra, a chain of mountains.

sièsta f.—from the Spanish, siesta, a rest taken after the mid-day meal.

sifílide f.—syphilis. Concealing it and causing it to spread is a crime subject to imprisonment. Art. 554, Italian Penal Code.

sigillàre—to seal.

sigíllo m.—seal. See apposizióne dei sigíli.

sígla f.—abbreviation; initial.

signoría f.—authority; dominion; lordship; power; governing body of medieval Italian republics; gentlemen as a class.

silènzio m. — silence; stillness. For tacit approval, see rinnovazióne tàcita del contràtto.

silurare—to torpedo.

silúro m.—torpedo.

silvicultúra f.—silviculture; cultivation of trees of the forest; forestry.

simonía f.—simony; traffic in the sacred; the sin of buying or selling ecclesiastical benefices.

simulazióne f.—simulation; feigning; counterfeiting; deception; a feigned or fictitious transaction; one which assumes the appearance of a pretended act without the reality.

simulazióne del contràtto—simulation of the contract. It does not produce any effect between the parties. If the parties wished to conclude a contract other than the apparent one, the dissimulated one has effect between them, so long as there subsist the requisites of form and substance. The simulation cannot be opposed by the contracting parties, or the assignees or creditors of the simulated transferor to third parties who have acquired rights in good faith from the apparent, nominal party to the contract, barring the effects of the transcription in a complaint for simulation. Third parties may make use of the simulation against the parties when it prejudices their rights. The simulation may not be opposed by the contracting parties against creditors of the nominal, apparent holder of rights who have effected acts of execution against the goods which were the object of the simulated contract. Testimonial proof of the simulation is admissible without limits, if the complaint is proposed by creditors, or third parties, and whenever it is directed to make use of the illegality of the dissimulated contract, even if it is proposed by the parties. Art. 1414-1417, 2652, Italian Civil Code.

simulazióne di reàto—simulation of a crime. Whoever, by complaint, accusation, petition or demand, even if anonymous or under false name, directed to the Judicial Authority or other Authority which has to report it, affirms falsely that a crime occurred, or simulates evidence of a crime, so that a penal proceeding may be initiated to ascertain it, is punished with imprisonment. Art. 367, Italian Penal Code.

sinallagmàtico—a contract imposing reciprocal obligations on the parties; a bilateral contract. See **bilateràle.**

sindacàle (collègio)—board of directors of a corporation. Art. 2397-2409, Italian Civil Code.

sindacàre—to audit official accounts; to control; to oversee; to unite; to combine.

sindacàto m.—syndicate; a combination of financiers and capitalists who carry out a particular enterprise or venture in common; an association of persons who have common interests to defend; the office of the mayor or syndics.

sìndaco m.—syndic; an advocate or defender; an auditor; one who manages business for a corporation or university; a corporate director; one who administers a bankrupt's affairs, similar to a trustee; the mayor of a commune or city.

sindicatóre m. — inspector; one who oversees and audits.

sinìstro m.—accident; disaster; misfortune.

sinìstro — left-handed; sinister; unlucky; damaging.

sipàrio m.—theater curtain.

siròcchia f.—sister.

sistèma f.—system.

sistèma tavolàre—tabular system. See **tavolàre (sistèma).**

sistemàre—to systematize; to reduce to a system; to arrange or regulate affairs.

sistemazióne f.—systemization; regularization.

sitibóndo—thirsty.

sitíre—to thirst.

sìto m.—site; musty smell.

sitofobía f.—sitophobia; aversion to food.

situàre—to situate; to put in place.

situazióne f.—situation; position.

slacciàre—to untie; to unlace; to free oneself from an annoyance.

slanciàre—to hurl; to fling; to launch with force.

slàncio m.—outburst; jump; impetous movement.

sleàle—disloyal. Also **disleàle.**

slítta f.—sledge.

slogàre—to dislocate. Also, **dislogàre.**

sloggiàre—to dislodge; to evict.

slòggio—See **afràtto.**

smàcco m.—affront; insult.

smània f. — craze; restless desire; burning wish; morbid agitation.

smanieràto—ill-mannered.

smanigliàre—to unshackle.

smantellàre—to dismantle.

smarriménto m. — loss; mislaying; fainting; swooning.

smarriménto di còsa determinàta—loss of a specific thing. A performance which has as its object a specific thing, is considered to have become impossible of performance even when the thing is lost without it being possible to prove its destruction. Art. 1257, Italian Civil Code.

smarriménto di títoli di crédito—loss of credit instruments. In the event of their loss or being stolen, the extinction of the debt represented by the instrument may be sought. They include: (a) instruments payable to order, (Art. 2016); (b) nominative instruments, (Art. 2027), and bearer instruments only as permitted by special laws, but not otherwise (Art. 2006), Italian Civil Code.

smarriménto, sottrazióne o distruzióne dell'asségno bancàrio e dell'asségno circolàre—loss, defalcation or destruction of a check and a cashier's check. In the event of the above, notification is made to the drawee and recourse had to the Tribunal at the place where the instrument is payable or the Praetor where the complainant has his domicile, demanding extinction of the debt represented by the instrument. Art. 69-74, 86, Asségni (Checks), Usual Laws, Appendix to Italian Civil Code.

smemoràto—forgetful.

smentíre—to belie; to contradict; to repudiate a statement.

smèrcio m.—sale; traffic.

sméttere—to put aside; to leave off; to abandon.

smilitarizzàre—to demilitarize.

smistaménto m.—the act of separating; separation.

smistaménto (stazióne di)—marshalling yard; a station or yard where the cars of freight trains are arranged and made up for proper distribution and routing to their destinations.

smistàre—to separate a mixture into its component elements.

smobilitàre—to demobilize.

smoderàto—excessive; immoderate.

smontàre—to dismount; to dismantle; to descend.

smòrfia f. — grimace; affectation; a book containing numbers corresponding to words, incidents and dreams, which can be used in playing the Italian lottery game of lotto.

smúngere—to dry; to exhaust. Also, emúngere.

smuòvere—to move with effort; to plough the ground.

smuràre—to take down the walls.

snazionalizzàre—to denationalize; to divest of national status or character and rights; to return a previously nationalized industry or business to private initiative.

snazionalizzazióne f. — denationalization.

snervàre—to enervate.

sobbórgo m.—suburb.

sobrietà f. — sobriety; moderation; temperance.

sòbrio—sober.

socchiúso—partially closed; ajar.

sòccida f.—a contract of agistment whereby two parties nurture a quantity of livestock, thereafter dividing their increase and other products as well as the profits derived. Art. 2170, Italian Civil Code. .

sòccida con conferiménto di pàscolo—a contract of agistment where one party, the soccidàrio, contributes livestock and the other, the soccidànte, provides the land for pasture. The soccidàrio has charge of the undertaking and the soccidànte controls the management of the enterprise. Art. 2186, Italian Civil Code.

sòccida parziària—a contract of agistment where both contracting parties contribute livestock in agreed quotas, and of which they become co-owners in proportion to their contribution. If the contract is not less than three years duration, should the major part of the livestock perish without fault of the soccidàrio, each of the contracting parties may withdraw from the contract if not otherwise stipulated. The loss must occur during the first half of the contracted period. Art. 2182-2185, Italian Civil Code.

sòccida sémplice—simple contract of agistment. Here, the soccidànte furnishes the livestock which is appraised without passing ownership to the soccidàrio, and the latter performs the work. The appraisal must indicate the number, breed, quality, sex, weight and age of the livestock and the relative market value. The appraisal serves as the basis for determining the share to be withdrawn by the soccidànte at the termination of the contract. Art. 2171-2181, Italian Civil Code.

soccidànte m.—a party to a contract of agistment. In the sòccida sémplice, he furnishes the livestock. In the sòccida con conferiménto di pàscolo, he provides the land for pasture. See the above titles.

soccidàrio m.—a party to a contract of agistment. In the sòccida sémplice, the soccidàrio performs the work. In the sòccida con conferiménto di pàscolo, he has charge of the undertaking. See the above titles.

sòccio m.—agister or agistor; one who pastures animals under an agreed contract of sòccida.

soccombénza f.—act of succumbing, of losing or being defeated.

soccómbere—to succumb; to lose; to admit defeat; to yield; to submit.

soccórrere—to succor; to aid; to assist; to help; to relieve.

soccórso m.—aid; help; relief.

soccórso (omissióne di)—omission or failure to render help. Whoever, finding an abandoned or lost child less than age ten, or other person incapable of providing for himself because of mental or physical illness, advanced age or other reason, fails to give immediate notice to the Authorities, is punished with imprisonment or fine. Subject to the same punishment, is one who finding a human body which may be or appears lifeless, or a person wounded, or otherwise in peril, fails to give necessary assistance and to give immediate notice to the Authorities. If said wrongful conduct causes personal injury, the punishment is augmented; if it causes death, the punishment is doubled. Art. 593, Italian Penal Code.

società f.—society; association of two or more persons engaged in a common pursuit; congregation; partnership. The partnership agreement is a contract whereby two or more persons contribute property or services to a common financial enterprise for the purpose of sharing the profits. Art. 2247, Italian Civil Code.

società a capitàle variàble—variable capital corporation. The capital of these corporations is not predetermined but varies in amount. Cooperatives are of this nature. See **società cooperatíve.**

società a responsabilità limitàta—limited responsibility partnership. Here, the partners are liable only to the extent of their capital contribution. The firm name must indicate that it is a partnership of limited responsibility. It is constituted by public Act and must be registered. Art. 2472-2497 bis, Italian Civil Code.

società all'èstero — foreign corporations. See **società costituíte all'èstero con sède nel territòrio dello stàto.**

società anònima—anonymous association; corporation. This is the former name for a stock corporation. It has been changed to società per azióni. See that title.

società con prevalènti interèssi stranièri—corporation with dominant foreign interests. It is subject to the rules of special laws which forbid or place under particular conditions the exercise of specific activities. Art. 2510, Italian Civil Code.

società controllàte—controlled corporations. These are subsidiary corporations controlled by a parent or holding company. Controlled corporations are those in which another corporation possesses a number of shares of stock sufficient to assure it of a majority of votes, or which by virtue of contractual ties, are under the dominant influence of another corporation. Art. 2359-2361, Italian Civil Code.

società cooperatíve—cooperative associations. They have a basis of mutual assistance and economic benefit. They include consumer groups as well as credit, construction, labor and production organizations. Their capital is variable and financial responsibility may be limited or unlimited according to their charter. The title of the cooperative must reflect the degree of responsibility. Art. 2511-2545, Italian Civil Code. See **società a capitàle variàbile.**

società costituíte all'èstero con sède nel territòrio dello stàto—foreign corporations with headquarters in the territory of the State. They are subject to Italian Law. Art. 2505, Italian Civil Code.

società costituíte nel territòrio dello Stàto con attivita all'èstero—domestic corporations with foreign activities. They are subject to Italian Law. Art. 2509, Italian Civil Code.

società di capitàli—capital stock corporations. They have a juridical personality and the corporate assets are used to pay its liabilities.

società d'interèsse nazionàle—national interest corporation. Also, **società per azióne di'interèsse nazionàle.** Art. 2461, Italian Civil Code.

società di mútua assicurazióne—mutual insurance associations. Their obligations are guaranteed by their total assets and they are governed by the rules established for cooperative associations of limited responsibility. Art. 2546-2548, Italian Civil Code.

società di persóne—association of persons or partnerships. The partners are jointly and severally liable without limit for firm liabilities. Art. 2267, Italian Civil Code.

società èstere con sède secondària nel territòrio dello stàto—foreign corporations with subsidiary offices in the territory of the State. They are subject to Italian Law regarding the inscription and filing of their charters in the Register of Businesses. They are also required to publish their budget and the names of those representing the corporation and to deposit their autographed signatures. Art. 2506, Italian Civil Code.

società èstere di típo divèrso da quélle nazionàli—foreign corporations of a different nature than the national ones. When these are other in nature than those regulated by the Civil Code, they are subject to the rules affecting stock corporations for registration in the Register of Businesses and the responsibility of the officers and managers. Art. 2507, Italian Civil Code.

società in accomàndita per azióni—corporation of limited responsibility. The accomandatàri members or shareholders have unlimited, joint and several responsibility for corporate debts. The accomandànti members or shareholders are limited in responsibility to the extent of their subscribed capital. It is formed by public Act and registered. Art. 2462-2471, Italian Civil Code.

società in accomàndita sémplice—simple partnership in accomàndita. It is similar to a limited partnership. The accomandatàri members are jointly and severally liable without limit. The accomandànti members are liable to the extent of their contributions. This type of partnership uses a firm name indicating its nature, and must be registered. Art. 2313-2324, Italian Civil Code.

società in nóme collettívo—partnership bearing a collective name. Here, all the partners are jointly and severally liable for the firm obligations without limit. The partnership engages in commercial activity and its charter must be filed in the Registry Office. Art. 2291-2312, Italian Civil Code.

società per azióni—stock corporation. Abbreviated S. p A., it is placed following the name or title of the corporation. Art. 2325-2461 Italian Civil Code.

società per azióni d'interèsse nazionàle—national interest stock corporation. Also, **società d'interèsse nazionàle.** Art. 2461, Italian Civil Code.

società sémplice—simple partnership or association. It is one created by a contract that is not subject to special legal requirements. It is used by those engaged in some economic activity for profit. Art. 2251-2290, 1350, Italian Civil Code.

sòcio m.—partner; associate; companion; member of a group or society.

sòcio occúlto—dormant, silent, sleeping partner.

sofisticàre—to adulterate or alter a substance or liquid; e.g. to adulterate foodstuffs or beverages.

soffítta f.—attic; garret.

soffittàre—to panel; to wainscot.

soffítto m.—ceiling; soffit. The expense for the maintenance and reconstruction of condominium ceilings, vaults and terraces are borne equally by the owners of the two floors, one over the other. The superior owner is charged with covering the pavement and the lower owner with the plastering, painting and decoration of the ceiling. Art. 1125, Italian Civil Code.

soggètto m.—subject; one placed under

the authority or dominion of some-one else; matter; theme; topic.

soggètto—lying under; lying below; subject to.

soggeziόne f.—subjection; submission; constraint; awe; timidity.

soggiacére—to be subject to; to succumb.

soggiόrno m.—sojourn; place of temporary stay. Where one is guilty of a crime against the personality of the State or against public order, or one committed for political motives or occasioned by particular social or moral conditions existing in a determined place, such guilty person may be enjoined from sojourning in one or more Communes or one or more Provinces designated by the judge. Art. 233, Italian Penal Code; Art. 653, Italian Code of Penal Procedure; Preventive Measures, Usual Laws, Appendix to Italian Code of Penal Procedure.

soggiόrno degli stranièri nello stàto—sojourn of foreigners within the State. See **stranièri (soggiόrno degli stranièri nello stàto)**.

solàio m.—terrace. The expense for the maintenance and reconstruction of condominium ceilings, vaults and terraces are borne equally by the owners of the two floors, one over the other. The superior owner is charged with covering the pavement and the lower owner with the plastering, painting and decoration of the ceiling. Art. 1125, Italian Civil Code.

solàrio m.—solarium.

solcàre—to plough; to furrow; to excavate.

sόlco m.—furrow; track; wrinkle.

solére—to be accustomed to; to be wont.

solèrte—diligent; industrious.

solidàle—joint and several.

solidarietà f.—solidarity; a joint and several obligation. See **obbligaziόni in sòlido**. Art. 1292-1313, Italian Civil Code. In penal matters, the obligation, *ex delicto* and for restitution is joint and several upon those con-

demned for the same crime. Art. 187, Italian Penal Code.

solidarietà tra condebitόri—joint and several obligation of co-debtors. Co-debtors are jointly and severally liable unless it is otherwise indicated by the law or the instrument in question. Art. 1294, Italian Civil Code.

sòlido—solid; firm; a joint and several obligation. See **solidarietà.**

solitàrio—solitary.

sòlito—usual.

sollecitaménte—carefully; diligently; with dispatch.

sollecitaménto m.—solicitation; instigation.

sollecitànte m.—solicitor.

sollecitàre—to solicit; to urge; to hasten forward; to expedite.

solleticàre—to tickle.

sollevàre—to raise; to lift; to move; to excite; to revolt; to alleviate; to cheer up.

sollevaziόne f.—elevation; rebellion; revolt; tumult.

sollièvo m.—alleviation; relief.

solúbile—soluble.

soluti retentio (Lat.)—retention of payment. The Civil Code provides that certain payments that have been made cannot be the subject of an action for restitution. These are: (a) by an apparent legatee, who in reality is holding as a trustee for others; once such person has transferred the property to the person intended by the testator, he cannot seek restitution unless he lacked capacity; (b) gambling debts, unless there has been fraud involved or the loser lacks capacity; (c) that which has been loaned voluntarily in furtherance of moral or social obligations, unless the loan was made by one lacking capacity; (d) a performance made against good custom and propriety, and (e) a payment made voluntarily in fulfillment of a barred or outlawed debt. Art. 627, 1933, 2034, 2035, 2940, Italian Civil Code.

solutivo—solutive; aperient; laxative.

264

solúto—dissolved.

soluzióne f.—solution.

solve et repete (Lat.)—pay (perform) and then seek restitution. Such a clause (clàusola limitatíva della proponibilità di eccezióni, Art. 1462, Italian Civil Code), when inserted in a contract requires the aggrieved party to first perform his own obligation to avoid default, and thereafter seek redress against the opposing party for any breach of contract or illegality. The clause is not effective against defenses or claims involving the validity of the contract or seeking its annulment or rescission. Also, see nullità del contràtto, azióne di rescissióne del contràtto and azióne di ripetizióne.

solvènte—solvent; able to pay just debts.

solvènza f.—solvency; ability to pay just debts as they mature. See insolvènza.

sòlvere—to dissolve; to solve.

sòlvere i creditóri—to settle with one's creditors.

somigliànza f.—resemblance.

somigliàre—to resemble.

sómma f.—sum; amount; addition; conclusion; compendium; summary.

sómma da pagàre—amount to be paid. Pecuniary debts are extinguished with money which is legal tender in the State at the time of payment and at its nominal value. If the amount due was fixed in money which is no longer legal tender at the time of payment, this must be done in legal currency, balanced to equal the value of the first. Where the amount to be paid in checks or drafts is written in letters and figures, the amount to be paid, in the event of difference in amount between the writing and figures, will be the amount written in letters. If the amount to be paid is written more than once in letters or figures, the amount to be paid in the check or draft will be the lesser sum. Art. 1277-1280, Italian Civil Code; Art. 9, Asségni (checks) and Art. 6, Cambiàle (Drafts), Usual Laws, Appendix to Italian Civil Code.

sommàrio m. — summary; compendium; abstract.

sommàrio—summary; brief; concise.

sommergíbile m. — submarine; submergible. Also, sottomaríno.

sommersióne f.—submersion; sinking. It is a criminal act to cause the same. Art. 428, 436, 449, 450, Italian Penal Code.

somministràre—to administer; to provision; to supply.

somministrazióne f. — provision; the act of supplying or furnishing.

somministrazióne (contràtto di)—an output, requirements and exclusive dealings contract. Art. 1559-1570, Italian Civil Code. Cf. Art. 2-306, Uniform Commercial Code.

somministrazióne a minóri di sostànze velenóse o nocíve — administering poisonous or harmful substances to minors. Whoever, being authorized in the sale or commerce of medicinals, delivers to a person under sixteen years of age, poisonous or narcotic substances, even pursuant to a medical prescription is punished with a fine. The person who sells or dispenses tobacco to a person under fourteen years of age is subject to a fine. Art. 730, Italian Penal Code.

somministrazióne al nemíco di provvigióni—supplying provisions to the enemy. Whoever, in time of war, supplies, even indirectly, the enemy State with provisions, or other things which may be used to the detriment of the Italian State, is punished with imprisonment. This disposition is not applicable to a foreigner who commits this act abroad. The punishment is applicable when the crime is committed to the detriment of a State which is allied or associated in war with the Italian State. Whoever instigates such acts or those enumerated in Chapter I and II of Title I of Crimes against the Personality of the State, even though done without intent or done negligently, is subject to the prescribed punishment. Art. 248, 268, 302, 310, Italian Penal Code. See Art. 241-293; 301-313, Italian Penal Code, for

Crimes against the Personality of the State.

somministrazióne di medicinàli guàsti (commèrcio o)—commerce in or supplying spoiled medicines. Whoever holds for commerce, places in commerce or supplies spoiled or imperfect medicines, is punished with imprisonment. Art. 443, Italian Penal Code.

somministrazióne di bevànde alcoòliche a minóri o a inférmi di ménte—supplying alcoholic beverages to minors or those mentally ill. Operators of inns or other public shops where food and beverages are sold, which supply, in a public place or one open to the public, alcoholic beverages to a minor of sixteen years, or to a person who appears to be mentally ill, or is in a manifest condition of psychic deficiency due to another illness, is punished with arrest. If drunkenness results from the act, the penalty is increased. Sentence imports suspension of the right to operate. Art. 689, Italian Penal Code.

somministrazióne di bevànde alcoòliche a persóna in stàto di manifèsta ubriachézza — supplying alcoholic beverages to a person in a manifest state of drunkenness. It is a violation punished with arrest. If the guilty party is an operator of an inn or other public shop for the sale of foods or beverages, the sentence will carry as punishment the suspension of the license to exercise the business. Art. 691, Italian Penal Code.

somministrazióne di medicinàli in mòdo pericolóso per la salúte pública—supplying medicines in a manner dangerous to public health. It is a crime punishable with imprisonment. Art. 445, Italian Penal Code.

somministrazióne di stupefacènti—supplying of narcotics. It is a crime punished with imprisonment. Art. 446, Italian Penal Code. See **stupefacènti (commèrcio clandestíno o fraudolènto di sostànze).**

sommissióne f.—submission.

sommòssa f.—uprising; riot; mutiny; instigation.

sónda f.—a thin instrument for sounding or measuring cavities in the human body.

sonería f.—the striking mechanism of clocks; a burglar alarm system.

sopiménto m.—the effect of being drowsy or sleepy; a soothing or calming effect.

sopíre—to begin to sleep; to allay; to calm; to soothe.

sopóre m.—sopor; drowsiness; lethargy; heavy sleep.

soporífero—soporific; that which induces sleep; a narcotic.

sopperíre—to provide for needs.

soppesàre—to calculate approximate weight by holding something in the hand.

soppiantàre—to supplant.

sopportàre—to support; to uphold; to sustain; to endure.

sopportazióne f.—support; endurance; assistance.

soppòrto m.—support; toleration.

sopprèssa f.—press; mangle.

soppressàre—to press; to squeeze.

soppressióne f.—suppression; abolition; overthrow; concealment; withholding from disclosure or publication.

soppressióne della persóna giurídica—extinction of the juridical (artificial) person. It is extinguished when its objective has been reached or it has become impossible. Partnerships are extinguished when all the partners are missing. See **estinzióne della persóna giurídica**, Art. 27, Italian Civil Code.

soppressióne, falsificazióne o sottrazióne di àtti o documénti concernénti la siurézza dello stàto—suppression, falsification or abstraction of Acts or documents concerning the security of the State. Whoever, in whole or in part, suppresses, destroys or falsifies, or otherwise takes with violence or artifice, or removes or diverts, even though temporarily, Acts or documents concerning the security of the State or other political interest of the State, whether internal or international, is punished with imprisonment. The death penalty is applied in cases provided by Military Law of war, if the act has compromised the preparation or efficiency for war of the State or its military operations. The penalties apply when the crime is committed to the damage of a foreign State allied or associated in war with the Italian State. Art. 255, 259, 268, 302, 21 (death penalty abolished), Italian Penal Code.

soppressióne di àtti véri—suppression or concealment of true (genuine) Acts. Whoever destroys, withholds or conceals, in whole or in part, a public Act or a genuine private writing is punished with imprisonment. Art. 490, 491, Italian Penal Code.

soppressióne di cadàvere — concealment of a cadaver. Whoever destroys, conceals or withholds a cadaver, or a part thereof, or withholds or scatters its ashes, is punished with imprisonment. The penalty is increased if the act is committed in cemeteries or other places of burial, deposit or custody. Art. 411, Italian Penal Code. See occultaménto di cadàvere.

soppressióne di corrispondènza (violazióne, sottrazióne e)—violation, abstraction and suppression of correspondence. Whoever obtains cognizance of the contents of closed or sealed correspondence not directed to him, or, abstracts or disturbs sealed or open correspondence not directed to him, for the purpose of taking cognizance thereof himself or for others, or, destroys or suppresses it, is punished with imprisonment, unless it is not otherwise foreseen as a crime by some other disposition of the law. If the guilty party, without just cause, reveals, in whole or in part, the contents of the correspondence and damage results from the act, the punishment is increased unless that act constitutes a more serious crime. The crime is punishable upon the complaint of the person damaged. This section applies to letters, telegraphic and telephonic communications. Art. 616-620, Italian Penal Code.

soppresióne di stàto (supposizióne o)—supposition or suppression of status. Whoever records in the State civil registers an inexistent birth is punished with imprisonment. A person is subjected to the same punishment, who suppresses the civil status of a new born child by concealing his birth. Art. 566, Italian Penal Code. Also, supposizióne o soppressióne di stàto. See alterazióne di stàto.

soppressióne di testaménto—suppression or concealment of a testament. A party who has suppressed, concealed or altered a testament which regulates the succession, is excluded from the succession as unworthy. Art. 463, subd. 5, Italian Civil Code.

sopprímere—to suppress; to conceal.

sopraddàzio m.—a duty imposed in addition to the ordinary one.

sopraddòte f.—an allowance which a bride brings in addition to her dowry.

sopraedificàre—to build above, especially, on a pre-existing building. Also, sopraelevàre.

sopraedificazióne f.—the act of building above another structure. See sopraelevazióne.

sopraelevàre—to build higher; to build on a pre-existing story.

sopraelevazióne f.—act of building higher or constructing on a pre-existing story. It is not permitted if the static conditions of the building do not permit it, if it prejudices the architectural appearance of the building, or notably diminishes the air and light of the lower floors. The builder must indemnify the other condominium owners in an amount equal to the actual value of the area of the new construction, divided by the number of floors, including those to be built, less the amount of his own share. He must, also, reconstruct the terrace which all, or part, of the condominiums had the right to enjoy. Art. 1127, Italian Civil Code.

sopraffàre—to overcome; to surpass.

sopraggiúngere — to arrive unexpectedly; to take unawares.

sopraggravàre—to overload; to surcharge.

soprallegàto—above cited; above mentioned.

sopralluògo m.—on the spot visit by a magistrate of the scene of a crime or place in dispute.

sopralluògo—on the spot.

sopranominàto—above named.

soprappagàre—to overpay. Also, sovrappagàre.

soprapprèzzo m.—a price beyond the normal price; overprice; a sum received for corporate stock issued at a price greater than its nominal value. Art. 2430, Italian Civil Code.

soprapprofítto m.—a greater profit made on a sale of merchandise for any reason.

sopràrbitro m.—an arbiter called to determine the correctness of a decision of other arbiters or arbitrators.

soprascàrpa m. — overshoe; rubber shoe.

soprassàlto m.—sudden attack; unexpected movement or attack.

soprassedére—to supersede; to forbear; to omit; to displace; to supplant; to replace; to postpone action.

soprasuòlo or soprassuòlo m.—topsoil; surface soil. See sottosuòlo.

soprastallía f.—the period of time a vessel is detained in excess of the normal period required to load and unload a vessel and for which extra compensation is given in proportion to the period of delay. Also, controstallía. See stallía—demurrage.

soprastaménto m.—delay; superiority; demurrer.

soprastànte—superintendent.

soprastàre — to stand above; to be superior; to defer; to linger; to superintend.

soprastruttúra f.—superstructure.

sopravanzàre—to exceed in number or measure; to jut out.

sopravvedére—to oversee; to supervise; to manage.

sopravveniènte m.—one who arrives unexpectedly; a posthumous child.

sopravveniènza f.—the act and effect of arriving unexpectedly or posthumously. See revocazióne per sopravveniènza di fígli. Art. 803, Italian Civil Code.

sopravveniménto—unforeseen event.

sopravveníre—to arrive unexpectedly.

sopravvènto m.—windward; the taking advantage over a person; having the upper hand or the best of it; the imposing of one's will over another.

sopravvenúta f.—unexpected arrival.

sopravvivènte m.—survivor.

sopravvivènza f.—surviving; survivorship; outliving. See commoriènza and premoriènza.

sopravvívere—to survive.

soprintendènte m. — superintendent. Also, sovrintendènte.

soprintendènza f. — superintendence; office of the superintendent. Also, sovrintendènza.

soprintèndere—to superintend. Also, sovrintèndere.

soprúso m.—abuse; overbearing act; act of taking unfair advantage of another.

sorbétto m.—ice-cream; sherbet; iced drink.

sorbíre—to sip.

sórdo m.—deaf.

sordomúto m.—deaf and dumb; deafmute. He may be disqualified from managing his own affairs. Art. 415, Italian Civil Code. See inabilitazióne.

sorèlla f.—sister. Marriages between sisters and brothers are prohibited whether they are german, consanguineous or uterine. Art. 87, Italian Civil Code. See germàni (fratèlli e sorèlle), unilateràli (fratèlli e sorèlle), uteríni (fratèlli e sorèlle) and consanguínei (fratèlli e sorèlle).

sorgènte f. — source; spring water; running water; headwaters. It is considered an immovable and part of real property. Art. 812, Italian Civil Code.

sórgere—to arise; to rise; to issue.

sorgíva f.—spring water; source of water.

sorpassàre—to surpass; to excel; to rise above; to overtake and pass on.

sorprèndere—to surprise.

sorprésa f.—surprise.

sorrègere—to sustain; to hold up; to bear up; to support.

sórso m.—sip; draught.

sòrta f.—sort; kind; species; class.

sòrte f.—sort; chance; luck; fate; destiny; capital or money given at interest.

sorteggiàre—to draw by lot; to assign by lot or chance.

sortéggio m.—drawing.

sortilègio m.—sorcery; witchcraft.

sortílego m.—sorcerer; wizard.

sortíre—to choose or draw by lots; to go out; to sally forth.

sortíta f.—assortment; choice; sortie; sudden issuing of troops from a besieged place to attack the enemy; gate of a fort; the entrance of an actor on stage.

sorvegliànza f. — surveillance; close watch; supervision.

sorvegliànza speciàle—special surveillance or supervision. It is a preventive measure taken against persons considered dangerous to public security and morality and members of the Mafia. Also, vigilànza speciàle. See misúre di prevenzióne, and misúre di prevenzióne cóntro la màfia, Usual Laws, Appendix to Appendix to Italian Code of Penal Procedure.

sorvegliàre—to conduct a surveillance; to maintain close watch; to inspect; to oversee; to supervise; to survey.

sorvolàre—to fly above; to soar.

soscrívere—to subscribe; to sign. Also, sotttoscrivere.

soscrizióne f.—subscription; signature. Also, sottoscrizióne.

sospèndere—to suspend; to hang up; to put a stop to.

sospendiménto m.—suspension.

sospensióne f.—suspension.

sospensióne condizionàle della péna—conditional suspension of punishment. Where a sentence of imprisonment is imposed for a determined period, or a money fine imposed, alone or jointly with the detentive penalty, the judge may order the suspension of the execution of the sentence for prescribed periods, depending upon whether the crime was a delitto or contravvenzióne. Art. 163, Italian Penal Code; Art. 590, Italian Code of Penal Procedure.

sospensióne dei procèssi—suspension of (civil) actions. These involve proceedings challenging the competence of a judge to hear a case in a civil case. Art. 48, 47, Italian Code of Civil Procedure. See regolaménto di competènza.

sospensióne del córso della prescrizióne—suspension of the running of prescription. It remains suspended in cases requiring the authorization of the Minister of Justice before proceeding (Art. 313), or of a suit deferred to another proceeding, and in every case in which suspension of the penal proceeding is imposed by a particular disposition of law. Art. 159, Italian Penal Code. See sospensióne della prescrizióne.

sospensióne del procediménto—suspension of the proceeding in a penal action. When the accused finds himself in such a state of mental infirmity to exclude his capacity to understand or to make free decisions, the judge may suspend the proceeding. Art. 88, Italian Code of Penal Procedure. See capacità d'intèndere e volére.

sospensióne del procèsso—suspension of the civil cause of action. Art. 295-298, Italian Code of Civil Procedure.

sospensióne della prescrizióne—suspension of prescriptive rights. They are suspended between certain parties bearing determined relationships to each other. Ex., (1) between spouses; (2) between a person exercising parental authority and those subject to it; (3) between guardian and minor or one interdicted from managing his affairs, till the final accounting; (4) between trustee and emancipated minor or one disqualified from managing his affairs; (5) between an heir and an accepted inheritance with benefit of inventory; (6) between persons whose property is subjected by law or judicial disposition to another's management and those exercising such management, till the rendering and definitive approval of the accounting; (7) between juridical persons and their managers or directors, while in office, for actions against them for which they may be responsible; (8) between a debtor, who has fraudulently concealed the existence of a debt, and a creditor, till the fraud is discovered. Art. 2941, 2942, Italian Civil Code. See **sospensióne del córso della prescrizióne.**

sospensíva f.—deferment; suspension.

sospensívo—suspensive; doubtful; uncertain.

sospéso—suspended; pendent.

sospettàre—to suspect.

sospètto m.—suspicion; suspect.

sospètto—suspicious; doubtful.

sospètto (legíttimo)—legitimate suspicion. It involves a suspicion of bias in a certain area which may impede a fair trial for one accused of a crime. Also, **suspicióne (legíttimo).** See **rimessióne dei procediménti,** Art. 55-60, Italian Code of Penal Procedure.

sospiràre—to breathe; to sigh.

sòsta f.—pause; cessation; stop; the stopping or parking by a driver of an unattended vehicle. Proper measures to avoid accidents must be taken by the driver of a vehicle or animal, during a protracted stoppage. Art. 115, Còdice della stràda (Code of the Road). See **stràde.**

sòsta (divièto di)—stopping or parking prohibited.

sostànza f.—substance; essence.

sostànze (pl.) f.—substances. Regard-

ing the poisoning, adulteration, supplying and commerce in foodstuffs, medicinals and narcotics the Penal Code specifies various punishments. Art. 439-448, 516, 518, Italian Penal Code.

sostégno m.—support; prop.

sostenére—to support.

sosteniménto m.—sustenance; maintenance; support.

sostenitóre m. (sostenitríce f.)—sustainer; maintainer.

sostentaménto m.—sustenance; maintenance.

sostentàre—to provide; to sustain; to maintain.

sostituíre—to substitute; to nominate a second person to take under a will if the one first named cannot or refuses to accept the inheritance.

sostitúto m.—substitute.

sostitúto del mandatàrio—substitute of the mandatary. The mandatary who, in the execution of a mandate, substitutes others to himself without being authorized, or, without it being necessary by the nature of his duties, is responsible for the work done by the substituted person. If the mandator had authorized the substitution without indicating the person to be substituted, the mandatary is liable only for his error in the choice. The mandatary is liable for the instructions he has imparted to the substitute. The mandator may act directly against the person substituted by the mandatary. Art. 1717, Italian Civil Code. See **mandànte** and **mandatàrio.**

sostituzióne f.—substitution; the nomination of a person to take under a will if the individual first named cannot or refuses to accept the inheritance as heir or legatee. See **sostitutizióne ordinària, sostituzióne volgàre** and **sostituzióne fedecommissària.**

sostituzióne di neonàto—substitution of a newborn child. See **alterazióne di stàto** and **supposizióne o soppressióne di stàto.**

sostituzióne di persóna—substitution of

person. Whoever, for the purpose of obtaining an advantage to himself or others, or causing damage to others, leads someone into error, and illegally substitutes his own person for that of another, or attributes to himself or to others a false name, or a false status, or a character to which the law attributes legal effects, is punished with imprisonment if the act itself does not constitute another crime against public faith and credit. Art. 494, Italian Penal Code.

sostituzióne fedecommissària—a testamentary disposition similar to a trust. The parents, the ascendants in direct line or the spouse of a person interdicted for mental incapacity or of a minor in a state of habitual mental infirmity, may make such a disposition. They may designate a son, descendant or a spouse to conserve and at death, to turn over the property, including the legitimate share (leggítima), to the person or institutions who, under supervision of the guardian, had the care of the interdicted person or minor. Art. 692-699, Italian Civil Code.

sostituzióne ordinària—ordinary substitution. The testator may substitute another person to take under a will if the person first designated cannot or refuses to accept the inheritance or bequest as heir or legatee. Art. 688-691, Italian Civil Code. Also, **sostituzióne volgàre** and **sostituzióne testamentària**.

sostituzióne testamentària—testamentary substitution. See **sostituzióne ordinària**.

sostituzióne volgàre—common substitution. See **sostituzióne ordinària**.

sottéchi—furtively; stealthily. Also, **sottòcchi**.

sotterfúgio m.—subterfuge.

sotterràneo—subterranean; below the the surface of the earth.

sotterràre—to bury; to inter.

sottòcchi or sottòcchio — furtively; stealthily. Also, **sottéchi**.

sottointendènte m.—sub-manager; assistant manager.

sottointèndere — to understand that which is not stated explicitly.

sottointéso—that which is understood implicitly, but not stated expressly.

sottomaríno m.—submarine. Also, **sommergíbile**.

sottomaríno—under water.

sottomissióne f.—submission.

sottopassàgio m.—underpassage.

sottopórre—to subject; to place under.

sottoposizióne f.—subjection; submission.

sottopósto—placed under; subject to; exposed (to a risk).

sottoscrítto—subscribed; signed.

sottoscrittóre m.—signatory.

sottoscrívere—to subscribe; to sign.

sottoscrizióne f.—subscription; the act of signing; collection of signatures for a specific purpose.

sottoscrizióne autenticáta della scrittúra privàta — authenticated subscription of a private document. The subscribed signature which is authenticated by a notary or other public official empowered to do so, will be recognized. The authentication consists in an attestation of the public official that the subscribed signature was affixed in his presence. The public official must first ascertain the identity of the subscribing person. Art. 2703, Italian Civil Code. See **autenticazióne della scrittúra privàta**.

sottoscrizióne di azióne—subscription to shares of stock of a corporation. Art. 2329, 2333, 2335, Italian Civil Code.

sottoscrizióne di testaménto ològrafo —subscription of a holographic will. Art. 602, Italian Civil Code. See **testaménto ològrafo**.

sottoscrizióne di testamènto púbblico— subscription of a public will. Art. 603, Italian Civil Code. See **testaménto púbblico**.

sottosuòlo m.—subsoil; ownership of land (surface soil) extends to the subsoil with everything that it contains, and the owner thereof may make any excavation or work that does not cause damage to his neighbor. This disposition does not apply to the objectives of the laws on mines, quarries and peat bogs. Equally excepted, are the limitations deriving from the laws on antiquities and fine arts, over waters, over hydraulic works and by other special laws. The owner of the surface soil cannot oppose the activities of third parties undertaken at such depth of the subsoil, or at such height in the space over the surface of the land, that he would have no interest in excluding them. Art. 840, 943, Italian Civil Code.

sottràrre—to abstract; to take away; to subtract; to withdraw; to withhold.

sottrazióne f.—subtraction; deduction; taking away; withholding; defalcation.

sottrazióne consensuàle di minorènni—consensual taking away of minors. Whoever takes away from a parent exercising parental authority, or from a guardian, a minor who has completed fourteen years of age, with the latter's consent, or detains him against the will of the said parent or guardian, is punished with imprisonment. The penalty is reduced if the act was committed for the purpose of matrimony; it is increased if it was committed for a lustful purpose. Art. 573, Italian Penal Code.

sottrazióne di cadàvere—withholding of a cadaver. See **distruzióne, soppressióne o sottrazióne di cadàvere.** Also, see **cadàvere (úso illegíttimo di).**

sottrazióne di còse comúni—taking or withholding of common property. The co-owner, partner or co-heir who, for the purpose of procuring a profit to himself or others, takes over possession of the common property, withholding it from the one who has its custody, is punished with imprisonment. Art. 627, Italian Penal Code.

sottrazióne di persóne incapàci—taking away of persons lacking capacity. Whoever takes away a minor of age fourteen, or a person of infirm mind from a parent exercising parental authority, from a guardian, or from a trustee of property (curator), or from one having his care and custody, is punished with imprisonment. The same penalty applies to one who takes away or detains a minor who has completed fourteen years, without his consent, for a purpose other than lust or matrimony. Art. 574, Italian Penal Code.

sottrazióne in bancaròtta fraudolènta—defalcation in a fraudulent bankruptcy. It involves one's act of having abstracted, destroyed or falsified, in whole or in part, the books or other records of accounts, or keeping them in such manner as to render impossible the reconstruction of the property of the bankrupt or the operations of his affairs, for the purpose of gaining an unjust profit to himself or others, or causing damage to the creditors. It is punishable with imprisonment. Art. 216, 219, 223, Falliménto (Bankruptcy), Usual Laws, Appendix to Italian Civil Code.

sottrazióne o dannegiaménto di còse sottopóste a pignoraménto o a sequèstro—taking away or damaging property placed under attachment or sequestration. It is a crime punished with imprisonment. It involves the taking away, concealment, destruction, dispersion or deterioration of a thing placed under attachment or sequestration, and entrusted to one's custody, for the sole purpose of aiding the owner of the property. Art. 334, Italian Penal Code.

soverchiàre—to surpass; to exceed; to overflow; to browbeat.

soverchiatóre m. (soverchiatríce f.)—overbearing person.

soverchiería f.—abuse of power; overbearing conduct.

sovèrchio m.—excess; that which is overabundant.

sovèrchio — excessive; superfluous; over-abundant.

sovraccàrico m.—overloaded.

sovranità f.—sovereignty.

sovràno m.—sovereign.

sovrastàre—to stand above; to be higher; to overcome.

sovrinendènte m. — superintendent. Also, **soprintendènte.**

sovrintendènza f. — superintendence; office of the superintendent. Also, **soprintendènza.**

sovveníre—to aid; to assist; to succor.

sovventóre m.—one who furnishes material aid and assistance.

sovventóri di bànda armàta—persons giving aid and assistance to an armed band. They are subject to imprisonment equally with those who promote, constitute or organize it. Art. 306, Italian Penal Code.

sovvenzióne f.—subsidy.

sovversióne f.—subversion.

sovversivísmo m.—the tendency to subvert the order of the State. See **propagànda ed apología sovversíva o anti-nazionàle.**

sovversívo m.—one who seeks to overthrow the government and alter its constitution; subverter.

sovversívo—subversive.

sovvertiménto m.—subversion; overthrow.

sovvertíre—to subvert; to overthrow.

sovvertíto—subverted; overthrown.

sovvertitóre 'm. (sovvertitríce f.)—subverter.

spacciàre—to sell; to sell at retail; to dispatch.

spàccio m.—a place or shop where goods are sold; retail shop; dispatch.

spàcco m.—split; crack; opening or slit in a dress along its length. Also, **sparàto.**

spàda f.—sword; swordsman; a spade in a game of cards.

spadaccíno m.—one adept at swordplay; a swaggering bully seeking swordplay.

spadronàre—to take over as the owner in an offensive manner.

spadroneggiàre—to order imperiously; to act as though one were the owner.

spalancàre—to throw wide open.

spalàre—to remove the props; to shovel away; in rowing, to feather the strokes.

spalleggiàre—to shoulder; to support; to sustain; to aid; to walk a horse with a good action.

spallétta f.—parapet; embankment.

spallièra f.—back of a chair or sofa.

spallière m.—the oarsman placed on the stern bench of a large rowboat.

spallína f.—epaulet.

spallóne m.—one who carries on the shoulder; a porter of contraband merchandise.

spalmàre—to smear; to tar; to grease.

spàlto m.—glacis; gentle slope or declivity; in a fort, the natural or artificial slope from the counterscarp to the open country.

sparagnàre—to save; to spare. See **risparmiàre**, which is in common use.

sparàgno m.—savings. See **rispàrmio.**

sparàre—to shoot; to discharge a firearm; to rip open; to disembowel; to unfurnish a house; to remove decorations.

sparàta f.—discharge of firearms; great promises; boasting.

sparàto m.—opening or slit in a dress along its length; opening in a shirt. Also, **spàcco.**

sparàto—a disemboweled animal.

sparatóre m. (sparatríce f.)—shooter.

sparatòria f.—an affray wherein firearms are discharged; a discharge of firearms; a harmless discharge of firearms.

sparecchiàre — to clear away (the table); to devour.

sparéggio m.—disparity.

spàrgere—to scatter; to spread.

spargiménto m. — effusion; pouring out; scattering.

sparíre—to disappear.

sparizióne f.—disappearance.

sparlàre—to speak ill of.

spàro m.—discharge of firearms; volley; opening in a dress.

spàrso—dispersed; scattered.

spartiménto m.—distribution; division; partition; sharing.

spartíre — to allot; to divide; to separate; to share.

spartizióne f.—division; separation.

sparúto—thin; wan.

sparvière or sparvièro m.—hawk; a mason's trowel.

spasimàre—to suffer acute pain; to have eager desire for a person.

spàsimo m.—spasm; a sudden, involuntary muscular contraction; acute pain; figuratively, an eager desire for a person.

spàsmo m.—spasm; convulsion. See spàsimo.

spassàre—to amuse.

spasseggiàre—to walk about.

spasseggiàta f.—a walk; a turn about.

spassionàto—dispassionate.

spàsso m.—amusement; pastime.

spàsso (a)—out of work; unemployed.

spauríre—to alarm; to frighten.

spavaldería f.—effrontery; impudence.

spavàldo—impudent; shameless.

spaventaménto m.—fright; terror.

spaventàre—to frighten.

spaventàto—frightened.

spavènto m.—fright; terror.

spaventóso—frightful.

spazzacamíno m.—chimney-sweep.

spazzanéve m.—a triangular contrivance placed in front of a locomotive to clear the snow in front of it on the tracks.

spazzàre—to sweep.

spazzavía m.—a triangular contrivance placed in front of a locomotive to clear the track of obstructions; a cowcatcher.

spazzíno m.—street sweeper.

spàzzo m.—ground; pavement.

spàzzola f.—brush.

spècchio m.—mirror.

spècie f.—species.

spècie (fár)—to make an impression; to surprise.

specificazióne f.—specification. A mode of acquiring property by transforming materials belonging to another to form something new, whether or not the material used may be able to regain its prior form. The one so transforming the material acquires title to it, but must pay the original owner the price of the material, except where the value of the material greatly surpasses the work involved, in which case the thing belongs to the owner of the material, who must pay the price of the work. Art. 940, Italian Civil Code.

spedíre—to ship or forward goods and merchandise; to dispatch; to expedite; to send (a letter).

spedíre una càusa—to hear a case and render judgment.

spedíre una ricètta—to fill a prescription.

spedizióne f.—expedition; dispatch; forwarding; shipment. It is a contract of mandate, whereby the shipper assumes the obligation of concluding, in his own name and on behalf of the mandator, a transportation contract and to fulfill the accessory operations. Art. 1737-1741, 1703, 1678, Italian Civil Code.

spedizióne in fórma esecutíva—issuance of judgments and orders in executive form. Judgments and other Orders or dispositions of the Judicial Authorities and Acts received from a notary or other public official in order to have the efficacy of an executive title (títolo esecutívo), leading to a forced execution, must, first, be provided with the executive formula, unless the law disposes otherwise. The issuance of the title (judgments and orders) in executive form may be made only to the party in whose behalf the disposition or stipulated obligation was made, or to his successors, with the indication at the bottom thereof, of the person to whom it is issued. The issuance in executive form, is headed: "Italian Republic. In the name of the Law," and the affixing by the court clerk, notary or other public official, of the following formula on the original or copy: "We command all Judicial Officials who may be requested and to whomever it may concern, to put into execution the present title, and to the Public Prosecutor to furnish assistance, and to all officials of public security to cooperate when legally requested." Art. 475, 474, Italian Code of Civil Procedure; Art. 153, Enabling Rules, Code of Civil Procedure. See título esecutívo and esecuzióne forzàta.

spedizionière m.—forwarding agent; shipper; the official at the Vatican who issues Papal Briefs and Bulls.

spegnàre—to redeem from a pledge or pawn.

spègnere—to extinguish; to put out; to quench.

spelàre—to peel; to pluck; in a figurative sense to fleece a person of his money; to remove hairs; to depilate.

spelàto—one who has lost his hair; fig., one who has been "plucked", or fleeced of his money.

spellàre—to excorciate; to remove the skin; to cheat money from a person.

spérdere—to lose; to waste.

spérdere la creatúra—to miscarry.

sperdiménto m.—dispersion; miscarriage.

sperdúto—lost; wasted.

spergiuraménto m.—false oath; perjury.

spergiuràre—to swear falsely.

spergiuratóre m. (**spergiuratríce** f.)—perjurer.

spergiúro m.—perjury; perjurer. See fàlso giuraménto della pàrte and fàlsa testimoniànza.

sperimentàre—to experiment.

speriménto m.—experiment.

spérma m.—sperm; seminal fluid.

speróne m.—spur; ram on a warship.

sperperaménto m.—dissipation; wasting.

sperperàre—to dissipate; to lose; to waste; to destroy.

sperpètua f. — calamity; misfortune; accident.

spèrso—lost; dispersed.

spésa f.—cost; expense; marketing or household expense.

spése di esecuzióne delle condànne e di manteniménto in càrcere—costs of executing the sentence and of maintenance in prison. Costs relative to execution of the sentence are borne by the State without right of recovery. Costs of maintenance in prison are borne by the prisoner with credit for work performed. Art. 612, Italian Code of Penal Procedure; Art. 145, Italian Penal Code. See anticipazióne delle spése and ricúpero delle spése processuàli anticipàte dallo stàto.

spése per il manteniménto del condannàto—costs for the maintenance of a condemned person. The condemned person is required to reimburse the State treasury the expenses for his maintenance in penal institutions and he responds for such obligation with all his personal and real property, present and future according to the rules of the civil laws. This obligation does not apply to those civilly responsible and is not transmitted to the heirs of the condemned. The State has a legal right of hypothecation over the property of the accused as a guaranty for the payment of: (1) pecuniary penalties and any other sum owed the State treasury; (2) costs of the proceeding; (3) costs relative to maintenance of the condemned in penal institutions; (4) costs sustained by a public health institute for care and food for the injured person during his infirmity; (5) sums owed as compensation for damages; (6) expenses advanced by defense counsel and fees owed him for his honorarium. Art. 188, 189, 191, Italian Penal Code.

spessóre m.—thickness.

spettàcoli oscèni (pubblicazióni e)—obscene publications and performances. It involves the making and introduction into the territory of the State, for the purpose of commerce or distribution or public display and circulation, writings, designs, pictures or other obscene objects and the offering of public, theatrical or cinematographic performances of an obscene nature. It is punished with imprisonment and fine. Art. 528, 529, Italian Penal Code.

spettàcolo m. — spectacle; performance; public exhibition; stage play.

spettàre—to belong to; to concern.

speziàle m. — apothecary; druggist; pharmacist.

spìa f.—spy.

spiàggia f.—beach; sea shore. It is part of the public domain. Art. 822, Italian Civil Code.

spiccàre—to detach; to unhook; to stand out; to be prominent; to pronounce clearly; to emit or dispatch.

spicciàre—to dispatch; to expedite.

spìcciolo m.—loose change.

spièdo m.—spit; spear.

spietàto—pitiless; cruel.

spìga f.—ear of corn.

spigionàre—to remain untenanted or unlet.

spigionàto—unrented; unleased.

spignoràre—to remove from attachment, pledge or lien.

spìgo m.—lavender.

spigolàre—to glean, to gather wheat left by reapers.

spigolàre, rastrellàre o raspollàre nei fòndi altrùi—gleaning wheat, raking or gleaning grapes on the lands of others. See **fùrti punìbili a querèla dell'offéso**, Art. 626, Subd. 3, Italian Penal Code.

spìlla f.—pin. See **spìllo**.

spillàtico m.—pin-money. Formerly, a contractual arrangement whereby a wife received an annual income from her dowry for small expenses and personal needs.

spìllo m. — pin; brad-awl; gimlet; probe.

spìllo di sicurézza—safety-pin.

spìna f.—thorn.

spìna dorsàle—spinal column.

spionàggio m.—espionage.

spionàggio di notìzie di cùi e stàta vietàta la divulgazióne—espionage of information whose divulgence has been prohibited. Whoever obtains, for the purpose of political or military espionage, information whose divulgence has been prohibited by the competent Authorities, is punished with imprisonment. The penalty of life imprisonment is applied if the act is committed in the interest of a State at war with the Italian State, or, if the act has compromised the war preparation or efficiency of the State, or military operations. Art. 258, 259, Italian Penal Code.

spionàggio polìtico o militàre—political or military espionage. Whoever obtains, for the purpose of political or military espionage, information which in the interest of the security of the State, or in any manner, should remain secret in the internal or international political interest of the State is punished with imprisonment. The penalty of life imprisonment is applied: (1) if the act is committed in the interest of a State at war with the Italian State; (2) if the act has compromised the war preparation or efficiency of the State, or military operations. Art. 257, 259, Italian Penal Code.

spodestàre—to deprive of power; to deprive of one's property; to dispossess. Also, **dispodestàre**.

spogliàre—to undress; to deprive; to despoil to divest; to plunder. Also, **dispogliàre**.

spòglio m.—act of divesting or despoiling. See **azióne di reintegrazióne** and Art. 1168, 1169, Italian Civil Code.

spoliazióne f.—spoliation; the act of despoiling or plundering; the appropriation of the property of others.

spolpàre—to remove the flesh from a bone; figuratively, to fleece someone.

spolverìna f.—dust cloak.

spolverìno m.—feather duster.

spònda f.—extreme side; edge; shore; strand; border; parapet; side of a cart.

276

spónde e àrgine (riparazióne di)—repairs to banks and dikes. When banks and dikes have been destroyed in whole or in part, or have been thrown down, or because of the natural variation in the course of the water it becomes necessary to construct new dikes or restorations and the owner of the land does not undertake to repair or construct them with diligence, each of the owners who have suffered or could suffer damage, may undertake such work, after first obtaining authorization from the Praetor on an emergency basis. The work is to be performed without causing damage to the owner of the land. All the proprietors who benefit by the work must contribute to the cost in proportion to the benefit each one obtains. Art. 915-917, Italian Civil Code.

spondàggio m.—wharfage.

sponsàli m. — betrothal; mutual promise of marriage. The promise of marriage does not produce a legal obligation to contract it nor to perfrom that which had been agreed. In the event that the marriage is not performed, the promisor may demand restitution of the gifts made by reason of the promise of marriage. A promise of marriage, mutually made by public Act, or private writing by a person in his majority or by a minor permitted to marry by reason of Art. 84, obliges the promisor who refuses without just cause to perform it, to compensate the other party for expenses incurred and for obligations contracted because of that promise. The damage is compensated within the limits which the expenses and obligations correspond to the conditions of the parties. Art. 79-81, 84, Italian Civil Code.

spontaneità f.—spontaneity; quality of being spontaneous. It is a mitigating circumstance in a crime, when before trial, one has spontaneously and effectively worked to remove or mitigate the damaging or dangerous consequences of the crime. Art. 62, 62 bis, Italian Penal Code.

spòrto m.—a projection in a building.

There is a presumption that such a projection belongs to the owner of the land and wall from which the projection appears. Art. 881, 905, Italian Civil Code.

spòsa f.—spouse; bride; betrothed.

sposalízio m.—nuptials; wedding.

sposàre—to marry.

sposàto—married.

spòso m.—spouse; husband.

spòsi (pl.) m. — married couple; spouses.

spossàre—to exhaust; to weaken.

spostàre—to remove from its place; to misplace; to transfer.

spostàto m.—one who is out of place socially or in his job; one who is debt-ridden.

sprànga f.—cross-bar; metal wire for mending china.

sprecàre—to squander; to waste.

spregévole—contemptible; despicable.

sprègio m.—contempt; disdain; scorn.

spregiudicàre—to be impartial; to be unprejudiced.

spretàre—to renounce the clerical life; to unfrock.

sprezzàre—to despise; to disdain; to contemn.

sprigionaménto m. — release from prison.

sprigionàre—to release from prison; to emit (gas).

spropiàre—to expropiate; to oust; to dispossess.

spropiazióne f.—expropiation.

spropòsito m.—absurdity; nonsense; excess.

sprovvedére—to leave unprovided.

spurgàre—to cleanse; to purge; to spit.

spúrgo di pózzi e di latríne—cleansing of wells and latrines. The cleansing of wells and latrines is at the expense of the lessor. Art. 1610, Italian Civil Code.

squílla f.—a tinkling bell attached to domestic animals.

squillàre—to sound loud and shrill.

squílli di trómba—blasts of a horn. It is a signal to order the dispersal of a crowd meeting in a public place which is involved in seditious manifestations. The dispersal is ordered with three, separate, formal orders of the Authorities, each preceded by a blast of the horn. Art. 23, Sicurézza Púbblica (Public Security), Tèsto Único (Unified Text) and Art. 25, Public Security Regulations, Usual Laws, Appendix to Italian Code of Penal Procedure. See **riunióni públiche.**

stabbiàre—to fold or enclose domestic animals so as to manure the ground.

stàbbio m.—the fold or enclosure for domestic animals.

stàbile m.—a house or piece of real property.

stàbile—settled; stable.

stàbili (bèni)—houses and lands.

stabiliménti e locàli assimilàti agli albèrghi—establishments and premises similar or conforming to hotels. The operators of health homes, establishments of public spectacles (shows), bathing pavilions, pensions (boarding houses), eating houses (restaurants), sleeping cars and similar places, have the same responsibility for things brought therein as an inn-keeper. Art. 1786, Italian Civil Code. See **responsabilità per le còse portàte in albèrgo.**

stabliménto m.—establishment; settlement; the act and effect of settling (peace); foundation.

stabulàrio m. — dog-pound; cattle-pound.

staccàre—to detach; to unhook.

staccàre il bollóre—to commence boiling.

staccàre la córsa—to begin the race.

staccàre le denúncie—to issue the denunciations or accusations; to denounce.

stàffa f.—stirrup; iron band.

staffétta f.—a courier or soldier on horseback or motorcycle who delivers orders; a pilot train or lomo-motive which precedes the principal one as a matter of precaution and safety.

stàgna f.—can. See **làtta.**

stagnàio m.—tinsmith. Also, **stagníno.**

stagnàre—to be stagnant; to stanch the flow of blood; to make water-tight; to line with tin.

stagnatúra f.—tin lining; tinning.

stagníno m.—tinsmith. Also, **stagnàio.**

stàgno m.—pond. See **làghi e stàgni.**

stàgno m.—tin.

stàgno—water-tight.

stàio m. (stàia f.)—a measure for cereals or dry foods; the area of ground required to produce a stàio of food.

stàlla f.—stable; stall. The distances to be observed between such a building and others of an offensive or dangerous nature from the boundary line of the property, must follow those set by the regulations and in the absence thereof, such measures necessary to preserve neighboring land from every damage to solidity, health and safety. Art. 890, Italian Civil Code.

stallía f.—demurrage; the period of time during which a vessel is detained for loading and unloading. See **controstallía** and **soprastallía.**

stàmpa f. — the press; impression; printing; stamp; punch; mould. Besides the responsibility of the author of a publication, the responsible director or vice-director of a newspaper issued at fixed times or otherwise, who fails to exercise the necessary control over its content to prevent the commission of crimes, is subject to punishment. Art. 57-58 bis, Italian Penal Code. See Art. 21, Constitution of the Italian Republic; Stàmpa, Usual Laws, Appendix to Italian Code of Penal Procedure.

stampàre—to print.

stampàti—printed materials. The sale, distribution or affixture in a public place or one open to the public, of writings or designs which the Authorities have ordered seized, is punishable with a fine. Art. 352, Italian Penal Code; also, Art. 663-664, idem.

stampàto—printed material.

stampàto alla màcchia—printed clandestinely.

stampatóre m. (stampatríce f.) — printer. He is responsible for the material published in a newspaper issued at fixed times or clandestinely, or otherwise, which may lead to crimes, in the event the writer is unknown or not chargeable, or the editor or responsible director is not indicated or chargeable. Art. 57-58 bis, Italian Penal Code. See **stàmpa.**

stampèlla f.—crutch. Also, **grúccia.**

stampería f. — printing shop; typographic shop. Also, **tipografía.**

stàmpo m.—stamp; punch.

stampóne m.—printer's proof sheet; galley proof. Also, **bòzza.**

stànga f.—bar; cross-bar; a long pole lowered to bar passage at street level and railway crossings; swing bar separating horses in a stable; a bar to hang clothes in a closet.

stànza di compensazióne — clearing house. An association of banks or credit institutions and exchanges for the adjustment and payment of daily balances among themselves. A presentation of a check to a clearing house is equivalent to a presentation for payment. Art. 34, Asségni (Checks), Usual Laws, Appendix to Italian Civil Code.

stàr del crédere — guaranty of payment. A del credere agent or factor is one, who in addition to his compensation, has a right to additional compensation for guaranteeing the execution of the transaction and its payment. Art. 1736, Italian Civil Code.

stàti emotívi o passionàli—states of emotion or passion. They do not exclude or diminish imputability for crime. Art. 90, Italian Penal Code; Art. 314, Italian Code of Penal Procedure.

stàto m.—condition; grade; state; status.

stàto civíle (ufficio di)—office of civil status. There is one in each commune or municipality. It maintains registers of citizenship, births, weddings and deaths. Art. 14, Stàto Civíle (Civil Status), Usual Laws, Appendix to Italian Civil Code; Art. 449-455, Italian Civil Code.

stàto di adottabilità (condizióni per lo) —conditions for the state of adoptability. Upon motion of the Public Prosecutor, the public and private institutions where a minor is sheltered, or a party having an interest therein, the Tribunal for Minors in the district in which minors under eight years of age are found, who are deprived of material and moral assistance by their parents or relatives held to provide for them, so long as such lack of assistance is not due to force majeure, may be declared adoptable. Art. 314/4-314/19, Italian Civil Code.

stàto d'incapacità procuràto mediànte violènza—state of incapacity procured by means of violence. Whoever, by means of hypnotic suggestion or during a dormant or drowsy condition, or by means of administering alcoholic or stupefying substances, or by any other means, puts a person, without his consent, in a state of being incapable of understanding or volition, is punished with imprisonment. Art. 613, 579, Italian Penal Code.

stàto di necessità nei fàtti illéciti— state of necessity in illicit facts. When the person committing a damaging act has been compelled by necessity to save himself or others from actual peril of grave damage to the person, which peril was not voluntarily caused by him, or was otherwise inevitable, an indemnity is due to the damaged party, whose measure is referred to the equitable assessment of the judge. Art. 2045, 2046, Italian Civil Code.

stàto di necessità nel reàto—state of necessity in crime. It is a mitigating circumstance to the act. A person is not subject to punishment for having been compelled by necessity to save himself or others from actual peril of grave damage to the person, which peril was not voluntarily caused by him, or was otherwise inevitable, provided that the act was proportionate to the peril. This disposition is not applicable to those whose lawful duty it is to expose themselves to the peril. Art. 54, 55, Italian Penal Code.

stàto e capacità delle persóne—status and capacity of persons. The status and capacity of persons and family relations are regulated by the law of the State to which they belong. Nevertheless, a foreigner if he performs an act for which he has no capacity under his national law, is considered as having capacity, if under Italian law, a citizen (of Italy) would have capacity, except when it pertains to family relations, of succession upon death, of gifts, or acts of disposition of real property situated abroad. Art. 17, et seq. Preliminary Dispositions.

stàto passívo del fallimento—state of liabilities in a bankruptcy. The clerk of the bankruptcy court prepares a chronological list of those creditors who demand to present their claims as liabilities of the bankrupt. It is then sent to the bankruptcy judge, who with the assistance of the trustee, after hearing the bankrupt and taking the necessary information, examines the claims and on the basis thereof, prepares the state of the liabilities in the bankruptcy. The judge indicates, specifically, the credits (claims) which are allowed, specifying if they are supported by priority, pledge or mortgage, and the credits (claims) which are disallowed, in whole or in part, summarily explaining the reasons for their total or partial exclusion and their relative guaranties. Art. 95, 92-94, 96-103, Falliménto (Bankruptcy), Usual Laws, Appendix to Italian Civil Code.

statúto m.—statute; charter; written law; a fundamental law which establishes the political order of a State.

statúto dei lavoratóri—the workers' charter. It contains the rules for safeguarding the liberty and dignity of workers, of union freedom and union activities in places of work and rules for their implementation. Art. 1-41, Statúto dei Lavoratóri, Usual Laws, Appendix to Italian Civil Code.

statúto delle associazióne—charter of associations and juridical persons. Associations, juridical persons and foundations must be established with a public Act. The establishing Act and the charter must contain the name of the organization, its purpose, capital and headquarters. Art. 14-16, Italian Civil Code.

stazionaménto m.—the parking of a vehicle.

stazionàre—to park a vehicle; to remain stopped in a place.

stazionàrio—stationary.

stazióne f.—station.

stàzza f.—a graduated rod for measuring the interior capacity of a vessel; the capacity, volume or tonnage of a vessel.

stàzzo m.—the measurement of vessel's capacity or tonnage; an enclosure for domestic animals. See **stàbbio**.

steccàta f.—blow with a stick.

steccàto m.—palisade; stockade.

stellàge m.—a premium contract on the exchange. See **contràtti di bórsa** and **contràtti stellàge**.

stellionàto m.—stellionate; the crime of fraudulently selling or mortgaging property that one does not own; the selling of the same property to different persons.

stèmma m.—coat of arms; crest; insignia.

stendàrdo m. — banner; standard; colors; principal insignia of an army.

stenografía f.—stenography. The minutes of a proceeding may be taken in shorthand or stenography. Art. 496, Italian Code of Penal Procedure.

sterilità f.—sterility.

sterilizzàre—to sterilize; to render sterile.

sterilizzazióne f.—sterilization.

sterminàre—to exterminate.

stermínio m. (sterminazióne f.)—extermination.

stíbio m.—antimony.

stillettàta f. — blow given with a stiletto.

stilètto m.—a type of dagger with a triangular blade.

stillicídio m.—drainage of waters. See scàrico delle àcque piovàne and scólo delle àcque.

stíllo m.—still; distillery. See alambícco and lambícco.

stíma f.—esteem; appraisal; evaluation.

stíme mòrte—appraisal of inanimate accessories to the land. See scòrte mòrte.

stíme víve—appraisal of live accessories to the land. See scòrte víve.

stipèndio m. — stipend; employee's wages; settled pay for services.

stípite m.—door post; stem without branches, but with fronds such as a palm; stock; lineage; relationship. See parentèla, Art. 74-77, Italian Civil Code.

stipulazióne f. — stipulation; agreement; contract. A stipulation or contract in favor of a third party is valid, so long as the stipulator has an interest therein. Art. 1411-1413, Italian Civil Code.

stírpe (s.), stírpe (pl.) f.—(Lat.—stirps, stirpes)—stirps; race; stock; lineage; the family of a person including ascendants and descendants. One taking the property of a descendent by representation acquires the succession *per stirpes*. Ex. Property is left by a parent to sons A and B. He is predeceased by son A who leaves two children, X and Z, who take A's share by representation. They each receive 25% of the estate, for a total of 50% and the balance of the 50% of the estate goes to B. Art. 469, 731, Italian Civil Code. See **reappresentazióne** and **càpi (per).**

stíva f.—the hold of a ship; handle of a plough.

stivàggio m.—the operation of putting goods in the hold of a ship.

stivàre—to place goods in the hold of a ship.

stivatóre m.—stevedore; a person engaged in the operation of loading and unloading a ship.

stòffa f.—stuff; fabric; material; the inyard qualities, character and abilities of a person.

stonacàre—to remove whitewash from a wall.

stonaménto m.—out of tune.

stonànte—dissonant; discordant.

stonàre—to be out of tune; to bewilder, in a figurative sense.

stonàta f.—the act and effect of being out of tune.

stonàta—out of tune; bewildered; confused.

stonatúra f.—out of tune; a thing, word, phrase or concept which is out of order; disorder; disharmony; discordance; dissonance.

stòrcere—to twist; to wrench; to unravel. Also, distòrcere.

stordíre—to stun; to astound.

stormíre—to rustle; to make noise.

stórmo m.—flock of birds; crowd.

stornàre—to turn aside; to turn back; to divert; to fall or run backwards as a car; to dissuade.

stornàre una partíta—to cancel and divert an entry in a ledger and carry it elsewhere.

stornàre una sómma—to divert a sum from a purpose to which it had been assigned.

stornàre un contràtto—to break a contract.

stórno m.—the act of diverting sums from a purpose to which they had been intended; a bird of the startling species; a lottery ticket sold out of turn.

storpiaménto m.—maiming; crippling. Also, **storpiatúra.**

storpiàre—to maim; to cripple. Also, **stroppiàre.**

storpiàto — crippled; maimed; deformed. Also, **stroppiàto.**

storpiàto m.—cripple; lame person. Also, **stroppiàto.**

storpiatúra m.—the act and effect of crippling; crippling; maiming.

stórpio m.—a lame person; hindrance.

stórpio—lame crippled.

stòrta f.—wrench; twisting; act of wrenching or twisting; curved sword; chemical retort.

stòrto—crooked; twisted; deformed.

stovíglie (pl.) f.—crockery and kitchen utensils.

stracciàre—to tear; to rend.

stracciàto—torn; one dressed in rags.

stràccio m.—rag; tatter; figuratively, a scrap of knowledge.

straccióne m.—one dressed in rags and tatters.

stràda (s.) f.—road; street; way.

stràde (pl.) f.—roads. If they belong to the State, they are part of the public domain, together with automobile highways, railroads, airdromes and acqueducts which belong to the State. Art. 822-824, Italian Civil Code; Stràde (Roads), Usual Laws, Appendix to Italian Civil Code.

stràde ferràte—railroads; railways. If they belong to the State, they are part of the public domain. Art. 822-824, Italian Civil Code; Ferrovíe (Railroads), Usual Laws, Appendix to Italian Civil Code; Blòcco stradàle (Road blockage), Usual Laws, Appendix to Italian Code of Penal Procedure.

stràge f.—carnage; massacre. See **devastazióne, sacchéggio e stràge.**

stragiudiziàle—extra-judicial.

stralciàre—to prune; to lop off.

strampalàto—extravagant; queer.

strangolàre—to strangle.

stranièra f.—foreigner. See **stranièro.**

stranièri (soggiórno degli stranièri nello stàto)—sojourn of foreigners within the State. Foreigners are required to present themselves, within three days of their entry into the territory of the State, to the Public Security Authorities in the place where they find themselves, to give notice of themselves and make a declaration of their sojourn. The same obligation is incumbent upon foreigners each time they transfer their residence from one commune of the State to another. Foreigners in transit who remain for pleasure within the territory of the State for a period not over two months, need only make the first declaration of entry. Art. 142-149, Tèsto único (Unified Text), Sicurézza Púbblica (Public Security), Usual Laws, Appendix to Italian Code of Penal Procedure. See **stranièri e apòlidi.**

stranièri e apòlidi—foreigners and stateless persons. Whoever gives lodging or entertainment to a foreigner or stateless person, by whatever designation, even if he is a relative or kinsman, or, for any reason takes him under his care, is required to communicate the particulars to the local Public Security Authorities within twenty four hours. This violation is a contravvenzióne punishable by arrest and fine. Art. 1, 2, stranièri e apòlidi, Usual Laws, Appendix to Italian Code of Penal Procedure; Art. 665, Italian Penal Code. See previous title.

stranièro m.—foreigner. The foreigner who is denied, in his own country, the effective exercise of the democratic liberties guaranteed by the Italian Constitution, has the right of asylum in the territory of the Republic under the conditions established by law. Extradition of the foreigner for political crimes is not permitted as it is not for citizens. Art. 10, 26, Constitution of the Italian Republic; Art. 13, Italian Penal Code; Art. 661-671, Italian Code of Penal Procedure.

stranièro convenúto—the foreigner as a defendant. He may be made a defendant before the judges of the

State. Art. 4, Italian Code of Civil Procedure.

stranièro (corruzióne del cittadíno da pàrte dello stranièro)—corruption of a citizen by a foreigner. See corruzióne del cittadíno da pàrte dello stranièro.

stranièro (espulsióne dello stàto)—expulsion of the foreigner from the State. See espulsióne dello stranièro dello stàto.

stranièro (matrimónio dello stranièro nello stàto)—marriage of the foreigner within the State. The foreigner who wishes to contract marriage within the State must present to the official of Civil Status a declaration from the competent Authority of his own country to the effect that, in conformance to the laws to which he is subject, there exists no impediment to the marriage. Art. 116, Italian Civil Code.

strapagàre—to overpay.

strappàre—to pull away; to snatch; to wrest.

strappazzàre—to overwork; to maltreat; to treat badly.

stràppo 'm.—the act of snatching or wresting. See scíppo and fúrto con stràppo. Art. 625, subd. 4, Italian Penal Code.

straripàre—to overflow.

strasciàre—to drag along.

strascinàre—to drag along the ground.

straziàre — to lacerate; to tear to pieces.

stràzio m.—laceration; figuratively, to cause atrocious moral pain.

strèga f.—witch.

stregóne m.—wizard.

strégua f.—measure; standard.

stremàre—to reduce to extremities.

strènna f.—New Year's gift; gift-book.

strèpito m.—loud noise; uproar.

stritolàre—to triturate; to grind down; to pound; to smash; to pulverize.

strofinàre—to rub; to polish.

strombazzàre — to trumpet; to proclaim.

strombettàre—to trumpet; to proclaim.

stroppiàre—to maim; to cripple. Also, storpiàre.

strozzàre—to strangle; to choke; to throttle.

strozzíno m. — a usurious money-lender.

struménti impignoràbili—instruments not subject to attachment. These include the instruments as well as the objects and books that are indispensable for the exercise of the profession, art or trade of the debtor. Art. 514, subd. 4, Italian Code of Civil Procedure. See impignoràbili (còse mòbili assolutaménte).

struménto m.—instrument; a public Act drawn by a notary; a writing.

struttúra f.—structure; construction.

stúdio m.—studio; study.

stúdio legàle—law office.

stupefacénte m.—stupefacient; a substance inducing stupefaction; narcotic.

stupefacènti (abúso di sostànze) — abuse of narcotic substances. Art. 729, Italian Penal Code. See abúso di sostànze stupefacènti.

stupefacènti (inabilitazióne per abúso abituàle)—disqualification to manage one's affairs because of habitual use of drugs. See persóne che pòssono èssere inabilitàte and inabilitazióne.

stupefacènti (commèrcio clandestíno o fraudòlento di sostànze)—clandestine or fraudulent commerce in narcotic substances. Whoever, in a clandestine or fraudulent manner, carries on commerce in narcotic substances, or holds them for the purpose of carrying on clandestine or fraudulent commerce, or supplies or procures to others such substances clandestinely and fraudulently, is punished with imprisonment. Art. 446, Italian Penal Code.

stupefàre—to make stupid or dull; to stupefy; to fill with stupor; to fill with amazement.

stupefazióne f.—stupefaction; the act and effect of stupefying.

stupràre—to ravish; to rape.

stupratóre m.—ravisher.

stúpro m.—ravishment; rape. See violènza carnàle.

subaccollàre—to transfer or assign to another, work which had been acquired under a contract of accòllo.

subaffittàre—to sub-lease.

subaffítto m.—sub-lease. The lessee may not sub-lease productive property without the consent of the lessor. The faculty of assigning the rented property comprises that of subleasing it; the faculty of subleasing does not comprise that of assigning it. If the lessor consents to the sub-lease of rural property, this is considered as a direct rental between the lessor and the new tenant. Art. 1624, 1649, Italian Civil Code. See sublocazióne o cessióne della locazióne.

subappaltàre—to sub-contract. See subappàlto and appàlto.

subappaltatóre m.—sub-contractor.

subappàlto m.—sub-contract. The contractor cannot sub-contract the execution of the work or service if he has not been authorized by the one for whom the work or service is being performed. The contractor, in order to have an action back against sub-contractors, under pain of forfeiting his rights, must communicate to them denunciations and complaints within sixty days of their receipt. Art. 1656, 1670, Italian Civil Code.

subàsta f.—a public auction sale.

subbissàre—See subissàre.

subbúglio m.—confusion; disturbance of public order.

subcomodàto m.—a loan for use sub-contract. It is a sub-contract to deliver to a third party personal or real property which one has received from a person for a time or a determined use, with the obligation of returning the identical property. The first receiver of such property cannot assign to a third party the enjoyment of the property without the consent of the bailor. Art. 1804, Italian Civil Code. See commodàto.

subenfiteùsi f.—subemphyteusis; subinfeudation. It is not permitted. Art. 968, Italian Civil Code. See enfiteùsi.

subentrànte—one who takes the place of another; assignee.

subentràre—to take the place of another; to succeed; to replace; to assign.

subingrèsso m.—the act of entering into or taking over the rights of another.

subíre—to undergo; to sustain; to be subjected to.

subissàre—to sink into ruin; to overturn or overthrow. Also, subbissàre.

subísso m.—great ruin of things which sink; ruin; destruction; vast quantity of things.

sublocàre—to sub-lease.

sublocatàrio m.—sub-lessee.

sublocazióne f.—sub-lease by a lessee of property he has rented.

sublocazióne o cessióne della locazióne—sub-lease or assignment of rented property. The lessee, unless there is agreement to the contrary, has the faculty to sub-lease the property rented to him, but cannot assign the lease contract without the consent of the lessor. With respect to personal property, the sublease must be authorized by the lessor or permitted by usage. Art. 1594, Italian Civil Code.

subornazióne f.—subornation. Whoever offers or promises money or other thing of value to a witness, expert or interpreter, to induce him to commit perjury, give false expert testimony or interpretation, is subjected to the same punishment, reduced by two-thirds, as provided by Art. 372 and 373, whenever the offer or promise is not accepted. The same disposition is applied whenever the offer or the promise is accepted, but the falsity is not committed. The sentence of condemnation carries with it the interdiction from public offices. Art. 377, Italian Penal Code. See fàlsa testimoniànza, Art. 372, Italian Penal Code and fàlsa perízia o interpretazióne, Art. 373, Italian Penal Code.

successióne f.—succession; the devolution of title to property by testament or operation of law. Art. 457, Italian Civil Code. See delazióne dell'eredità.

successióne (apertúra della)—opening of the right of succession. It occurs at the moment of death, in the place of the last domicile of the deceased. Art. 456, Italian Civil Code.

successióne dello stàto—succession of the State. In the absence of other successors to an estate, the inheritance devolves upon the State. Such acquisition operates as of right, without necessity of acceptance, and cannot be renounced. The State does not respond for the debts of the estate beyond the value of the property acquired. Art. 586, Italian Civil Code.

successióne legíttima—legitimate or intestate succession. In this case, the estate devolves upon the spouse, the legitimate and natural descendants, to the legitimate ascendants, to collaterals and other relatives and to the State, in the order and according to the rules established in the present Title. Art. 565, Italian Civil Code.

successióne necessària—necessary succession. It is a quota of a descendant's estate reserved by law to certain persons in his family, which they can elect even against the provisions of the testator's will. See legittimàri, Art. 536, 537, Italian Civil Code.

successióne particolàre — particular succession. It is a testamentary disposition or bequest to a named person called a legatee. Art. 588, Italian Civil Code.

successióne testamentària—testamentary succession. It relates to a disposition by testament of all or part of a testator's property. Art. 587, et seq., Italian Civil Code.

successióne universàle—universal succession. Testamentary dispositions, whatever be the expression or denomination used by the testator, are universal dispositions and attribute the quality of heir, if they comprise the totality or a quota of the testator's property. The other dispositions are particular dispositions to a legatee. The indication of specific property or of a mass of property, does not exclude that the disposition is by universal right, when it results that the testator has meant to assign those properties as a quota of his patrimony or estate. Art. 588, Italian Civil Code.

successóre—successor.

successòrio—that which regards a succession or inheritance.

successòrio (pàtto) — agreement regarding an inheritance. It is null and void. See pàtto successòrio, Art. 458, Italian Civil Code.

succursàle—branch office.

suddétto—above-mentioned.

súddito—subject; dependant; one who owes allegiance to a government and is under its protection; one under the dominion of a sovereign.

suffràgio m.—suffrage; the right of voting; vote.

suggestióne f.—suggestion. It is a mitigating circumstance when a person has acted at the suggestion of a crowd in tumult, so long as it is not a meeting or assembly forbidden by law or the Authorities, and the person so acting is not a criminal or an habitual or professional violator or delinquent by tendency. Art. 62, subd. 3, Italian Penal Code.

suggestióne ipnòtica — hypnotic suggestion. Whoever, by means of hypnotic suggestion or while a person is in a dormant or drowsy condition, or by administering alcoholic or narcotic substances, or by any other means, puts a person, without his consent, in a state of incapacity to comprehend or to will his acts, is punished with imprisonment. Art. 613, Italian Penal Code.

suicídio m.—suicide.

suicídio dell'assicuràto—suicide of the insured. Where this occurs before two years have passed from the stipulation of the contract, the insurer is not held to payment of the sums involved, unless there is an agreement to the contrary. Art. 1927, Italian Civil Code.

suicídio (istigazióne o aiúto al)—instigation or aid to suicide. Whoever causes others to commit suicide or reinforces the purpose of others to commit suicide, or, in any way, facilitates its execution is punished with imprisonment. If the suicide does not occur, the penalty is less, provided that from the attempted suicide there is derived a grave or most grave personal injury. The penalties are augmented if the person who is instigated or incited or aided is a minor less than age eighteen or a person of infirm mind, or who finds himself in a condition of psychic deficiency by reason of another infirmity or because of abuse of alcoholic or narcotic substances. Art. 580, 579, Italian Penal Code.

sui juris (Lat.)—competent; not under a legal disability or guardianship.

sunnominàto—above-named.

suòcera f.—mother-in-law.

suòcero m.—father-in-law.

suòla f.—shoe sole.

suòlo m.—shoe sole; soil; surface soil; the soil as well as the sub-soil and all plantings and buildings attached or annexed thereon, even though temporarily, are considered as immovables and real property. Art. 812, 840, 934, Italian Civil Code.

superfície f. — superficies; surface; everything on the surface of a parcel of land or a building so as to constitute a part of it.

superfície (costituzióne del diritto di) —constitution or establishment of the right of superficies. The owner of land may constitute the right of building and maintaining a structure, above or below ground, in favor of others who will acquire the property thereto. Likewise he may transfer ownership of existing structures, separately from the ownership of the land. If the constitution of the right of superficies is for a determined

time, the right is extinguished with the expiration of the time agreed and the owner of the land becomes the proprietor of the structure. The right to construct on the land of others expires by prescription due to protracted non-use for twenty years. There cannot be constituted or transferred ownership in plantings separately from ownership of the land. Art. 952-956, Italian Civil Code.

supèrstite m.—survivor.

supèrstite—surviving.

supleménto m.—supplement.

supplènte m.—substitute; deputy.

suppletòrio—supplementary. See **giuraménto suppletòrio** — supplementary sworn testimony.

súpplica f.—petition.

supplicànte m.—supplicant; petitioner.

supplízio m. — severe punishment; death penalty; torture.

supposizióne f.—supposition; substitution.

supposizióne o soppressióne di stàto— supposition or suppression of status. Whoever records in the State civil registers an inexistent birth is punished with imprisonment. A person is subjected to the same punishment, who suppresses the civil status of a new born child by concealing his birth. Art. 566, Italian Penal Code. Also, **soppressióne di stàto**. See **alterazióne di stàto**.

suppósto—supposed; imagined.

suppósto reàto—supposed crime. See **reàto suppósto erroneaménte e reàto impossíbile.**

surrogàre—to surrogate; to subrogate; to substitute; to put one in place of another.

surrogàto m.—substitute.

surrogatória—a surrogate or substitute action. See **azióne surrogatória** and Art. 2900, Italian Civil Code.

surrogazióne f.—subrogation; substitution.

surrogazióne (pagaménto con)—payment with right of subrogation. See **pagaménto con surrogazióne.**

suspicióne f.—suspicion.

suspicióne (legíttimo)—legitimate suspicion. It involves a suspicion of bias in a certain area which may impede a fair trial for one accused of a crime. Also, **sospètto (legíttimo).** See **rimessióne dei procediménti,** Art. 55-60, Italian Code of Penal Procedure.

sussidiàre—to subsidize.

sussidàrio—subsidiary; auxiliary.

sussídio m.—subsidy; help.

sussídio al fallíto e alla famíglia—subsistence for the bankrupt and his family. See **aliménti al fallíto e alla famíglia.**

sussistènza f.—subsistence.

sutúra f.—suture.

svalutàre—to devalue.

svalutazióne f.—devaluation.

svéglia f.—alarm clock.

svegliàre—to awaken.

svéglio—wide awake.

svelàre—to unveil; to uncover; to reveal; to disclose.

sveniménto m. — act of fainting or swooning.

sveníre—to faint; to swoon.

svòlgere—to unfold; to develop; to clear; to explain.

svòlta f.—a point in the road where it turns into another.

svoltaménto m.—the act of turning or unwrapping.

svoltolàre—to roll around; to overturn.

T

tabàcco (véndita or somministrazióne di)—sale or dispensing of tobacco. Whoever sells or dispenses tobacco to a person under fourteen years of age is subject to a fine. Art. 730, Italian Penal Code. See **somministrazióne a minóri di sostànze velenóse o nocíve.**

tàcca f.—notch; cut; blemish; stature.

tàcche o tàglie di contrasségno — notches or tallies as countersigns. The ones that correspond to countersigns for comparison serve as full proof, between those who make use of them in that way, to prove the supplying of things they provide or receive at retail. It is a rudimentary method of keeping a record of what is due between a creditor and debtor. Notches were cut in two staves, known as tallies. One was given to the creditor who supplied the goods, and the other was given to the debtor who received it. The notches were proof of the units of goods exchanged. Art. 2713, Italian Civil Code. Also, **tàglie o tàcche di contrasségno.**

tàcco m.—heel of a shoe.

tafferúglio m.—quarrel; uproar; scrimmage.

tàglia f.—the price on someone's head; ransom; cutting; notch; impost; tax; tallage.

tàglie o tàcche di contrasségno — notches or tallies as countersigns. See **tàcche o tàglie di contrasségno,** Art. 2713, Italian Civil Code.

tàglio m.—the act of cutting something or oneself; cut of material; cut.

tàglio (véndere a)—sale at retail.

tàglio (veníre a)—to come at the opportune time.

taglióne m.—retaliation; reprisal. It is derived from the Lex Talionis (Lat.), the law of retaliation, which involves the infliction of the same kind of injury upon the wrongdoer as he inflicted upon the victim.

tàlamo m.—the nuptial bed.

talèd m.—Jewish prayer shawl.

talióne m.—retaliation; reprisal. See **taglióne.**

talloncíno m.—detachable coupon.

tallóne m.—heel.

tamponàre—to close a wound with a tampon of cotton or gauze.

tampóne m.—tampon; a mass of cotton or gauze used to fill a natural or artificial cavity.

tàna f.—den; hole; figurativley, a hovel.

tanàglia (tanàglie pl.)—pincers. Also, tenàglia.

tànfo m.—mouldy smell.

tàppa f.—a stop for rest and food.

tappàre—to plug; to stop; to cork.

tàrga f.—shield; an architectural ornament in the shape of a shield; metal plate with an inscription; an automobile license plate.

tarí m.—ancient Sicilian and Neapolitan money, the name of which is of Arabic origin.

taríffa f.—tariff; list or schedule of prices; a schedule of goods upon which duty is imposed upon importation into a country.

taríffa penàle—schedule of penal fees. It covers a wide range of fees payable to witnesses, experts, magistrates, judges, clerks, defense of accused persons, etc., relative to the administration of criminal justice. Taríffa Penàle (Schedule of Penal Fees), Usual Laws, Appendix to Italian Code of Penal Procedure.

tarsía f.—inlaid work.

tartàna f.—tartan, a single masted vessel with lateen sail.

tartassàre—to abuse; to harass; figuratively, to play an instrument badly.

tàsca f.—pocket.

tàso m.—tartar; sediment.

tàssa f.—tax duty; impost; fee; assessment.

tassàbile—taxable.

tassàmetro m.—taxi meter.

tassàre—to tax; to assess; to fix the price of merchandise.

tassativaménte—invariably; precisely; specifically.

tassatívo—that which determines or establishes or prescribes without deviation.

tassí m.—taxi.

tàsso m.—rate of interest or discount. Also, sàggio. See interèsse et seq.

tastaménto m.—the act of feeling or touching.

tastàre—to feel; to touch.

tastatúra f.—the order of the keys on a keyboard (of a piano).

tastièra f.—keyboard of an instrument such as a piano.

tàttica f.—tactic or or tactics; arrangement or order; the art of disposing and maneuvering military or naval forces in battle.

tavolàre (sistèma)—tabular system. The Germanic method of recording or registering rights in real property. An account or table of title to real property is kept together with the ownership and transference thereof as may occur. This system of registration is used in the provinces of the Italian Alto Adige, near the Austrian border.

teàtri (rappresentazióne abusíve)—unlawful theater performances. Whoever performs dramas or other theatrical performances in public, or gives theatrical productions in public, of any kind, without first having advised the Authorities, is punished with arrest or fine. One who allows the public performance of motion picture films without first submitting them to review by the Authorities, is subjected to the same penalty. If the act is committed against the prohibition of the Authorities, the pecuniary and detentive penalties are applied together. Whoever opens or keeps open places of public spectacle, entertainment or assembly, without having observed the prescriptions of the Authorities for public safety, is punished with arrest and fine. Art. 668, 681, Italian Penal Code.

tedésco m.—German.

tégolo m. (tégola f.)—roof tile.

telecomunicazióni f. (s. & pl.)—long distance communication.

telèfoni (intercettàre o impedíre communicazióni) — interception or obstruction of telephone communications. Such interception cannot be made without the authorization of the Judicial Authorities. Art. 226, 339, Italian Code of Penal Procedure.

telèfono (molèstia o distúrbo per mèzzo

del)—molestation or disturbance by means of the telephone. Whoever, in a public place or one open to the public, or by means of the telephone, by insolence or for other reprehensible motive, causes one molestation or disturbance is punished with arrest or fine. Art. 660, Italian Penal Code.

telegràmma m.—telegram. It has the probatory effect of a private writing, if the original was delivered to the sending office, and was subscribed by the sender, or if it was delivered there even without the subscription of the sender. Art. 2705, Italian Civil Code.

telegràmma (conformità tra originàle e riproduzióne del)—conformity between the original and copy of the telegram. The copy of the telegram delivered to the addressee is presumed, till proof to the contrary, to be in conformity with the original. The sender, if he has compared the original of the telegram with the copy according to the dispositions of the regulations, is presumed to be free from fault for differences between the original and the copy. Art. 2706, Italian Civil Code.

tellúrico—pertaining to or proceeding from the earth.

tellúrico (moviménto)—movement of the earth; earthquake; slow and continuous rise and fall of the ground.

temerarietà f.—temerariousness; the act of being temerarious; heedless; rash; reckless; an action having no ground or just cause. In a transaction entered into without just cause, if one of the parties had knowledge of his groundless claim, the other party may demand the annulment of the transaction. Art. 1971, Italian Civil Code; Art. 96, Italian Code of Civil Procedure.

temeràrio — temerarious; heedless; rash; reckless; groundless (action).

temeràrio (giudízio)—groundless cause of action. Also, líte temerària.

tempestivaménte—at the appropriate time.

tempestívo—that which is done at the appropriate time; opportune.

tèmpo del pignoraménto—time for attachment (of property)—An attachment cannot be made on holidays, nor prior to 7 A.M. and after 7 P.M., during the period of October 1st, to March 31st; and from prior to 6 A.M. and after 8 P.M. during the period April 1st to September 30th, except upon authorization of the Praetor. An attachment commenced within the prescribed hours may continue to completion. Art. 519, 147, Italian Code of Civil Procedure.

tèmpo di guèrra—time of war. For the purposes of the penal law, under the denomination of *time of war*, is included, also, the period of imminent danger of war which precedes it. Art. 310, Italian Penal Code.

tèmpo (efficàcia della légge nel)— effect of the law on time. The law does not dispose but for the future; it has no retroactive effect. Collective work contracts may establish for their effect a date prior to their publication, so long as it does not precede the date of the agreement. Art. 11, Preliminary Dispositions.

temporàle m.—storm.

temporàle—temporal.

temporeggiàre—to temporize; to procrastinate.

temúto—feared.

tenàglia f.—pincers. Also, tanàglia.

tendènza f. — tendency; inclination; propensity.

tendènza a delínquere—tendency to commit crime. A person is so declared, even though not a recidivist or habitual or professional criminal, who commits a non-culpable crime against the life or individual safety of another, even though the act is not one of the crimes against the person set forth in Art. 575-593, of this Code. Art. 108, 109, 133, Italian Penal Code. See capacità a delínquere.

tentatívo m.—attempt; effort; endeavor; trial; experiment.

tentatívo di conciliazióne—attempt or

effort at conciliation. If the nature of the case permits, the examining judge, at the first hearing, must seek to conciliate the parties, arranging, when necessary, for their personal appearance. The attempt at conciliation may be renewed at any time during the hearing. When the parties are reconciled, minutes of the concluded agreement are drawn up. These minutes constitute an executive title or order which may be enforced by a sale of property. Art. 185, 474, Italian Code of Civil Procedure; Art. 88, Enabling Rules, Italian Code of Civil Procedure.

tentàto—attempted; experimented.

tentàto delítto—attempted crime. One which falls short of its accomplishment, although overt acts towards its commission were performed by the accused. Art. 56, Italian Penal Code. Also, **delítto tentàto**.

tentazióne f.—temptation.

tentennàre—to shake; to waver; to hesitate; to vacilate.

tènue—tenuous; slender; thin.

tenúta f.—capacity; holding; keeping; a rural possession or estate.

tenúta (bàssa)—half dress uniform.

tenúta (grànde)—full dress uniform; civilian full dress.

tenúta dei líbri—the keeping of the books of a business; bookkeeping.

tenúta della contabilità—keeping of accounts. All the written accounts must be kept according to the rules of orderly bookkeeping, without blank spaces, without interlineations and without transpositions in the margins. There cannot be erasures, and if some cancellation is necessary, it must be done in such a manner that the cancelled words are legible. Art. 2219, Italian Civil Code.

tenutàrio m.—one who has possession; a landed proprietor.

tergiversàre—to tergiversate; to use subterfuge; to practice evasion; to change attitude and opinion concerning a subject.

tèrgo m.—back; spine of a man or animal; the back of anything.

tèrmine m. — term; limit; duration; boundary; end; a fixed or determined period of time or prescribed duration. Art. 1183-1187, 1457, 2963, Italian Civil Code; Art. 152-155, Italian Code of Civil Procedure; Art. 14, Italian Penal Code; Art. 180-183 bis, Italian Code of Penal Procedure.

tèrmine (contràtti a)—time contracts; contracts on exchange markets where payment is due at a certain time, usually the end of the current month or the following one. See **contràtti di bórsa.**

tèrmine (decadènza del)—termination of a period of time. Although a period of time has been fixed in favor of a debtor, the creditor may immediately demand performance if the debtor has become insolvent, or by his acts has diminished the guarantees he had given, or has failed to give the guarantees he had promised. Art. 1186, Italian Civil Code.

tèrmine ordinatório—limitation of time ordered by a judge. The judge, prior to the expiration of a time limit, may abbreviate or postpone the limitation, ex officio, provided it had not been set under penalty of a default. The postponement cannot be for a period longer than the original limitation. Further postponement cannot be granted except for particularly grave reasons and upon proper grounds. Art. 154, Italian Code of Civil Procedure.

tèrmini (azióne per apposizióne di)— action to fix boundaries. If the boundaries between contiguous lands are missing or have become unrecognizable, each of the owners has the right to demand that they be placed or be reestablished at common expense. Art. 951, Italian Civil Code; Art. 8, subd. 2, Italian Code of Civil Procedure.

tèrmini (còmputo dei)—computation of time. In computing time by days or hours, the initial day or hour is excluded. In computing time by months or years, the common calendar is used. Holidays are computed in the period of time. If the due date falls on a holiday, said maturity date is postponed to the following day which is not a holiday. Art. 155, Italian Code of Civil Procedure; Art. 1187, 2963, Italian Civil Code; Art. 14, Italian Penal Code; Art. 180-183 bis, Italian Code of Penal Procedure.

tèrmini di prescrizióne (cómputo dei) —computation of the limits of prescription. The limits of prescription contemplated by the present Code and other laws is computed according to the common calendar. The day on which the period of prescription starts is excluded from computation and the last day is included. If the period of prescription expires on a holiday, it is deferred to the following non-festive day. Prescription by months is determined in the month of expiration and on the day of the month corresponding to the day of the initial month. If the due month of expiration does not have such a date, then the termination of time is completed on the last day of that same month. Art. 2963, Italian Civil Code; Art. 155, Italian Code of Civil Procedure; Art. 14, Italian Penal Code; Art. 180, Italian Code of Penal Procedure.

tèrmini legàli e tèrmini giudiziàri— legal and judicial limitations of time. The time limitations for the effectuation of the documents of the trial are established by law; they may be established by the judge even under penalty of default, only if the law expressly permits it. The limitations established by law are imposed by order (of the judge) except where the law has expressly declared them to be peremptory. Art. 152, Italian Code of Civil Procedure.

tèrmini perentòri—peremptory time limitations. Peremptory time limitations, may not be abbreviated or postponed, not even upon agreement of the parties. Art. 153, Italian Code of Civil Procedure.

tèrmini (restituzióne in)—restoration to a legal right after default to exercise it within the prescribed period of time. Art. 183 bis, Italian Code of Penal Procedure.

terràzza f.—terrace; a raised level space on top of a house, surrounded by a parapet or railing; flat roof.

terràzzo m.—a terrace smaller than a terrazza; a small terrace extending from the external wall of a house to which access is gained through one or more large doors which open to the pavement. See **làstrici solàri.**

terremòto m.—earthquake.

terremòto, guèrra, insurrezióne, tumúlti popolàri—earthquake, war, insurrection, popular tumults or riots. Except for a contrary agreement, the insurer is not obligated for damages caused by telluric or earth movements, war, insurrection or by popular tumults or riots. Art. 1912, Italian Civil Code.

terréno m.—ground; land; soil.

terréno—earthly; pertaining to the earth as opposed to celestial; terrestrial; worldly.

terréno (piàno)—ground floor.

territorialità (princípio di)—principle of territoriality. This principle demands that all the substantive and procedural laws within the territory of a State must be observed by citizens and foreigners alike, and that foreign laws have no applicability within the State except as allowed by international treaties and conventions. Art. 17-31, Preliminary Dispositions.

territòrio (competènza civíle per)— civil territorial jurisdiction. See **competènza civíle per territòrio.**

territòrio (competènza penàle per)— penal territorial jurisdiction. See **competènza penàle per territòrio.**

tèrzo m.—a third part; a third party in a controversy. See **opposizióne di tèrzo.**

tèsi f.—thesis.

tesorería f.—treasury; office which collects and pays out money.

tesorière m.—treasurer.

tesòro m.—treasure. It is any personal property of value which is hidden or buried, of which no one can prove to be the owner. Treasure belongs to the owner of the land upon which it is found. If the treasure is found upon the land of another, even though discovered by chance, half belongs to the owner of the land and half to the finder. The same disposition is applied if the treasure is found in the personal property of another. Art. 932, Italian Civil Code.

tèssera f.—mark; sign; tally; identification card; small piece of mosaic.

tèssere—to weave.

tessitúra f. — texture; weaving; in music the extension or compass of the voice or instrument.

testaménti speciàli — special testaments. When a testator finds himself in exceptional and difficult circumstances and he cannot avail himself of the ordinary forms of wills, the law authorizes the use of more simple wills for the disposition of property. These are: (a) testaménto a bórdo aeromóbile (testament executed aboard an aircraft); (b) testaménto a bórdo nàve (testament executed aboard ship); (c) testaménto dei militàri e assimilàti (testament of military personnel and auxiliaries); (d) testaménto fàtto in luògo contagióso o per càusa di púbblica calamità o d'infortúnio (testament made by reason of public calamity or disaster). Art. 609-619, Italian Civil Code.

testaménto m.—testament. It is a revocable written Act whereby a person disposes of all his property or part thereof after his death. It is revocable during his lifetime, the dispositions made by him to take effect after his death. Art. 587, 601, Italian Civil Code and Art. 26, Preliminary Dispositions.

testaménto a bórdo aeromòbile—testament executed aboard an aircraft. The disposition applicable to wills executed aboard a ship also pertain to a will made aboard an aircraft. Such a will is received by the commander of the craft in the presence of one, or where possible two witnesses. Art. 616, Italian Civil Code. See **testaménto a bórdo nàve.**

testaménto a bórdo nàve—testament executed aboard ship. When made aboard a ship at sea, the testament may be received by the ship's commander. That of the commander may be received by the officer next in line of command. A testament made at sea must be in original and duplicate original, subscribed by the testator in the presence of two witnesses and the person receiving it. If the testator or witnesses cannot subscribe, the reason therefore must be indicated. The testament is preserved with the ship's papers and entered in the log-book. Such a testament losses its validity three months after the testator has debarked at a place where a testaway. Art. 611, 612, 615, Italian Civil ment can be executed in the usual Code.

testaménto congiuntívo o recíproco—joint or mutual will. A testament cannot be made in the same writing by two or more persons, neither for the benefit of a third party or with reciprocal dispositions. Art. 589, 635, Italian Civil Code.

testaménto dei militàri e assimilàti—testament of military personnel and auxiliaries. The will of military personnel and persons who accompany them in the armed forces of the State, may be received by an officer or military chaplain, or an officer of the Red Cross, or an officer of the Association of Italian Knights of the Sovereign Order of Malta, in the presence of two witnesses; it must be subscribed by the testator, by the person who receives it and by the witnesses. If the testator or the witnesses cannot subscribe, the reason which has prevented the subscription must be indicated. The will must be transmitted as soon as possible to General Headquarters, and thence to the appropriate Ministry, which will order it deposited in the notarial archives of the testator's place of domicile or last residence. Such a will losses its effectiveness three months after the testator returns to a place where it is possible to make a testament in the ordinary forms. Art. 617, 618, Italian Civil Code.

testaménto fàtto in luògo contagióso o per càusa di púbblica calamità o d'infortúnio—testament made in a place overrun by contagious illness or made by reason of public calamity or disaster. When a testator cannot avail himself of the ordinary forms of wills because he finds himself in a place overrun with illness reputed to be contagious, or by reason of public calamity or disaster, his will is valid if received by a notary, by the Praetor or Judge of Conciliation of the locality, by the mayor or his deputy or a minister of religion, in the presence of two witnesses of the age not less than sixteen. The will is written and subscribed by the person who receives it, and also subscribed by the testator and the witnesses. If the testator or witnesses cannot write, the reason must be indicated. Such a will loses its effectiveness three months after the cessation of the reason which prevented the testator from using the ordinary forms. Art. 609, 610, Italian Civil Code.

testaménto (fórme ordinàri di)—ordinary forms of testaments. The forms of ordinary testaments are the holographic (ològrafo) will and the will by Act of a notary. The testament by Act of a notary is either public or secret. Art. 601, Italian Civil Code.

testaménto ològrafo—holographic will. The holographic will must be entirely written, dated and subscribed in the testator's hand. The subscription must be placed at the end of the dispositions. If it is made without indicating the name and surname, it is nonetheless valid when it indicates with certainty the person of the testator. The date must contain the indication of the day, month and year. Proof of the inaccuracy of the date is admitted only when it is necessary to judge the capacity of the testator, the priority of dates among a number of wills, or of other questions to be decided on the basis of the time of the will. The holographic will, destroyed, torn or cancelled, in whole or in part, is considered revoked in whole or in part, unless it can be proven that it was destroyed, torn or cancelled by a person other than the testator, or it can be proven that the testator

had no intention to revoke it. Art. 602, 684, Italian Civil Code.

testaménto púbblico—public will. The public will is received by the notary in the presence of two witnesses. The testator, in the presence of the witnesses, declares his will to the notary, which is reduced to writing under preparation of the notary himself. He then reads the will to the testator in the presence of the witnesses. Mention is made in the testament of each of these formalities. The will must indicate the place, the date and hour of its receipt and subscription and that it was subscribed by the testator, the witnesses and the notary. If the testator cannot subscribe, or can do so only with great difficulty, he must declare the reason, and the notary must mention this declaration prior to reading the document. For the will of a mute, deaf person or deaf-mute, the rules established by the notarial law are observed for public Acts made by these persons. Where the testator is incapable of reading, there must be four witnesses to the will. Art. 603, Italian Civil Code.

testaménto recíproco — reciprocal or mutual will. See **testamento congiuntívo o recíproco.**

testaménto segréto—secret will. It may be written by the testator or by a third party. If it is written by the testator, it must be subscribed by him at the end of the dispositions; if written in whole or in part by others, or if it is written by mechanical means, it must bear the subscription of the testator on each half page, together or separate. The testator who can read but cannot write, or who has been unable to affix his subscription when he was having his own dispositions written, must also declare to the notary who receives the testament, that he has read the will and add the reason which has prevented him from subscribing it. This fact is mentioned in the document receiving it. Whoever does not know how, or cannot read, cannot make a secret will. The paper on which the dispositions are drawn, or the one serving as envelope, must be sealed with an impression, so that the testament may not be opened or extracted without breakage or alteration. The testator, in the presence of two witnesses, personally delivers the paper so sealed to the notary, or has it sealed in the manner above indicated in the presence of the notary and witnesses, and declares that his testament is contained in that paper. The Act of receipt of the document is written on the paper in which the testament is written or enveloped or upon another envelope prepared by the notary and sealed by him, which indicates the fact of delivery and the declaration of the testator, the number and the impression of the seals and the participation of the witnesses and all the formalities. The document must be subscribed by the testator, the witnesses and the notary. If the testator cannot, due to any impediment, subscribe the Act of delivery, that which has been established regarding a testament must be observed by public Act. All the above must be done in sequence without proceeding to other acts. Art. 604, 605, 607, Italian Civil Code.

testàtico m.—numeration by head; poll tax.

testatóre m. — testator; one who executes a will and disposes of his property.

testatríce f.—testatrix. See **testatóre.**

tèste m. & f.—witnesses. Also, **testimòne** and **testimònio.**

testé—just now; lately.

testificàre—to testify.

testificazióne f.—act of giving testimony; attestation.

testimòne m. & f.—witness.

testimòne auricolàre — auricular witness; one who has heard with his own ears.

testimòne reticènte—reticent witness. See **reticènza** and **fàlsa testimoniànza.**

testimoniàle m.—testimonial proof; the parol evidence adduced by one of the parties. See **pròva testimoniàle.**

testimoniàle—testimonial; pertaining to testimony.

testimoniànza f.—testimony; evidence; deposition; proof; attestation.

testimoniànza fàlsa—false testimony. See **fàlsa testimoniànza.**

testimoniàre—to testify; to attest.

testimònio m.—witness.

testimònio a càrico—witness for the prosecution.

testimònio a discàrico—witness for the defense.

testimònio a scàrico or testimònio di scàrico—witness for the defense.

testimònio oculàre—eye-witness.

tèsto m.—text; earthen pot-lid; flowerpot; a terracotta baking disc or pan.

tétto m.—roof.

timóne m. — rudder; wagon shaft; handlebar of a bicycle.

timoneggiàre—to steer.

timonièra f. — wheelhouse; a small structure above deck containing the steering wheel.

timonière m.—steersman.

timóre f.—fear; a feeling of apprehension of contemplated evil or harm; a sentiment of respect and reverence for those in authority or those endowed with dignity or worth.

timóre riverenziàle—reverential fear; a sentiment of profound respect for those in authority or rank, mingled with apprehension of displeasing them. Such a fear, by itself, is not a ground for annulling a contract. Art. 1437, Italian Civil Code.

típo m.—type; model; printing type.

típo di campióne—type of sample. See **véndita su campióne e su típo di campióne**—sale by sample and by type of sample.

tipografía f. — typography; printing house.

tipogràfica (esercízio abusívo dell' àrte)—unlawful exercise of the typographic art. Whoever, without the permission of the Authorities, or without observing the prescriptions of the law, exercises the art of ty-

294

pography or lithography, photography or any of the arts of printing or mechanical or chemical reproduction in multiple copies, is punished with arrest and fine. Art. 662, Italian Penal Code.

tipògrafo m.—typographer; printer.

tirapièdi m.—executioner's assistant.

tiraprànzi m.—dumb-waiter. Also, calaprànzi.

tiràre—to drag; to draw; to pull; to fire (a shot); to deliver (a blow).

tiràre avànti—to get ahead or along in one's affairs.

tíro m.—throw; draught or act of drawing; shot (of a gun).

tíro a ségno—target practice; target range used for practice shooting.

tísi f.—phthisis; consumption.

tirocínio m.—apprenticeship. See apprendista and Art. 2130-2134, Italian Civil Code for provisions relative to duration of apprenticeship, compensation, certification and rules applicable.

titolàre—to give a title; to call one a bad name.

titolàre—titular; nominal.

titolàto m.—a titled person.

tìtoli all'órdine—instruments payable to order. They are transferred by indorsement. Any condition attached to the indorsement is void. Likewise a partial indorsement is invalid. Art. 2008-2020, Italian Civil Code.

tìtoli al portatóre—instruments payable to bearer. They can be negotiated by mere delivery and do not require an indorsement. Art. 2003-2007, Italian Civil Code.

tìtoli di crédito—documents of title; instruments of credit; evidences of debt; securities; shares of stock; commercial paper such as promissory notes, bills of exchange, drafts and checks; bank notes; treasury bonds; government obligations; bills of lading; warehouse receipts. Art. 1992-2027, Italian Civil Code.

tìtoli nominatívi—nominative instruments; instruments bearing the owner's name, which are registered by the issuer and are transferable by notation of the name of the new purchaser on the instrument and in the issuer's register, or by the issuance of new instruments to the new holder. They can also be transferred by indorsement, authenticated by a notary or an exchange broker. Art. 2021-2027, Italian Civil Code.

tìtoli (usurpazióne di tìtoli o di onóri)—usurpation of titles or honors. Whoever unlawfully wears in public the uniform or insignia of a public office or employment, or of a political, administrative or judicial body, or of a profession for which a special qualification is required by the State, or unlawfully wears the ecclesiastic habit in public is punished with a fine. The same penalty is applied to a person who arrogates ranks or academic grades and titles, decorations or other public honorary insignia, or the quality inherent in any of the offices, positions or professions indicated in the above dispositions. Art. 498, Italian Penal Code.

tìtolo m.—title; right to property; the name of a work; a chapter heading.

tìtolo di rèndita—an instrument, which is evidence of income due to the possessor, such as a bond, whether private or public.

tìtolo esecutívo — executive title or order; an instrument which when executed may lead to a forced sale of property of a debtor by the creditor. Examples are judgments and orders, commercial paper and Acts received by a notary or other public official authorized by law relative to money obligations. The instrument must be for an obligation which is certain, liquidated and collectible. Art. 474, Italian Code of Civil Procedure.

tollerabilità delle immissióne—tolerability of introduction (of smoke or heat onto neighboring land). See **immissióne di fúmo o di calóre nel fóndo vicíno.**

tollerànza (àtti di) — tolerated acts. The acts performed with the toleration of others may not serve as the basis for the acquisition of possession. Art. 1144, Italian Civil Code.

tollerànza per difètto di qualità— toleration with respect to defect in quality. See mancànza di qualità.

tómba f.—tomb; place of sepulcher or burial. See vilipèndio delle tómbe— contempt or disparagement of tombs.

tontína f.—tontine; from the Italian banker, Tonti who devised a plan whereby a group of persons pooled their capital, receiving life annuities, with the agreement that the shares of those who died passed to the survivors. This principal is also employed in some forms of life insurance.

toponomàstica f. — toponomy; the naming or nomenclature of places and regions. Toponomàstica, Usual Laws, Appendix to Italian Civil Code.

tórba f.—peat.

torbièra—peat bog. Peat bogs are part of the patrimony of the State. Art. 826, Italian Civil Code.

torrènte m.—torrent; mountain stream. Mountain streams and currents are part of the public domain. Art. 822, Italian Civil Code.

tòrto—bent; crooked; twisted.

tòrto m.—wrong; injury; harm; that which is against right or reason.

tortúra f.—torture.

tósa f.—girl; lass.

tosàre—to clip; to shear.

tòsco m.—poison.

tòssico m.—poison.

tòsto m.—toast, derived from the English.

tòsto—quickly; immediately.

tot (Lat.)—so many; an indeterminate number of things.

traboccàre—to overflow; to incline downward.

tràccia f.—trace; track; trail; footprint; mark sign; vestige.

tradiménto m.—betrayal; treason.

tradiménto (a)—traitorously.

tradiménto (àlto)—high treason. The President of the Republic is not responsible for acts committed in the discharge of his duties except for high treason or attempts against the Constitution. In such case, he is charged by Parliament in joint session, by absolute majority of its members. The Constitutional Court sits in judgment. Art. 90, 134, Constitution of the Italian Republic.

tradiménto (mangiàre il pàne a)—to eat bread traitorously, i.e., to live at the expense of others.

tradíre—to betray; to deceive.

tradíto—betrayed.

traditóra f.—traitress. Also, traditríce.

traditóre m.—traitor.

traditríce f.—traitress. Also, traditóra.

tradizióne m.—tradition; delivery of merchandise; transmission.

tradótta f.—a train used exclusively for the transportation of soldiers.

tradótto—translated.

tradúrre—to translate; to interpret; to transfer; to transport.

traduttóre m. (traduttríce f.)—translator.

traduzióne f.—translation; transportation or banishment to a penal colony.

traènte m.—drawer of a draft or bill of exchange. See emittènte—maker of a vàglia cambiàrio; maker of a promissory note.

traènte—drawing; attractive.

trafficànte m.—trader; merchant; trafficker.

trafficàre—to trade; to traffic; to engage in commerce.

tràffico m.—traffic; trade; commerce; movement.

trafíggere—to transfix.

trafóro m.—a boring; piercing; openwork; tunnel.

trafugàre—to carry off secretly or by stealth; to hide.

trafúgo m.—concealed person; stowaway.

traghétto m.—ferry.

tragittàre—to ferry across; to travel through.

tragítto m. — journey between two places; crossing.

traguardàre—aim; to level; to sight; to observe through a levelling instrument.

traguàrdo m.—aim; level; sight; the sight on an instrument or firearm to guide the aim towards an objective point; in sports events, the finish line or winning point.

traiettòria f.—trajectory.

tràina f.—the irregular motion of a horse which half-canters with his forelegs and trots with the rear ones.

tràina (alla)—under tow, referring to a boat being dragged along by a rope.

trainàre—to drag; to haul.

tràino m.—dray; sledge; train; load; body of a carriage.

transazióne f.—transaction; compromise. It is a contract whereby the parties by making reciprocal concessions, terminate a legal controversy or dispute already started, or anticipate and forestall a future dispute which may arise between them. The transaction must be reduced to writing to have effect. Art. 1965-1976, Italian Civil Code. See **compromésso.**

trànsfuga m.—deserter who passes over to the enemy; one who passes from one political party to the opposition.

transigènte — tolerant; indulgent; yielding.

transígere—to compromise; to come to terms.

transitòrio—transitory; transient dispositions added to a new law to regulate the passage from the old to the new, and which end their effect when the new law is in full vigor.

tranvài m.—tram; trolley-car. Also, **tranvía.**

trapassàre—to surpass; to overpass; to overstep; to pass away; to die.

trapiantàre—to transplant.

trapiànto terapeútico — therapeutic transplant. The removal and setting aside of organs and parts of a cada-ver for transplanting to humans. Trapiànto Terapeútico, Usual Laws, Appendix to Italian Civil Code.

tràppola f.—trap; pitfall; snare.

tràrre—to draw; to pluck; to pull; to reap.

tràrre una cambiàle—to draw a draft or bill of exchange.

trasandàre—to neglect; to omit; to pass over.

trasbordàre—to transfer merchandise or persons from one vessel to another, or from a train or car to another.

trascrizióne f.—transcription; recording; the writing required by law to be placed in a special register so that it be made public by recording it; recording of real property. Art. 2643-2696, Italian Civil Code. See **regístro di trascrizióne.**

trascinàre—to drag; to draw along; to draw out.

trascórrere—to pass hastily through time; to pass over; to glance through.

trascrívere—to transcribe, to record data in public registers as required by law.

trasferíbile—that which can be transferred; transportable.

trasferiménto m.—transfer.

trasferíre—to transfer; to pass a thing from one person to another.

trasfèrta f.—transfer; to remove from one place to another; the transfer of a public official.

trasformazióne f. — transformation; change.

trasformazióne delle società—change in the legal structure of partnerships. A public Act must evidence the resolution to change a partnership bearing a collective name, or a limited partnership (in accomàndita sémplice) into a stock corporation, a corporation of limited responsibility or into a limited responsibility partnership. Art. 2498-2500, Italian Civil Code.

traspòrti (attentàti alla sicurézza dei) —attempts against the security of transports. See attentàti alla sicu-rézza dei traspòrti.

traspòrto m.—transport; carriage; con-veyance; ecstasy; rapture.

traspòrto di còse—carriage or trans-portation of things. Art. 1678, 1683-1702, Italian Civil Code. See lèttera di vettúra, léttera di traspòrto aèreo and pòlizza di càrico. Re transport of things by air. Art. 950-964, Italian Navigation Code. See avaría.

traspòrto di persóne — carriage or transportation of persons. The car-rier is responsible for accidents which befall the person of the trav-eler during the voyage or trip and of the loss or damage to the things that the traveler brings with him, if he does not prove to have taken all suitable measures to avoid damage. Clauses which limit the responsibil-ity of the carrier for accidents which befall the traveler are void. Art. 1678, 1681, 1682, Italian Civil Code. Re transport of persons by sea. Art. 396-418, Italian Navigation Code. Re transport of persons by air. Art. 940-949, Italian Navigation Code. See avaria.

tràtta f.—a draft or bill of exchange in which the drawer designates a drawee who is to pay the amount in-dicated therein at a fixed time; com-mon expression for such a draft; impressed; dragged forcibly.

tràtta di schiàvi—forcible taking of slaves. It is a crime against personal liberty. See achiavitú and Art. 600-604, Italian Penal Code.

trattàrio m.—drawee of a draft or bill of exchange.

trattatíva f.—negotiation.

trattatíve a responsabilità precontrat-tuàle—negotiations and pre-contract-ual responsibility. The parties, in the development of negotiations and in the formation of the contract, must act in good faith. The party who knows or should know of the exist-ence of a cause of invalidity in the contract, and has not given notice to the other party, is held to compen-sate the damage suffered by the other, who, without fault, relied on the validity of the contract. Art. 1337, 1338, Italian Civil Code.

trattazióne f. — treatment; handling; management; conduct; conduct of a hearing or trial and its procedure.

trattoría f.—an establishment where meals may be obtained by the public; restaurant.

trattórie (depòsito in)—deposit or bail-ment in eating houses or restaurants. Their responsibility for a guest's property is similar to that of a hotel keeper as a bailee. They are respon-sible for things left in their care. Art. 1786, 1783-1785, Italian Civil Code. See depòsito in albèrgo.

travagliàre—to toil; to work hard; to distress; to torment; to afflict.

tràve f.—beam; girder; rafter; timber.

travestiménto m.—disguise; the act of changing clothes.

travestíre—to change clothes in order not to be recognized; to disguise; to travesty.

travestíto—disguised.

tràvi nel múro comúne—beams in a common or party-wall. Each co-owner may use the common wall to support the timbers of the contiguous building under construction. Art. 884, Italian Civil Code.

traviàre—to deviate or go astray from a virtuous life.

traviàta f.—a worldly woman; ex., Vio-letta, the principal character in Verdi's opera, La Traviata.

traviàto m.—one who has strayed from a virtuous life.

travisaménto m.—disguise. It is one of the aggravating circumstances in the commission of the crimes of theft and robbery. Art. 624, 625, 628, Ital-ian Penal Code.

travisàre—to disguise; to make things appear other than they are; to dis-tort.

travòlgere—to overthrow; to upset.

travolgiménto m.—overthrow.

trébbia f.—flail; instrument for thresh-ing grain by hand.

trebbiàre—to thresh.

298

trebbiatóio m.—threshing machine.

trebelliàna f. — trebellanic portion, named after a Roman Consul; it pertained to the part of the inheritance which a fiduciary or trustee of property under a will could detain. See **sostituzióne fedecommissària.**

trégua f.—truce; suspension of hostilities for a determined period; partial armistice; respite.

tremàre—to tremble; to quake; to quaver; to quiver; to shake; to shiver; to flicker.

tremarèlla f.—trembling with fear.

trevière m.—rigger; one who adjusts the fitting of the rigging of ships.

tribórdo m.—the starboard side of a vessel; the side of the ship to the right of a person looking forward towards the bow. In Italian marine usage, this word is usually replaced by the wórd drítta. See **babórdo**—port side.

tribúna f.—a platform from which orators speak; stage or box for spectators at public assemblies, sporting events and races.

tribunàle m.—tribunal; court of justice; it is a collegial body of three judges. It has limited jurisdiction in civil and penal cases. Art. 9, 163-310, Italian Code of Civil Procedure; Art. 42-48, Ordinaménto Giurisdizionàle (Jurisdictional Governance of the Judiciary), Usual Laws, Appendix to Italian Code of Civil Procedure; Art. 30, 31, Italian Code df Penal Procedure. See **competènza civíle, et seq.,** and **competènza penàle, et seq.**

tribunàle (competènza del)—jurisdiction of the Tribunal. It possesses jurisdiction of crimes other than those tried by the Court of Assizes and which are not granted to the Praetor. Art. 30, 29, 31, Italian Code of Penal Procedure.

tribunàle delle àcque púbbliche — tribunal for public waters. It is a section of the Court of Appeals and has jurisdiction, in the first instance, regarding controversies over waters in the public domain. Art. 140, 141, Tribunàli Delle Àcque Púb-

bliche (Tribunals for Public Waters), Usual Laws, Appendix to Italian Code of Civil Procedure; Art. 64, Ordinaménto Giurisdizionàle (Jurisdictional Governance of the Judiciary), Usual Laws, Appendix to Italian Code of Civil Procedure.

tribunàle fallimentàre — bankruptcy tribunal or court. It has the power to declare a bankruptcy and to control all its proceedings. Art. 23, 24, 9, Falliménto (Bankruptcy), Usual Laws, Appendix to Italian Civil Code. See **competènza del tribunàle fallimentàre.**

tribunàle per i minorènni — tribunal for minors. There is instituted a Tribunal for Minors at every headquarters of a Court of Appeals or a section thereof, comprised of a judge of the Court of Appeals, who presides over it, by a judge of a Tribunal and by two citizens, a man and a woman, meritorious in social assistance, chosen among practitioners of biology, psychiatry, criminal anthropology, pedagogy and psychology, who have completed thirty years of age. The Procurator of the Republic at the Tribunal for Minors, institutes a penal action for all crimes committed by minors not over age eighteen within the territory of the Court of Appeals or the section thereof in which a Tribunal for Minors exists. That Tribunal has jurisdiction of such crimes. It also has civil jurisdiction in matters affecting parental authority, guardianship, interdiction, conduct of business and the admission to insane asylum of mentally affected minors of age twenty-one and to their discharge. Art. 1-32, Tribunàli per i Minorènni (Tribunals for Minors), Usual Laws, Appendix to Italian Code of Penal Procedure; Art. 311-314, 314/2-314/28, 315-337, 343-389, 397, 414, 416, Italian Civil Code; Art. 40, Enabling Rules, Italian Civil Code.

tribunàle superióre delle àcque púbbliche—superior tribunal for public waters. It has appellate jurisdiction in all cases decided in the first instance by the Tribunàle Delle Àcque Púbbliche (Tribunal for Public Waters). Art. 139, 140-144, Tribunàli Delle Àcque Públbliche (Tribunals for Public Waters), Usual Laws, Appendix to Italian Code of Civil Procedure.

tribunàli amministratívi regionàli—regional administrative tribunals. They are organs of administrative justice of the first instance. Their territorial divisions are regional and comprise provinces which make part of individual regions. Their headquarters are in the principal cities of the regions. A separate section with special governance is also instituted for the Trentino-Alto Adige region with headquarters in Bolzano. Art. 1-53, Tribunàli Amministratívi Regionàli, Usual Laws, Appendix to Italian Code of Civil Procedure.

tribunàli militàri di bórdo—military (naval) tribunals aboard vessels. Defense counsel before military tribunals aboard vessels may be chosen only from among the officers of the Navy or other forces embarked on board the naval vessels on the spot. If the vessel is in a port or roadstead of the State, defense counsel may be chosen, also, from among the practicing lawyers and procurators there. Art. 54. Militàri (Military), Usual Laws, Appendix to Italian Code of Penal Procedure.

tribunàli militàri territoriàli — territorial military tribunals. Defense counsel before these tribunals may be chosen from among officers, inferior in service, residing in the place where the tribunal has its headquarters If the accused is of the grade of captain or above, defense counsel may be chosen from among superior or general officers, so long as their grade is inferior to that of the president of the tribunal. If the officer to act as defense counsel does not reside in the place where the tribunal has its headquarters, he may be chosen when the president of the tribunal regards that such circumstance will not produce delay in the determination of the trial or some other disadvantage. This measure is not reviewable. Practicing lawyers and procurators may also be chosen as defense counsel if they

reside outside the headquarters place of the tribunal, provided the foregoing dispositions are observed. Art. 53, Militàri (Military), Usual Laws, Italian Code of Penal Procedure.

tributàrio—tributary; dependent; subject to tribute; subject to taxes.

tribúto m.—tribute; tax; duty.

trinàcria f.—Trinacria, the ancient, classic name of Sicily.

trinàcrio m.—Sicilian.

trívia f.—the moon, poetically.

triviàle — trivial; belonging to the cross-roads or streets; pedestrian; low; vulgar.

trívio m.—cross-roads; place where three roads meet.

trovàre—to find.

trovatèllo m.—foundling.

truccàre—to transform the appearance with color, wigs and make-up.

truccàto—transformed; made-up (cosmetically).

truccatúra f.—that which is applied to transform the appearance; make-up.

trúcco—make-up; a game played on the ground with large wooden balls; a deception.

trúffa f.—a cheat; a swindle. It is the crime committed by one who with artifice and deception, induces another into error, for the purpose of obtaining for himself or others, an unjust advantage or profit, thus causing damage to the other. Art. 640, Italian Penal Code.

truffatóre m. (truffatríce f.)—swindler.

tumúlto m.—tumult; commotion; riot; uproar. Regarding the responsibility of an insurer for damages caused by tumults, see **terremòto, guèrra, insurrezióne, tumúlti popolàri.**

tumúlto (rifiúto di prestàre la pròpria òpera in occasióne di)—refusal to lend assistance in the event of a tumult. Whoever, in the event of a tumult or a public disaster, or a common danger, or during the very act that a crime is being committed, refuses, without just cause, to lend his own assistance and cooperation, or to give the information or the facts which may be requested of him by a public official or by a person charged with a public office, during the exercise of their functions or service, is punished with a fine. If false information or facts are given by the culpable party, he is punished with arrest and a fine. Art. 652, Italian Penal Code.

turbaménto m. — confusion; disturbance; perturbation; agitation. Disturbance of religious ceremonies and funeral services are punished with imprisonment. Art. 405, 406, 409, Italian Penal Code.

turbàre—to disturb; to disturb possession; to cause damage or annoyance to the possessor of property to deprive him of peaceful enjoyment.

turbàta libertà degli incànti—disturbed freedom of auctions. Whoever, by violence or threats, or by gifts, collusion, or other fraudulent means, impedes or disturbs competition in public auctions, or private auctions on behalf of Public Administrations, or puts off or sends away the offerors, is punished with imprisonment and fine. Art. 353, 354, Italian Penal Code.

turbatíva f.—an act which disturbs possession of property.

turbatíva violènta del possèsso di còse immòbili—violent disturbance of the possession of real property. It is a crime punishable with imprisonment and fine to disturb with violence to the person, or with threats, another's peaceful possession of real property. Art. 633 punishes the acts of invading public or private lands and buildings and occupying them. Art. 634, 633, Italian Penal Code.

túrpe—depraved; disgraceful; nasty; obscene; shameless.

turpilòquio m.—scurrilous and obscene language. The use of such language, which is contrary to public decency, in a public place or one open to the public, is punished with a fine. When acts contrary to public decency are committed in the above places, the punishment is arrest or fine. Art. 726, Italian Penal Code.

tutèla f.—tutelage; guardianship; the protection granted by law to minors, their persons and property. Art. 343-389, Italian Civil Code.

tutèla dei dirítti—protection of rights. Art. 2643-2969, Italian Civil Code.

tutelàre—to safeguard; to protect.

tutelàre (adj.)—tutelary; having the position of guardian or protector.

tutóre m.—guardian. He is charged with the care of the person of the minor, represents him in all civil acts and administers his property. Art. 357, Italian Civil Code. See protutóre.

U

ubriachézza f.—drunkenness; state of being drunk; inebriation. Whoever, in a public place or one open to the public, is found in a state of manifest drunkenness, is punished with arrest or fine. The penalty of arrest is also imposed upon a wrongdoer, if the act is committed by one who has already been sentenced to a non-culpable crime against the life or safety of an individual. Penalty is increased in the case of habitual drunkenness. Art. 688, Italian Penal Code.

ubriachézza (stàto di manifèsta)—state of manifest drunkenness. A person in this condition cannot testify in judicial proceedings. He may be excluded from the court or hearing room. When found in a flagrant state of manifest drunkenness, the officials and agents of judicial police or public force, may arrest him. Art. 159, 426, 236, Italian Code of Penal Procedure; Art. 688, Italian Penal Code.

uccídere—to kill; to murder; to slay.

uccisióne f.—killing; slaughter.

uccisióne o danneggiaménto di animàli altrúi—killing or damaging animals belonging to others. Whoever, without necessity, kills or renders useless, or causes to be impaired, animals of another, is punished with imprisonment or fine at the complaint of the person damaged. The penalty of imprisonment is augmented if the act is committed upon three or more head of cattle gathered in a herd or flock, or upon bovine or equine animals even if not gathered in a herd. One who commits the act over flying creatures surprised on lands owned by him and at the moment in which they are causing damage, is not punishable. Art. 638, Italian Penal Code.

udiènza f.—audience (granted by an authority); hearing; sitting.

udiènza civíle—civil hearing. It refers to the preliminary hearing as well as the trial before the full court in the civil hearing. The hearing in which the case is tried is public, but the judge may clear the court and hold hearings behind closed doors for reasons of State security, public order or of good morals. The judge exercises police powers for the maintenance of order and decorum and may remove anyone contravening his orders. The preliminary hearings before an examining magistrate are not public. The parties and their counsel may attend the hearings but are not heard, unless they obtain from the judge, through counsel, authority to intervene. The parties and their counsel cannot submit their statements of fact for the minutes unless permitted by the judge. Art. 127-130, Italian Code of Civil Procedure; Art. 84, Enabling Rules, Italian Code of Civil Procedure. See **azióne civíle.**

udiènza penàle—penal hearing. The hearings during arguments of counsel before the Courts of Assizes, the Tribunals and Praetors are public under penalty of nullity. The President of the Court or the Tribunal or the Praetor may order that the arguments of counsel or some portions thereof, take place behind closed doors, when due to publicity, by reason of the nature of the facts, or the quality of the persons, said arguments may prejudice the security of the State, the public order or ranted curiosity, or when there are good morals, or may excite unwar-manifestations on the part of the public which may disturb the tranquility of the arguments. The Presi-

dent or Praetor may order all the arguments be held behind closed doors for reason of public health in a time of spreading epidemic diseases or other contagious diseases. When it is ordered to proceed behind closed doors, no one, for any reason, may be admitted to the hearing room, except those who have the duty or right to be in attendance. The order prescribing that the arguments or portions thereof be held behind closed doors, is issued during a public hearing; it is revoked only when the reasons for the order have ceased, with the statement of the President or Praetor which is to be inserted in the minutes of the hearing. The doors of the hearing room are reopened immediately after the revocation. Art. 423-436, Italian Code of Penal Procedure. See **dibattiménto** and **azióne penàle.**

uditóre m.—auditor; one who is admitted to a university course but who receives no credit; hearer; listener; one who examines accounting records and verifies a balance sheet; a starting rank in the Italian judiciary.

uditòrio m.—audience.

ufficiàle—official. Also, **officiàle.**

ufficiàle m.—officer; official. Also, **officiale.**

ufficiàle giudiziàrio — judicial officer. He is a court official who serves court documents and legal papers for judges and parties and makes attachments and seizures. Ufficiàli Giudiziàri (Judicial Officers), Usual Laws, Appendix to Italian Code of Civil Procedure.

ufficiàle púbblico—public official. See **púbblico ufficiàle.**

ufficiàre—to officiate. Also, **officiàre.**

uffício m.—office; charge; duty.

uffício del bóllo e registro—a State Office which controls the collection of judicial fees and the affixing of stamps on legal documents.

uffício del catàsto—office of real property assessments. The public office where the register of assessed valuation of real property for tax purposes is kept together with the identity of the owners.

uffízio m.—office; charge; duty.

uguagliànza f.—equality.

uguagliàre—to make equal.

uguàle—equal; uniform; the same.

ugualitàrio m.—egalitarian.

ulterióre—ulterior; that which is beyond; that which is beyond what is seen.

único azionísta—sole shareholder. In case of the insolvency of a stock corporation, when the shares of stock are owned by one shareholder, he is liable for corporate liabilities without limit, during the period he held the stock. Similarly, in the case of insolvency of a limited partnership, the sole remaining partner is liable for partnership liabilities without limit, during the period he held all the quotas of capital contributions. Art. 2362, 2497, Italian Civil Code.

unilateràle—unilateral; one-sided; the opposite of bilateral.

unilateràli (fratèlli e sorèlle)—unilateral brothers and sisters. These are those born of the same father and different mothers, or of the same mother and different fathers. The first are called consanguineous (Lat. consanguineus), and the latter uterine (Lat. uterinus). See **germàni (fratèlli e sorèlle)**, **uteríni (fratèlli e sorèlle)** and **consanguínei (fratèlli e sorèlle)**.

unióne f.—union; act of uniting or joining two or more things into one. It is one of the methods of acquiring property. Art. 922, 939, Italian Civil Code.

unióne e commistióne—union and commixtion. When properties of different owners are united or commingled so as to form one whole, but are separable without notable deterioration, each preserves the property in his own things, and has the right to obtain its separation. If not separable, it becomes common property in proportion to the value of each one's property. However, when one of the things may be regarded as the prin-

cipal one or is of superior value, even though it serves the other as ornament, the owner of the principal thing acquires the property to the whole. He must pay to the other the value of the thing that is united or commingled; but if the union or commingling came about without his consent through the work of the owner of the accessory thing, he is only obliged to correspond for the lesser sum between the gain in value brought to the principal thing and the value of the accessory thing. Art. 939, Italian Civil Code.

unità colturàle (mínima) — minimal unit of cultivation. See **mínima unità colturàle**.

universalità di mòbili—universality of movables (personal property). The plurality of things which belong to the same person and have a unitary destination is considered universality of movables. The single things composing the universality may form the object of separate acts and jural relations. Art. 816, Italian Civil Code.

univoco—having one meaning only.

uragàno m.—hurricane.

urgènza f.—urgency.

urgènza (provvedimènti d')—urgent measures for relief. See **provvedimènti d'urgènza**.

úrgere—to urge; to press.

urlàre—to howl.

úrna f.—urn; ballot-box.

úrto m.—violent collision of two bodies in motion or where one is in motion and the other stationary.

úrto tra veícoli — collision between vehicles. See **scóntro tra veícoli** or **circolazióne di veícoli**.

usànza f.—usage; custom.

uscière m.—door-keeper; usher; the title of a court official who formerly served court documents and legal papers of judges and parties and made attachments and seizures, but is now referred to as **ufficiàle giudiziàrio**.

úscio m.—door; outside door; entrance.

uscíta f.—exit; outcome.

úso (úsi pl.)—use; usage; custom. Art. 1, 8, 9, Preliminary Dispositions, and Art. 1368, 1374, Italian Civil Code. See consuetúdine and úso.

úsi cívici—civic use or usages. It denotes the collective rights of people to enjoy rights in the property of others, be it public or private. Some of these rights are the right to cut wood, right to pasturage, the right to fish and similar rights enjoyed by people of a community by custom. See diritti demaniàli su bèni altrúi.

úsi della Bórsa di Milàno—Usages of the Milan Stock Exchange. The usages and customs of the Milan stock Exchange relative to contracts on that exchange. Úsi della Bórsa di Milàno, Usual Laws, Appendix to Italian Civil Code.

úsi locàli—local usages; they are observed with regard to the exercise of the servitude over water rights, and in certain assignments and releases of rentals of houses and lands. Art. 1084, 2924, Italian Civil Code.

úsi normatívi—norms or standards of usage. The determination of the usages and customs of commerce. The determination of the general usages of commerce belongs to a permanent special commission established at the Ministry of Industry and Commerce. Úsi Normatívi, Usual Laws, Appendix to Italian Civil Code.

úso—use; the right to the limited use of another's property to meet one's own needs. Whoever has the right to use a thing, may use its natural profits to serve the needs of himself and his family. The needs must be ascertained according to the social condition of the holder of the right. Art. 1021-1026, Italian Civil Code. See usufrútto.

úso abusívo di sigílli e struménti véri—unlawful use of seals and true instruments. Whoever, having procured the true seals or true instruments destined to a public authentication or certification and makes use thereof to another's damage, or to his own gain or that of others, is punished with imprisonment and fine. Art. 471, Italian Penal Code.

úso legíttimo delle àrmi—legitimate use of arms. A public official is not punishable, when, in the discharge of his official duty, he uses or orders the use of arms or of any other means of physical coercion, when constrained by the necessity to repel violence or to overcome resistance to the Authorities. Art. 53, 51, 52, Italian Penal Code.

ustrína f.—crematorium.

usucapióne f.—adverse possession; one of the methods of acquiring title to property by long, continued possession for the period of time prescribed by law. Art. 922, 923, 1158-1167, Italian Civil Code.

usufrútto m.—usufruct. It is the right to enjoy the property of another and to derive profit or utility therefrom without altering its substance or affecting its economic destination. It is created by law, by contract or by will and may be acquired by adverse possession. Its duration cannot eccede the life of the usufructuary nor last more than thirty years in the case of a juridical person. The usufructary may assign his right of enjoyment for a time certain or for the duration of the usufruct, unless prohibited at the creation of the usufruct. The owner of the property must be notified at the time of the assignment or the usufructuary will be jointly and severally liable with the assignee. Art. 978-1020, Italian Civil Code. See quàsi usufrútto.

usufrútto congiuntívo—joint usufruct; one held by a number of persons jointly. Art. 678, Italian Civil Code. See usufrútto.

usufrútto successívo—successive usufruct; it cannot be granted except in favor of those, who at the death of a testator are first in line to enjoy it. A grantor may reserve a usufruct to himself, and after him to the benefit of another or even a number of persons, but not successively. Art. 698, 796, Italian Civil Code. See usufrútto.

usúra f. — usury. Originally, usura (Lat.), in the Civil Law, meant interest or money given for the use of

304

money. Now, it refers to charging an excessive and usurious rate of interest, the rate not being specified. It is a crime which involves taking advantage of a borrower's needs by a lender who receives and accepts the promise of a usurious rate for a loan of money or personal property. Art. 644, Italian Penal Code; Art. 1284, Italian Civil Code. See **interèssi legàli** and **interèssi usuràri.**

usuràio m.—usurer. Also, **usurière.** See **feneratóre.**

usuràrio—usurious. See **feneratízio.**

usurière m.—usurer. Also, **usuràio.** See **feneratóre.**

usurpàre—to usurp; to appropriate with violence or fraud.

usurpazióne f.—usurpation; appropriation with violence or fraud.

usurpazióne di fúnzioni púbbliche—usurpation of public functions. Whoever usurps a public function or the faculties inherent in a public employment is punished with imprisonment. The same punishment is applied to a public official or employee who having received notice of the disposition which terminates or suspends his functions or faculties, continues to exercise them. Art. 347, Italian Penal Code.

usurpazióne di immòbili altrúi—usurpation of the real property of others. Whoever, in order to appropriate, in whole or in part, the real property of another, removes or alters the boundaries, is punished with imprisonment or fine. Art. 631, Italian Penal Code.

usurpazióne di potére político o di comàndo militàre — usurpation of political power or military command. Whoever usurps a political power or persists in exercising it wrongfully, is punished with imprisonment. The same punishment is applied to one who unlawfully assumes a high military command. If the act is committed in time of war, the guilty party is punished with life imprisonment if the act has compromised the outcome of military operations. Art. 287, Italian Penal Code.

usurpazióne di títoli o di onóri—usurpation of titles or honors. Whoever unlawfully wears in public the uniform or distinctive signs of a public office or employment or of a political administrative or judicial body, or of a profession for which a special qualification is required by the State, or unlawfully wears in public the ecclesiastic habit, is punished with a fine. The same punishment is applied to one who arrogates academic dignities or grades, titles, decorations or other public honorary insignia, or the qualities inherent in some offices, employments or professions indicated in the previous disposition. Art. 498, Italian Penal Code.

uteríni (fratèlli e sorèlle)—uterine brothers and sisters. They are those born of the same mother but different fathers. See **germàni (fratèlli e sorèlle), unilateràli (fratèlli e sorèlle)** and **consanguínei (fratèlli e sorèlle).**

útero m.—uterus.

útile m.—profit; gain.

utilizzazióne dei segréti di stàto—utilization of state secrets. The public official or one in charge of a public service who uses to his own profit or that of another, inventions or scientific discoveries or new industrial applications, which he knows by reason of his office or service, and which should remain secret in the interest of the security of the State, is punished with imprisonment. Art. 263, Italian Penal Code.

utroque (Lat.)—both. It was contained in the expression indicating one to be a doctor in both the Civil and Canon law.

uxoricída m.—one who murders his own wife.

uxoricídio m.—the killing of a wife by her husband. Art. 577, 575, 576, 61, Italian Penal Code. See **omicídio.**

V

vacànte—vacant; empty; unoccupied; an unoccupied post or office.

vacànza f.—vacancy; vacation; holiday.

vacàre—to be vacant; to be unoccupied; to relinquish an office; to adjourn; to recess.

vacatio legis (Lat.)—exemption from the law. It is the period of time that elapses between the promulgation of a law and the date of its becoming effective, which is after the fifteenth consecutive day from its promulgation by the President of the Republic. Art. 73, Constitution of the Italian Republic; Art. 10, Preliminary Dispositions, Italian Civil Code. See promulgazióne.

vacazióne f.—a work period of two hours comprising the work unit upon which is based the compensation of an expert, technical expert, interpreter and translator for performance rendered in both penal and civil matters. Períti ed Ausiliàri del Giúdice (Exprets and Auxiliaries of the Judge), Usual Laws, Appendix to Italian Code of Civil Procedure.

vagabondàggio m.—vagabondage; the state of being a vagabond; state of idle wandering; one who habitually does not work. See vagabóndo.

vagabóndo—vagabond; idler. He is one of a class of persons who endanger public security or morality and is subject to a public admonition by the Quaestor. Art. 1, et seq., Measures of Prevention, Usual Laws, Appendix to Italian Code of Penal Procedure. See diffída.

vàglia m.—money order. See vàglia postàle.

vàglia f.—merit; worth; valor.

vàglia cambiàrio—promissory note; sometimes also referred to as pagherò and cambiàle. Art. 100-105, Cambiàle (Drafts), Usual Laws, Appendix to Italian Civil Code. See cambiàle tràtta.

vàglia postàle—postal money order. See asségno circolàre.

vagliàio m.—sieve maker.

vàglio m.—sieve; boulter, a long fishing line with several hooks.

vagóne m.—railway car.

vàio m.—gray squirrel, or the color of its fur; miniver, a fur of white or spotted white and gray used for trimming.

vàio—spotted white and black.

valànga f.—avalanche. It is a crime punishable with imprisonment to cause an avalanche or to damage protective works against it. Art. 426, 427, Italian Penal Code.

vàle (Lat.) m.—farewell.

vàle (estrèmo)—last farewell to the departed.

valènte — capable; skillful; valiant; valorous.

valentía f.—the state of being capable, skillful or valiant.

valére—to be worth; to cost; to merit.

valóre m.—value; valor; commercial paper; negotiable instrument; worth.

valúta f.—cost; price; monetary value.

valúta in contànti—value in cash.

valúta in cónto—value on account.

valúta in garanzía—payment guaranteed. See giràta a título di pégno.

valúta in pégno — payment under a pledge. See giràta a título di pégno.

valúta intésa—agreed sum; agreed net value.

valúta per incàsso—payment for collection. See giràta per incàsso o per procúra.

valutàre—to appraise; to estimate; to value.

valutazióne f.—appraisal; estimate; valuation.

valutazióne delle pròve—evaluation of the proofs. Art. 116, 117, Italian Code of Civil Procedure. See pròva.

vàmpa f.—blaze; flame.

vànga f.—spade.

vàno m.—door or window space; empty space.

vàno—empty; useless; vain.

vantàggio m.—vantage; superiority.

vantàre—to boast; to praise.

vapóre m.—steam; vapor. See gètto pericolóso di còse.

varàre—to launch.

varcàre—to cross over; to pass over.

vascèllo m.—a former three masted ship of war. Today, the word appears in the title of capitàno di vascèllo, captain of the vessel.

vaticinàre—to divine; to predict; to prophesy.

vaticinazióne f.—prediction. Also, vaticínio.

vaticínio m.—prediction. Also, vaticinazióne.

vècchia f.—old woman.

vecchiàia f.—advanced age. See abbandóno di persóne minóri o incapàci—abandonment of minors or incompetents.

vècchio m.—old man.

vècchio—old.

véce f.—functions; office; substitute.

vedétta f.—look-out.

veditóre m.—customs examiner; observer.

védova f.—widow. Art. 45, 89, 140, 149, Italian Civil Code.

vedovànza f.—widowhood.

vedúta f.—view. See lúci, vedúte o prospètti.

véglia f.—vigil; watch; evening; evening party.

vegliàrdo m.—old man.

vegliàre—to be awake; to keep watch; to be vigilant.

veícolo m.—vehicle. See circolazióne di veícoli—movement of vehicles.

véla f.—sail; canvas; ship.

velàre—to veil; to cover; to conceal; to hide.

velàrio m.—awning; tent.

veleggiàre—to sail.

veléno m.—poison; venom; figuratively, spite or malice.

velière or velièro m.—sailing ship.

vellúto m.—velvet.

vélo m.—veil; gauze.

véna f.—vein; blood vessel; mood; underground spring of water; oats.

venàle—venal.

vendémmia f.—vintage; the gathering of grapes.

véndere—to sell.

vendétta f.—vendetta; revenge.

vendíbile—saleable; alienable; venal.

vendicàre—to avenge; to vindicate.

véndita f.—sale; a contract of sale and transfer of a thing or right in exchange for a purchase price. Also, compravéndita. Art. 1470-1547, Italian Civil Code.

véndita a còrpo—sale (of real property) by mass. When the price of real property is determined by mass and not by measurement or dimension, even though the latter was indicated, there shall be no diminution or addition to the price except if the real dimension be less or more than a twentieth part of that indicated in the contract. In case an increase would have to be paid, the buyer has the option to withdraw from the contract or pay the supplement. Art. 1538, Italian Civil Code.

véndita a mèzzo di commissionàrio—sale by means of a commission agent. When the Praetor deems it opportune, he may order that attached property be turned over to a commission agent so that he may proceed with its sale. In the same disposition, the Praetor, having heard an appraiser where necessary, fixes the minimum sale price and the total amount at which the sale is to be executed, and he may require an indemnity bond of the commission agent. If the value of the property is based on stock exchange or market prices, the sale may not be made at a price less than the quoted price. Art. 532, Italian Code of Civil Procedure; Art. 1474, Italian Civil Code. See esecuzióne forzàta and pignoraménto.

véndita a misúra—sale (of real property) by dimension. When a piece of real property is sold with specification of dimension or size, and at a fixed price based on an amount for each parcel, the buyer has the right to a reduction in price if the dimension of the real property is less than that indicated in the contract. If the dimension is more, the buyer must supplement the price, but can withdraw from the contract if the excess surpasses the twentieth part of the dimension specified. Art. 1537, Italian Civil Code.

véndita a pròva—sale on approval. It is presumed to be made on the basis of conditions which may render the contract effective or subject to rescission, and that the property has the qualities agreed upon or be fitted for the use to which it is destined. The test of approval must be executed within the time and according to the provisions of the contract or of usage. Art. 1521, 1353, Italian Civil Code. Cf. Art. 2-326, Uniform Commercial Code.

véndita a tèrmine—sale at a set term of time. Here, title passes to the buyer and payment of the price or delivery of the goods is deferred. Art. 1376, 1470, Italian Civil Code; Cf. Art. 2-310, Uniform Commercial Code.

véndita a tèrmine di títoli di crédito—time sale of securities. In the sale of securities at a set term or period of time, interest and dividends collectible after the conclusion of the contract and before the expiration of the term, if recovered by the seller, are credited to the buyer. Whenever the sale involves shares of stock, the right to vote belongs to the seller up to the moment of delivery. The right of option inherent in securities sold on time belongs to the buyer. The seller, whenever the buyer requests within the appropriate time, must place the buyer in a position to exercise the right of option, or he must exercise it on account of the buyer if the latter has furnished the necessary funds. In lieu thereof, the seller must execute the sale of the option rights for the account of the buyer through a broker or credit institution. At least two days prior to the expiration of the term, the buyer must furnish to the seller the sums necessary to make the payments on the unredeemed securities. If at the termination of the term, the parties agree to extend the execution of the contract, there is owed the difference between th original price and the current one on the date of expiration, except for the observance of different usage. Art. 1531-1536, Italian Civil Code.

véndita all'àsta—auction sale. See incànto and incànto púbblico.

véndita con incànto—sale by auction. Art. 576-591, Italian Code of Civil Procedure.

véndita con pàtto di riscàtto—sale with agreement to redeem back the property. See pàtto di riscàtto, Art. 1500-1509, Italian Civil Code.

véndita con risèrva del domínio—conditional sale; an installment sale where the title remains with the seller until final payment has been made by the buyer when title passes to him. Also, **véndita con risèrva della proprietà, riservàto domínio** and **domínio riservàto**. Art. 1523-1526, Italian Civil Code.

véndita con risèrva della proprietà—conditional sale; an installment sale where the title remains with the seller until final payment has been made by the buyer when title passes to him. Also, **véndita con risèrva del domínio, riservàto domínio** and **domínio riservàto**. Art. 1523-1526, Italian Civil Code.

véndita con risèrva di gradiménto—sale with reservation of satisfaction. When things are sold with a reservation of satisfaction on the part of the buyer, the sale is not perfected until such time as the satisfaction is communicated to the seller. If the examination of the thing is to be made at the seller's place, the latter is released, whenever the buyer does not proced within the time established by the contract or usage, or, in their absence, within a convenient time fixed by the seller. If the thing is at the buyer's place, and he does not declare himself within the time above indicated, the thing is considered to be to his satisfaction. Art. 1520, Italian Civil Code.

véndita cumulatíva di piú immòbili—cumulative sale of a number of real properties. If two or more parcels of real property have been sold under the same contract for the same total price with indication of the measure or dimension of each parcel and it is found that the quantity is less in one and more in the other, compensation will be made, after due agreement, for a supplement or diminution in price. The right of the seller to a supplement and that of the buyer to a diminution in price is prescribed within one year of the delivery of the realty. Art. 1540, 1541, Italian Civil Code. Also, **véndita in blòcco.**

véndita di animàli—sale of animals. In the sale of animals, the guarantee against faults or defects is regulated by special laws, or, in lieu thereof, by local usage. If neither of these deal with it, the rules of the Civil Code on sales will be followed. Art. 1496, Italian Civil Code.

véndita di còse altrúi—sale of another's property. If at the time of contract, the thing sold was not the property of the seller, the latter is obligated to procure its acquisition for the buyer. The buyer becomes its owner at the moment in which the seller acquires the property from its rightful owner. Art. 1478, Italian Civil Code.

véndita di còse futúre—sale of future things. In a sale whose object is a future thing, the acquisition of the property therein is realized as soon as the thing comes into existence. If the objects of the sale are trees or products of the soil, the property is acquired when the trees are cut or the products severed. Whenever the parties have not wished to conclude an aleatory contract, the sale is void if the thing does not come into existence. Art. 1472, Italian Civil Code. Cf. Art. 2-105, 107, Uniform Commercial Code.

véndita di còse immòbili—sale of real property. Art. 1537-1541, Italian Civil Code. See **véndita a còrpo** and **véndita a misúra.**

véndita di còse mòbili—sale of personal property. Art. 1510-1519, Italian Civil Code.

véndita di còse mòbili e luògo di conségna—sale of personal property and place of delivery. In the absence of agreement or use to the contrary, the delivery of the thing takes place at the place where it was located at the time of sale if the parties were aware of it; or in the place where the seller had his domicile or his place of business. Except agreement or usage to the contrary, if the thing sold must be transported from one place to another, the seller is freed from the obligation of delivery by placing the thing into the possession of a carrier or shipper; the expenses of transport are to be borne by the buyer. Art. 1510, Italian Civil Code. Cf. Art. 2-503, 504, 601, 602, 705, Uniform Commercial Code.

véndita di eredità—sale of inheritance. The one who sells an inheritance without specifying its content and extent, is not bound except to guarantee his own quality as heir. The sale must be made by a document in writing or it is void. The seller is held to supply the necessary documents on his part to render effective before third parties, the transmission of all the rights comprised in the inheritance. If the seller has received the profits or interest from some property or has obtained some credit or payment from the inheritance, or has sold some property thereof, he must reimburse the buyer, unless there is agreement to the contrary. The buyer must reimburse the seller for the amounts the latter has paid for the debts and taxes of the inheritance and must also answer for what would be owed him from the inheritance itself, save agreement to the contrary. The buyer, if there is no agreement to the contrary, is jointly and severally liable with the seller to pay the debts of the estate or inheritance. Art. 1542-1546, Italian Civil Code.

véndita di màcchine utènsili—sale of appliances. It is applicable to new appliances for domestic and kitchen use, or those for production, of a determined value, which are sold with reservation of title, or by installment or deferred payment, or leased with option to buy, or under an agreement transferring title to the lessee as a result of payment of the installments. Véndita di Màcchine Utènsili, Usual Laws, Appendix to Italian Civil Code.

véndita di sostànze alimentàri non genuíne cóme genuíne—sale of nongenuine food-stuffs as genuine. Whoever places on sale, or otherwise places in commerce as genuine, food-stuffs that are not genuine, is punished with imprisonment or fine. Art. 516, Italian Penal Code.

véndita forzàta—forced sale. It transfers to the party acquiring the property at a forced sale, the rights over the property which belonged to the one subjected to the expropriation, save the effects of good faith possession. However, the rights acquired by third parties over the thing are not opposable to the acquiring party, if the same rights do not have effect in prejudice of the attaching creditor or the creditors intervening in the execution. Art. 2919-2929, Italian Civil Code; Art. 501-508, 620, Italian Code of Civil Procedure.

véndita in blòcco—mass sale (of realty). If two or more parcels of real property have been sold under the same contract for the same total price with indication of the measure or dimension of each parcel and it is found that the quantity is less in one and more in the other, compensation will be made, after due agreement, for a supplement or diminution in price. The right of the seller to a supplement and that of the buyer to a diminution in price is prescribed within one year of the delivery of the realty. Art. 1540, 1541, Italian Civil Code. Also, véndita cumulatíva di piú immòbili.

véndita in dànno—prejudicial sale. It refers to a forced sale where a buyer has failed to fulfill the obligation of paying the price. See esecuzióne coattíva.

véndita internazionàle di bèni mòbili materiàli—international sale of material or corporeal personal property. It was adopted at an international convention at the Hague on July 1, 1964. Véndita Internazionàle, Usual Laws, Appendix to Italian Civil Code.

véndita (proméssa di) — promise to sell; contract to sell goods. It is not a present sale but one to sell in the future. It may be enforced. Art. 2932, 1478, Italian Civil Code. Cf. Art. 2-106, Uniform Commercial Code.

véndita sènza incànto—sale without auction. Art. 570-575, Italian Code of Civil Procedure.

véndita su campióne e su típo di campióne—sale by sample and by type of sample. If a sale is made by sample, it is understood that this must serve as the exclusive standard of comparison for the quality of the merchandise, and in such case, any defect whatever gives rise to a right in the buyer to rescind the contract. However, whenever it results from agreement or usage that the sample is to serve only to indicate in an approximate manner the quality of the merchandise, rescission can be demanded only if the defect compared to the sample is notable. In every case, the action is barred unless the buyer gives notice of the defects to the seller within eight days of their discovery unless a different time was set by the parties or by the law. Art. 1522, 1495, Italian Civil Code.

véndita su documénti e con pagaménto cóntro documénti—sale by documents and with payment against documents. In a sale by documents (of title), the seller is freed of the obligation of delivery by remitting to the buyer the title (document) representing the merchandise and the other documents agreed by contract, or in lieu thereof, by usage. Except by agreement or contrary usage, payment of the price and accessories must be made in the place where delivery of the documents is made. When the documents are regular, the buyer cannot refuse payment of the price by alleging objections relative to quality and the state of things, unless these result to have already been demonstrated. If the sale involves things in transit and among the documents delivered to the buyer is comprised a policy of insurance against the risks of transport, the risks to which the merchandise is exposed from the moment of delivery to the carrier fall upon the buyer. This disposition is not applicable if the seller at the time of the contract had knowledge of the loss or damage and concealed them in bad faith from the buyer. When payment of the price is to be made through a bank, the seller cannot turn to the buyer till after refusal made by the bank itself and verified by the act of the presentation of the documents in the manner established by usage. The bank which has confirmed the credit to the seller may only interpose objections deriving from the incompleteness or irregularity of the documents and those relating to the relationship confirming the credit. Art. 1527-1530, Italian Civil Code. Cf. Art. 1-301; Art. 2-503, 504, 513, 514, Uniform Commercial Code.

ventàglia f.—visor or opening in a helmet.

ventàglio m.—fan.

ventièra f.—ventilator. See **ventilatóre**.

ventilatóre m.—ventilator; opening in a building to permit the circulation of air; a fan operated by motive power.

ventúra f.—fortune; luck.

ventúro—that which is to come, such as the coming week or month.

verbàle—verbal; pertaining to words; minutes. See **procèsso verbàle**.

vérga f.—rod; switch; staff of authority.

verífica f.—verification; confirmation; inspection. Also, **verfiicazióne**.

verífica del passívo—verification of liabilities. See **verificazióne dello stàto passívo**.

verífica e pagaménto dell'òpera—inspection and payment for work. See **dirítto di verífica**.

verífica nel córso di esecuzióne dell' òpera—inspection during the course of execution of the work. The one for whom work is being done has the

right to review the work during its performance and to verify and inspect its state at his own expense. Art. 1662, Italian Civil Code.

verificazióne f.—verification; confirmation; inspection. Also, **verífica**.

verificazióne della scrittúra privàta—verification of private writings. Art. 214-220, Italian Code of Civil Procedure.

verificazióne dello stàto passívo—verification of liabilities (in bankruptcy). Art. 96, Falliménto (Bankruptcy), Usual Laws, Appendix to Italian Civil Code.

vessàre—to oppress; to vex.

vessatòrio—oppressive.

vessatóre m. (vessatríce f.) — oppressor.

vessatríce (léggi)—oppressive laws.

vestíti (impignorabilità di)—non attachableness of clothing. They are absolutely not subject to attachment. See **impignoràbili (còse mòbile assolutaménte)**.

vettóre m.—a carrier of goods or persons under a contract of carriage. Art. 1678, 1681, Italian Civil Code. See **traspòrto di persóne** and **traspòrto di còse**.

vettúra f.—carriage; coach; conveyance; vehicle; railway car; rental of beasts of burden or carriage.

vettúra (lèttera di)—bill of lading. See **lèttera di vettúra**.

vetturàle m.—carrier; carter.

vetustà f.—ancient.

vetústo—very old (person); ancient.

viaggiatóre m. (viaggiatríce f.) — traveler; passenger. The carrier is responsible for accidents which affect the person of the passenger during transportation and for the loss or damage caused to things which the passenger carries with him. Art. 1681, Italian Civil Code.

viaggiatóre (commésso) — travelling salesman. Art. 2210-2212, Italian Civil Code.

viàggio m.—journey; voyage.

viàggio (bigliétto di)—trip ticket;

ticket for a journey. The traveler pays for his transportation and his payment is evidenced by the trip ticket, representing the contract of carriage.

vicènda f. — incident; vicissitude; change; affair; business.

vicènda (a)—in turn; mutually.

vicinàle—neighboring.

vicinàle (stràda)—Country road serving neighboring rural farms and habitations.

vicinànza f.—neighborhood. Also, vicinità.

vicinità f.—neighborhood. Also, vicinànza.

vícolo f.—alley; lane; passage; dead-end.

vidimàre—to authenticate.

vidimazióne f. — authentication. Art. 2216-2218, 2421, Italian Civil Code.

víe funiculàri (passàgio coattívo di)—compulsory passage of funicular railways. See passàgio di víe funiculàri.

vigènte—in effect; in force.

vigilànza f. — vigilance; supervision; watchfulness.

vigilànza speciàle — special surveillance or supervision. It is a preventive measure taken against persons considered dangerous to public security and morality and members of the Mafia. Also, sorveglianza speciàle. See misúre di prevenzióne, and misúre di prevenzióne cóntro la màfia.

vigilànza sui detenúti — supervision over prisoners. At least once a month, the Procurator of the Republic must visit the judicial prisons in his territory to oversee the prisoners. The Praetor has an equal obligation over the prisons within his territorial jurisdiction. Art. 13, Enabling Rules, Italian Code of Penal Procedure.

vigilànza sull'esecuzióne delle péne—supervision over the execution of punishments. The execution of detentive punishments is supervised by the judge. He determines admis-sion to outside work and renders opinion regarding admission to conditional freedom or release. The supervising judge visits the penal institutions every two months to ascertain enforcement of the laws and regulations. He reports the results of his visits to the Ministry of Justice. Art. 144, Italian Penal Code; Art. 4, Càrceri (Prisons), Usual Laws, Appendix to Italian Code of Penal Procedure.

vigilàta (libertà)—supervised liberty or release. See libertà vigilàta.

vígile m.—guard.

vígile—watchful.

vígile urbàno—municipal guard; policeman.

vígili (pl.) m.—firemen.

vigília f.—vigil; watch; eve before a holiday.

vigliàcco m.—coward.

víle—vile; cowardly.

vilipèndio m. — contempt; disparagement; scorn; slight.

vilipèndio alla bandièra o ad àltro emblèma dello stàto—disparagement of the flag or other emblem of the State. Art. 292, Italian Penal Code.

vilipèndio alla nazióne italiàna—disparagement of the Italian nation. When done publicly, it is punished with imprisonment. Art. 291, Italian Penal Code.

vilipèndio della Repúbblica—disparagement or contempt for the Republic, the legislative assemblies or one of them or the Government, the Constitutional Court, the judicial system or the armed forces of the State. Art. 290, Italian Penal Code.

vilipèndio delle tómbe — act of disparagement or contempt towards tombs. Whoever, in cemeteries or other places of burial, commits an act of disparagement or contempt to a tomb, sepulchre or urn, or of things destined to the worship of the deceased, or for the protection or ornament of cemeteries, is punished with imprisonment. Art. 408, Italian Penal Code.

vilipèndio di cadàvere—disparagement

of a cadaver. Whoever commits acts of disparagement or contempt over a cadaver or over his ashes, is punished with imprisonment. If the culpable person disfigures or mutilates the cadaver, or commits on it acts of brutality or obscenity, in any manner, he will be punished with a longer term of imprisonment. Art. 410, Italian Penal Code.

violazióne f.—violation; infringement; transgression.

violazióne dègli òbblighi di assistènza familiàre—violation of the obligations to render family assistance. Whoever, abandoning the domestic domicile, or in any manner by maintaining a conduct contrary to order or morals of the family, withdraws from the obligations of assistance inherent in the parental authority, or from the quality of spouse, is punished with imprisonment or fine. The same penalties are applied to one who: (1) embezzles or wastes the property of a minor child or of a ward or of a spouse; (2) neglects to provide the means of subsistence to minor descendants or minors otherwise unable to work, to ascendants, or to a spouse from whom he is not legally separated through his fault. Art. 570, Italian Penal Code. Art. 143, Italian Civil Code.

violazióne di domicílio—violation of the domicile. It is committed by one who introduces himself into the habitation of another or in a place of private residence or appurtenances thereto, against the express or tacit permission of whoever has the right to exclude him, or introduces himself therein clandestinely or with deception. Art. 614, Italian Penal Code.

violazióne di sepólcro—violation of a tomb. Whoever violates a tomb, a burial place or funerary urn is punished with imprisonment. Art. 407, Italian Penal Code.

violazióne di sigilli—violation of seals. Whoever violates the seals affixed by disposition of law or by order of the Authorities for the purpose of assuring the conservation or suitability of a thing, is punished with imprisonment. Art. 349, Italian Penal Code.

violazióne, sottrazióne e soppressióne di corrispondènza — violation, abstraction and suppression of correspondence. Whoever obtains cognizance of the contents of closed or sealed correspondence not directed to him, or, abstracts, or disturbs sealed or open correspondence not directed to him, for the purpose of taking cognizance thereof himself or for others, or, destroys or suppresses it, is punished with imprisonment, unless it is not otherwise foreseen as a crime by some other disposition of the law. If the guilty party, without just cause, reveals, in whole or in part, the contents of the correspondence and damage results from the act, the punishment is increased, unless the act constitutes a more serious crime. The crime is punishable upon the complaint of the person damaged. This article applies to letters, telegraphic and telephonic communications. Art. 616-620, Italian Penal Code.

violénza f. — violence; compulsion; force. Violence is a ground for annulling a contract, even if it was exercised by a third party. It is related to common law duress, and must be of such a nature as to cause an impression on a judicious person and to make him fear exposing himself or his property to an unjust and great harm. Regard must be had in this matter to the age, sex and condition of the person. Art. 1434-1436, Italian Civil Code.

violènza carnàle — carnal violence. Whoever, with violence or threats, compels another to submit to carnal knowledge, is punished with imprisonment. Subject to the same penalty is one having carnal knowledge of a person, who at the time of the act; (1) has not reached age fourteen; (2) has not reached age sixteen, when the wrongdoer is the ascendant, or guardian or other person to whom the minor is entrusted for reasons of care, education, instruction, supervision or custody; (3) is mentally ill, or not in condition to resist by reason of psychic or physical inferiority, even if the condition is independent of the act of the wrongdoer; (4) has been deceived by the wrongdoer taking the place of another. Art. 519, Italian Penal Code. See **seduzióne con proméssa di matrimònio comméssa da persóna coniugàta.**

violènza, dòlo, erróre nel testaménto— violence, fraud, error in the testament. The testamentary disposition may be challenged by anyone having an interest therein, when it is the effect of error or mistake, of violence or of fraud. Art. 624, Italian Civil Code.

violènza, ed erróre nel matrimònio— violence and error in marriage. The marriage may be challenged by the spouse whose consent was extorted by violence or produced by exceptionally serious fear deriving from causes external to the spouse. It may also be challenged by that spouse whose consent was given through effect of error on the identity of the person or essential error or mistake over the personal qualities of the other spouse. Mistake over the personal qualities is essential whenever, bearing in mind the conditions of the other spouse, it is ascertained that the spouse would not have consented if said qualities had been exactly known and provided the error concerns: (1) the existence of a physical or psychic illness or of a sexual anomaly or deviation sufficient to impede the fulfillment of conjugal life; (2) the existence of a sentence for a nonculpable crime with imprisonment for not less than five years, except in case of intervening rehabilitation before the celebration of the marriage. The annulment action may not be instituted before the judgment has become irrevocable; (3) a declaration of habitual or professional delinquency; (4) the circumstance that the other spouse has been convicted of crimes concerning prostitution with punishment of not less than two years. The action of annulment cannot be instituted before the judgment has become irrevo-

cable;; (5) a state of pregnancy caused by a person other than the subject of the mistake. The action may not be instituted if there has been cohabitation for a year after the violence, or the causes which determined the fear have ceased, or the mistake has been discovered. Art. 122, 128, 129, 129 bis, Italian Civil Code. See **matrimònio putatívo.**

violènza física— physical violence. See **costringiménto físico.**

violènza o minàccia ad un púbblico ufficiàle— violence or threat to a public official. It is a crime punishable with imprisonment to use violence or threat to a public official or one charged with a public service to compel him to perform an act contrary to his duties, or to omit an act of office or of the service. An act is also punishable if committed to compel one of the aforesaid persons to perform an act of their office or service, or to influence it in any manner. Art. 336, Italian Penal Code.

violènza o minàccia ad un Còrpo político, amministratívo o giudiziàrio— violence or threat to a political, administrative or judicial body. It is a crime punishable with imprisonment to use violence or threat to one of the foregoing bodies, or one of their representatives, or any public Authority constituted collegially, to impede, in whole or in part, even temporarily, or to disturb their activity in any manner. Art. 338, Italian Penal Code.

violènza o minàccia per costríngere a comméttere un reàto— violence or threat to constrain one to commit a crime. Whoever uses violence or threat to constrain or compel others to commit an act constituting a crime, is punished with imprisonment. The punishment is augmented if the acts are performed by the use of arms, or by a disguised person, or by more than one person in concert, or by anonymous writing, or in a symbolic manner, or by employing intimidating force derived from secret associations, whether existent

314

or presumed. Art. 611, 339, Italian Penal Code.

violènza privàta — private violence. Whoever, by violence or threat constrains others to do, to tolerate or to omit a thing is punished with imprisonment. The punishment is augmented if the acts are performed by the use of arms, or by a disguised person, or by more than one person in concert, or by anonymous writing or in a symbolic manner, or by employing intimidating force derived from secret associations, whether existent or presumed. Art. 610, 339, Italian Penal Code.

viràre—to veer; to heave to; to turn about.

visièra f.—visor; fencing mask.

vísita doganàle—customs inspection.

víso m.—face; countenance; visage. A permanent disfigurement of the face is considered a serious personal injury and an aggravating circumstance punishable with imprisonment. Art. 583, Italian Penal Code.

vísta f.—sight; faculty of sight; view; appearance.

vísta (a)—at sight, with reference to the payment of a draft.

vistàre—to affix a visa; to authenticate; to certify.

vísto m.—a visa; an official certification of a passport, document or commercial book.

vísto—seen; examined; considered.

víta f.—life; sustenance necessary to life; waist or body of a dress.

víta (assicuraziόne sulla)—life insurance. See assicuraziόne sulla víta.

víta (delítti cόntro la)—crimes against life. See delítti cόntro la persόna—crimes against the person.

víta (matrimόnio in imminènte perícolo di)—marriage made in imminent peril of life. In case of imminent peril to life of one of the spouses, the officer of Civil Status may celebrate the marriage without publication and without assent, if requested, provided the parties swear that no impediments exist not susceptible of dispensation. Art. 101, Italian Civil Code.

víta (perícolo di)—danger to life. If serious personal injury is inflicted leading to illness endangering life, it is punishable with imprisonment. Art. 593, Italian Civil Code.

vitalízio—life annuity; life interest. See rèndita vitalízia.

víte—vine; screw.

víttima f.—victim.

vítto m.—food; victual. It is part of the compensation of a worker. Domestic servants receive food in addition to compensation. Cost for food furnished a debtor and family during the last six months has priority in claims. Art. 2121, 2242, 2751, Italian Civil Code.

viviseziόne f.—vivisection. Together with other experiments, it is forbidden on warm-blooded vertebrate animals (mammals and birds) when it does not have the purpose of promoting the progress of biology and experimental medicine. They are performed in scientific Institutes and laboratories of the State and those approved by it. Vivisection of dogs and cats is normally forbidden unless indispensable for experiments of scientific research and it is absolutely impossible to use animals of other species. Animàli (Proteziόne Degli) (Animals—Protection of), Usual Laws, Appendix to Italian Code of Penal Procedure.

vízi del consènso—defects of assent or agreement. The contracting party whose assent was given in error, extorted by violence or obtained by fraud, may seek the annulment or rescission of the contract pursuant to dispositions of the Civil Code. Art. 1427, Italian Civil Code.

vízi della còsa comodàta—defects in the thing loaned for use. If the thing loaned for use has such defects which may cause damage to the one using it, the bailor must make compensation whenever, knowing the defects in the thing, he has not warned the bailee. Art. 1812, Italian Civil Code. See comodànte and comodatàrio.

vízi della còsa locàta—defects in leased property. If at the moment of delivery, the leased property is impaired by defects which appreciably diminish its suitability for the use agreed, the lessee may ask for the rescission of the contract, or a reduction in payment, unless it is for defects known by him, or easily recognizable. The lessor must compensate the lessee for damages derived from the defects of the thing, unless he proves to have not known of the defects at the moment of delivery and without negligence on his part. Art. 1578, Italian Civil Code.

vízi della còsa vendúta—defects in a thing sold. The seller must guarantee that the thing sold is free of defects which render it unsuitable for the use to which it is destined, or which appreciably diminish its value. The agreement limiting or excluding the guarantee has no effect, if the seller has, in bad faith, concealed from the buyer, the defects of the thing. Art. 1490, Italian Civil Code.

vízi dell'òpera nell'appàlto—defects of work under a contract for work or services. The contractor is held to the guarantee against irregularity and defects in the work. The guarantee is not effective if the one for whom the work is done has received the work and the irregularities or defects were known by him or were easily recognizable, provided that they were not concealed in bad faith by the contractor. Art. 1667, Italian Civil Code. See appàlto.

vízio parziàle di ménte—partial defect of the mind. One who, at the moment of the commission of the act was, by reason of infirmity, in such a state of mind to diminish greatly, without excluding it, the capacity to comprehend or to will, responds for the crime committed, but the punishment is diminished, Art. 89, Italian Penal Code. See capacità d'intèndere e di volére.

vízio totàle di ménte—total defect of the mind. One is not chargeable, if at the moment of the commission of the act, he was, by reason of infirmity, in such a state of mind to exclude the capacity to comprehend or to will. Art. 88, Italian Penal Code. See capacità d'intèndere e di volére.

vocazióne f.—vocation, calling.

vocazióne ereditària—the call to accept an inheritance. It devolves by law or by testament and cannot be disposed by agreement. Acceptance is done by a public Act or document or by private writing by the one called to the inheritance or has assumed the title of heir. An acceptance under conditions, or terms, or partially, is void. Art. 475, 457, 458, Italian Civil Code.

vóci corrènti—current voices; reports; rumors; hearsay. Witnesses must not depose or testify regarding public rumors or hearsay concerning the facts at issue in the trial. It is, also, forbidden under pain of nullity to read reports of public rumors regarding facts at issue in the trial. Art. 349, 464, Italian Code of Penal Procedure. See bócca d'altrúi and sentíto díre.

volàtile—volatile.

volàtili m.—winged or flying creatures. The killing of winged creatures is not punishable when they are surprised on one's lands and at the moment they are causing damage to it. Art. 638, Italian Penal Code.

volére—to will; to wish; to want; to intend; to require. See capacità d'intèndere e di volére.

volére m.—will; wish. Also, volontà.

volontà f.—will; wish; desire; determination; operation of the mind; volition; power of choosing. See volére and capacità d'intèndere e di volére.

volontària giurisdizióne — voluntary jurisdiction. It involves jurisdiction of the court over proceedings and hearings of a non-adversary nature. Art. 706-805, Italian Code of Civil Procedure.

voltàre—to turn; to turn around; to turn over.

voltàta f.—a turn in the road; curve; change of direction.

voltúra f.—assignment; transfer.

voltúra catastàle—recording or transcription of a transfer of an interest in real property from one person to another in the real property records.

volúta f.—volute; spiral; ornamental scroll of a capital.

voluttà f.—sensual pleasure or luxurious enjoyment.

voluttuàrio—pertaining to sensual or luxurious enjoyment.

voluttuóso—voluptuous.

votànte m.—voter.

votàre—to vow; to cast a vote.

votazióne f.—the act of voting; the results of the voting; suffrage.

vóto m.—vow; votive offering.

vuotàre—to empty.

vuòto—empty.

Z

zaffàre—to plug; to stop.

zàffo m.—bung; stopper.

zàino m.—knapsack.

zàmpa f.—claw; paw; talon.

zampíno m.—little claw or paw; this word is used to indicate one who "butts in," or intrudes into a matter, usually furtively. He is said to put the zampíno or little claw into it.

zàna f.—basket; cradle; cheat; trick.

zanàio m.—basket maker.

zanaiuòlo m.—basket carrier; porter.

zanàta f.—basket-full.

zànca f.—leg; shank.

zanèlla f.—street gutter.

zàngola f.—churn.

zànna f.—tusk.

zannàta f.—piece of foolishness.

zànni m.—buffoon.

zàttera f.—raft.

zavòrra f.—ballast.

zàzzera f.—long, flowing hair.

zécca f.—mint.

zecchière m.—one who supervises the mint; a worker at the mint.

zía f.—aunt.

zibaldóne m.—medley; notebook containing random notes.

zibellíno m.—sable.

zibíbbo m.—raisin; dried sweet grape.

zíi m.—uncles and aunts. Marriage cannot be contracted between uncle and niece or aunt and nephew. Art. 87, 117, Italian Civil Code.

zimbèllo m.—decoy; lure.

zío m.—uncle. See zíi.

zitèlla f.—young, unmarried girl.

zólfo m.—sulphur.

zóne di esclusíva nel contràtto di agenzía—zones of exclusion in a contract of agency. The principal cannot avail himself of more agents in the same area simultaneously and in the same field of activity, nor may the agent assume to represent more competing businesses in the same area and in the same field of activity. Art. 1743, Italian Civil Code.

zòppo—lame.

zúcca f.—gourd.

zúcchero m.—sugar.

zúcco—name of a Sicilian wine.

zúffa f.—affray; battle; conflict; fight.

zúppa f.—soup.

zúrigo f.—Zurich.